The Newbery Companion

The Newbery Companion

Booktalk and Related Materials
for Newbery Medal and Honor Books

Second Edition

John T. Gillespie
Corinne J. Naden

2001
Libraries Unlimited
A Division of Greenwood Publishing Group, Inc.
Greenwood Village, Colorado

LIBRARIES UNLIMITED
A Division of Greenwood Publishing Group, Inc.
7730 East Belleview Avenue, Suite A200
Greenwood Village, CO 80111
1-800-225-5800
www.lu.com

Library of Congress Cataloging-in-Publication Data

Gillespie, John Thomas, 1928-
      The Newbery companion : booktalk and related materials for Newbery Medal and
Honor books / John T. Gillespie, Corinne J. Naden.--2nd ed.
         p. cm.
      Includes bibliographical references and indexes.
      ISBN 1-56308-813-4
      1. Newbery Medal--Bibliography. 2. Children's literature, American--Bibliography. I.
Naden, Corinne J. II. Title.

Z1037.A2 G55 2001
[PS490]
016.813'5099282--dc21

126- 9467   00-045092

Contents

1950s

1960s

1970s

1980s

1990s

2000s

Preface

The most prestigious annual prize in children's literature in the United States and perhaps in the world is the Newbery Medal. Named after the English publisher and bookseller John Newbery (1713–1767), one of the pioneers in establishing juvenile literature as an important branch of publishing, it honors the most distinguished children's book published in America during the year preceding the award. Begun in 1922, the award's importance and stature have grown through the years. Teachers, other educators, librarians, and parents are all familiar with the golden facsimile of the medal that adorns the dust jackets of winners and the silver medallion on the Honor Books. Parents often purchase copies or borrow copies from librarians for their children, teachers frequently make assignments involving these titles, and librarians scramble for copies as soon as the award winners are announced in January of each year.

Many books have been published about the Newbery winners, their authors, and the Honor Books, formerly known as the "runners-up." It is the purpose of this book to combine in one volume information that is found in several sources, to expand on the brief plot outlines usually given, and to update data through 2001. It is hoped that this book will not only supply information about the medalists and Honor Books and where further information about them can be located, but also furnish hints on how these books can be introduced to young readers and give suggestions for related follow-up reading titles.

The work is arranged chronologically, beginning with the first award in 1922 for *The Story of Mankind* by Hendrik Van Loon and ending with Richard Peck's 2001 winner *A Year Down Yonder*. Preceding this material is a brief introduction to John Newbery and his publishing record plus a history of the award and a description of how the winners are chosen. For each winner there is a paragraph that introduces the author, supplies information on the author's other literary works, and often tells of the origins and inspiration behind the writing of the prizewinner. This is followed by material arranged under the following six headings:

Plot Summary: For each title there is a detailed analysis of the plot, covering all key incidents and introducing and identifying all of the important characters. In each case, an effort has been made to retain, as much as possible, the atmosphere, feeling, and point of view of the author.

Themes and Subjects: This section identifies major themes covered in the text as well as important people, places, and time periods. It is hoped that this material will facilitate the use of these books in a variety of situations.

Incidents for Booktalking: Passages suitable for reading aloud or retelling to stimulate interest in the book are identified with pagination in the hardcover edition indicated for quick retrieval. Pagination in paperback editions is usually the same.

Related Titles: Additional titles (usually five) that are related to the prizewinner, either by theme or subject, are listed with basic bibliographic information and brief annotations. It is hoped that these can be used during booktalks or in giving suggestions for follow-up reading.

About the Book and Author: Such standard biographical sources as the Something About the Author series, the Junior Book of Authors series, and Contemporary Authors series are listed to provide sources for additional information about the book and author. Each is identified with full bibliographic information, including relevant page numbers. In each list, there is at least one entry where the reader can locate the medal-winning author's acceptance speech. Whenever appropriate, related nonprint material (e.g., screen adaptations, audio cassettes) are also included. Additional information, particularly magazine articles, can be obtained by consulting such periodical indexes as *Readers' Guide*, *Library Literature*, and *Education Index*.

Honor Books: There is a plot summary for each of the year's Honor Books. Although shorter than the summaries for the medal winners, each covers the major plot developments, the important characters, and the primary themes.

There follows a general bibliography of works about John Newbery, the prize, its recipients, and the award-winning books. The book ends with an index listing all of the children's books mentioned in the text, the authors, and subjects.

As well as supplying coverage on award winners from 1997 through 2001 and providing material related to these titles, this second edition updates the bibliographic information on the winners as well as related titles. International Standard Book Numbers have been added. Out-of-print titles in the "Related Titles" sections have been removed and newer suitable titles have been added. The "About the Book and Author" sections have also been expanded with the inclusion of newer reference sources.

A few of the plots have appeared in part or in their entirety in the series of "Plot" books that the authors have written for R. R. Bowker, a Reed Reference Publishing Company. All are copyrighted by Reed Elsevier, Inc., and the copyright dates are included in the list below.

From *Juniorplots*, copyright 1967:

- *Rifles for Watie*
- *Shadow of a Bull*
- *It's Like This, Cat*
- *Miracles on Maple Hill*
- *A Wrinkle in Time*
- *I, Juan de Pareja*

More Juniorplots, copyright 1977:

- *Sounder*
- *Roll of Thunder Hear My Cry*
- *The Slave Dancer*
- *Summer of the Swans*
- *M. C. Higgins the Great*
- *Julie of the Wolves*
- *The Bronze Bow*

Juniorplots 3, copyright 1987:

- *Jacob Have I Loved*
- *The Hero and the Crown*

Juniorplots 4, copyright 1992:

- *Maniac Magee*

Introducing Books, copyright 1970:

- *The Witch of Blackbird Pond*

Middleplots 4, copyright 1994:

- *Dear Mr. Henshaw*
- *Missing May*
- *Shiloh*
- *Number the Stars*

In addition to thanking R. R. Bowker for their kind permission to reprint the above material, the authors thank the many others who have helped in the preparation of this book, particularly the staff of the Children's Room at the Donnell Branch of the New York Public Library and the very helpful librarians in the Instructional Materials Center of the Library at the C. W. Post Center of Long Island University in Greenvale, New York.

It is our sincere hope that this volume will be a useful tool in bringing together young readers and quality books.

John T. Gillespie
Corinne J. Naden

 # Introduction

John Newbery—The Man and the Medal

Before John Newbery and other contemporary bookmakers began publishing children's books that would delight as well as inform, the few books written specially for children were pedantic, gloomy, and often frightening in their descriptions of death and the wages of sin. They were religious in nature and warned incessantly and unrelentingly of hellfire and damnation without revealing any hint of the joy and adventure of childhood. Their main purpose was to produce obedient, God-fearing youngsters who were prepared, by living lives of saintliness and goodness, to go to heaven in the afterlife.

One work that was extremely popular for many years was *A Token for Children* (1671–1672) by James Janeway. The nature of its contents are apparent in its subtitle, "being an exact Account of the conversion, holy and exemplary Lives and joyful Deaths of several young children." Another example was Isaac Watts's *Divine Songs Attempted in Easy Language for the Use of Children* (1715), which, in one of its most familiar poems, admonishes children to follow the example of the busy bee, "For Satan finds some Mischief still: For idle Hands to do."

One source of inexpensive reading material for the common reader was the chapbook—cheap, poorly made books and pamphlets, sold usually for a penny by traveling salesmen called chapmen. These slim volumes, usually 16 to 64 pages in length, offered access to bowdlerized versions of folk and fairy tales and other imaginative literature. Some popular subjects were retold Bible stories, along with simplified versions of old romances about folk heroes such as Robin Hood, Dick Whittington, and St. George. Many of the stories from the *Arabian Nights*, in addition to fairy tales (particularly those of Charles Perrault, such as *Little Red Riding Hood*, *Bluebeard*, and *Cinderella*), also became standard fare. One characteristic of the chapbook was the frequent use of illustration, usually badly carved woodcuts that were recycled for economy's sake into different books, regardless of the appropriateness of the pictures to the subject matter. Although these chapbooks were intended for a mass adult reading audience, children found this often-forbidden reading material attractive and appealing.

Two adventure stories, Daniel Defoe's *Robinson Crusoe* (1719) and Johnathan Swift's *Gulliver's Travels* (1726), the latter intended originally as a social satire, were also taken over by this mass market. They then appeared in distorted, adulterated versions available from these enterprising peddlers who not only frequented country fairs and other public gathering places but also were the forerunners to the modern door-to-door salesmen.

Whenever chapbooks were available, children delighted in these stories of imagination and adventure even though they were not the intended audience. As Darton states in his pioneer history of children's literature, "Before 1744, children with imaginative minds still had to steal in order to satisfy their free desires. Nothing cheerfully original was offered to them, nor were there facilities for them to look for it."[1]

The year 1744 was chosen by Darton because in that year John Newbery published his first book for the amusement of children, *A Little Pretty Pocket-Book*. Although Newbery was not the only pioneer to publish children's books, he was best known because of the diversity of his products as well as their quantity and quality. Because early children's books were ill-made and cheaply produced, many titles have disappeared entirely, although we do have records that, as early as 1740 (four years before *Pocket-Book*), Thomas Boreman, a London publisher, issued the first of a 10-volume set of miniature books for children, *Gigantick Histories*. The first is an imaginative story of two giants, Gog and Magog, whose statues stood in Guildhall. Newbery, however, retains the title of the first British publisher of children's books, not only because he established this form of publishing as a serious business venture, but also because of the superiority of his books and his influence on later publishers.

John Newbery was born in 1713, the son of a modest farmer, at Waltham Saint Lawrence (his grave can be visited in the churchyard there), a remote village in Berkshire County, England. Largely self-educated, Newbery left the farm when he was about 16 and became the assistant of William Carnan, a printer in Reading, England. After Carnan's death in 1737, Newbery married the printer's widow and later became a partner in the business, publishing some of his own books. Late in 1743 or early 1744, he and his family moved to London and soon set up shop at the sign of the "Bible and Sun," 65 St. Paul's Churchyard. In addition to newspapers and adult titles, he began issuing volumes in his *Juvenile Library*, a series of tiny books attractively bound with colored paper over boards. Newbery became well known in the London literary establishment and numbered as his friends such luminaries as Samuel Johnson and Oliver Goldsmith, for whom he also frequently acted as beneficiary during lean times. Goldsmith has been rumored to be the author of *Little Goody Two-Shoes* (1765), although this has never been proven. In his *The Vicar of Wakefield* (published by Newbery's nephew Francis), Goldsmith furnishes us with a thinly disguised portrait of Newbery when the Vicar, Mr. Primrose, receives a visit from "the philanthropic bookseller on St. Paul's Churchyard, who has written so many little books for children: he called himself their friend, but was the friend of all mankind." Samuel Johnson calls him "Jack Whirler" in a portrait written for *The Idler*. He refers to Newbery's active and preoccupied nature when he says, "When he enters a house, his first declaration is that he cannot sit down, and so short are his visits that he seldom appears to have come for any other reason but to say he must go."

Newbery was probably as successful a purveyor of patent medicines as he was a printer. In fact, after his death his son spent most of his time in the medicine business and left the publishing to his stepbrother. One of their most successful products was Dr. James's Fever Powder, advertized as a cure for numerous and varied ailments. Newbery was not above unashamedly advertising these wares in his publications. For example, in *Little Goody Two-Shoes*, one of Newbery's last books for children, the father of the heroine "was forced from his family and seized with a violent Fever in a place where Doctor James's Powder was not to be had and where he died miserably."

During his lifetime, Newbery probably published 20 to 30 books for children, many of which he wrote himself, although credit to specific authors is never given. The first, *A Little Pretty Pocket-Book*, was published at 6 pence, and for 2 pence more one received either a pincushion for girls or a small ball for boys. These toys were half red and half black. For each good deed, a pin was to be placed on one side, and for a bad one, in the other. Thus the book lived up to its blurb that stated, it "will infallibly make Tommy a good Boy and Polly a good Girl." The contents included letters from Jack the Giant-Killer (one for boys, another for girls), a songbook using each letter of the alphabet, poems for each of the seasons, and "Select Proverbs for the Use of Children."

This book was followed by many additional titles including *The Lilliputian Magazine*. Although it was small—truly Lilliputian in size—the term *magazine* was a misnomer because it appeared in 1751 in a single volume without further installments. Its full title was *The Lilliputian Magazine, or the Young Gentleman's and Lady's Golden Library, being an Attempt to Mend the World, to render the society of Man More Amiable and to Establish the Plainness, Simplicity, Virtue and Wisdom of the Golden Age*. Actually, the contents consisted of a delightful collection of stories, riddles, jokes, and games.

Other books by Newbery introduced children to Nurse Truelove; Wogog the giant; Tommy Trip and his dog, Jouler; Abraham Aesop and his fables; Zig Zag, who could communicate with birds and animals; Tom Telescope, a budding scientist; and Giles Gingerbread, who learned his alphabet by eating each day a gingerbread cake with letters stamped on it.

Newbery's most enduring and endearing character appeared in *The History of Little Goody Two-Shoes; Otherwise Called Mrs. Margery Two-Shoes* (1765). On the title page is the observation, "See the Original Manuscript in the Vatican at Rome, and the Cuts By Michael Angelo." The story tells how, after his landlord dies, Farmer Meanwell, his wife, and his daughter Margery and son Tommy are forced off their land by cruel Sir Timothy Gripe and his lessee, Farmer Graspall. The parents also die, and both children are left alone. "They were both very ragged, and Tommy had two shoes, but Margery had but one. They had nothing, poor things, to support them (not being in their own parish) but what they picked from the hedges, or got from the poor people." Eventually, through the kindness of others, Tommy is sent to seek his fortune at sea, and Margery, after learning the alphabet from other children, sets herself up as a tutor and later becomes a principal in a dame school. She has further adventures, including being accused of witchcraft and trying in various ways to prevent cruelty to animals. She becomes betrothed to a wealthy squire. At her wedding, a stranger appears. It is Tommy, who has prospered overseas. After several years of happy married life, Margery's husband dies. She continues her good works, even giving charity to Timothy Gripe and Graspall when they suffer financial setbacks.

The novel was a great success and went through many editions under the imprint of John Newbery's successors. Although he died in 1767, Newbery's legacy lived on. Under various names and changes of ownership, his publishing firm lasted into the twentieth century (as did Dr. James's Fever Powder). His most important legacy, however, is the concept that children need and deserve imaginative, pleasurable, and attractive books to read, and that publishers have an obligation to produce them. It is therefore understandable that Frederic Melcher used the name of John Newbery to adorn a medal dedicated to excellence in children's literature.

Frederic Gershon Melcher (1879–1963) was a distinguished American bookman who, during his life, served as coeditor of *Publishers Weekly* for 40 years and was chairman of the board of directors of the R. R. Bowker publishing company, which also issued *Library Journal,* and later, *School Library Journal.* His abiding interest in literature for children was shown in many ways, including organizing a committee in 1917 when he was the chairman of the American Booksellers Association, which resulted in the establishment of Children's Book Week. During the American Library Association 1921 convention in Swampscott, Massachusetts, Melcher spoke to the Children's Librarians' Section and proposed that an annual medal be awarded for the most distinguished contribution to American literature for children. He proposed that it be named after John Newbery, who, in his words, was "the first bookseller who saw the possibilities in publishing books particularly for children." He insisted, "The machinery for making the awards, the methods of announcing them and of honoring the winners was to be wholly in the hands of the children's section of the ALA." He also generously offered to contribute a bronze medal to the winner. The proposal was approved and the incoming executive empowered to carry it out.

For the first award, nominations were asked from the membership. A total of 212 votes were cast, 163 for Henrik Van Loon's *The Story of Mankind*, with Charles Hawes's *The Great Quest* coming in second with 22 votes. The final decisions were made by officers and four prominent children's librarians. In addition to the winner, five other titles were chosen as "runners-up," a designation changed to "Honor Books" in 1971.

The Newbery Medal was designed by René Paul Chambellan, a young but prominent sculptor, who later also designed the Caldecott Medal. In the center of the face of the Newbery Medal, there is an open book on which are the words "For the Most Distinguished Contribution to American Literature for Children." Around the rim are the words "John Newbery Medal" and "Awarded annually by the Children's Librarians' Section of the American Library Association" (although the name of the section has changed through the years, the inscription has not). On the reverse side, enclosed in a wreath, are the figures of a man standing (representing the author), and a girl sitting on his right and a boy on his left, both with arms outstretched signifying their desire to receive the author's gifts. In 1956, it was decided that gold-colored facsimile seals of the medal could be placed on medal winners, and in 1971, silver seals were made available for Honor Books.

The first award was presented at the Detroit conference of ALA in 1922. At that time, Mr. Melcher expanded on what he saw as the purpose of the award. He said it was "to encourage original and creative work in the field of books for children. To emphasize to the public that contributions to the literature for children deserve recognition as do poetry, plays or novels. To give to those librarians who make it their life to serve children's reading interests, an opportunity to encourage good writing in the field."

It was soon found that using the popular vote was both an ungainly and inaccurate method of establishing winners, and after three years, it was decided to use a committee for this purpose. After the Caldecott Medal was established in 1937, this committee selected the medal winners and Honor Books for both awards, but this, too, proved ungainly and unsatisfactory. Since 1979, after the 1980 winners were chosen, separate committees have been used for deciding each award.

Throughout the years the composition of this committee has changed. Currently, the Newbery Award Committee consists of 15 members that are chosen or elected annually. Of these, 8 are elected by the membership of the Association for Library Service to Children: 7 from a slate of at least 14 candidates, and a chair from a slate of at least 2 candidates. The remaining 7 members are chosen by the vice president (president elect) to achieve balance and diversity on the committee. Nominees must be able to attend both the midwinter and annual summer conferences of ALA and have access to newly published children's books.

During the year, the committee members read and evaluate new books and suggest possible winners to the chair. This information is shared with other members by sending out lists of recommended books. At the ALA midwinter conference, in January or February, the formal procedures of voting take place. After generally discussing the strong contenders, a vote is taken with each committee member listing three books in order of preference. Using a rating scale of four points for a first choice, three points for a second, and two for third, the votes are tallied. At least eight first-place rankings are necessary as well as an eight-point or more lead over the book that has the next highest number of points. If there is no clear winner, further discussions and balloting resume until a winner is chosen. At this point the committee decides if there will be Honor Books, and if so, the number and the titles.

For the first 27 years of the award, the results of the voting were kept secret until the formal announcement at the summer ALA conference. Because secrecy was difficult to maintain over such a long period of time, announcements are now made at a press conference during the midwinter meeting. However, one of the highlights of the large summer ALA conference is the awards banquet at which the medals are formally presented and the author delivers the much-anticipated acceptance speech.

The terms, definitions, and criteria involved in the Newbery Award have also been codified through the years. The following statements are excerpted from a statement adopted by the Association for Library Service to Children in January 1978 and revised in January 1987:

> The Medal shall be awarded annually to the author of the most distinguished contribution to American literature for children published in the United States during the preceding year. There are no limitations as to the character of the book considered except that it be original work. . . . The Award is restricted to artists who are citizens or residents of the United States. Books in all forms of writing (e.g., fiction, poetry, nonfiction) are eligible, but books originally published in another country are not.

In amplifying these statements, the phrase "contribution to American literature for children" refers to "a book for which children are the potential audience. . . . Children are defined as persons of ages up to and including fourteen."

The term *distinguished* is defined as "marked by eminence and distinction; noted for significant achievement; marked by excellence in quality; marked by conspicuous excellence or eminence; and individually distinct."

Under the term *criteria*, committee members are asked to consider:

Interpretation of the theme or concept

Presentation of information, including accuracy, clarity, and organization

Development of plot

Delineation of characters

Delineation of setting

Appropriateness of style

Following these general criteria, there is an amplification that states: "The committee need not expect to find excellence in each of the named elements. The book should, however, have distinguished qualities in all of the elements pertinent to it." A "Note" following the basic criteria also states, "The committee should keep in mind that the award is for literary quality and quality of presentation to children. The award is not for didactic intent or for popularity."

A review of the literature shows that during its history, the award has not only garnered praise but also its share of criticism. Some think that the medal winners are too conservative in style and content and would like to see greater divisity and innovation. Others maintain that there is an amazing degree of similarity in the content and themes of the winners—so much so that it is possible to create a profile of the typical Newbery Medal winner. Presenting this point of view, Martha Parravano wrote in the July/August 1999, issue of *Horn Book* (see Bibliography) of the characteristics that would be present in the "quintessential Newbery book." In summary, the book is a work of fiction that has as its central character an older but preadolescent child. This hero (the central character is usually a boy) faces a series of problems and hurdles that are caused by both internal and external conflicts; however, during the process of overcoming these obstacles, he gains greater self-knowledge and maturity. Ironically (and prophetically), the next year's (2000) winner (*Bud, Not Buddy*), contained all these characteristics.

In spite of these caveats, for more than 75 years, librarians, educators, parents, and children have given thanks to the many dedicated individuals who have contributed to making this award so important and significant. Through their efforts, adults and children have been made aware of books of lasting value and importance, and their authors have been suitably rewarded.

Notes

1. Books about John Newbery and the Newbery Medal, including Harvey Darton's *Children's Books in England*, 3d ed. (Cambridge 1982) are found in the Bibliography.

1920s

Van Loon, Hendrik Willem. *The Story of Mankind*. Illustrated by the author. Boni and Liveright, 1921, o.p.; new ed., 1985, $32.95: 0-87140-171-1; pap., $13.95: 0-87140-156-8. (Grades 7–12)

The winner of the first Newbery Award, Hendrik Willem Van Loon (1892–1944), was born in Rotterdam, Holland, and came to the United States in 1903, where he studied at Harvard and Cornell. An accomplished writer and artist, he wrote many distinguished biographies for adults, including those of Rembrandt and Johann Sebastian Bach. For young people, he produced a series called *Books for Instruction*, which included *The Story of the Bible* (1926), *The Story of America* (1927), and *The Story of Mankind*. At the time of publication, noted children's literature critic Anne Carroll Moore called this prizewinner "the most influential children's book for many years . . . a book that bids to revolutionize the writing and illustrating of history and biography." As predicted, its influence on the writing of informational books for children has been enormous with many authors inspired by Van Loon's taste, comprehensiveness, humor, and depth. Overcome with the praise showered on him, Van Loon wrote, "I humbly wonder that I even wrote it for it was a fiendish job, and now that people are saying good things about it, I wonder whether it can be all true?"

Plot Summary

In his foreword to his award-winning nonfiction work, Hendrik Willem Van Loon expands on his notion that "History is the mighty Tower of Experience, which Time has built amidst the endless fields of bygone ages. It is no easy task to reach the top of this ancient structure and get the benefit of the full view. There is no elevator, but young feet are strong and it can be done. . . . Here I give you the key that will open the door. . . . When you return, you too will understand the reason for my enthusiasm."

From this beginning, Van Loon, a well-known writer and lecturer, traces the steps of human development from prehistoric days to the more modern concerns of the space age in the later years of the twentieth century. Acclaimed as a revolutionary approach to the subject at the time of its publication, *The Story of Mankind* brims with the enthusiasm of its author. Such enthusiasm involved in storytelling delights and excites both the author and the reader.

The latest edition contains 75 chapters. It begins by setting the stage, which discusses what we do and do not know about the beginnings of humankind. From the half-ape, half-monkey creature that evolved during that long period came a rather unattractive mammal that Van Loon describes as the great-great-grandfather of the human race. Slowly, ever so slowly, thousands and thousands of years passed. Human ancestors progressed and grew, learned to make fire, and learned to survive.

From these slow beginnings, Van Loon delves into the complicated and progressive civilization of the Egyptians and how a French general, in 1798, quite by accident solved the problem of the ancient Egyptian picture language known as hieroglyphics, which means "sacred writing." From the fascinating story of the rise and fall of Egypt and the building of the pyramids, the reader is taken to the second center of Eastern civilization, Mesopotamia, the country between the two rivers—the Euphrates and the Tigris. From there we travel to the Sumerians, whose clay tablets recount the tale of the great Semitic melting pot.

Through the story of Moses, the Phoenicians, the Indo-Europeans, and finally to the land of Greek civilization, the journey continues. There we tarry awhile as Van Loon explains the intricacies of Greek self-government, whose laws still affect humankind today. From Greece, we travel to the glories and the spectacle of Rome and Carthage and the awesome story of the all-powerful Roman Empire.

In telling the story of Rome, Van Loon explains how it became the center of the Christian Church and goes on to other religions, such as Islam. Mohammed, who became the prophet of millions of followers of Islam, nearly conquered the entire known world for the greater glory of Allah, the one true god.

From there, history follows Charlemagne, king of the Franks, who would become Holy Roman Emperor and nearly brought back the ideal of a world empire. Then came long periods of religious wars, the Crusades, and finally the Middle Ages, an era of pioneering settlement and the growth of the medieval city.

From this long, often dark period emerged the Renaissance, when once more people dared to be happy and speak of a rebirth of civilization. Manuscripts and art flourished, preserved through all the centuries for the enjoyment of modern civilization.

Then in the fifteenth century, humans began to explore in great numbers, traveling the globe to push knowledge to its limits. The so-called New World came to the attention of the old, and gigantic migrations began that changed the face and history of the earth. With these new explorations, ancient worlds were revealed, such as the civilizations of China. The mysterious vast lands of Russia emerged as a force.

In the eighteenth century, Europeans began to hear of a revolution across the waters, ending in the birth of a new nation that was destined to become a world leader in a very short time. Inventions and discoveries linked the world through communications and made it ever smaller and smaller. The age of science was ushered in, with great benefits for all humankind. Unfortunately, science also aided the extent of destruction that could be unleashed when humans disagreed. Colonial expansion, bitter wars, exploitation, and an explosion of killing and inhumanity culminated in World Wars I and II. Beginning with the rise of the Nazis in Germany and ending with the terrifying destruction of the atom bomb, the peace built on medieval foundations came crashing down around the world and changed it forever.

From the ashes of World War II, the countries of the world entered a new phase of wariness and distrust. Having the power to annihilate everything and everyone, they lived in mistrust, worry, and doubt. In an effort to end this uncertain period, world leaders formed an organization known as the United Nations, which sadly has never quite lived up to the hopes for an end of world destruction and a path of world peace.

The story of humankind continues, now reaching into space, still exploring, still filled with the same curiosity and spirit of adventure that our ancestors must have felt long ago when they emerged from the terrifying mist of a newly forming world. But for Van Loon, as fascinating as are human adventures in space, more fascinating still is our earthly home, where all astronauts and all adventurers must return. Science and technology have made the planet a shrinking world, but Van Loon feels that humankind has the capacity to work together to avert disaster for the common good. He believes humankind will prevail.

Themes and Subjects

This nonfiction history of the growth of civilization reads more like a story than a history. It is filled with the excitement of a storyteller as he unravels the mysteries of how civilizations grew and died and led to discovery and adventure. He traces the important steps that culminated in the development of different countries and world order. It is a work of nonfiction and a book of information that is fun to read.

Incidents for Booktalking

Depending on the era under discussion, any chapter in the *The Story of Mankind* will serve as an exciting, informative introduction to history. See, for example, the story of Moses, leader of the Jewish people (pp. 38–41); the conflict of Rome and Carthage (pp. 88–104); Charlemagne's story (pp. 144–49); the teachings of Buddha and Confucius (pp. 241–50); revolution in America (pp. 328–33) and in France (pp. 334–48); global war (pp. 514–23); into space (pp. 554–59).

Related Titles

Kate Morgan's *The Story of Things* (Walker 1991, $15.95: 0-8027-6919-5) is a slim volume that outlines a history of civilization.

More Plants That Changed the World (Atheneum 1985, $13.95: 0-689-31099-4) by Joan E. Rahn tells how plants and their products such as papyrus, rubber, tea, and opium have affected the world's culture.

The important events of the twentieth century are covered in double-page spreads and a month-by-month arrangement in Simon Adams's *Junior Chronicle of the 20th Century* (DK 1997, $39.95: 0-7894-2033-3).

The basic history of the world from the big bang theory to the present is given in the lavishly illustrated *In the Beginning: The Nearly Complete History of Almost Everything* (DK 1995, $19.95: 0-7894-0206-8).

Carol Gelber's *Masks Tell Stories* (Milbrook 1993, $23.90: 1-56294-224-7) explores the meaning and uses of masks in various cultures.

About the Book and Author

Commire, Anne, ed. *Something About the Author.* Vol. 18. Gale, 1980, pp. 284–92.

Brown, Muriel W., and Rita Schoch Foudray. *Newbery and Caldecott Medalists and Honor Book Winners: Bibliography & Resource Material Through 1990.* 2d ed. Neal-Schuman, 1992, pp. 422–25.

Kunitz, Stanley J., and Howard Haycraft, eds. *Twentieth-Century Authors.* Wilson, 1942, pp. 1447–48.

May, Hal, ed. *Contemporary Authors.* Vol. 117. Gale, 1986, p. 453.

Miller, Bertha M., and Elinor Field, eds. *Newbery Medal Books: 1922–1955 with the Author's Acceptance Papers and Related Material.* Horn Book, 1955, pp. 10–16.

Peterson, Linda K., and Marilyn L. Solt, eds. *Newbery and Caldecott Medal and Honor Books: 1922–1981.* Hall, 1982, pp. 13–14.

Silvey, Anita, ed. *Children's Books and Their Creators.* Houghton, 1995, p. 663.

Van Loon, Gerard Willem. *Story of Hendrik Willem Van Loon.* Lippincott, 1972.

Honor Books 1922

Bowen, William. *The Old Tobacco Shop: A True Account of What Befell a Little Boy in Search of Adventure.* Illustrated by Reginald Birch. Macmillan, 1921, o.p. (Grades 4–7)

This fantasy-adventure, set in the late nineteenth century, starts and ends in a river town in the eastern United States with many fantastic stops in between. Freddie, a small boy, is sent to buy tobacco at the shop of hunchback Toby Littleback. There he meets Littleback's spinster aunt, Amanda, and encounters the store's guardian, a life-size wooden statue of Mr. Punch, Littleback's look-alike. Soon Toby, Amanda, and Freddie become fast friends and Toby goes to a play that depicts the frightening adventures of the mute local churchwarden. One day Freddie secretly disobeys Toby's instructions not to smoke a special magic tobacco and finds that he and his friends, including Mr. Hanlon, are suddenly transported to a leaky ship, the *Sieve.* They embark on a incredible voyage to Correction Island on the Spanish Main and are captured by pirates, who imprison them, first in the Low Dungeon and later in the more terrifying High Dungeon. When the churchwarden persuades the pirates to breathe in his Odour of Sanctity, they melt, and Freddie and friends escape with their treasure. In the City of Towers, they buy magical hourglasses from Shiraz, the Persian rug merchant. Shiraz turns each into what he or she most wants to be: both Toby and Mr. Punch lose their hunchbacks; Amanda becomes a beautiful queen with three children; Churchwarden takes on the appearance of a saintly person; Mr. Hanlon is turned into a tall, handsome man; and Freddie becomes an adult. Later they meet the Old Man of the Mountain who releases them from Shiraz's enchantment so they can face reality again. Freddie falls ill and sinks into a coma. When he awakens he is back home in bed. The trip had been a tobacco-induced dream. Back with his friends, Freddie hears Amanda say, "There's no place like the Old Tobacco Shop. . . . I wouldn't exchange it for a palace if you'd give it to me."

Colum, Padraic. *The Golden Fleece: And the Heroes Who Lived Before Achilles.* Illustrated by Willy Pogany. Macmillan, 1983, $17.00: 0-02-723620-X. (Grades 4–8)

This masterful retelling of the most important early Greek myths (excluding those told by Homer) is the work of the great Irish folklorist and poet, Padraic Colum. It begins with Jason's youth, and how his father Aeson places the boy in the care of the centaur Chiron to escape the wrath of Aeson's wicked brother, King Pelias of Iolcus. As a man, Jason receives a promise from Pelias that he will be made king if he is able to journey to Colchis and bring back the Golden Fleece that King Aeates guards. A mighty ship is built named the *Argo* after its builder Argus. Jason takes as his crew, known as the Argonauts, the strongest men in Greece, including Orpheus, Hercules, and Theseus. During the voyage, they amuse themselves by retelling such ancient myths as the stories of the world's creation; of Demeter, her daughter Persephone, and the creation of the seasons; and of the Golden Maid, Pandora, and the box she owned, which contained all the evils imaginable. After many adventures, Jason is able to obtain the Golden Fleece, chiefly through the help of the princess Medea, who betrays her father King Aeates, and is responsible for the death of her brother, all for her love of Jason. The further adventures of many of the Argonauts (Orpheus and Euridice, Theseus and the Minotaur, and the labors of Hercules) are retold as well as the story of Jason's desertion of Medea because of his love for Glauce, and of Medea's rage that brought death to the maiden, leaving Jason to reign alone in Iolcus, the city where for years young men came to view and wonder at the Golden Fleece.

Hawes, Charles Boardman. *The Great Quest.* Illustrated by George Varian. Little, Brown, 1921, o.p. (Grades 7–9)

For 20-year-old Josiah (Joe) Woods, the quiet summer of 1826 in the town of Topham, Massachusetts, changes suddenly when suave, arrogant Cornelius Gleason comes to town. Joe, an orphan, works for his prosperous Uncle Seth Upham, along with Sim Muzzy and a Frenchman, Arnold Lamont, in Seth's general store. Gradually Cornelius (Neil), who is returning to Topham, supposedly wealthy, after being forced to leave years ago because of his wild behavior, gains such power over Seth that the shop owner sells all his property to buy a brig called the *Adventure.* Neil sets out on a crazy scheme to gain a fortune on a mysterious quest that will take them first to Cuba and then to the coast of Africa. Joe, Sim, and Arnold have no choice but to join in the venture. Soon, however, Neil's true villainy is revealed, but Seth seems powerless to withstand him and the dangerous crewmen that are Neil's followers. In Havana, Arnold and Joe narrowly escape a plot to kidnap them for a press gang (Sim is not so fortunate). They now are wary of Neil's every move. At the mouth of a river in central Guinea, a small band including Joe, Neil, Arnold, Seth, and some of Neil's henchmen leave the ship and safari to a jungle hut where the object of Neil's quest, a cache of jewels, is hidden. A tribe of hostile natives lays siege to the hut. Under this mental pressure of confinement, Seth goes berserk and is killed by the natives. Through the help of Faith Parmenter, whose missionary father was also killed in the uprising, Joe, Neil,

Faith, and the rest get back to the ship, where they hastily set sail. Neil wants to convert the *Adventure* into a slaver, but Joe, through a duel, asserts himself as rightful owner. Joe and Faith find that they are attracted to each other, but tragedy again strikes. Off the coast of South America, the ship is wrecked and Neil drowns. Arnold, who reveals he has hidden resources, gives the newly married Joe and Faith money to return to Topham, where Joe discovers that Seth had secreted enough money to enable him to buy back the general store and start a new life with his bride.

Marshall, Bernard, G. *Cedric the Forester*. Appleton, 1921, o.p. (Grades 7–9)

Set in England during the reigns of Plantagenet kings Henry II, Richard II, and John, this swashbuckling, rousing adventure of sieges, warfare, and derring-do, contains more than its share of dated expressions, such as "gadzooks," "forsooth," and "methinks." Through his adroit use of the crossbow, 16-year-old Cedric, the son of a peasant forester, saves the life of Richard, nicknamed Dichon, son of Lord Mountjoy, when the young man's life is threatened by the Mountjoy's neighboring enemy, Lionel of Carleton. In gratitude, Lord Mountjoy makes Cedric Dichon's squire, and accepts him as part of the family. While at the manor, Cedric improves his martial skills and is taught reading and writing by Lady Katherine. The two young men share many adventures. Together they rescue Geoffrey of Carleton and his mother Lady Elizabeth from outlaws, ending the long feud between their families. Cedric continues to show endurance, courage, and phenomenal abilities as a strategist, fighting both in Scotland and Wales. In one foray, a castle is besieged and relief secured through the use of a secret tunnel. As reward for his part in the Battle of the Eagles in Wales, Cedric becomes Sir Cedric and is given the manor of Grimsby, the land of a knight killed in battle. Later in life, the two friends are reunited to help draft the Magna Carta, a document designed to curb the powers of King John. To gain necessary support for the inclusion of articles that would guarantee the right of the common people, Cedric and his friends disguise themselves as palmers and kidnap an abbot. Satisfied that his wishes have been met, the gallant Cedric together with the other nobles compel the king to sign the document at Runnymede.

Meigs, Cornelia. *The Windy Hill*. Macmillan, 1921, o.p. (Grades 5–7)

Fifteen-year-old Oliver Peyton and his 13-year-old sister, Janet, are spending a summer with their usually affable cousin, Jasper, at his estate in Medford Valley near the New England coast. Instead of the quick, mild-mannered Jasper they knew in the past, they find that he has become irritable, impatient, and preoccupied. Upset with these developments and Jasper's plan to introduce him to Eleanor Brighton, another relative, whom the boy imagines to be horrid, Oliver and Janet decide to return home. In their wanderings, they happen on a cottage inhabited by a kindly, wise beekeeper and his daughter Polly, who is about Oliver's age. Both Oliver and Janet become friends with the beekeeper and his charming daughter. They also meet an unpleasant neighbor, Anthony Crawford, a hard-eyed man whom they later realize is responsible for Jasper's problems. Anthony, it appears, is another of their cousins. Through underhanded methods, he has already seized part of Jasper's lands and is now demanding more. A storm causes severe flooding in the valley, and because of Anthony's neglect, water breaks through the dike on his property and threatens the entire valley. That night Oliver also learns that the beekeeper is actually another of Jasper's cousins, Tom Brighton, and Polly is the Eleanor he dreaded to meet. All three of the cousins, the young people, and the men of the neighborhood work all night and successfully battle the flood. When Oliver points out how evil and unjust his actions are, Anthony is so overcome with remorse and guilt that he leaves the valley the next morning with his family. Uncle Jasper is now free of worry and, once again, can relax and enjoy the company of Oliver and Janet.

Newbery Winner 1923

Lofting, Hugh. *The Voyages of Doctor Dolittle*. Illustrated by the author. Frederick A. Stokes, 1922: o.p; Delacorte, 1988, $15.95: 0-385-29663-0; pap., Dell, $3.99: 0-440-41240-4. (Grades 3–6)

Hugh Lofting (1886–1947), the author of 12 books about Dr. Dolittle, was born in England; he came to the United States in 1912. While serving in the trenches during World War I, he invented Dr. Dolittle to amuse his two children, Elizabeth and Colin, in the letters he wrote home. Impressed with the role that animals played in the war, he felt they required the same attention when wounded as humans. As he states, this inspired him to imagine an "eccentric, country physician with . . . a great love of pets who decides to give up his human practice for the more difficult, sincere, and attractive therapy of the animal kingdom." The doctor first appeared in book form in 1920 in *The Story of Doctor Dolittle*. In appreciation of Lofting's work, Henle Dean Fish states, "Doctor Dolittle is a good man for children to know because he stands for kindliness, patience, and reliability, mixed with delightful humor, energy, and gaiety." Lofting believed that any notable book for children is also enjoyable for grown-ups to read. This is certainly true of the delightful Dolittle stories.

Plot Summary

In this second series of fantasies, Tommy Stubbins of Puddle-by-on-the-Marsh, England, introduces the novel by telling of how he came to meet Doctor John Dolittle, the remarkable physician who can talk to animals. It is 1839, some five years after the doctor has made many voyages and has become a famous, although not rich, naturalist.

Tommy is the nine-and-a-half-year-old son of the village cobbler, Jacob. The boy is distressed one morning to find a squirrel with a broken leg. He is advised by his friend the mussel-man to find Doctor Dolittle, a "naturalist," who will attend to the little creature. Tommy takes the squirrel in search of the good doctor and finds him quite by accident. He bumps into him in the rain. Dr. Dolittle is a round little man wearing a shabby high hat and a kind face. They go to the doctor's friendly but rather strange home to dry off and tend to the squirrel. Tommy is fascinated at once, especially when he enters the doctor's home to see a spotless white duck hopping down the stairs and carrying a lighted candle in her right foot. Her name is Dab-Dab.

From this auspicious beginning, Tommy becomes an assistant to the friendly, eccentric doctor and enters his household of animals. Probably the most fascinating is Polynesia, the 200-year-old West African parrot that the doctor left behind when he returned to England, thinking that the bird would be homesick away from her native land. Not so, for Polynesia finds her way to England and the doctor is overjoyed.

Polynesia teaches Tommy the language of the animals. He is also present when Luke the Hermit is accused of murder. Tommy actually becomes a very important part of the trial, for there is no "human" eyewitness and things look very bad for Luke. However, there *is* a witness to the crime. It is Luke's bulldog, Bob. Because Tommy is able to translate Bob's language and give an explanation of what took place, the wrongful charges against Luke are dropped. When it is time for Doctor Dolittle to plan another voyage, Tommy becomes part of the crew, which also includes Polynesia, Chee-Chee the monkey, and Jip the dog. Before they leave, however, they are joined by the crown prince of Jolliginki, Bumpo Kahbooboo, who is now studying at Oxford University. Bumpo needs a rest from his studies and decides to go with them. Next, they discover three stowaways, who by that time are quite willing to be put ashore. They are Matthew Mugg, the now freed Luke, and his wife. Another stowaway, seaman Ben Butcher, is also discovered and, on Polynesia's advice, locked up until they reach land.

Their destination is Spidermonkey Island, a floating island off the coast of South America, where they hope to find Long Arrow, the world's other great naturalist, who has disappeared. On the way, they stop for supplies at Monteverde. But they have no money because the doctor has given what he had to Luke. Dr. Dolittle bets the bullfight promoter that if he wins in the bullring, all bullfights will be banished. He gets into the ring with five bulls at once. Because the good doctor has already talked to the bulls and they have agreed to cooperate, he wins the fight and bullfighting is forever banished. Meantime, Bumpo has placed some side bets on Dr. Dolittle so they can get supplies.

At sea once more, they catch a Silver Fidget, a fish that speaks some English. He tells the good doctor to find the Great Glass Sea Snail, who will aid him in speaking the language of shellfish, which Dolittle much wishes to do. But their ship runs into a storm and is wrecked. However, friendly dolphins push the remains to Spidermonkey Island.

With the help of a Jabizri beetle, Dr. Dolittle and his companions find the cave where Long Arrow and his companions are trapped. They release them and go to the Popsipetel Indian village, where they discover that the people have never seen fire and are suffering because of it. The doctor introduces fire to the village. When the people explain that they are also suffering because their island is floating south to the cold Antarctic, Dolittle calls some whales to push the island back into the tropics.

Although Dr. Dolittle is a peace-loving man, he leads the fight when the Bagjagderags, from the other side of the island, attack. Polynesia aids in their victory by calling in millions of Black Parrots, which give nasty bites to the enemy. Impressed with this show, the enemy gives up and joins forces with Long Arrow's people. They all insist that Dr. Dolittle be made king. Against his wishes, he is coronated King Jong Thinkalot. The shouts and cheers of the people are so loud during the coronation that a great stone on the edge of a volcano becomes loose and crashes right into the hollow center of the island, causing it to sink somewhat. The water does not cover the island, though, which is quite fortunate.

In all the confusion, however, Dr. Dolittle discovers what he has been searching for—the Great Glass Sea Snail. However, it begins to look as though Dolittle is destined to spend the rest of his life on the island, so beloved is he by his new subjects. Once again, Polynesia comes to the rescue. At her suggestion, the Great Glass Sea Snail offers to carry all of them back to England.

It is a fascinating trip indeed as they are transported by the snail, which is 70,000 years old. On the way, Dr. Dolittle has a fine time studying the bottom of the ocean. As Tommy explains, "It was a thrilling and ever-changing show."

At journey's end, the crew finds itself back in fog-shrouded, merry old England. There is some grumbling about the weather, of course, but all in all, according to Polynesia and the others, they are glad to be back to the "beastly climate." Besides, Dr. Dolittle is quite confident that when they reach his home, Dab-Dab will have a nice fire burning in the kitchen and a fine pot brewing on the stove. Fortunately, they will be just in time for four o'clock tea.

Themes and Subjects

This is fantasy filled with humor and originality, and its rather strange happenings actually follow a kind of marvelous logic. Dr. Dolittle is a genuinely lovable character, filled with goodness and kindness toward all living things, but especially to animals. The adventures are wildly imaginative. In recent years, the book has been maligned for its treatment of Bumpo. Although the author seems at first to regard this black character as an object of ridicule, principally for his many malapropisms, he is actually a figure of much affection, never treated condescendingly by Dr. Dolittle. It becomes clear throughout the novel that Bumpo is a man of intelligence and common sense and is equal in every way to the others. Terms that might be regarded as offensive today have been deleted from more recent editions.

Incidents for Booktalking

Almost every scene in this humorous fantasy is a fine introduction to the daffy, wonderful world of Dr. Dolittle. See especially: Tommy enters the doctor's house for the first time (pp. 19–23); Polynesia returns (pp. 33–40); the dog on the witness stand and the trial of Luke the Hermit (pp. 111–25); Dr. Dolittle in the bullring (pp. 184–92); the landing on Spidermonkey Island (pp. 233–38).

Related Titles

A king sends a 12-year-old messenger to poll the country about the meaning of delicious in Natalie Babbitt's *The Search for Delicious* (Farrar, 1969, $16.00: 0-374-36534-2; pap., $3.95: 0-374-46536-3).

In L. Frank Baum's classic *The Wizard of Oz* (Macmillan, 1998, $29.00: 0-8057-8623-6), Dorothy, in her dreams, leaves Kansas to visit the Emerald City. This is one of many editions available.

Marvin, a mouse, and two friends leave their home in Macy's and travel to a summer camp in Vermont in *The Great Summer Camp Catastrophe* (Dial, 1992, $13.99: 0-8037-1106-9) by Jean Van Leeuwen.

A motley gang of murderous bilge rats attacks Redwall Abbey in *Redwall* (Philomel, 1987, $21.95: 0-399021424-0) by Brian Jacques. One of a growing series.

Troubles begin for 12-year-old Ian when he sprouts wings in Bill Brittain's *Wings* (Harper, 1945, pap., $4.50: 0-06-440612-1).

About the Book and Author

Berger, Laura Standley, ed. *Twentieth-Century Children's Writers*. 4th ed. St. James, 1995, pp. 599–600.

Blishen, Edward. *Hugh Lofting*. Bodley Head, 1968.

Brown, Muriel W., and Rita Schoch Foudray. *Newbery and Caldecott Medalists and Honor Books: Bibliographic & Resource Material Through 1990*. 2d ed. Neal-Schuman, 1992, pp. 266–68.

Chevalier, Tracy, ed. *Twentieth-Century Children's Writers*. 3d ed. St. James, 1989, pp. 608–9.

Collier, Laurie, and Joyce Nakamura, eds. *Major Authors and Illustrators for Children and Young Adults*.Gale, 1993, 6 vols., pp. 1506–9.

Commire, Anne, ed. *Something About the Author*. Vol. 15. Gale, 1979, pp. 180–84.

Green, Roger. *Teller of Tales*. Watts, 1965.

Hedblad, Alan, ed. *Something About the Author*. Vol. 100. Gale, 1999, pp.160–63.

Helbig, Alethea K., and Agnes R. Perkins, eds. *Dictionary of American Children's Fiction, 1859–1959*. Greenwood, 1986, p. 308 (bio.), pp. 552–54 (book).

Kunitz, Stanley J., and Howard Haycraft, eds. *The Junior Book of Authors*. Wilson, 1951, pp. 198–200.

Mahoney, Bertha E. *Illustrators of Children's Books, 1744–1945*. Horn Book, 1947, p. 335.

Miller, Bertha M., and Elinor Field, eds. *Newbery Medal Books: 1922–1955 with the Author's Acceptance Papers and Related Material*. Horn Book, 1955, pp. 17–27.

Peterson, Linda K., and Marilyn L. Solt, eds. *Newbery and Caldecott Medal and Honor Books: 1922–1981*. Hall, 1982, pp. 15–17.

Senick, Gerard J., ed. *Children's Literature Review*. Vol. 19. Gale, 1990, pp. 202–31.

Silvey, Anita, ed. *Children's Books and Their Creator*. Houghton, 1995, pp. 415–16.

Newbery Winner 1924

Hawes, Charles B. *The Dark Frigate*. Atlantic Monthly Press, 1923, o.p. Illustrated by Warren Chapell. Little, Brown, 1971, $21.45: 0-316-35096-6. (Grades 7–10)

The untimely death of Charles B. Hawes (1889–1923) when he was only 35 robbed children's literature of an amazing talent—a writer of historical adventures that rival *Treasure Island* for re-creating the bold seafaring life of both buccaneers and honest seafaring men. Hawes was born in Clifton Springs, New York, grew up in Maine, and attended Bowdoin College. Always interested in writing, he edited two important children's magazines of the time, *Youth's Companion* and *Open Road*. His other important book for young readers, *The Mutineers* (1923, o.p.), though set in a different period, shares many plot similarities with *The Dark Frigate*. It, too, tells of a mutiny on a ship in which those in command are killed. Eventually the protagonists outwit the pirates and regain control of the ship. Denied the personal recognition he deserved, he was awarded the Newbery Award posthumously.

Plot Summary

The story takes place in seventeenth-century England during the reign of Charles I. Philip Marsham's mother died when he was just a toddler. Since that time he has been a sailor, a veteran of many voyages on the London ketch on which his father was master. He could climb the ship's rigging before he could walk. Although he was schooled in reading and writing by the good Dr. Josiah Arber, young Phil endured his lessons with ill-concealed impatience. He wished to learn mathematics only because it would aid him in navigation on the seas.

At the age of 19, Phil comes down with a fever, which prevents him from sailing with his father. On that voyage, the ketch flounders on the high seas and is lost.

Moll Stevens had been caring for young Phil during his bout with the fever. But when she learns that his father, whom Moll had expected to marry, has been lost at sea, the young man is turned out on his own. Phil leaves to wander the countryside. In doing so, he gets into a fight in an inn with a man named Barwick, who is about to punish Paul with dirty unfair tactics. But the fight is interrupted by Sir John Bristol, who asks the cause. Barwick says that Phil is a poacher. For this, Phil expects prison at the very least. However, Bristol says that no matter what the cause, a fight should be fair, and so it is, with Bristol's help. Phil leaves, thinking he has met no fairer man than Bristol, with the exception of his own father.

It seems only natural for Phil to head once again to the sea. He signs on with Captain Francis Candle for the voyage of the *Rose of Devon*. The ship is a frigate, a fine, tall vessel with carvings on bow and stern, a band of crimson down its length, and billowing sails. But the sides of the tall ship are painted black, giving it a dark, shadowy appearance.

The *Rose of Devon* is not long at sea before it hits a storm. Darkness comes and the winds and rain only increase. During the storm, Philip saves the life of fellow sailor Martin. When the storm lets up somewhat the next day, the *Rose of Devon* sights a ship in distress, and although somewhat in distress itself, goes to its aid. Instead of taking on fellow sailors, the *Rose of Devon* is captured by pirates, with the Old One, Tom Jordan, in charge.

Phil has no choice, of course, but to serve with the pirates, which he does for many months. During the journey, he has many adventures and run-ins with Jordan, whom he begrudgingly admires for his intelligence if not for his criminal ways, and there is a fight between Captain Candle and one of the pirates. The old captain is killed.

Although the voyage with the pirates seems to last forever for Phil, at last the ship reaches land and anchors at an island in the Bahamas. This is Phil's chance to escape. Sighting an English ship in the harbor, he swims out to it and is brought before the captain, an Englishman named Winterton of His Majesty's ship *Sybil*. Phil explains that he is the late boatswain of the *Rose of Devon* frigate. He tells Winterton that he himself is not a pirate, but that the ship was captured and Captain Candle was killed. He says that he has been forced to serve and asks only that he be taken back to England.

Because of Phil's warning that an attack by the pirates will occur at any time, Winterton is able to dash Jordan's plans and bring the pirates to justice in England. However, for a time it looks as though Phil himself will be caught in the pirates' web, for indeed he had served on the ship with them and was part of the crew. In the end, however, he speaks in his own defense and is further defended by the scoundrel captain of the pirates, Tom Jordan himself, who corroborates Phil's story of being forced to take part in the pirates' voyage. Although Phil is against all that the pirate captain stands for, he is forced to admire his bravery and honesty in this situation. Tom Jordan sways the verdict. The court finds 14 of the pirates guilty as charged, and one is acquitted—Philip Marsham.

Phil then parts company with these pirate men and never sees them again. He hears later that they were marched to the gallows. But he is now a free man once more on the streets of London.

First, he seeks out the man of honor that he remembers from before the voyage, Sir John Bristol. Sir John is overjoyed to see him and accepts him as a friend into his home. More good fortune soon befalls Philip Marsham, for in time he inherits a fortune left to him by his father's father, the Reverend Dr. Marsham of Little Grimsby.

But Phil's adventures are far from over, for he goes off to war with Sir John Bristol to fight for the king against Oliver Cromwell. But the king's cause is lost and Phil, who loses his own fortune, is ready to turn his back on England.

Instead, he goes again to the harbor of Bideford, where first he left on his sea adventure years before. He asks what ship he sees in the harbor and is told that it is the *Rose of Devon*. Unbelieving, Phil asks where the ship is heading and is told that the *Rose of Devon* sails for Barbados.

Philip Marsham pays for his passage with gold and sails for the second time from England in the *Rose of Devon*, the old dark frigate of his youth.

Themes and Subjects

This is an old-fashioned tale of derring-do, of buccaneers and pirate ships, and raging seas, a swashbuckling adventure in the old vein. History and a fast-paced nautical background keep the reader engrossed in this lively tale of seventeenth-century skullduggery mainly on the high seas. The seafaring way of life is depicted in vivid detail. Even the pirate captain has something to be admired in the way he stands up for Phil and tells the truth of his reluctant participation in the voyage of the *Rose of Devon*. Honor has an important place in this story, shown by Phil himself, by Sir John Bristol, and by the pirate captain.

Incidents for Booktalking

By far the most engrossing scenes in this adventure take place on the high seas. See, for example: at sea in the storm (pp. 83–87); Phil saves Martin (pp. 88–91); the taking of the ship by pirates (pp. 96–100); the death of Captain Candle (pp. 110–14); the pirate feast (pp. 121–28).

Related Titles

In Kristiana Gregory's *Orphan Runaways* (Scholastic, 1998, $15.95: 0-590-60366-3), two brothers run away from a San Francisco orphanage in 1879 to look for an uncle in the gold fields.

Leon Garfield's novel *Young Nick and Jubilee* (Delacorte, 1989, $13.95: 0-385-29777-7) is set in the eighteenth century and tells of two orphans who are duped by a pickpocket pretending to be their father.

Oliver is kidnapped by the pirate Captain Scratch in Sid Fleischman's *The Ghost in the Noonday Sun* (Greenwillow, 1989, $16.00: 0-688-08410-9).

A young runaway couple is captured by pirates and sold into slavery in Cynthia Voigt's *On Fortune's Wheel* (Macmillan, 1990, $17.00: 0-689-31636-4).

Exquemelin and the Pirates of the Caribbean by A. O. Exquemelin and edited by Jane Shuter (Raintree, 1995, $24.26: 0-8114-8282-0), first published in 1684, tells a true first-person narrative account of seventeenth-century piracy in the West Indies.

About the Book and Author

Berger, Laura Standley, ed. *Twentieth-Century Children's Writers*. 4th ed. St. James, 1995, p. 441.

Brown, Muriel W., and Rita Schoch Foudray. *Newbery and Caldecott Medalists and Honor Books Winners: Bibliographic & Resource Material Through 1990*. 2d ed. Neal-Schuman, 1992, pp. 186–87.

Chevalier, Tracy, ed. *Twentieth-Century Children's Writers*. 3d ed. St. James, 1989, pp. 435–36.

Helbig, Alethea K., and Agnes R. Perkins, eds. *Dictionary of American Children's Fiction, 1859–1959*. Greenwood, 1986, pp. 207–8 (bio.), pp. 121–22 (book).

Miller, Bertha M., and Elinor Field, eds. *Newbery Medal Books: 1922–1955 with the Author's Acceptance Papers and Related Material*. Horn Book, 1955, pp. 28–32.

Peterson, Linda K., and Marilyn L. Solt, eds. *Newbery and Caldecott Medal and Honor Books: 1922–1981*. Hall, 1982, pp. 17–18.

Ward, Martha, ed. *Authors of Books for Young People*. 3d ed. Scarecrow, 1990, p. 315.

Newbery Winner 1925

Finger, Charles. *Tales from Silver Lands*. Illustrated by Paul Honore. Doubleday, 1924, $17.00: 0-385-07513-8. (Grades 5–8)

In his late teens, Charles Finger (1869–1941) left his home in England to become a merchant seaman. He traveled to South America, where he roamed for ten years, and later went adventuring in Mexico, Canada, and prospecting in the Klondike Gold Fields of Alaska. Other pursuits involved being an editor, music director, and railroad manager. This Renaissance man eventually settled in Arkansas and began his writing career at age 50. From his travels in South America, he recalled folktales and legends, which he told to his children. Their favorites were published as *Tales from Silver Lands* and a companion volume, *Tales Worth Telling* (1927, o.p.). Both capture the atmosphere and culture of South America, while retaining the qualities of good storytelling. He wrote both fiction and nonfiction for children and adults. One of his juvenile novels is *Courageous Companions* (1929, o.p.), the story of an English boy who sailed around the world with Magellan.

Plot Summary

The 19 tales in this volume stem from the author's travels throughout South America at the beginning of the twentieth century. They are stories of fairy folk, giants, and witches; of people under the sea; and of eerie enchantments and ways to break them.

Some of the stories contain colorful descriptions of the place in which the tale was heard and sometimes of the storyteller. In all the stories, the atmosphere and the flavor of the land are well preserved.

Magic is an important feature in several of these tales. In "The Magic Knot," a lad named Borac, said by some to be the son of a king, is found in a basket at the side of a lake by a man who is gathering fruit. The man takes the baby home to join his wife and three children. Borac grows up as one of them, although his sight is better than that of his foster brother and sisters, and he seems to know things the others do not. One day when they are mountain climbing, they see an owl about to attack a dove. When Borac tries to climb the mountain to save the dove, a condor flies by and drops a white feather. Borac catches it and is able to fly and save the dove. In doing so, he finds a fine thread that contains an odd knot. All the children have fun with the magic feather. One day a little boy and then a little girl vanish in the village. Everyone is terrified. But a wise old woman gives Borac advice and he follows a great bird of evil to the hiding place where all the people who have disappeared are hidden. With his magic knot, Borac is able to bind up the evil bird forever and rescue the people. That is why today no birds in the air harm humans.

Some tales tell how things happen. In "The Humming-Bird and the Flower," the hummingbird relates how it came to have so beautiful a dress. At one time long ago, when all hummingbirds were gray, a black panther walks in the woods and steps on a nest of mice, killing the babies. Although the panther apologizes to the mother mouse, she means to get back at him. One day when the panther is asleep, the mother mouse seals his eyes with gum and mud so he cannot tell day from night. The panther is very angry and asks the hummingbird to kill the mouse, but the hummingbird will not. Then the panther asks the hummingbird to pick the gum and mud from his eyes so he can see. The hummingbird agrees if the panther will tell her where she can get a beautiful dress, for the panther travels much and knows a great deal of things. So the hummingbird picks out the gum and mud and the panther can see again. He tells the hummingbird from what flowers and other objects to choose the colors for her dress. And that is why the hummingbird looks as it does today.

In "Na-Ha the Fighter," the people in the far south near Cape Horn are at the mercy of the wild folk who live under the sea. Sometimes the Cape Horn people can live in peace, but sometimes the undersea folk rise up and drag them down beneath the waves. There is no resisting them. The people are helpless and they watch in horror as others are taken down into the water and bound to great rocks with ties of kelp. One day the undersea people attack a strong youth named Na-Ha. Although he fights valiantly, he is overcome and dragged to the bottom. But the following morning Na-Ha walks out of the sea saying that he wandered a while after the battle until he came to a cave door and entered. Inside was a woman with golden hair. She told him that the way to free his people was the way of white death. She gave him a great seashell with which he could blow away the undersea people. First, he tells his people to go far away, for when he blows the great shell, the land will freeze. Unwillingly the people leave, and Na-Ha remains. Na-Ha blows a great blast through the shell and the sea becomes a place of great white ice. In the biting cold, the undersea people shrivel, becoming the seals they are today.

Hunapu and Balanque are "The Hero Twins," so alike that the first wears a crimson feather and the second a blue one to tell them apart. One day they meet a sad old man and woman who tell them of the fearful giants that have taken away their children. The twin brothers go into the land of the giants. Soon they run into a monstrous fellow who sings this song: "My name is Cakix, Yukub-Cakix, And all men fear me!" But the twins shout, "We come to make an end of you." The giant is astonished at first, but because he closes his eyes when he turns his head, he cannot see them. Hunapu hits the giant in the chin with his bow and arrow. When the giant roars with pain, the twins tell him that it is his teeth that are causing him trouble. They promise to take out the teeth, which are the giant's strength, and replace them. Soon, they have pulled out all the giant's teeth, but the twins replace the teeth with grains of corn. In a short time, the monster dies of starvation, and one of the giants is gone.

Other tales are reminiscent of European folktales, with wolves and witches and animals and birds of all kinds in every story.

Themes and Subjects

All the standard subjects of folktales are contained in this 19-story collection—witches and evil spirits, enchantments, good overcoming evil, giants and those who slay them, and stories of how animals got their color or abilities. Each story carries the unique flavor of the region from which it comes.

Incidents for Booktalking

Each of the tales differs and each has its own special enchantment. See, for example, how animals got their tails in Honduras (pp. 1–13); how the twins killed the giant Cabrakan (pp. 92–98); and the exciting story of the witch with such an appetite that she swallows huge turtles whole (pp. 143–55).

Related Titles

In an attractive format, well-known storyteller Verna Aardemare tells fables and folktales from various parts of Africa in *Misoso: Once upon a Time Tales from Africa* (Knopf, 1994, $19.00: 0-679-83430-3).

Julius Lester has many excellent collections of Uncle Remus's stories suitable for re-telling or reading. The latest, *The Last Tales of Uncle Remus* (Dial, 1994, $18.99: 0-8037-1303-7), contains 39 folktales.

Tales Alive! Ten Multicultural Folktales with Activities (Williamson, 1995, $15.95: 0-913589-79-9) by Susan Milord combines a variety of tales from around the world with some stimulating craft projects and other activites.

Information about the Incas and their civilization is given followed by a collection of Inca and Peruvian legends in *Myths and Legends of Incas* (Cavendish, 1991, $9.99: 1-85435-267-9) by Daniele Kuss.

With a text in both English and Spanish, Lois Ehlert's *Moon Rope: A Peruvian Folk-tale* (Harcourt, 1992, $14.95: 0-15-201616-3) tells how Fox persuades Mole to accompany him on a trip to the moon.

About the Book and Author

Berger, Laura Standley, ed. *Twentieth-Century Children's Writers*. 4th ed. St. James, 1995, p. 441.

Brown, Muriel W., and Rita Schoch Foudray. *Newbery and Caldecott Medalists and Honor Book Winners: Bibliography & Resource Material Through 1990*. 2d ed. Neal-Schuman, 1992, pp. 134–36.

Chevalier, Tracy, ed. *Twentieth-Century Children's Writers*. 3d ed. St. James, 1989, pp. 337–38.

Commire, Anne, ed. *Something About the Author*. Vol. 42. Gale, 1986, pp. 77–85.

May, Hal, ed. *Contemporary Authors*. Vol. 119. Gale, 1987, p. 109.

Miller, Bertha M., and Elinor Field, eds. *Newbery Medal Books: 1922–1955 with the Author's Acceptance Papers and Related Material*. Horn Book, 1955, pp. 33–38.

Peterson, Linda K., and Marilyn L. Solt, eds. *Newbery and Caldecott Medal and Honor Books: 1922–1981*. Hall, 1982, p. 18.

Ward, Martha, ed. *Authors of Books for Young People*. 3d ed. Scarecrow, 1990, pp. 226–27.

Honor Books 1925

Moore, Anne Carroll. *Nicholas: A Manhattan Christmas Story*. Illustrated by Jay Van Everen. Putnam, 1924, o.p. (Grades 3–5)

For maximum enjoyment, this fantasy requires some knowledge of New York City landmarks, both past and present. At Christmas time, a Brownie and a Norwegian Troll, hiding in the Children's Room of the New York Public Library on Fifth Avenue, are surprised when an eight-inch-high boy arrives through a window and introduces himself as Nicholas. In his long blue breeches, short jacket, French helmet, and Dutch wooden shoes, he has arrived from Europe to explore the city at Yuletide. Brownie introduces him to several people who become his friends, including: Lucky, a gardener and writer; the kindly Ann Carraway; and John Moon, a young man around the age of 20 who is a veteran of World War I. These friends share many adventures. They explore New York's Fifth Avenue, the Waldorf, and Brentano's Book Store; listen to carols at Trinty Church; hear stories about early Christmases in the city; and talk to Washington Irving and Mary Mapes Dodge. Nicholas learns to greet the famous library lions, Leo Astor and Leo Lenox. At a gala Christmas party, real-life people mingle with storybook characters such as Sinbad the Sailor, Palmer Cox's Brownies, Alladin, and Boy Wizard. Nicholas enjoys engaging in winter sports, riding the subway, and taking a trip on the Staten Island Ferry, and also visits friends of Ann Carraway in Portland, Maine. Nicholas spends Valentine's Day walking across Brooklyn Bridge with Ann and attending a gathering with the Queen of Hearts and the Toy Soldier. On Washington's birthday, another friend, Jimmy Blair, tells him about the Revolution and shows him the historical sites associated with it. Just before Easter, an enlightened and happy Nicholas sails for France.

Parrish, Anne, and Dillwyn Parrish. *The Dream Coach*. Illustrated by the authors. Macmillan, 1924, o.p. (Grades 3–5)

In this fantasy are four stories, each of which begins in real life and then describes the effects of the arrival of a magical coach drawn by 100 misty horses that bring dreams to four different sleepless children. In the first, the King's abused little daughter receives seven white dreams and in each she is something white—a cloud, a lamb, and a butterfly. In the end, she becomes a playmate of lovely white angels. The second tells of Goram, a Norwegian boy, who is left alone by his mother when she goes to the village for winter supplies. There is a violent snowstorm and Goram makes a snowman that, in his dream, comes alive along with a teapot and the Queen from a deck of playing cards. A bored little Chinese Emperor is the central character of the third. He catches a bird and places him in a cage, but now the bird will not sing. In his dream, the Emperor becomes the caged captive of the birds, and through this experience, learns the value and beauty of freedom. Awakening, he frees the little bird. In the last, a French boy named Philippe visits his grandparents, a cousin, and an effusive uncle, Pablot. In his dream, Philippe's grandmother becomes Grandmother Rain; his uncle, Uncle Wind; his cousin, the spring; and his grandfather, who has white hair and beard, Grandfather Snow. Together, the four of them produce flowers. These stories, reminiscent of Hans Christian Andersen's tales, contain many examples of the poetic use of language and illustration.

Newbery Winner 1926

Chrisman, Arthur Bowie. *Shen of the Sea*. Illustrated by Else Hasselriis. Dutton, 1925, $16.99: 0-525-39244-0. (Grades 4–7)

Arthur Chrisman (1889–1953) was born on a farm near White Post, Virginia. As a youngster, he not only loved nature and the outdoors but also filled his days writing and telling stories. In college, he studied electrical engineering at

Virginia Polytechnic Institute. He was always fascinated with Chinese history, customs, and folktales, and he spent several years in California exploring the state and absorbing the culture and literature of both China and India. He became friendly with a Chinese shopkeeper and, from him, heard many other folktales. From this large collection, he chose 16 to be included in *Shen of the Sea*. Two other collections followed: *The Wind That Wouldn't Blow* (1927, o.p.) and *Treasure Long Hidden* (1941, o.p.). Though set in exotic places and times, these tales deal with such universal themes as love, hate, avarice, hope, and fear. He is also noted for his clear, brisk prose and use of humor. His motto was a favorite Chinese proverb: "Walk slowly, perhaps the river will have receded when you come to it."

Plot Summary

This book contains stories from Chinese folk material. These 16 classic tales are amusing and appealing. They convey the philosophy that has guided and influenced the lives of the Chinese people for generations upon generations. Synopses of three of these classic tales follow to give the spirit and flavor of this entertaining book.

In "Shen of the Sea," a man asks his gardener, Wu Chang, if the sea has ever broken through its restraining walls and flooded Kua Hai City, which stands on a plain in northern China. As he asks, the speaker gazes from his beloved city over the Bay of the Sharp-Horned Moon.

Wu Chang is astonished to discover that his master does not know the story of Chieh Chung and the bottle that he buried, perhaps in this very garden. His action saved Kua Hai City from the invasion of the sea. Chieh Chung, explains the gardener, was the first king of Wa Tien, and he invented writing. One day long ago, when the sea was much higher than it is now, the Shen, demons of the sea, got together and decided that they needed more room for themselves because their sea was too small. Because they were mighty, they decided to take some land and make it into sea.

After looking over likely spots, they see Kua Hai and enter the garden of the palace. King Chieh Chung is astonished to see them with their codfish-like mouths, but he politely asks what they want. When he hears that they want his city and the plain that surrounds it, he is most distressed and asks for time to take his people to safety.

The Shen say that they can wait until the cypress tree is in flower, and then they prepare to depart. But it is too late in the day, for the moisture has left the land, and no Shen can exist without moisture. Chieh Chung suggests that they make themselves much smaller and jump into a crystal water bowl. When they do, the king quickly pours the water containing all the Shen into a bottle and closes the mouth securely.

The king saves the city. Years and years later, ambassadors from afar come to visit the great king. A foolish servant, trying to make sure that all is in readiness for the visitors, comes across the jade bottle and uncorks it. The king is upset, but because he knows that the cypress tree *never* blooms, he believes his city to be safe. The water demons hasten toward the garden, where they see the brightly colored garments of the ambassadors drying on the trees. The Shen believe they are the flowers of the cypress tree. They call in the ocean, which covers the land, and thousands die.

King Chieh Chung escapes and is grief-stricken. Hour after hour he sits, until one day he cries aloud that he has a plan to regain his city. He begins to write his plan on parchment. The curious Shen turn themselves into red stones at the root of the lily in the crystal bowl so that they can spy upon his plan. Quickly Chieh Chung thrusts them once more into the bottle and captures six of them. The seventh is so small that he throws the demon back into the sea. The small demon speeds away and takes the sea with him, saving the city once more.

The six Shen, says the gardener, may be buried deep in a jade bottle under this very garden.

In "The Rain King's Daughter," King Ta Lang is worried because the people of Shen Su are starving. A famine lays heavy upon the land. Ta Lang summons all his wise men, who tell him that the famine is brought about by the Shen of Falling Water, Yu Shin. The Shen is angry, says one. But another says that a rat is eating all the food. Most agree, yes, the cause is a rat. They also agree that the rat is in the mountain called Che Chou.

So a huge wooden rat trap is built at the end of the mountain. But the famine continues. Next, the wise men say that a spear must be thrust through the heart of the rat. So a giant wooden spear is constructed. In making the giant flint for the giant spear, a fire starts and the whole mountain is ablaze. Splendid, thinks the king, no rat can live through that.

Sure enough, the rains come, and while it rains for seven days, the king's son is born. At the same time a basket is found in the garden containing a tiny girl. How she got there is a mystery. The wise men tell the king to name his son Tou Meng (Give Thanks) and to keep the girl and name her Chai Mi (Enables Us to Live). She is the daughter of the Rain King and will marry Tou Meng.

When they are grown, Chai Mi finds a roll of parchment that says the enemy is marching upon the city. Tou Meng and the other men leave to fight. With the men gone, the women of the city soon see an immense enemy army across the raging river. Chai Mi realizes that King Ta Lang and his men marched off so hastily that they left their armor behind. The enemy knows that the men have left and believe that they can march on the city. Suddenly the enemy sees 1,000 archers carrying their spears! As was the custom, they are all wearing false faces.

The enemy has no recourse but to surrender. When King Ta Lang and his men return to learn that Chai Mi and the women have saved the city, they are astounded! But the king's chief general is very jealous and reminds the king that, according to law, no maiden can put on the king's armor.

The king hears the news with grief but agrees that Chai Mi must lose her head. Whether or not he would have done so will never be known, for suddenly the king's boat sinks and he is gone. Queen Chai Mi and King Meng rule over the city for many a year.

In "As Hai Low Kept House," Hai Lee saves his money for many years until he and his little brother, Hai Low, are able to come down from the mountains and buy a tiny house near Ying Ling toll road. That is near the King's road, and it is said that "he who lives on the King's road has seen the whole world."

Hai Low keeps house and Hai Lee tends the fields. The small hovel is a palace to the two brothers because they have always lived in a cave.

One day as Hai Low tends the house, a fox dashes under the floor. Hunters soon arrive chasing the fox. When they ask to dig under the house for the fox, Hai Low refuses, for his brother has told him that he must always tend their little home carefully and let no harm come to it. No matter what the hunters do, including an offer of money, Hai Low refuses. The hunters finally leave, although the fox stays under the floor. But when Hai Lee returns, he does not praise his brother for saving the house. Instead, he says that the fox is an enemy and should be gone from their home.

The next day two men come to the house with crossbows. Hai Low offers them rice and tells them to dig for the fox. But these crafty men believe Hai Low to be stupid.

Bidding him turn their backs while they dig for the fox, they manage to make off with all the brothers' money. Hai Lee, however, is able to retrieve it and tells his brother never to let another stranger in the house.

The next day an old man knocks, but Hai Low sends him away. Once again, his brother is angry, for it seems that Hai Low has chased off their own grandfather, Hai Ho, who is wealthy and was about to make the brothers his heirs. But because they have another wealthy grandfather, Hai Lee tells his brother to ask next time before he sends someone away.

Soon a well-dressed man appears. Hai Low asks if the man is his grandfather. The man turns out to be the governor, who is insulted by the question. Hai Lee tells Hai Low not even to open his mouth next time.

The next day, Hai Low sees their stable door open and a stranger come out leading Hai Lee's donkey. Hai Low opens his mouth but says nothing. Now, Hai Lee is really angry because someone stole his donkey. He tells his brother to shoot the next stranger near the stable.

Sure enough, a stranger appears and Hai Low shoots him in his hat. Hai Lee is nearly hysterical when he returns, for the stranger is an ambassador and has said his country will now declare war. Just be polite next time, Hai Lee says, and chase the hat.

The next day, a great company of men appear with a gilded sedan. As a breeze carries a hat from the sedan, Hai Low chases it. The men chase him, but Hai Low hides. When he returns to his home that night, his brother tells him the hat belongs to his royal majesty and that anyone who touches it must be put to death. He tells Hai Low to crawl under the bed and stay there.

The next day, soldiers come and burn the house. Hai Low dares not leave and would surely have died if his brother did not save him. Next time, says his brother, throw water on the fire. When Hai Low sees a fire the very next day, he throws water on it and puts out a traveler's meal. Hai Lee insists that his brother catch up to the traveler, return his dry stick of wood, and apologize.

Hai Low is bound to find the stranger. As he travels, a crowd gathers behind him. When they enter the capital city, the king, How Wang, a most unpopular man, thinks an enemy army is coming to get him. He calls for his horse and vanishes.

The generals immediately surrender to their new king and place a crown upon Hai Low's head. Hai Low is now king and his housekeeping days are over.

Themes and Subjects

These amusing stories catch the spirit of Chinese life and thought. Beneath their sometimes witty, always wise charm is the practical philosophy that so influences Chinese life. They are written in the classic way of folktales by an author who has studied the ancient literature and history of China for many years. His storytelling is a rare gift that can be enjoyed by readers of all ages.

Incidents for Booktalking

Any of these classic tales brings out the charm, humor, and flavor of the folk story. See, for example, how Ching Chi, China Cha, and the child Ah Mee all have a hand in the invention of printing (pp. 17–28); the history of a merry, clever rascal called Meng Hu (pp. 42–57); how King Cheng Chang abolished knives, forks, and spoons and invented chopsticks of wood (pp. 58–69); how an orphan finds a father in the emperor (pp. 70–80); the story of a kingdom saved by four generals (pp. 81–97); the tale of Radiant Blossom, the loveliest of maidens (pp. 111–21).

Related Titles

Myths from South American Indian tribes—such as why the rainbow is bent—are included in Natalia M. Belting's *Moon Was Tired of Walking on Air* (Houghton, 1992, $16.95: 0-395-53806-8).

Ten spooky ghost stories, some based on folktales, are included on Patricia C. McKissack's *The Dark Thirty: Southern Tales of the Supernatural* (Knopf, 1992, $12.00: 0-679-89006-8).

Michael J. Rosen's *How the Animals Got Their Colors* (Harcourt, 1992, $14.95: 0-15-236783-7) explains such phenomena as the spots on leopards.

Robert D. San Souci's *Larger Than Life* (Doubleday, 1991, $10.95: 0-385-32180-5) is a collection of tall tales featuring such heroes as Paul Bunyan and Old Stormalong.

Mysterious Tales of Japan (Putnam, 1996, $18.95: 0-399-22677-X) by Rafe Martin, is a collection of 10 haunting folktales about the spiritual powers in nature.

About the Books and Author

Berger, Laura Standley, ed. *Twentieth-Century Children's Writers*. 4th ed. St. James, 1995, pp. 345–46.

Brown, Muriel W., and Rita Schoch Foudray. *Newbery and Caldecott Medalists and Honor Book Winners: Bibliographic & Resource Material Through 1990*. 2d ed. Neal-Schuman, 1992, p. 64.

Chevalier, Tracy, ed. *Twentieth-Century Children's Writers*. 3d ed. St. James, 1989, pp. 194–95.

Commire, Anne. *Yesterday's Authors of Books for Children*. Vol. 1. Gale, 1977, pp. 94–96.

Kunitz, Stanley J., and Howard Haycraft, eds. *The Junior Book of Authors*. Wilson, 1951, pp. 69–71.

Miller, Bertha M., and Elinor Field, eds. *Newbery Medal Books: 1922–1955 with the Author's Acceptance Papers and Related Material*. Horn Book, 1955, pp. 39–42.

Peterson, Linda K., and Marilyn L. Solt, eds. *Newbery and Caldecott Medal and Honor Books: 1922–1981*. Hall, 1982, p. 20.

Ward, Martha, ed. *Authors of Books for Young People*. 3d ed. Scarecrow, 1990, p. 126.

Honor Books 1926

Colum, Padraic. *The Voyagers: Being the Legends and Romances of Atlantic Discovery.* Illustrated by Wilfred Jones. Macmillan, 1925, o.p. (Grades 5–8)

By a high tower on the coast of Portugal, Prince Henry the Navigator listens to wise men who tell him about the exploration of the Atlantic Ocean. They begin with the legend of the magic island of Atlantis, where, in the center, is a mountain on which Evenor dwelled. Evenor's daughter married Poseidon and one of their 10 sons was Atlas, the fabled ruler of this land. In "The Voyage of Maelduin," the noble Maelduin sails from Ireland with 17 companions to seek the man who slew his father. Blown off course, they have a series of adventures on exotic islands, including one where giant eagles renew their lives through preening. When he finally finds his father's killer, his experiences have subdued him enough that Maelduin forgives him, so they can live in peace. The voyages of St. Brendon include stays on various strange islands. On one island, the ship's cat miraculously brings them a freshly killed salmon to eat each day, and on another day he meets the wretched Judas Iscariot. "The Children of Eric the Red" deals with the exploits of such adventurers as Leif the Lucky and of the land he explored named "Wineland the Good" because of the grapes he found there. A section called "The Great Admiral" tells of the different voyages of Christopher Columbus, and in "The Fountain of Youth," the story of Ponce de Leon is retold. There are also stories about the early history of Virginia, including that of the marriage of John Rolfe to Pocahantas, the daughter of the Indian chief Powhatan. Many years after Henry's death, two students, one a mapmaker, visit the tower and talk to Amerigo Vespucci. When Vespucci leaves, they decide to use the word "America" as the name for the new world.

Newbery Winner 1927

James, Will. *Smoky, the Cowhorse.* Illustrated by the author. Scribner, 1926, o.p.; Simon, 1972, $12.95: 0-684-12875-6. (Grades 6–10)

In his autobiographical writings including *Lone Cowboy: My Life Story*, Will James (1892–1942) claimed that he was born in Montana. His mother died when he was a year old and his father was killed handling cattle when he was four. Adopted by a French Canadian trapper and prospector, Jean Beaupre, James states that he was entirely self-educated. The truth is less romantic. James was born in Quebec, Canada, as Joseph Ernest Dufault and attended a Catholic primary school in Montreal. After serving in the U.S. Army during World War I, he attended the California School of Fine Arts in San Francisco and the Yale School of Fine Arts. Both fact and fiction agree that he spent much of his life as an adventurer, earning his living as a cowhand, rodeo rider, and stunt man in Hollywood. An accomplished artist, he was always fascinated with the life on the range and claimed that his happiest times were spent as a cowboy. Commenting on his writing, he stated, "I only tell of the true life and happenings with the cowboy and his work."

Plot Summary

The biography of Smoky the cowhorse can be told in several parts: his birth and freedom on the open range; his gentle handling by cowboy Clint, who trains him as a first-class cow pony; his capture and terrible treatment; his years as an outlaw; his life on top of the rodeo circuit; and his reunion with Clint and return to the high mountain range of his youth.

Although Smoky would grow up to become the color of his name, he is born jet black, an uncertain little colt trying to stand on wobbly legs. It is not long, however, before he begins to understand that the gentle shoving of his mother means that he should try to stand up on those shaky legs.

The world is exciting, strange, and fun to Smoky during those early days on the high mountain range of his birth. An occasional tangle with a coyote or prickly porcupine is about all that worries him. So, it is quite a shock when he sees his first human at branding time.

By the time Smoky is nearly five, he is strong, tall, and handsome. That is when he meets cowboy Clint, the bronc buster of the Rocking Ranch outfit. Clint loves horses and is gentle with them, even though he has to be firm to teach them what they need to know. Patiently, he begins with gentleness to tame the wild and strong young horse, and a bond develops between them. Saddling is perhaps the hardest part. Smoky just does not take to it at all, but Clint is patient as always and in time, Smoky accepts the saddle. Clint is careful to teach the horse but never to break his spirit. After Clint is badly hurt in a range accident and Smoky saves him, the two become more inseparable than ever.

The years pass, and one day Smoky is lost in a terrible winter storm. Clint tries to find him but to no avail. He searches everywhere. Spring roundup comes, then summer and fall, and still no Smoky. He has many adventures, but the worst is that he is captured by a mean cowboy identified only as BREED. The man wants to kill Smoky's wild spirit and vows to do so. Instead, when the man's cruelty goes too far and he is about to shoot Smoky, the big horse turns on him and tramples him.

From that terrible experience, Smoky becomes famous as the bucking horse with murder in his eyes. No cowboy can stay on him and his fame on the rodeo circuit grows. He is known as The Cougar and billed as a man-hating bucking outlaw. There is no horse in the state or any other that can compete with this smoke-colored dangerous animal.

The years pass, and Smoky's fame as The Cougar begins to recede a little as he slows down, and indeed his distaste for humans seems to slow down a little, too. Finally, useless to the rodeo circuit, the great horse is sold to a livery stable man for $25. This time he is given the name of Cloudy.

The life seems to have gone out of Smoky. His abhorrence is gone but so is his desire for living. When the day's work is done, all he cares about is the little grain that he is given and rest. Lots of boys and girls and grown-ups come to ride him. One day a young girl takes him out for a ride, and Smoky collapses. The girl wants to help him, but the stable man tells her that he has turned the old horse out on the range. The truth is that he has sold Smoky to a man who buys old horses and kills them for chicken feed.

Instead, however, Smoky is sold once again, a saddle put on his back once more, and his new owner finds all sorts of work for the old horse. Soon the days run into weeks and it seems as though Smoky's misery will never end.

Then the rodeo comes to town. The cowboys gather and take turns talking about the famous horse known as The Cougar. One of the cowboys points out Smoky and remarks that he is the same color as The Cougar. One cowboy in the crowd is Clint, who looks twice at the old horse. There is something about that old broken-down animal that bothers Clint. He begins to ask questions. Finally, he learns who owns the horse and what treatment he has been given over the past few months. First, Clint gets the sheriff involved to ensure that no horse will be treated in such a way again, and then he goes in search. Finally, at the end of a line of railroad cars, Clint finds a bale of hay, a barrel of water, and an old smoke-colored horse.

Oh, how Smoky's life changes! For two months, Clint works on him. He gets Smoky a warm box stall filled with the best hay. He buys preparations that will help to restore life to that old worn coat and body. But it all seems hopeless, for Smoky is listless and uncaring.

Then, little by little, there is a change—a small spark of the old spirit in the horse's eyes, a slight difference in the luster of his coat, a little more meat on those thin bones. And then, one marvelous day, when Clint is talking to him, Smoky actually cocks his ear!

From that time on, Smoky grows stronger and better and more like himself. As the days grow longer and the sun gets warmer, Smoky starts walking around in the sunshine, with Clint leading him. Sometimes Smoky goes out on his own, but always at sundown he returns to Clint.

But although he has recovered so well, Smoky's heart is not repaired, for Clint realizes that the old horse never nickers anymore, a sure sign of a decline in spirit. Clint reasons that perhaps the terrible treatment he has endured has broken him forever. "Somebody must of stretched that pony's heartstrings to the breaking point," says Clint.

Perhaps the kind thing to do is to return old Smoky to the high mountain of his youth to let him live out his remaining time in that gentle land. With a heavy heart, Clint leads Smoky to the high mountain and watches him for a time. Smoky seems undecided whether to join the other horses on the mountain range or to stay with Clint. Finally, a horse nickers and Smoky decides. Sadly, Clint watches him go and then leaves. Someday, he hopes he will come back and see if the old horse is alright, to see if the old horse has found his heart again. The days pass and Smoky never leaves the cowboy's mind. And then, one bright early morning, as Clint sticks his head out his cabin door, he hears a nicker. He drops his water bucket in surprise as he sees his cowhorse standing in front of him slick and shiny and full of spirit. His heart has come to life, and he has come home.

Themes and Subjects

This is an animal story showing the courage and heart of a special horse and the bond of friendship and love that can develop between animal and human. Although not treated as a cartoon character, the horse is given feelings and emotions that are carefully and feelingly portrayed. The author also gives a realistic portrait of the world of the cowboy and the rodeo circuit. Contrasted nicely are the kindness and caring of the cowboy Clint against the thoughtless cruelty of other humans who come in contact with Smoky.

Incidents for Booktalking

Any of the following scenes can introduce the reader to the great horse Smoky and his brave spirit. See especially: Smoky's early days in the high mountain range (pp. 1–21); Smoky and the lion (pp. 42–44); Smoky meets Clint (pp. 85–98); Smoky learns to carry a rider (pp. 116–24); the separation (pp. 224–34); life on the rodeo circuit (pp. 240–51); Smoky and Clint are reunited (pp. 300–09).

Related Titles

Another classic horse story is Anna Sewell's *Black Beauty* (Putnam, 1945, $14.95: 0-448-06007-8; pap., $7.95: 0-448-11007-5), which tells of a horse's experiences with many owners in nineteenth-century England.

An additional classic is John Steinbeck's *The Red Pony* (Viking, 1959, $15.95: 0-670-59184-X), about Jody growing up on a California ranch where he gets his first horse.

In S. E. Hinton's *Taming the Star Runner* (Delacorte, 1988, $14.95: 0-440-50058-3; pap., Dell, $4.99: 0-440-20479-8), a tough delinquent is sent to his uncle's ranch, where he encounters a wild horse named Star Runner.

A hostile and resentful Native American teenager is sent to live with a rancher in Colorado in *Bearstone* (Atheneum, 1989, $17.00: 0-689-31496-5; pap., Avon, $4.50: 0-380-71249-0) by Will Hobbs.

The Original Adventures of Hank the Cowdog (pap., Puffin, $6.95: 0-14-130377-8) by John R. Erickson is the first of several hilarious stories about a dog in charge of security on a Texas ranch.

About the Book and Author

Amaral, Anthony A. *Will James: The Last Cowboy Legend*. University of Nevada, 1980.

Bell, William C. *Will James: The Life and Work of a Lone Cowboy*. Northland, 1987.

Berger, Laura Standley, ed. *Twentieth-Century Children's Writers*. 4th ed. St. James, 1995, pp. 486–87.

Brown, Muriel W., and Rita Schoch Foudray. *Newbery and Caldecott Medalists and Honor Book Winners: Bibliographic & Resource Material Through 1990*. 2d ed. Neal-Schuman, 1992, p. 215.

Chevalier, Tracy, ed. *Twentieth-Century Children's Writers*. 3d ed. St. James, 1989, pp. 491–92.

Commire, Anne, ed. *Something About the Author*. Vol. 19. Gale, 1980, pp. 148–65.

James, Will. *Lone Cowboy: My Life Story*. Scribner's, 1930.

Kunitz, Stanley J., and Howard Haycraft, eds. *The Junior Book of Authors*. Wilson, 1951, pp. 169–71.

Miller, Bertha M., and Elinor Field, eds. *Newbery Medal Books: 1922–1955 with the Author's Acceptance Papers and Related Material*. Horn Book, 1955, pp. 44–48.

Peterson, Linda, K., and Marilyn L. Solt, eds. *Newbery and Caldecott Medal and Honor Books: 1922–1981*. Hall, 1982, pp. 21–22.

Smoky. Fox, 1966. Film, 103 min.

Ward, Martha, ed. *Authors of Books for Young People*. 3d ed. Scarecrow, 1990, p. 367.

Newbery Winner 1928

Mukerji, Dhan Gopal. *Gay Neck, the Story of a Pigeon*. Illustrated by Boris Artzybasheff. Dutton, 1927, $15.99: 0-525-30400-2. (Grades 4–7)

Dhan Mukerji (1890–1936) was born in Calcutta, India, to a high-caste family. At the age of 14, he was initiated into the Brahmin priesthood and, after attending the University of Calcutta, came to the United States at 20, where he graduated from Stanford University. Though he wrote and lectured for adults in the field of comparative literature, his most lasting accomplishments are in children's literature. In his writings he enjoyed being able to explain Hindu folklore, culture, and philosophy in language suitable for young people. The book he was most proud of was *Hindu Fables for Little Children* (1929, o.p.). He also enjoyed writing about wildlife and its relationship to the environment. Prophetically, he voiced contemporary concerns when he wrote, "You cannot destroy one species of animal without upsetting the balance of life. Life is a whole." Two other themes that are prominent in his writings, and found in *Gay Neck*, are the bond between human beings and other living creatures and the healing power of prayer and meditation.

Plot Summary

Gay Neck, destined to become a brave and exceptional carrier pigeon, was born in Calcutta, India. His young master, the author of this tale, named him Chitra (painted in gay colors)—griva (neck), or Gay Neck. Sometimes he was also called Iridescence-throated. When Gay Neck was born, however, he was tiny, shivering, and not at all attractive. But he was very quick-witted. From his mother, he had inherited wisdom, and from his father, alertness and bravery.

About the age of two weeks, when his feathers are beginning to change from gray-blue to glossy aquamarine, Gay Neck begins to learn how to fly. Even though he is a bird, flying does not come easily. Finally, with coaxing from his mother and his young master, and nudging from his father, Gay Neck gingerly takes to the air. As the days pass, the young pigeon takes longer and higher flights.

Soon, the boy begins to teach Gay Neck a sense of direction. Within a week, he can return to his home from as far as 15 miles away. Mukerji decides it is time for a trip down the Ganges in a boat. He takes Gay Neck and his parents along. But a terrible storm occurs and Gay Neck's father is lost, although his mother and the young pigeon are saved.

That summer Mukerji's father takes the family up in the Himalayas to the small village of Dentam. There, Mukerji continues to train Gay Neck and his other pigeons in the art of direction. The boy is aided in this endeavor by his friend Radja, a 16-year-old Brahmin priest, and old Ghond, who teaches Mukerji much about the jungle.

The Himalayas are also home to the hawk. One terrible day, in trying to defend her youngster, Gay Neck's mother is attacked by a hawk and is killed. Gay Neck is so frightened that he disappears. With the help of Radja and Ghond, Mukerji sets out to find his beloved bird. Finally, they reach the lamasery of Buddhist monks. They are told that the young pigeon was indeed there but has gone away again. One of the monks tells Mukerji that Gay Neck came because he was filled with fear, but now the fear has gone and the bird is healed.

Mukerji and his friends return to the village of Dentam, where they find Gay Neck in his nest at Mukerji's home. The young boy is overjoyed. However, his joy is short-lived, for Gay Neck disappears again the following morning. Once more, Mukerji and his friends travel back to the lamasery. They are reunited with Gay Neck, who at this point in the story tells the reader of his fears and flight to the lamasery and how he is saddened by all the killing and inflicting of pain by birds and beasts on one another.

Mukerji and Gay Neck return to Calcutta, where rumors of the approaching World War I abound. In preparation, Mukerji decides to give his beloved bird training in case Gay Neck is asked to become a carrier for the British War Department. Mukerji feels that Gay Neck's experience flying in the Himalayas should be a great asset. As the training progresses, Gay Neck establishes himself as the leader of Mukerji's flock of pigeons. Finally, his intelligence and courage make him the recognized leader of all the pigeon flocks in the city.

After Gay Neck is mated and has youngsters of his own, he is called to serve in World War I. Along with Ghond, Gay Neck leaves Calcutta for Bombay. Mukerji cannot go because he is underage. Ghond and Gay Neck are sent to Europe, where they are trained to carry messages for the Indian army in France. Twice the courageous bird carries important messages back to headquarters from the front lines.

But his most dangerous assignment is behind the German lines, where Ghond is sent to find an ammunition dump. After locating it, he makes a map of the site and attaches the note to Gay Neck's leg. The bird makes the difficult journey back to his own lines, but is followed part way and shot at by an airplane. The bullets break his wing and injure his leg, and Ghond is also injured trying to return from enemy territory.

Although Gay Neck's injuries heal, he will no longer fly. The courageous bird knows that he has recovered from a broken wing and wounded leg, but nothing will induce him to fly again. Each time he hops into the air, terrible noises surround him and flaming bullets fly before his eyes. His wings are paralyzed with fear. In addition, he cannot fly without the presence of Ghond, who must also recover from his wounds.

And so the two heroes are sent home to recuperate in mind and body. Ghond returns to the lamasery in the Himalayas to find solace in prayer and meditation. Mukerji tries his best to help the brave bird lose his fear and return to normal. He has Gay Neck examined by bird doctors, who declare that nothing is wrong with him. Yet, he will not fly. He will not even help in the nesting of his young ones.

On Ghond's advice, Mukerji puts Gay Neck in one cage, his wife in another, and heads north. After staying in Dentam for a time, Mukerji leaves Gay Neck's wife behind and sets out for Singalila with Gay Neck and a caravan of Tibetan ponies. Mukerji hopes that when Gay Neck has recovered, he will be inspired to return to his wife and help her hatch the newly laid eggs.

Mukerji and Gay Neck are reunited with Ghond at the lamasery. The lama tells Mukerji that to cure Gay Neck of his fears, the young man must seat Gay Neck on his shoulder each dawn and sunset and recite: "Infinite courage is in all life. Each being that lives and breathes is a reservoir of infinite courage. May I be pure enough to pour infinite courage into those whom I touch!"

Mukerji does as he is bid for about 10 days. Then, one day as Mukerji and the lama are meditating, Gay Neck walks out of his cage and looks at the sunset. Slowly and softly, he opens one wing and then the other as if to salute the setting sun.

The following morning, Gay Neck is not in his cage. After a terrible fight with a murderous buffalo in the area, which Ghond is forced to kill, Mukerji and Ghond return to the village of Dentam. They are thrilled to discover that Gay Neck has been home for three days! Their days in the monastery have healed both Ghond and Gay Neck in mind and spirit. The disease of fear and hate that they had caught on the battlefields of war is gone from both. Now the brave Ghond and the courageous Gay Neck can live their lives in peace and happiness.

Themes and Subjects

This is a story of courage, love, friendship, and devotion to duty. It also points out the mental horror of war and what it can do to both human and animal. The reader learns a good deal about the training and experiences of carrier pigeons, as well as their contributions during World War I. It also details the life of a young Indian boy of high caste during the early years of this century, but *Gay Neck* is mainly a story of bravery, friendship, devotion, and love. The moral behind the story is that humans and animals are indeed brothers and sisters.

Incidents for Booktalking

Any of the incidents involving Gay Neck's growth, care, and training will be of interest to the reader. See especially: Gay Neck's birth and early development, including learning to fly (pp. 22–27); the trip on the Ganges (pp. 31–33); Gay Neck is lost in the Himalayas (pp. 52–69); the carrier pigeon goes to war (pp. 130–41); Gay Neck is injured and learns fear (pp. 157–62); the healing process in the Himalayas (pp. 175–79, 190–91).

Related Titles

Tom and Orville become friends when they train pigeons together in Charlotte Towner Graeber's *Grey Cloud* (Macmillan, 1979, $13.95: 0-02-736910-2).

Eleven-year-old Mary wants to enter her pigeon in a race in France in this English story set in the 1930s, *Speedwell* (Candlewick, 1992, $14.95: 1-56402-112-2) by Ann Turnbull.

In *The Year of the Panda* (Harper, 1990, $14.89: 0-690-04866-1) by Miriam Schlein, a Chinese farm boy cares for an orphaned baby panda.

The Sixth Sense and Other Stories (Greenwillow, 1988, $12.95: 0-688-08129-0) by Jessie Haas is a collection of tales about the bonds between man and animals.

A wide range of subjects—from fireflies to moose—by such authors as Beverly Cleary and Betsy Byars are included in *A Newbery Zoo: A Dozen Animal Stories* (Delacorte, 1945, $16.95: 0-385-32263-1) edited by Martin H. Greenberg and Charles G. Waugh.

About the Book and Author

Berger, Laura Standley, ed. *Twentieth-Century Children's Writers*. 4th ed. St. James, 1995, pp. 684–85.

Brown, Muriel W., and Rita Schoch Foudray. *Newbery and Caldecott Medalists and Honor Book Winners: Bibliographic & Resource Material Through 1990*. 2d ed. Neal-Schuman, 1992, pp. 303–4.

Chevalier, Tracy, ed. *Twentieth-Century Children's Writers*. 3d ed. St. James, 1989, pp. 703–4.

Commire, Anne, ed. *Something About the Author*. Vol. 40. Gale, 1985, pp. 150–58.

Helbig, Alethea K., and Agnes R. Perkins, eds. *Dictionary of American Children's Fiction, 1859–1959*. Greenwood, 1986, p. 364 (bio.), pp. 176–77 (book).

Miller, Bertha M., and Elinor Field, eds. *Newbery Medal Books: 1922–1955 with the Author's Acceptance Papers and Related Material*. Horn Book, 1955, pp. 49–64.

Senick, Gerard J., ed. *Children's Literature Review*. Vol. 10. Gale, 1986, pp. 127–236.

Ward, Martha, ed. *Authors of Books for Young People*. 3d ed. Scarecrow, 1990, p. 513.

Honor Books 1928

Snedeker, Caroline Dale. *Downright Dencey*. Illustrated by Maginel Wright Barney. Doubleday, 1927, o.p. (Grades 5–7)

The main action in this novel takes place in the town of Nantucket on Nantucket Island during the years immediately following the War of 1812. Dionis Coffyn (nicknamed Dencey), a strong-willed, sensitive young girl, is growing up in a stern, spartan Quaker household with a usually absent father, Tom, captain of a whaler, and a dominating, God-fearing mother, Lydia, who genuinely feels that her inflexible and severe treatment of Dencey will make her daughter a better person. One day on her way to school, Dencey is so angered by some boys calling names that she throws a stone and wounds young Sam Jetson, a vagabond youth who lives on the outskirts of town with the village drunk, Indian Jill, supposedly his mother. The next day, filled with remorse, she again confronts Sam, hoping to win forgiveness, first by offering him a precious seashell given to her by her father, and then by presenting him with her equally precious copy of *Pilgrim's Progress*. He demands, as well, that Dencey teach him to read, and so whenever possible, Dencey guiltily spends time after school with Sam, whom she grows to like. When Lydia finds out, Dencey is confined to her room on a diet of bread and water until she promises never to see Sam again. Dencey stubbornly refuses, and only through the intervention of kindly Aunt Lovesta does Lydia partially relent. Tom falls under the influence of an unscrupulous magician, Professor Snubnose. To prevent Tom's departure from the island with this charlatan, Dencey ventures out into a violent snowstorm. Tom finds her on the deserted moors, and half-dead himself, drags her back home. Through this act of heroism, he is accepted into the Coffyn family and gradually becomes transformed. Although he finds out that Indian Jill is not his true mother, he tries to rehabilitate her and, through these acts of caring, embraces the Quaker faith. With Captain Coffyn's help, he becomes a cabin boy on a whaler. Dencey and Tom, now known as Tom Seaman, pledge their love and look forward to marriage after he returns. A sequel is *The Beckoning Road* (Doubleday, 1929, o.p.).

Young, Ella. *The Wonder-Smith and His Son: A Tale for the Golden Childhood of the World*. Illustrated by Boris Artzybasheff. Longmans, 1927, o.p. (Grades 5–7)

These 14 Irish legends were gathered by the author from the cottagers and fishermen of Gaelic-speaking County Clare of Ireland. They deal with the exploits of the folk hero Gubbaun Saor, also known as Mamamaun or Cullion the Wonder Smith. In the story on how he gained his trade, three master builders came to town and promised to create a masterpiece, provided that no one looked on while they were working. Unfortunately, someone did, and the three craftsmen were turned into birds that immediately flew away. Luckily, the Gubbaun Saor happened by and completed the job. In another story, "How the Gubbaun Saor Got His Son," he laments that he only has a daughter, Aunya, and—clever though she may be—he would like a son. He meets a woman who has only a son but would like a daughter. They trade, but the Gubbaun soon realizes he has been cheated because his new son, Lugh, wants only to sit basking in the sunlight. Later the Gubbaun decides to find a wife for his son and promises a treasure to the prospective bride who will use the money wisely. All three finalists fail the test because the first would spend it, the second would simply lock it up, and the third would use bargaining techniques that disqualify her. The most exciting series of stories deals with Gubbaun and his son in the bleak land of Balor, the god of darkness and death, where they have been summoned to build the most magnificent house ever constructed. Balor plans on eventually killing the builder and Lugh. Through the wiles of Aunya, who is able to trick Balor's emissaries, they are saved. The many full-page illustrations of Boris Artzybasheff help convey the mystery, magic, and grandeur of these tales.

Newbery Winner 1929

Kelly, Eric P. *The Trumpeter of Krakow*. Illustrated by Angela Pruszynska. Doubleday, 1928, o.p.; Macmillan, 1966, $17.00: 0-02-750140-X; pap., Aladdin, $4.95: 0-689-71571-4. (Grades 6–9)

While working in France as a teacher of English during World War I, Eric P. Kelly (1884–1960) met some Polish emigrés and became fascinated with their native land. After the armistice, he went to Poland to deliver food and supplies, and there learned the language and explored the country. Later, during the school year 1925–1926, he became a Kosciuszko Foundation scholar and lectured at the University of Krakow. He and the city formed a mystical bond. He stated that there was "a kind of vibration that issues from the city of Krakow that arouses a very tumult in my heart . . . the Polish people start me vibrating with the most exquisite pleasure [and] the same thing is true with the buildings in the city." This fixation with Krakow is revealed in the author's intricate reconstruction within the novel of life in the city during the fifteenth century with detailed descriptions of customs, life, and landscapes. For young people he wrote two other novels about Polish cities, *The Blacksmith of Vilno* (Doubleday, 1930, o.p.) and *The Golden Star of Halich* (Doubleday, 1931, o.p.).

Plot Summary

The story begins in fifteenth-century Poland in the city of Krakow. For many many years, the Charnetski family has secretly guarded the legendary Great Tarnov crystal, a gem of enormous beauty and value. However, through the years so many tales have been spun about this fabulous crystal that many people regard it as a legend and do not believe that it exists at all.

One day, a servant in the service of Andrew Charnetski sees his master hiding the inordinate jewel in a pumpkin. The knowledge that the crystal actually exists spreads throughout the land, even reaching the ears of Russia's leader, Ivan. Most anxious to have this extravagant wealth, Ivan sends Bogdan the Terrible, a brigand also known as Peter of the Button Face, to steal the jewel from the Charnetskis. As Andrew and his family, which includes 15-year-old Joseph, are traveling from Ukraine, Button Face attacks them and attempts to steal the crystal. He is unsuccessful and the Charnetskis flee to Krakow, where Andrew hopes to be able to deliver the gem to the king.

Although the Charnetski family had expected to stay with a cousin in Krakow, they are dismayed to discover that she has fled the city. However, when Joseph saves a young girl, Elzbietka, from a mad dog, she offers them lodgings right above her home, which she shares with her alchemist uncle, Nicholas Kreutz.

Andrew becomes a night trumpeter in the Church of Our Lady Mary in Krakow. Each hour during the night, the Heynal—a hymn to Our Lady—is sounded from the balcony high up in the church tower. Joseph is learning to become a substitute trumpeter. One night while Andrew is in the tower, Button Face ransacks the Charnetski home. Although Kreutz chases him away, the crystal is gone. Naturally, Andrew and his family assume that Button Face has taken it. However, some months later, Button Face and his men attack the church demanding the gem. It happens that Joseph is in the church tower with his father that night. When Button Face orders him to play the Heynal, Joseph does so in a slightly unusual manner. When Elzbietka hears this odd playing, she senses that something is wrong and calls for help. Button Face is driven off.

Obviously, Button Face does not have the crystal. Actually, it is in the hands of the alchemist Kreutz. Urged on by his conniving assistant Johann Tring, Kreutz believes that the great gem will give him the power to convert base metal into gold. Elzbietka becomes more and more frightened by her uncle's strange actions. She warns Joseph of possible danger. She also tells him that if she ever hears him play the Heynal straight through without stopping at the broken note, she will know that he is in trouble once again and will find help.

Button Face stages another attack in the church, desperate to find the famous crystal. He overcomes Andrew in the church tower. During the attack, Joseph plays the Heynal straight through as the prearranged signal with Elzbietka. She hears the signal and immediately calls for help from Jan Kanty, the priest. The good Kanty sends the guards to their rescue.

In the meantime, Kreutz and his evil assistant start their experiments to change base metal into gold. Put into a trance by Tring, Kreutz looks into the crystal and believes he sees the sought-after formula. But when the two men attempt the experiment, they instead start a fire that eventually destroys a good part of the city of Krakow. The Charnetski family escapes harm, but sometime later Kreutz is found wandering around the city and he seems out of his senses. He has the crystal under his robe.

The following day, Jan Kanty, along with Andrew and Joseph, take the crystal to the king, who has just returned to the city after being gone for a long period. Just as the exchange is made, a crazed Kreutz rushes to the king and snatches the crystal from his hands. He flings the gem into the Vistula River.

Even though the gem is of great beauty and value, the king decides to let it remain in the river bed where it fell. The crystal has brought enough suffering and trouble to Krakow.

According to the story, the gem still lies on the river bed, never disturbed, although many have sought it. Andrew Charnetski rebuilt his house in Ukraine and, with Elzbietka and the broken alchemist, went there to live. Tring was never seen again. Joseph went on to the university and eventually returned home to marry Elzbietka and to manage his father's lands.

Themes and Subjects

Suspense and action move this story of life in fifteenth-century Poland. Belief in superstition and the practice of alchemy—turning metal into gold—is skillfully woven into the plot. Good and evil are plainly exemplified by the Charnetskis and Elzbietka on one side and Tring and Button Face on the other. This story combines adventure, self-sacrifice, and mystery against a medieval backdrop.

Incidents for Booktalking

The most interesting passages in the novel give a flavor of medieval life in Poland. See, for example: market day in Krakow (pp. 7–16); Joseph saves Elzbietka from the dog (pp. 29–31); Jan Kanty hires Andrew as a trumpeter (pp. 48–58); the trumpeter's duties in the tower (pp. 74–81); Kreutz and his assistant practice alchemy (pp. 86–93); Button Face attacks (pp. 107–16); Elzbietka hears Joseph's signal (pp. 141–55).

Related Titles

W. S. Kuniczak's *The Glass Mountain* (Hippocrene, 1992, $16.95: 0-7818-0552-X) features 26 tales and fables from Poland about devils, princesses, peasants, and villains.

Esther Hautzig's *A Gift for Mama* (pap., Puffin, $3.95: 0-14-032384-8) is set in Poland during the 1930s and centers on Sara, who is determined to buy her mother a gift for Mother's Day.

In fourteenth-century Poland, a sickly boy is accused of being a werewolf in Gloria Skurzynski's *Manwolf* (Clarion, 1981, $10.95: 0-395-30079-7).

A young Jewish boy lives inside the Warsaw ghetto during World War II in Uri Orlev's *The Island on Bird Street* (Houghton, 1984, $16.00: 0-395-33887-5; pap., $5.95: 0-395-61623-9).

In Jane Yolen's time-warp story *The Devil's Arithmetic* (Viking, 1988, $15.99: 0-670-81027-4), a young girl is transported back to Warsaw during the Holocaust.

About the Book and Author

Berger, Laura Standley, ed. *Twentieth-Century Children's Writers*. 4th ed. St. James, 1995, pp. 511–12.

Brown, Muriel W., and Rita Schoch Foudray. *Newbery and Caldecott Medalists and Honor Book Winners: Bibliographic & Resource Material Through 1990*. 2d ed. Neal-Schuman, 1992, p. 220.

Chevalier, Tracy, ed. *Twentieth-Century Children's Writers*. 3d ed. St. James, 1989, pp. 506–17.

Commire, Anne. *Yesterday's Authors of Books for Children*. Vol. 1. Gale, 1977, pp. 165–66.

Helbig, Alethea K., and Agnes R. Perkins, eds. *Dictionary of American Children's Fiction, 1859–1959*. Greenwood, 1986, p. 227 (bio.), p. 504 (book).

Kunitz, Stanley J., and Howard Haycraft, eds. *The Junior Book of Authors*. Wilson, 1951, pp. 176–78.

Miller, Bertha M., and Elinor Field, eds. *Newbery Medal Books: 1922–1955 with the Author's Acceptance Papers and Related Material*. Horn Book, 1955, pp. 65–73.

Peterson, Linda K., and Marilyn L. Solt, eds. *Newbery and Caldecott Medal and Honor Books: 1922–1981*. Hall, 1982, pp. 24–25.

Ward, Martha, ed. *Authors of Books for Young People*. 3d ed. Scarecrow, 1990, p. 389.

Honor Books 1929

Bennett, John. *The Pigtail of Ah Lee Ben Loo*. Illustrated by the author. Longmans, 1928, o.p. (Grades 4–7)

These 18 stories are written either in rhyming verse or in standard prose. All are generously illustrated by the author with intriguing "comical" silhouettes that convey the wit and humor of the subject matter. The title story is in verse and involves a rich banker, Li Ching, and his lovely daughter, Ting-a-Ling. A poor neighbor, the laundry man Ah Lee Ben Loo, is infatuated with Ting-a-Ling, and when he serenades her she returns his love. Ah Lee's rival is a wicked, wealthy mandarin who plots to remove Ah Lee from the competition. He learns that Ah Lee's 15-foot queue is in violation of a law that states no queue can be longer than the king's. Ah Lee is sent to prison. In despair, Ting-a-Ling takes off in a boat, but as it passes the prison Ah Lee lowers himself onto it by using his hair as a rope ladder. In the process he is forced to cut off his pride and joy, but the lovers are reunited and live happily ever after.

In "The Astonishing Story of the Caliph's Clock," a powerful Caliph decides that he needs a new clock after he continually arrives late for such important events as breakfast. A traveling Yankee peddler sells him a special clock with the guarantee that it will produce daylight savings. The new clock becomes the official timepiece of the city. However, soon there is a conflict with the sundials and nature's indicators, such as the cock's crow in the morning. In no time, confusion reigns and no one knows what is the real time. When the newfangled clock runs down, the Caliph is persuaded not to rewind it so the city can return to the peaceful bliss of not really caring what time it is. The author, John Bennett, is also the author of the classic historical novel first published in 1896, *Master Skylark: A Story of Shakespeare's Time* (pap., Airmont, $1.95).

Gag, Wanda. *Millions of Cats*. Illustrated by the author. Coward-McCann, 1928 o.p; Putnam, 1952, $11.95: 0-698-20091-8; pap., Sandcastle, $4.95: 0-698-20637-1. (Grades Preschool–2)

This picture book was designated a Newbery Honor Book in 1929, nine years before the Caldecott Award was established. Told in fairy-tale style, beginning with "Once upon a time," this delightful book is a perfect marriage of folk-like black-and-white illustrations and a simple text that uses the repetitive verse about "hundreds and thousands and millions and billions and trillions of cats." It tells the story of an elderly lonely couple who wish to have a cat as a companion. The husband sets out and comes to a hill covered with cats. Unable to decide which is the prettiest, he takes them all home to his wife, who promptly points out that they are unable to feed such a vast number of cats. The couple decide to let the cats choose which is the prettiest, which leads to a ferocious quarrel. When the husband and wife return to the scene of the battle, they discover only one cat left, a frightened little kitten who claims that it survived because it was too ugly to matter to the rest of the cats. The couple take the kitten in, feed it, and shower it with love until, in their eyes, it becomes the prettiest cat in the world.

Hallock, Grace T. *The Boy Who Was*. Illustrated by Harrie Wood. Dutton, 1928, o.p. (Grades 6–8)

This historical fantasy consists of 10 episodes that relate to the history of the Italian coastal area around Naples, which includes Capri, Sorrento, Ravello, Pompeii, and Amalfi. At Feast of Corpus Christi in 1927, a young artist climbs the mountains at Ravello and encounters a black-haired young Italian goatherd, Nino, who leads him to a spot where he can see all of the Bay of Naples. As Nino poses for the artist, he shows him his wood carvings that illustrate important events in the history of the area. In each of the stories that span 3,000 years of history, he appears as the goat boy. He first re-creates the story of the sirens who sang about the Phoenicians and their search for tin, and were later destroyed when Odysseus, on his voyage to Capri, defied them by placing wax in the ears of his crew members. He tells of the construction of a massive temple to Poseidon and of Miriam, a Jewish slave girl, who escaped the destruction of Pompeii by running from the city on the day that Vesuvius erupted. One story involves a local incident pertaining to the Children's Crusade to free the Holy Land, and another tells of the escape from the Byzantines of a wounded Goth hero. The victorious strategies of Robert the Wise are recalled in a story about the war between the Normans and the Saracens, and in another tale, the fleet of the Turks under Barbarossa is destroyed in a storm before they can destroy Amalfi. The emergence of the Carbonari in the early 1800s is recalled in an incident where Garibaldi captures a prince to prove that he is sincere in his desire to free Italy from the French. These vignettes bring to life some interesting aspects of Italian history that might be unfamiliar to many readers.

Meigs, Cornelia. *Clearing Weather*. Illustrated by Frank Dobias. Little, Brown, 1928, o.p. (Grades 6–9)

After the American Revolution, old Thomas Drury, head of the once-prosperous shipbuilding Drury family of Branscomb, Massachusetts, finds himself on the verge of bankruptcy because most of the family fortune has been used to finance the revolutionary cause. An additional threat comes from the unprincipled Darius Corland, Thomas's creditor, and the wicked lawyer, Joseph Ryall, who are arousing community opposition so they can take over the business. Thomas's nephew, Nicholas Drury, age 19, is determined to save the family business. When he helps a French adventurer, Etienne Bardeau, escape arrest, Nicholas is rewarded with documents indicating that Corland helped the British during the Revolution. Uncle Thomas becomes ill, and Nicholas and his friend, Michael Slade, take over the business. After making the people of Bransomb copartners, they build the *Jocasta*, a forerunner of the clipper ship, with the intent of mounting a trading expedition. Under the leadership of Captain Douglas, the crew, including Michael, sails first to the West Indies and then decides that greater riches lie around Cape Horn, trading with American Indians, and eventually with the Chinese. The trip is filled with adventure. At one point the ship is trapped on a sandbar and surrounded by hostile Indians, but luckily, a friendly Indian, grateful for kindnesses he has received, indicates a hidden channel that, at the full moon's high tide, allows them a narrow escape passage. They survive violent storms and pirate attacks and eventually arrive back home with an abundant cargo including riches from Canton. Through Etienne's efforts, the wicked Corland is forced to flee to England. The Drury shipyard is saved and the townspeople happily share in the profits of the venture.

Moon, Grace. *The Runaway Papoose*. Illustrated by Carl Moon. Doubleday, 1928, o.p. (Grades 4–6)

This novel, set in the southeastern United States of the 1920s, effectively introduces the Indian life and culture of the period. In descriptions and illustrations, it also interestingly portrays the flora and fauna of these desert regions. While a Pueblo Indian tribe is traveling through the desert to a new home, they are attacked by outlaw Indians. In the confusion, young Nah-tee, whose parents are members of the tribe, wanders out of camp and becomes lost. She finds an Indian shepherd boy, Moyo, who promises to take her on his pony to the great mesa, the destination of her tribe. During their trip they encounter a violent storm and flash flood, forcing them to spend the night in a cave used by mountain lions. After meeting an old man, Naybi, they discover a fortune in turquoise in an abandoned Pueblo cliff dwelling. Before leaving them, Naybi tells them to deliver the stones to Lampayo, the Pueblo chief. Continuing their journey, they are helped by two other youngsters, Chi-wee, a Pueblo girl, and Loki, a Navajo boy, but are kidnapped by the wicked Su-hu-bi, the next in line after Lampayo for the tribal leadership. They are sold to a trader with instructions to take them far away, but Chi-wee, who has escaped capture, rounds up some friends, and after pursuing the outlaws, frees her friends. Nah-tee is reunited with her parents at the mesa, and the villainy of Su-hu-bi is exposed. In a happy ending, Nah-tee's father, a member of the tribe that used to live in the deserted cliff dwelling, is named the new successor to Lampayo.

Whitney, Elinor. *Tod of the Fens.* Illustrated by Warwick Goble. Macmillan, 1928, o.p. (Grades 6–10)

This boisterous adventure story takes place in Boston, England, during the early fifteenth century, when England was expanding its merchant marine and increasing its continental trade in wool. The central character is a brawny rogue of about 20, Tod, who leads a band of 12 merry scoundrels who live in rude huts in the swampy lands around this coastal town. Their chief sport is to make game of unfortunate travelers who happen into their territory. One such wanderer calls himself Dismas, but is actually Prince Hal, who later becomes Henry V. Only Tod recognizes the disguised prince but keeps silent about his discovery. Dismas enjoys being part of Tod's merry, carefree life, and soon embarks on a private escapade that, he promises, will make fools of the townspeople of Boston. On five different occasions in different disguises, he enters the town and steals the five keys of the city's coffer. Suspicion for the thefts falls on the honest councilman Sir Frederick Tilney, whose beautiful 14-year-old daughter, Johanna, is preoccupied with her betrothal to Gilbert Branche, son of another merchant adventurer. Sir Frederick's maritime enterprises have placed him in direct competition with the Hanseatic League, whose members wish to discourage his expansionist activities. This supposedly will be accomplished by having one of their members, Ranolf, kidnap Johanna. Under false pretenses she is lured to a church, where she accidentally finds the hidden five keys. Another subplot centers on two dishonest councilmen who wish to steal the town's treasure. In time, all is set straight: Johanna and Gilbert are reunited, the keys and treasure are restored to the town, and Dismas reveals himself as their prince. Tod accepts an offer from Sir Frederick to become captain of a new ship that will help establish Britain's mastery of the seas.

1930s

Field, Rachel. *Hitty: Her First Hundred Years*. Illustrated by Dorothy P. Lathrop. Macmillan, 1929, $17.00: 0-02-734840-7. (Grades 4–7)

The house in which Rachel Field (1894–1942) was born in the quaint village of Stockbridge, Massachusetts, became for a time a museum that contained the paintings of another American original and onetime resident of Stockbridge, Norman Rockwell. After college at Radcliffe, Rachel Field moved to New York, where she did editorial work. While browsing through an antique store on West Eighth Street in Greenwich Village one day, she and her friend, Dorothy Lathrop, were intrigued with a wooden doll they discovered that was more than 100 years old—a real museum piece. Unable to afford the purchase price, "We went our separate ways and tried to think no more about her and her very brown and wise old face." However, the image of the doll haunted both of them and soon became the inspiration for a novel. As each chapter was written, Miss Field sent it to Albany, where Miss Lathrop supplied the illustrations. Other works for young people followed, including *Calico Bush* (see "Honor Books," 1932, p. 56).

Plot Summary

"The antique shop is very still." So began the remarkable adventures of an extraordinary doll named Hitty, who was made from a small piece of mountain ash wood more than a century ago. Today, Hitty sits in the window of the antique shop in New York City, where she is admired by one and all. However, shoppers would be even more admiring if they knew of her extensive travels and adventures.

After Old Peddler carves Hitty from the small piece of wood he has brought across the sea from Ireland, she is given to seven-year-old Phoebe Preble, who lives with her family along the seacoast in the state of Maine. Phoebe's father is a sea captain. Although Phoebe adores Hitty and takes good care of her, she tends to be careless, as little girls sometimes are. One day, Phoebe hides Hitty in her muff and takes her to church on Sunday. When Phoebe nods off, Hitty falls out of the muff and is left on the floor when the service is over. That is the first of Hitty's adventures, frightening to be sure. Some days later the church sexton finds her and she is returned to an adoring Phoebe.

That adventure, however, is mild compared to what is to follow. When Captain Preble cannot find a cook for his next sea voyage and therefore cannot set off after whales, he talks his wife into becoming the new cook for this trip. In that way, the Preble family, along with Hitty and Andy, the chore boy, go to sea on the *Diana-Kate*.

Sea life takes some getting used to, but Hitty rather enjoys it, especially as one of the sailors makes her a small sea chest to hold her possessions. But all is not well aboard the *Diana-Kate*, and Captain Preble soon experiences trouble with the crew. After a successful whale run, fire breaks out in the blubber room and the crew and the Prebles are forced to abandon ship. This is an especially frightening experience for Hitty, for as they are leaving the ship, the small doll falls into the sea. Miraculously, she floats to a nearby island where, of all things, the Prebles have also landed and Andy finds her.

Hitty hardly has time to relax after being reunited with Phoebe when some unfriendly island natives appear. Their chief spies Hitty and wants her. The Prebles have no choice but to hand her over, and so Hitty is carried away.

Her luck holds out, however, for some time later Andy once again comes to the rescue. Just before the Prebles are rescued, Andy, who has seen where Hitty was hidden, gets her back for a brokenhearted Phoebe.

The Preble family adventures to India, where an entirely foreign lifestyle begins for Hitty. She is being carried in Phoebe's hand when the girl falls asleep and drops her in the streets of Bombay. Hitty never sees Phoebe or the Prebles again.

That misery is further complicated by the fact that Hitty now falls into the hands of a snake charmer. Soon, however, she is bought by a missionary couple and spends the next couple of years in the relatively uneventful company of Little Thankful.

Life is somewhat quiet and dull until Little Thankful's parents decide that the climate would be better for her in the United States. So the little girl and Hitty sail to Philadelphia, where they will live with Little Thankful's grandparents.

Glad as she is to return home, Hitty is most unhappy to discover that she does not make an impressive showing against the dolls of Little Thankful's chums in Philadelphia. In fact, Little Thankful is ashamed of her and stuffs her out of sight in a horsehair sofa. It is a long time before she is rescued by Little Thankful's cousin, Clarissa Pryce, in whose care Hitty spends some of the most pleasant years of her life.

Clarissa is a frail, quiet ten-year-old and a Quaker. During Hitty's life with her, she has the honor of meeting the poet John Greenleaf Whittier. He even composes "Lines to a Quaker Doll of Philadelphia" in her honor. Also during this time, Hitty learns that the country is at war, North against South, and a solemn air settles over the Quaker household and the city.

Near the end of the Civil War, Clarissa is sent away to boarding school and Hitty finds herself in camphor. Two years pass, during which the box in which she has been packed is moved from Philadelphia to distant cousins in New York. She is uncovered by Miss Milly Pinch, who is visiting the Van Rensselaer family of New York City. Miss Pinch is a dressmaker and is determined to show off her skills by making little Hitty a fashion plate. It is like a butterfly emerging from a cocoon, for Hitty undergoes a magical transformation. She becomes a doll of fashion.

Hitty is now the property of Isabella Van Rensselaer, an attractive child with a temper and high spirits. Hitty rather enjoys her stay with Isabella. She even meets a gentleman more famous than Whittier. He is Charles Dickens, and Hitty is quite proud of being introduced.

One disastrous New Year's Eve, Hitty is stolen from Isabella by a rowdy bunch of boys. She comes into the possession of an Irish cab driver's family, who give her to their cousin Katie, who lives in Rhode Island. Katie is a sickly child, and Hitty is glad that she can be a comfort to her.

Unfortunately for Hitty, she is next dumped in a hayloft, where she spends some time until she is rescued by a painter, Mr. Farley. He spruces up Hitty to look attractive once more and uses her to keep little girls calm and quiet while he paints their portraits. In this manner, Hitty becomes an artist's model.

As Mr. Farley's traveling companion, Hitty sees a good bit of the United States, including the South. Hitty becomes part of the Cotton Exposition in New Orleans, where she is dressed as a beautiful bride. At the Exposition, a young girl named Sally Loomis is so enchanted with Hitty that she steals her. Sally, who hides Hitty, is later told by her father that the newspapers have printed an article about the valuable doll stolen from the Exposition.

Later, at a Sunday service, Sally becomes so guilty about stealing the valuable Hitty that she runs down to the river and throws her in, wicker basket and all. In time, Hitty is rescued by two boys, who take her to the little sister of one of the boys. Her name is Car'line. Soon, Hitty's real identity is realized and she is returned to New Orleans, where she had been stolen from the Exposition.

Mr. Farley, the artist, is said to have returned to New York, so Hitty is sent packing once more. But when he cannot be located, she is headed for the Dead Letter Office, a terrible fate. Instead, she falls into the hands of one of the postmen and ends up at the church fair.

Hitty is bought at the fair as a present for Great-Aunt Louella who lives in Boston. From there, she is taken by Miss Pamela Wellington, who adds Hitty to her famous doll collection. Fate takes over once again, when Hitty is flipped out of the car in which Miss Pamela is riding. She is found and transferred to Portland, Maine, to Carrie's restaurant. It is about this time that people begin referring to Hitty as an antique.

From the restaurant, Hitty finds herself at auction, where she is sold for $53 to an old gentleman. And so, Hitty returns to New York and is now in the antique shop on Eighth Avenue. The shop belongs to Miss Hunter, and the old gentleman had been asked to buy some items for the shop when he was in New England.

Hitty becomes well-known in the neighborhood as she sits in the front window and is admired by all. Life may not be as adventurous as it once was, but it is pleasant and busy. Besides, Hitty has had quite enough adventures for a century-old doll made of well-seasoned mountain ash.

Themes and Subjects

This is a pleasant old-fashioned story seen through the eyes of a doll. Bits of history and Americana abound as Hitty goes from one adventure to another. Different personalities emerge in the little girls who own Hitty for a time. The doll itself shows spunk and charm as her lifestyle changes, which she accepts with great courage and strength.

Incidents for Booktalking

Any of Hitty's marvelous perils will delight readers and serve as a good introduction to this plucky doll's character. See: lost in the church (pp. 7–12); Hitty goes to sea (pp. 37–45); taken by the native chief and rescued by Andy (pp. 69–71, 74–80); lost in Bombay with the snake charmer (pp. 84–92); the pleasant years with Clarissa (pp. 109–20); Hitty becomes a doll of fashion and meets Charles Dickens (pp. 131–41).

Related Titles

In Richard Kennedy's *Amy's Eyes* (Harper, 1985, $14.89: 0-06-023220-X), Amy's doll, Captain, comes alive and runs away to sea, where Amy joins him for some high adventure.

A tiny red-haired man leaves his home among the chickens and travels throughout Rhode Island, where he has a series of adventures in Stephen Manes's *Some of the Adventures of Rhode Island Red* (Lippincott, 1990, $10.95: 0-397-32348-4).

Fantasy and reality mix in William Mayne's *Hob and the Goblins* (Dorling Kindersley, 1994, $12.95: 1-56458-713-4) when a house sprite adopts a family and tries to save them from goblins.

For a younger audience, two dolls celebrate Christmas together in Tasha Tudor's *The Dolls' Christmas* (McKay, 1979, $6.95: 0-8089-102603).

For a more mature audience, readers are taken to a world where dolls come alive in the British fantasy *Through the Doll's House* (pap., Dell, $3.25: 0-440-40433-9) by Jane Gardam.

About the Book and Author

Berger, Laura Standley, ed. *Twentieth-Century Children's Writers*. 4th ed. St. James, 1995, pp. 341–42.

Brown, Muriel W., and Rita Schoch Foudray. *Newbery and Caldecott Medalists and Honor Book Winners: Bibliographic & Resource Material Through 1990*. 2d ed. Neal-Schuman, 1992, pp. 131–34.

Cech, John, ed. "American Writers for Children, 1900–1960." In *Dictionary of Literary Biography*. Vol. 22. Gale, 1983, pp. 170–76.

Chevalier, Tracy, ed. *Twentieth-Century Children's Writers*. 3d ed. St. James, 1989, pp. 334–36.

Commire, Anne, ed. *Something About the Author*. Vol. 15. Gale, 1979, pp. 106–13.

Helbig, Alethea K., and Agnes R. Perkins, eds. *Dictionary of American Children's Fiction, 1859–1959*. Greenwood, 1986, p. 160 (bio.), pp. 220–21 (book).

Kunitz, Stanley J., and Howard Haycraft, eds. *The Junior Book of Authors*. Wilson, 1951, pp. 123–26.

May, Hal, ed. *Contemporary Authors*. Vol. 109. Gale, 1983, p. 132.

Peterson, Linda K., and Marilyn L. Solt, eds. *Newbery and Caldecott Medal and Honor Books: 1922–1981*. Hall, 1982, pp. 29–31.

Senick, Gerard J., ed. *Children's Literature Review*. Vol. 19. Gale, 1990, pp. 62–81.

Silvey, Anita, ed. *Children's Books and Their Creators*. Houghton, 1995, pp. 238-39.

Ward, Martha, ed. *Authors of Books for Young People*. 3d ed. Scarecrow, 1990, p. 226.

Honor Books 1930

Adams, Julia Davis. *Vaino: A Boy of New Finland*. Illustrated by Lempi Ostman. Dutton, 1929, o.p. (Grades 6–9)

This novel, set during the Finnish Revolution of World War I that freed the country from oppressive Russian rule, not only evokes the proud spirit of the revolutionary movement after the declaration of independence in 1917, but also incorporates many stories from the Finnish national epic, the *Kalevala*. These stories are told by Vaino's mother, Fru Lunberg, as she sits knitting before their huge stove. Many of the war incidents are based on facts gathered during the author's many visits to Finland. Fru Lunberg lives near Helsingfors with her three children: young Vaino; his sister, Anniki, an 18-year-old university student; and an older brother, 20-year-old Sven. Both Sven and Anniki are active in the White revolutionary forces. Early in the story, Vaino and his mother hide a Russian named Vladimir who is fleeing the Red troops, and later Vaino becomes part of a dangerous mission to secure arms and ammunition from a German U-boat. When Sven is forced into hiding, Vaino, on skis, smuggles supplies to his brother and his comrades in hiding and they are reunited with Vladimir, who has now become a staunch ally. After Vaino leaves, Sven and his friends are forced to flee and suffer incredible hardships during a journey across ice fields to Estonia. Good news comes from Anniki, who has married her fellow revolutionary Scarelius, but in Helsingfors, Vaino and his mother are under suspicion for their activities and, when the city becomes a battleground, are forced to move twice to escape detection. Eventually the forces of liberty prevail, and Vaino witnesses the victorious army of Mannerheim enter Helsingfors.

Eaton, Jeanette. *A Daughter of the Seine: The Life of Madame Roland*. Harper, 1929, o.p. (Grades 7–10)

This is a fictionalized biography of the French Revolutionary patriot and writer Jeanne Manon Philipon Roland de la Platiere (1754–1793), who became known simply as Madame Roland. She was the daughter of a Paris engraver who encouraged his daughter's interest in music, painting, and literature. As a young girl, she told her grandmother, "I'll call myself daughter of the Seine," and as an adult she often said that the river was part of her soul. As a young woman she became interested in the radical ideas of Jean Jacques Rousseau and the movement for equality. She shared these enthusiasms with her husband, whom she married in 1780. After the outbreak of the Revolution, she formed a salon of followers, who later became known as the Girondists. Under the constitutional monarchy, her husband became minister of the interior, a post he held after the monarchy was overthrown. Madame Roland both directed her husband's career and influenced the important politicians of the period. Gradually she and her husband became alienated from the more radical party of the revolutionaries, the Jacobins, which included Danton and Robespierre. The breach culminated in her arrest in June 1793. During her time in prison, she studied English, corresponded with her friends, and wrote her memoirs, *Appeal to Impartial Posterity*. On November 8, 1793, after five months in prison, she was sent to the guillotine. Her last words were, "O, Liberty, what crimes are committed in thy name!" This biography, rich in details of the period, successfully brings to life one of the most interesting and tragic figures of the French Revolution.

McNeely, Marian Hurd. *The Jumping-off Place*. Illustrated by William Siegal. Longmans, 1929, o.p. (Grades 6–9)

In 1910, the author and her husband homesteaded in South Dakota. She has used the same time, setting, and many of her experiences to tell the story of the four Linville youngsters and their fight for the land. When their guardian, Uncle Jim, dies, the four Linvilles, Becky, 17, Dick, 15, and the young ones, Phil and Joan, decide to leave their home in Platteville, Wisconsin, and live on the land for which Uncle Jim had filed a claim on the Rosebud Reservation in South Dakota. Luckily, their uncle has left detailed instructions on how to survive in this environment. With these and the help of Mr. and Mrs. Cleaver, who live in the nearby town of Dallas, South Dakota, they begin their homesteading, hoping that they will be able to last the 14 months required to validate their claim. They purchase farm animals, supplies, and equipment, and sow some crops to get them through the winter. Becky and Dick convert part of a barn for living quarters, but the youngsters encounter many obstacles, both natural and man-made. Drought and severe wind storms, plus encounters with rattlers and general weariness, take their toll. There is also trouble with the Welps, a family that is squatting on part of their land hoping to drive the Linvilles from the land and claim it as their own. When their crops fail, and their money is almost gone, the Linvilles seem defeated until Mr. Cleaver arranges for Becky to teach at a prairie school. After she helps her students through a terrible blizzard, the neighbors band together to help the youngsters and drive off the Welps. With this assistance, they are now assured of proving their claim when it comes due in July.

Miller, Elizabeth Cleveland. *Pran of Albania*. Illustrated by Maud Petersham and Miska Petersham. Doubleday, 1929, o.p. (Grades 7–9)

At the close of World War I, the author spent some time in Albania with the Red Cross. From these experiences she used the same settings and time period to tell this story of steadfast love and family devotion set against a backdrop of political strife, savage battles, and a gallant people's resistance to Slavic domination. Pran, a 14-year-old girl, lives in the mountains of Albania with her mother, Lukja, her father, Ndrek, and her younger twin brothers, Nik and Gjon. While gathering branches in the woods, Pran meets a handsome young man, Nush, who saves mischievous Nik's life when he falls into a turbulent river. She finds Nush attractive and later meets him during a feast day. When Pran goes to the town of Skodra on an errand, she sees him again, now disguised as a Moslem. He interprets distant signal fires as indications of an impending Slavic attack and she warns her villagers in time. Because of attacking Slavs, Pran's family, now without Ndrek who is away fighting, move to Skodra where they care for Dil, a girl of Pran's age, and later her younger brother and sister, Noz and Lul. When Pran goes to the front to deliver supplies to her father, she once more sees Nush, who has been wounded, and overhears a Slavic plan of attack, which she is able to battle. Back home, Pran learns that she has been betrothed to marry, and caring only for

Nush, she takes an oath of virginity. At a council meeting that Pran attends, she persuades the elders to maintain a truce called a *bessa* to end blood feuds between warring tribes. Nush, who belongs to one of these rival families, is now free to openly declare his love for Pran. The girl also discovers that Nush was the man her father had named as her betrothed. The story ends with the happy, traditional marriage of Pran and Nush.

Swift, Hildegarde Hoyt. *Little Blacknose*. Illustrated by Lynd Ward. Harcourt, 1929, o.p. (Grades 3–5)

Little Blacknose is the nickname of the first locomotive ever made for the New York Central Railroad. This account traces its life story from its creation in the West Point Foundry in New York City in 1831 to its placement on exhibit in Grand Central Station in 1928. Blacknose begins his career on a Hudson River ferry boat that takes him from New York to Albany. On land, he is promptly insulted by a horse who is scornful of the idea that this ugly machine with a hump in its middle could take its place. Soon, however, Blacknose is fueled up and ready to begin his first trip. Later in a formal ceremony, he is named DeWitt Clinton and becomes the first locomotive to lead an excursion from Albany to Schenectady. In time, his supremacy is threatened by the arrival of John Bull, a larger, more powerful engine from England. On the gala excursion day, John Bull suffers problems with his supply pipe and Little Blacknose saves the day by pulling three of the coaches to Schenectady at the great speed of 19 miles per hour. In time, the two engines become fast friends instead of rivals. Eventually, Little Blacknose is pensioned off, but there are still days of glory ahead. At the 1893 World's Fair in Chicago he is placed on display, and 35 years later finds his place in Grand Central Station. This highly anthropomorphized account unfortunately presents an overly emotional and didactic version of what was an interesting chapter in American railroad history.

Young, Ella. *The Tangle-Coated Horse and Other Tales: Episodes from the Fionn Saga*. Illustrated by Vera Brock. Longmans, 1929, o.p. (Grades 5–8)

This collection of 14 tales tell about the life of the legendary Irish hero, Fionn McCool, and of his comrades and foes. Fionn's mother was Moorna and his father, Uail, chief of the Clann Bassna, slain by Goll who took away the family's land. Fionn spent his earliest years learning in the forest from his guardian, an old woman named Bovemall. Here he was taught nature crafts and learned of his ancestry, but from an ancient fisherman, he learned about language and verse. As a youth, he finds a magic sword in the woods that belonged to his father and eats of the Salmon of Knowledge. Conn, the High King of Ireland, posts a reward for anyone who can challenge the evil Allyn and prevent him from destroying the king's castle, Tara. Equipped with his sword and an enchanted clock, Fionn confronts Allyn. The monster breathes deadly lightning but Fionn uses his cloak to deflect it. Allyn knows he is defeated and flees but Fionn pursues him to the death. As a reward he receives the traditional land of his family, the lordship of the Fianna of Ireland. Here he receives pledges of allegiance from all, including Goll. For many years Fionn and his companions live in the palace of Aloon, which had been built for his mother. A beautiful deer he has been hunting suddenly turns into a young woman, Saba, who becomes his wife. But in a few months the Dark Shadowy One casts a spell over her and takes her away. Seven years later, Fionn finds a young boy in the woods and realizes that it is his son, whom he names Usheen. In the title story, Fionn follows a shaggy-coated, shambling horse to the Land-Under-Wave and there discovers that the horse is actually the enchanted stallion that belongs to the epic hero, Mananann. In the final story, Usheen learns how to be a hero like his father, then retreats to live in a monastery with Saint Patrick, the bringer of Christianity to Ireland. Thus ends the Irish age of fable and legend.

Newbery Winner 1931

Coatsworth, Elizabeth. *The Cat Who Went to Heaven*. Illustrated by Lynn Ward. Macmillan, 1930, $16.00: 0-02-719710-7; pap., $4.95: 0-02-042580-5. (Grades 4–6)

This brief fantasy set in Japan tells of an artist's cat named Good Fortune whose devotion to the Lord Buddha and his teachings leads to her acceptance by the Buddhist priests into the faith, even though the faith claims that the cat is the only animal that denies the Buddha's teachings. The author, Elizabeth Coatsworth (1893–1986), was a seasoned world traveler who lived for one year in the Orient (1916–17), where she gained memories and impressions that helped in the writing of this book. She wrote,

> Its main inspiration was the Buddhist temples of Borobodur, in Java. Among the many carvings on its terraces are some of the animal rebirths of Buddha, which very much took my imagination. Many years later, I was to read translations of the rebirths and string them together on the thread of a Japanese legend. Later, Tom Hanforth sent me a print, which, like the temple scroll, showed a cat coming to mourn the death of Buddha.

From these ideas came this moving book, which is one of the most enduring of the author's 90 books for young people.

Plot Summary

A long time ago in Japan, a young artist was very poor. No one had bought one of his paintings for a long time. Now he sits dreaming of the rice cakes his housekeeper will buy at the market with his few last pennies. But when she returns, he is dismayed to learn that she has not bought rice cakes at all. Instead, she returns with her shopping basket full of—a cat! Why has she done such a thing, he cries! The housekeeper says that she heard of a little boy who had drawn pictures of cats and then went on to become a great artist.

Although he is hungry, the artist calms down and accepts the cat into his household. He has to admit that she is a pretty little thing, with white fur, big yellow eyes, and yellow and black spots. He remembers that three-color cats are supposed to bring good luck, and so he names her Good Fortune.

Good Fortune proves to be a very neat, polite, and well-behaved cat. She accepts the small portion of food that the artist can give her and keeps out of his way when he is working. In time, the artist has to admit that Good Fortune is, indeed, a very special cat. One day he sees her catch a bird and then release it unharmed from beneath her paws.

The days pass, the artist works, and still no one comes to buy his paintings. Then one day, the housekeeper excitedly tells the artist that the priest from the temple has come to see him. The artist is astounded. What does the priest want with him? Quickly, he gives the only thing of value he still owns, a vase, to the housekeeper and tells her to sell it and then buy tea and cakes for the guest.

The priest informs the artist that he has been chosen, from among other artists whose names had been put on slips of paper, to paint the death of Lord Buddha for the temple. This is a great honor, and the priest has brought the first payment for such a work with him.

The poor artist and the housekeeper nearly cry for joy when the priest leaves. Then, he hears a curious noise. Good Fortune is purring for joy, sounding as loud as the housekeeper! Painting the death of the great Buddha is very serious business, and so the young artist is determined to understand the Buddha before he begins to paint him. On the first day of his contemplation of the Buddha, the artist imagines him as Siddhartha, the young Indian prince. He pictures the young prince as he readies himself to compete with other young princes for the hand of his bride. Siddhartha wins the princess without ill feeling from his rivals.

On the second day of his contemplations, the young artist, with Good Fortune at his side, reflects upon the renunciation of Siddhartha. He sees how the young prince becomes aware of the world's suffering and renounces his princely garments, giving up the royal world of his youth.

During all this time, Good Fortune sits silently by in encouragement. It becomes a habit for the artist and Good Fortune to begin each morning by praying together to the Buddha.

The artist finally decides that he will paint the procession of animals who all paid homage to the Buddha. He knows that this means he cannot paint a cat, for of all the animals, only the cat refused to pay homage to the great Buddha and so was refused the doors of Paradise.

With Good Fortune watching silently, the artist paints the Buddha at his death and those who came to see him. Then, it is time to paint the animals. He begins with the snail because the snail was the first creature to sacrifice itself to the Buddha. When the snail is painted, Good Fortune views it and seems to say that it is a very snail-like snail.

Next comes the great body of the elephant, and when it is finished, Good Fortune stands awestruck. After that comes the beautiful, wild horse, and once again Good Fortune approves, gazing at his work with admiration.

It is time now to paint the swan, and although it is a beautiful swan, Good Fortune looks slightly as though the artist might better spend his time painting something else. The ugly but powerful buffalo comes next. Good Fortune looks on approvingly, although with just the slightest dissatisfaction.

After a good deal of reflection, the artist paints the dog for the picture. He is very proud of the finished animal, but that day Good Fortune will not even enter the room to view it.

The Banyan deer, who was filled with the spirit of the Buddha, is a worthy animal to be represented in his drawing. Good Fortune does come to view it but says nothing. She seems to be asking why there is no room in his painting for a cat.

Instead, the artist adds a monkey. All the time the little cat grows sadder and sadder. After the tiger is added, the artist says to Good Fortune that he would gladly add the cat to his painting if he could. But, after all, the cat is the one animal who would not pay homage to the Buddha and so has not received the Budda's blessing. Good Fortune mews and mews with a bowed head like a child.

When the picture is finished, the young artist knows that it is very good indeed. And yet he is not satisfied. Something is missing. As he hears Good Fortune's plaintive mewing from the kitchen, he knows what he must do. Picking up his best brush, he draws a magnificent cat.

The artist calls the housekeeper and the cat into the room to view his completed masterpiece. Good Fortune looks at the artist with complete joy in her eyes and then falls dead of sheer joy on the floor.

The priest comes to view the painting on the following day. But when he sees the cat, his eyes harden. "Did you not know that the cat did not receive the Buddha's blessing?" he asks. The artist replies that he knew. "Then each person must suffer the consequences of his acts," says the priest. The painting is to be burned on the next day.

The artist's future is ruined. No one will come to him for a painting ever again. And yet, he does not regret his actions, not when he thinks of the great happiness that, for a moment, he had brought to Good Fortune's eyes.

Early the next morning the artist hears the sounds of people coming to his house. They bade him follow them to the temple. There his picture hangs with incense and candles before it. But the young artist cannot believe his eyes! In the painting, the Buddha has stretched out his arm in blessing. Under his hand kneels the tiny figure of a cat, its little white head bowed in adoration.

Themes and Subjects

This is a beautiful and tender story of how humility and devotion brought good fortune for a young artist in the miracle of the Buddha. It points out the compassion of the artist who, although desperately needing the money and recognition that this painting will bring him, cannot ignore his loving companion, the cat. This unselfish act of including the cat in the painting brings about the miracle of the Buddha and brings fame to the young man. This gentle story of a long ago time and a faraway place illustrates a love for all animals.

Incidents for Booktalking

Many passages in this book demonstrate the gentleness and compassion of the story. See: the artist first accepts the cat (pp. 3–4); the cat releases the bird (p. 8); the artist gets the commission to paint the death of the Buddha (pp. 9–10); the cat approves of the snail painting (p. 22); the cat admires the horse (pp. 26–28); the cat will not view the dog (pp. 36–38); the artist paints the cat and Good Fortune dies with happiness (pp. 52–54); the miracle of the Buddha (pp. 61–62).

Related Titles

Molly Bang retells a Japanese version of the Orpheus story in *Dawn* (Morrow, 1983, pap., $3.95: 0-688-10989-6).

At first Keifi is unhappy at the thought of spending three months with her grandparents in rural Japan in Romer Godden's *Great Grandfather's House* (Greenwillow, 1993, $18.00: 0-689-11319-2).

Japanese geography, history, and culture are covered in Richard and Sheila Tames's *Japan* (Watts, 1994, $20.00: 0-8167-2115-7).

Ten unusual dream-related stories from around the world are included in Laurence Yep's *Tree of Dreams: Ten Tales for the Gardens of Night* (Troll, 1994, $13.95: 0-8167-3498-4).

Nine stories that the author heard as a child in Shanghai are found in Linda Fang's *The Ch'i-lin Purse: A Collection of Ancient Chinese Stories* (Farrar, 1994, $16.00: 0-374-31241-9; pap., $4.95: 0-374-41189-1).

About the Book and Author

Berger, Laura Standley, ed. *Twentieth-Century Children's Writers*. 4th ed. St. James, 1995, pp. 223–26.

Brown, Muriel W., and Rita Schoch Foudray. *Newbery and Caldecott Medalists and Honor Books Winners: Bibliographic & Resource Material Through 1990*. 2d ed. Neal-Schuman, 1992, pp. 69–73.

Cech, John, ed. "American Writers for Children, 1900–1960." In *Dictionary of Literary Biography*. Vol. 22. Gale, 1983, pp. 94–101.

Chevalier, Tracy, ed. *Twentieth-Century Children's Writers*. 3d ed. St. James, 1989, pp. 216–19.

Coatsworth, Elizabeth. *Personal Geography: Almost an Autobiography*. Stephen Green, 1976.

Commire, Anne, ed. *Something About the Author*. Gale, 1970, Vol. 2, pp. 65–68; 1989, Vol. 56, p. 26.

Evory, Ann, and Linda Metzger, eds. *Contemporary Authors (New Revision Series)*. Vol. 4. Gale, 1981, pp. 141–43.

Harte, Barbara, and Carolyn Riley, eds. *Contemporary Authors (First Revision Series)*. Vols. 5–8. Gale, 1969, pp. 230–31.

Hedblad, Alan. *Something About the Author*. Vol. 100. Gale, 1999, pp. 62–67.

Helbig, Alethea K., and Agnes R. Perkins, eds. *Dictionary of American Children's Fiction, 1859–1959*. Greenwood, 1986, pp. 106–7 (bio.), pp. 89–90 (book).

Hopkins, Lee Bennett, ed. *More Books by More People*. Citation Press, 1974, pp. 95–99.

Kunitz, Stanley J., and Howard Haycraft, eds. *The Junior Book of Authors*. Wilson, 1951, pp. 71–73.

Miller, Bertha M., and Elinor Field, eds. *Newbery Medal Books: 1922–1955 with the Author's Acceptance Papers and Related Material*. Horn Book, 1955, pp. 88–98.

Peterson, Linda K., and Marilyn L. Solt, eds. *Newbery and Caldecott Medal and Honor Books: 1922–1981*. Hall, 1982, pp. 34–35.

Riley, Carolyn, ed. *Children's Literature Review*. Vol. 2. Gale, 1976, pp. 51–64.

Silvey, Anita, ed. *Children's Books and Their Creators*. Houghton, 1995, p. 151.

Ward, Martha, ed. *Authors of Books for Young People*. 3d ed. Scarecrow, 1990, p. 134.

Honor Books 1931

Adams, Julia Davis. *Mountains Are Free*. Illustrated by Theodore Nadejen. Dutton, 1930, o.p. (Grades 7–9)

This historical novel, set principally in fourteenth-century Switzerland during the struggle for independence against Austria, features, but does not highlight, the famous apple-cleaving feat of William Tell. Bruno, a 13-year-old orphan, is being reared by the Tells but leaves their impoverished household to seek his fortune as a page for the cruel Sir Rupprecht von Lowenhokie in Austria. At the castle of the Duke of Valberg, he meets the charming Lady Zellina, a year his junior. Lady Zellina is the ward of the Duke, the heiress to an immense fortune and the fiefdom of Rathwyl, and the girl Sir Rupprecht hopes to marry. Bruno also meets the minstrel jester, Kyo, who is devoted to Zellina. Rupprecht is summoned to fight in Austria, and therefore wants to marry Zellina immediately. Kyo, Bruno, and the miserable Zellina flee and make their way to Switzerland, where the girl is adopted by a friendly Swiss family. Years pass, but the oppressed mountaineers, under the control of the tyrannical bailiff, Gessler, are still fighting for their freedom. Bruno witnesses the scene in which Gessler forces Bruno's hero, William Tell, to shoot an apple from his son's head. After Tell escapes from the ship that is taking him to prison, Bruno sees Tell kill Gessler. Bruno is also either an observer or participant in other important events of the revolution. The Austrians sent a well-equipped army to put down the rebellion, but they are no match for the canny mountaineers. Both Rupprecht and the Duke of Valberg are killed, but Zellina decides to postpone the claim to her Austrian fortune to stay in Switzerland and marry Bruno.

Best, Herbert. *Garram the Hunter: A Boy of the Hill Tribes*. Illustrated by Erick Berry. Doubleday, 1930, o.p. (Grades 5–8)

In writing this story set in precolonial Africa, the author has relied on information collected while he was an English civil servant in the area. Garram, son of the tribal chieftain, Warok, in a hill region of Africa, has gained the nickname "the hunter" because of his amazing abilities stalking jungle animals with his faithful dog, Kon. His foolish cousin, Menud, son of Garram's wealthy scheming uncle, Sura, is jealous of Garram's prowess and plans to frame him for stealing goats. Taking the advice of the village high priest, The Rainmaker, Garram flees to a nearby walled city, Yelwa, where the Fulani live ruled by a Moslem emir. With the help of Kon, the boy circumvents two plots to assassinate the Emir, first by the well-intentioned Ibrahim and second by an evil Grand Vizier. Garram wins the favor of the Emir and secures a pardon for Ibrahim. Sensing problems at home, Garram leaves Yelwa and is intercepted by a messenger from The Rain-maker, telling him that his uncle and nephew have seized power and that his father will be executed in the morning. He kills a leopard and, wearing the skin over his armor, frightens the prison guards and frees his father. Order is restored, and while the elders are deliberating the fate of Sura and Menud, word comes that enemy tribes, the Fulani of the East, are approaching. Despite the treachery of Menud, who has revealed a secret pass to the enemy, Garram and his tribesmen win a victory over the invaders and, later, when the Fulani are trapped on a narrow path, the final victory is achieved by The Rainmaker and the women of the village, who roll stones on the enemy from a cliff above. Both Sura and Menud are killed in the battle. The victory is complete when reinforcements arrive from Yelwa under the leadership of a grateful Ibrahim.

Gray, Elizabeth Janet. *Meggy MacIntosh.* Illustrated by Marguerite de Angeli. Doubleday, 1930, o.p. (Grades 6–9)

This novel, first set in Edinburgh and later in North Carolina, spans more than a year in the life of its plucky, determined young heroine, Meggy MacIntosh. Orphaned, 15-year-old Meggy, whose family supported Bonny Prince Charlie's ill-fated attempt to claim the throne of Scotland, has been given a home by her aunt and uncle, Sir Douglas and Lady Keith in Edinburgh. Their daughter, Veronica, plans to elope with Ewan MacNeill, the son of another wealthy Scottish family, and sail on the brigantine, *Bachelor of Leith,* to the colony of North Carolina. When Veronica loses her courage, Meggy gathers her small inheritance and some jewels, and takes her place. Later, at sea, when she is discovered, Ewen is furious, but the indomitable Meggy is soon a favorite aboard ship and becomes friendly with a Miss Cameron, who is taking her brother's sons to Holy Quarter, their plantation. On land, Meggy plans to find her idol, the legendary Flora MacDonald, who helped Prince Charlie escape from Scotland, but when she reaches Wilmington, she finds that Flora and her family are strong Loyalists and have moved into the backwoods. Meggy stays for a time with a Clayton family who are Whigs, or American patriots, and then stays at Holy Quarter with the Camerons. Through the help of David Malcolm, the attractive cousin of the Claytons, and Ewen, who has matured somewhat toward Meggy, the girl finally travels into the timberlands and stays with Flora. Meggy travels with a bound girl, Tibbie McNabb, whose freedom Meggy has bought with her last ruby. Although Flora is as warm and pleasant as Meggy anticipated, she finds that there is no place for her and Tibbie in Flora's household and that, particularly because of growing fondness for David, her allegiances really lie with the freedom-seeking Whigs. She and Tibbie go to Cross Creek, the Malcolm plantation, where they nurse David's ailing mother. There, she and Mrs. Malcolm await the return of Mr. Malcolm and David, who are now fighting as part of the rebelling patriot forces. Meggy has irrevocably cast her lot with the Revolutionaries.

Hewes, Agnes Danforth. *Spice and the Devil's Cave.* Illustrated by Lynn Ward. Knopf, 1930, o.p. (Grades 7–10)

This story, set in Lisbon in the late 1490s, combines real and fictional characters. The action centers about the home and workshop of a kindly Jewish financier and mapmaker, Abel Zabuto, and his wife, Ruth. Into this setting comes a group of people who, like Abel, are intent on opening the spice trade to the East by way of the Cape of Good Hope, also known as the Devil's Cave. They include Bartholomew Diaz, Vasco da Gama, and Ferdinand Magellan, a precocious page from the court of King Manoel. They are joined by a young, handsome Venetian, Nicolo Conti, who is also eager to enter the spice trade. One night a frightened waif seeks refuge in Abel's home. At first, she is too terrified to speak, but a seafarer named Shander recognizes her as Nejmi, the daughter of a European spice trader father, and an Arab mother, who were both murdered by Arabs in the Near East. With Shander's help, she escapes from slavery, and comes to Lisbon as a stowaway.Through her knowledge of trade routes, and Abel's ability to create maps, the king is persuaded to support an exploratory voyage by Vasco da Gama. While awaiting the return of Gama, Nicolo, now enamored of Nejmi, becomes a regular visitor at Abel's home. Together with Shander he buffaloes a plot led by the Venetian ambassador to steal Abel's valuable maps. The quiet of the Zabuto household is also disrupted by news that the Jews in Portugal, like their counterparts in Spain, might face expulsion. Though Gama returns triumphant from his voyages, Abel decides that because of his uncertain future, he and his wife must leave Portugal. After the couple witness the joyful wedding of Nicolo and Nejmi, they secretly depart, leaving their house and belongings to the newly married couple. This novel portrays a fascinating period in history by combining historical fact, including material on the prevalent persecution of Jews, with a tale of adventure, romance, and intrigue.

Hubbard, Ralph. *Queer Person*. Illustrated by Harold von Schmidt. Doubleday, 1930, o.p. (Grades 5–7)

The author, a specialist in Native American lore, has incorporated much of this fascinating knowledge into this tale of Indian life in central Montana before the arrival of Europeans. On a cold winter morning, clad only in a worn buffalo robe, a four-year-old deaf-mute child wanders into the village of the Pikuni, who are members of the Blackfoot tribe. Though rejected by all and named "Queer Person," he is eventually adopted by another of the group's outcasts, an old woman named Granny. She teaches him sign language and, after she uses her folk medicines to cure the chief's son-in-law, both Granny and Queer Person gain stature in the tribe and the boy becomes friendly with the chief's daughter, Singing Moon. When he is 16, Queer Person suffers severe headaches, and large worm-like balls of wax fall from his ears. He can now hear, though he tells no one but Granny, who secretly teaches him to speak. He wishes to reveal his secret particularly because he has fallen in love with Singing Moon, but Granny bids him be silent until the time comes to prove himself as a warrior. Four years later, when the chief's seven-year-old son, Sun Pipe, is kidnapped by the Crows, and Singing Moon is promised as the bride to his rescuer, it is Queer Person's time to act. In disguise, he enters the Crow village and finds a half-dead Sun Pipe prepared to be a human sacrifice. Queer Person is discovered and, to win freedom for himself and Sun Pipe, must perform the Porcupine Dance of running across a course of slippery buffalo heads. Should he fall he will be shot through with arrows until he looks like a porcupine. He is successful and in a second and last trial, kills an old warrior in single combat. After leaving the village in triumph he later learns that the old warrior was his dissolute father, who had allowed Queer Person to be abandoned when he was believed to be deaf and dumb. Queer Person returns to his home with the Pikunis, now worthy of the hand of Singing Moon in marriage.

Lide, Alice Alison, and Margaret Alison Johansen. *Ood-le-uk, the Wanderer*. Illustrated by Raymond Lufkin. Little, Brown, 1930, o.p. (Grades 7–9)

This story tells how a fearless young man is able to establish contact between his people, the Eskimos of coastal Alaska, and the fierce Tschuktschi tribe in Siberia across the Bering Strait. Ood-le-uk, the timid, puny son of Kotuk, the Eskimo village chief, one day finds on the shore a case that contains a metal cross, which he places about his neck as a good luck charm. While on a tribal hunt, Ood-le-uk becomes separated from his group and is swept away on an ice flow. Later he kills a walrus and uses the carcass to fashion a small kayak. Blown off course, he lands in Siberia and is befriended by Valetka, the headman of the Tschuktschi tribe, and his son Etel, a boy of Ood-le-uk's age. When the tribe's shaman wants to sacrifice Ood-le-uk to stop a plague in the area, the presence of his cross saves him because the tribe members, recently converted to a primitive Christianity, do not want to kill a fellow believer. In the three years he stays with the Tschuktchi, he has many adventures. Through his cunning and courage, he saves a reindeer herd from the wolves, and at a great local fair, he and Etel are narrowly saved from gypsies when a Christian priest intervenes. When the tribe is struck by famine, the two boys travel north into the feared Land of Spirits in search of food. They find mammoth meat, frozen hundreds of years ago. Through this discovery, they save the tribe from starvation. Ood-le-uk builds a large sailing vessel and, accompanied by Etel and others, sails for his home. Now a mature leader of men, he is welcomed by his tribesmen. In time, he and Etel build more boats and soon a thriving trade route is created across the Bering Sea.

Malkus, Alida Sims. *The Dark Star of Itza: The Story of a Pagan Princess*. Illustrated by Lowell Houser. Harcourt, 1930, o.p. (Grades 7–9)

Based partly on fact, this historical novel accurately re-creates the everyday life, warfare, religion, and festivals in the Yucatán peninsula around A.D. 1250, when the Mayan civilization was at its height. In the prosperous city of Chichén Itzá, Nicte is the pupil and daughter of Hol Chan, the high priest. She hopes one day to marry her father's best pupil, the young priest Itzam Pesh, who is also a skilled builder. In spite of Nicte's dire predictions, their king Chac Zib Chac accepts an invitation from neighboring King Hunac Ceel to attend a religious festival in his city of Mayapan. There the impetuous, irresponsible Chac Zib Chac becomes infatuated with King Hunac Ceel's betrothed, the beautiful princess Kantol, and kidnaps her, taking her back with him to Chichén Itzá. With his ally, Pantemit, a Toltec prince who is secretly in love with Nicte, Hunac Ceel attacks and conquers Chichén Itzá. For his help Pantemit is given the city to rule. Itzam fights gallantly and is able to trade Chac Zib Chac's life for the release of Kantol, but when he is taken prisoner and sent to Mayapan, he must leave behind his beloved Nicte and her father. As the years pass, Pantemit, still hoping for Nicte's love, rebuilds the war-torn city. However, a severe drought produces crop failures and famine in the land. If Pantemit will cease his cruel practice of making human sacrifices, Nicte agrees to offer herself to be cast into the Sacred Well as the sacrificial bride of the Rain God. Nicte's father alerts Itzam, who has escaped from Mayapan, and he is able to rescue Nicte as she falls into the murky waters. The two lovers succeed in escaping from the city to a land far from the control of Pantemit.

Parrish, Anne. *Floating Island*. Illustrated by the author. Harper, 1930, o.p. (Grades 3–5)

In a lovely canary-yellow Doll House in a toy store lives the Doll family: Mr. and Mrs. Doll; their three children, William, Annabel, and Baby Doll; and their black servant, Dinah the Cook. There are also four plaster models of foods on paper plates that have become the family pets. They are Lobby, the lobster; Finny, a fish (complete with slices of lemon); Chicky, a chicken; and Pudding. One day, Uncle Harry enters the Toy Shop and buys the Doll House to be sent by ship to the tropic island where his darling niece Elizabeth and her family live. Unfortunately there is a shipwreck, and although all the humans are saved by a passing ship, the Doll House is swept ashore onto an island. Here, William, Annabel, and Dinah become separated from Mr. and Mrs. Doll and Baby Doll. The remainder of the book recounts their efforts to be reunited. For example, after William is helped by friendly crabs to find the beach where his parents and Baby Doll are living, he endures a series of narrow escapes from such creatures as a hostile land crab and a ferocious crocodile when he ventures into the jungle to find his sister. Dinah's adventures include confrontations with a thieving seagull and a group of helpful monkeys. Finally all the family, including their plaster pets, are reunited. The Dolls light a fire on the beach and are rescued by sailors from a passing ship. Dinah, however, decides to remain on the island with her friends, the monkeys. Through the use of footnotes and many black-and-white illustrations, the author introduces scientific information about the flora and fauna of a tropical island. Unfortunately, stereotypic treatment of Dinah in words and pictures, plus the slow action and the dated writing style, limit this book's present-day use.

Newbery Winner 1932

Armer, Laura. *Waterless Mountain*. Longmans, 1931, o.p.; Knopf, 1993, $11.95: 0-679-20233-1. (Grades 4–7)

Laura Armer (1874–1963) was an accomplished artist in three media: film, painting, and writing. She was born Laura Adams in Sacramento, of pioneer stock that had driven an ox team across the prairies and mountains to settle in California. She studied art at the California School of Design in San Francisco, and later married her fellow art student, Sidney Armer. When she was about 50, she made her first trip to northern Arizona and photographed the life and culture of the Navajo people. Several visits later, she produced a film of a Navajo ritual, *Mountain Chant,* in the native language and rendered 100 sand paintings for the House of Navajo Religion in Santa Fe, New Mexico. Her first novel, *Waterless Mountain*, was published when she was 57. It is the story of a young Navajo boy who dreams of one day becoming a medicine man. Without a hint of condescension or stereotyping, the author treats her Native American subjects as intelligent, sensitive human beings. The very words she chooses to depict their everyday life comes from their point of view, one that encourages truthfulness and respect, and the illustrations by her and her husband reinforce these impressions.

Plot Summary

Younger Brother is an eight-year-old Navajo boy in Arizona in the 1920s. He lives near Waterless Mountain with his parents, Elder Brother, and Baby Sister. Everyone in the family has a job. His father works with turquoise and silver, his mother weaves rugs, his brother hunts, and Younger Brother himself tends his mother's sheep. As for the baby, her job seems to be swinging in her cradle, to which she is tied, and greeting all the family with smiles and giggles.

One day Mother takes Younger Brother to the trading post for the first time, and there he meets the first white man he has ever seen. He is Big Man, a trader. The white man becomes a friend to Younger Brother. On another occasion, Mother, Baby Sister, and Younger Brother visit the trading post at Christmastime. Although they do not know what Christmas means, it is an exciting experience for them all, especially when Younger Brother sees Santa Claus.

When Younger Brother looks into the face of his new friend, Big Man, he senses that all medicine men are beautiful no matter their skin color. That is Younger Brother's mission in life, to be a medicine man. At his young age, he is already learning the seriousness of this vocation from his mother's brother, called Uncle. As Younger Brother herds the sheep, he begins to sense that he is being aided and guided by nature's creatures such as Yellow Beak, the eagle. The members of his family slowly realize that the young boy has a special gift, and they encourage his spirituality and oneness with the beauties of nature. Uncle teaches him the stories and songs of his Navajo people. When Older Brother and Night Chant marry, Younger Brother participates in the ceremony.

All these events help to bring Younger Brother closer in spirit to the gods, known as Yays. When he is alone watching the sheep, the boy meditates on earth's mysteries. He becomes one with the creatures of the earth. He makes up a song when he sees the deer dancing, and the bees eat jam from his lips. Uncle instructs him in the stories of his people. He learns of Spider Woman, who taught all Navajo women to weave, and of the ancient Holy People who inhabited the land of the Navajo long, long ago. He also learns of Turquoise Woman of the Western Sea and of her husband, the Sun Bearer. Uncle gives Younger Brother the sacred name of Little Singer. The name, however, must be kept a secret until he is grown.

The years pass, and Younger Brother is now 12 years old with his own pony to ride as he watches the sheep. Although he is happy with his family and with his increasing duties helping Uncle to prepare for special ceremonies, Younger Brother becomes restless. He believes that he must travel to the west, to reach the Western Ocean where he will find Turquoise Woman, who is calling him.

Younger Brother starts out on his journey, sometimes traveling alone and sometimes in the company of a young white boy. He does not find the ocean but at last he reaches the Western Mountains. There he places a prayer stick, asking for help in in finding the trail westward and reaching the wide waters of the ocean.

Big Man comes to Younger Brother's aid in his search for Turquoise Woman. His friend takes his parents, Baby Sister, and Younger Brother in a train behind the "fire horse." When they arrive in Santa Barbara, Father demonstrates his skills in silverwork for the curator of the museum there and Mother shows her talent for weaving rugs. Younger Brother realizes his dream when he looks out across the water to an island in the distance. This must be where Turquoise Woman lives. After sending her a bead offering, Younger Brother fills a water jar to take back to Uncle from this special place.

When Younger Brother returns home, he and Uncle climb Waterless Mountain. Sometime later, with Younger Brother's help, four jars are discovered in a cave in the mountain. The jars contain 20 deerskin masks believed to have come from the time of the Indian migration known as the Long March in 1863. Uncle and Younger Brother participate in the ceremonies that follow to celebrate this precious discovery. The celebrations culminate on the sixth day in the ceremony of the whirling logs. Everything is in readiness for the all-night dance of the Yays, which ends the ceremonies.

Younger Brother has a new understanding of the ways of his people, and a new song is born in his heart. He understands the song of his people and the pain of all that is beautiful. Younger Brother faces the new day with the feeling of new power rising in him as he takes his place among the medicine men of his people.

Themes and Subjects

Waterless Mountain is a slow-moving, episodic story of everyday life for the Navajo in the early years of the twentieth century. Small incidents and events are faithfully portrayed, generally from the point of view of the Navajo. Through the growth of Younger Brother as a medicine man, the traditions and religious beliefs of the Navajo are vividly conveyed. There is much introspection and mysticism shown in the lives of the Navajo people. What the story lacks in adventure, it makes up in poetic verse that depicts the beauty and understanding of nature felt in the Navajo community.

Incidents for Booktalking

Essentially an episodic story, any of the following scenes can well serve as an authentic look into the heart of the Navajo culture. See: Younger Brother and Yellow Beak (pp. 9–14); Younger Brother and his friend the bee (pp. 21–22); the dance of the deer (pp. 26–27); Christmas at the trading post (pp. 60–66); Big Man and the giant dragonfly (pp. 71–73); Younger Brother goes west (pp. 91–98); riding behind the fire horse (pp. 124–29); the discovery of the masks on Waterless Mountain (pp. 170–77).

Related Titles

A young Navajo girl sees her culture destroyed by Spanish slavers in Scott O'Dell's *Sing Down the Moon* (Houghton, 1970, $16.00: 0-395-10919-1; pap., Dell, $4.99: 0-440-80271-7).

A 12-year-old boy is adopted by the Shoshoni in 1855 in Kristiana Gregory's *The Legend of Jimmy Spoon* (Harcourt, 1990, $15.95: 0-15-200506-4; pap., $5.95: 0-15-243812-2).

Jane L. Curry's *Back in the Before Time* (Macmillan, 1987, $15.00: 0-689-50410-1) contains a loose narrative that links traditional tales from many native tribes of California.

A young white boy is captured by Indians and, after becoming a true tribe member, is suddenly returned to his parents in Conrad Richter's *Light in the Forest* (Knopf, 1966, $23.00: 0-394-43314-9; pap., Fawcett, $4.99: 0-449-70437-8).

In Anthony Hill's novel set in Australia, *The Burnt Stick* (Houghton, 1995, $12.95: 0-395-73974-8), a boy of mixed parentage is taken from his Aborigine mother and sent to a white missionary community.

About the Book and Author

Armer, Laura. *In Navajo Land*. McKay, 1962.

Bowden, Jane A., ed. *Contemporary Authors*. Vols. 65–68. Gale, 1977, pp. 31–32.

Brown, Muriel W., and Rita Schoch Foudray. *Newbery and Caldecott Medalists and Honor Book Winners: Bibliographic & Resource Material Through 1990*. 2d ed. Neal-Schuman, 1992, p. 15.

Chevalier, Tracy, ed., *Twentieth-Century Children's Writers*. 3d ed. St. James, 1989, pp. 30–31.

Commire, Anne, ed. *Something About the Author*. Vol. 13. Gale, 1978, pp. 2–6.

Kunitz, Stanley J., and Howard Haycraft, eds. *The Junior Book of Authors*. Wilson, 1951, pp. 8–9.

Mahoney, Bertha E. *Illustrators of Children's Books 1744–1945*. Horn Book, 1947, p. 268.

Miller, Bertha M., and Elinor Field, eds. *Newbery Medal Books: 1922–1955 with the Author's Acceptance Papers and Related Material*. Horn Book, 1955, pp. 99–104.

Peterson, Linda K., and Marilyn L. Solt, eds. *Newbery and Caldecott Medal and Honor Books: 1922–1981*. Hall, 1982, pp. 40–41.

Ward, Martha, ed. *Authors of Books for Young People*. 3d ed. Scarecrow, 1990, p. 21.

Honor Books 1932

Allee, Marjorie Hill. *Jane's Island*. Illustrated by Maitland de Gorgoza. Houghton, 1931, o.p. (Grades 5–8)

Fresh from her first year of college in Chicago, 17-year-old Ellen McNeill is excited at the prospect of spending the summer on an island off the coast of Maine as a companion to Jane Thomas, the 12-year-old daughter of the head biologist at the Woods Hole marine laboratory. Jane, a lively, attractive girl, is, like her father, keenly interested in science. She dreams of an island where there are no rules and she can live her life as she pleases, independent of others' rules and expectations. Ellen meets many of the other people connected with the laboratory including two boys—Jane's old brother, Walter, whose job is to collect specimens, and Jim Harrison, a graduate student also from Chicago who is attracted to Ellen. Also present are Miss Wareham, a retired biologist who has been connected with the laboratory for many years, and a lame German scientist, Dr. Fritz Von Bergan, an unpleasant, sullen man who is secretly trying to disprove Dr. Thomas's findings about planaria, small aquatic creatures. During a beach party that the usually anti-social Dr. Van Bergen attends, he tries to swim a narrow channel between two islands that can become dangerous because of tidal currents. Hampered by his disability, he begins floundering. First Jane and then Ellen swim out and save him, but characteristically he is discourteous and surly in his feeble attempt at showing appreciation. However, when the two girls are stranded on an island after a blanketing fog rolls in, he proves himself by, in turn, rescuing them. Dr. Thomas becomes ill and Dr. Von Bergen must take over the planaria project. He carries it to a satisfactory finish even when the conclusions prove that Dr. Thomas's theories were correct and his wrong. It has been an exciting summer for Ellen, one in which she has learned a great deal about science and people.

Davis, Mary Gould. *The Truce of the Wolf and Other Tales of Old Italy*. Illustrated by Jan Van Everen. Harcourt, 1931, o.p. (Grades 4–7)

Six of the seven tales included in the charming volume are versions of old Italian legends. The seventh, "The Tale of Nanni," is original. In it, a self-willed, intelligent donkey, Nanni, spends the first two years of his life with the kindly Elizabetta. Then, regretfully, she sells him to Benedetto, a shoemaker, because she no longer has work for him to perform. Benedetto uses Nanni on his many trips selling shoes. One night as he is returning from one of these trips, Nanni stops suddenly on the road and Benedetto hears groaning. It is the padre, who has fallen and hurt himself. While Benedetto cares for the injured priest, Nanni goes to the home of Elizabetta and brings back help, thus gaining the title of the wisest donkey in Italy.

In the title story, the town of Gubbio is beset with a marauding wolf that has killed two of the town's children. The inhabitants decide to seek the aid of soldiers, but the padre suggests that they send for Sir Francis of Assisi instead. The holy man ventures alone to the lair of the wolf and confronts the savage beast. The wolf is overcome by this man of peace and the two reach a bargain: the townspeople will feed the wolf if he will stop his attacks. The animal holds out his paw as a sign of agreement and accompanies St. Francis into the city where he lives until dying of old age. In a third, "The Boar Who Was a Man," a witch places an enchantment on a childless couple, causing them to have a boar instead of a human child. Their son is intelligent and learns to speak. When he marries, the witch relents and allows him to be a man from sundown to sunrise provided that his wife tells no one of these transformations. But she does, and the boar reverts to being a boar 24 hours a day. The wife, as punishment for tattling, is turned into a little green frog who repeats everything the boar says.

Field, Rachel. *Calico Bush*. Illustrated by Allen Lewis. Macmillan, 1931, $16.00: 0-02734610-2; pap., Aladdin, $4.50: 0-689-82285-5. (Grades 4–7)

This novel spans a period of one year—from summer 1743 through spring 1744—in the life of orphaned 12-year-old Marguerite Ledoux, who was originally bound for France but was set ashore at Marblehead, Massachusetts, when plague broke out on the ship. The plague killed her beloved Uncle Pierre. She has now become a bound-out girl indentured to the Sargent family until her eighteenth birthday. The Sargents are Joel, his wife Dolly, and six children including pesky 13-year-old Cabeb, twins Becky and Susan, age six, and Debby, a baby of eight months. Joel's younger brother, Ira also accompanies them. From Marblehead, the family along with their young servant—whom they call Maggie (the Sargents loath anything French or overly refined)—board the *Isabella B.* to take them to a house Joel has bought on Penobscot Bay in Maine. They arrive to find that marauding Indians have burned the house. The crew and the neighbors erect a new log cabin, and a roof raising party commemorates the event.

Marguerite becomes fond of the Jordans who live offshore on Sunday Island, particularly old Aunt Hepsa, who understands and sympathizes with the young girl. Their first year in Maine is an eventful one. Marguerite's quick thinking saves the children when they encounter a bear in the woods; Indians attack and drive off their cattle; and in spite of Aunt Hepsa's help, the baby Debby dies of burns when she crawls into the fire. While gathering cones in the woods at Christmastime, Marguerite encounters an Indian who speaks some French. As a token of friendship, she gives him a brass button she had saved from her uncle's coat. In the spring, while both Caleb and Ira are absent, Joel breaks a leg and is confined to bed. At this moment, Indians arrive. Marguerite creates a diversion by tearing up fabric into strips and nailing them to a flagpole. As the Indians and children dance around this maypole, her friendly Indian arrives and leads the others back into the woods. Single-handedly, she saves the family. As a gesture of gratitude, Joel Sargent offers Marguerite her freedom and ship's passage to Quebec, but she decides to stay with the only family she has. The title comes from the name of a tenacious bush that, like Marguerite, seems to thrive in spite of adversity.

Lathrop, Dorothy P. *The Fairy Circus*. Illustrated by the author. Macmillan, 1931, o.p. (Grades 1–4)

This brief, almost plotless fantasy contains delicate black-and-white and color illustrations in which the fairies are pictured as delicate, childlike creatures with pointy ears and transparent wings. After having seen a real circus, the fairies decide that they are capable of staging their own, although a great deal of improvisation will be necessary. First they use everyday woodland creatures for their animals: turtles become elephants, weasels are camels, chipmunks are tigers, shrews act as trained dogs, the little newts—known as red efts—are the performing seals, and the toad portrays a hippopotamus. Fireflies become the lighting engineers, and everyday articles become props. Cobwebs make natural tightropes for fairy performers and can also be used by acrobats and trapeze artists. Fairy jugglers use dandelion puffs for juggling balls, and others ride the backs of frogs into the pond for a stagy water show. The climax occurs when the fairies' queen appears, and her subjects mount a magnificent circus parade in her honor. This imaginative, quaint variation on the traditional circus might still have some appeal for naive children who are in awe of the real thing.

Lownsbery, Eloise. *Out of the Flame*. Illustrated by Elizabeth Tyler Wolcott. Longmans, 1931, o.p. (Grades 6–9)

This novel, set at the court of Francois I of France during the early days of the Renaissance, covers roughly a six-year period from 1529 to about 1535. Its central character is young Pierre de Bayard, nephew and namesake of a great knight. Pierre serves as a court page, but because he is a ward of the king, he is treated like one of the other royal children and is taught by their tutors, Master Fabri and the king's sister, Marguerite, Queen of Narvarre. Pierre loves learning, but also longs to become a loyal, courageous knight like his uncle. The king's two older sons, Francois, the Dauphin, age 11, and Henri, who is Pierre's age, almost 10, return to the court after spending three years in a dungeon as hostages of the Spanish king, Charles V. Henri is changed by these experiences and is moody and mentally disturbed. He publicly bullies and degrades Pierre and the boy becomes confused about his proper response. He wants to be a loyal subject but he questions the value of devoting one's life to serving a person whom he is growing to despise. The court dwarf, Jak, whose life he has saved, becomes his confidant and advisor. Meanwhile the court is alive with intellectual and social activities, all of which Pierre witnesses. Such famous people as Rabelais, Sir Thomas More, and Erasmus come to the court and the children visit the small villa where da Vinci spent his last days. There, they pursue da Vinci's notebooks. While on a vacation on Navarre, Henri is kidnapped by pirates but is rescued thanks to Pierre's quick thinking. When Pierre in turn is captured, he is saved by some North American Indians who have been brought to France by Jacques Cartier. In time, Henri marries Catherine de'Medici, and Pierre, who always preferred learning to jousting, becomes a scholar at the court of Magdaleine, the king's daughter, now the bride of James V of Scotland.

Tietjens, Eunice. *Boy of the South Seas.* Illustrated by Myrtle Sheldon. Coward, 1931, o.p. (Grades 4–7)

Set in the South Sea Islands during the early twentieth century, this is the story of Teiki and how he learns to appreciate and preserve his Polynesian culture. When Teiki is 10 he falls asleep in a lifeboat on an English trading schooner that has stopped at one of the Marquesas Islands where his father, a widower, is chief. Fearful of continuing on to Tahiti, he swims ashore at the island of Moorea where he is taken in by a kindly woman and sent to school. Teiki becomes dissatisfied with the lazy, nonproductive life of the natives but, one day, he meets an old hermit who lives in isolation on a ledge and sleeps in a hollow banyan tree. The old man, also a native of Teiki's island, is a master carver who uses the legends of the ancient people of the South Seas as subjects. Teiki learns of his heritage and becomes a master carver. He is lowered into a secret cave by the old man, where he explores the ancient burial place of the Moorean kings. The boy is so terrified by the experience that, when he tries to find an exit, he falls and breaks a leg. While it is healing, Teiki feels that he hears the old man calling him. He returns to the hermit's ledge and finds that the man is dying. He follows directions and destroys the hermit's personal god, his tiki, so he can die in peace. Before dying, the old man leaves his valuable carvings and collection of artifacts to Teiki and directs the boy to contact an anthropologist in Hawaii. Teiki finds shelter in a cave and manages to survive a hurricane that destroys the old banyan tree. Teiki notifies the anthropologist, and at the end of the story, is preparing to leave Moorea to accept a position as a helper in a Hawaiian museum that preserves the culture of his people.

🏵 Newbery Winner 1933

Lewis, Elizabeth Foreman. *Young Fu of the Upper Yangtze*. Illustrated by Kurt Wiese. Winston, 1932, o.p.; Holt, 1973, $18.95: 0-8050-0549-8. (Grades 5–8)

In 1917, Elizabeth Lewis (1892–1958) was sent to China by the Methodist Woman's Board. She taught in several major Chinese cities and absorbed the country's culture and ambiance. By the time she came home for medical reasons in 1921, China and its people had become an obsession with her. Through her remaining years she continued to be moved by the "inherent greatness" of the Chinese and their country. In *Young Fu of the Upper Yangtze*, she writes about a 13-year-old country boy who, accompanied by his widowed mother, ventures to Chungking to become apprenticed to a coppersmith. In a companion volume, *Ho-Ming, Girl of the New China* (1934, o.p.), she tells of a girl who must free herself of her restrictive, old-fashioned background to get an education in public nursing. Both books sympathetically portray China in the 1920s in transition from being an ancient, superstition-bound culture to becoming a modern nation. A glossary is appended, giving meanings and pronunciations of difficult Chinese words.

Plot Summary

At the age of 13, Young Fu and his widowed mother, Fu Be Be, move to Chungking from their village in rural China. Young is delighted with his first sights of the busy city. He knows, however, that his mother is not so happy. She hates to leave their farm where she has spent her life. But with the death of Young's father and his grandfather as well, there is no man left in the family to tend the fields. The head of their village told Fu Be Be that there was an opening in Chungking for a coppersmith's apprentice at the shop of Tang. So Young and his mother have come to the city, where he is to spend the next three years learning the coppersmith's trade.

Young Fu and Fu Be Be move into the one room that they can afford to occupy. The young boy soon meets their upstairs neighbor, Wang, an elderly gentleman who has the title of Scholar. The following morning, Young's apprenticeship begins.

Young's first lesson is to tend the fire, an important task that no one wants to do. Besides the other two apprentices, five journeymen work in the shop. Each has had at least three years of experience.

On his first day as an apprentice, Young sees a foreigner, who comes into the shop. It is an amazing event because his mother tells him that foreign barbarians are to be avoided.

The days and weeks go by and Young takes on more duties in the coppersmith shop. Most of all, he likes to run errands, because he gets to see the delights of the big city. He runs across harshness and cruelty, too, such as the way coolies are treated by wandering soldiers. Young becomes wary of the military.

One day, in a conversation with Wang Scholar, Young admits that he wishes to learn to read and write. Wang invites him upstairs and asks why he wants to learn. Young answers that if can read and write, he will earn more money. Wang is not happy with his answer, although he promises he will educate the boy.

After about a year of his apprenticeship has passed, Young admires a large watch in a jeweler's shop. The shopkeeper, Hsui, compliments him on his good taste and says the boy can take the watch home if he will sign a paper that says he will pay the sum of five dollars when he makes his fortune. Young signs.

His mother is horrified when he returns home. How will he ever be able to pay off such a debt? A chastened Young comes up with a plan. As the New Year approaches he visits relatives of his mother's who, she told him, live across the Yangtze. Seeing snow for the first time, he fills some baskets with it. He returns to the city where he sells the snow, calling it Winter Dragon's Breath, as good fortune for the New Year. In this clever manner, Young is able to pay off his debt.

One evening Young is on the streets when he sees a foreign hospital ablaze with fire. He watches from a hiding place as a yellow-haired foreign woman helps people to escape the flames and then is trapped herself on the second floor. No one helps her. Young admires her courage as she attempts to climb to the roof to safety. He leaves his hiding place and shows her the way to the roof.

The women is grateful and promises to send him money in the morning. Young replies that he wants no money, surprising even himself. Others say he is crazy to help a foreigner, but Young replies that foreigners do not seem so different after all.

The foreign woman sends five dollars to Young Fu. He spends one-half of a dollar to buy the woman a small kettle from Tang's shop in appreciation. The woman is delighted with the fine gift and begins to bring her trade to Tang.

Young has many adventures as he learns the trade of a coppersmith, including living through the terrible plague of cholera that grips the city. When his friend Li at the shop comes down with the disease, Young asks the help of his foreign lady friend.

One day Tang asks Young to accompany him downriver to deliver some fine brasses. There is always the danger of river bandits, but Young is thrilled at the prospect of the trip. An escort of soldiers will go along. On the return trip, bandits board their boat. Although the chief bandit demands payment of $300 from Tang, he does not realize that he is standing on a pile of rags, under which is Young with the silver that was payment for delivery of the brasses. The boy endures the agony of the man's weight in pain and silence. Young has saved Tang much money, and the coppersmith vows he will not soon forget his bravery.

This is a time of great unrest in China, as the centuries-old culture comes in contact with the new. Although the Nationalists are in control, Young hears talk of a coming Communist change. When unrest occurs, the military assumes control, and Young knows that they can be ruthless.

Once when Young is sent outside the city gates on an errand, he returns too late to reenter the city and must spend the night on the outside. He goes to the dwelling of Old Mother Ling and her husband and they grant him refuge. But during the night, the Yangtze River breaks through the restraints holding the waters back and all are in danger of losing their lives. Young Fu bids them to quickly tie their most prized possessions together and takes them to high ground. Many perish in the flooding but Young and the old people are safe. He finds his friend, the yellow-haired foreign lady, and she takes in the elderly Chinese couple.

Time passes and Young is now past 18 years old. He proves himself even more to Tang by apprehending a burglar and solving the mystery of a theft in the shop. Although he is often chastised by Tang when his work is not as the master wishes, he also proves a diligent and talented apprentice.

Finally, one day the master coppersmith asks the young man to stay with him while his mother is away visiting relatives. Tang tells Young that he has trusted him as a son and has watched him grow and develop with great pride. If Young continues to improve and grow into manhood, Tang promises that within the year he will recognize the boy as his own son by adoption. With this, of course, will come the burden of responsibility.

Young Fu can hardly sleep that night as he thinks back on the more than five years of his apprenticeship since his arrival in the city of Chungking. He happily awaits his mother's return to tell her of his good fortune. Tomorrow he will prove to master Tang just how good a coppersmith he can be!

Themes and Subjects

This is both the story of a young boy's maturation and the history of a country undergoing turmoil and change. Although not directly related to the outcome of the story, the history does give a vivid picture of life in China before the Communist revolution. Important underlying themes of this book are hard work, dedication, and always doing one's best at whatever task is presented. Although Young's adventures seem more luck and circumstance than the result of maturation on his part, the boy's wit, honesty, and compassion do add to his good fortune.

Incidents for Booktalking

Descriptions of the city and Chinese countryside, as well as the day-to-day life of a coppersmith apprentice will serve as fine introductions to a look at pre-Communist life in China. See: Young's first impression of Chungking (pp. 1–5); Young's first visit to the coppersmith shop (pp. 16–20); Young sees his first foreigner (pp. 29–35); a coolie is abused by the military (pp. 40–45); Wang Scholar begins the lessons (pp. 53–56); Young gets into trouble over the watch (pp. 71–74) and solves his problem with snow (pp. 79–87); Young saves the foreign lady (pp. 93–100); the trip downriver where Young saves the silver (pp. 127–42).

Related Titles

In nineteenth-century China, a 15-year-old boy and a young girl engage in activities to overthrow the Manchu government in *Rebels of the Heavenly Kingdom* (Dutton, 1983, $14.99: 0-525-66911-6; pap., Puffin, $4.99: 0-14-037610-0) by Katherine Paterson.

In Amy Tam's *The Moon Lady* (Macmillan, 1992, $16.95: 0-02-788830-4; pap., Aladdin, $5.95: 0-689-80616-7), a grandmother in the United States remembers her childhood in China.

In World War II China, young Tien Pao sets out with his pig to be reunited with his parents in Meidert De Jong's *The House of Sixty Fathers* (Harper, 1956, $15.89: 0-06-021481-3; pap., Trophy, $4.95: 0-06-440200-2).

Ten-year-old Shao Shao is growing up in World War II Shanghai when it was occupied by the Japanese in *In the Eye of War* (McElderry, 1990, $14.95: 0-689-5050305) by Margaret and Raymond Chang.

When the Japanese invade China during World War II, Ashley Anderson flees China for India in Michael Morpurgo's *King of the Cloud Forests* (Viking, 1988, $12.95: 0-670-82069-5; pap., Puffin, $3.95: 0-14-032586-7).

About the Book and Author

Berger, Laura Standley, ed. *Twentieth-Century Children's Writers*. 4th ed. St. James, 1994, p. 398.

Brown, Muriel W., and Rita Schoch Foudray. *Newbery and Caldecott Medalists and Honor Book Winners: Bibliographic & Resource Material Through 1990*. 2d ed. Neal-Schuman, 1992, p 257.

Chevalier, Tracy, ed. *Twentieth-Century Children's Writers*. 3d ed. St. James, 1989, pp. 583–84.

Commire, Anne. *Yesterday's Authors of Books for Children*. Vol. 7. Gale, 1978, pp. 242–44.

Helbig, Alethea K., and Agnes R. Perkins, eds. *Dictionary of American Children's Fiction, 1859–1959*. Greenwood, 1986, p. 291 (bio.), pp. 587–88 (book).

Kunitz, Stanley J., and Howard Haycraft, eds. *The Junior Book of Authors*. Wilson, 1951, pp. 195–96.

Miller, Bertha M., and Elinor Field, eds. *Newbery Medal Books: 1922–1955 with the Author's Acceptance Papers and Related Material*. Horn Book, 1955, pp. 107–13.

Trosky, Susan M., ed. *Contemporary Authors*. Vol. 137. Gale, 1992, pp. 272–73.

Ward, Martha, ed. *Authors of Books for Young People*. Scarecrow, 1990, pp. 432–33.

Honor Books 1933

Burglon, Nora. *Children of the Soil: A Story of Scandinavia*. Illustrated by E. Parin d'Aulaire. Doubleday, 1932, o.p. (Grades 4–7)

    Set in Sweden in the early part of the twentieth century, this is an episodic novel about two poor, talented children and their loving mother who overcomes their adversities by industry and hard work. Since their father disappeared after going to sea two years before, Nicolina Salstad, a fourth-grader, and her younger brother, Gulklumpen, a second-grader, have been living alone with their mother, Olina, on a small piece of rented property owned by the Colonel. The family makes a meager living selling some of the milk their two goats produce, and bartering with the products of Olina's and Nicolina's spinning and weaving. They suffer many setbacks: the land that they try to cultivate is poor; the crab trap they earn for weeding a potato patch washes out to sea during a storm; Nicolina loses in a school contest when her weaving is judged second to the superior work of a gentry girl; and later the gentry's mother rejects a tapestry she commissions from Nicolina. Their triumphs more than compensate for these disappointments. Gulklumpen wins a cup in a ski jumping competition against much older boys and begins carving wooden figures that can be sold to tourists. As a reward for saving a gentry baby from a sow, he receives new clothes and a knife. Nicolina also takes first prize at the fair for her weaving. Through these windfalls, the family acquires two cows, a lamb, and some ducklings. Although Gulklumpen gives credit for their good fortune to a little tomte, or elf, that he believes lives in a small house he has built for him on their property, it is actually their diligence and perseverance that brought them hope for a brighter future.

Meigs, Cornelia. *Swift Rivers*. Illustrated by Forrest W. Orr. Little, Brown, 1932, o.p. (Grades 6–8)

In 1835, Chris Dahbert, a 17-year-old orphan, is living with his mean-spirited, ill-tempered Uncle Nels Anderson, a prosperous Swedish farmer in the Goose Wing River section of Minnesota. When he is locked out of his uncle's house, Chris goes to live with his aged grandfather, Alexis Dahbert, who lives simply in a modest cabin on a large track of forest land. To supplement his grandfather's meager income, Chris decides to float logs from this land down the river to the St. Louis market, hundreds of miles away. He is helped by Eric Knudson.Together they ready a log boom that includes the beautiful walnut from the front of the cabin. In the spring, the logs are flowed down the Mississippi where Eric returns home and Chris hitches his logs to the raft of the respected Pierre Dumenille, who is part Indian and part French. The journey down the river is filled with adventures and danger. There is tension and anxiety that the logs will be lost when Chris and his friends must run hazardous rapids. When another pilot, Joe Langford, becomes ill with a fever, he loses control of the logs and the raft breaks up on a shoal above St. Louis at Lone Tree Crossing. Most of the logs are recovered including the treasured walnut, which Chris and coworker Stuart Hale retrieve by visiting the village of some hostile Indians. Finally they arrive at St. Louis where the logs are sold for a good price. The walnut is bought by a businessman who will have it carved as a figurehead for his ship. Chris plans to repeat the log run next year and with the accumulated profits, he will attend school to get a proper education.

Swift, Hildegarde Hoyt. *The Railroad to Freedom: A Story of the Civil War*. Illustrated by James Daugherty. Harcourt, 1932, o.p. (Grades 5–8)

This fictionalized biography covers the life of Araminta Harriet Ross (later Tubman) from roughly age 13 in 1833 to the end of the Civil War. Harriet, nicknamed Minty, was born into a loving slave family on the Maryland plantation, Broadacres, owned by kindly "Marse" Henry Carter, mistress "Miss Annie," and a son, the profligate, cruel, young master George. Harriet's family consists of her mother, Old Rit, the plantation cook, her father Dabby Ben, and her older brother, Benjie. When only 13, Harriet innocently incurs the anger of George, who, in his father's absence, sells Harriet to his Cousin Susan. Harriet is cruelly mistreated, and when her only friend Emily, Susan's kindly sister, leaves for the North, Harriet, a high-spirited, courageous girl, escapes back to Broadacres. There, Henry Carter welcomes her back. In time, she grows into a valuable, robust farmhand and lumberyard worker, but after the Master's untimely death, Harriet is fearful of her future under the brutal stewardship of George, particularly after he forces her to marry John Tubman, a man she despises. In a desperate move, she plans her escape. Aided by a neighboring plantation owner, Dr. Arnold, she accidentally connects with some Quakers who operate the Underground Railroad. They smuggle her first to Wilmington and then to Philadelphia, where she is taken in by

Emily. From the North, Harriet leads many expeditions into the South to help slaves escape, earning her the nickname Moses. Among the more than 300 people she helps to freedom are her parents, her brother Benjie, and his family. During the Civil War, she acts as a scout, a riverboat pilot, and a nurse. During one foray, she is forced to shoot a Southern spy, whom, she discovers, is her hated enemy Master George. At war's end she returns to Broadacres. The plantation, ravaged by Northern looters, is now deserted except for old and feeble Miss Annie and one former slave. Sadly Harriet tells them of George's death. This is an exciting, action-filled account that sympathetically portrays the plight of pre-Civil War blacks and the horrors of slavery.

❁ Newbery Winner 1934

Meigs, Cornelia. *Invincible Louisa: The Story of the Author of "Little Women."* Little, Brown, 1933, $18.45: 0-316-56590-3; pap., Scholastic, $2.50: 0-590-41937-4. (Grades 5–7)

When Cornelia Meigs (1884–1973) was a child, she often turned to *Louisa Alcott's Life, Letters and Journals* for hope and direction. This woman's life never ceased being an inspiration for her. As she states, "When difficulties and perplexities seemed almost too many to face, I have deliberately got down [this volume] and read a page or two, for the stimulation of courage which such reading never fails to bring." With her indomitable courage and efforts to win comfort and security for her family, Louisa May Alcott was indeed "invincible." During her long career, Miss Meigs was not only a distinguished teacher and scholar at her alma mater, Bryn Mawr College in Pennsylvania, but also a prolific author of more than 40 books. Beginning with *The Kingdom of the Winding Road* (o.p.) in 1915, she created a number of distinguished books, many of which were prize-winners. Along with her Newbery Medal Winner, three of her other books were Newbery Honor Books. They are: *The Windy Hill* (see "Honor Books," 1922, p. 6), *Clearing Weather* (see "Honor Books," 1929, p. 35) and *Swift Rivers* (see "Honor Books," 1933, p. 63).

Plot Summary

Little Women, the classic by Louisa May Alcott, is the story of the March sisters, Meg, Jo, Beth, and Amy. Published in 1868, the book was based on the author's real family, which included Bronson and Abigail May Alcott and their four daughters, Anna, Louisa, Elizabeth, and May. *Invincible Louisa* recounts the life, in fictionalized form, of this famous author, portrayed as Jo in *Little Women*, the unconquerable, spirited girl whose writing talent brought her fame and the money her family desperately needed.

Louisa, the second child, is born in Germantown, Pennsylvania, on November 29, 1832, shortly before the Alcotts moved to Philadelphia. The family eventually grows to four daughters and experiences many moves. They know much love and happiness, but never peace and security, until Louisa's writing career begins to pay off. Her mother, Abba May, a quiet, staid young woman from Boston, marries charming but unusual Bronson Alcott, a scholar and teacher with only the slightest of education and the biggest of dreams. At the time of Louisa's birth, her father is running a small school in Germantown.

Unfortunately, although Bronson is a dedicated teacher, even with his somewhat unorthodox ideas, he has no head for administration or finance, and so the school in Germantown flounders. The Alcott family moves on to another school in Philadelphia that proves no better, and in 1834 they move to Boston.

Louisa finds the new city fascinating, and for the first time she meets members of her own family, mainly her mother's relatives, including the formidable and wealthy Aunt Hancock. In her youth, Louisa's aunt had married John Hancock, whose bold signature heads the list of signers of the Declaration of Independence.

Soon enough, Bronson's newest attempt at founding a school fails, and in 1840, the family is on the move again. This time they go to Concord, Massachusetts, where the last of the Alcott girls, known as May, is born. The father never had the heart to try another school, and so he works at any odd job in an effort to support the family. The mother does what work she can, leaving the girls' education to Bronson. Despite their usually desperately poor situation, the girls are taught to give what little they have to the poor—and they do.

In early 1842, Bronson sails off for England, where he is invited to see a school named after him by people who agree with his somewhat unorthodox ideas of education. He returns that October with two men and a young boy. The new arrivals are to live with the Alcotts until the spring, when they will all begin another "new life." Louisa is now 10 years old.

In the spring, the Alcotts and their houseguests move into an empty farmhouse near Harvard, which they call Fruitlands. This is to be the great experiment. It is, in fact, an effort at commune living, very much like the communes that sprang up among young people in the 1960s and 1970s. During this time, Louisa learns that her family aided runaway slaves in this period leading to the Civil War.

The experiment at Fruitlands fails eventually, mainly because of a disagreement with the Englishmen, who feel that Bronson should be willing to give up his family for the true cause of common living. Bronson refuses, but it breaks his spirit and he becomes ill. In 1844, the Alcotts return to Concord and then move to Boston.

In 1845, they go back to Concord to a house they name Hillside, now known historically as Wayside. Here Louisa begins to write and entertain the family with her plays, so charmingly described in *Little Women*. When she turns 14, she goes to school for a year for the first time in her life since her education, as well as her sisters, has remained in the hands of their father.

In 1848, the Alcotts move again, this time back to Boston where Mrs. Alcott has been offered employment and her brother has offered the family his house in which to live. In 1852, Louisa's first story is printed, and three years later her first book *Flower Fables* appears. Louisa May Alcott could be said now to be an author.

The Alcott family next moves to Walpole, New Hampshire, in the year that Louisa's first book is published. From this experience, she makes an important decision. She must go out on her own if she is to make a serious career of her writing. And so, untrained and inexperienced, she sets out to live in Boston alone.

Louisa sees her family as often as she can while she devotes herself to her writing. In 1857, the Alcotts move again, this time to Concord, where it is hoped that Elizabeth, who has never fully recovered from a bout with scarlet fever, will regain her health. However, Elizabeth dies the following year. The closely knit family will never be the same again. The family unit is further changed in 1860, when Anna marries John Bridge Pratt.

Through the years of the Civil War, Louisa works on her writing and volunteers as a hospital aide in Washington, D.C. From this experience, she writes "Hospital Sketches," which is well received. In 1863, the sketches are printed as a book. But

Louisa has more than a book to remember her hospital service, for she contacts typhoid and is seriously ill for a long period. When at last she is able to go home to Boston to recuperate, her father comes to see her with the news that Anna has had a baby boy.

Louisa's next book *Moods* is published in 1864. Next, she travels through Europe as nurse and companion to an invalid friend of the family. After a long stay, during which she forms a close relationship with a young Polish man named Ladislaw Wisniewski, Louisa returns home to write the novel that will bring her lasting fame. It is called *Little Women*. The first part of the book is published in 1868. Louisa has never had so much money in her life.

The years pass quietly and pleasantly in Concord, Boston, and sometimes visiting abroad. Louisa writes a number of novels after that, including *Jo's Boys*, published in 1886, and her last, *A Garland for Girls*, which was published in 1888.

With steadily worsening illnesses through the years, Louisa May Alcott dies on March 6, 1888. Unknown to her, her father died just shortly before. She was not yet 56 years old.

Themes and Subjects

Like Alcott's famous novel *Little Women*, this is a story of a close, loving family whose members experience all the tears and joys of day-to-day living and put up with the foibles and foolishness of the family members. The Alcotts were not to know great joy and gaiety throughout their lives, but they cherished the love and warmth they shared and handled adversity with quiet dignity. The courageousness with which they face the death of a young daughter is especially well done. This is also the story of a shy young women's courage as she shoulders the responsibilities of caring for her family. Well expressed are the inner resources that young Louisa calls upon as she slowly and painstakingly labors with her writing, never giving up when it looks as though she will never meet with success. *Invincible Louisa* is the story of a real-life heroine who would not be conquered by life's adversities.

Incidents for Booktalking

A number of episodes will serve to introduce the reader to the Alcott family and to Louisa, the real-life heroine. See: Louisa remembers her first trip to Boston (pp. 19–23); Bronson returns from England with strangers and they go to Fruitlands (pp. 39–47); the Alcotts leave the commune (pp. 62–69); Louisa becomes a hospital aide and falls ill (pp. 135–60); her writing career begins in earnest (pp. 173–76); the death of Elizabeth (p. 116); Louisa returns from Europe and *Little Women* is published (pp. 201–10).

Related Titles

Laura Ingall Wilder's *West from Home* (Harper, 1974, $15.89: 0-06-024111-X; pap., Trophy, $5.95: 0-06-44008-6) is a collection of letters that the author wrote to her husband when she visited San Fransisco in 1915.

Angel Carpenter and Jean Shirley have written a fine biography of a writing wizard in *L. Frank Baum: Royal Historian of Oz* (Lerner, 1992, $21.50: 0-8225-4910-7).

The creator of *Charlotte's Web* is highlighted in a well-researched and moving biography, *E. B. White: Some Writer!* (Macmillan, 1992, $13.95: 0-606-06341-2) by Beverly Gherman.

The author, Eve Bunting, tells about her childhood in Ireland, her immigration to the United States, and her writing career in *Once Upon a Time* (Owen, 1995, $14.95: 1-878450-59-X).

In *The Moon and I* (Messner, 1992, $12.95: 0-671-74166-7; pap., Morrow, $4.95: 0-688-137040-0) by Betsy Byars, the famous author talks about her life and writing and also about Moon, a black snake that visited her back porch.

About the Book and Author

Berger, Laura Standley, ed. *Twentieth-Century Young Adult Writers*. St. James, 1994, pp. 446–48.

Brown, Muriel W., and Rita Schoch Foudray. *Newbery and Caldecott Medalists and Honor Book Winners: Bibliographic & Resource Material Through 1990*. 2d ed. Neal-Schuman, 1992, pp. 290–92.

Chevalier, Tracy, ed. *Twentieth-Century Children's Writers*. 3d ed. St. James, 1989, pp. 674–75.

Commire, Anne, ed. *Something About the Author*. Vol. 6. Gale, 1974, pp. 167–69.

Helbig, Alethea K., and Agnes R. Perkins, eds. *Dictionary of American Children's Fiction, 1859–1959*. Greenwood, 1986, pp. 339–40 (bio.).

Kinsman, Clare D., and Mary Ann Tennenhouse, eds. *Contemporary Authors*. Vols. 9–12. Gale, 1974, pp. 613–14.

Kunitz, Stanley J., and Howard Haycraft, eds. *The Junior Book of Authors*. Wilson, 1951, pp. 217–19.

Miller, Bertha M., and Elinor Field, eds. *Newbery Medal Books: 1922–1955 with the Author's Acceptance Papers and Related Material*. Horn Book, 1955, pp. 114–26.

"Newbery Medal Acceptance Material." *Horn Book* 10, no. 3 (May/June 1934): 217–20.

Peterson, Linda K., and Marilyn L. Solt, eds. *Newbery and Caldecott Medal and Honor Books: 1922–1981*. Hall, 1982, pp. 50–51.

Silvey, Anita, ed. *Children's Books and Their Creatlors*. Houghton, 1995, pp. 454–55.

Ward, Martha, ed. *Authors of Books for Young People*. 3d ed. Scarecrow, 1990, p. 483.

Honor Books 1934

Berry, Erick. *The Winged Girl of Knossos*. Illustrated by the author. Appleton, 1993, o.p. (Grades 6–8)

This novel incorporates Greek mythological characters, Cretan history, and archeological findings into an exciting story set in Bronze Age Crete. The heroine is a high-spirited, adventurous girl, the beautiful Inas, the daughter of Daidalos, the famous sculptor, architect, and inventor. The ruler of Crete is King Minos, for whom Inas's father has constructed his palace, the Labyrinth. His daughter, Ariadne, is a dear friend of Inas and when Ariadne falls hopelessly in love with Theseus, the handsome Athenian slave, Inas helps him break out from his prison by using black thread to indicate an escape route. The lovers flee and successfully escape Crete. Inas is a fearless athlete and enjoys participating in many activities usually associated with boys like bull-vaulting, but she is also keenly interested in her father's many inventions and his recent work involving gliders. Like many scientists in history, Daidalos is accused of sorcery by a populace incited by the jealous Kres, a goldsmith. He and Inas flee to the island of Siceli. Minos is slain in an effort to bring Daidalos back to Crete, and Inas returns to Crete with her rescuer, Kadmos, the attractive son of King Minos's fleet commander. Because of problems on the island of Crete, Inas, now betrothed to Kadmos, must leave the island immediately. Using Daidalos's gliders, which become their wings, they float in the sky to a small boat that transports them to Greece where Ariadne and Theseus will give them shelter. This novel is enriched by the author's illustrations based on Minoan illustrations and her afterword, which completes the story according to Greek legends.

Colum, Padraic. *The Big Tree of Bunlahy: Stories of My Own Countryside*. Illustrated by Jack Yeats. Macmillan, 1933, o.p. (Grades 4–7)

Simon the Huntsman and other residents of the town of Bunlahy in which the author grew up told him many enchanting stories in the shade of their famous old tree. The 13 stories included in this anthology are a selection of these tales. In "The First Harp," an old couple lives together but are lonely and miserable. One day they find a giant whale's skeleton on the beach. The wind makes strange, exotic sounds as it whispers through the bones. The old man copies this idea by making a frame of pine wood and placing strings across it through which the wind passes and makes noises. In time, he tightens the strings and begins striking them to make different sounds. The music he creates brings happiness to the couple and to the lives of others. When this harp playing cures the King's illness, the monarch rewards the man and his wife with great riches. The instrument becomes known as a harp and the man is Cendfind, the first harpist in Ireland.

Another story, "King Cormac's Cup," tells of a good but gullible and foolish king who is so enamored of a juggler's silver branch with golden apples that he will give anything to possess it. The juggler gives him the silver branch on the condition that he be granted three requests. The first is to take away the king's son, the second his daughter, and the third his wife. In each case the unhappy king complies because "a promise is a promise." When the king tries to follow his wife, he finds himself in an enchanted land. The Lord of the Palace, who is really the juggler, explains that it is the Land of Wonders, and taking pity on King Cormac, returns his family to him. The Lord also gives him a magic cup that breaks when it hears a lie and mends when truth is told. With it King Cormac can test the value of others and can no longer give away the things he has for things that are brought him.

Gag, Wanda. *The ABC Bunny*. Illustrated by the author. Putnam, 1978, $15.95: 0-698-20000-4; pap., $6.99: 0-698-30000-9. (Grades Preschool–1)

This simple alphabet book recounts in rhyming couplets the adventures of a bunny as he encounters a series of objects and animals and undergoes several different aspects of nature, each of which highlight a different letter. For example, "F for frog—he's fat and funny; 'Looks like rain,' says he to Bunny; G for gale! H for Hail; Hippy-hop goes Bunny's tail." The book begins with a predictable "A for Apple" but ends surprisingly with "Z for Zero" and the request to close the book. During his day-long excursion the bunny encounters such animals as a frog, a quail, a porcupine, and a squirrel before jumping into his burrow on "X for eXit." All of the illustrations are large black-and-white lithographs. The only color in the book is red, which is used for each of the uppercase letters. Both sets of endpapers are used to reproduce an ABC song including music using many of the words and rhymes found in the book. As in her many other classic picture books, Wanda Gag has produced a wonderful marriage of picture and text.

Hewes, Agnes D. *Glory of the Seas*. Illustrated by N. C. Wyeth. Knopf, 1933, o.p. (Grades 7–10)

Set in Boston during the 1850s, this historical novel weaves together two plot elements. The first is the development of clipper ships and the passenger service from the East Coast around Cape Horn to California. These beautiful, tall-masted ships deserve their nickname—the Glory of the Seas. The second is the enforcement of the Fugitive Slave Law of 1850, which provided for the return of escaped slaves between states. Young John Seagrave, a clerk in the counting house of Pinckney and Fay, is enthusiastic about the future of the clipper ships and also about Sue, the daughter of his employer Mr. George Fay. He has seen the clippers being built in the shipyards of Donald McKay and has just learned that McKay's ship *Flying Cloud* has completed the passage to California in a record 89 days. John lives with his uncle, Asa Wentworth, a federal judge and an abolitionist who resigns his position rather than enforce the Fugitive Slave Law. When John and Uncle Asa help a runaway slave, Jasper, escape, John discovers a business arrangement between Mr. Fay and an orphaned boy named Benny Paradiso. Mr. Fay is illegally recapturing slaves and importing them using Benny's pigeons as messengers. He plans to use the largest clipper ship afloat, the *Great Republic,* for his next shipment. When the ship catches fire in New York harbor, Mr. Fay is killed while trying to put out the blaze. Both Uncle Asa and John decide to move to California where Asa will try to influence the political affairs of the young state and John will go into business. The two book passage on the rebuilt *Great Republic,* and Sue, who is now John's fiancee, promises to join him when he gets settled.

Kyle, Anne. *The Apprentice of Florence*. Illustrated by Erick Berry. Houghton, 1933, o.p. (Grades 6–10)

This story, set chiefly in Florence from roughly 1452 through 1454, re-creates the bustling, energetic, exciting world of the Italian Renaissance. After his father has been missing for four years, 16-year-old Nemo leaves his home in Tuscany for Florence to seek information from his father's former employer, the wealthy silk merchant, Messer Bardo. Although he learns nothing about his father, he becomes Messer Bardo's apprentice and meets his son, the profligate Everardo, and his pretty, adventurous daughter, Clarice. One night when he is drunk, Everardo kills a young nobleman, Corso Corsi. Both Nemo and Clarice witness the crime but remain silent to protect their friend. When Nemo and Everardo are sent on business to Constantinople, Clarice dons men's clothes and accompanies them. There the Grand Vizier realizes that Nemo's father once saved his life, and gives the boy a valuable ring as a token of appreciation. It is 1453 and the city is under siege by the Turks. Everardo is wounded and he and Clarice escape while Nemo remains behind to fight. Later when Nemo is captured he gains his freedom by showing the Vizier's ring. He finds passage home to Italy, and in Genoa the boy learns from a youngster named Christopher Columbus that his father is alive but very ill. They are reunited before his father's death. Back in Florence, Nemo is accused of the Corsi murder. When Clarice persuades her brother to sign a confession and accept banishment as punishment, Cosimo de'Medici orders Nemo's release. The bribe from Nemo of a rare manuscript of the *Iliad* he had found in Constantinople also helped. Messer Bardo accepts Nemo as his surrogate son and perhaps his future son-in-law.

Schmidt, Sarah L. *New Land*. Illustrated by Frank Dobias. McBride, 1933, o.p. (Grades 6–9)

This novel is set in the western Wyoming plains during the 1930s when farmers barely scratched a living from the earth and the study of agriculture was becoming a science. Seventeen-year-old Sayre Morgan, along with her twin brother, Charley, her father and a little sister, Hitty, arrive in Upham, Wyoming, to live in an unproved homestead claim given to Mr. Morgan by his former associate, Parson. Sayre's hopes for a smooth beginning to a better life are dashed when they have difficulty transferring the claim. Undaunted, Sayre and family begin working the land. She studies agriculture part time and Charley goes back to school where he is soon in competition with Frank Hoskins, the handsome son of the local store owner, the manipulative Franklin Hoskins. This growing hostility leads to a fistfight which Charley wins.

Sayre begins raising chickens and turkeys, but someone attempts to steal her poultry using a hook attached to a fishing rod that is later traced to Mr. Hoskins's store. Later the Morgan's hay is found to contain alfalfa weevils and an embargo is temporarily placed on all hay from the region. The community turns against the Morgans and Sayre tries to discover who is sabotaging their efforts to succeed. René Osgood, Frank's girlfriend, confesses that she tried to support Frank by the attempted turkey theft and that Frank had placed the infected alfalfa in the Morgan's hay. Later the conflicts and hostility between Frank and Charley are resolved when the two boys are trapped in a terrible blizzard and Frank risks his own life to save Charley. Sayre and Charley form a partnership now confident that they will secure ownership of their land. In spite of many obstacles and hardships, the Morgans have succeeded in carving out a satisfactory new life.

Singmaster, Elsie. *Swords of Steel*. Illustrated by David Hendrickson. Houghton, 1933, o.p. (Grades 7–10)

This novel, which deals with the Civil War and the years preceding it, is set in Gettysburg, Pennsylvania, where the author spent her childhood and absorbed both the atmosphere and history associated with the area. In 1859, John Deane is 12 years old and living with his father, David, his grandfather, called "Gran'sir," and older twin sisters, Sue and Sallie. With the help of a black servant, Nicholas, he is training a colt, Lady Gay, and paying attention to Maggie Swift, the grand-daughter of Nicholas's employer. John is heartbroken when Nicholas is caught by slave catchers and sent south to be sold. Later John learns that his father, an agent for a carriage company, is also a conductor on the Underground Railway. Mr. Deane and John travel to Harper's Ferry where they help a slave escape and witness the raid of the abolitionists under John Brown. War comes and John's father joins the cavalry. The beaux of Sue and Sally also enlist. When the war reaches Pennsylvania, Gran'sir and John are balked in an attempt to deliver supplies to Union troops, and Lady Gay is taken. The Confederates seize their house and lock John in the basement. To John's amazement, the troop's cook is his former friend, Nicholas, who smuggles food and clothing to the boy. When the house becomes a Confederate hospital, John helps nurse the wounded. Later he hears President Lincoln at the dedication of the Gettysburg cemetery where he delivers his famous address. John's father is captured and as a result of a prisoner exchange is sent home from Andersonville prison. John is allowed to join the army, where he witnesses the events of the final days of the war. He returns home hoping to complete his education, marry Maggie, and help heal the wounds his country has suffered.

Snedeker, Caroline Dale. *The Forgotten Daughter*. Illustrated by Dorothy Lathrop. Doubleday, 1933, o.p. (Grades 7–10)

Set in second-century B.C. Rome and its environs, this novel faithfully captures the history, customs, and culture of the times. After Chloe is abandoned by her father, the Roman centurion Laevinus, and following the death of her Greek-born mother, she becomes a scorned and battered slave girl in the Villa Caracinia where she is abused by her master Davus. Her only comfort is the attention she receives from a fellow slave, her mother's former friend, Melissa, who tells the girl of her origins and heritage. Together they re-create in song and story the idyllic life on Lesbos, before Chloe's mother and Melissa were taken captive and sent to Rome. When Laevinus fell in love with Chloe's mother he had installed her in his villa, where Chloe was born, but after his wife's death he never returned. Aulus Cornelius Maro, the son of the owners of the neighboring Villa Cornelia, returns home to escape capture by the forces of those Romans opposed to the extensive land reforms proposed by the tribune Tiberius Gracchus, whom they have murdered. Chloe, now 17, rescues Aulus when he falls into an animal trap and the two fall in love. A plague in Rome kills Laevinus's new wife and children, and for solace he returns to the villa after years of absence. Here he is amazed to meet his daughter Chloe. Laevinus's parents were opposed to his marriage to a Greek and had reported to him that both his wife and his daughter had died. Delighted to be united with a daughter he had believed was dead, he is pleased to help arrange a marriage between Chloe and Aulus.

❧ Newbery Winner 1935

Shannon, Monica. *Dobry*. Illustrated by Atanas Katchamakoff. Viking, 1934, o.p.;
pap., Puffin, $4.99: 0-14-036334-3. (Grades 4–7)

Monica Shannon (1905–1965) was born in Ontario, Canada, but spent most
of her life in the United States. During part of her childhood she lived on a ranch
in Montana's Bitterroot Valley. After receiving a degree in library science, she
worked in the Los Angeles Public Library and began a career in writing. *Dobry* is
the last of the five books she wrote for children. The others include *Tawnymore*
(Viking, 1931, o.p.), the story of a half-breed boy and his encounter with pirates,
and an enchanting collection of stories, *California Fairy Tales* (Viking, 1926,
o.p.). During her childhood in Montana, the author absorbed the customs and listened to the folktales of the Bulgarian immigrants who worked on her father's
ranch. Although these formed part of the inspiration for *Dobry*, she also relied on
incidents in the life of her illustrator, Atanas Katchamakoff. From these sources,
she wrote this inspiring story of a young Bulgarian peasant boy who aspires to be
a great sculptor.

Plot Summary

A young peasant boy named Dobry lives in a small village in the European land of
Bulgaria. His father died fighting in World War I and Dobry lives with his mother,
Roda, and his grandfather. His home is typical of Bulgarian peasant life. The family's
quarters are on the second floor, the oven is in the yard, and the oxen occupy the first
floor. The small house is heated by a *jamal*, a tile fireplace.

This episodic, plotless story tells of his life and growth and the daily village
happenings.

Dobry enjoys his homelife and his village. He has plenty of everything—food,
work, and play—and he delights in the many festivals that involve the whole village.
There is always so much to do. On the first snow of the year, he digs tomatoes from a
storage mound and then gets a stomachache from overeating. His friend is Neda, the
shoemaker's daughter. With her, he makes a trip to the mill along with Grandfather.
Dobry draws a picture of Neda's pig and delights in watching the village storks as they
leave for the season.

Dobry's grandfather is a farmer and householder and as such is an important man
in the village. His mother is almost as devoted to the soil as she is to her son. She respects and worships the fields in which they toil and that give them the bread for their
table. Naturally, she expects that Dobry will continue in the tradition of the family and
become a tiller of the fields also.

As much as Dobry loves his home and his life, as he grows older, his feelings start to
change. He does not want to remain in the fields. Instead, he wishes to become a sculptor.

Dobry's mother cannot understand how her son could wish to give up his heritage. She cannot imagine another life. But, oddly enough, Grandfather, the farmer,
does understand, for he shares some of his grandson's feelings.

As Dobry grows older, he assumes new duties. He replaces the village herdboy
and spends many days by himself. He watches over the flock while he happily draws
and carves. The *jamal* maker, a Macedonian named Maestro Kolu, shows Dobry
where he can get clay for his models.

Then on Christmas Eve a fresh snow covers the land. Dobry and his family and friends sing their favorite carols and go to sleep to await the holiday. Everyone in the village sleeps late on Christmas morning—everyone but Dobry. He rises early and with a rough charcoal sketch he has made, he sets out in the snow to create a nativity scene. He piles a small mountain of snow in the corner of the courtyard and creates the Holy Family. His figures are peasants, Joseph looking much like Dobry's own grandfather and Mary like his friend Neda. Dobry fashions the animals as well and then decides that his work is good.

When Grandfather rises and tends to his chores on Christmas morning, he comes upon the nativity scene and sinks to his knees, overcome by its beauty. Roda joins him in silence. Neither of them have ever seen such a nativity scene. It is so well done, with such love and talent, that all who see it kneel before it in wonder. When news spreads throughout the village of such a wondrous thing, people come from miles around to see it.

Then it is the New Year and family and friends sit around the table while Grandfather tells their fortune for the coming months. When it is the schoolmaster's turn to speak, he tells Dobry that as his New Year present, he is giving the boy a small room in the school where he may take one hour from his studies each day to work in clay.

But at this point, Dobry's mother, Roda, interrupts. She takes from her pocket a handful of gold coins. She explains that she has saved these coins from her wedding dress and other garments. Now she gives them to her son so that he may go to the city of Sofia, where he will study to be an artist. He will go in the spring, she tells him.

In the spring, when the gypsy bear has returned to the village, which signifies that all villagers must bathe in the river, Dobry, now 16 years old, prepares to begin his art education in Sofia. Young Neda is sad that he must leave, but she tells him that he will be a great man—a great artist—when he returns. "Your grandfather says you will be," she tells him.

Dobry replies, "Of course. That's why I'm going. And that's why I'm coming back, too, Neda."

Themes and Subjects

This is an episodic, essentially plotless tale that is most memorable for its depiction of peasant life in a small Bulgarian village. The customs and clothes as well as the food and daily activities of the villagers are well portrayed. Such incidents as Dobry gorging himself on cold tomatoes that he digs out of the snow and then suffering a colossal stomachache add flavor to the otherwise static flow of action. Dobry and Grandfather are the most memorable, but the appeal of the story falls more heavily on the ethnic culture than on the characters themselves.

Incidents for Booktalking

For a warm look into peasant life in a small European village, see: Dobry gets a stomachache from eating too many tomatoes (pp. 19–22); Dobry and Neda string peppers (pp. 35–36); Dobry and Neda go to the mill with Grandfather (pp. 49–66); the dancing bear (pp. 91–95); Dobry creates the nativity scene (pp. 145–48).

Related Titles

In *Sister Shako and Kolo the Goat: Memories of My Childhood in Turkey* (Lothrop, 1994, $14.00: 0-688-13271-5), Vedat Dalokoy, a former mayor of Ankara, tells of growing up in rural Turkey.

A young girl living in the Middle Ages changes places with her brother so she can become a knight in Tamora Pierce's *Alanna: The First Adventure* (Atheneum, 1983, $16.95: 0-689-3099-5; pap., Random, $4.99: 0-614-28945-9).

In eighteenth-century Japan, a boy runs away to become an apprentice in a puppet theater in Katherine Paterson's *The Master Puppeteer* (Harper, 1976, $15.00: 0-690-00913-5; pap., Avon, $2.95: 0-380-53322-7).

Edward Fenton's *The Refugee Summer* (Delacorte, 1982, $10.95: 0-385-28854-9) is set in Greece in 1922 where a youngster becomes involved with refugees fleeing the Turks.

For older readers, *Against the Storm* (Little, Brown, 1992, $14.95; 0-316-36078-3) by Gaye Hicyilmaz tells of the terrible conditions Mehmet and his family face when they move to Ankara.

About the Book and Author

Berger, Laura Standley, ed. *Twentieth-Century Children's Writers*. 4th ed. St. James, 1995, pp. 869–70.

Brown, Muriel W., and Rita Schoch Foudray. *Newbery and Caldecott Medalists and Honor Book Winners: Bibliographic & Resource Material Through 1990*. 2d ed. Neal-Schuman, 1992, p. 375.

Chevalier, Tracy, ed. *Twentieth-Century Children's Writers*. 3d ed. St. James, 1989, p. 880.

Commire, Anne, ed. *Something About the Author*. Vol. 28. Gale, 1982, pp. 186–87.

Helbig, Alethea K., and Agnes R. Perkins, eds. *Dictionary of American Children's Fiction, 1859–1959*. Greenwood, 1986, p. 466 (bio.), p. 130 (book).

Kunitz, Stanley J., and Howard Haycraft, eds. *The Junior Book of Authors*. Wilson, 1951, pp. 272–73.

Miller, Bertha M., and Elinor Fieldeds. *Newbery Medal Books: 1922–1955 with the Author's Acceptance Papers and Related Material*. Horn Book, 1955, pp. 127–34.

"Monica Shannon." *Horn Book* 11, no. 1 (March/April 1935): 73–81.

Peterson, Linda K., and Marilyn L. Solt, eds. *Newbery and Caldecott Medal and Honor Books: 1922–1981*. Hall, 1982, p. 135.

Ward, Martha, ed. *Authors of Books for Young People*. 3d ed. Scarecrow, 1990, p. 639.

Honor Books 1935

Rourke, Constance. *Davy Crockett*. Illustrated by James MacDonald. Harcourt, 1934, o.p. (Grades 7–10)

This fascinating biography, now sadly out of print, recounts the life of America's folk hero, Davy Crockett, with authentic details enlivened by reconstructed dialogue. Born in the wilderness of Tennessee to a poor frontiersman's family in 1786, he was given his first rifle at age eight and was soon supplementing the family diet with plenty of squirrel and possum. At 12 he was bound to a German farmer as a cattle driver and at 14 earned money as a wagoner. When only 16, he hired himself out to work on a neighboring Quaker's farm to repay one of his father's debts. There he received his only formal education. When still 19, he married Polly Finley and began raising his family, supplementing his meager farmer's income by selling furs of the many animals he hunted. After gaining attention as an Indian fighter during the Creek Indian War of 1813–1814, he entered politics, fighting unsuccessfully in Washington to pass a land bill that would help the squatters of West Tennessee. Intrigued by the idea of settling in Texas, and eager to help in the Texas Rebellion of 1835 against Mexico, he traveled south with a trusted band of followers. Close to the town of Bexar, he and other fighters took refuge from a Mexican attack in a fortified mission, the Alamo. Here he died gallantly on March 6, 1836. In two final chapters, the author tells of the sources she used in writing the book and also recounts some of the tall tales that surround Crockett's life. The author has succeeded admirably in separating fact from fiction to create an accurate portrait of this famous American pioneer. In addition, both the political and the everyday life of frontier days come to life in this gripping account. Realistic black-and-white drawings also enliven the text.

Seeger, Elizabeth. *The Pageant of Chinese History*. Illustrated by Bernard Watkins. Longmans, 1934, o.p. (Grades 6–10)

This one-volume history of China appeared in several revisions during its 20-year publishing history. The end coverage varied with each edition, the later ones ending with the Civil War and the establishment of the Communist regime. In addition to the salient facts, this account includes material about the people and their customs, character, family life, humor, philosophy, and religion. Chapter 1 begins in "Mythical Times," thousands of years before the birth of Christ, and traces the early history of China through such leaders as the Emperor Huang Ti, who built roads, studied the stars, and developed writing beyond its early rudimentary forms. According to legend, his wife found that by rewinding the cocoon of the worm that fed on mulberry leaves, a long thread could be produced that could be woven into a new material, silk. Coverage continues through the Chou Dynasty (1122–255 B.C.) and the contribution of Lao-tse and Confucius and the empire of Shi Huang Ti (246–210 B.C.), noted chiefly by the building of the Great Wall. The Tang and Sung dynasties brought prosperity and a development of the arts, which ended with the harsh rule of the Mongols (1280–1368), during which Europeans became interested in trading with China and Marco Polo made his historic visit that lasted from 1275 to 1292. After the stable Ming dynasty (1368–1644), the Manchu people from Manchuria invaded and established a dynasty that lasted until 1912. During this period there were many clashes with western powers and unscrupulous merchant traders. The people, under the leadership of Sun Yat Sen, became involved in an extended rebellion that ended with the defeat of the Manchu establishment and the creation of the Chinese Republic in 1911. The last emperor, a six-year-old boy named Pu Yi, abdicated on February 12, 1912, and modern China was born.

Van Stockum, Hilda. *A Day on Skates: The Story of a Dutch Picnic*. Illustrated by the author. Harper, 1934, o.p. (Grades 2–4)

This story is set in Holland more than 60 years ago when girls wore peaked caps and long shirts, boys were in pantaloons, and both wore wooden clogs. It tells the story of nine-year-old twins, Afke and her brother Evert, and their adventures when their village of Elst had its first winter freeze. When the ice becomes thick enough for safety, their teacher announces that on Friday the class will go on a daylong skating picnic. Each brings skates and a tasty lunch. The day provides some unforeseen surprises and expeditions. While skating in front of the others, Evert stumbles on the ice and falls into a fishing hole. Fortunately he is quickly pulled to safety and given dry clothes by neighborly Mrs. Sjollema whose hospitality also involves making fresh pancakes for all. Later, when the class stops to visit a historic church, Evert and three other boys are accidentally locked in the tower after the others leave. One of the fast-thinking boys begins tolling the ancient bells and soon help is on the way. Both children arrive home tired but with many thrilling stories to tell their parents. This charming, old-fashioned story is enhanced by numerous illustrations (many are full-page and in color) that re-create the idealized Holland of 200 years ago.

❧ Newbery Winner 1936

Brink, Carol Ryrie. *Caddie Woodlawn*. Illustrated by Kate Seredy. Macmillan, 1935, o.p.; Macmillan, 1973 (Illus. by Trina S. Hyman), $16.00: 0-02-713670-1 (Grades 4–6)

Carol Ryrie Brink (1895–1981) was born in Moscow, Idaho, the daughter of the town's mayor. Orphaned at age eight, she went to live with her aunt and grandmother. She stated, "I was quite a spoiled child but I could be bribed to do almost anything if Gram would tell me a story. The stories I liked best were the ones she told about her own childhood in Wisconsin when she was a little girl named Caddie Woodhouse." Later she realized that, "If I had liked them so much, why shouldn't other children like them, too?" This was the genesis of this delightful pioneer story that takes place in 1864 and tells of 11-year-old Caddie, "as wild a little tomboy as ever ran the woods of western Wisconsin." Her flair for depicting realistic family relationships, and for re-creating the past is also demonstrated in the sequel *Magical Melons* (pap., Aladdin, $3.95), which contains 14 more stories about Caddie and her brothers. Another popular book by this author is *Baby Island* (pap., Aladdin, $3.95), the delightful story of two girls who take care of a lifeboat full of babies after they are shipwrecked on a desert island.

Plot Summary

Along with her brothers, 11-year-old Caddie can get into an amazing number of scrapes and adventures in this fictionalized account of events that actually occurred to the grandmother of the author. Red-haired Caddie lives in the rolling hills of western Wisconsin during the pioneer days of the mid-1800s. She counts as her friends the band of Native Americans that live across river from the settler's community. Her parents had feared these people when the Woodlawns first arrived from Boston some seven years earlier. Caddie had feared them, too, especially when she first saw Indian John. She was standing in the village store and Indian John was so amazed at the color of her hair that he picked her up to stare. Since then a strange kind of friendship had grown up between the two. He is always leaving her odd bits of carvings and once he made her a tiny doll with a buckskin dress. Caddie, whose real name is Caroline Augusta, is different from her sisters. Both she and her sister Mary had been frail and ill when the family arrived from Boston. After Mary died, her father begged her mother to let Caddie grow up free and running wild with her brothers instead of being kept in the house learning to be a lady like the other Woodlawn girls. And so Caddie Woodlawn grew strong and brown and as handy as the boys.

Talk around the dinner table is often of the Civil War, which seems very far away from western Wisconsin. Closer at hand is the talk about Indian massacres. But Father says there is nothing to fear from the Native Americans that live across the river. Others are not so sure.

Anything out of the ordinary is a great event for the Woodlawn children and so they are especially delighted when they get word that Uncle Edmund is arriving on the next steamer. Caddie and her brother Warren are dismayed to learn that they cannot go along in the wagon to pick him up because there just is no room. But not to meet Uncle Edmund is unthinkable, so Warren and Caddie fly across the fields on Betsy, the black mare, and are there to greet their uncle along with everyone else.

Caddie is especially unhappy when Uncle Edmund leaves this time because he takes his dog Nero with him. Caddie has grown to love Nero and had hoped her uncle would leave him behind. Some time later, Uncle Edmund writes that Nero has run away and Caddie is heartbroken.

Soon after Uncle Edmund's visit, it is time for school. Miss Parker the schoolteacher is dismayed to enter the room to find Caddie and Obediah Jones kicking each other and pulling hair. Caddie says that Obediah refused to take his feet off the desk so she hit him with a ruler. Obediah says he can do anything he wants. All the children instantly realize that this moment will decide whether defiant Obediah or the small young schoolteacher will rule the classroom this year. Miss Parker gives Obediah a smack on the backside and tells him to leave and never come back, or come back in five minutes prepared to act like a gentleman. Obediah leaves. A few minutes later he is back. His hair is combed, and Miss Parker is boss.

As winter wears on and snow piles higher, Saturdays are free for sleigh riding and skating. And for the second time that year, Caddie nearly drowns. Her brother Tom, an expert skater, warns her that the ice looks thin. But Caddie, of course, does not listen and ventures out. The ice breaks and she goes under. Brother Warren screams but it is cool-headed Tom who rescues his sister.

One evening in midwinter, Father comes home with the frightening news of a possible Indian uprising. The men at the tavern say that the Indians are gathering and will soon strike. Although Father does not believe that such a strike will come from their friends, he knows that they must take precautions. At daybreak, the settlers meet at the Woodlawn farm to defend themselves if need be. But the day and night pass without incident. Children and adults grow restless with fear and boredom.

Finally, Caddie overhears a conversation among some of the settlers. One of the men suggests that they go out and attack the Indians first. Then they will all be able to go home and rest peacefully. They know that Caddie's father will not agree and so they decide not to tell him of their plan.

Caddie decides that she must warn Indian John and her friends. Taking Betsy, she rides to the Indian camp and seeks her friend. He listens to her story and returns Caddie to her home, where they meet her father and Caddie tells him of the settlers' plan. Indian John assures Father that they have no intention of attacking them. They shake hands.

One day Indian John comes to see Caddie. He is going west on a trip and he leaves his scalp belt with her. Grim as it is, the children regard it more with curiosity than horror and in his absence give a show to exhibit it! John also finds and rescues Nero, who has made his way back to his home in Wisconsin.

Time passes and eventually the Woodlawns receive the news that the war has ended. They also hear the sad news that President Abraham Lincoln has been assassinated.

When summer comes, the Woodlawns receive another visitor on the steamer. It is Mother's cousin Annabelle Grey. She arrives with trunks and boxes and tiny buttoned shoes. She fascinates the seven Woodlawn children with her fantastic tales of the city of Boston. During their cousin's visit, Caddie and her siblings play some silly tricks on the city girl. For this, Caddie is punished, but it makes her realize that perhaps it is time to act a little more grown up and put away the practical jokes.

Before Annabelle departs, Father receives a letter from England, home of his ancestors. It says that an uncle whom Father has never seen has died and left him the title and estates. To claim them, however, the family must go to England to live and give up their American citizenship. Mother agrees immediately. She and Caddie's older sister, Clara, think about being presented to the Queen. Father is silent, and Caddie knows she does not want her future to be in a strange land.

Father calls the family together and says they must all vote on such an important decision. In the end, the vote is to stay—even from Clara and Mother! Caddie Woodlawn will remain a pioneer and an American.

Themes and Subjects

This is a fictionalized account of a true pioneer life on the Wisconsin prairie. Although the despair of her mother and older sister, Caddie Woodlawn is the delight of her father, who watches her grow as strong and spirited as her brothers. This is a little girl who would rather plow a field than bake a cake. Full of mischief and pranks, Caddie nevertheless realizes a time when she should begin to put away the silliness of childhood and act with a little more responsibility. She shows courage and resourcefulness when she rides into the Indian camp to warn them of an impending raid. Also depicted are the closeness of a pioneer family and their simple joys in everyday life.

Incidents for Booktalking

Most of the story is composed of small happenings or vignettes in the life of this pioneer family. See: Caddie and her brothers go swimming without their clothes (pp.

1–5); Caddie meets Indian John (pp. 7–8); meeting Uncle Edmund (pp. 28–32); Uncle Edmund takes Nero (pp. 45–47); Caddie fights with Obediah (pp. 57–62); Caddie nearly drowns (pp. 65–68); Caddie warns her friend of an impending attack (pp. 119–28).

Related Titles

Eleven-year-old Anne gradually wins the heart of her foster mother in Lucy Maud Montgomery's *Anne of Green Gables* (pap., Harper, $5.95: 0-694-01251-3), the first in an extensive series.

Timid nine-year-old Elizabeth Ann spends a summer with relations in Vermont in Dorothy Canfield Fisher's classic *Understood Betsy* (pap., Avon, $1.50: 0-380-01595-1).

In Robert Burch's *Ida Early Comes over the Mountain* (Viking, 1980, $14.99: 0-670-39169-7; pap., Avon, $2.50: 0-380-57091-2), a young woman brings happiness to four motherless children.

D. Anne Love's *Bess's Log Cabin Quilt* (Holiday, 1995, $15.95: 0-8234-1178-8; pap., Dell, $3.99: 0-440-41197-1) tells of an 11-year-old girl living in frontier Oregon who hopes to win a quilt contest to help save her family's house.

Addie is disappointed when her cousins do not fit into pioneer farm life in Laurie Lawlor's *Addie's Long Summer* (Whitman, 1992, $12.95: 0-8075-0167-0).

About the Book and Author

Berger, Laura Standley, ed. *Twentieth-Century Children's Writers*. 4th ed. St. James, 1995, pp. 145–46.

Brown, Muriel W., and Rita Schoch Foudray. *Newbery and Caldecott Medalists and Honor Book Winners: Bibliographic & Resource Material Through 1990*. 2d ed. Neal-Schuman, 1992, pp. 47–49.

Brink, Carol R. *Caddie Woodlawn*. Public Media Video, 1995. Videocassette.

———. *Caddie Woodlawn*. VHS Library Video, 1989. Videocassette, 116 min. ($19.95)

———. *Caddie Woodlawn*. Read by Roslyn Alexnder. Recorded Books, 1994. Audiocassettes, 6 hrs., 15 min. ($42.00)

———. *Caddie Woodlawn*. SVE and Churchill Media, 1993. Kit includes book, video, audiocassettes, overheads, and guides. ($149.00)

———. *Caddie Woodlawn*. Children's Television International (Book Bird Series, no. 15). Videocassette, 15 min. ($24.95)

Chevalier, Tracy, ed. *Twentieth-Century Children's Writers*. 3d ed. St. James, 1989, pp. 132–33.

Commire, Anne, ed. *Something About the Author*. Gale, 1971, Vol. 1, pp. 34–35; 1982, Vol. 27, p. 36.

Evory, Ann, and Linda Metzger, eds. *Contemporary Authors (New Revision Series)*. Vol. 3. Gale, 1981, p. 92.

Hedblad, Alan. *Something About the Author*. Vol. 100. Gale, 1999, pp. 32-35.

Helbig, Alethea K., and Agnes R. Perkins, eds. *Dictionary of American Children's Fiction, 1859–1959*. Greenwood, 1986, pp. 69–70 (bio.), p. 78 (book).

Hopkins, Lee Bennett, ed. *More Books About More People*. Citation Press, 1974, pp. 53–59.

Kunitz, Stanley J., and Howard Haycraft, eds. *The Junior Book of Authors*. Wilson, 1951, pp. 45–46.

Peterson, Linda K., and Marilyn L. Solteds. *Newbery and Caldecott Medal and Honor Books: 1922–1981*. Hall, 1982, pp. 57–58.

Senick, Gerard J., ed. *Children's Literature Review*. Vol. 30. Gale, 1993, pp. 1–17.

Silvey, Anita, ed. *Children's Books and Their Creators*. Houghton, 1995, pp. 84-85.

Ward, Martha, ed. *Authors of Books for Young People*. 3d ed. Scarecrow, 1990, pp. 84–85.

Honor Books 1936

Gray, Elizabeth Janet. *Young Walter Scott*. Viking, 1935, o.p. (Grades 6–8)

This fictionalized biography of Sir Walter Scott covers a period of seven years, from age 10 to 17 (roughly 1781 through 1788). Because of a illness that produced a lifelong limp, he is sent as a child from his home in Edinburgh to live at the family farm at Sandyknowe with his Aunt Janet and grandmother. At age 10 he goes back to live with his lawyer father, mother, and several siblings, including an older, John, and a younger brother, Tom, with whom he gradually develops a great friendship. At first he is sent to a special private school, which he detests. After the family unsuccessfully tries a tutor, Wattie (his nickname) joins John at High School. Gradually he gains scholastic honors, including surpassing the very bright Davy Douglas. Unfortunately this involves stealing Davy's special button, a talisman that seems to bring him good luck. Wattie overcomes his handicap and resents being treated any different than other boys. He and his friends frequently engage in street fights called *bickers* with other neighborhood gangs. In one, his arch rival, the feared Green-Breeks, is seriously wounded by an unfair tactic used by young Tom. Luckily, Green-Breeks recovers, and in time becomes friends with Wattie. While he grew up to be a robust, athletic man, he also grew into a young man well versed in literature with a particular ability to write verse. At age 15, he became apprenticed to his father while still pursuing his consuming interests in literature and Scottish history. In that year, he achieved one of his great ambitions—a meeting with the great Scottish poet, Robert Burns. By age 17, Walter was a more confident, accomplished young man poised on the verge of adulthood and the beginning of a period of great creativity.

Seredy, Kate. *The Good Master.* Illustrated by the author. Viking, 1935, o.p.; pap., Puffin, $4.99: 0-14-030133-X. (Grades 4–6)

This novel, set in pre-World War I Hungary, is based partly on childhood experiences of the author. Young Jansci is eagerly awaiting the arrival of his young cousin from Budapest who is coming to live with him, his mother, and his kindly father, Marton Nagy, a man of such gentleness and wisdom that he has gained the nickname the Good Master. Cousin Kate (he is disappointed that it is not a boy) proves to be a perfect hellion sent by her widowed schoolteacher father to their remote farm in the plains because he is no longer able to cope with her audacious behavior. True to form, on her first day at the Nagys, she causes the horses on the farm wagon to bolt and race through town; later she climbs onto the living room rafters and dangles dangerously above the heads of her new family. However, gradually she is tamed under the guidance of the loving family and that of her good-natured cousin, Jansci, with whom she becomes good friends. She experiences many adventures including unmasking a fake freak at a country fair, being saved from drowning by Jancsi when swept downstream in a swiftly flowing river, helping to avert a dangerous cattle stampede, fishing for crawfish, and escaping from a band of marauding gypsies who attempt to kidnap her. She also absorbs the wonderful culture and traditions of this area like coloring and distributing eggs at Easter and listening to engrossing folktales. On the eve of December 6, Mikulas (Father Christmas) arrives on his sleigh to distribute presents in the neighborhood. Kate and Jansci accompany him on his rounds. Mikulas is impressed when the two children give up their presents for others more needy. Back home, Mikulas is discovered to be really Kate's father, newly arrived from Budapest. He is so pleased with his daughter's transformation that he is easily persuaded to stay to open a school in the village. There are further adventures of Kate and Jansci in *The Singing Tree* (see Honor Books, 1940, p. 105).

Sperry, Armstrong. *All Sails Set: A Romance of the Flying Cloud.* Illustrated by the author. Winston, 1935, o.p. (Grades 5–7)

This story is told as a reminiscence by a 97-year-old sailor, Enoch Thatcher, who recalls his first sea voyage, taken when he was only 15 years old. The story begins in East Boston when, at the death of his father, a failed sea merchant, Enoch is forced to leave school to help his widowed mother. He becomes a student draftsman in Donald McKay's shipyard where the massive new clipper ship, the *Flying Cloud,* is being built. He becomes so intrigued with the ship that, after its launching, McKay arranges to have Enoch become an apprentice seaman under Captain Creesy on her maiden voyage from New York to San Fransisco and then to China. On board ship, Enoch makes some friends and some enemies. His friends include the second mate, Mister Andrews, and the other apprentices, particularly good-natured Brick Warner. His chief enemies are the first mate, a surly bully named Mister Jones, and a seaman, Jeeter Sneed, who swears vengeance on Enoch after the boy knocks him down in a fistfight. Although he remembers a few happy times like the hazing he received from "Father Neptune" and other crew members when they cross the Equator, life is generally arduous and at times very dangerous. The storms become more and more violent and the seamen are increasingly discontented. Capitalizing on these conditions, Sneed leads an abortive mutiny and is later placed in irons. During a massive storm rounding the Cape of Good Hope, Brick is swept overboard and Enoch grieves the loss of his friend. Sneed escapes and Enock discovers him below decks trying to destroy the ship by starting a fire. Sneed dies in the fire but Enoch, though severely burned, is able to turn in the alarm and save the ship. With great fanfare, San Fransisco is reached. The time is a record 89 days and 21 hours. Unfortunately, Enoch is not well enough to continue to China but will be sent home on another ship carrying with him an engraved gold nugget as a sign of appreciation from Captain Creesy and the men of the *Flying Cloud.*

Stong, Phil. *Honk the Moose.* Illustrated by Kurt Wiese. Dodd, Mead, 1935, o.p. (Grades 3–5)

During one of the coldest winters ever experienced in Minnesota, two young friends, Waino and Ivar, return home from an unproductive day of hunting and skiing. Both long for the day when they will bag a moose. As they warm themselves at the stove in the livery stable where Ivar's father boards horses and mules, they hear a strange honking sound, and on exploring find a huge, mournful moose with large spreading antlers in one of the stalls. In spite of their efforts, he will not leave, and even Ivar's father, Mr. Ketonen, cannot make him budge. When Mr. Ryan the local policeman is also unsuccessful, the mayor and city council are called to solve the crisis. They agree to pay temporarily for feeding the moose, now known as Honk. However, when Honk leaves the stable, on his return he finds the door is locked. Back at the stable, the boys lure him with food to shelter under the town bandstand but he follows them back into town. An exasperated mayor once more allows Honk into the livery stable where he stays until returning to the wild in the spring. The following winter, however, he reappears ready to accept another winter's free board and room. This humorous, believable story successfully avoids personifying Honk while painting an affectionate portrait of a rural Finnish settlement in Minnesota 60 years ago. It is lavishly illustrated with drawings, many of them in color.

Newbery Winner 1937

Sawyer, Ruth. *Roller Skates.* Illustrated by Valenti Angelo. Viking, 1936, $15.00: 0-670-60310-4; pap., Puffin, $3.99: 0-14-030358-8. (Grades 4–7)

Ruth Sawyer (1880–1970) was a woman of many talents and interests. As a student at Columbia's Teacher's College, she majored in folklore and storytelling. Later she taught school in South America and Cuba, was a reporter for the *New York Sun*, and started the first storytelling program at the New York Public Library. Her passion for storytelling is revealed in her many collections of folktales and in the book *The Way of the Storyteller* (pap., Penguin, $9.95). When she was 10 and living in New York City, her parents went abroad for a year, leaving young Ruth to explore the city on her roller skates. From these memories, she wrote her prize-winning novel about the energetic, independent, and strong-willed Lucinda Wyman and her adventures. Miss Sawyer states that many of the characters in this novel—such as Trinket, Tony Coppicco, Mr. Gilligan, Mr.

Night Owl, and Uncle Earle—were based on real people. Lucinda's story is continued in *The Year of Jubilo* (Viking, o.p.), in which the family moves to a cottage on Penobscot Bay in Maine after the death of Mr. Wyman.

Plot Summary

The time is the 1890s in New York City. Independent, imaginative Lucinda Wyman, age 10, is about to spend a year with family friends. Her parents must go to Italy for her mother's health. (Lucinda will stay with the Misses Peters, one a chubby and sweet seamstress and the other a hardy schoolteacher.) Lucinda was very nearly shipped off to Aunt Emily, who was rebuffed that her niece was not staying with her and concerned because the Misses Peters "have no social position." When Lucinda's mother hesitated after reading Aunt Emily's letter, Lucinda put her 10-year-old foot down, declaring that she would not stay with Aunt Emily and that was that.

So begins a year of growing up in the pleasantly informal household of the Misses Peters. Especially important to friendly Lucinda are the adventures she has while roller skating all over the New York City neighborhood formed by Broadway, Eighth Avenue, and Bryant Park. One of her special new friends is Patrick Gilligan, a friendly hansom cab driver who helps Lucinda move her belongings into the Peters home and also invites her to his own home for tea and griddlecakes with Mrs. Gilligan. Mr. Gilligan points out to Lucinda that it would have been a shame if they had never gotten acquainted for they are just the right age to be friends—she past 10 and Mr. Gilligan past 50.

Lucinda is also especially fond of the Browdowskis. They live in the upstairs apartment and their golden-haired daughter is called Trinket, a pet name. Because they are neighbors, Lucinda asks if she can "borrow" Trinket sometimes. Mrs. Browdowski does not quite know what to make of that request at first, but after looking over Lucinda she thinks her child will be safe.

Thanksgiving is an especially fine time for Lucinda. Never has she had so many invitations to dinner! Mr. and Mrs. Gilligan ask; along with Miss Lucy from downstairs and her godmother, Aunt Ellen Douglas McCord; as well as Mr. Collyer, who christened her; and others too. In the end, though, she accepts her godmother's invitation because it is the only one she can accept without terribly offending Aunt Emily, even though she really did not want to go. Unfortunately for Lucinda, she roller skates to Aunt Ellen's, bumps into a fat man, and scrapes her knees. Her stockings are ruined. After she is sponged off and repaired, Lucinda suggests that they cut the stockings into stocks and she is none the worse for wear.

There is so much to do as the year passes. To make money for Christmas presents, Lucinda takes a job walking Pygmalion, a dog, and she tutors an old woman in English. Lucinda calls her Princess Zayda because of her unusual-looking apartment. There is the circus and picnics in the vacant lot and lots of new friends such as the local policeman and Tony, the young man who runs his father's fruitstand.

There is sadness for Lucinda, too, in that exciting year. One day she goes to "borrow" Trinket to go to the circus, but Mrs. Browdowski says the little girl has a cold and can't go out. When the cold does not get better, Lucinda suggests they call a doctor even though she knows the young couple is very poor. Finally, Lucinda is able to get her own family doctor, Dr. Hitchcock, to see Trinket, but it is too late and the little girl dies.

Lucinda grows up a little after that as she realizes how much Trinket meant to her parents in a way that Lucinda herself never experienced from her own busy mother and father. When the year is up and her parents are about to return, Lucinda knows that she will be very happy to see them and to be back with them again. But she knows she is different, too, a little more grown up. She has learned to reach out to people. She is not quite as impulsive or restless as she was a year ago. She is not quite the "difficult" child that her parents left behind. She has made friends on her own, not through her family. Her awareness of people and the city has broadened. She is certain that all her life she will never be quite as happy again as she has been during this wonderful, growing-up year in New York City.

Lucinda will face what comes, but for right now she thinks that every single spring it would be terrific to be just 10 years old, never any older. That's what she calls a perfectly elegant idea!

Themes and Subjects

This is the story of a young girl's growing-up time. Always restless and impulsive, ever the concern of her wealthy parents, Lucinda gradually becomes aware of realistic life around her. She is touched by the friendliness and goodness of new friends that she meets on her own. She is especially touched by the devotion of the young couple who lose their young and precious daughter. The many references to events and culture of the times add a realistic flavor to the novel, giving it a good sense of the late nineteenth century in New York City.

Incidents for Booktalking

Any of Lucinda's adventures in New York City can serve as an exciting introduction to this look at old-style, big city life through the eyes of an engaging heroine. See: Lucinda meets Mr. Gilligan (pp. 7–23); getting to know Patrolman M'Gonegal and Bryant Park (pp. 27–28); Lucinda meets Trinket and the Browdowskis (pp. 32–35); getting acquainted with Shakespeare (pp. 47–64); the Thanksgiving adventure (pp. 85–101).

Related Titles

Sidney Taylor's *All-of-a-Kind Family* (pap., Dell, $4.50: 0-440-40059-7) gives an appealing, moving picture of growing up Jewish in New York City's Lower East Side.

In Nina Bawden's warm, often humorous novel *Humbug* (Clarion, 1991, $13.95: 0-395-62149-6), eight-year-old Cora discovers the difference between truth, lies, and humbug.

Lexie reluctantly agrees to have a joint party with an unpopular classmate to celebrate their birthdays in Lisa Eisenberg's *Happy Birthday, Lexie* (Viking, 1991, $12.95: 0-670-83553-6).

Elana Rose Rosen, an extraordinary youngster, introduces herself and her New York City neighbors in the delightful *Scooter* (Greenwillow, 1992, $15.00: 0-688-09376-0) by Vera B. Williams.

In 1910, a Jewish orphan who lives in a tenement in New York City is thrilled at the thought of of spending two weeks on a farm in Johanna Hurwitz's *Faraway Summer* (Morow, 1998, $15.00: 0-688-15334-8).

About the Book and Author

Berger, Laura Standley, ed. *Twentieth Century Children's Writers*. 4th ed. St. James, 1995, pp. 841–43.

Brown, Muriel W., and Rita Schoch Foudray. *Newbery and Caldecott Medalists and Honor Book Winners: Bibliographic & Resource Material Through 1990*. 2d ed. Neal-Schuman, 1992, pp. 352–55.

Cech, John, ed. "American Writers for Children, 1900–1960." In *Dictionary of Literary Biography*. Vol. 22. Gale, 1983, pp. 294–99.

Commire, Anne, ed. *Something About the Author*. Vol. 17. Gale, 1979, pp. 207–11.

Haviland, Virginia. *Ruth Sawyer*. Walck, 1965.

Helbig, Alethea K., and Agnes R. Perkins, eds. *Dictionary of American Children's Fiction, 1859–1959*. Greenwood, 1986, p. 454–55 (bio.), p. 436–37 (book).

Kunitz, Stanley J., and Howard Haycraft, eds. *The Junior Book of Authors*. Wilson, 1967, pp. 266–67.

Lesniak, James G., ed. *Contemporary Authors (New Revision Series)*. Vol. 37. Gale, 1992, pp. 394–96.

Miller, Bertha M., and Elinor Field, eds. *Newbery Medal Books: 1922–1955 with the Author's Acceptance Papers and Related Material*. Horn Book, 1955, pp. 145–56.

"Newbery Award Acceptance Material, 1937." *Horn Book* 13, no. 4 (July/August 1937): 251–56.

Peterson, Linda K., and Marilyn L. Solt, eds. *Newbery and Caldecott Medal and Honor Books: 1922–1981*. Hall, 1982, pp. 60–61.

Sawyer, Ruth. *The Way of the Storyteller*. Viking, 1962.

Senick, Gerard J., ed. *Children's Literature Review*. Vol. 36. Gale, 1995, pp. 134–66.

Silvey, Ania, ed. *Children's Books and Their Creators*. Houghton, 1995, pp. 574-75.

Ward, Martha, ed. *Authors of Books for Young People*. 3d ed. Scarecrow, 1990, p. 623.

Honor Books 1937

Bemelmans, Ludwig. *The Golden Basket*. Illustrated by the author. Viking, 1936, o.p. (Grades 2–4)

This book, which was a Newbery Honor Book before the creation of the Caldecott Medal, is noteworthy for its many black-and-white sketches and full-color paintings of the sights of the Belgium city of Bruges. It also features a brief appearance by one of Mr. Bemelman's most delightful creations, the red-headed schoolgirl named Madeleine. In 1925, Mr. Coggeshall, an Englishman, takes a business trip to Bruges accompanied by his two daughters, Celeste and Melisande. They stay in an inn called the Sign of the Golden Basket and there they become friends with the hotel keeper, his wife, and his son Jan, as well as several guests. They visit the famous Bruges tower with its museum and carillon and get a detailed history of the building. They watch the French chef, Monsieur Carnewal, create his delicacies, and soak their hotel room's carpet playing submarine with Jan.

While riding on a canal in Jan's new rowboat, the boat capsizes and the girls are rescued by none other than the mayor of Bruges. Other incidents include catching flies to feed Jan's pet frog and visiting a cathedral where they encounter a dozen little girls from their school who are also visiting this important landmark. One of them is Madeleine. The pleasant visit comes to an end and the girls must return home.

Bianco, Margery. *Winterbound*. Viking, 1936, o.p. (Grades 7–9)

Set in a rural Connecticut farmhouse during the Great Depression, this charming family story tells how four young people cope during their mother's absence of several months. While her husband is away on a two-year archaeological expedition, Mrs. Ellis moves her family of four out of the city to a farmhouse to save money. Kay, the oldest at 19, misses the city at first, but the others, 16-year-old Gerry, short for Margaret, and the younger children Martin and Caroline, adjust easily. Penny, their mother, is forced to travel to the Southwest with a niece who is found to have a spot on her lung, but before she leaves, she hires a widow, Mrs. Cummings, to oversee the household. She becomes so domineering and unpleasant that Kay dismisses her after paying the promised advance of $40. On their own, the young siblings cope nicely in spite of meager finances and inconveniences like keeping the wood stove alight during very cold weather. They make several friends including their neighbors, the Rowes. Kay, who is an artist, sells her manuscript for a picture book to a publisher and Gerry helps a young working couple who have just had a baby. To further increase their income, they answer an advertisement from a writer seeking a quiet place to live and take in a winter boarder, Miss Emily Humbold, and her dog, Arabella. While out for a walk, Gerry helps Jane Bassett, a girl her age, who has been thrown from her horse. Later the family meets Jane's young, wealthy brother, Charles, who is their landlord. When their mother returns in the spring, she finds a happy and flourishing family with Gerry now working part time in a greenhouse and Kay deeply in love with Charles.

Hewes, Agnes D. *The Codfish Musket*. Illustrated by Armstrong Sperry. Doubleday, 1936, o.p. (Grades 7–10)

 This complex story set at the beginning of the nineteenth century shifts locales from Boston and Washington to points west on the American frontier. Dan Boit is one of the crowd in Boston that meets the *Columbia*, the first American ship to sail around the world. Inspired by stories of trading furs and other commodities with the Chinese, he takes a job with storekeeper and arms dealer, Israel Cotton, a friend of his grandfather's. When a large lot of firearms bearing the codfish trademark are stolen, Dan suspects Tom Gentry, a mysterious young Englishman. These suspicions are confirmed when he interrupts a second robbery. There is a scuffle, and Tom escapes. Dan is sent to Washington to learn if war with Spain is near and to find markets for the Kentucky rifle. Here he finds a diary and returns it to its owner, President Jefferson. Later he becomes the President's secretary, replacing Meriwether Lewis, who is with William Clark exploring the newly claimed Northwest. After the Louisiana Purchase, Dan is sent to the frontier to deliver a message to Lewis about the establishment of forts in the area. On the journey Dan discovers that Gentry is the leader of a gang that is selling guns, including those with the codfish marking, to the British who are arming the Indians. In turn, the Indians are using them to terrorize the American trappers. In a shootout the gang is dispersed and most of them killed. In the spring of 1804, Dan delivers the message to Lewis and returns to Washington. He has used every form of transportation available—foot, horseback, Conestoga wagon, pack train, and flatboat. He has seen the vast frontier and returns hopeful for its dynamic future.

Jones, Idwal. *Whistler's Van*. Illustrated by Zhenya Gay. Viking, 1936, o.p. (Grades 4–7)

 This adventure story set in rural Wales shortly after World War I introduces the reader to the clever, rowdy gypsies, or Rommanies, and their life on the road. Fourteen-year-old Gwilyn lives on a farm in Wales with his grandfather, Taid, and Gwilyn's sister, Myfi. Each spring the gypsies pause close to their home and when they whistle, Taid, a wealthy farmer and scholar, begins to act strangely. When another spring arrives, Taid suddenly disappears in a pony cart just before the whistling begins. When the whistling starts, Gwilyn joins the gypsies hoping to find his grandfather. The whistlers are the Ringos: a grandmother, named Gammer, and twin brothers Natty, a superb horseman, and Jubal, a quiet expert artisan. During the month he spends with the Ringos, Gwilyn has many adventures during which he learns about gypsy life, their handicrafts, their music, and their shrewdness. Under the tutelage of Natty, he is taught horsemanship and at an outdoor fair, he unexpectedly excels at boxing. He also discovers the great conflict and differences that exist between the gypsies and the landed folk, called Georgios. At the annual meeting of the gypsies, the Sirnihatch—during which there is a great horse race—Gwilyn is reunited with his grandfather, who confesses that he is a Ringo who had settled down after his marriage, but that, this spring, had heeded the irresistible call of the road. Practicing what Natty has taught him, Gwilyn wins the great race. Taid refuses the honor of being king of the gypsies and instead turns over this position to Natty. Taid and Gwilyn return home but Gwilyn promises to return to the gypsies for six months of every year.

Lenski, Lois. *Phebe Fairchild: Her Book*. Illustrated by the author. Stokes, 1936, o.p. (Grades 4–6)

In trying to present an accurate picture of life in Connecticut in the 1830s, the author, in her preface, mentions the extensive research involved and the great variety of sources consulted. This painstaking effort results in a great deal of historical detail that sometimes, unfortunately, obscures the simple plot. Ten-year-old Phebe Fairchild is sent by stagecoach from her home in New Haven to live with relatives inland at Winton, Connecticut, while her mother and father, a sea captain, sail to England on her father's ship. Her large new family lives on a farm and includes Uncle Jothan and Aunt Betsy Fairchild, their five children, Grandmother Fairchild, and Aunt Hannah, the spinster sister of Captain Fairchild. Phoebe brings her favorite book with her, *Mother Goose*. At first Aunt Hannah, who like Grandmother is a hidebound puritan, opposes such trashy, sinful reading material, in the same way she objects to Phebe's colorful, pretty clothes, but in time she softens her convictions somewhat.

Phebe's independent, spirited ways often cause trouble. For example, she is caught impersonating her wealthy great-aunt Pettifer and her grandiose manner and dress. Sent to apologize, Phebe finds her great-aunt less imposing and more human than expected, and has a fine visit learning about the childhood of her father. With the help of the peddler Jeremiah, Phebe brings together her Uncle Benjamin and his girlfriend, Lucy Rogers, and is responsible for bringing home her sick friend, Christopher Ross, whom Aunt Hannah nurses back to health. Phebe's visit has brought many changes to her as well as to her many relatives.

Rouke, Constance. *Audubon*. Illustrated by James MacDonald. Harcourt, 1936, o.p. (Grades 7–10)

In this biography that covers the entire life of John James Audubon, the author has brought to life this talented, hardworking, impractical, and engaging artist. The 12 color plates that are included give an interesting sample of his work. Born in what is now Haiti in 1785, Audubon spent his childhood in France, where he haunted the woods and forests, watching and sketching birds. In 1803, he was sent by his father to the family estate, Mill Grove, near Philadelphia, where he continued to draw birds. He married Lucy Bakewell in 1808, and the young couple moved to the small river town of Louisville, where Audubon often neglected his various jobs to pursue his passion of finding and painting birds. A failure at business, Audubon moved to Louisiana where his wife was a governess and founded a private school where the artist sometimes taught. In 1826, Audubon went first to Scotland and then to England hoping to find a publisher for his work. Between 1827 and 1838, the life-sized paintings were published in folio parts under the collective title, *Birds of America*. The set contained a total of 425 colored engravings from his watercolors. Now a recognized artist, he returned to America and moved with his family to the northern part of Manhattan on the Hudson River, an area called "Minnie's Land."

He worked on a smaller edition of his great work and continued to make trips into the wilderness to collect specimens and paint. He was working on another giant project on the quadrupeds of North America when he died in 1851. It was completed by his sons Victor and John. His work remains one of the great achievements in American art and ornithology. The author has shown that Audubon's life was as colorful as his paintings.

Newbery Winner 1938

Seredy, Kate. *The White Stag*. Illustrated by the author. Viking, 1937, $14.99:
0-670-76375-6; pap., Puffin, $4.95: 0-14-031258-7. (Grades 4–7)

While growing up in Budapest, Hungary, Kate Seredy (1896–1975) studied art at the local academy and listened to Magyar tales recited by her father, a famous storyteller. After she emigrated to the United States in 1922, she made her living as an artist and illustrator, until May Massee, at Doubleday, suggested that she write and illustrate a book about her childhood in Hungary. The result was *The Good Master*, a Newbery Honor Book for 1936 (see p. 81), that told of a horse farm in the plains of Hungary where "the good master" lived with his son, Jancsi, and rambunctious niece, Kate. This story is continued in an Honor Book for 1940, *The Singing Tree* (see p. 105), in which the master's family, the Nagys, survive the horrors of World War I. The favorite story of Kate Seredy's father was "the legend of the White Stag, the story of unbroken faith in a great purpose." She also states, "It is an ageless and immortal story: one of the great legends of mankind. To a young child it is a fairy story, to a growing child it speaks of romance and adventure." It demonstrates "unshakable belief in a guiding hand from above and faith in one's powers."

Plot Summary

Based on the oral telling of the founding of Hungary, the story begins in Asia. "The early history of the Hungarian (Magyar) race is a matter of learned dispute. Their own traditions declare them to be descendants of the horde which sent forth the Huns from Asia in the fourth century."

Long ago, the mighty old hunter Nimrod made a prophecy. After years of wandering, he and his people found themselves in a cold and barren land. Somewhere he knew there was a region for them that was rich in greenery and filled with fertile pastures. Asking for a sign from the powerful Hadur, Nimrod killed his faithful horse and stretched his arms to the sky. A great eagle, the holy bird of Hadur, appeared. Hadur had spoken. To the west, in a region between two rivers, Nimrod's people would find their promised land.

Soon after, Nimrod's sons, Hunor and Magyar, appear. They have returned from a hunt, and Hunor tells of seeing and following a great white stag. Nimrod dies and his sons build a great tomb in his honor. Now the leadership of their people has passed to the sons.

Nimrod's sons and their people leave the wild Asian land, looking always for the magic white stag. Will it appear to lead them to the promised land? One day toward dusk, when the brothers return again from a hunt, they see the white stag, which seems to float on the rolling mist. The brothers follow him and come to the edge of a misty blue lake. It is there that Nimrod's people remain for several years.

Hunor and Magyar meet two moonmaidens, strange fairylike creatures who live in birch trees and are never seen in daylight. The brothers marry the moonmaidens, who are named Tunde and Cilla by Damos, the blind boy of the tribe. Hunor and Tunde have a son called Bendeguz, destined to become the White Eagle and father of Attila, the Red Eagle.

When 15 years pass, it is time for the tribe to move once again. But this time the once-united people will split. The most spirited and adventuresome among them will follow Hunor, who is far more reckless than his brother. Hunor fears no one but has no pity for those who are weak. Young Bendeguz is as fierce and fearless as his father. Magyar is the gentle and serious brother, and those of a like nature will follow him.

The tribe divides and the followers of Magyar settle on a divided strip of land in eastern Europe. The Magyars are content to stay there, but the restless followers of Hunor, known now as Huns, must move on to the west. The Huns grow ever more fierce and cruel as they grow wealthy. They seem more interested now in conquering and killing than they are in gaining their promised land, as Nimrod had prophesied.

Bendeguz, called the White Eagle, meets Alleeta, daughter of King Ashkenaz, the leader of a homeless, wandering people called Cimmerians. The Cimmerians unite with the Huns and accept Bendeguz as their leader. Bendeguz and Alleeta marry, but she dies when their son, Attila, is born. That night, Damos, now old and a prophet, declares that Attila, the Red Eagle, will lead the people into the promised land.

On the night of his wife's death and his son's birth, all feelings die in Bendeguz and he raises his son, Atilla, without love or tenderness. His heart has turned to stone. In like manner, when Attila is grown, he becomes a warrior utterly ruthless in battle. The Huns call him the Red Eagle, but his father calls him Attila, the Scourge of God. That cry is echoed throughout Europe, from land to land.

Long years of ruthless battles and killing pass. At last, with Attila as leader, the Huns gain their long promised land. During a blinding snowstorm, they follow the white stag through a pass in the Carpathian Mountains. The land before them seems enchanted. Attila and his now elderly father gaze in wonder at the forests and fields. The Huns know that they have come home, and they build an altar to honor Hadur, the first altar they have built since leaving the Magyars. When it is done, Attila the Conqueror, king of the promised land, lifts his sword as his oath of protection for his people.

Themes and Subjects

This is an old-style epic tale of heroes and the mighty in battle. It is dramatic in the telling and emphasizes the strength and weaknesses of the leaders as they set out to fulfill the prophecy of a promised land for the people. Through a long and dangerous journey, Attila, the ruthless warrior, leads them to their home, according to legend, the land of Hungary.

Incidents for Booktalking

Many heroic scenes highlight this tale of the founding of Hungary. See: the prophecy of Nimrod (pp. 9–18) and the sighting of the white stag (pp. 19–25); the brothers follow the stag to their first resting place and to the moonmaidens (pp. 32–42); Bendeguz, the White Eagle, is born (p. 43); Bendeguz meets Alleeta and the Red Eagle is born (pp. 50–64); Attila follows the white stag and leads his people through a pass (pp. 80–86).

Related Titles

The customs, lifestyle, amusements, and occupations of the people of Hungary are covered in Jetty St. John's *A Family in Hungary* (Lerner, 1988, $15.95: 0-8225-1683-7).

Nancy Ekholm Burkert's *Valentine and Orson* (Farrar, 1989, $16.95: 0-374-38078-3) is a stunning retelling in verse of the old folktale of twins separated at birth, one raised in poverty and the other in wealth.

Puzzles and folklore are combined in *Stories to Solve: Folktales from Around the World* (Greenwillow, 1985, $17.00: 0-688-04303-8) by George Shannon.

A princess sends three cousins on a yearlong quest to win her hand in Eric A. Kimmel's *The Three Princes: A Tale from the Middle East* (Holiday, 1994, $15.95: 0-8234-1115-X).

Bernard Evslin has written about many of the famous Greek heroes from mythology. Included are *Hercules* (Morrow, 1984, $16.00: 0-688-02748-2) and *Jason and the Argonauts* (Morrow, 1986, $16.00: 0-688-06245-1).

About the Book and Author

Berger, Laura Standley, ed. *Twentieth-Century Children's Writers*. 4th ed. St. James, 1995, pp. 861–62.

Brown, Muriel W., and Rita Schoch Foudray. *Newbery and Caldecott Medalists and Honor Book Winners: Bibliographic & Resource Material Through 1990*. 2d ed. Neal-Schuman, 1992, pp. 366–68.

Cech, John, ed. "American Writers for Children, 1900–1960." In *Dictionary of Literary Biography*. Vol. 22. Gale, 1983, pp. 198–306.

Chevalier, Tracy, ed. *Twentieth-Century Children's Writers*. 3d ed. St. James, 1989, pp. 870–71.

Collier, Laurie and Joyce Nakamura. *Major Authors and Illustrators for Children and Young Adults*. Gale, 1993, 6 vols., pp. 2065–67

Commire, Anne, ed. *Something About the Author*. Vol. 1. Gale, 1971, pp. 192–93.

Fadool, Cynthia. *Contemporary Authors*. Vols. 57–60. Gale, 1976, p. 517.

Helbig, Alethea K., and Agnes R. Perkins, eds. *Dictionary of American Children's Fiction, 1859–1959*. Greenwood, 1986, pp. 461–62.

Kunitz, Stanley J., and Howard Haycraft, eds. *The Junior Book of Authors*. Wilson, 1951, pp. 270–71.

Mahoney, Bertran E. *Illustrators of Children's Books, 1744–1945*. Horn Book, 1947, p. 357.

Miller, Bertha M., and Elinor Field, eds. *Newbery Medal Books: 1922–1955 with the Author's Acceptance Papers and Related Material.* Horn Book, 1955, pp. 157–65.

"Newbery Medal Acceptance Material, 1938." *Horn Book* 14, no. 4 (July/August 1938): 226–29.

Peterson, Linda K., and Marilyn L. Solt, eds. *Newbery and Caldecott Medal and Honor Books: 1922–1981.* Hall, 1982, p. 66.

Senick, Gerard J., ed. *Children's Literature Review.* Vol. 10. Gale, 1986, pp. 162–82.

Silvey, Anita, ed. *Children's Books and Their Creators.* Houghton, 1995, p. 588.

Ward, Martha, ed. *Authors of Books for Young People.* 3d ed. Scarecrow, 1990, p. 637.

Honor Books 1938

Bowman, James Cloyd. *Pecos Bill.* Illustrated by Laura Bannon. Little, Brown, 1937, o.p. (Grades 4–8)

This tall tale in biographical format tells how Pecos Bill rightfully deserves to be called "the greatest cowboy of all time." While journeying through Texas by covered wagon with his parents and 17 siblings, four-year-old Bill is bounced out of the wagon close to the Pecos River. He is raised to manhood by a pack of coyotes who name him Cropear. With them, he learns how to communicate with all animals, survive in the wilderness, and run like lightning. When he is finally found by his brother Chuck (short for Chuckwagon because of his appetite), Bill is persuaded to leave the wilds and become a cowboy. In no time he revolutionizes the world of cowpunching through such innovations as inventing a lariat to rope animals and by devising the first system of branding to denote ownership of cattle. He also helped cowboys use their leisure time by creating games like bulldogging and hog-tying as well as developing the rodeo and the Wild West Show. He tames the dreaded outlaw band, the Devil's Cavalry, by using his wild animal friends to frighten them. As well as developing the first perpetual motion ranch on Pinnacle Mountain where upkeep requires practically no work (for example, he teaches cattle to jump out of their skins), he tames the wildest, most powerful horse in the West, a white stallion originally named Pegasus whom he renames Widow Maker. When he lassos and redirects a ferocious cyclone, one of the geographical results is the creation of the Grand Canyon. While selling his Pinnacle Mountain ranch to an English couple, he falls in love with their daughter, a vivacious would-be cowgirl named Slue-Foot Sue. However, when Sue tries to ride Widow Maker on their wedding day and is thrown with such power that she spends several days in space, she decides the West is not for her and the marriage is called off. Gradually farmers begin to take over the land, and so, after supervising the greatest roundup of all time, Pecos Bill rides off into the sunset never to be heard from again.

Robinson, Mabel L. *Bright Island.* Illustrated by Lynd Ward. Random, 1937, o.p. (Grades 6–9)

This novel, set off the coast of Maine during the 1930s, covers one year in the life of 16-year-old Thankful Curtis, a high-spirited, independent girl who has lived all her life with her family on Bright Island. She has been schooled by her mother, a no-nonsense Scottish woman, in a household that includes her farmer father, Jonathan. Her four older brothers have all married and left for the mainland and her beloved Gramp has recently died. Thankful's closest friend on the island is Dave Allen, a hardworking young man who once lived with the Curtis family. Her parents have decided that Thankful must take her senior year at a fashionable boarding school on the mainland where, they hope, some of her rough edges will be smoothed. The transition from a home where there is neither plumbing nor electricity to the highly structured, proper life in the school is not without problems, but Thankful soon adjusts successfully. Through the help of her roommate, Selina, a popular girl who at first resents her, Thankful learns to dress properly. She soon begins to shine scholastically, and wins the favor of her teachers, particularly the young Latin instructor, Orin Flecher, who at the close of the school year makes a proposal of marriage, which she refuses. She attends many social functions and gets over a crush she has on a pampered rich boy. Gradually she learns social graces and how to evaluate people on inner strengths rather than superficial traits. Though successful academically, Thankful decides at the end of the school year not to continue her education but to return to her beautiful island and the family and friends she knows and admires. It is here she plans to stay after marrying the man she loves, her childhood friend, Dave Allen.

Wilder, Laura Ingalls. *On the Banks of Plum Creek.* Illustrated by Garth Williams. Harper, 1937, $15.95: 0-06-025470-5. (Grades 3–7)

This, the fourth of the "Little House" books, takes place in the mid-1870s and covers a period of two and one-half years in the lives of the Ingalls family. Charles and Caroline Ingalls and their three children, obedient, quiet Mary, age eight; adventurous, daring Laura, age seven; and the baby Carrie, move to Minnesota by covered wagon to homestead and farm. In exchange for their two horses and a colt, Pa buys a stretch of land on the banks of Plum Creek complete with a sod house and stable. Living underground is an arduous feat for the family but the pioneer life has its compensations. Swimming in the creek is a great recreation in spite of the leeches, and in the fall Mary and Laura enjoy the forbidden joys of sliding down the haystack. After their first winter, the family begins to prosper. Pa works as a day laborer and is able to buy a cow and two horses, and in the spring he borrows enough money to build a two-room farmhouse for the family. Laura, because of her mischievous and outspoken nature, sometimes gets into trouble, but this family is united by their love and devotion to each other. Laura and Mary go to school and meet other girls including the unpleasant Nellie Oleson, and on Sundays the family begins going to church. Tragedy strikes in the fall at harvesting time when a sky full of grasshoppers descends, eats all their wheat, and lays enough eggs to destroy next year's crop. Pa is forced to walk 300 miles and spend several months away from home to find harvesting work in order to support his family and make payments on the lumber. He comes home in time for a joyful Christmas reunion with his family. The next year is a lean one for the Ingalls but their amazing grit and courage carry them through. Pa narrowly escapes death during a blizzard in which he is lost for three days, but he is saved and the family spends their third Christmas on Plum Creek confident that the worst is over and the new year will be a better one. The sequel, *By the Shores of Silver Lake*, was an Honor Book in 1940 (p. 105).

Newbery Winner 1939

Enright, Elizabeth. *Thimble Summer*. Illustrated by the author. Holt, 1938, o.p.; Harcourt, 1995, $11.95: 0-03-015686-6; pap., Dell, $3.50: 0-440-80227-X. (Grades 3–6)

Elizabeth Enright (1909–1968) began her career in publishing as an accomplished book illustrator, but later decided to supply the words as well as the pictures for one of her books, *Kintu, A Congo Adventure* (1935, o.p.). Buoyed by its success, she next wrote the award-winning *Thimble Summer*, the story of a long, hot summer in rural Wisconsin during the Great Depression, as experienced by the bold, mischievous, nine-year-old Garnet Linden. Incidents used in the book were derived from the author's experiences as a child on her uncle's farm in the Midwest during a drought, and from stories she heard from her mother and grandmother about their childhoods. Best known for her episodic family stories, the author wrote several books about the Melendy family of four motherless children growing up in New York City, beginning with *The Saturdays* (Holt, 1941, $12.95). Her novel *Gone-Away Lake* (1957) (see "Honor Books," 1958, p. 216) tells of the experiences of Julian and Portia exploring a swamp, where they encounter two unusual recluses. The story is continued in *Return to Gone-Away* (Holt, 1961, o.p.).

Plot Summary

It seems as though the rains will never come to Wisconsin that summer. Garnet Linden, nearly 10 years old, cannot remember such a dry spell on the farm. The corn is drying up and the oats are turning yellow before their time. Garnet knows her father is very worried about the drought. Every evening he stands outside looking at the night sky. Then he shakes his head and says, "No rain tonight." However, Garnet knows he is most worried about the mounting bills. If a farmer can't sell crops, there will be no money to pay bills. Garnet knows that among other things, her father wants money to replace their old dilapidated barn.

Garnet and her best friend Citronella Hauser, from the farm down the road, talk about the drought. They also look at catalogues that come in the mail, trying to decide what they will buy if they ever have the money.

One evening after supper, Garnet and her 11-year-old brother, Jay, go down to the swimming hole to cool off. Even the water is warm. As they explore the sandy flats along the water before returning home, Garnet finds a small silver thimble half buried in the sand. She picks it up and decides it must be magic. Jay just laughs.

But maybe the thimble *is* magic. Later that night, Garnet awakens, feeling something strange is about to happen. And it does. It rains! Jay and Garnet run out in the rain like wild animals for the pure joy of the drought's end.

Things definitely improve on the farm after that, and the welcome rains continue. During one rainy afternoon, Garnet and Citronella visit Citronella's great-grandmother, Mrs. Eberhardt, who is very, very old. Sitting in her rocking chair in her little room in Citronella's house, she tells the girls a long-ago story. She describes the wilderness of the Wisconsin countryside when she was young. She talks of her 10th birthday when she went into Elly Gensler's Emporium and saw a pretty imitation coral bracelet. Elly told her it was worth one dollar, but he would sell it to her for 50¢. She promised to come back for it when she had the money. Her father promised to take her back for the bracelet for her birthday that August. But when her birthday came, her father was too busy to take her to town, so she left her little brother to pick berries by himself and walked the long, hot way. She was heartbroken to discover that the bracelet had been sold after all. When she returned home, her little brother had become lost. After a long time, they found him, but she was ashamed of her behavior in leaving him. That Christmas, she received a coral bracelet from her father.

The magic of the thimble continues, and before long, a letter arrives for Garnet's father saying that the government is going to loan them some money to put up a new barn! This proves to be a very exciting time for Garnet because she gets to help in making the lime that is needed for the new building. After much pestering, her father says that she and Jay can go along to the kiln, about two miles away in a thick wood, where they will stay up all night because the fire must be fed every 10 or 15 minutes. Garnet's father and Mr. Peabody do most of the feeding and Garnet falls asleep, but it is an exciting time nevertheless.

One day a stranger arrives on the farm, a young boy hardly older than Jay. His name is Eric and he has no home or family. He says he is just hitchhiking. Garnet's father offers him work with building the new barn. Eric accepts and soon becomes almost a member of the family. Garnet decides that she likes having two brothers.

Eric proves to be a great help on the farm. He even helps her and Citronella build a treehouse, where the girls often spend hours talking and dreaming and making up stories for each other's entertainment. Tired of the treehouse one day, the girls decide to go into town to the library for some new books. They happen upon Mr. Freebody in his truck and he takes them to town.

Garnet loves the smell of the library. The girls say hello to Miss Pentland, the librarian, who often confuses Garnet's name and calls her Ruby. The two girls lose themselves in the wonderful worlds they find in such stories as *The Jungle Book* and *Duchess Olga, or the Sapphire Signet*. So engrossed are they that they do not notice the passage of time. When they realize that the light has faded outside, they discover that they are locked in the library! It is midnight before they hear the reassuring voice of Mr. Freebody. Both the girls' fathers have been scouring the town looking for them. Miss Pentland is very upset, not knowing how she could have missed them when she locked up. The girls are none the worse for wear, and Garnet rather wishes they could have spent the whole night in the library.

As the long days of August pass, the new barn is taking shape nicely. Soon it is harvest time and Garnet, along with everyone else on the farm, is busy with picking and packing and canning and threshing. One day while Garnet is working on the oat stacks, she falls asleep and nearly brings the pile of oats down on top of her. Eric rescues her, but Jay gets angry and tells her to stay home and help their mother because "threshing isn't something girls should be monkeying with."

Garnet is furious with her brother and vows never to feel the same way about him again. When she stomps back to the house, she discovers that her mother is entertaining. This makes Garnet more angry than before. She decides there is no place for her and so she leaves. Once out on the road, she remembers Eric's stories of hitchhiking and decides that she can do that too. She first gets a ride with a man and his wife who are going to New Conniston, 18 miles away. The wife turns out to be a singer. When she tries out "Rock of Ages," Garnet is sure her tremendous voice will blow her out of the window!

Garnet has a fine time in New Conniston seeing the sights until she discovers that she has lost her money. This time she gets a ride with a trucker who is going near her farm. On the way, Garnet helps him to recover some ornery chickens and in return, he gives her a wayward hen.

After she is dropped off near home, Garnet meets Mr. Freebody, who tells her that she has not been missed because her father thought she was at the house and her mother thought she was working with her father. Mr. Freebody gives her a kindly lecture about stopping to think a little more before she does something. He knows she is a spirited youngster and he doesn't want to change that, but he doesn't want anything to happen to her either. Garnet promises.

Home once more, with Jay forgiven, it is time for the big fair that Garnet has been looking forward to all summer. She is entering her prize pig, Timmy. The fair is a wonderful experience for them all, but especially for Garnet. She was right about Timmy for he wins a blue ribbon.

Home on the farm, Garnet is so happy with her life that she runs out into the field. There, to the astonishment of Griselda, the finest of Jersey cows, Garnet turns handsprings up and down the pasture.

Themes and Subjects

Adults who discuss this story with children should stress that it was published in 1939 at a time when hitchhiking, if not encouraged, was certainly not the universally forbidden activity for youngsters that it is today. Aside from the fact that Garnet hitchhikes and accepts rides with strangers, this is a warm, reassuring story of farm and family life in the American Midwest. There is a sense of cooperation and sharing among all family members and a willingness to help others, as when the stranger, Eric, appears and is readily accepted when he proves willing to do his share. There is also a nice sense of sharing of life's experiences between the generations, as when Citronella's great-grandmother tells the girls the story of the coral bracelet and her 10th birthday.

Incidents for Booktalking

A number of scenes portray the warm sense of Midwestern farm life and the love of friends and family. See: Garnet goes swimming with Jay and finds the thimble (pp. 10–12); it rains (pp. 14–16); Mrs. Eberhardt's 10th birthday story (pp. 18–29); working the kiln (pp. 33–38); Eric arrives (pp. 39–49); Garnet and Citronella are locked in the library (pp. 54–62); Timmy wins a blue ribbon (pp. 115–19).

Related Titles

Life is difficult when Lacey returns with her mother to the North Carolina mountain village where she was born in *Return to Bitter Creek* (Viking, 1986, $12.95: 0-670-80783-4; pap., Puffin, $4.99: 0-14-032223-X) by Doris B. Smith.

In Isabelle Holland's *The Journey Home* (Scholastic, 1990, $13.95: 0-590-43110-2; pap., Apple, $2.95: 0-590-43111-0), two orphaned girls start life anew in the second half of the nineteenth century when they are adopted by a couple in Kansas.

Lindsay has problems adjusting to her life in New York City but she finds new friends because of a Siamese cat in C. S. Adler's *Courtyard Cat* (Clarion, 1995, $13.95: 0-395-71126-6).

Set in 1899, the eighth and the last of the Great Brain series is, as usual, narrated by J. D., who laments his brother's plots and schemes in John D. Fitzgeralds's *The Great Brain Is Back* (Dial, 1995, $14.99: 0-8037-1346-0).

Using an English setting, Hilary McKay writes about the four enterprising, delightful Conroy sisters in *The Exiles* (Macmillan, 1992, $16.00: 0-689-50555-8) and *The Exiles at Home* (Macmillan, 1994, $16.00: 00-689-50610-4).

About the Book and Author

Berger, Laura Standley, ed. *Twentieth-Century Children's Writers*. 4th ed. St. James, 1995, pp. 323–24.

Brown, Muriel W., and Rita Schoch Foudray. *Newbery and Caldecott Medalists and Honor Book Winners: Bibliographic & Resource Material Through 1990*. 2d ed. Neal-Schuman, 1992, pp. 125–27.

Chevalier, Tracy, ed. *Twentieth-Century Children's Writers*. 3d ed. St. James, 1989, pp. 317–18.

Commire, Anne, ed. *Something About the Author*. Vol. 9. Gale, 1976, pp. 61–62.

Enright, Elizabeth. *Thimble Summer*. SRA McGraw Hill, 1985. Audiocassettes. ($21.33)

Fadool, Cynthia. *Contemporary Authors*. Vols. 61–64. Gale, 1976, pp. 179–80.

Helbig, Alethea K., and Agnes R. Perkins, eds. *Dictionary of American Children's Fiction, 1859–1959*. Greenwood, 1986, p. 150 (bio.), pp. 517–18 (book).

Kunitz, Stanley J., and Howard Haycraft, eds. *The Junior Book of Authors*. Wilson, 1951, pp. 113–14.

Mahoney, Bertha E. *Illustrators of Children's Books, 1744–1946*. Horn Book, 1947, p. 306.

"Newbery Medal Acceptance Material, 1939." *Horn Book* 15, no. 4 (July/August 1939): 231–35.

Peterson, Linda K., and Marilyn L. Solt, eds. *Newbery and Caldecott Medal and Honor Books: 1922–1981*. Hall, 1982, pp. 69–70.

Senick, Gerard J., ed. *Children's Literature Review*. Vol. 4. Gale, 1982, pp. 67–77.

Silvey, Anita, ed. *Children's Books and Their Creators*. Houghton, 1995, pp. 225-26.

Ward, Martha, ed. *Authors of Books for Young People*. 3d ed. Scarecrow, 1990, pp. 211–12.

Honor Books 1939

Angelo, Valenti. *Nino*. Illustrated by the author. Viking, 1938, o.p. (Grades 4–6)

In this episodic novel, the author re-creates scenes from his own childhood in Italy and re-creates the simple, innocent life of villagers in turn-of-the-century Italy. This is the story of Nino's childhood in the little Italian village of Massarosa where the boy lives with his mother, Allinda, and grandfather. When Nino was still a baby, his father migrated to America and days become special when they receive a letter from him. Nino's family is poor materially but rich in their many friends and their loving relationships. Julio, son of the neighboring Ditto family, is a mischievous lad who is Nino's age and his best friend. One day the two families have dinner together and using Signor Ditto's donkey cart and later a rowboat, travel to Viareggio where Nino has his picture taken to send to his father. Nino is proud to take part in a religious procession to a hill chapel, but the shoes he is obliged to wear cramp his feet. With his grandfather, Nino helps pick and sort olives and watches the miller press them to make olive oil. Later, with Julio, he sees Julio's father stomp on grapes to make the wine of which he is so proud. Both families attend a country fair during which Signor Ditto is defeated when he wrestles the gypsies' bear. Nino receives a pig that he keeps as a pet and he and Julio partake of the delicious food their mothers prepare for such occasions as Christmas and Easter. When Nino is eight, a letter arrives from his father that contains money for his family's passage to America. Eager and excited, the three leave behind their friends and country hoping to find happiness and prosperity in the New World.

Atwater, Richard, and Florence Atwater. *Mr. Popper's Penguins*. Illustrated by Robert Lawson. Little, Brown, 1938, $16.95: 0-316-05843-2; pap., Dell, $3.50: 0-316-05842-4. (Grades 3–5)

Mr. Popper, an affable, absent-minded house painter, lives at 432 Proudfoot Avenue in the small town of Stillwater, with his wife and two children, Janie and Bill. His humble, quiet life is interrupted with the arrival of a gift from Admiral Drake, the Antarctic explorer to whom Mr. Popper had written a fan letter. It is a penguin, whom Mr. Popper names Captain Cook. The bird soon captivates both the Popper household and the entire community. To accommodate Captain Cook, the Poppers have to make many adjustments, including converting the ice box into a ersatz Antarctic home and purchasing expensive canned shrimp for food. When Captain Cook develops a seemingly incurable case of loneliness, the local aquarium donates another penguin, named Greta. Soon there are 10 little additions to the family, which leads to further expenses for buying fresh fish (preferred over the canned shrimp) and installing an ice-making machine to convert the basement into a suitable environment. Faced with imminent bankruptcy, Mr. Popper hits on a wonderful idea. He trains the penguins and soon they are a sell-out attraction in theaters across the nation, billed as Popper's Performing

Penguins. Unfortunately, in Boston Mr. Popper mistakes the Royal Theater for the Regal. In the confusion, the penguins create such a disturbance during a trained seal act that the police are called and both Mr. Popper and his penguins are sent to jail. There they are visited by Admiral Drake who suggests a happy solution to everyone's problems. In the spring, he and Mr. Popper will take the penguins to the North Pole to establish the first penguin colony in the Arctic. After almost 60 years this book remains a favorite in part because its ridiculous, exaggerated situations are tempered by a genial humor represented by the easygoing Mr. Popper. Robert Lawson's illustrations add to the fun.

Crawford, Phyllis. *"Hello the Boat!"* Illustrated by Edward Laning. Holt, 1938, o.p. (Grades 4–7)

In addition to a pleasant, uncomplicated plot, this lighthearted saga of the Doak family and their trip down the Ohio River in 1817 contains facts about life on the river and outlying settlements, history of the area, tall tales about Mike Fink, and an encounter with a real historical personage, General William Henry Harrison, later to become the ninth president of the United States. In March 1817, the Doak family—father, mother (known as Miss Biddy) and their children, 16-year-old Susan, 14-year-old Steve, and 10-year-old David—leave their home in Pittsburgh to resettle on a farm near Cincinnati. Mr. Doak has made arrangements for them to travel with all their belongings and a menagerie of farm animals by rented storeboat, selling goods and supplies during their journey and sharing in the profits at the end. At first the trip is smooth and pleasant and business is good. At one of their stops, Susan meets and is attracted to Simon Winthrop, a young man on his way to Cincinnati to study law, and at another, an exuberant old riverman name Pappy signs on as a crewman. At one point they successfully navigate rapids and at two of their many stops the family attends a traveling show and meets friendly Indians. Before reaching their destination, Susan discovers that the $3,000 they have earned is missing from their cash box and so is Pappy. They arrive in Cincinnati in time for a gala Fourth of July celebration during which Pappy appears with the missing money. He had spotted the robber, an ancient enemy, and tracked him down. The happy ending is complete when Father accepts a job offer to become the manager of a manufacturing company, Pappy agrees to help operate the farm, and Susan and Simon become engaged.

Eaton, Jeanette. *Leader by Destiny: George Washington, Man and Patriot.* Illustrated by Jack Manley Rose. Harcourt, 1938, o.p. (Grades 7–10)

As the title suggests, this fictionalized biography takes the position that George Washington did not actively seek to become a great leader of his country but instead the responsibility and the eventual attendant glory were thrust upon him by fate and circumstance. The book begins in 1747 when Washington is 15 and ends with his death at Mount Vernon in 1799. This book covers both his personal and public life. For example, the author leads the reader to believe that the true love of his life was Sally Fairfax, the wife of his neighbor in Virginia. She left for England when Washington was about 40. Of her departure, he says, "Darling of my life—goodbye!" Although all the facts have been authenticated by painstaking research and there are many quotes from existing documents, letters, and journals, the book also contains passages of Washington's imagined inner thoughts and invented dialogue. Many of Washington's contemporaries are brought to life in the book, from his neighbors and friends in Virginia like George Mason and the Lee family to the leaders of the Revolution such as Patrick Henry, Alexander Hamilton, and Thomas Jefferson. All the important events and accomplishments of his adult life are covered, including his participation in the French and Indian Wars, his role as delegate to both the first and second Continental Congresses, his appointment as chief of the Continental Army, his part in the war and the victory at Yorktown, and his contributions to leading the new government under the Constitution through its initial trials. Of the book, one reviewer stated, "The human portrayal of Washington makes this biography of enduring interest." The text is nicely complemented by more than 20 full-page detailed drawings of people and places mentioned in the book.

Gray, Elizabeth Janet. *Penn*. Illustrated by George Gillett Whitney. Viking, 1938, o.p. (Grades 7–10)

With an emphasis on his formative years, the author, herself descended from Quakers, retells the life of this courageous leader, colonist, and fighter for religious freedom and tolerance. In 1644, William Penn was born to a wealthy family in London, England. While at Oxford his outspoken fight for the individual's right to worship as one pleased led to expulsion. When he was 22, while managing his family's estates in Ireland, Penn met a Quaker preacher, Thomas Loe, and became a member of this peaceful but persecuted religion. Afterward he was imprisoned many times for writing and preaching about Quakerism. Soon he realized that the only way for him and other Quakers to escape this oppressive persecution was to emigrate to America. As payment of a debt owed his father, Charles II gave him a tract of land between New York and Maryland. In 1682, he and his followers arrived on their land, named Pennsylvania, or Penn's Woods. As governor, he put into practice the teachings of the Quakers. He also signed a treaty with the Indians, who called him Onas, that was so fair that the Indians never attacked the colony. The constitution of Pennsylvania later served as a model for the country's constitution. After the end of the reign of James II, the colony was placed under royal control for two years, but was returned to Penn in 1694. After a stay in England he returned in 1699 to tend to problems involving the government, piracy, and trade. He returned to England in 1701, suffered a debilitating stroke in 1712, and died there in 1718. He had lived long enough to see his colony grow and prosper—a suitable testament to his courage and convictions.

1940s

 Newbery Winner 1940

Daugherty, James. *Daniel Boone*. Illustrated by the author. Viking, 1939, o.p. (Grades 5–9)

Multitalented James Daugherty (1889–1974) began studying art as a child. When his family moved from North Carolina (where he was born) to Washington, D.C., the young man studied art at the Corcoran Art School, and later, when his father was transferred to London as part of the Department of Agriculture, he studied there for two years. He was exclusively an illustrator of books until the editor, May Massee, persuaded him to try writing as well. His first effort was the charming *Andy and the Lion* (Viking 1938, $13.95; pap., Puffin, $4.99), an amusing modern picture book version of Androcles and the Lion. Although he had already illustrated Stewart Edward White's *Daniel Boone* in 1926, he wrote and illustrated his own prizewinning version in 1939. Of this book, Anne Carroll Moore wrote, "It has pioneer flavor and authenticity. Only a pioneer at heart who has seen freedom at a crossroads could have reached back more than 100 years with so warm a handclasp for the Pioneer of the Wilderness," and the noted artist Lynd Ward wrote in an appreciation of Daugherty's work, "His talent is firmly rooted in American experience . . . his voice speaks out for the values of democratic life."

Plot Summary

Daniel Boone is a very early American folk hero. He was born on November 2, 1734, in Berks County, Pennsylvania, and died on September 26, 1820, in St. Charles, Missouri. Even in his own lifetime, his fame as a frontiersman had spread around the world. Famed poet Lord Byron devoted seven stanzas to Boone in "Don Juan." Boone is most noted as the hero who helped blaze a trail through the Cumberland Gap, which is a notch in the Appalachian Mountains near the juncture of Kentucky, Tennessee, and Virginia.

This is a fictionalized account of the life of Daniel Boone, emphasizing his wandering spirit and concentrating on both his trailblazing activities and the many troubles that the frontier settlers encountered during that time with Native Americans, whose land was often being invaded.

As a young boy, one of 11 children, Daniel and his family, who were English Quakers, leave Berks County and head west in their Conestoga wagons, as did so many others, looking for a new and better life. They cross the Potomac River at Harpers Ferry and enter the Shenandoah Valley, eventually settling along the North Carolina frontier.

Although young Daniel has very little formal schooling, he does learn to read and write. He also learns the trade of blacksmithing and joins a company of North Carolina riflemen that was patrolling the frontier. At one time, his group comes under the command of a young colonel named George Washington.

As a young man, Boone marries his childhood sweetheart, Rebecca Bryan. In 1773, Boone and his family head for Kentucky but encounter hostile Cherokees and are forced to turn back. Boone's son James is killed in the fighting. Although many trappers and explorers had entered what became Kentucky, Boone is generally noted as its discoverer because in 1767, he traversed a short way through the Cumberland Gap on a hunting trip. He returned two years later with some hunting companions and spent some time trapping and hunting.

In 1775, Boone and others are asked by the Richard Henderson's Transylvania Company to blaze a trail through the Cumberland Gap. The company had plans to establish Kentucky as a fourteenth British colony. Boone and his men encounter great difficulties but are able to build the Wilderness Road from eastern Virginia into the Kentucky interior. It later became the main route that opened up the West to exploration and settlement.

As a consequence of the Wilderness Road, many new settlements are able to open up in the region. Among them is Boonesborough, to which Boone moves his wife and their daughter in 1775. Their arrival marks the first permanent settlement there and Boone's wife and daughter were probably the first white women to live in the area.

Kentucky never does become the fourteenth colony, and in fact is made a county of Virginia. A leader in defending Boonesborough against Native American attack, Boone becomes a captain in the county militia. In 1778, Boone is captured, but the Shawnee chief, Blackfish, admires Boone so much that he adopts him. Five months later, Boone is able to escape unharmed and returns to Boonesborough in time to warn the settlers that an attack is coming. When it does come that September, the settlement is able to withstand the 10-day siege.

Boone spent all his life hunting and trapping and following the wilderness trails. Ever restless, in the years following the American Revolution, he surveyed the land along the Ohio River. He settled in what is now West Virginia for a few years, and then in 1799 followed his son Daniel west to Missouri, in the Louisiana Territory. There, he continued to hunt and trap until his death. By that time, all the world knew of the exploits of the frontier hero, Daniel Boone.

Themes and Subjects

In fictionalized, somewhat romanticized form, this book sketches the life of the trailblazer named Daniel Boone. Much is made of his free spirit and courage, and although the character of the man never comes alive, the book does portray an adventurous period in American history.

Incidents for Booktalking

See any of the following scenes for a glimpse of frontier life: the Boone family moves west (pp. 14–15); in the command of George Washington (pp. 17–18); Boone moves his family to Boonesborough (pp. 49–66).

Related Titles

There are several other recommended biographies of Daniel Boone, the famous wilderness scout, including Jim Hargrove's *Daniel Boone: Pioneer Trailblazer* (Children's Press, 1985, $14.40: 0-516-03215-1); Seamus Cavan's *Daniel Boone and the Opening of the Ohio Country* (Chelsea, 1991, $19.95: 0-7910-1309-X); and for younger readers, Keith Brandt's *Daniel Boone: Frontier Adventures* (Troll, 1983, $17.29: 0-89375-843-4).

Laurence Santrey's *Davy Crockett: Young Pioneer* (Troll, 1983, $10.79: 0-89375-848-5) tells the story of another frontier scout.

The famous expedition across America is told in *Meriwether Lewis and William Clark* (Children's, 1991, $28.20: 0-516-03061-2) by Christine A. Fitzgerald.

David Kherdian's *Bridger: The Story of a Mountain Man* (Greenwillow, 1987, $12.95: 0-688-06510-4) is a novel based on two years in the life of the famous trapper and explorer.

Life on the changing frontier and its history are covered in text and excellent large illustrations in *Frontier Living* (Harper, 1976, $26.00: 0-690-01064-8) by Edwin Tunis.

About the Book and Author

Berger, Laura Standley, ed. *Twentieth-Century Children's Writers*. 4th ed. St. James, 1995, pp. 273–74.

Brown, Muriel W., and Rita Schoch Foudray. *Newbery and Caldecott Medalists and Honor Book Winners: Bibliographic & Resource Material Through 1990*. 2d ed. Neal-Schuman, 1992, pp. 90–93.

Chevalier, Tracy, ed. *Twentieth-Century Children's Writers*. 3d ed. St. James, 1989, pp. 263–65.

Commire, Anne, ed. *Something About the Author*. Vol. 13. Gale, 1978, pp. 26–29.

Kunitz, Stanley J., and Howard Haycraft, eds. *The Junior Book of Authors*. Wilson, 1951, pp. 88–90.

Locher, Frances C., ed. *Contemporary Authors*. Vols. 73–76. Gale, 1978, pp. 153–54.

Mahoney, Bertha E. *Illustrators of Children's Books, 1744–1945*. Horn Book, 1947, pp. 296–97.

Miller, Bertha M., and Deborah A. Straub, eds. *Newbery Medal Books: 1922–1955 with the Author's Acceptance Papers and Related Material*. Horn Book, 1955, pp. 176–91.

"Newbery Medal Acceptance Material, 1940." *Horn Book* 16, no. 4 (July/August 1940): 231–46.

Peterson, Linda K., and Marilyn L. Solt, eds. *Newbery and Caldecott Medal and Honor Books: 1922–1981*. Hall, 1982, pp. 73–74.

Silvey, Anita, ed. *Children's Books and Their Creators*. Houghton, 1995, pp. 187–88.

Ward, Martha, ed. *Authors of Books for Young People*. 3d ed. Scarecrow, 1990, p. 170–71.

Honor Books 1940

Meader, Stephen W. *Boy with a Pack*. Illustrated by Edward Shenton. Harcourt, 1939, o.p. (Grades 5–8)

During the 1930s, Stephen Meader was one of the foremost writers of historical fiction for young readers, with more than 30 titles to his credit. This novel deals with 17-year-old Bill Crawford and his journey in 1837 from his home in New Hampshire to seek a new life in Ohio. To sustain him on the trek, he has spent his entire savings on a small trunk load of "notions" (everything from calico and combs to ribbons and fishhooks) to peddle to strangers he meets. In Vermont, he frees a half-grown hound puppy from a trap. Bill now has a traveling companion he names Jody. He is almost cheated out of his pack of wares by an unscrupulous accordion-playing horse thief, Alonzo Peel, but on the voyage along the Erie Canal, he earns a little money working as a horse driver on the boat *Mohawk Tiger* for its owner Buck Owen. On board, Bill also meets the young, pretty cook, Mary Ann Bennett, who is also intent on starting a new life in Ohio. Because Bill helps bring Peel to justice, he is rewarded with a splendid black mare, Martha. Continuing his trek, Bill has encounters with a traveling circus, a marauding black bear, and two ruffians who disguise themselves as an old lady and a blind man to dupe unsuspecting victims. Bill has another mouth to feed when Martha gives birth to a foal, Bub.

In Ohio, Bill happens on a station on the Underground Railroad operated from the farmhouse of a devout Quaker family, the Halseys. Risking his own life and future, Bill transports a young black boy, Banjo, to a stop on the railroad where he can reach safety in Canada. In the big sprawling expanse of Ohio, Bill decides to set down roots particularly when he finds Mary Ann working as a cook in a gristmill where, coincidentally, they need the services of another worker.

Robinson, Mabel. *Runner of the Mountain Tops: The Life of Louis Agassiz*. Illustrated by Lynd Ward. Random, 1939, o.p. (Grades 6–9)

The author once lived in a house in America where Agassiz was a frequent visitor. She heard so many stories about him and his accomplishments that she felt she had to write his biography. As she says in this book's preface, "I seem always to have known him." This complete account of his life deals equally with his personal life and his contributions to science. The famous naturalist and geologist was born in Switzerland in 1807. After studying at universities in Zurich, Erlangen, Heidelberg, and Munich, Agassiz accumulated Ph.D. and M.D. degrees, the latter at the insistence of his family who wanted him trained for a profession. Although he practiced medicine briefly, his real interest lay in scientific research.

In Paris he studied fossil fish and wrote several volumes on the subject of such importance that he gained an international reputation. For 14 years he taught natural history at the University of Neuchatel where he also wrote papers on glacial movements and deposits, work that established the concept of the Ice Age. He came to the United States in 1846, leaving his wife and three children behind. Two years later, after his wife died in Europe, Agassiz decided to remain in America and accepted a professorship of zoology and geology at Harvard University. His children joined him and he later married Elizabeth Cary in Cambridge. A very popular and influential teacher, he helped to establish the concept of field studies. His own expeditions included one from Boston to California to study the Atlantic and Pacific coasts. Before his death in 1873, he achieved one of his greatest dreams, the opening of the Agassiz Museum at Harvard.

Seredy, Kate. *The Singing Tree*. Illustrated by the author. Viking, 1939, o.p.; Peter Smith, 1992, $19.00: 0-8446-6588-6; pap., Puffin, $5.99: 0-14-03454304. (Grades 4–7)

This sequel to *The Good Master* (see "Honor Books," 1936, p. 81) continues the story of Kate, now age 12; her beloved gentle uncle, Marton Nagy; and his son Jansci, age 13, on Marton's sheep and horse ranch in the Hungarian plains. At the wedding of their neighbors, Mari Vidor and Peter Hodi, news comes of the Archduke's assassination, which plunges Europe into World War I. At first the war means little to them, but gradually its effects are felt. Men are conscripted into the army including Kate's father, Sandor, and the newly married Peter. Sandor is taken prisoner by the Russians and young, homesick Peter deserts and is hidden by Kate and Jansci until he realizes he must return to his unit. After Marton is also drafted, Jancsi becomes the manager of the farm. He is helped by the well-liked village storekeeper, Uncle Moses Mandelbaum, whose son, a rabbi, was one of the first casualties of the war. Jansci is granted permission to use six Russian prisoners of war to work the harvest. They soon become family favorites, particularly the burly, fun-loving Grigori. In the summer of 1916, Jansci and Kate journey to bring Jansci's maternal grandparents to the safety of the ranch. During the trip they find Marton wounded in an army hospital. He is suffering from amnesia but when Kate shouts his name his memory returns and he is able to accompany them back to the ranch. Soon they are joined by Mari, her baby, and six German refugee children ranging in age from 6 to 12. At war's end, Marton talks about the wonderful singing tree he and his comrades saw on the Russian front—a tree so filled with singing birds that it seemed alive with music. Everyone hopes that brotherhood and peace will prevail in the future.

Wilder, Laura Ingalls. *By the Shores of Silver Lake*. Illustrated by Garth Williams. Harper, 1939, $15.95: 0-06-026416-0; pap. Scholastic, $2.50: 0-590-01401-3.(Grades 4–8)

During the two years that have elapsed since the end of *On the Banks of Plum Creek* (see "Honor Books," 1938, p. 93), the Ingalls family has not prospered. A bout of scarlet fever has blinded the eldest daughter, Mary, and the crops have been so poor that Pa decides to accept an offer from Aunt Docia to accompany her to the Dakota Territory where her husband, Hiram, is a contractor for the railroad. Here Pa will work as combined storekeeper and bookkeeper for Hiram at a handsome wage of $50 per month. When he is settled, the rest of the family—Ma; Laura, now 12 ½; younger sister Carrie; and the family's new addition, baby Grace—travel by rail to join him.

At first they live in a shanty close to the railroad camp, but close to the beautiful Silver Lake. Their family life is enlivened by Pa having to cope with horse thieves and a pay dispute among the men. Laura forms friendships with Hiram's two children, Lena and Jean, and rides their ponies.

In the fall when the camp closes down, Pa moves the family to a surveyor's house where he has the job of caring for the camp's tools. They are soon joined by homesteaders from Iowa, newlyweds Mr. and Mrs. Boast. The two families spend a happy winter and greet the new year of 1880 together. In the spring, a steady stream of settlers passes through the territory and the Ingalls make a little money renting rooms and selling meals. From one of their visitors, they learn of a college for the blind in Iowa, and the family, particularly Laura, hopes to earn enough money to send Mary there. In the meantime, Pa files his own homesteading claim. He builds both a store in the town site of De Smet and a humble family home on his property a mile out of town. On moving day, Laura sees two young men in a wagon driven by a pair of beautiful horses. One is Almanzo Wilder, the man Laura is destined to marry. The series is continued in *The Long Winter*, a 1941 Honor Book (p. 112).

Newbery Winner 1941

Sperry, Armstrong. *Call It Courage.* Illustrated by the author. Macmillan, 1940, $16.00: 0-02-7860302. (Grades 4–6)

The author-illustrator Armstrong Sperry (1897–1976) was born in New Haven, Connecticut, where he was surrounded by the lore and the life of the sea. His grandfather had followed the sea as a livelihood and enthralled the young boy with his stories of adventures in remote lands. Most memorable was his account of being wrecked in Bora Bora, where he spent months with the natives. After studying at several art academies including the Yale School of Fine Arts, and serving in the Navy during World War I, Armstrong Sperry fulfilled his ambition to visit the lands described by his grandfather. He spent two years in the French-owned islands of the South Pacific, and, during one voyage to Tahiti, he found a schooner to take him to Bora Bora. Many of his books were inspired by these adventures, including the Newbery Honor Book *All Sails Set* (see "Honor Books," 1936, p. 81), the story of the first voyage of the famous Clipper Ship, the *Flying Cloud.* Of *Call It Courage,* in which a young Polynesian boy conquers his fear of the sea, Sperry wrote:

> I had been afraid that perhaps in *Call It Courage,* the concept of a spiritual courage might be too adult for children, but the reception of this book has reaffirmed a belief I have long held: that children have imagination enough to grasp any idea, and respond to it, if it is put to them honestly and without a patronizing pat on the head.

Plot Summary

This is a tale of a time long ago in the South Seas, when the Polynesians were great in number and fierce in heart. These people worshipped courage, and so they were much shamed by the behavior of Mafatu, son of the Great Chief of Hikueru. Although his name meant Stout Heart, Mafatu was deeply afraid of the sea and his people branded him a coward.

Mafatu's fear of the sea stems from a terrible event 12 years before, when he was just a child of three. It was the time of the great hurricanes. His mother had taken him out in the canoe to search the barrier reef for sea urchins. At the first signs of a hurricane coming in, others call to her, but she does not heed their warnings. Mother and child are caught in the storm and the craft capsizes. Mafatu's mother is able to drag him onto a piece of coral. The boy lives but she dies.

Since that time, Mafatu has been afraid of the sea. He can bear the silence of his people as they look at him, but he cannot bear the silence of his father, Tavana Nui, and the shame in his eyes.

Mafatu knows that his fear will keep him from ever earning his proper place in the tribe as the son of the chief. Instead, he must stay at home making spears and nets. He is very good at his work, but it is not the work of a brave tamer of the sea. Even his only friend, Kana, grows disgusted with him. Kana talks of a run of bonitos out on the reef. Tomorrow all the boys will go after them. That is their job, says Kana. "Won't it be fun?" he asks. Mafatu can only remain silent as Kana walks away.

Then one night, Mafatu hears the other boys calling him a coward. Unable to bear the shame any longer, Mafatu, with his little yellow dog, Uri, decides to conquer his fear or die in the attempt. Either way will be better than being branded a coward.

With outrigger canoe, some drinking nuts, and a fish spear, Mafatu and Uri set off on the feared ocean. Before long they run into a Pacific storm. Although the storm is terrifying and he loses the drinking nuts and spear, Mafatu and Uri survive.

Time passes and boy and dog are growing unbearably thirsty as they drift on the ocean. Suddenly they hear the cry of an albatross. It is Kivi, the albatross with the shortened leg whom Mafatu befriended on his island home. Kivi is leading them to land.

Almost by an unseen hand, Mafatu and Uri are led to shore on a deserted volcanic island. Their long period of isolation begins. There are breadfruit and wild banana trees, coconuts, and fresh water. There is also a wild boar, which Mafatu vows to kill for meat. He will make a necklace from the tusks so that when he returns home everyone will know that he was brave enough to kill a wild boar single-handedly. Then his father, Tavana Nui, will be filled with pride.

Day after day, Mafatu works on building a new canoe for their homeward trip. One day, quite by accident, he comes upon a Sacred Place, a great stone idol to the gods. He realizes with horror that he has landed on a Forbidden Island, where eaters-of-men make terrible sacrifices to the Varua Ino. As he is about to leave, he sees a sharp-edged spear on the sacred platform. Dare he take it to use for food and protection? What will happen to him if he approaches the sacred idol? With every ounce of bravery he can muster, Mafatu approaches the idol and succeeds in grabbing the spear. He has scored another victory.

Each day as he works and plans for his return home, Mafatu finds new confidence in himself and in his skills. With much patience and work, he fashions himself a knife from a whale's rib. One morning as he and Uri are fishing, a hammerhead shark slowly begins to circle. As the hammerhead attacks Mafatu's fish trap, Uri slides into the water. Emboldened by fear for his dog, Mafatu jumps into the water and kills the shark. Later, he realizes that he could never have done that for himself. He did it to save the life of Uri, his beloved dog and companion. He feels humble but full of pride.

Now comes the test of the wild boar. Carrying his spear, he charges the animal as it lunges at him. Bracing himself, Mafatu times his spear thrust perfectly. Although he is knocked to the ground by the blow, he quickly leaps to his feet in joy. He has killed the wild boar! "Do you hear me?" he shouts to his father far away. "I, your son, have killed a boar!" His triumph is complete. He is all Polynesian now, filled with the ancient fierceness of his people. With pride he puts the boar's tooth necklace about his throat.

The canoe is finished and boy and dog prepare to leave their island place. But another trial is in store as he has a terrible battle with an octopus. Then, before they can depart, the eaters-of-men return to the island. From a hiding place, the boy watches as they perform their ritual homage to the idol. But he is spotted and pursued.

Mafatu and Uri make it to the canoe with the savages in pursuit. Using all the sailing skills he knows, the boy skims over the ocean to freedom. Long days pass as Mafatu tries to return to his home and his father. Without water, boy and dog are suffering and he fears he has been deserted. But he knows that he no longer fears the sea. When all seems lost, Mafatu sees his albatross. He has come home. A crowd gathers on the beach. Mafatu has enough strength to stagger onto the beach and show his fine necklace, Uri at his feet.

His father catches him as he falls from exhaustion. Tavana Nui says to his people, "Here is my son come home from the sea. Matfatu, Stout Heart. A brave name for a brave boy!"

That is the tale still told by the people of Hikueru as they gather at their evening fires to speak of bravery and courage.

Themes and Subjects

This is a strong and simple tale of bravery and courage combined with a spirit of adventure. Although Mafatu says he will conquer the sea to erase the shame in his father's eyes, it is really the boy's own fear that he is out to conquer. The great sense of pride that he experiences stems from his sense of freedom from his own terrors. His spirit has been liberated and will never be chained again. In telling the story of conquering one's own personal demons, the author also points out how resourcefulness and keeping one's wits can help to solve the most terrifying of problems. The story also gives a feeling of the customs and strong beliefs of an ancient island people.

Incidents for Booktalking

Most of the book deals with Mafatu's personal fight to rid himself of his fears and to preserve his own life and that of his beloved dog. Important passages are: Mafatu and Uri are terrified by the storm (pp. 24–28); they land on the volcanic island (pp. 30–34); Mafatu decides to kill the wild boar (pp. 41–42); he stumbles upon the idol and takes the spear (pp. 46–50); he is chased by the eaters-of-men (pp. 82–88).

Related Titles

Marcia Brown's *Backbone of the King* (University of Hawaii, 1984, $9.95: 0-8248-0963-7) is based on a Hawaiian legend of a boy who wants to help his exiled father.

As seen through a child's eyes, *To Find the Way* (University of Hawaii, 1985, $12.95: 0-8248-1376-6) by Susan Nunes tells of the voyage of the ancient Polynesians from Tahiti to Hawaii.

Tim finds a buried model ship and uncovers details of a romantic tragedy in Robert Westall's *Stormsearch* (Farrar, 1992, $14.00: 0-374-37272-1).

A lost six-year-old is cared for by a female badger in turn-of-the-century Saskatchewan in Allan W. Eckert's *Incident at Hawk's Hill* (Peter Smith, 1996, $19.50: 0-8446-6848-6).

When his father becomes ill, nine-year-old Ben must leave school and return to his home in the Oregon Territory in Avi's *The Barn* (Orchard, 1994, $14.95: 0-531-068661-7; pap., Avon, $4.99: 0-380-72562-2).

About the Book and Author

Berger, Laura Standley, ed. *Twentieth-Century Children's Writers*. 4th ed. St. James, 1995, pp. 897–98.

Brown, Muriel W., and Rita Schoch Foudray. *Newbery and Caldecott Medalists and Honor Book Winners: Bibliographic & Resource Material Through 1990*. 2d ed. Neal-Schuman, 1992, pp. 396–98.

Chevalier, Tracy, ed. *Twentieth-Century Children's Writers*. 3d ed. St. James, 1989, pp. 912–13.

Collier, Laurie, and Joyce Nakamura. *Major Authors and Illustrators for Children and Young Adults*. Gale, 1993, 6 vols. pp. 2185–88.

Commire, Anne, ed. *Something About the Author*. Vol. 1. Gale, 1971, pp. 204–5.

Kinsman, Clare D., ed. *Contemporary Authors: Permanent Series*. Vol. 1. Gale, 1975, p. 592.

Kunitz, Stanley J., and Howard Haycraft, eds. *The Junior Book of Authors*. Wilson, 1951, pp. 279–80.

Mahoney, Beth E. *Illustrators of Children's Books, 1744–1945*. Horn Book, 1947, p. 362.

Miller, Bertha M., and Elinor Field, eds. *Newbery Medal Books: 1922–1955 with the Author's Acceptance Papers and Related Material*. Horn Book, 1955, pp. 192–207.

Peterson, Linda K., and Marilyn L. Solt, eds. *Newbery and Caldecott Medal and Honor Books: 1922–1981*. Hall, 1982, pp. 77–78.

Silvey, Anita. Ed. *Children's Books and Their Creators*. Houghton, 1995, pp. 617–18.

Sperry, Armstrong. *Call It Courage*. Chivers North America, 1987. Audiocassettes, 120 min.

————. *Call It Courage*. Read by George Guidall. Recorded Books, Inc. Audiocassettes, 135 min. ($18.00)

————. *Call It Courage*. Walt Disney Home Video, 1981. VHS videocassette, color, 24 min. ($79.00)

Ward, Martha, ed. *Authors of Books for Young People*. 3d ed. Scarecrow, 1990, pp. 664–65.

Honor Books 1941

Carr, Mary Jane. *Young Mac of Fort Vancouver*. Illustrated by Richard Holdberg. Crowell, 1940, o.p. (Grades 7–9)

This fine historical novel contains many authentic details on the fur trade, early coastal settlements, and the life of West Coast Indians. It is set in 1832, chiefly at Fort Vancouver, on the Columbia River where the city of Vancouver, Washington is now situated. Donald McDermott, nicknamed Young Mac, is the son of a deceased white fur trader, Big Mac, and White Cloud who was the daughter of a Frenchman and a Cree woman. It was his father's wish that Young Mac be sent for an education from the Indian settlement beside the Red River where he had been living, to Dr. John McLoughlin at Fort Vancouver, an important trader of the Hudson's Bay Company. At the fort, Young Mac wins a fight with the fort's young bully, Antoine. One day Bluebelle, the horse that Young Mac is exercising, trips and the boy is injured in the fall. He is taken to the hut of the old medicine man, Three Gulls, who nurses him. When the old man dies of the plague, Young Mac is seized by other Indians who blame him for Three Gull's death. A friendly squaw, Yellow Bird, helps him to escape, and back at the fort, he too becomes ill with the plague. While recuperating, he becomes reconciled with Antione, who graciously allows the young boy to take his place and ride Bluebelle in a big race, which he wins. During his stay at Fort Vancouver Young Mac learns to prefer the white man's way of life over the more primitive Indian culture he absorbed as a child. He travels east to locate his grandfather in Quebec and with his help goes to Edinburgh to study medicine. Ten years later he returns a doctor and is reunited with Mia, an attractive convent-trained girl he had rescued from Indian slavery years before. The future looks promising for both of them.

Gates, Doris. *Blue Willow*. Viking, 1940, o.p.; pap., Puffin, $4.95: 0-14-03092401. (Grades 4–6)

This novel, set during the Great Depression, tells of the Larkin family—father, stepmother, and 10-year-old Janie. After Mr. Larkin was forced to abandon his farm in the Dust Bowl, the family has become migrant workers in the San

Joaquin valley. Janie misses the stability of a permanent home and lasting friendships but she has one prize possession, a plate with blue willow trees painted on it that had belonged to her mother.

The family moves into an abandoned clapboard shack a few miles from the work camps. There Janie meets the Romero family and becomes friends with their young daughter, Lupe. Janie spends a magical day visiting the County Fair with the Romeros. She also enrolls in the local school, where the teacher, Miss Peterson, takes a special interest in her. In a stroke of good fortune, Janie's father wins $75, the second prize in the county cotton-picking contest and is able to buy secondhand tires for the car and a coat for Janie.

Unfortunately, their good fortune ends. Mrs. Larkin becomes dangerously ill and Mr. Larkin is unable to pay the rent on the cottage, which is collected by the evil, dishonest Bounce Reybourn, foreman for landowner Mr. Anderson. Janie gives Bounce her beloved plate as partial payment.

Before the Larkins move on, Janie decides she must have one last look at the plate. She visits Mr. Anderson in his home. This friendly man is unaware that rent has been collected on the shack, and when he learns that Bounce has been pocketing the money illegally, he fires his foreman and asks Mr. Larkin to take his place.

In time, Mr. Larkin builds an adobe cottage with running water and a fireplace. Janie's blue willow plate is given a special place of honor on the mantelpiece.

This well-loved book, written from the author's personal experiences with migrant workers, portrays effectively both a strong loving family and the difficult, uncertain lives of migrant workers.

Hall, Anna Gertrude. *Nansen.* Illustrated by Boris Artzybasheff. Viking, 1940, o.p. (Grades 6–9)

Using original sources, the author has faithfully re-created the inspiring life story of Fridtjof Nansen (1861–1930). One of Norway's national heroes, Nansen excelled as a scientist, Arctic explorer, statesman, and humanitarian. Even as a boy, Nansen was a well-rounded individual with a wide range of aptitudes including abilities in all forms of science and skills in a variety of sports, particularly championship skiing. After college, to further his knowledge of his special interest in the Arctic regions, he sailed on the sealer, the *Viking,* for his first trip into northern waters. Here he began his lifelong study of Arctic ocean currents, ice movements, land formations, and animal life. After serving as curator of the natural history collection of the Bergen Museum, he and five other men faced incredible odds by crossing Greenland from east to west. From his study of ice floes, Nansen believed that the North Pole could be reached by drifting in ice through the polar basin. In the specially designed ship named *Fram,* he set out to prove this theory on July 21, 1893. When the ship became hopelessly imbedded in slow-moving ice, he, along with another team member, Hjalmar Johansen, ventured out by sledge. Though turned back by severe ice and cold, he came closer to reaching the pole than anyone before him. He and his friend were forced to spend an entire winter in a crudely constructed hut barely tall enough to stand in. By a stroke of luck, the two were found by members of another expedition and were able to return safely to Norway, days before the *Fram* also arrived.

Nansen continued to pioneer the science of oceanography and in later years distinguished himself further as a statesmen. His untiring efforts on behalf of the League of Nations to help the refugees caused by the war and the Russian Revolution earned him a Nobel Peace Prize in 1922. This book admirably brings to life the man whose motto was "There is always a way to do the thing that must be done."

Wilder, Laura Ingalls. *The Long Winter*. Illustrated by Garth Williams. Harper, 1940, $15.99: 0-06-026460-8. (Grades 4–8)

> This continuation of *By the Shores of Silver Lake* (see "Honor Books," 1940, p. 105), covers an eight-month period, from October 1880 through May 1881, in the lives of the Ingalls family—Ma, Pa, and their four daughters—Mary, who is blind; Laura, now 13; Carrie; and baby Grace. In the fall of 1880, there are several signs that the coming winter will be a tough one including a prediction from a wise Indian that winter will last a grueling seven months. After the first blinding blizzard in October when the cattle are almost lost, Pa Ingalls heeds the signs and moves his family from their homesteading shack into his empty store building in the nearby town of De Smet, South Dakota, where about 75 other souls, including the brothers Almanzo and Royal Wilder, plan to wait out the winter. Soon the snowstorms and blizzards begin. Because it is impossible to clear the railway lines, train service is canceled until spring. Now completely isolated, the community begins using up its precious food supply. The Ingalls home becomes completely covered with snow and is accessible only by tunnels. When the coal supply is exhausted, the family, including Laura, must twist hay into miniature logs to keep the fire going. Precious wheat is ground daily into flour using the coffee mill. Close to starvation, Pa manages to purchase a little seed wheat from the Wilder boys. When Lorenzo realizes the severity of the situation for his neighbors, he and teenager Cap Garland drive a sled and horses south where a homesteader, Mr. Anderson, is reported to have wheat. Despite horrendous weather during which both almost lose their lives, the two return to De Smet with a precious load of wheat. In May, the first train arrives. Along with building supplies, it has a carload of food intended for immigrants. The starving settlers are able to commandeer it, and fortunately the next day, the regular supply train arrives, with Christmas parcels from the East for the Ingalls, including a still-frozen turkey. Their May Christmas is the best ever. Laura's story is continued in *Little Town on the Prairie*, a 1942 Honor Book (p. 118).

❦ Newbery Winner 1942

Edmonds, Walter D. *The Matchlock Gun*. Illustrated by Paul Lantz. Putnam, 1941, $16.95: 0-399-21911-0; pap., Paperstar, $4.95: 0-698-11680-1. (Grades 3–6)

> Walter D. Edmonds (1903–1998) was born on his father's farm in Boonville in the Mohawk Valley of upstate New York. His interest in the history of this region, coupled with his unusual writing talent, produced a series of excellent adult historical novels, including *Rome Haul* (pap., Syracuse University, $13.95) and *Drums Along the Mohawk* (pap., Bantam, $3.95), both of which became successful motion pictures. Edmonds claims that he never specifically writes for children: "My stories published as such were originally written for adults and for the most part saw print in adult magazines."
>
> Such was the case of *The Matchlock Gun*. The story is based on a happening many years before that involved the Shepherd family of Ilion, New York. Intrigued by the idea, Edmonds thought that "the incident would work into a short

story, and I wrote for permission to try it. This tale was so sound and the incident had such a feeling for truth in it that it wrote itself in a couple of days." Appearing first under the title "The Spanish Gun" in *The Saturday Evening Post*, it was discovered by a book editor who persuaded him that it would make a good book for children. With the handsome illustrations of Paul Lantz, it has subsequently become a children's classic.

Plot Summary

In the 1750s, when New York State was still a British colony, Teunis and Gertrude Van Alstyne lived near Albany with their young children, 10-year-old Edward and plump 6-year-old Trudy. Through Trudy, who would come to be known as the best spinster—meaning someone who spins—in the whole Hudson Valley, this story of real people came to be told.

Teunis was a Dutchman, like most of the settlers around Albany. Gertrude's family came from the Rhine River region in Germany.

As the story opens, Teunis, a captain in the militia, is preparing to leave his family for a short time. Every so often he is called to duty, patrolling the area looking for raiding Indian parties. Edward thinks that his father looks very fine in his blue uniform coat, but just once he wishes that when the elder Van Alstyne goes away he would take the Spanish gun with him.

The huge Spanish gun hangs over the fireplace and is longer than a grown man is tall. His father can hardly lift it. He explains to Edward that such a gun has to be fired by touching the priming with fire, like a cannon. It is called a matchlock gun, and Edward's great-grandfather, Dygert, brought it with him all the way from Holland. Edward says, "He bought it in Bergom op Zoom to bring to the wild America." Young Trudy laughs and says, "Bergom op Zoom!"

Once again, instead of the Spanish gun, Teunis Van Alstyne takes his musket on patrol. It is November and rain is falling when he leaves. He tells his wife, Gertrude, not to worry. Indian raiding parties surely have not come so far. Besides, the militia will be stationed at the bridge, so their home will be safe. If she gets lonely, says her husband, she should take the children and go to his mother's. She lives some distance away in a brick house that is like a fort.

Gertrude Van Alstyne doubts that she will act on her husband's suggestion. She knows that her mother-in-law does not think very highly of her simply because she does not have a "van" to her name.

After their father leaves, Edward and Trudy go up to bed in their loft. As their mother tucks them in, she assures the children that nothing will harm them and their father will soon return. Edward tells his mother that if Indians come, he will come down from the loft and help her.

The skies are clear by the next morning when Gertrude goes out to milk their two cows. She is uneasy and hopes that her husband will come home soon. She decides to stay outside much of the day so that no Indian raiding party can sneak up on the family.

After lunch, a rider appears in the person of John Mynderse, a neighbor. He tells Gertrude that her husband will probably not return this night either. Indians have burned the upper settlements and some people have been killed, so the militia must stay on duty. Teunis has sent a message that she and the children should go to his mother's big house.

That afternoon the children and Gertrude go out for a walk in the fields. As young Trudy runs about shouting "Bergom op Zoom!" Edward knows that his mother is worried. When they return to the house, she tells her son that she believes the Indians are near. She does not want to make the journey to the big house and feels that they should stay at home. However, she asks Edward if he would be afraid to fire his great-grandfather's Spanish gun.

Edward replies that he would not be afraid but that he is not strong enough to hold the gun. His mother replies that she has a plan. First, she takes down the huge gun from above the fireplace. She tamps in the powder, although she really has no idea how much should be used. Then she bids Edward find two bullets, which he does, and she loads the gun.

With Edward's help, she props the huge gun across the table aimed at the door. Then she bolts the cabin blinds and sends Trudy off to bed.

Next, Gertrude tells Edward that she is going outside to see if the Indians are coming near. She tells him that if there is trouble, she will call out his name in Dutch—*Ateoord*. If he hears that name, he must fire the gun. He must not fire it under any other circumstances. Edward says that he understands and will obey.

Gertrude goes out into the twilight pretending to pick beans. Down in the valley she can see smoke and realizes that the Van Alstyne's big house is on fire. The Indians must be near.

Suddenly, Gertrude sees the raiding party on her land. There are five of them, but they have not yet seen her. They are heading straight for the house. As fast as she can, Gertrude runs for the house. The Indians see her and close in. They are too close and Gertrude realizes she may be killed, and the children as well.

As she runs onto the stoop of the cabin with the Indians in close pursuit, she screams "Ateoord!" At that moment, she feels a terrible pain in her shoulder, as the tomahawk thrown by the first Indian finds its mark. Gertrude falls to the floor.

In the next second, Gertrude hears a tremendous roar and sees the figures of the Indians behind falling to the ground. She knows that Edward has fired the Spanish gun.

As for Edward himself, he remembers only hearing his mother's call. Almost unaware, he puts a flame to the great gun and hears the tremendous roar. He is nearly knocked unconscious as the gun lands on top of him, but he is aware that Trudy is crying.

Edward wiggles out from under the heavy gun. With Trudy's help, they drag their mother away from the now burning cabin. He and Trudy sit down together between their lifeless mother and the dead Indians.

Some time later, their father returns with other militiamen and finds them in that position. Gertrude is still unconscious. Trudy is asleep, and Edward sits with the great gun across his legs.

Teunis tends to his injured wife. She will get well, although her shoulder will be forever crippled from the tomahawk injury. Grandmother Van Alstyne has survived the fire in the big house. Edward is a great hero for having fired the Spanish gun. As the militiamen admire his courage, Trudy wakes up and solemnly points to Edward. "Bergom op Zoom!" she says.

Themes and Subjects

This is an old-fashioned, historical tale of courage and family life in the wilderness of colonial America. It shows a time when people had only themselves to depend on and children were often called upon to be brave beyond their years. The Van Alstynes are ordinary people who behave in an extraordinary way to save themselves and their home. *The Matchlock Gun* points up the best in the pioneer spirit.

Incidents for Booktalking

Much of interest in this short story centers on the Spanish gun. See: Teunis explains how the gun works to his son (pp. 4–5); Gertrude explains her plan to Edward and asks if he can fire the gun (pp. 26–30); Edward's mother gives him instructions (pp. 33–34); the firing of the gun (pp. 44–45). For insights into colonial life, see: Edward and Trudy go to bed in the loft (pp. 10–14); Gertrude talks with her children about slavery (pp. 17–18); a rider comes by (pp. 19–22); Teunis returns home (pp. 49–50).

Related Titles

To escape hostile Indians, Dewey Martin and his grandmother travel downstream on a homemade raft in *Trouble River* (pap., Puffin, $4.50: 0-14-034243-5) by Betsy Byars.

When 14-year-old Henry Desant lies about reports of a white girl being brought up by Indians, an amazing adventure begins in *I Tell a Lie so Often* (pap., Farrar, $3.50: 0-374-43539-1) by Bruce Clements.

In 1839, on the Ohio frontier, 11-year-old Nathan runs afoul of a renegade killer in Cynthia C. DeFelice's *Weasel* (Macmillan, 1990, $15.00: 0-02-726457-2).

Two orphans in the late eighteenth century have the prospect of surviving the winter with a runaway Indian and his grandson in Betty Levin's *Brother Moose* (Greenwillow, 1990, $12.95: 0-688-09266-7).

In eighteenth-century Maine, Matt learns woodland skills from the Indians in Elizabeth Speare's *The Sign of the Beaver* (Houghton, 1983, $16.00: 0-395-33890-5; pap., Dell, $5.50: 0-440-47900-2).

About the Book and Author

Berger, Laura Standley, ed. *Twentieth-Century Children's Writers*. 4th ed. St. James, 1995, pp. 315–17.

Brown, Muriel W., and Rita Schoch Foudray. *Newbery and Caldecott Medalists and Honor Book Winners: Bibliographic & Resource Material Through 1990*. 2d ed. Neal-Schuman, 1992, pp. 117–18.

Chevalier, Tracy, ed. *Twentieth-Century Children's Writers*. 3d ed. St. James, 1989, pp. 310–11.

Commire, Anne, ed. *Something About the Author*. Gale, 1971, Vol. 1, pp. 81–82; 1982, Vol. 27, pp. 86–93.

Evory, Ann, and Linda Metzger, eds. *Contemporary Authors (New Revision Series)*. Vol. 2. Gale, 1981, pp. 199–200.

Fuller, Muriel, ed. *More Junior Authors*. Wilson, 1963, p. 73.

Helbig, Alethea K., and Agnes R. Perkins, eds. *Dictionary of American Children's Fiction, 1859–1959*. Greenwood, 1986, p. 144 (bio.), pp. 330–51 (book).

Matchlock Gun. SRA., n.d. Videocassette.

Miller, Bertha M., and Elinor Field, eds. *Newbery Medal Books: 1922–1955 with the Author's Acceptance Papers and Related Material*. Horn Book, 1955, pp. 208–24.

"Newbery Medal Acceptance Material, 1942." *Horn Book* 18, no. 4 (July/August 1942): 263–75.

Peterson, Linda K., and Marilyn L. Solt, eds. *Newbery and Caldecott Medal and Honor Books: 1922–1981*. Hall, 1982, pp. 81–82.

Sarkissian, Adele, ed. *Something About the Author: Autobiographical Series*. Vol. 4. Gale, 1987, pp. 167–80.

Silvey, Anita, ed. *Children's Books and Their Creators*. Houghton, 1995, p. 219.

Ward, Martha, ed. *Authors of Books for Young People*. 3d ed. Scarecrow, 1990, p. 204.

Honor Books 1942

Foster, Genevieve. *George Washington's World*. Illustrated by the author. Scribner, 1941, o.p. (Grades 5–9)

In six chronologically arranged chapters, the author outlines George Washington's life and also tells about contemporary events and people around the world. Beginning with "When George Washington Was a Boy (1740–1755)," such personalities as Daniel Boone, John Adams, John Hancock, Benjamin Franklin, Frederick the Great, Louis XV, and Voltaire are introduced. In the section covering 1756 through 1763, Chinese Emperor Ch'ien Lung closes Canton to foreign traders, the Seven Years War is fought, George III scolds his American colonies, and Catherine becomes Empress of the Russians. While Washington was farming his land (1763 to 1776), Watt works on his steam engine, Pompeii is unearthed, California is settled, Boston has a tea party, and the Continental Army is formed. During the years of the Revolution from 1776 through 1783, some important events are the writing of the Declaration of Independence, Washington crossing the Delaware and wintering at Valley Forge, John Paul Jones stating that he has not yet begun to fight, and the signing of a peace treaty with England in 1783. When Washington again became a private citizen (1783–1789), Thomas Jefferson begins his stay in Paris, Benjamin Franklin witnesses the first aviators to go up in a balloon, Beaumarchais and Rousseau are spreading revolutionary ideas, Catherine becomes "the Great," and the Constitution of the United States is written. While Washington is president (1789–1799), the French Revolution is fought culminating in the beheading of Louis XVI and Marie Antoinette and Europe's declaration of war against France, Napoleon emerges as a leader and conquers Italy, the Rosetta Stone is discovered, and Eli Whitney invents the cotton gin. Washington dies at Mount Vernon in December, 1799, the end of an era and the beginning of a new America.

Gaggin, Eva Roe. *Down Ryton Water*. Illustrated by Elmer Hader. Viking, 1941, o.p. (Grades 7–10)

This first-person narrative begins in June 1608, when our hero, Matt Over, is about to celebrate his fifth birthday. It ends about 20 years later. The novel successfully mixes fact and fiction with real and imaginary characters in an effective re-creation of the story of the Pilgrims. The Separatists of Scrooby, Nottinghamshire, are fearful that the frequent visits from the troops of King James presage a crackdown on their errant religious ways and prepare to flee to the Netherlands under the leadership of William Brewster and William Bradford. At night they steal out of their homes, the men walking through the swamps and the women and children being carried in small boats down Ryton Water to the Boston Strand, where they board a ship. Matt's family includes his father Matthew Over, a farmer; his mother, Orris, who prides herself on her herb garden and takes cuttings with her; baby Memby; an adopted eight-year-old daughter, impulsive Winover; and Orris's eight-year-old brother, Uncle John Brodie. The Pilgrims stay in the Netherlands for 12 years during which Matthew prospers and becomes a Dutch citizen, baby Nicolas is born, and Orris's herb garden flourishes. Fearful of renewed persecution from King James, many, including the Overs, decide to emigrate to the New World. The Over women are left in England, while Matthew and Matt sail on the *Mayflower,* landing on Cape Cod in November 1620. The next year the women arrive, the colony begins to prosper, and the family spreads out. John Brodie and Winover marry and move to Boston and Memby and Nicolas each marry into a Dutch family in New Amsterdam. Matt marries and stays in Plymouth where his mother's herb garden is thriving once again.

Lenski, Lois. *Indian Captive: The Story of Mary Jemison*. Illustrated by the author. Lippincott, 1941, o.p. (Grades 4–7)

This fictionalized biography covers the first two years of Mary Jemison's life with the Seneca Indians. In the spring of 1758, word reaches the pioneer families in eastern Pennsylvania that the Seneca Indians—accompanied by their French allies—are raiding settlements and slaughtering homesteaders. Thomas Jemison does not heed the warnings, and on April 5, he and his family are captured by Senecas and some Frenchmen. Later, his 12-year-old daughter Mary, nicknamed Molly, is separated from her family and taken first to Fort Duquesne and later to a Indian settlement called Seneca Town in southern Ohio. Here, she is taken care of principally by two sisters, stern, unfriendly Squirrel Woman and kindly, beautiful Shining Star. She is adopted by the sisters' family to take the place of their brother, killed by white men. During her first five months as a captive, Mary, now known as Corn Tassel because of her blond hair, gradually learns the Seneca language and grows to respect the Indian culture. When it appears that the French at Fort Duquesne will try to rescue her, she is hastily moved to the main Seneca settlement, Genesee Town, situated in present-day upper New York State. Here she comes under the influence of a strong, loving woman named Earth Mother and a 18-year-old fellow captive, Josiah Johnson, whose Indian name is Turkey Feather. Josiah makes a daring escape and Mary wonders if she too should also try to rejoin the white settlers. However, when the white trader Felle-nash visits Genesee Town and tells her that the other members of the Jemison family were slaughtered, she realizes that there is no hope of resuming her former life. The English, now allied with the Senecas against the French, make an offer to buy Mary out of captivity. In a dramatic scene, she refuses the offer and decides to remain with her adopted family. This exciting narrative, filled with authentic background information, is based on the memoirs of Mary Jemison, written when she was 80 years old.

Wilder, Laura Ingalls. *Little Town on the Prairie.* Illustrated by Garth Williams. Harper, 1941, $15.95: 0-06-026450-0. (Grades 5–8)

This novel, which covers almost two years (spring 1881 through 1882), con-tinues the saga of the Ingalls family: Pa, Ma, and daughters Mary, Laura, Carrie, and Grace, and their lives as homesteaders in and around the town of De Smet, South Dakota. In the spring the family returns to the homestead after the long winter, and Laura takes a job sewing shirts in the dry goods store at 25¢ a day for six weeks to help the family finance a college education for Mary (who is blind). After Pa sells a heifer, sufficient money has been collected to send Mary to a school for the blind in Iowa. When the family moves back to town for the winter, Laura's social life prospers and 19-year-old Almanzo Wilder begins paying at-tention to her. On Friday nights, the townspeople organize a series of "literaries" consisting of spelling bees (Laura is bested only by her father), charades, musical evenings, and similar programs. Unfortunately, at school, Laura and Carrie are unfairly picked on by their teacher Miss Wilder, Almanzo's sister, who has been unduly influenced by another student, the spiteful Nellie Oleson. The problem is solved when Miss Wilder leaves at the end of term. Another summer is spent on the claim where Laura continues her studies. She hopes to get a teaching certifi-cate when she is 16 to earn money for Mary's education.

Back in town for the winter, Laura is again sought out by Almanzo who be-gins walking her home from social events including the November revival meet-ings. Later he takes her sleigh riding. At the December School Exhibition, Laura so impresses everyone with her recitations, particularly in American history, that the next day, Mr. Brewster, from a neighboring district, offers her a teaching posi-tion in a new school 12 miles away. For financial reasons the school is open only two months a year, but the pay is $20 a month—a huge sum for Laura. A teacher's examination is hastily arranged, which she passes easily, and with understandable apprehension, Laura begins to prepare for her new job. Followed by *These Happy Golden Years*, a 1944 Honor Book (p. 128).

Newbery Winner 1943

Gray, Elizabeth Janet. *Adam of the Road.* Illustrated by Robert Lawson. Viking, 1942, $17.99: 0-670-10435-3; pap., Puffin, $4.99: 0-14-03246-X. (Grades 4–7)

Elizabeth Gray (1902–1999), also known as Elizabeth Gray Vining, pursued three careers during her life. She was a writer, a teacher, and a librarian. Some-times these careers intersected when, for example, she became the tutor to the Crown Prince of Japan in 1946. Her four years in the royal palace became the subject of one of her most successful adult books, *Windows for the Crown Prince* (pap., Tuttle, $9.95), published in 1952. She has received four Newbery Awards, first as a Medal Winner for *Adam of the Road*, and three times for Honor Books. The Honor Books are the novel *Meggy MacIntosh* (see "Honor Books," 1931, p. 49) and two important biographies, *Penn* (see "Honor Books," 1939, p. 100), and *Young Walter Scott* (see "Honor Books," 1936, p. 80). The settings for *Adam of the Road* were explored by the author while she was doing research for *Penn* in England. In the Chiltern Hills, she found the inspiration that she later tapped to create this story about 11-year-old Adam and his minstrel father, Roger Quartermayne, which is set in Chaucer's England. In discussing the values in historical novels, Gray states that a significant work "gives us a perspective on the present and may help us to chart the future. It gives us a profound sense of being part of a long chain of life that went on years before us and will go on years after us."

Plot Summary

In 1294, 11-year-old Adam leaves his school at St. Alban's Abbey and with his minstrel father, Roger Quartermayne, sets out to travel about southeastern England for nearly a year. Their adventures end at Oxford in the spring of 1295.

Adam's father is no ordinary minstrel, for he can play the viol and recite long involved romances about historical figures. Adam plays the harp, which his father taught him when he was a young boy. When Roger arrives at the school to pick up Adam, he tells him they will first go to London with Sir Edmund de Lisle, for whom Roger is now minstrel. Adam is anxious to get started, although he is sad to leave his dear friend Perkin.

Adam and his father, along with Adam's dog, Nick, set out for London on the road. Roger tells his son that the road "is a kind of holy thing. It brings all kinds of people and all parts of England together."

Once on the road with Sir Edmund's party, Adam meets his daughter, the pretty Margery. When he and Nick get tired on the journey, Lady Richenda allows them both to ride in the carriage with her and Margery.

Once at Sir Edmund's townhouse outside of London, Adam is lonely. He misses his friend Perkin, and Roger is often in the company of Sir Edmund. No one pays any attention to him, except that he is constantly snubbed by the boy, Hugh.

Adam and his father remain at the home of Sir Edmund until August and the wedding of Emily de Lisle. After that, Roger will not be needed until Christmas, so father and son get ready to take to the road. However, the night before they are to leave, Roger loses all his money, and worse still, his wonderful horse, Bayard, to Jankin, another minstrel. This means that Adam and his father, along with Nick, will be traveling through England on foot, carrying their instruments and their clothes.

Their first stop is London, where they run into Jankin once more. The minstrel takes a fancy to Nick, a silky red spaniel with a special talent for tricks. He offers to match pennies for him, but Roger refuses. Adam does not like Jankin and is afraid that he will not treat Nick kindly.

After London, Adam, Nick, and Roger set out for Winchester. The greatest fair in all of England, St. Giles Fair, is held there every September. After being caught in a rainstorm, they stop at an inn. During the night, Jankin steals Nick and leaves Bayard, who is now lame, in the dog's place. Adam and Roger take out after the scoundrel.

Adam spies Jankin with his dog, but Jankin gets away with Adam in hot pursuit. Adam and his father become separated in the chase. Adam learns that Roger has set off for Farnham and he follows. The separation turns into several months for both must travel on foot and there is little in the way of communication. But Adam finds out that he is truly his father's son, for he takes care of himself by singing and telling tales, just as his father does. In this way, he earns his food and a place to sleep.

Adam has many adventures and some scary times, too. Once, a merchant with whom he is traveling for a time is robbed by an outlaw knight. Adam manages to escape and helps the merchant by getting the sheriff to save him. The boy also makes many friends along the way—among them a ferryman, a parish vicar, and a plowman. But still he cannot find Nick or his father. Adam's travels take him through history as well. Along the way, he meets an old man who talks about the signing of the Magna Carta by King John in 1215.

It is near Christmas when Adam returns to the de Lisle House, where he hopes to find Roger because he knew that his father was to return there in December. But Roger has gone. He has left a message for Adam to stay at the de Lisle until he can travel with someone who is going to Ludlow, where Roger will pick him up later.

Sometime after Christmas, Adam bumps right into the scoundrel Jankin. He demands to know the whereabouts of Nick. The wicked minstrel tells him the dog chewed his leash and ran away. Adam is not sure whether to believe him. Then Jankin says he lost Nick near Gorhambury, which is near St. Alban's. Adam thinks Nick has gone back to the Abbey looking for him.

After a long and tiring journey, Adam, his beloved Nick, and his friend Perkin are reunited. The little dog returned to his home, just as Adam thought he would.

In April, Adam and Nick go to the city of Oxford looking for Roger. At last, father and son are reunited. Roger tells Adam that the Warden of Merton has heard good things of him and offers the boy a place at Oxford.

Adam declines. "I am a minstrel," he says. "I want to be on the road with you."

Themes and Subjects

This is a lively and absorbing story of thirteenth-century England, giving a flavor of life on the open road. Adam is depicted as an independent, quick-witted lad who, when faced with adversity, uses his skills and the lessons learned from his father to fulfill his goals. Adams shows compassion for animals and a need for the companionship of the friend he left behind. The relationship between father and son is more comradeship than adult to child, although the bond of affection between them is deep. Historical facts are unobtrusively woven into the story, giving a light but pleasing picture of the colorful life of the wandering minstrel.

Incidents for Booktalking

Any of a number of scenes will provide a fine introduction to this picture of England in the thirteenth century. See: Adam, Roger, and Nick leave on their journey (pp. 43–52); Adam is lonely (pp. 69–71); Jankin steals Nick (pp. 125–35); Adam loses his father (pp. 149–59) and finds the sheriff (pp. 177–90); he meets minstrels (pp. 217–31); Adam and Nick are reunited (pp. 293–95).

Related Titles

In a fantasy by Elaine Marie Alphin, *Tournament of Time* (pap., Bluegrass, $3.95: 0-9643683-0-7), a homesick American girl in England is transported back in time and solves the mystery of the princes in the Tower.

Lord Justin is about to fight in his first tournament in Joe Lasker's *A Tournament of Knights* (Harper, 1986, $12.95: 0-690-04541-7; pap., Trophy, $5.95: 0-06-443192-4), a novel set in medieval England.

In sixteenth-century England, even Elizabeth I attends the famous fair in the novel *Bartholomew Fair* (pap., Morrow, $3.95: 0-688-11501-2) by Mary Stolz.

Jane Yolan's *The Dragon's Boy* (Harper, 1990, $14.95: 0-06-026789-5) is a retelling of the boyhood of King Arthur, as is T. H. White's *The Sword in the Stone* (Putnam, 1993, $22.95: 0399-22502-1; pap., Dell, $4.99: 0-440-98445-9) for an older audience.

For better readers, Frances Temple's *The Ramsay Scallop* (Orchard, 1994, $18.95: 0-531-06836-6) tells about 14-year-old Eleanor and a pilgrimage with her betrothed, Thomas, through France in 1299. Several of their fellow travelers also tell their stories.

About the Book and Author

Adam of the Road. Live Oak Media, 1980. Audiocassette, 61 min.

Berger, Laura Standley, ed. *Twentieth-Century Young Adult Writers.* 4th ed. St. James, 1994, pp. 668–69.

Brown, Muriel W., and Rita Schoch Foudray. *Newbery and Caldecott Medalists and Honor Book Winners: Bibliographic & Resource Material Through 1990.* 2d ed. Neal-Schuman, 1992, pp. 173–74.

Chevalier, Tracy, ed. *Twentieth-Century Children's Writers.* 3d ed. St. James, 1989, pp. 1000–1001 (under "Vining") .

Commire, Anne, ed. *Something About the Author.* Vol. 6. Gale, 1974, pp. 93–95.

Helbig, Alethea K., and Agnes R. Perkins, eds. *Dictionary of American Children's Fiction, 1859–1959.* Greenwood, 1986, pp. 550–51 (bio.), pp. 4–5 (book).

Kunitz, Stanley J., and Howard Haycraft, eds. *The Junior Book of Authors.* Wilson, 1951, pp. 143–45.

Miller, Bertha M., and Elinor Field, eds. *Newbery Medal Books: 1922–1955 with the Author's Acceptance Papers and Related Material.* Horn Book, 1955, pp. 225–41.

"Newbery Medal Acceptance Material, 1943." *Horn Book* 19, no. 4 (July/August 1943): 205–20.

Peterson, Linda K., and Marilyn L. Solt, eds. *Newbery and Caldecott Medal and Honor Books: 1922–1981*. Hall, 1982, pp. 85–86.

Silvey, Anita, ed. *Children's Books and Their Creators*. Houghton, 1995, pp. 281–82.

Ward, Martha, ed. *Authors of Books for Young People*. 3d ed. Scarecrow, 1990, p. 282.

Vining, Elizabeth. *Windows for the Crown Prince*. Lippincott, 1952.

Honor Books 1943

Estes, Eleanor. *The Middle Moffat*. Illustrated by Louis Slobodkin. Harcourt, 1942, o.p.; pap., Dell, $3.25: 0-440-80176-1. (Grades 3–6)

This sequel to *The Moffats*, set during World War I , focuses on 10-year-old Jane Moffat, who, because she is sandwiched between her 16-year-old sister, Silvie, and brothers Joey, 13, and Rufus, age 6, considers herself to be the middle Moffat. The four youngsters live with their widowed mother, a dressmaker, in the quiet town of Cranbury, Connecticut. In this charming, homey novel, Jane emerges as a lovable, imaginative girl whose best intentions often go awry. For example, Jane's musical recital on the family's newly acquired organ ends disastrously when Jane's furious pumping dislodges a nest of moths. However, she later single-handedly leads a crusade to retrieve broken objects (including her skates) that a procrastinating neighbor, Wallie Banks, has promised to fix. At Christmastime, she softens Rufus's disappointment at not getting a pony by writing him an apology from Santa Claus, and at a benefit performance of "The Three Bears," she steals the show by accidentally wearing the head of her costume backwards. Later, Jane shares many adventures with her best friend Nancy Stokes, and discovers that she has a hidden talent: Jane Moffat is actually a basketball whiz capable of throwing perfect baskets. The unifying element in this novel is Jane's friendship with the town's oldest inhabitant, 99-year-old Civil War veteran, Hannibal B. Buckle, and her unstinting efforts to make sure he reaches his centenary. This involves such thoughtful actions as always carrying an umbrella in case she might meet Mr. Buckle in the rain. When the sought-after birthday arrives, Jane presents him with a bouquet of 100 bluets she has picked, and after the celebration, is rewarded by riding home with him in his shiny limousine. The third book about the Moffats, *Rufus M.*, was an Honor Book in 1944 (p. 127).

Hunt, Mabel Leigh. *Have You Seen Tom Thumb?* Illustrated by Fritz Eichenberg. Lippincott, 1942, o.p. (Grades 5–8)

This is a somewhat fictionalized account of the life of the midget Charles Sherwood Stratton, who as General Tom Thumb became one of the foremost attractions of the show business entrepreneur P. T. Barnum. In November of 1842, Barnum, proprietor of Barnum's American Museum, a fancy sideshow in New York City, contacts the Stratton family in Bridgeport, Connecticut, with an offer they cannot refuse—to make their tiny son (only 25 inches tall) one of his theatrical attractions. Although Charley is only five and an American, he is billed with true theatrical hyperbole as "a dwarf 11 years of age, just arrived from England" at his hugely successful debut. His singing and dancing routines so outshine the others in the show like the Albino lady, an educated dog, and the bearded woman, that he soon embarks on an extended tour of Europe with Barnum. Although the English court is in official mourning, Charley pays several visits to Buckingham Palace where he enchants Queen Victoria. In addition to other luminaries in England, the young man gives a command performance for Louis Philippe in France. After three years he returns to America, where there are further tours, one of which helps Barnum out of bankruptcy caused by unwise real estate investments. After a brief courtship, he marries another midget under contract to Barnum, the lovely Lavinia Waren. During his honeymoon in 1863, Carley meets President Lincoln. Now prosperous from his thousands of appearances including four tours of Europe, he builds a home in Bridgeport, which contained an apartment filled with appropriately sized miniature furniture. He continues to perform almost to his death in 1883, when he was only 45. His eulogies rightfully call him a show business legend.

Newbery Winner 1944

Forbes, Esther. *Johnny Tremain*. Illustrated by Lynd Ward. Houghton, 1943, $15.00: 0-39-506766-9; pap., Dell, $3.99: 0-440-22827-1. (Grades 7–10)

Esther Forbes (1891–1967) wrote only one novel for young people, *Johnny Tremain*, but this is considered by many critics to be the best juvenile American historical novel ever written. Forbes was born in Massachusetts and grew up in New England, where she absorbed the atmosphere of early American history. She became an editor for Houghton Mifflin and began her own career writing both fiction and nonfiction for adults. In 1942, she received a Pulitzer prize for her masterful biography, *Paul Revere and the World He Lived In* (Peter Smith, 1992, $20.00; pap., Houghton, $9.80). While working on this book, she became interested in an incident concerning a horse boy who told Paul Revere of his discovery that British troops were being sent out of Boston on April 18, 1775. This story, coupled with her growing fascination with the life of apprentices during the period, led to the creation of Johnny, a handicapped orphan who became an apprentice silversmith and hero during the American Revolution. Of her historical writing, Forbes said that she tried to tell "not merely what was done but why, and how people felt." Not only did she accomplish these aims in this novel, but as the *New York Times* reported, "With *Johnny Tremain* she proved her conviction that children can grasp mature writing much better than some writers and publishers believe."

Plot Summary

Fourteen-year-old Johnny Tremain is an orphan who works as an apprentice to a Boston silversmith in the late eighteenth century. Because his employer, Mr. Lapham, does not take much interest in the shop, Johnny has pretty much the run of the place. He is a clever, bright, and talented lad with an inclination to be arrogant and bossy toward the other apprentices, whom he orders about. His employer's daughter-in-law, Mrs. Lapham, likes Johnny, however, and gives him favored treatment in the household.

Then tragedy strikes. John Hancock has commissioned a silver piece, which Johnny is rushing to finish. Dove, an apprentice who dislikes Johnny, gives him a defective cup. While Johnny is working on the silver, the cup breaks and the molten material burns Johnny's right hand badly. He can no longer work as a silversmith and he is very bitter because now he is reduced to the lowly position of errand boy.

Unwilling to continue as errand boy but knowing he must support himself, Johnny seeks another trade. He remembers his dead mother's advice to ask the assistance of a wealthy relative, merchant Jonathan Lyte, if he ever needs help. To prove the relationship to Lyte, his mother had given him a silver cup with a distinctive crest.

Johnny is sorely disappointed when he confronts Lyte with the cup and is charged as a theif by the dishonest merchant. However, he is proven innocent by Lapham's granddaughter, Priscilla, and by Rab Silsbee, who works for the *Boston Observer*, a weekly newspaper that backs the cause of liberty for the colonies.

Johnny moves into the attic room over the print shop with Rab, who is a few years older than Johnny, and goes to work for the paper. The work proves far more exciting than Johnny had thought because Rab's uncle, to whom he is an apprentice, is a Son of Liberty working for freedom from Great Britain. Among the paper's subscribers are such patriots as Paul Revere, John Hancock, and Sam Adams. Sometimes these men hold meetings in the very attic room where Johnny and Rab sleep.

Johnny's days become more and more entwined with the exciting political happenings in Boston and the colonies. When the statesmen meet in the attic room and plan the Boston Tea Party, Johnny, Rab, and other boys are enlisted to help. They dress as Indians and dump tea into the harbor in retaliation for what they consider unfair taxation.

After the Boston Tea Party, the colonials know that the British will exact revenge for their daring act. The whole town of Boston will be punished somehow. Nevertheless, there is much pride among Johnny and the other young apprentices on the morning after when they wander about the city, small spots of paint still behind their ears. They nurse their sore muscles with pride in a job well done and for a good cause. As for Paul Revere, he has already left the city on horseback for New York and Philadelphia to spread the word of what has been accomplished here.

After that day, Johnny Tremain becomes the eyes and ears of the patriots as he wanders about the city of Boston and gleans information he overhears from the British soldiers stationed there. Actually, Johnny comes to know and like some of the soldiers.

The British, angry over the Boston Tea Party, retaliate by closing the harbor of Boston and quartering more soldiers in town. As tension mounts, Johnny learns of the British plans to advance upon Lexington and Concord. He gives the information to Paul Revere, who sets out to warn the colonists of the impending attack. Rab goes to Lexington to drill with the minutemen of his hometown. Fighting breaks out and the Revolution has begun. When Johnny, in disguise, goes to Lexington to find Rab, he discovers that his young friend has been fatally wounded in battle. Before he dies, Rab gives Johnny his musket. He never had a chance to fire it because the British shot first. Johnny tells his young friend that he will take good care of the musket, even though he knows that with his crippled hand, it is useless to him.

Saddened by Rab's loss, Johnny finds some consolation in the advice of Doctor Warren. He examines Johnny's hand and declares that he can cut through the scar tissue and free Johnny's thumb so that it will be useful once again. Perhaps he will never be a great silversmith, but he will be able to hold a gun and fight for the cause of freedom for his country—and for Rab.

When fighting breaks out, the Lyte family, who are sympathetic to the British cause, take the ship to London. Before leaving, Lavinia Lyte, the merchant's beautiful daughter, tells Johnny that he is indeed the great-nephew of her father.

Johnny will take his place with the fighters for freedom, a young boy grown older by the times. Caught up in a cause that is larger than himself, he regains the self-confidence lost in his accident. Now he is Johnny Tremain, the patriot.

Themes and Subjects

This is a realistic historical novel with a dramatic sense of the excitement of the times and an authentic flavor to the accounts of the patriots. Johnny Tremain is a believable character, intelligent, and talented, but with the flaws of arrogance and disdain for those he considers beneath him. But he learns to overcome the bitterness of his crippling accident and is caught up in a cause of liberty that is larger than his own needs. By the book's end, he has grown in stature and self-confidence. The author depicts a fine sense of Boston in the late 1770s and furnishes a dramatic look into the personalities of the leading patriots as the American Revolution is about to begin. Through the years, *Johnny Tremain* has gained a well-deserved reputation as an American classic.

Incidents for Booktalking

The author, a noted historian, flavors the events leading to and following the Boston Tea Party and life in colonial Boston with realistic drama. See: Johnny's accident (pp. 31–38); he meets Rab (pp. 46–49); the meeting with merchant Lyte (pp. 65–69); the Boston Tea Party (pp. 120–28); Paul Revere's spy system (pp. 183–86); the death of Rab and the gift of the musket (pp. 249–50); Johnny becomes a fighting patriot (pp. 151–56).

Related Titles

Jonathan learns about the realities of war when he joins a band of colonists in *The Fighting Ground* (Lippincott, 1984, $12.95: 0-397-32073-6) by Avi.

Leonard Wibberley's *John Treegate's Musket* (pap., Farrar, $3.95: 0-374-43788-2) is a novel about Peter Treegate and the events immediately preceding the Revolutionary War.

In Scott O'Dell's *Sarah Bishop* (Houghton, 1980, $16.00: 0-395-29185-2), the only survivor of a British attack on her Tory family seeks refuge in the wilderness.

A young black boy tries to buy freedom for himself and his mother with money his father earned during the Revolution in James Collier and Christopher Collier's *Jump Ship to Freedom* (pap., Dell, $5.99: 0-440-91158-3), the first book of a trilogy.

For a slightly younger audience, Jean Fritz began her series of lively biographies of famous Americans with *And Then What Happened, Paul Revere?* (Putnam, 1973, $14.95: 0-698-20274-0). With this group also use Ron Goor and Nancy Goor's account of the capital of Colonial Virginia, *Williamsburg: Cradle of the Revolution* (Atheneum, 1994, $15.95: 0-689-31795-6).

About the Book and Author

Berger, Laura Standley, ed. *Twentieth-Century Young Adult Writers*. 4th ed. St. James, 1994, pp. 218–19.

Brown, Muriel W., and Rita Schoch Foudray. *Newbery and Caldecott Medalists and Honor Book Winners: Bibliographic & Resource Material Through 1990*. 2d ed. Neal-Schuman, 1992, pp. 139–41.

Cech, John, ed. "American Writers for Children, 1900–1960." In *Dictionary of Literary Biography*. Vol. 22. Gale, 1983, pp. 176–78.

Chevalier, Tracy, ed. *Twentieth-Century Children's Writers*. 3d ed. St. James, 1989, pp. 354–55.

Collier, Laurie and Joyce Nakamura. *Major Authors and Illustrators for Children and Young Adults*. Gale, 1993, 6 vols., pp. 849–57.

Commire, Anne, ed. *Something About the Author*. Vol. 2. Gale, 1971, pp. 108–10.

Forbes, Esther. *Johnny Tremain*. Blackstone Audio Books, 1994. Audiocassettes. ($44.95)

———. *Johnny Tremain*. Critic's Choice, 1957. VHS videocassette, color, 80 min. ($14.77)

———. *Johnny Tremain*. Library Video (Disneys's Great-American Epics), 1997. VCR videocassette, 93 min. ($19.95)

Fuller, Muriel, ed. *More Junior Authors*. Wilson, 1963, p. 88.

Hedblad, Alan. ed. *Something About the Author*. Vol. 100. Gale, 1999, pp. 74–77.

Helbig, Alethea K., and Agnes R. Perkins, eds. *Dictionary of American Children's Fiction, 1859–1959*. Greenwood, 1986, p. 167 (bio.), p. 255 (book).

Kinsman, Clare D., ed. *Contemporary Authors (Permanent Series)*. Vol. 1. Gale, 1975, p. 216.

Miller, Bertha M., and Elinor Field, eds. *Newbery Medal Books: 1922–1955 with the Author's Acceptance Papers and Related Material*. Horn Book, 1955, pp. 242–54.

Nasso, Christine, ed. *Contemporary Authors (New Revision Series)*. Vols. 25–28. Gale, 1977, p. 241.

"Newbery Award Acceptance Material, 1944." *Horn Book* 20, no. 4 (July/August, 1944): 261–70.

Peterson, Linda K., and Marilyn L. Solt, eds. *Newbery and Caldecott Medal and Honor Books: 1922–1981*. Hall, 1982, pp. 88–89.

Senick, Gerard J., ed. *Children's Literature Review*. Vol. 27. Gale, 1992, pp. 57–74.

Silvey, Anita, ed. *Children's Books and Their Creators*. Houghton, 1995, pp. 247–48.

Telgen, Diane, ed. *Authors and Artists for Young Adults*. Vol. 17. Gale, 1995, pp. 89–96.

Ward, Martha, ed. *Authors of Books for Young People*. 3d ed. Scarecrow, 1990, p. 236.

Honor Books 1944

Estes, Eleanor. *Rufus M*. Illustrated by Louis Slobodkin. Harcourt, Brace, 1943, $15.95: 0-15-26915-3; pap., Dell, $3.50: 0-440-40192-5. (Grades 3–6)

This, the third volume about the enterprising Moffat family (see *The Middle Moffat*, in "Honor Books," 1943, p. 122), concentrates on the youngest Moffat, imaginative, impulsive seven-year-old Rufus and his harmless escapades during the last year of World War I in the small town of Cranbury, Connecticut. The first episode introduces Rufus and his three older siblings and tells how he received his first library card—by entering the library from a coal chute during closing hours and frightening the poor librarian half to death. In a subsequent adventure Rufus, who has been knitting a washcloth at school for soldiers, disobeys his teacher and delivers his in person to a soldier on a troop train. His reward is a postcard signed "Joe" thanking him. When he sees his neighbor's player piano in operation, he is convinced that an invisible man is at work, until its owner disillusions him with the commonplace truth. Rufus is convinced that the eyes he sees gleaming in one of the huge sewer pipes lying on his street belong to a ferocious beast, but the prowler is discovered to be only their family pet, Catherine-the-Cat. During the winter the Moffats's pipes freeze. When Rufus finds a gold mine of 90¢ buried in a piece of ice, he is able to pay for the thawing procedure by giving their kindly and compassionate neighbor, Mr. Spec Cullom, 5¢ for his work. In the spring, Rufus plants a Victory Garden but becomes so impatient at the slow growth of the seeds, that he digs up his beans to make sure they are sprouting. Later, at the local midway, the gruff, kindly operator of the merry-go-round gives the boy a magical but dizzying ride on his favorite horse, Jimmy. Rufus's one venture into ventriloquism ends in disaster when his exasperated teacher first sends him to the cloakroom and later to the principal, who fortunately excuses him with just a lecture. The book ends on a joyful note, the signing of the Armistice and the promise of good times ahead.

Sauer, Julia L. *Fog Magic*. Illustrated by Lynd Ward. Viking, 1943, o.p.; pap., Puffin, $3.99. (Grades 4–7)

This atmospheric fantasy takes place in twentieth-century Nova Scotia in a fishing village. Fog often blankets the area, giving the imagination free reign to picture that swirling vaporous shapes are living beings inhabiting a dream world. A single member of each generation of the Addington family has a mystical affinity with the enveloping fog that often surrounds their village of Little Valley. Eleven-year-old Greta Addington does not realize that she has this gift. On sunny days when she walks to the deserted village of Blue Cove she finds only ruins of abandoned homes, but on foggy days she is transported back to Victorian days to the flourishing village that once existed there. In this dream world, Greta meets a girl her age, Retha Morrill, along with Retha's mother Laura, who seems to sense Greta's strange powers. She becomes involved with the residents of this thriving village that existed 100 years before and hears about the servant girl, Ann, who was falsely called a thief; of a legless foreign sailor who lives there; and of the faithful bride of a sea captain who, after his death, took command of his ship so that she could return his body to dry land for a proper burial. During her visit to Blue Cove on her 12th birthday, Laura gives her a kitten. Greta realizes that because she is maturing, her magical village will no longer appear to her but she later learns that her father had, in his generation, similar experiences. Her memories of Blue Cove and the kitten will be reminders of this fascinating land she visited as a child.

Wilder, Laura Ingalls. *These Happy Golden Years*. Illustrated by Garth Williams. Harper, 1943, $15.95: 0-06-026480-2. (Grades 5–9)

This, the seventh of the autobiographical novels in the Little House series, covers the years 1882 through 1884. In this story, Laura Ingalls teaches at three different schools (each school term is only of two or three months duration), and is courted by and ultimately married to young, attentive Almanzo Wilder. When only 15, Laura begins teaching school to raise money to help in the education of her blind older sister, Mary. Her first schoolhouse is an abandoned claim shanty where she has five pupils, three older than herself. She lodges with the unpleasant Brewster family. Mrs. Brewster is a nasty, brooding, unstable woman who frightens Laura, especially late one night when Laura sees her roaming the house carrying a huge knife. Mr. Brewster spends most of his time in the barn and their only child, John, is neglected and fractious. Laura's only relief occurs on Fridays when Almanzo faithfully rides out to bring her into town for the weekend. Finally, the term is over and Laura returns home having learned much about how to run a classroom and teach even unruly pupils. Because she has studied independently in the evenings, she is able to resume her schooling without problems. During the next two years, Laura's life follows a predictable pattern of studying, earning money sewing, helping at home, and teaching grade school during the winter months. In spite of Laura's outward displays of independence and disinterest, her relationship with Almanzo deepens. He takes her for sleigh rides in the winter and buggy rides in the summer. She helps break in a pair of wild colts he owns, and in turn he pays her tuition at a new singing school they both attend. A few months after Almanzo has presented her with a garnet and pearl engagement ring, they marry in a simple ceremony. The next day the couple move into the home Almanzo has built on his land claim and they begin creating their own "little house on the prairie."

Yates, Elizabeth. *Mountain Born*. Illustrated by Nora S. Unwin. Coward, 1943, o.p. (Grades 4–6)

This quiet, bucolic novel traces the cycle of birth, life, and death as seen through the experiences of a young boy, Peter, who lives with his parents, Martha and Andrew, and their elderly hired hand, Benji, on a modest sheep farm. During the lambing season, Andrew brings into the house a newborn black ewe lamb that he thinks is dead. But Benji gives her the breath of life and together with Martha, they revive the little creature. They give him to six-year-old Peter who adopts him as his cosset, or pet lamb. Soon the animal gains in strength and becomes completely attached to the young boy who feeds and cares for him. The lamb, now named Biddy, gradually assumes a leadership role in the flock and leads them through the annual farm rituals in which Peter is also beginning to participate, like tail-docking, shearing, dipping to rid them of fleas, pasturing, and culling in which the older sheep and the unwanted rams are sold to market. When Biddy is sheared for the first time, the grandmother of Peter's friend Mary weaves him a sturdy coat from the warm, pungent wool. When he is placed in charge of the flock for the first time, Peter unfortunately fails the test by falling asleep and letting the sheep roam. However, Benji and their sheepdog Rollo save the day, and Peter never forgets the lesson he has learned.

Five years pass, and Biddy, now approaching old age, gives birth to a black ewe after having only white rams in previous years. At shearing time, Biddy's wool is once again used to make a new coat for Peter, one that will take him into young adulthood. During a sudden unseasonable snowstorm, Biddy leads the flock to safety, but the exertion takes its toll and she dies peacefully in Peter's arms. He accepts this loss and takes comfort in the coat that Biddy has provided for him, along with the young ewe that he has grown to love.

Newbery Winner 1945

Lawson, Robert. *Rabbit Hill*. Illustrated by the author. Viking, 1944, $15.99: 0-670-58675-7; pap., Puffin, $4.50: 0-14-031010-X. (Grades 2–5)

Robert Lawson (1892–1957), the famous author-illustrator, was the first person to win both the Newbery and Caldecott Awards. The latter was given to him in 1941 for *They Were Strong and Good* (Viking, 1940, $14.00), a picture book of biographies of some of his ancestors who contributed to this country in their own small ways. After Lawson and his wife built Rabbit Hill in 1936, a house in rural Connecticut, he decided to write a story about the problems of owning a home and how the animals ate everything in their garden. However, as he said in a BBC Radio talk in 1956, soon "the little ones had taken over the book entirely and apparently were writing their own story." In the sequel to *Rabbit Hill*, *The Tough Winter* (pap., Puffin, 1979, $3.95), the rabbit, Uncle Analdas, predicts a severe winter, but his relatives, Father Rabbit and Little Georgie, hope he is wrong. The animals learn that the kindly Folks on the hill are leaving, but a storm strikes before they can leave and their cat, Mr. Muldoon, is trapped in an iced-over snowdrift. Fortunately, the animals are able to free him. A caretaker arrives with a vicious dog that attacks the burrow where Porkey the woodchuck is trying to hibernate. Phewie the skunk saves the day by discharging his odoriferous golden mist onto the dog. Finally spring arrives in time for the animals to greet the return of Folks and enjoy the prospects of a glorious summer.

Plot Summary

The Hill is fairly teeming with excitement. Little Georgie tumbles down the Rabbit burrow to tell his parents the good news. "New Folks coming!" he shouts. This is indeed exciting for all the Animals on the Hill. It has been some years since the Big

House has been filled. New Folks may mean a good garden. Food has been scarce for the Animals, as the shiftless people who were the last tenants had not planted a garden at all.

But "New Folks coming!" sings Little Georgie, and everyone perks up—Porkey the Woodchuck, and Gray Fox, Gray Squirrel, Willie Fieldmouse, Phewie the Skunk, and even Mole. Of course, Mother Rabbit worries a little about the new arrivals. They could have Dogs or Cats, they might set traps, they might even have Boys! However, Mother is known to be a worrier. Father is a bit more philosophical. He speaks of a wondrous future in a felicitous and bountiful era. Father is a Southern Gentleman and always sounds like that. In fact, his talk of the Kentucky bluegrass of his youth often becomes just a bit tiresome to the Animals on the Hill.

More and more signs of the approaching new tenants appear. Father says such signs are extremely auspicious for their lovely little piece of Connecticut. However, Mother continues to worry. She is also upset because she has been planning to ask old Uncle Analdas down from Danbury for the summer. All this worry causes Father to say that perhaps this is indeed a good time for a visit from Uncle Analdas. He needs a change of scenery, and besides, as the oldest living relative of the family, he will have good advice in case the New Folks turn out to be difficult people.

Unfortunately, Father has so many pressing matters on tap that he cannot make the journey to fetch Uncle Analdas. That duty must fall to Little Georgie.

Mother starts to worry all over again, but Little Georgie is certain he can safely make the rather dangerous journey. With dire warnings from Father about Dogs and other such perils, he sets off. He is generally alert and careful, but soon he becomes preoccupied with a tune that has been flitting around his head: "New Folks coming, oh my!" He does not notice Old Hound until he can feel the Dog's hot breath. Little Georgie has a close call, but he makes it to Uncle Analdas and returns with him to the Hill. Not long after, all the Animals of the Hill have picked up the "New Folks coming" refrain, and its joyous notes can be heard for miles around.

The Big House appears ready for its new occupants. The great day dawns. The moving vans appear. Then comes the car of the New Folks! There is a pipe-smoking Man, a good sign; a Lady; a stout woman called Sulphronia; and, oh my, a gray Cat! However, fears about the latter, whose name is Mr. Muldoon, are soon calmed when it can be seen that he is rather large, rather old, and rather contented. He is obviously harmless.

The Animals' joy continues to grow over the next few days as the New Folks show promising signs of being friendly, kind, and considerate to all living creatures. The Man puts a sign on the road that says "Please Drive Carefully on Account of Small Animals." This is auspicious indeed. And they are obviously going to plant a garden! As far as Father is concerned, the very best news is that they are planning to plant some Kentucky bluegrass.

The Animals are delirious with happiness. They are even happier when they overhear the Man telling Louie Kernstawk that he wants no walls built to keep out the animals. And he tells Tim McGrath, the planter, that there will be no traps or fences or poisons in the garden to protect the vegetables. Louie and Tim think the Man is crazy. There will be no garden left at all when things start to grow.

As the garden progresses, the Animals on the Hill look forward to Dividing Night. At this time, they will meet to decide what Animal will get what vegetable as it grows. The decisions are largely made on taste and need and must not be violated. Phewie the Skunk and Gray Fox act as judges, because they are not vegetarians and can be counted on to be fair in all decisions. In this manner, all the vegetables grown in the garden of the New Folks will provide the Animals with an abundant supply of food. It is a most happy time.

Their happy meeting is interrupted with the dreaded sound of car brakes screeching on the Black Road. The car hits something and drives off. The New Folks rush from the Big House to the road and pick up a small lifeless form. The Lady looks very sad. To the horror of the Animals, Mother soon discovers that Little Georgie is missing.

There is grief all over the Hill, for Little Georgie was their most beloved. Mother takes to her bed and Father is inconsolable. Days pass and even the approach of Midsummer's Eve, when the garden vegetables will first be ready for raiding, does nothing to lift the spirits of the Hill.

One evening Willie Fieldmouse bounds into their midst screaming, "I've seen him! I've seen Little Georgie!"

It is surely a miracle. As Willie Fieldmouse peered into the windows of the Big House, he saw Little Georgie being tenderly nursed by the Lady. He was sitting right on her lap! And Mr. Muldoon was scratching Little Georgie's neck! Little Georgie seemed in fine shape, says Willie, except that his hind legs appeared to be in bandages. For the few next days, Willie Fieldmouse reports, as he peers through the window, on the progress of Little Georgie, who spends most evenings resting in the Lady's lap.

Just as happiness and relief are returning to the Hill, however, a feeling of dread overtakes the Animals when a huge crate appears in the garden. Uncle Analdas thinks it contains traps and guns. Maybe the New Folks were only pretending to care for Little Georgie. Perhaps they are going to make an example of him. Perhaps the huge crate contains a gallows to hang poor Little Georgie as a lesson for them all to stay away.

Then one night, as the moon shines on the garden and the Lady sits with the dozing Mr. Muldoon, Uncle Analdas boldly steps out on the lawn demanding the return of Little Georgie. From the lap of the startled Lady leaps Little Georgie, all well and healed. He and Uncle Analdas and even Mr. Muldoon leap about the lawn in happiness.

In the midst of all this joy, the Man approaches and lifts the tarpaulin from the huge crate. He uncovers a statue of St. Francis of Assisi, protector of Animals. All about the saint's feet are stone likenesses of the Animal inhabitants of the Hill. And at their feet is a pool of clear water. Around the pool are flat stones on which all sorts of real vegetables have been placed. Words cut into the stone read: "There is enough for all."

After much munching and chewing by the Animals, they begin a stately procession around the garden while Man and Lady and Cat silently watch. When the procession stops, Red Buck makes this announcement: "We have tasted their salt, we have drunk their water, and all are good. From now on this is forbidden ground."

And so it was. Each evening throughout the summer a banquet was laid at the pool's edge. Each morning the stones were empty and neatly swept clean. Each night Red Buck, Phewie, and Gray Fox patrolled the premises to keep out marauders. Mother and others packed away the abundance of food for the winter months. And Man and Lady had a flourishing garden.

Tim McGrath just shook his head and said to Louie, "I can't understand it. No fences, no traps, no poisons, and nothing is touched. I got all them things and still they eat everything. Must be Beginner's Luck." "Must be," Louie agreed.

Themes and Subjects

The author has created a warm, lively, and amusing fantasy that centers on little animals of the field and wood in the Connecticut countryside. It shows how, in this case, kindness to all creatures is rewarded a hundredfold and all are served. Although the Animals of the Hill take on the obviously human characteristics of speech and exhibit such human traits as pomposity and cantankerousness, they remain true to their living and eating habits. Like humans, they try to follow order in their society, such as strictly adhering to the rules of Dividing Night. There is a magical spirit on Rabbit Hill, and it is this spirit of love, friendship, and kindness that forms the strong bond among the animals and between them and the New Folks.

Incidents for Booktalking

The following interactions between the Animals can serve as fine introductions to the inhabitants of the Hill: Father and Porkey the Woodchuck discuss the possibility of new arrivals (pp. 15–18); Willie Fieldmouse and Mole talk about the New Folks (pp. 21–24); Phewie and Red Buck have a serious discussion concerning "garbidge" (pp. 24–25); Mother and Father discuss Cats and Dogs (pp. 29–31). See also the following for examples of the kindness the New Folks show toward the Animals of the Hill: the Man puts out a "Please Drive Carefully" sign (pp. 77–78); the Man and Lady tell Louie there will be no traps in the garden (pp. 81–84); the Folks take care of Willie Fieldmouse when he nearly drowns (pp. 87–94); and Man and Lady rescue the lifeless form of Little Georgie from the Black Road (pp. 101–2).

Related Titles

A mouse named Pearl sets out to save her brother from a pet store python in Frank Asch's *Pearl's Promise* (Delacorte, 1984, $12.95: 0-385-29321-6). Also see *Pearl's Pirates* (Delacorte, 1987, $13.95: 0-385-29546-4).

In Timothy Foote's *The Great Ringtail Garbage Caper* (Houghton, 1980, $6.70: 0-395-28759-6), a group of raccoons revolts when the garbage collectors in a summer resort become too efficient.

Three young mice brothers take charge of a farmhouse that has been ruled by cats in Dick King-Smith's humorous *Three Terrible Trins* (Crown, 1994, $15.00: 0-517-59828-0).

Ben, Kate, and Foster make super scarecrows to combat the birds and beasts that steal the local corn in Betty Levin's *Starshine and Sunglow* (Greenwillow, 1994, $14.00: 0-688-12806-8).

A lemming named Bubber discovers that he cannot swim and therefore tries to prevent his companions from marching into the sea in Alan Arkin's *The Lemming Condition* (Harper, 1976, $12.95: 0-06-020133-9; pap., Trophy, $9.00: 0-06250048-1).

About the Book and Author

Berger, Laura Standley, ed. *Twentieth-Century Children's Writers*. 4th ed. St. James, 1995, pp. 556–57.

Brown, Muriel W., and Rita Schoch Foudray. *Newbery and Caldecott Medalists and Honor Book Winners: Bibliographic & Resource Material Through 1990*. 2d ed. Neal-Schuman, 1992, pp. 235–38.

Cech, John, ed. "American Writers for Children, 1900–1960." In *Dictionary of Literary Biography*. Vol. 22. Gale, 1983, pp. 231–40.

Chevalier, Tracy, ed. *Twentieth-Century Children's Writers*. 3d ed. St. James, 1989, pp. 561–62.

Collier, Laurie and Joyce Nakamura. *Major Authors and Illustrators for Children and Young Adults*. Gale, 1993. 6 vols., pp. 1414-17.

Commire, Anne. *Yesterday's Authors of Books for Children*. Vol. 2. Gale, 1978, pp. 222–41.

Fuller, Muriel, ed. *More Junior Authors*. Wilson, 1963, pp. 189–90.

Hedblad, Alan. ed. *Something About the Author*. Vol. 100. Gale, 1999, pp.142–46.

Helbig, Alethea K., and Agnes R. Perkins, eds. *Dictionary of American Children's Fiction, 1859–1959*. Greenwood, 1986, p. 286 (bio.), pp. 421–22 (book).

Hearn, Michael Patrick. "Who Was Robert Lawson?" *Teaching and Learning Literature with Children and Young Adults* (Sept./Oct. 1997): 48–57.

Lawson, Robert. *At That Time*. Viking, 1947.

——. *Rabbit Hill*. Read by Barbara Caruso. Recorded Books, 1997. Audiocassettes, 180 min. ($18.00)

Mahoney, Bertha E. *Illustrators of Children's Books, 1744–1945*. Horn Book, 1947, pp. 331–32.

"Newbery Award Acceptance Material, 1945." *Horn Book* 2, no. 4 (July/August 1945): 233–42.

Peterson, Linda K., and Marilyn L. Solt, eds. *Newbery and Caldecott Medal and Honor Books: 1922–1981*. Hall, 1982, p. 93

Silvey, Anita. ed. *Children's Books and Their Creators*. Houghton, 1995, pp. 395–96.

Ward, Martha, ed. *Authors of Books for Young People*. 3d ed. Scarecrow, 1990, pp. 421–22.

Honor Books 1945

Dalgleish, Alice. *The Silver Pencil*. Scribner's, 1944, o.p.; pap., Puffin, $4.99: 0-14-034792-5 (Grades 5–8)

This largely autobiographical novel tells of the childhood and young adult years of Janet Laidlaw. It takes place in a variety of settings and spans the early years of the twentieth century ending in the early 1920s. When the novel begins, Janet is nine and growing up in Trinidad with a sickly English mother and a loving Scottish father. After her father's sudden death, Janet and her mother move to England where Janet attends school, makes friends, and wins several juvenile prizes for her stories. She is looking forward to entering college, when, at age 16, she and her mother return to Trinidad. To prepare for a career in teaching, Janet attends the Clark Training School in Brooklyn. She meets and falls in love with Stephen Monroe who later jilts her. The remainder of the novel tells of her teaching career, her discovery of Nova Scotia where she refurbishes a beach house, her many friends including other love interests, and the crippling arthritis that often confines her to bed, but also fortuitously gives her the opportunity to resume her writing. She always uses a silver pencil that was a gift from her father many years before.

Foster, Genievieve. *Abraham Lincoln's World*. Scribner's, 1944, o.p. (Grades 5–8)

This book is actually a continuation of the author's *George Washington's World* (see "Honor Books," 1942, p. 116), another Newbery Honor Book. Coverage in that volume that ends in 1799 and this book starts with the beginning of the nineteenth century. As in other books in this series, this book shows what is happening around the world and in the United States during the life of its principal subject, in this case Lincoln. For example, in the section, "When Abraham Lincoln was born," there is coverage of the career of Napoleon; the burning of Moscow; the youth of Simón Bolivar; the War of 1812; Andrew Jackson, the Indian fighter; and the early years of William Gladstone. The subjects and persons discussed span a wide spectrum of subjects including politics, business, the arts, and science. Many original sources are quoted or reprinted in full, such as, for example, a letter from Harriet Beecher Stowe to her husband about antislavery riots in Cincinnati. All are complemented by the author's delightful, often witty illustrations.

Eaton, Jeanette. *Lone Journey: The Life of Roger Williams*. Harcourt, 1944, o.p. (Grades 7–9)

This is a fictionalized biography of the famous fighter for religious freedom and for the separation of church and state, Roger Williams (1604–1683). As a young teenager in England, Williams embraced the Puritan faith, a denomination that was out of favor at the time. After becoming an outspoken Puritan minister, he learned that a plan was afoot to place him on trial. To avoid possible incarceration or worse, he and his wife sailed for Boston where he again became unpopular through his teachings on the separation of powers and his crusade to improve the treatment of the Indians. In 1836, he was banished from Boston and fled into the wilderness where the sachem of the Narragansett Indians sold him a tract of land he called New Providence. Through his efforts, this newly founded colony of Rhode Island became a landmark of democracy and religious freedom. This is an excellent biography of the first American to demand that the government should be the instrument of the people, working for the greatest good for the greatest number. The book is enhanced by full-page woodcuts by Woodi Ishmael.

Estes, Eleanor. *The Hundred Dresses*. Harcourt, 1944, $16.00: 0-15-237374-8; pap., Voyager, $6.00: 0-15-642350-2. (Grades 3–5)

Poor Wanda Petronski is the butt of her classmates' taunts and derision. She is motherless, comes from a "foreign" Polish immigrant family, and wears the same faded blue dress to school every day. Although classmate Maddie sometimes feels a tinge of pity, she does nothing to stop the cruel behavior of her friends, particularly Peggy. One day, Wanda responds to their teasing by stating that she owns 100 dresses. Only after the Petronskis move away is the winner of the class art contest revealed—it is Wanda for her drawings of 100 different, attractive dresses. When Mr. Petronski writes to the teacher, Miss Mason, in broken English about the cruelty his daughter has suffered, Peggy and Maddie are so stricken by conscience that they write to Wanda. At Christmastime she responds in a tone that indicates that she has forgiven them for their unthinking behavior. This touching moralistic tale is effectively illustrated by Louis Slobodkin.

Newbery Winner 1946

Lenski, Lois. *Strawberry Girl*. Illustrated by the author. Lippincott, 1945, $16.00: 0-397-30109-X; pap., Trophy, $4.95: 0-06-440585-0. (Grades 4–6)

During the more than 40 years that Lois Lenski (1893–1974) was active in publishing, she wrote and illustrated almost 80 of her own books for children, and another 50 books written by other people. She was particularly proud of a series of regional novels that dealt with the poorer elements in American society and how they made a living. The first of these was *Bayou Suzette* (Stokes, 1943, o.p.) and the second was *Strawberry Girl*, which takes place in the early 1900s when Florida was becoming an important fruit-growing state. *Strawberry Girl* centers on the feud between two "Cracker" families, one thrifty and hardworking and the other shiftless and undependable. About the young heroine of the book, the author said in an interview in 1946:

> Birdie Boyer . . . is a real little girl I saw plowing in a sandy field in Florida. Little did I dream when I snapped her photograph and talked to her, that she would make friends for me all over the country and return to me nearly three years later, bearing the Newbery Medal in her hand!

Like the other books in the series, this novel is notable for its realistic portrayal of hardship and poverty. It champions conventional values like hard work and education while supplying authentic details both in background locales and dialect. For example, such colorful expressions as "gettin' biggity," "plumb good," and "right purdy" abound in the book.

Plot Summary

The Boyer family, descendants of Anglo-Saxons from the Carolinas, Georgia, and West Florida, move into a frontier community of Florida's lake region in the early 1900s. Known as Crackers, the family consists of Mother and Father; Birdie, age 10; her big sister and brother, Dixie and Buzz; and her little sister and brother, Dovey and Bunny.

The Boyers have moved into the old Roddenberry house, a frontier home deserted for years. Their aim is to grow vegetables and fruits to sell, including strawberries, which will be Birdie's special project.. Their frontier neighbors, the Slaters, think they are crazy. Anyone knows you cannot grow enough fruits and vegetables—including strawberries—in Florida to make a living. The only way to make any money at all is by selling cows for beef. At least that is what Mrs. Slater tersely tells Ma Boyer when she comes for a first look-see at the new neighbors.

In the eyes of Ma Slater, the ways of the newcomers are different, and therefore to be feared. The Slater family has little in the way of comforts, even the rather primitive comforts of the Boyer home. Their life is hard, primarily because Pa Slater has a drinking problem and usually squanders what little money he makes. In addition to the parents are a 12-year-old boy known as Shoestring; two little girls, Essie and Zephy; and two older boys, Gus and Joe.

Trouble starts almost immediately between the two families. The Boyers put up fences to keep their cows penned up at night. The Slaters let their animals run loose all the time. Naturally, it is not long before Birdie's coveted strawberry patch, in which she has worked so many hours, is trampled by the Slater livestock. When Shoestring sees the new fences that Birdie's pa is planning to put around the strawberry plants, he warns Birdie that his own father will only tear them down—just as soon as he starts drinking.

It seems that the trouble with the Slaters never ends. A few days later the Boyer family is awakened in the night to find Slater hogs wallowing in their fields. When Pa goes off angry, Birdie is afraid that he will kill one of the Slater hogs; then they will really have trouble.

But the next morning at the church All-Day Sing and dinner, the fathers of the two families seem to get along well, and Birdie relaxes. She does not relax for long, however, because she is soon furious when Shoestring puts a snake in her hat. It seems that no one can get along with Slaters!

On the next Saturday, it is Birdie's turn to go to town with her mother and father. She is going to get a new summer hat. Pa goes off about his business, and Birdie and Ma go to Miss Liddy's, the millinery. While Birdie waits for her new hat, she sees Shoestring in the dry goods store. He tells her that he is buying three new pairs of overalls because his pa is going to get money for a steer he brought to the butcher. She tells him that her pa is buying barbed wire for a new fence.

When it is time to go home, Birdie meets Shoestring again. He has no new overalls and his mother and little sisters are crying. Pa Slater got the money for the steer and gambled and drank it away in the saloon. The Boyers give the sad Slater family a ride home.

At last, the long hot summer ends. It is time for the Boyers to grind the cane from which will come syrup to sell and brown sugar and molasses to eat all year. Pa sends out word of the grinding and neighbors come from miles around to help. That evening there is a candy pull.

The next morning the Boyers find that their new wire fence has been cut and cattle have plowed right through Birdie's precious strawberry field. Pa does not do or say anything, but the next Saturday he goes to town again. Birdie, Dovey, and Buzz go with him. He finds Slater in the saloon, where he has long been drinking, and the two men have a loud argument over property rights. Buzz and Gus Slater also have a fight; Buzz gets a black eye, but Gus gets thrown in jail.

The fence is quickly repaired and just as quickly, the Slaters threaten that no one will stop them from driving their cattle through the Boyer's property to the lake. But when they drive up to the fence and watch Ma Boyer sprinkling flour on the strawberry plants, they back away. They think she is sprinkling poison.

Relative peace reigns, the strawberries ripen, and the Boyers pick their crop and take it to market. Things remain peaceful through the winter until spring comes and it is time to round up the cattle and brand them. After an argument over the ownership of a spotted calf, which Pa Boyer claims, three of the Slater hogs are found dead. Birdie is sure her father has killed them in revenge. Soon after, the Boyers get a note warning that they will be burned out. And soon after that, the Boyer's beloved mule, Semina, is poisoned.

Sometime later, Birdie is helping to paint their house when she smells smoke. The piney woods are on fire. The Boyers save their home, although the Slaters refuse to help, but the schoolhouse burns down in the fire. Birdie and the rest of her family never want to see any of the Slaters again. However, one day the little Slater girls appear in the yard with an invitation from their mother to come to dinner. It seems that Pa Slater, when drunk, shot off all the heads of their chickens, so Ma Slater has to cook them all at one time.

The Boyers go to the dinner, as do other neighbors. The two mothers talk over their troubles, and Ma Slater admits that her husband wanted to burn out the Boyers so they would go back to Caroliny. Ma Boyer tells her that they have no intention of going back anywhere; this is their home.

About a week later, Shoestring arrives at the Boyer place in the middle of the night to ask for help. Ma and the young ones are ill with fever and the father and oldest sons are off somewhere. Birdie and her mother go immediately. They care for the sick woman and girls for several days. Shoestring says nothing, but he helps them in any way he can.

Pa Slater and his sons return to find the Boyers in his house. He orders them out until Shoestring stands up to his father and explains what has happened and how the Boyers have saved his family while he was off on his shiftless ways.

A near-miracle occurs when Pa Slater goes to the preacher's camp meeting and is converted. He later explains to the Boyers how much of a part they had in his seeing the light. He has given up drinking and meanness and aims to be a good neighbor in thanks for all they have done for his family. He allows as how times are changing, land will be fenced in, and he may just take a job with the phosphate company nearby.

Shoestring tells Birdie that he will be going to school as soon as the new schoolhouse is finished. His father has admitted his mistakes in not wanting the older boys to get any book learning. Birdie says she will help him with his lessons.

When the school opens with Miss Annie Laurie Dunnaway as the new teacher, Birdie arrives with a bunch of red roses. She introduces Shoestring to the teacher by his rightful name, Jefferson Davis Slater.

Birdie returns home that evening to a great surprise. Her parents have been in town and returned with a parlor organ for the Strawberry Girl who has worked so hard.

Birdie is happy but dismayed because she does not know how to play the organ. Ma suggests that the new teacher might just be willing to give her lessons. In the meantime, Ma Boyer sits down in front of the new organ and plays them an inspiring tune.

Themes and Subjects

Although this award winner was written more than a half-century ago and set in a little-known backwoods region of Florida in the early 1900s, its themes are as valid today as then. It speaks of the value of learning to love one's neighbors even though their ways may be different than your own. *Strawberry Girl* is a lesson in tolerance. It shows how the unknown—different ways of speaking or acting—can embarrass or frighten people, causing them to react in strange and even hostile ways, as when Ma Slater condemns the Boyers for being "biggety" because they have things she does not have and live their lives in ways that seem to contradict hers. It takes up the little discussed, especially for the time in which it was written, subject of addiction—in this case, Pa Slater's abuse of alcohol—and shows how the destructive actions of a parent profoundly affect the way in which a family interacts with themselves and others. One of the author's objectives in writing *Strawberry Girl* was to show how people live in different—and generally little-known—parts of the United States. In doing so, as in this portrayal of the people known as Crackers, she also allows the reader to see how environment shapes people's lives and beliefs.

Incidents for Booktalking

A number of episodes will serve to introduce the reader to the unfamiliar, colorful ways of speaking and acting in the backwoods Florida of long ago. See: Ma Slater visits the Boyers and calls them "biggety" (pp. 7–13); Birdie and Shoestring discuss their families' opposite ways of farming (pp. 14–20); the Boyer children go to school and run into the Slater boys (pp. 28–38); the fathers of both families meet at the church sing and Birdie discovers a snake in her hat (pp. 42–47); Pa Slater drinks away the money for Shoestring's overalls (pp. 58–65); folks come for the cane grinding at the Boyers (pp. 80–89); Birdie and her mother help the ailing Ma Slater and her children (pp. 169–83).

Related Titles

A series of episodes describe a year in the life of a young girl growing up in West Virginia in Cynthia Rylant's *A Blue-Eyed Daisy* (Bradbury, 1985, $15.00: 0-02-777960-2).

Nine-year-old Vinnie suffers from grief and loneliness in Katherine Paterson's *Flip-Flop Girl* (Dutton, 1994, $14.99: 0-525-67480-2; pap., Puffin, $3.99: 0-14-037679-8).

Because 11-year-old Lena Rosen is the only Jewish child in her neighborhood, her life is different than that of her friends in Anne Mazer's *Moose Street* (Knopf, 1991, $13.00: 0-679-83233-5).

In Niki Yektai's *The Secret Room* (Orchard, 1992, $14.99: 0-531-08606-2), Katharine Ontwater and her family move to upstate New York, where she and her brothers are subjected to a strict governess.

For an older audience, Brent Ashabranner's nonfiction *Children of the Maya: A Guatemalan Indian Odyssey* (Putnam, 1990, $14.95: 0-399-21707-X) tells about of Mayan immigrants who have become migrant workers in Florida.

About the Book and Author

Berger, Laura Standley, ed. *Twentieth-Century Children's Writers*. 4th ed. St. James, 1995, pp. 565–66.

Brown, Muriel W., and Rita Schoch Foudray. *Newbery and Caldecott Medalists and Honor Book Winners: Bibliographic & Resource Material Through 1990*. 2d ed. Neal-Schuman, 1992, pp. 248–54.

Cech, John, ed. "American Writers for Children, 1900–1960." In *Dictionary of Literary Biography*. Vol. 22. Gale, 1983, pp. 241–51.

Chevalier, Tracy, ed. *Twentieth-Century Children's Writers*. 3d ed. St. James, 1989, pp. 573–75.

Collier, Laurie, and Joyce Nakamura. *Major Authors and Illustrators for Children and Young Adults*. Gale, 1993, 6 vols. pp. 1442–47.

Commire, Anne, ed. *Something About the Author*. Gale, 1971, vol. 1, pp. 142–43; 1982, vol. 26, pp. 134–42.

Hedblad, Alan. ed. *Something About the Author*. Vol. 100. Gale, 1999, pp. 150–55.

Helbig, Alethea K., and Agnes R. Perkins, eds. *Dictionary of American Children's Fiction, 1859–1959*. Greenwood, 1986, pp. 289–90 (bio.), pp. 497–98 (book).

Huck, Charlotte. S. "Lois Lenski." *Catholic Library World* (Feb. 1968): 346–50.

Kunitz, Stanley J., and Howard Haycraft, eds. *The Junior Book of Authors*. Wilson, 1951, pp. 193–94.

Lenski, Lois. *Journey into Childhood: The Autobiography of Lois Lenski*. Lippincott, 1972.

———. *Strawberry Girl*. 1988, McGraw-Hill. Audiocassettes. ($21.33)

Miller, Bertha M., and Elinor Field, eds. *Newbery Medal Books: 1922–1955 with the Author's Acceptance Papers and Related Material*. Horn Book, 1955, pp. 268–87.

"Newbery Award Acceptance Material, 1946." *Horn Book* 22, no. 4 (July/August 1946): 276–94.

Peterson, Linda K., and Marilyn L. Solt, eds. *Newbery and Caldecott Medal and Honor Books: 1922–1981.* Hall, 1982, pp. 96–97.

Senick, Gerard, ed. *Children's Literature Review.* Vol. 26. Gale, 1992, pp. 817–25.

Silvey, Anita. ed. *Children's Books and Their Creators.* Houghton, 1995, pp. 402–03.

Trosky, Susan M., ed. *Contemporary Authors (New Revision Series).* Vol. 41. Gale, 1994, pp. 264–68.

Ward, Martha, ed. *Authors of Books for Young People.* 3d ed. Scarecrow, 1990, pp. 427–28.

Honor Books 1946

Henry, Marguerite. *Justin Morgan Had a Horse.* Rand, 1945, o.p.; pap., Aladdin, $3.95: 0-689-71534-X. (Grades 4–7)

In the introduction to this historical novel, the author states, "This is the story of a common ordinary little work horse which turned out to be the father of the famous family of American horses . . . the Morgan horses." The book begins in the late 1700s when Vermont teacher Justin Morgan and singing master Joel Goss travel to West Springfield, Massachusetts, to collect on a debt owed Justin. The payment is in the form of two horses, a large colt and a nondescript pony named Little Bub. The older horse is sold but Joel takes over the upbringing of the pony in his after school hours. The horse proves to possess both remarkable strength for his size and a special talent for racing. Joel and Bub are separated when Justin moves, taking his horse with him, and Joel is apprenticed to a miller. Years pass, and Joel finishes his apprenticeship and serves in the cavalry during the War of 1812. In 1817, Joel locates Bud, now a broken-down workhorse. Joel nurses him back to health and Bub, now named Justin Morgan, has the honor of carrying President Monroe during a parade in Plattsburg. The sepia-toned illustrations by Wesley Dennis add to the book's appeal.

Means, Florence Crannell. *The Moved-Outers.* Houghton, 1945, o.p.; pap., Walker, $6.95: 0-8027-7386-9. (Grades 5–8)

The writing of this historical novel was motivated by the shameful treatment of West Coast Japanese Americans during World War II. The story centers on the Ohara, a Japanese American family that is living in Cordova, California, when the Japanese attack Pearl Harbor in 1941. Mr. Ohara owns a nursery and flower shop. He and his wife have four children—Tad, who is in the army; Amy, in college; and Sue and her brother Kim, two popular, successful high-school seniors. The story is told from Sue's viewpoint. After some of the townspeople show open hostility, Mr. Ohara is sent to an internment camp in North Dakota. In February 1942, Sue, Kim, and their mother are sent first to a temporary camp close to home and then to barracks surrounded by barbed wire in Amache, Colorado. Life in both camps is made more livable for Sue by the presence of another family from their area, the Itos. The Itoses' son Jiro and Sue gradually grow to love each other.

At the end of the book, in 1943, Kim and Jiro enlist in a Japanese American army unit and Sue, along with Tomi, Jiro's sister, leaves the camp to attend college. Both families yearn for a better life after the war.

Shippen, Katherine B. *New Found World.* Viking, 1945, o.p. (Grades 5–8)

This attractively illustrated history chronicles the story of Latin America from the earliest times to the slow, painful struggle for liberation from the colonial powers, Spain and Portugal, and the emergence of today's independent countries. Following a brief geographic introduction that highlights the land and its flora and fauna, there are separate chapters on the history and characteristics of each of the ancient civilizations such as the Caribs, the Aztecs, the Mayans, and the Incas. Subsequent chapters deal with the voyages of Columbus and other explorers, the career of Cortes and his conquest of Mexico, Pizarro and invasion of Peru, the subjugation of other native tribes, and the search for El Dorado. The coming of Christianity is chronicled and several chapters are devoted to the struggle for independence. There is also some coverage on the arts in Latin America that includes music and literature. The text is enhanced by illustrations by C. B. Falls, several maps, and a chart, "Six Centuries in America," that covers the years from 1400 through 1942.

Weston, Christine. *Bhimsa, the Dancing Bear.* Scribner, 1945, o.p. (Grades 4–6)

Set in contemporary India, this tale, chronicles the adventures shared by two boys, one Western and the other a native Indian, along with an amazingly talented tame bear. One evening David is resting in a garden while his servant, Lal, is asleep under a tree. Suddenly through the underbrush David hears noises of someone approaching. It is a native Indian boy, Gopala, and his trained bear, Bhimsa, who seems to understand human language. Gopala, who has been separated from his family, has been earning a meager living wandering around the countryside entertaining people with his music making and Bhimsa's incredible dancing. Disguising himself as a native with the cloth from the turban of the sleeping Lal, David joins them. Together they share a series of improbable adventures including their escape from a young tyrant named Prince by hiding in a cart carrying hides, their capture by and amazing deliverance from robbers, and their survival of an encounter with a tiger. Gopala is eventually reunited with his family and David is persuaded to return home. These fantastic incidents are humorously illustrated by Roger Duvoisin.

Newbery Winner 1947

Bailey, Carolyn. *Miss Hickory.* Illustrated by Ruth Gannett. Viking, 1946, o.p.; pap., Puffin, $3.99: 0-14-030956-X. (Grades 3–5)

Carolyn Bailey (1875–1961) was born in Hoosick Falls, New York, and lived all of her life in the Northeast, where most of her work is situated. Before entering publishing, where she worked as both an author and an editor, she taught school in several places including New York City. She wrote more than 70 books for young people, notably a series on colonial life and crafts in this country.

Miss Hickory is a sharp-tongued plain-spoken doll who possesses all of the necessary survival qualities of a true New Englander when she is left alone for the winter. The author, in her Newbery Award acceptance speech, said that she had many dolls as a child but the first Miss Hickory was made by her grandmother, presumably from a colonial design. She said, "I found Miss Hickory a stout companion. We lived under a lilac bush. Then she must have broken, and the years forgot her." Sometime later, while the author was isolated in Florida on a writing assignment and ill with hay fever, she remembered her childhood doll and began to write a book about Miss Hickory. This proved to be the author's most lasting success, and through the years Miss Hickory has joined other famous toys in literature such as Pinocchio and Paddington.

Plot Summary

Miss Hickory is not at all pleased when Crow makes a call to her tidy home one day in late September. She lives in a corncob house under a lilac tree in the yard of Great-granny Brown near Temple Mountain in New Hampshire. Miss Hickory, who had once been part of a tree, has a hickory nut for a head, inked-on eyes and mouth, and an apple-wood twig body. As usual, with the severe New Hampshire winter approaching, she expects to spend the long cold days on Great-granny Brown's kitchen windowsill with young Ann dropping in nearly every day with useful items for her house.

Now, however, Crow, who truly loves gossip, has come to tell her the shocking news. Great-granny Brown and all the family are going to spend the winter in Boston! Even young Ann will go to school there. They have forgotten all about Miss Hickory.

Although Miss Hickory refuses at first to believe Crow's dreadful news, she realizes that if it is true, she will have to move. She cannot survive the cold New Hampshire winter under a lilac bush in a corncob house. But first she will check with Mr. T. Willard-Brown. He will tell her the true facts.

The following day, Miss Hickory sets out to find Mr. T., a wandering barn cat and hunter of some renown. Not only does Mr. T. confirm her worst fears, but he tells her that Granny and the rest of the family have already left for Boston. Out of kindness because they are good friends, Mr. T. offers Miss Hickory the use of his barn home all winter.

Miss Hickory objects that she was not born to live in a barn and prepares to return home to her lilac bush to figure out what to do. Then Mr. T. drops another bombshell. It seems that Chipmunk, seeing the deserted corncob house, has already moved in and taken it over. He is there for the winter.

Near tears but too proud to give in, Miss Hickory sits under the rose trellis to contemplate her plight. She sits so long that a first dusting of snow lands on her cap. Then along comes Crow again.

Assuring Miss Hickory that change is good for everybody, he tells her he has found her a new home and he will fly her there. And so he does, right up the hill on McIntosh Lane where he deposits a startled Miss Hickory into a roomy, empty nest in an apple tree. Robin will not need it until spring.

Miss Hickory's first chore in her new surroundings is to find herself some clothes for the winter. This she does and fashions a new outfit from moss and larch tree cones, with fern fronds for soft underwear. Thus attired, she bumps into Squirrel, who lives in a hole at the foot of her apple tree and finds Miss Hickory quite enchanting.

Now it is November and one day Miss Hickory engages in conversation with Hen-Pheasant, a drab little creature who is quite depressed because Cock has driven her out of her home. It seems he does so every autumn and Hen-Pheasant can do nothing about it. All the other Hen-Pheasants are in the same fix and very depressed.

Very well, declares Miss Hickory, what you must do is band together so that no cock will dare to drive you out of your homes. You must form a Ladies Aid Society and start making a bed quilt, which will occupy you through the winter and keep you busy and safe.

Now it is late December and Squirrel tells Miss Hickory that she must not miss the celebration in the barn. Miss Hickory has never heard of such a thing. But Squirrel assures her that something wonderful happens every Christmas Eve at midnight.

Because Miss Hickory has never really trusted Squirrel anyway, she decides to go to sleep early on Christmas Eve. But she wakes with moonlight on the snow so dazzling that she gets out of bed to see what is happening. Down from Temple Mountain comes a procession—robins and bluebirds and fawns and crows and all manner of animals. Miss Hickory goes to the barn in spite of herself, and at midnight the Christmas star enters. The next morning Miss Hickory wonders if what she saw was real. Now it is February, which brings an unexpected thaw. Ground Hog sees his shadow. He also sees Miss Hickory, who is so startled by his size that she runs off, right into the Ladies Aid Society of the Hen-Pheasants. When Miss Hickory tells them what she saw, the Hen-Pheasants moan about six more weeks of winter.

Now it is March and spring is in the air. Miss Hickory feels it in her twig arms and legs. And who turns up but her old friend Crow, who invites her to take a flight with him. Against her will, Miss Hickory rides on Crow's back as he takes her about the countryside to see the first beginnings of spring. When he brings her back to her tidy nest home, she declares that it is time to make herself some spring clothes.

Newly outfitted, Miss Hickory returns home one day to find that Robin has reclaimed his nest and is not about to give it back. Desperate at first, Miss Hickory finds that Squirrel's home at the bottom of the tree is now empty. Very likely he has moved. This will be a pleasant home for her.

Miss Hickory steps into the dark hole only to find that Squirrel has not moved. He is still inside but in a very weak condition because he has forgotten where he stored all his nuts for the winter and is now very hungry.

Miss Hickory tells Squirrel that he is a brainless wastrel. This so angers Squirrel that he takes a good look at her hickory nut head and bites it off.

Miss Hickory stumbles out of Squirrel's home feeling strangely alert and rather in good spirits even without her head. She decides to climb to the very top of the old apple tree that had been her home, shedding her clothes as she goes. What a feeling of freedom and joy!

Higher and higher she climbs, feeling more and more as though she truly belongs in that old apple tree. She feels almost as though she is budding. Finally, tired from her climb, she pushes her headless self into the wide upper crotch of the tree and rests.

Now it is May. Young Ann and the family have returned from Boston. But Ann is dismayed to find that the corncob house in which Miss Hickory lived is in ruins and Miss Hickory is gone. Her friend Timothy-of-the-Next-Farm says he will make her another playhouse and that she is too old to play with dolls.

Ann protests that Miss Hickory was not a doll but a real person and a friend. Timothy shakes his head but suggests a walk through the orchard. They marvel at the pink and white beauty of the New Hampshire apple orchard and stop beneath an elderly McIntosh tree. Old Crow is calling from the top of the tree and Timothy climbs up to see what he wants. When he reaches the top he calls for Ann to come see what he has found.

Carefully, Ann climbs to the top of the old tree. "Look," says Timothy, pointing to the most flowery of all the branches on the tree. "It's a scion. It's growing like anything! Who put it there?"

Ann learns that a scion is a new graft put into an old tree to start it blooming and bearing again. Timothy doesn't understand how this new graft got there, but he is sure that it will grow and start the old tree growing again, too.

Ann is happy now, for she has recognized the new graft as her own Miss Hickory. One day, she knows, Miss Hickory will give her old friend a big red apple.

Themes and Subjects

This is a delightful fantasy that enters the country of a child's imagination and preserves the rhapsodies of childhood. It depicts the charm of a New Hampshire winter from an angle that humans never know. Crow, Squirrel, and Hen-Pheasant display their particular true characteristics, and Miss Hickory remains faithful to the staunchness of her tree ancestry and the proud independence of those who survive the sometime harsh realities of winter in New England. Humor, friendship, and pride abound in this imaginative tale of the indestructible Miss Hickory. It shows a refreshingly original awareness of the countryside and its remarkable outdoor residents.

Incidents for Booktalking

The real essence of this charming tale can be found in the vivid personalities of its animal characters. See: Mr. T. Willard-Brown as he tells Miss Hickory the truth of her plight (pp. 20–23); Crow tries to help find a new home (pp. 25–30); Squirrel hunts for nuts (pp. 32–35); Hen-Pheasant is distressed (pp. 40–46); the runaway fawn (pp. 54–60). For the humor of Miss Hickory's staunch New England character, see: Miss Hickory refuses to believe Crow's news (pp. 11–15); Miss Hickory fashions a winter outfit and meets Squirrel (pp. 35–39); Miss Hickory goes to the barn on Christmas Eve (pp. 71–77); Miss Hickory greets spring from Crow's back (pp. 88–92).

Related Titles

Rumer Godden has written many stories about dolls, including *The Doll's House* (pap., Puffin, $4.99: 0-14-030942-X), the story of a little 100-year-old Dutch doll, her family, and the English family to which they belong. Another Godden story, *The Story of Holly and Ivy* (Viking, 1985, $16.89: 0-670-80622-6; pap., Puffin, $4.95: 0-14-050723-X), is a sentimental tale about an orphan named Ivy, a Christmas doll named Holly, and a childless couple.

In one of the most famous tales for children, Geppetto finds a piece of wood and carves it into a marionette in Carlo Collodi's *The Adventures of Pinocchio*. Two fine editions are Putnam, 1996, $15.95: 0-448-41479-1 and pap., Puffin, $3.50: 0-14-035037-3.

In the simple, moving *Goldie the Dollmaker* (Farrar, 1969, $8.95: 0-374-32739-4; pap., Sunburst, $4.95: 0-614-28743-X) by M. B. Goffstein, Goldie lavishes her love on the beautiful dolls she makes and the expensive Chinese lamp she purchases.

Directions for making dolls out of washrags, gloves, and old fabrics are given in Sheila McGraw's *Dolls Kids Can Make* (Firefly, 1995, $19.95: 1-895565-75-8).

About the Book and Author

Berger, Laura Standley, ed. *Twentieth-Century Children's Writers*. 4th ed. St. James, 1995, pp. 53–55.

Brown, Muriel W., and Rita Schoch Foudray. *Newbery and Caldecott Medalists and Honor Book Winners: Bibliographic & Resource Material Through 1990*. 2d ed. Neal-Schuman, 1992, pp. 21–23.

Chevalier, Tracy, ed. *Twentieth-Century Children's Writers*. 3d ed. St. James, 1989, pp. 51–53.

Commire, Anne, ed. *Something About the Author*. Vol. 14. Gale, 1978, pp. 18–23.

Helbig, Alethea K., and Agnes R. Perkins, eds. *Dictionary of American Children's Fiction, 1859–1959*. Greenwood, 1986, pp. 33–34 (bio.), p. 348 (book).

Kunitz, Stanley J., and Howard Haycraft, eds. *The Junior Book of Authors*. Wilson, 1951, pp. 14–15.

Locher, Frances C., ed. *Contemporary Authors*. Vols. 73–76. Gale, 1978, pp. 37–38.

Miller, Bertha M., and Elinor Field, eds. *Newbery Medal Books: 1922–1955 with the Author's Acceptance Papers and Related Material*. Horn Book, 1955, pp. 288–99.

Miss Hickory. Live Oak Media, 1972. Audiocassette, 49 min. ($22.95)

"Newbery Medal Acceptance Material, 1947." *Horn Book* 23, no. 4 (July/August 1947): 239–49.

Peterson, Linda K., and Marilyn L. Solt, eds. *Newbery and Caldecott Medal and Honor Books: 1922–1981*. Hall, 1982, p. 100.

Silvey, Anita, ed. *Children's Books and Their Creators*. Houghton, 1995, pp. 445.

Ward, Martha, ed. *Authors of Books for Young People*. 3d ed. Scarecrow, 1990, p. 30.

Honor Books 1947

Barnes, Nancy. *The Wonderful Year*. Messner, 1946, o.p. (Grades 4–6)

This novel takes place during the early part of the twentieth century and centers on the Martin family: a vivacious, creative mother, a lawyer father who suffers from ill health, and their delightful daughter, 11-year-old Ellen. At first Ellen is dismayed to learn that the family is moving from Kansas because of her father's illness and resettling on an undeveloped fruit range in Colorado. However, the events surrounding their settling into a new life soon become a new adventure for Ellen.

First, they live in a tent until a comfortable cabin can be constructed for them. In no time they become friendly with the neighbors, the Erringtons, whose 15-year-old son Ronnie develops a close, brotherly relationship with Ellen. Together the two youngsters share many experiences during the summer such as bicycling and fishing in the area, getting lost, and celebrating Ellen's birthday. In the fall, Ellen is upset to learn that the family is moving once again, this time to nearby Mesa where her father will again practice law and Ellen will attend school. The change is painful for Ellen but gradually she adjusts. Ronnie suddenly reappears to stay with the Martins while he attends agricultural school. In all, it has been a wonderful year.

Buff, Conrad, and Mary Buff. *The Big Tree*. Viking, 1946, o.p. (Grades 4–7)

This is the story of Wawona, a giant sequoia, that is now at least 5,000 years old, the oldest living thing on earth. The story begins when Wawona is a seedling. During his story (the tree is personified and feels human emotions like pain and joy), references are made to events that are happening in other parts of the Earth. For example, he is 800 when the pyramids are being built in Egypt and 3,000 years old when Christ is born. Details are given concerning the ways in which the lives of such animals as a chipmunk, bear, and skunk are changed by contact with the tree. One disaster occurs when, during a violent storm, an old pine tree falls against Wawona, dealing him a crippling blow. After three years, the pine rots and falls away, allowing the big tree once more the freedom to grow.

In the twentieth century, the tree fears for his life at the hands of loggers, but suddenly the cutting and sawing stop. The big tree has been saved by becoming one of the attractions in a park where he is protected by rangers. It is here that Wawona continues to stand noble and proud. This book contains outstanding illustrations by the authors.

Fisher, Cyrus. *The Avion My Uncle Flew*. Appleton, 1945, o.p. (Grades 5–8)

This fast-paced adventure story set in France shortly after World War II features a 12-year-old American hero, Johnny Littlehorn, who is recovering from a crippling accident in which he fell from a pony on his father's Wyoming ranch. Johnny's mother is from a French family that owns property in the countryside of France. When Mr. Littlehorn is assigned to Paris for a postwar liaison mission, the entire family travels to France where Johnny hopes to increase his knowledge of the language and regain the use of his injured leg. In Paris, he meets Albert, the hotel doorman, and the rather sinister Monsieur Fischfasse, alias Simonis, who appears unusually interested in purchasing the family property. When Johnny visits his Uncle Paul Langres, a glider enthusiast, at the family home events become more exciting and dangerous. Johnny becomes friendly with the red-headed twins, Charles and Suzanne Neilhas, and together they uncover a plot devised by the town's mayor (who is actually a wartime collaborator), Albert, and Simonis (later unmasked as a Nazi agent), to steal a fortune in bank funds buried on the Langres property. In addition to being a thrilling spy story, this novel teaches the reader (and Johnny) many French words and expressions.

Jewett, Eleanore M. *The Hidden Treasure of Glaston.* Viking, 1946, o.p. (Grades 5–8)

This historical novel takes place in England at the monastery of Glaston during the years 1171–1172 when King Henry II was on the throne. When Sir Hugh de Morville is required to make a pilgrimage to Jerusalem to atone for his part in the murder of Thomas à Becket, he leaves his crippled 13-year-old son Hugh at the monastery to await his return. At Glaston, Hugh who can read and write, helps in the scriptorium under the watchful eye of Brother John. He also meets Dickon, a boy his age who has lived his entire life in the monastery. Together the two boys explore the many passages and caverns under the abbey. They encounter a deranged old hermit, Bleheris, who tells them stories of King Arthur, who supposedly lived in the area, and of the Holy Grail. They find an old sword that they believe to be Excalibur and uncover an ancient manuscript that might be part of the abbey's most important treasure, a book about the Grail. Hugh has a vision that leads to the discovery of the bones of King Arthur and Queen Guinevere and later, when he saves Brother John from a fire that destroys the monastery's sacred book, he sees in another vision the Holy Grail. This results in the instant healing of his crippled leg. When Hugh's father returns, the boy decides to stay at the monastery to reconstruct *The Book of the Holy Grail* while Dickon becomes Sir Hugh's squire.

Maxell, William. *The Heavenly Tenants.* Harper, 1946, o.p.; reprint, Parabola, 1992, $13.95: 0-930407-25-3. (Grades 5–7)

This fantasy set first in rural Wisconsin and later in Virginia combines fantasy with a lesson in astronomy. The Marvell family consists of mother and father and four children: 11-year-old Roger, sister Heather, age eight, and the five-year-old twins, Tim and Tom. On the night before the family is scheduled to leave their Wisconsin farm to spend three weeks with Grandmother in Virginia, Mr. Marvell points out to the children the various constellations in the sky that make up the signs of the zodiac. The following morning they leave, not knowing that the caretaker, Old August, to whom they have entrusted the care of their farm animals, is suffering from a bad case of rheumatism and is unable to fulfill his chores. The next night in Virginia, Mr. Marvell notices that the zodiac constellations have disappeared from the sky. At the same time, neighbors in Wisconsin note that that a peculiar glow is emanating from the Marvells' barn. When Old Augus is well enough to visit the property, he finds it inhabited with strange creatures like a glowing lion who acts as the weathervane, two fish larger than men, a white bull, and a bowman with a silver arrow. When the Marvells return, they also find evidence that their property has been visited by heavenly beings who have cared for their animals in their absence. That night Mr. Marvell sees that the constellations have returned to the sky.

Newbery Winner 1948

Du Bois, William Pène. *The Twenty-One Balloons.* Illustrated by the author. Viking, 1947, $15.99: 0-670-73441-1; pap., Puffin, $4.99: 0-14-032097-0. (Grades 5–8)

William Pène du Bois (1916–1993) was a hugely successful author-illustrator who won a number of awards during his life. In addition to receiving the Newbery

Award, two of his books, *Bear Party* (pap., Puffin, $3.99) and *Lion* (Viking, 1956, o.p.), were Caldecott Honor Books. He was born in New Jersey but received his elementary school education in France. By the time he arrived back in the United States at age 14, he already was firmly interested in the fantastic, the unconventional, and such imaginative forms of entertainment as the circus. Many of these interests surface regularly in both his writing and his illustrations.

The Twenty-One Balloons is cast in this mold. It is a zany journey, a mixture of fantasy and science that is filled with amusing characters. Its sometimes nightmarish qualities are softened by the wonderful illustrations that are perfectly matched to the story. The author claims that his ability to illustrate machinery with such loving detail comes from his lasting interest in the novels of Jules Verne. In spite of its fantastic element, the novel is rooted in fact. In 1883, most of the South Sea Island of Krakatoa was destroyed in a volcanic eruption that supposedly produced the loudest sound ever heard on Earth. Reading the novel produces other sounds in children, the sound of laughter at the amazing antics of Professor William Waterman Sherman.

Plot Summary

This most unusual fantastic voyage begins when Professor William Waterman Sherman, weary after 40 years of teaching arithmetic to young boys in San Francisco, decides to spend his first year of retirement traveling by balloon. His plan is to build a giant balloon and float about the Earth out of touch with everybody and everything, leaving his destination to the winds. It does not exactly work out that way.

After leaving San Francisco on August 15, 1883, a sick and exhausted Professor Sherman is fished out of the Atlantic Ocean on September 8 by Captain John Simon and the crew of the *S.S. Cunningham*. They find the professor floating around in the sea amidst a lot of broken planks and 20 empty ascension balloons. Even more extraordinary, the professor will tell no one of his adventures, or of how he set off on the Pacific Ocean and ended up in the Atlantic only three weeks later. Sherman insists that he will relate his fantastic tale only in the auditorium of the Western American Explorers' Club in San Francisco, of which he is a member. No one can dissuade him from this vow, not the mayor of New York City nor the president of the United States.

There is much scolding and prodding and pleading, but to no avail. Finally, the president, who is just as anxious to hear the story as anyone else, offers Professor Sherman his private train to travel across the country to San Francisco. Sherman accepts.

As the presidential train heads toward the West Coast, public curiosity reaches a fever pitch and San Francisco is in a turmoil as to how best to greet this returning hero. Actually, no one is quite sure of why or how he is a hero, but surely he must be. The city decides on a balloon motif: bright miniature balloons are everywhere, including a revived fashion in ladies' dress called the "round look." There is a slight mishap when so many balloons are attached to the cupola of the American Explorers' Club building that the cupola itself takes off and drifts onto a snug little Indian reservation, where the inhabitants turn it into a new house for the chief.

At long last, after much handshaking and cheek kissing and now possessing a key to the city, Professor Sherman arrives at the American Explorers' Club and begins his most extraordinary tale.

He explains to his enraptured audience how he came upon the idea for a year of quiet balloon travel; how he worked on his giant balloon, which he christened the

Globe; and how he planned each detail for his comfort and safety for a year's solitude. And how it all went wrong very quickly. On the seventh day of his journey, a seagull punctures a sizable hole in the balloon. Despite all efforts, the balloon crashes onto a small island, and the professor finds himself a new citizen of Krakatoa.

There really is a Pacific island of Krakatoa, only 18 square miles in size. In 1883 a volcanic eruption, the biggest of all time, reduced the island to half of its 1,400 feet elevation above sea level. But the professor has arrived before the explosion to find a most extraordinary civilization on this remote place, a civilization that none of its members wish disclosed to the rest of the world. In fact, the professor is told that he will be spending the rest of his life on Krakatoa.

Actually, it isn't as bad a sentence as it seems at first. He is told that eight years before, a young sailor was shipwrecked on the uninhabited island. He crawled into what he thought was a cave, only to discover it was a diamond mine. He became the richest man in the world! Deciding to create his own desirable civilization, he builds a raft, sets out to sea, is picked up by a ship, returns to San Francisco (with diamonds in his pocket, of course), and picks out 20 families each with a boy and a girl between the ages of three and eight. Each family has some special interest, such as music or architecture, so that future generations will not be bored on this small island.

Now this hand-picked civilization enjoys an extraordinary life on this supposedly uninhabited spot. Everything has been carefully thought out. Each of the 20 families, known only as Mr. and Mrs. A. or Mr. and Mrs. G, owns and operates a restaurant, for instance, so that each night the other 19 families dine out. There are 20 days to the Krakatoan month and 18 months to the Krakatoan year. Each restaurant serves different food; for instance, Mr. and Mrs. A. run an American restaurant, Mr. and Mrs. C. offer Chinese food, and so on. In other words, the island is run by a Restaurant Form of Government.

All this is quite extraordinary indeed to the professor, who nonetheless is beginning to feel that he might very well be content to spend his days on this unusual place. Surprise comes upon surprise, but the most unusual of all is the Giant Balloon Life Raft.

Although the inhabitants of the island have no wish to leave their ideal existence, they are aware that the constant rumblings from the volcano may one day mean disaster. As a precaution, they have carefully constructed an engineering marvel, a Giant Balloon Life Raft capable of lifting 20 families to safety in a remarkably short time. The balloon raft is to be lifted by 20 giant ascension balloons. Of course, this marvel, although built, has never been tried.

It is indeed Professor Sherman's fate to have landed on the island just before the biggest explosion of all time. When it comes, the inhabitants and the professor race to the Giant Balloon Life Raft and safely take off away from danger. The force of the gigantic explosion pushes the life raft aloft at tremendous speeds.

Each family, of course, has parachutes for safe landing, but because there was no time for a parachute to be made for the professor, he must try to land this gigantic raft. He crashes into the Atlantic, where the ship picks him up and the world learns of this incredible adventure.

When the professor's tale is finished, the audience is astounded. But what will he do now, someone in the audience asks. Professor Sherman grins and rolls up his coat sleeves to show the diamond cuff links he was able to take from the island. He says he will sell them, building a second balloon, this time with a seagull catcher, and he will finally spend one full year of truly delightful solitary living—in a balloon!

Themes and Subjects

This marvelous fantasy, written in 1947, hints at the Atomic Age and forecasts space travel to come. In much the same manner as *The Wizard of Oz*, it creates an entirely fantastic, although plausible, other world and civilization where things function in an orderly, believable manner, even if completely topsy-turvy from the usual, everyday world of Earth. The people that the professor meets on Krakatoa are like people anywhere except that their imaginations have created a different world, a world that, no matter how strange to the uninitiated, works for them. This is pure fantasy but it is highly imaginative, creative fantasy. One can marvel at the author's ingenuity or his vision of the Atomic Age, but the reader should never lose sight of the main reason that *The Twenty-One Balloons* is such a delight. It is just pure fun.

Incidents for Booktalking

Almost any page can introduce the reader to the marvelous imagination that created life on Krakatoa. See: San Francisco prepares for the professor's arrival (pp. 19–31); Professor Sherman builds his balloon (pp. 39–45); the landing on Krakatoa (pp. 52–59); explaining the Restaurant Government (pp. 87–93); the Moroccan house of marvels (pp. 95–111); a ride in the airy-go-round (pp. 116–33); the fantastic explosion (pp. 158–72).

Related Titles

Noah uses a silver powder to shrink himself and his friend Nate to the size of toys in *Back in Action* (Holiday, 1991, $13.95: 0-8234-0897-3) by Elvira Woodruff.

A mischievous sprite is accidentally transported from Scotland to Canada and his pranks cause serious problems for the Volnik family in Susan Cooper's *The Boggart* (McElderry, 1993, $15.00: 0-689-50576-0).

Ten-year-old James meets a creature made of recycled garbage in an old dump in Peter Dickinson's *The Box of Nothing* (Delacorte, 1988, $14.95: 0-385-29664-9).

In Diane Duane's *So You Want To Be a Wizard* (Delacorte, 1983, $14.95: 0-385-29305-4), Nita and friends embark on a journey to retrieve the *Book of Night and Moon*.

Nine-year-old Omri receives a magical tin medicine cabinet that can bring toy plastic figures to life in *Indian in the Cupboard* (Doubleday, 1985, $15.95: 0-385-17060-2; pap., Avon, $4.99: 0-380-60012-9), the first of a popular series by Lynne Reid Banks.

About the Book and Author

Berger, Laura Standley, ed. *Twentieth-Century Children's Writers*. 4th ed. St. James, 1995, pp. 304–5.

Block, Ann, and Carolyn Riley, eds. *Children's Literary Review*. Vol. 1. Gale, 1976, pp. 62–67.

Brown, Muriel W., and Rita Schoch Foudray. *Newbery & Caldecott Medalists and Honor Book Winners: Bibliographic & Resources Material Through 1990*. 2d ed. Neal-Schuman, 1992, pp. 108–11.

Chevalier, Tracy, ed. *Twentieth-Century Children's Writers*. 3d ed. St. James, 1989, pp. 298–99.

Collier, Laurie, and Joyce Nakamura. *Major Authors and Illustrators for Children and Young Adults*. Gale, 1993, 6 vols., pp. 1853–57.

DuBois, William Pene. *The Twenty-One Balloons*. Read by John McDonough. Recorded Books, 1997. Audiocassettes, 320 min. ($26.00)

Estes, Glenn E., ed. "American Writers for Children Since 1960: Fiction." In *Dictionary of Literary Biography*. Vol. 52. Gale, 1986, pp. 27–37.

Harte, Barbara, and Carolyn Riley, eds. *Contemporary Authors (First Revision Series)*. Vols. 5–8. Gale, 1969, p. 318.

Helbig, Alethea K., and Agnes R. Perkins, eds. *Dictionary of American Children's Fiction, 1859–1959*. Greenwood, 1986, pp.139–40 (bio.), p. 539 (book).

Kunitz, Stanley J., and Howard Haycraft, eds. *The Junior Book of Authors*. Wilson, 1951, pp. 102–4.

Mahoney, Berta E. *Illustrators of Children's Books, 1744–1945*. Horn Book, 1947, p. 302.

Metzger, Linda, and Deborah A. Straub, eds. *Contemporary Authors (New Revision Series)*. Vol. 17. Gale, 1986, pp. 113–14.

Miller, Bertha M., and Elinor Field, eds. *Newbery Medal Books: 1922–1955 with the Author's Acceptance Papers and Related Material*. Horn Book, 1955, pp. 300–17.

"Newbery Acceptance Material, 1948." *Horn Book* 24, no. 4 (July/August 1948): 235–49.

Olendorf, Donna, ed. *Something About the Author*. Vol. 68. Gale, 1992, pp. 178–82.

Peterson, Linda K., and Marilyn L. Solt, eds. *Newbery and Caldecott Medal and Honor Books: 1922–1981*. Hall, 1982, pp. 104–5.

Silvey, Anita. ed. *Children's Books and Their Creators*. Houghton, 1995, pp. 212–13.

Ward, Martha, ed. *Authors of Books for Young People*. 3d ed. Scarecrow, 1990, p. 196.

Honor Books 1948

Besterman, Catherine. *The Quaint and Curious Quest of Johnny Longfoot, the Shoe-King's Son*. Bobbs, 1947, o.p. (Grades 3–5)

This comic fantasy, a variation on a Polish folktale, is enhanced by the imaginative illustrations of Warren Chappell. It tells of the adventures of Johnny when he is sent by his father, a master cobbler, to visit his Uncle Lucas Longfoot, who proves to be so miserly that he saves his tears to be used instead of salt. Johnny encounters Barnac the Cat who promises him gold if he is able to secure the seven-league boats that are hidden on Coral Island. Johnny builds a barge, and accompanied by another cat as Captain and an unwilling Uncle Lucas, sets sail on his quest. He is able to mollify some amazing sea creatures that attack his boat, and from one, Mr. Shark, he obtains a magical Sea Passport. After a severe storm, Johnny is cast up on an isolated shore and the villainous Uncle Lucas is able, through trickery, to locate the boots and other treasures and set sail on the barge for home. Through the use of his Sea Passport, Johnny is escorted back to the boat by friendly sea creatures. There he finds a becalmed Uncle Lucas who is willing to repent and change his ways. After other adventures, Johnny is able to present the boots to Barnac and claim his reward.

Bishop, Claire H. *Pancakes-Paris*. Viking, 1947, o.p. (Grades 3–5)

This novel is set in Paris a few months after the end of World War II. Food and other commodities are still very scarce for civilians but everyone is still looking forward to celebrating Mardi Gras. Ten-year-old Charles, a hungry French schoolboy, gives two American soldiers in a jeep some needed directions, and as a reward, they give him a box of Aunt Jemima pancake mix. Unable to read the English directions, he travels to the American Embassy for help. Not only does he get a French translation but the two soldiers escort him back to his home. There is a further problem when he discovers that he has no grease with which to fry the pancakes. Fortunately, once again, the soldiers again rescued him by arriving at his home with all the necessary ingredients and other food so that Charles, his family, his friends, and the soldiers can enjoy the best Mardi Gras feast since before the war.

Courlander, Harold, and George Herzog. *The Cow-Tail Switch, and Other West African Stories*. Holt, 1947, o.p. (Grades 3–7)

This book consists of 17 simple tales from West Africa that run the gambit from realistic stories to several with talking animals including two concerning Anansi, the trickster. In the title story, Ogaloussa, a hunter, disappears in the jungle one day. Gradually his family forgets about him until Puli, a son who was born after Ogaloussa'a departure, asks after his father. This results in a search in the jungle by his other sons. His skeleton is found but by using magical powers, each of his sons contributes to bringing his father back to life. Ogaloussa wants to reward the son most responsible for his return to life by giving him a handsome switch made by braiding the hair of a cow's tail. The choice is difficult but he gives it to Puli. The reason? Puli asked for him and "a man is not really dead until he is forgotten." Each story is illustrated with an authentic drawing by Madye Lee Chastain.

Henry, Marguerite. *Misty of Chincoteague*. Macmillan, 1990, $15.00: 0-02-743622-5; pap., Simon, $3.95: 0-689-82170-0. (Grades 4–7)

This exciting horse story is based on real people and events that the author experienced while visiting Chincoteague Island off the coast of Virginia. This is the site of the annual Pony Penning Day when residents round up the wild ponies (supposed descendants of Spanish horses shipwrecked there centuries ago) that live on neighboring Assateague Island, and swim them to Chincoteague Island where the foals are sold to support the local fire department.

Maureen and Paul Beebe, two youngsters who live with their grandparents, have been doing odd jobs after school and have saved $100, which they hope is enough to buy Phantom, a wild three-year-old horse that has always escaped capture. When Phantom is captured along with her foal, the youngsters' hopes run high, and in time, they are allowed to purchase both horses. The two become extremely attached to both the mother and her easily tamed foal, who is now called Misty. Phantom responds to the youngsters but to others she is untamable. The following year, Paul is able to ride her to victory against the local champion. However, he realizes that she belongs in the wild, and releases her to return to Assateague with her mate, the stallion, the Pied Piper. Wesley Dennis's black-and-white drawings add authentic details to this story.

Treffinger, Carolyn. *Li Lun, Lad of Courage*. Abington, 1947, o.p. (Grades 4–7)

This short novella tells of Li Lun, a courageous 10-year-old Chinese boy, and his bravery in fulfilling the difficult task his father has assigned him. Growing up on Blue Shark Island off China where all the men turn to the sea for their livelihood, Li Lun angers his father when he refuses to go on a fishing trip that will test his manliness. As punishment, the father gives his son seven grains of rice and banishes him to the top of barren Lao Shan, the Sorrow Mountain, where he must grow seven times that amount of rice or become a fisherman. After receiving advice from an ancient wise man, Sun Ling, who remembers how rice was grown in the past, Li Lun reluctantly climbs the mountain, taking along some rich soil and a supply of food.. He is there for almost four months, the maturation time for rice. By the end of this time, only one plant has survived such natural enemies as seagulls and rats. But that seventh plant has prospered and produced more than the necessary crop. In a temple ceremony, the lad is praised for his great courage and endurance and is asked to teach others how to grow rice so that the island can became more economically self-sufficient. This charming fable is illustrated by the renowned artist, Kurt Weise.

Newbery Winner 1949

Henry, Marguerite. *King of the Wind*. Illustrated by Wesley Dennis. Rand, 1948, o.p.; Macmillan, 1990, $15.00: 0-02-743629-2; pap, Aladdin, $3.95: 0-689-71486-6. (Grades 5–8)

Marguerite Henry (1902–1997) is world famous for a series of exciting horse stories, many of which were based on fact and are the result of painstaking research to gather authentic background material. Before winning the Newbery Award, two of her works were cited as Honor Books. The first is *Justin Morgan*

Had a Horse (see "Honor Books," 1946, p. 140), and the second, *Misty of Chincoteague* (see "Honor Books," 1948, p. 153), was inspired by the wild horses who live on Assateague Island. Both of these books were beautifully illustrated by Wesley Dennis, who also supplied the inspiration for *King of the Wind*. He told the author about an Arabian stallion of the early eighteenth century that survived cruel and abusive treatment to become one of the sires of such thoroughbred racehorses as Man o' War. The story moves from Morocco to France and ends in England—three settings that required an enormous amount of research to re-create, but as the author said in her Newbery acceptance speech, she became enthralled with the story of a horse "who had rubbed shoulders with sultans and kings, cooks and carters." Both publishers and family were initially against the project, partly because all three of the novel's main characters, Agba, the stableboy, Sham, the horse, and Grimalkin, the cat, are unable to speak. Happily, Marguerite Henry and her amazing illustrator Wesley Dennis prevailed.

Plot Summary

One of the greatest of American thoroughbred horses was Man o' War, known affectionately as Big Red. In 1920, Man o' War won both the Preakness at Pimlico in Baltimore, Maryland, and the Belmont Stakes at Elmont, New York, two legs of the famed Triple Crown. The last leg of the Triple Crown is the Kentucky Derby at Churchill Downs, which was won that year by a now-forgotten horse named Paul Jones.

Big Red's owner, Samuel Riddle, retired the horse from racing at the height of his career in perfect condition. Riddle said the valiant horse needed no more victories to prove his superiority. After all, Big Red could trace his bloodlines all the way back to the great Godolphin Arabian some 200 years before. *King of the Wind* is the story of that legendary horse who had no pedigree at all.

Long, long ago in Morocco, a young stable boy named Agba, who is unable to speak, has charge of 10 of the Sultan's prized horses. He feeds, waters, and exercises them, polishes their coats, and cleans their stalls.

One day a spindly foal is born to one of the mares in the stable. On his hind heel is a small white spot, which the boy recognizes as an emblem of swiftness. For his red-gold coat, Agba silently names him Sham, which is Arabic for sun. But the chief of the grooms, Signor Achmet, is not happy with the foal because of a mark on its chest, called the wheat ear. Achmet warns that ill luck will befall the royal stables. Despite Achmet's warnings that the sickly foal will die, he lives and grows under Agba's tender care. Within a year he is strong and fleet, although small.

One day Agba and five other young stable boys are summoned to the Sultan and told that they will accompany six horses sent as a gift to the boy king of France, Louis XV. Each boy will remain in France to care for his horse as long as the animal lives, then return to Morocco. Only the most perfect horses in the Kingdom of Morocco will be chosen as such a fine gift. The horses will be selected by color—one must be a bay whose coat is touched with gold—and by proportions.

Agba knows Sham is the right color for his coat is indeed touched with gold, but does he have perfect proportions? Carefully and with heavy heart, the boy measures the young horse. Indeed, he measures perfectly! His neck is long for running.

With Sham, Agba makes the journey to France carrying the horse's pedigree with him. The young king is not much impressed with the gift, especially when Sham steps on his foot. In retaliation, the small horse is turned over to the chief of the kitchen for whom he will draw a cart to market. Agba remains with him.

Sham proves a troublesome horse whom only Agba can gentle, and the cook sells him. In search of his horse, young Agba flees to Paris where he finds Sham, now in the cruel care of a carter. The carter allows the boy to live in his shed because he can use him to work. Sham is so cruelly treated that he is noticed by an Englishman from London, who buys the animal for his son-in-law. The Englishman takes pity on the boy as well and the two are soon on their way to England.

The Englishman's son-in-law does not take kindly to riding, so Sham is sold to the keeper of the Red Lion Inn. Agba is not allowed to accompany the horse and when he goes to the stables to see him, he is accused of being a horse thief and sent to jail. At the jail, the constable finds Sham's pedigree in Agba's possession and rips it up.

Meantime, the housekeeper of the Englishman who originally brought Sham to London misses the little horse and decides to visit him at the Red Lion Inn. She learns that Agba is in jail. When she goes to see him, she is given a ride by the son-in-law of the Duchess of Marlborough. He is the Earl of Godolphin.

The kindly Earl frees Agba, buys Sham, who by now is sick and weak, and takes them all, including Agba's new friend, Grimalkin the cat, to his stables at Gog Magog. There Sham is nursed back to health. But the horse displeases his lordship in a fight with the stable's prize horse, and Agba, Sham, and Grimalkin are sent out on their own again.

After about a year of wandering the countryside, Agba is amazed when a shiny red van appears from Lord Godolphin's estate. It seems that a foal has been born to the stable's prize mare, Roxana. The foal has grown to become the most fleet of horses. And he looks exactly like Sham! Now the lord wants Sham to come back and sire a whole new and noble breed of horses.

At last, Sham is to be honored for his worth. Above his stall is hung the sign—The Godolphin Arabian. Sham fathers three sons in all, who prove to be great racers. When the King and Queen of England come to the horse meet to see the famous Sham, it is Agba who rides in the saddle for it is only Agba who can gentle the spirited animal. When his three sons win their races and the Queen asks for the pedigree of Sham, the Earl of Godolphin replies, "His pedigree has been lost. It is written in his sons."

Sham, the Godolphin Arabian, lived until age 29. His body was buried at the stable of Gog Magog. The names of his offspring became known the world over. His bloodlines continue, including Man o' War, the greatest racer of his time.

Agba, the stable boy who could not talk, left for Morocco on the night Sham died.

Themes and Subjects

This is a touching story of devotion and love between boy and animal. It speaks to the kindness of the human spirit and to the meanness as well. It shows how the courage and steadfastness of one person, in this case a small boy who could not speak, bolstered the strength and strong heart of a gallant animal. The speed and stamina of a little horse without a pedigree could not be denied, nor could the loyalty of a little boy. The author has presented a gentle story of friendship and love and the soaring of spirit, both human and animal.

Incidents for Booktalking

The gentleness of the boy Agba and the fiery spirit of the horse called Sham are excellent introductions to this tale of courage and devotion. See: the foal is born (pp. 30–32); Agba tends the growing colt (pp. 42–44); Sham steps on the king's foot and is sent away in disgrace (pp. 74–76); Agba searches for Sham in Paris (pp. 83–87); Agba goes to jail (pp. 111–14); Sham returns to Gog Magog as a hero (pp. 152–56).

Related Titles

Heather Brown struggles to ride in the Grand National in Enid Bagnold's *National Velvet* (Morrow, 1985, $18.00: 0-688-05788-8; pap., Avon, $4.50: 0-380-71235-0).

Sarah must make some tough decisions when she wants to acquire a new horse in Jessie Haas's *A Horse Like Barney* (Greenwillow, 1993, $13.00; 0-688-12794-0).

Chris runs away with a horse to save its life in Lynn Hall's *The Something-Special Horse* (Macmillan, 1985, $13.95: 0-684-18343-9).

Herds of Thunder, Manes of Gold (Macmillan, 1986, $15.95: 0-385-24642-0) edited by Bruce Coville is a collection of poems, stories, and book excerpts about horses by well-known writers.

Cynthia Rylant's *Every Living Thing* (Macmillan, 1985, $14.00: 0-02-777200-4) contains 12 short stories about the effects birds and animals have on people.

About the Book and Author

Berger, Laura Standley, ed. *Twentieth-Century Children's Writers*. 4th ed. St. James, 1995, pp. 447–49.

Brown, Muriel W., and Rita Schoch Foudray. *Newbery and Caldecott Medalists and Honor Books Winners: Bibliographic & Resource Material Through 1990*. 2d ed. Neal-Schuman, 1992, pp. 187–89.

Cech, John, ed. "American Writers for Children, 1900–1960." In *Dictionary of Literary Biography*. Vol. 22. Gale, 1983, pp. 217–22.

Chevalier, Tracy, ed. *Twentieth-Century Children's Writers*. 3d ed. St. James, 1989, pp. 443–44.

Collier, Laurie, and Joyce Nakamura, eds. *Major Authors and Illustrators for Children and Young Adults*. Gale, 1993, 6 vols. pp. 1098–2001.

Commire, Anne, ed. *Something About the Author*. Vol. 11. Gale, 1977, pp. 131–32.

Evory, Ann, and Linda Metzger, eds. *Contemporary Authors (New Revision Series)*. Vol. 9. Gale, 1983, pp. 261–62.

Hedblad, Alan. ed. *Something About the Author*. Vol. 100. Gale, 1999, pp. 122–26.

Helbig, Alethea K., and Agnes R. Perkins, eds. *Dictionary of American Children's Fiction, 1859–1959*. Greenwood, 1986, pp. 212–13 (bio.), pp. 274–75 (book).

Henry, Marguerite. *King of the Wind*. Read by Davina Porter. Recorded Books, 1993. Audiocassettes, 240 min. ($26.00)

———. *King of the Wind*. Read by David McCallum. BDD Audio Publishing, 1998. Audiocassettes, 200 min. ($18.99)

———. *King of the Wind*. Library Video. VHS Videocassette, 101 min. ($14.95)

Kinsman, Clare D., ed. *Contemporary Authors*. Vols. 17–20. Gale, 1976, pp. 335–36.

Kunitz, Stanley J., and Howard Haycraft, eds. *The Junior Book of Authors*. Wilson, 1951, pp. 156–57.

Miller, Bertha M., and Elinor Field, eds. *Newbery Medal Books: 1922–1955 with the Author's Acceptance Papers and Related Material*. Horn Book, 1955, pp. 318–34.

Nakamura, Joyce, ed. *Something About the Author: Autobiographical Series*. Vol. 7. Gale, 1989, pp. 91–108.

"Newbery Medal Acceptance Material, 1950." *Horn Book* 26 (January/February 1950): 9–24.

Olendorf, Donna, ed. *Something About the Author*. Vol. 67. Gale, 1992, p. 92.

Peterson, Linda K., and Marilyn L. Solt, eds. *Newbery and Caldecott Medal and Honor Books: 1922–1981*. Hall, 1982, p. 108.

Senick, Gerard J., ed. *Children's Literature Review*. Vol. 4. Gale, 1982, pp. 104–16.

Silvey, Anita. ed. *Children's Books and Their Creators*. Houghton, 1995, pp. 304–5.

Ward, Martha, ed. *Authors of Books for Young People*. 3d ed. Scarecrow, 1990, p. 324.

Honor Books 1949

Bontemps, Arna. *The Story of the Negro*. Knopf, 1948, o.p. (Grades 5–8)

This personalized, informal history of African Americans was revised and updated several times until its fifth edition, which extends the coverage to the late 1960s. This account begins with the early history of blacks in Africa and tells of the important civilizations of Ghana, Songhay, and Mandingo. It tells of the expulsion of the Moors from Spain and their return to Africa, where they created the impressive city of Timbuctoo, a center of learning that contained a magnificent library. The dark days of slavery and the horrifying conditions on slave ships are poignantly re-created with graphic descriptions of the French-controlled slave plantations in Haiti and the successful revolt of Toussaint L'Ouverture much later.

Slavery in the United States is traced with emphasis on such leaders as Frederick Douglass, Phillis Wheatney, Nat Turner, Harriet Tubman, and other leaders of the emancipation movement. The Civil War, Jim Crowism, and the importance of such leaders as W. E. B. DuBois and Booker T. Washington are discussed. For coverage in the twentieth century, the author includes material on black artists like Paul Robeson, the Montgomery bus boycott involving Rosa Parks, and the emergence of a new type of leadership personified by Martin Luther King, Jr. As an appendix, there is a 20-page chronology that traces important events in black history from before Christ to the 1960s.

Gannett, Ruth Stiles. *My Father's Dragon*. Random, 1986, $14.95: 0-394-88460-4. (Grades 2–4)

This comic fantasy, which ushered in a series that includes *Elmer in the Dragon* (pap., Knopf, $3.99), relies on absurd situations and fast action for its continued popularity. Young Elmer Elevator, the author's father, is told by a alley cat about a baby winged dragon who is held captive on Wild Island and forced to act as a flying ferry across a river there. Resolving to free the dragon, Elmer stows away on a ship bound for neighboring Tangerina Island. There, using a bridge of stones that connects the islands, Elmer is able to reach Wild Island, but before he is able to rescue the dragon, he encounters a series of wild animals each wishing to dispose of young Elmer. However, one by one, he is able to pacify them. For example, a savage rhinoceros is placated when Elmer shows him how to keep his tusk clean by using toothpaste and a brush. At last, he is able to free the dragon and together they fly off to Tangerina Island before going home. The book contains maps of both islands and a number of humorous illustrations by Ruth Christman Gannett.

Holling, Holling C. *Seabird*. Houghton, 1973, $18.00: 0-395-18230-1; pap., $7.70: 0-395-18230-1. (Grades 4–6)

This story of four generations of the seafaring Brown family of New Bedford is also a history of American shipping from 1832 to the middle of the twentieth century. It is unified by the presence of a carved talisman, Seabird, that remains through the story as the good luck charm of the Brown family. In 1832, 14-year-old Ezra Brown is the ship's boy on a whaler that is miraculously saved from crashing into an iceberg by following the flight pattern of a seagull. To commemorate this occasion, he carves a gull using two walrus tusks as wings joined together by pieces of amber and coral. Much later, when Brown's son, 10-year-old Nate, is serving as his cabin boy, Nate saves Seabird when the statue is thrown overboard by a vindictive bos'n. Nate later becomes, like his father, the captain of a clipper ship. His son, James, prefers working with machinery and becomes an important designer of steamships. His son, Ken, becomes a pilot with a new form of transportation, the airplane. The book ends with the great-grandson of Ezra soaring through the clouds accompanied by the family mascot, Seabird. This oversized book is filled with many stunning full-page illustrations by the author plus many small detailed drawings that border the pages.

Rankin, Louise. *Daughter of the Mountains*. Puffin, 1993, pap., $4.99: 0-14-036335-1. (Grades 4–6)

Set in Tibet and India during the mid-twentieth century, this novel re-creates the color and atmosphere of the these exotic locales. The narrative is enhanced by the black-and-white drawings of Kurt Wiese. More than anything in the world, 10-year-old Momo, a Tibetan girl whose mother owns a teahouse, longs to have a red-gold Lhasa terrier as her pet. She is overjoyed when passing mule train leader gives her an orphaned puppy of this breed whom she names Pempa. However, in time another trader on his way to India steals Momo's beloved dog. With great courage and no money, the young girl sets out to find the thief and retrieve her dog. Through the kindness of many people and after many adventures, she makes her way to Calcutta, where she learns that Pempa has been bought by an English couple, Sir Hugh and Lady Paton. After listening to her story, the Patons generously return the dog to Momo, while also assuring her a safe journey home and providing a new and better job for Momo's father as a caretaker of a building along the Great Trade Route.

1950s

de Angeli, Marguerite. *The Door in the Wall*. Illustrated by the author. Doubleday, 1949, $16.95: 0-385-07283-X; pap., Dell, $4.50: 0-440-22779-8. (Grades 3–6)

Marguerite de Angeli (1889–1987) was originally intent on a career as an opera singer until she chose married life, and happily for her admirers turned her attention to her other interests, drawing and writing. During her life, she wrote and illustrated more than 20 books for young readers. Although many of her stories are set in the past, their central themes and conflicts surround universal childhood problems and concerns. For example, *Thee, Hannah!* (Doubleday, 1970, $14.95) tells of a nine-year-old Quaker girl growing up in Philadelphia before the Civil War, who rebels, in a gentle, innocent way, against wearing the drab, plain clothing of the Quakers. The Viking story, *Black Fox of Lorne* (p. 209), was a Newbery Honor Book in 1957.

The Door in the Wall, the poignant historical novel set in the England of Edward III, tells how a crippled boy who is haunted by fear not only grows to accept his handicap but actually triumphs over it. The central character, Robin, was inspired by a handicapped neighbor of the de Angelis who, in spite of the paralysis that had crippled him at age 10, became an accomplished musician, teacher, and cabinetmaker. The story of how he found his own private "door in the wall," meaning an adjustment to his problems that allowed him to triumph over them, inspired de Angeli to write about Robin and his journey from anger and rebellion to acceptance. The book is touchingly illustrated by the author.

Plot Summary

As plague rages through the city of London in the thirteenth century, 10-year-old Robin, son of Sir John de Bureford and Lady Maud, prepares to leave his home. It is the custom for boys of his age and station to prepare for knighthood in the household of another knight. He will learn to be of service to his liege lord, to be courteous, gentle, and strong of heart.

Robin's father, Sir John, has already left the castle to fight in the Scottish wars. His mother, too, must leave before John-the-Fletcher comes to escort young Robin to the household of Sir Peter de Lindsay. Lady Maud has been called to serve as lady-in-waiting to the Queen. She leaves Robin in the care of trusted servants until his own escort arrives.

The day after his mother departs, Robin falls ill. Although it is not the plague, his legs are affected and he cannot walk. When Dame Ellen, who is to care for him, comes down with the dreaded plague, Brother Luke arrives to take the boy to the monastery of St. Mark's where they will watch over him and send a letter to his father telling him what has happened. As they set out on their journey, Brother Luke asks the boy if there is a door in the wall that surrounds his father's garden. When Robin replies that there is, the friar says, "Always remember that. Thou hast only to follow the wall far enough and there will be a door in it." Robin is puzzled by his words.

At St. Mark's, Robin is well cared for, although he is not always an agreeable patient. Frustrated and often impatient, he sometimes lashes out at those who would help him, but the friars are patient and kind. In time, Robin is instructed in the art of carving figures and objects from wood, at which he becomes quite proficient. Seeing another boy whose wounded legs require him to use crutches, Robin helps one of the friars to fashion a pair of crutches for himself and is thus able to move about with far more ease.

By the end of summer, the plague is dying out and a letter is received from Robin's father. He is shocked by the news of his son's plight and asks that Robin, in the care of Brother Luke and John-go-in-the-Wynd, be taken to the castle of Sir Peter de Lindsay, where he was to have been tutored in knighthood duties. Sir John cannot come for the boy now because he is still engaged in war, and Lady Maud is not able to leave the service of the ailing Queen.

The three start out on their journey, which will take them through Oxford, with Robin alternately walking on his crutches and riding in the saddle. At one point, they miss a fork in the road and are obliged to spend the night in the open. Luke finds an old rotted tree trunk that will shelter the boy from the elements and there he spends a relatively comfortable night.

The next night of their journey, the three find themselves at a rundown inn near the edge of Heathcot. Although they do not like the looks of the two ruffians sitting about the fire, they have no choice but to take lodging. Robin is very tired from their journey, but he awakens in the night to the loud voices of the ruffians and realizes that they are plotting to rob his companions of their money. He awakens them and the three are able to steal away.

At last the trio arrives in Oxford where a country fair is in progress. Robin begs to be allowed to watch the festivities for a time. He is especially fascinated with the Punch and Judy show.

On the road once more, they stop for a night with a friendly woodcutter and his wife before embarking on the last leg of their journey. Finally, they see the castle of Sir Peter de Lindsay before them.

Sir Peter, still recovering from war wounds, his wife, and children welcome Robin and his companions. When Robin tells Sir Peter that he will never become a knight in this condition, the knight says, "Each of us has his place in the world. If we cannot serve in one way, there is always another. If we do what we are able, a door always opens to something else." Once again, Robin is puzzled by the reference to a door.

Once the newcomers are settled, Robin begins instructions for his duties as page. These include shooting lessons, Latin study, and overseeing others in attending to the lady of the household. Time passes and by late October, Robin has grown strong despite his useless legs. His arms are sturdy from swimming lessons and Brother Luke compliments him on his lively mind and good wit.

As winter approaches, fog envelops the castle each day, making it difficult for watchmen to be on guard against enemies. The castle of Sir Peter is in danger of attack at any time from the Welsh, who have long wanted this strong fortification. It appears that they may succeed, for one morning the Welsh attack and take the town outside the castle. Robin does not see how anyone could storm such a impenetrable fortress. He is told that the castle inhabitants can be starved out. Indeed, that danger appears likely when the water supply from a well becomes dangerously low.

Someone must go for help to the castle of Sir Hugh Fitzhugh, cousin to Sir Peter. But who can be spared? All the watchmen are needed at their posts.

Robin volunteers. He will dress as a poor shepherd. If he is stopped, no one will think anything of his errand. But how will he cross the river? Robin declares that he is strong enough to swim across.

The boy is allowed to leave on his dangerous journey. With great difficulty in the biting cold, he is able to navigate the treacherous river with his crutches strapped to his back. And when an enemy guard stops him on the other side, Robin pretends to be a poor shepherd boy. The guard warms him by the fire and sends him on his way.

Robin finds the cottage of John-go-in-the-Wynd's mother. John has been visiting the old woman. Now he bids Robin to rest while he travels the rest of the way for help. When John returns, he tells the boy that he has given the message to Sir Hugh and help is on the way to the Lindsay castle.

The castle is freed and young Robin is acclaimed a hero for his bravery. But an even happier moment occurs when word comes that the Scottish wars have ended. On Christmas Eve, Robin is keeping watch from the castle tower when he sees a company of knights and men-at-arms heading toward the castle. Robin sees his father, Sir John, and the King and Queen, too. Surely, Lady Maud must be in the company as well!

Although he is nervous at first about how his parents will view him with his crutches, Robin's fears vanish at their warm and loving greeting. Nothing is said of his crutches or useless legs.

Soon Robin learns that he is to have an audience with the King. His pride swells when the King spreads a jeweled collar onto Robin's shoulders and praises his courage. "You are a true son of a noble father," says the King. "Though but a youth, you have shown courage a man might be proud to call his own."

Even with all his happiness, Robin must ask his father an honest question. "Mind you not that I must go thus, bent over, with these crutches to help me walk?"

His father replies that the boy's courage, craftsmanship, and spirit shine so brightly that he cannot see whether his legs are misshapen or not. And his mother declares that it is a comfort to know that wars will never take him. Now that the plague and wars are over and the Queen is well, they will all return to their home in London and Brother Luke will accompany them to become Robin's tutor.

When Robin wakes from sleep at dawn after all the excitement, he asks Brother Luke in bewilderment what has happened. The friar replies that it is Christmas and Sir Robin has found the door in the wall.

Themes and Subjects

This historical tale set in thirteenth-century England is based on a childhood experience of the author. "When you come to a stone wall, if you look far enough, you will find a door in it." The drama and pageantry of medieval life are portrayed well, as are the cares and feelings of the common folk of the day. Robin's disability is realistically and unsentimentally presented as is his gradual growth from an uncooperative child to a courageous and imaginative young man. This is a fine, lively presentation of medieval European life that conveys the theme that everyone has a place in the world and is able to contribute his or her own special talents in some way. It also points out that some children must learn to live with a disability and that with encouragement and reassurance, they can find their own rewarding place in the world.

Incidents for Booktalking

So many passages in this dramatic tale give a warm, realistic flavor of life in thirteenth-century England. Use any of the following for a discussion of life in those ancient times: Robin antagonizes Dame Ellen who comes to care for him in the castle (pp. 9–12); Brother Luke interests Robin in carving (pp. 20–22); Robin is angry at the crippled boy (pp. 23–24); Robin learns to swim (pp. 36–37); the three spend a night in an inn and are nearly robbed (pp. 52–57); they reach the castle of Sir Peter (pp. 64–70); Robin volunteers for a dangerous mission to save the castle (pp. 84–96).

Related Titles

Set in Elizabethan England, Beth Hilgartner's *A Murder for Her Majesty* (Houghton, 1986, $13.95: 0-395-4151-2; pap., $5.95: 0-395-61619-0) tells how a young girl must disguise herself as a boy to escape her father's murderers.

A young mute named Dummy is an abused servant on a farm near Sherwood Forest before he joins Robin Hood's band and discovers his true identity in *Robin's Country* (Knopf, 1995, $13.00: 0-679-84-332-9) by Monica Furlong.

In Paul Fleischman's *The Half-a-Moon Inn* (Harper, 1980, $14.89: 0-06-021918-1), the mute boy falls into the clutches of an evil crone, Miss Grackle.

A robber's daughter meets Birk, son of her father's rival, in Astrid Lindgren's *Ronia, the Robber's Daughter* (pap., Puffin, $3.95: 0-14-031720-7), a novel set in the Middle Ages.

Lubrin Dhu defends his clan against the invading Romans in Rosemary Sutcliff's *Sun Horse, Moon Horse* (Dutton, 1978, $9.95: 0-525-40495-3), a story that takes place in ancient Britain.

About the Book and Author

Block, Ann, and Carolyn Riley, eds. *Children's Literary Review*. Vol. 1. Gale, 1976, pp. 52–54.

Brown, Muriel W., and Rita Schoch Foudray. *Newbery & Caldecott Medalists and Honor Book Winners: Bibliographic & Resource Material Through 1990*. 2d ed. Neal-Schuman, 1992, pp. 96–98.

Cech, John, ed. "American Writers for Children, 1900–1960." In *Dictionary of Literary Biography*. Vol. 22. Gale, 1983, pp. 110–25.

Chevalier, Tracy, ed. *Twentieth-Century Children's Writers*. 3d ed. St. James, 1989, pp. 271–72.

Commire, Anne, ed. *Something About the Author*. Gale, 1971, Vol. 1, pp. 76–77; 1982, Vol. 27, pp. 61–73.

de Angeli, Marguerite. *Butter at the Old Price: The Autobiography of Marguerite de Angeli*. Doubleday, 1971.

———. *Door in the Wall*. Read by Roger Rees. BDD Audio Publishing, 1998. Audiocassettes, 180 min. ($16.99)

Evory, Ann, and Linda Metzger, eds. *Contemporary Authors (New Revision Series)*. Vol. 3. Gale, 1981, p. 160.

Hedblad, Alan. ed. *Something About the Author*. Vol. 100. Gale, 1999, pp. 74–77.

Helbig, Althea K., and Agnes R. Perkins, eds. *Dictionary of American Children's Fiction, 1859–1959*. Greenwood, 1986, pp. 126–27 (bio.), p. 134 (book).

Hopkins, Lee Bennett, ed. *More Books by More People*. Citation Press, 1974, pp. 115–19.

Kunitz, Stanley J., and Howard Haycraft, eds. *The Junior Book of Authors*. Wilson, 1951, pp. 96–97.

Mahoney, Bertha E. *Illustrators of Children's Books, 1944–1945*. Horn Book, 1947, p. 298.

Marguerite de Angeli. Profiles in Literature, 1976. Videocassette.

Miller, Bertha M., and Elinor Field, eds. *Newbery Medal Books: 1922–1955 with the Author's Acceptance Papers and Related Material*. Horn Book, 1955, pp. 335–53.

Peterson, Linda K., and Marilyn L. Solt, eds. *Newbery and Caldecott Medal and Honor Books: 1922–1981*. Hall, 1982, p. 111.

Silvey, Anita. ed. *Children's Books and Their Creators*. Houghton, 1995, pp. 190–91.

Ward, Martha, ed. *Authors of Books for Young People*. 3d ed. Scarecrow, 1990, p. 175.

Honor Books 1950

Caudill, Rebecca. *Tree of Freedom*. Illustrated by Dorothy Morse. Viking, 1949, o.p. (Grades 6–9)

This pioneer story, told from the viewpoint of 13-year-old Stephanie Venable, takes place in 1780 close to Harrod's Fort in Kentucky, then still part of the colony of Virginia. The Venable family, Jonathan, Bertha, and their five children, travel from North Carolina by foot to homestead on Jonathan's 400-acre plot of land. Stephanie and her older brother, 16-year-old Noel, help their parents build a cabin, plant a small crop, and begin a modest farm with the animals they brought—a cow and some pigs and chickens. Stephanie is particularly proud of the little apple tree she calls her tree of freedom that she is growing from a seed brought with her. Without any close neighbors except the peculiar Lonesome Tilly and still fearful of Indian attacks, the family feels isolated and uses their inner resources to remain strong and united. They are devastated to learn that there is a rival claim on their land made by a man who is a British sympathizer. The Revolutionary War reaches the frontier and changes their lives when, at the instigation of the British, Indians increase their raids and Jonathan becomes a courier to Governor Jefferson in Williamstown. Noel crosses the Ohio and joins Colonel George Rogers Clark on an expedition against the Indians that leads to a victory at Chillicothe. Left alone with the children, Stephanie and her mother continue to improve their simple home by such activities as chinking the complete cabin against the oncoming winter. Father and son return, Noel with news that the rival claim is unfounded and Jonathan with enough money to buy another 1,000 acres. With a bright future assured, Stephanie and Noel plan on returning east to continue their schooling.

Coblentz, Catherine Cate. *The Blue Cat of Castle Town*. Illustrated by Janice Holland. Longmans, 1949, o.p. (Grades 4–7)

This fantasy, told in the form of a legend, is supposedly based on true happenings in Castle Town, Vermont, where the blue kitten who learns the river's song about idealistic beauty teaches this to the various inhabitants of the town so each "can sing one's own song" and the cat can find a permanent home. He teaches the song to the town's many craftsmen and they soon incorporate grace and elegance in their creations. Ebenezer Southmayd, the pewterer, learns the song, and creates an outstanding teapot before his death. John Gilroy shows what he has learned from the cat in weaving twin tablecloths of great loveliness that use scenes of the town in the design, making the most out of linen rather than ordinary wool. Thomas Royal Dake learns the song and uses his savings and his skill to design and build a church pulpit that is considered the finest in the state. The cat narrowly escapes being killed by Arunah Hyde who objects to this emphasis on quality and workmanship and prefers to make money from shabby products. Zerual Guernsey, a lonely, unattractive girl who has been saddened by her mother's death also hears the kitten's song. Inspired by the song's beauty, Guernsey creates an amazing carpet so beautiful that it is chosen to hang in the New York's Metropolitan Museum of Art. Incorporated into the design is the figure of the little blue cat, who at last has found a permanent home.

Foster, Genevieve. *George Washington*. Illustrated by the author. Scribner, 1949, o.p. (Grades 3–5)

Described as "An Initial Biography," this easily read account uses short sentences and a simple vocabulary to cover the salient events in Washington's life. Growing up on a tobacco plantation in Virginia, young George was influenced by his elder half-brother, Lawrence. As a teenager, he went to live with Lawrence at his home, Mount Vernon, named after the admiral under whom Lawrence served. George mastered the skill of surveying and became a junior member of the party that mapped a wilderness tract of land west of the Blue Ridge Mountains for Lord Fairfax. As a major in the army, George distinguished himself in the French and Indian War, and after his return married the widowed Martha Custis and settled at Mount Vernon. Along with other members of the Virginia House of Burgesses like Patrick Henry, he objected to the unfair taxes that George III was levying on the Colonies. An official delegate at the First Continental Congress, Washington later became the leader of the Virginia forces. After the Second Continental Congress, Washington became commander in chief of the entire army of the revolutionaries. After eight years of war during which he led his troops to final victory, he was anxious to return to Mount Vernon and resume his farmer's life. However, once again, he was asked to serve his country and became its first president. He was inaugurated in New York City on April 30, 1789, and served two terms, the last spent mired in controversy about America's relations with revolutionary France. Turning the office over to his successor, John Adams, he returned to Mount Vernon where he died in December 1799. Though simply written, this account includes recent findings about Washington and omits the stories that lack authenticity. The author's illustrations include a floor plan of Mount Vernon.

Havighurst, Walter, and Marion Havighurst. *Song of the Pines*. Illustrated by Richard Floethe. Winston, 1949, o.p. (Grades 6–9)

The "Land of the Free" series of historical novels celebrates the contributions of various immigrant groups to American life. This story deals with the role of Norwegians in Wisconsin's lumbering industry during the mid-nineteenth century. In Norway, Nils Thorsen, 15 and orphaned, hears about the many opportunities awaiting new immigrants in America from Cleng Peerson, a pioneer who has returned temporarily after great successes in the New World. Fired with enthusiasm, Nils, a trained knife-sharpener, stows away on a ship but is discovered. However, when he prevents a serious boating accident, as a reward he is given passage in exchange for work. On board, he becomes friendly with Mr. and Mrs. Svendsen and their three children, Kisten,15, Helvor, 11, and Lisa, 5. After docking in New York City, he accompanies the Svendsens to the Koshkonong Lake area of southern Wisconsin. Nils helps them substantiate their land claim and defeat an unfriendly neighbor, Aaron Finch. After the Svendsens are secure in their new log cabin, Nils takes his grindstone and heads into lumbering country where he sees men handling logs awkwardly with crowbars. Remembering that loggers use cant hooks back in Norway, he fashions one for their use. He soon has a large demand for them and forms a successful business with Luke Sampson, a blacksmith. On his way back to the Svendsens in the spring, Nils visits Cleng Peerson, finding that Peerson has Lisa Svendsen is his custody. After being taken by Indians, Lisa had been turned over to Peerson by Red Otter, an Indian brave, to repay a kindness that Mrs. Svendsen had shown him. When they reach the Svendsen cabin, there is a great celebration made even happier by the news that a set of grandparents will soon arrive from Norway.

Montgomery, Rutherford. *Kildee House*. Illustrated by Barbara Cooney. Doubleday, 1949, o.p. (Grades 3–6)

> This novel, set in a redwood forest on a mountain in northern California, features a quiet, shy bachelor, Jerome Kildee, some interesting neighbors, and a number of fascinating animals. When former stonemason Jerome retires to his 100 acres in the forest, he builds a small house with a giant redwood serving as the back wall. Soon he begins sharing his humble dwelling with a number of animals including a family of spotted skunks under the floor, and in the tree above, a raccoon he calls Old Grouch who has just brought home a new mate. In a short period of time, more offspring arrive and soon Jerome has more than 50 young animals living with and around him. He meets the nearby Eppy family and becomes friendly with one of their children Emma Lou, a hotheaded, independent girl who dislikes Donald Roger Cabot because his dog hunts Jerome's animals and has already caused the death of Old Grouch's new bride. This resentment changes when Donald helps Emma Lou care for a fawn Jerome has rescued and also gives Jerome a helping hand with his household chores. Soon the two youngsters become friends. Jerome and Emma Lou become so alarmed at the rapid rise of the animal population around Kildee House that they stop and calculate the number of animals that will be around in the future if the population growth goes unchecked. It is staggering. Something must be done. Donald suggests that good homes be found for some of them. They begin an advertising campaign, and soon zoos and large estates answer with offers of help. In no time, things are back to normal, and Jerome can again enjoy his retirement.

❀ Newbery Winner 1951

Yates, Elizabeth. *Amos Fortune, Free Man*. Illustrated by Nora S. Unwin. Dutton, 1950, $15.00: 0-525-25570-2. (Grades 5–8)

> From an early age, Elizabeth Yates (1905–) had always wanted to be a writer. Her most productive years, however, came after her marriage and a 10-year stay in England with her businessman husband. When they returned to the United States because of her husband's failing eyesight, they bought a little old farmhouse in Peterborough, New Hampshire. In the nearby town of Jaffrey Center, she attended a lecture sponsored by the Amos Fortune Forum and soon became curious about the life of this former slave who had inspired such admiration. In the local churchyard she found the grave of Amos Fortune and of his wife Violet. His gravestone reads: "Sacred to the memory of Amos Fortune who was born free in Africa, a slave in America, he purchased liberty, professed Christianity, lived reputable and died hopefully Nov. 17, 1801." Her curiosity piqued, she began her research on this amazing man's life in Jaffrey Town History, where she found ample material on the last 20 years of his life but little on his earlier life. This began a search through town histories, vital statistics, and early books and records to try to reconstruct his complete life. In her Newbery acceptance speech, she said of the slave trade that although some of the Africans who were captured

by the traders were "princes and poets, men and women who had attained distinction by birth or their own prowess, they were all subjected to the same grim journey, the same inhuman treatment, and they were all sold on the wharves of our coastal cities." Later, in an interview, she said of Amos Fortune, "His life was a life of freedom, once gained, well lived, of self-reliance and great faith."

Plot Summary

This is a story based on the life of a man who was born a prince in Africa, became a slave in Boston, and died a free man in New Hampshire. It is also the story of the mark his life made on, and the respect he won from, the small community of Jaffrey, where he died in 1801.

In the equatorial forest of Africa in 1725, people in the village of At-mun-shi prepare for their dance to welcome the planting of corn. Fifteen-year-old At-mun, son of the chief, dances gracefully before his people. Suddenly, slavers descend upon the village, and At-mun is clapped into irons and led away. He sees his sister, Ath-mun, with arms outstretched as he leaves.

The journey to the slave ship is long and dreadful. Eventually, 350 black people are captured and put aboard the *White Falcon* for the horrid, cramped, frightening journey by sea to the port of Boston in the New World. The slaves are chained so tightly together in the hold that they must sleep spoon fashion, and they receive no food if they misbehave in any way. At-mun is aware that he has said goodbye to his native land for the last time.

The terrible voyage takes two torturous months. The harsh treatment and scarce food cause the young man to remember less and less of his life as a prince of the village. "I am a king," he repeats over and over. "I am At-mun."

The first port in the New World is in the Carolinas, where a third of the slaves are deposited. Then the ship sails north along the coast, arriving in Boston in July 1725. For the first time in months, At-mun's chains are removed and he is given a pair of trousers. He is sold at auction to a Quaker named Caleb Copeland, who names him Amos.

Copeland's Quaker wife is aghast when he returns home with a slave boy, because Quakers are against slavery. Her husband explains that he bought him because he knew he would be treated kindly in their home. They agree that in time he will be given his freedom.

In the Copeland household, Amos learns to read and write, to tend the children, and to do chores about the house. He lives in the Copeland house for 15 years, until he is grown. Whenever Copeland speaks to him of freedom, Amos says he does not yet want it. Copeland is a protector to the young man, who is not yet ready to part with the family.

Unfortunately, Caleb Copeland dies before he can give Amos his certificate of freedom, so he is sold along with the Copeland's other belongings, even though Copeland's wife does not want that to happen. Ichabod Richardson, a tanner in Woburn, purchases Amos.

Richardson is a stern but good man who tells his wife that he will give Amos his freedom in time, after he earns what had been paid for him. In 1763, Richardson and Amos make a bargain that he will be freed in 1769. In May 1769, after Richardson's death, his wife honors the agreement, and Amos becomes a free man.

Amos builds a homestead in Woburn and establishes a tanning and carpentry trade. In 1775, he buys the slave Lily, thereby freeing her, and she becomes his wife. Although Lily dies within the year, she does so as a free woman.

Later, Amos sees another slave girl named Lydia, who walks only with the aid of a crutch. He remembers that his sister in far-off Africa had been lame, too. After saving for three years, Amos buys Lydia. Like Lily before her, Lydia dies soon after she is free.

Taking the name of Amos Fortune, he journeys to New Hampshire in 1779. He settles first in the town of Keene and late in the year, he marries once more, this time to the former slave Violet. He is also able to free her young daughter Celyndia. Later, Amos sets up his tanning operations in the town of Jaffrey. At first he is not welcome. But with hard work, Amos is able to build up his tanning business and adds more room to the family's cabin. People who come to deliver hides to Amos often linger to talk to him.

Amos's work week stretches from Monday to Saturday, taking off only on Sunday for church and rest. Eight years after his arrival in Jaffrey, Amos becomes a member of the church he attends so faithfully. It is a great day for him. "What a pity he isn't white," one of the elders comments, "he could do so much for the church."

Amos is happy in Jaffrey, but he longs for a piece of land he can call his own. But every time he has saved the money, it always seems as though someone else is in need of it. Finally, when he seems about to give the money he has saved to a needy family, his wife hides the money, saying that he has earned the right to land for himself and his family. Amos goes up on the mountain to seek the answer to his problem. When he comes down, he tells Violet that he is going to buy the land. So, in 1789, now 80 years old, Amos Fortune becomes a landowner.

Citizen Amos Fortune also becomes a respected member of the Jaffrey community. At his death in 1801, he leaves his savings of $243 to the town for the education of its sons and daughters. He also requests that a silver communion service be bought for the church, which continues in use for many years.

Two handsome headstones, honoring Amos Fortune and his wife Violet, stand in the churchyard in Jaffrey, New Hampshire.

Themes and Subjects

This is a vividly told and dramatic re-creation of the life of a man who lived simply and with honor. The stark horrors of slavery are contrasted with the simple goodness of the slave and with the kindness and care shown by some of his captors. The author presents a moving story that reminds the reader of the worth of good people who live their days with affection and deep love for others. Amos Fortune emerges as a noble man with the love of freedom deeply etched in his soul. The dignity of the human spirit is well portrayed. This is a life not soon forgotten.

Incidents for Booktalking

The scenes of slavery are vividly portrayed and serve as a stark introduction to the life of this good man. See: At-mun is taken from his African home (pp. 7–13); the terrible journey to the New World (pp. 22–29); Amos is sold (pp. 30–33); Amos sees his reflection in a mirror for the first time (pp. 63–64); Amos gains his freedom (pp. 66–68).

Related Titles

In simple, moving prose, the Jamaican-born poet James Berry tells how in 1807, Ajeemah and his son Atu are kidnapped by slave traders and are sold separately to neighboring plantations in Jamaica, in *Ajeemah and His Son* (Harper, 1991, $13.95: 0-06-021044-3).

Harriette Gillam Robinet's *If You Please, President Lincoln* (Atheneum, 1995, $15.00: 0-689-31939-X) tells of a nightmarish trip in 1863 of 14-year-old Moses to a Haitian island.

The African Mask (Clarion, 1994, $15.00: 0-395-67295-3) by Janet E. Rupert is set 900 years ago in the Nigerian city of Ife and tells about Layo, a girl who loves making pottery and of the arranged marriage that changed her life.

Ann Cameron's version of *The Kidnapped Prince: The Life of Olaudah Equiano* (Knopf, 1995, $16.00: 0-679-85619-6) is a shortened, modernized version of the agonizing autobiography of a young African prince who was made a slave at age 11 and spent another 11 years as a slave in England and America.

Suzanne Jurmain's *Freedom's Sons: The True Story of the Amistad Mutiny* (Lothrop, 1998, $15.00: 0-688-11072-X) re-creates this fascinating chapter in American history with special focus on the nobility of Cinque and his men.

About the Book and Author

Amos Fortune. SRA, n.d. Videocassette.

Berger, Laura Standley, ed. *Twentieth-Century Young Adult Writers*. 4th ed. St. James, 1994, pp. 721–23.

Brown, Muriel W., and Rita Schoch Foudray. *Newbery and Caldecott Medalists and Honor Book Winners: Bibliographic & Resource Material Through 1990*. 2d ed. Neal-Schuman, 1992, pp. 463–65.

Chevalier, Tracy, ed. *Twentieth-Century Children's Writers*. 3d ed. St. James, 1989, pp. 1072–74.

Commire, Anne, ed. *Something About the Author*. Vol. 4. Gale, 1973, pp. 235–37.

Ethridge, James M., and Barbara Kopala, eds. *Contemporary Authors*. Vols. 1–4. Gale, 1967, pp. 1032–33.

Evory, Ann, ed. *Contemporary Authors First Revision Series*. Vol. 6. Gale, 1986, p. 570.

Helbig, Althea K., and Agnes R. Perkins, eds. *Dictionary of American Children's Fiction, 1859–1959*. Greenwood, 1986, pp. 583–84.

Hopkins, Lee Bennett, ed. *More Books by More People*. Citation Press, 1974, pp. 236–38.

Kunitz, Stanley J., and Howard Haycraft, eds. *The Junior Book of Authors*. Wilson, 1951, pp. 303–05.

Miller, Bertha M., and Elinor Field, eds. *Newbery Medal Books: 1922–1955 with the Author's Acceptance Papers and Related Material*. Horn Book, 1955, pp. 353–71.

Nakamura, Joyce, ed. *Something About the Author: Autobiographical Series*. Vol. 6. Gale, 1988, pp. 279–96.

"Newbery Medal Acceptance Material, 1951." *Horn Book* 27, no. 4 (July/August 1951): 262–78.

Olendorf, Donna, ed. *Something About the Author*. Vol. 68. Gale, 1992, pp. 236–38.

Peterson, Linda K., and Marilyn L. Solt, eds. *Newbery and Caldecott Medal and Honor Books: 1922–1981*. Hall, 1982, pp. 114–15.

Silvey, Anita. ed. *Children's Books and Their Creators*. Houghton, 1995, p. 699.

Ward, Martha, ed. *Authors of Books for Young People*. 3d ed. Scarecrow, 1990, p. 771.

Yates, Elizabeth. *My Diary; My World*. Westminster, 1981.

———. *My Widening World*. Westminster, 1983.

———. *One Writer's Way*. Westminster, 1984.

Honor Books 1951

Eaton, Jeanette. *Gandhi: Fighter Without a Sword*. Illustrated by Ralph Ray. Morrow, 1950, o.p. (Grades 7–10)

This is the life story of the great gentle Mohandas K. Gandhi of India, who was known to his people as Mahatma, or "Great Soul." It begins in a small town in western India, where Gandhi was attending school. He had already been married, by arrangement, for two years to Kasturbai. Even as a youngster he wondered why the foreign British should be occupying his land. The account covers his college days in England and his 21 years in South Africa where he first became the champion of thousands of downtrodden Indian workers.

After moving to India he led the famous political, nonviolent movement to end foreign oppression, and bring self-government and democracy to India. Though he gained world recognition, he lived a spartan life, existing on the most frugal diet and wearing only peasant clothes he wove himself. The book is filled with wonderful anecdotes about this heroic man. For example, he once appeared before the King of England clad only in his famous cotton robe and loin cloth. When questioned by an embarrassed friend about the appropriateness of this clothing, he replied that it was proper because the king wore enough clothes for two. He tried unsuccessfully to unite the warring factions of Hindus and Moslems and was keenly disappointed when his country was partitioned into two states,

India and Pakistan, at the time of the British exodus. When he was assassinated in 1948 by a Hindu extremist, his physical possessions were a loincloth, worn sandals, and his spectacles, but as the author states, "No one ever bestowed such gifts. He had brought freedom to a great people and had shown humanity the path to brotherhood and peace."

Hunt, Mabel Leigh. *Better Known As Johnny Appleseed*. Illustrated by James Daughtery. Lippincott, 1950, o.p. (Grades 6–8)

Only a few facts are known about John Chapman (1774–1845), better known as Johnny Appleseed. He was born in Massachusetts, spent his youth there, and started west when he was 18. In Pennsylvania he worked as an orchardist and gave apple tree saplings to families traveling west. Later he journeyed into the Ohio area, sowing his own seeds as he went. For 40 years he roamed the Midwest, caring for his orchards and helping others to begin their own. He also carried with him medicinal herbs, religious pamphlets by Swedenborg, and a bagful of stories. With his peculiar dress, unusual religious persuasion, and strange habits and eccentricities, he became well-known in the region. In time he was considered a folk hero about whom many stories were told. The first part of this book covers the factual information of his early years. The second contains nine stories about him, each named after a variety of apple that he might have planted during his travels, like Fall Wine, Nonesuch, and Northern Spy.

In the second story, "Front Door," Johnny is carrying a dappled fawn that he has found snagged in a patch of creepers. He happens on a young mail carrier, Andrew McIlvain, and the two swap stories and become friends. Together they travel into town where everyone makes a fuss over the fawn and Andrew invites Johnny into his home to accept his hospitality. The third part of the book describes the last part of his work and his death. The animated, spirited illustrations of James Daugherty, along with a helpful map of Johnny's travels, add to the book's appeal.

Judson, Clara Ingram. *Abraham Lincoln, Friend of the People*. Illustrated by Robert Frankenberg. Follett, 1950, o.p. (Grades 5–8)

This fictionalized biography of Abraham Lincoln begins when he is a child in 1813 on his father's farm in Knob Creek, Kentucky, and ends at Ford's Theater on April 15, 1865, when he was assassinated by John Wilkes Booth. In addition to black-and-white illustrations, 14 color prints are interspersed throughout the text. These are taken from the massive dioramas of the Chicago Historical Society, which were completed in 1941 and made by the Works Progress Administration under the sponsorship of the Chicago Board of Education. The account covers the salient points in this great president's life including his early stint as a postmaster and rail splitter. After studying law he became prominent in Illinois state politics, and served for consecutive terms in the state legislature before moving to Springfield and marrying Mary Todd in 1842. He joined the Republican party in 1856, became an opponent of slavery, and opposed Douglas. He accepted the party's nomination for the senatorial race, with a speech that contains the prophetic words, "A house divided against itself cannot stand." His eventual election as president was a signal for the South to secede. Determined to preserve the Union at all costs, he ordered that Fort Sumter be fired on and the country was plunged into the Civil War. He issued his own Emancipation Proclamation and called for national unity and healing in his noble speech delivered at the soldier's cemetery at Gettysburg in 1863. He was considered a statesman of vision and humanity, a remarkable politician, a great storyteller, a skillful lawyer, a devoted husband and father, and a friend of the people.

Parrish, Anne. *The Story of Appleby Capple*. Illustrated by the author. Harper, 1950, o.p. (Grades 1–5)

This is a complex, clever alphabet book in which each of the chapters is devoted to a different letter, with an alliterative narrative to illustrate the sound. For example, the "B" chapter contains the sentence, "Aunt Bella's bulb is blooming and her bird in his bird cage bursts into song." The text is accompanied by many cartoon-like illustrations, many of which are full-page. As well as teaching the alphabet, there is a connecting story and a large cast of characters. Five-year-old Appleby Capple, Apple for short, is on his way to Aunt Bella's birthday party for Cousin Clement who will be 99. Cousin Clement loves painting butterflies, but because he has never seen or painted a zebra butterfly, Apple decides that this will be his uncle's birthday present. He gets lost and has a series of adventures that include being chased by a crocodile, finding an elephant that has escaped from a zoo, meeting a monkey named Jocko, and saving a caterpillar that spins a cocoon on the boy's coat. When his relatives and friends realize that Apple is lost, they set out to find him. Some of the people who participate in these escapades are absent-minded Uncle Francis, Mr. Perkins, the patient postman, and the Indian squaws Prickly Pear and Pinkfeather. During these episodes, Cousin Kate of the booming voice and great woolen wigs marries a birdwatcher named Mr. Rollo Roberts. The muddle ends happily when all are reunited and Apple makes an entrance riding his elephant. Great Uncle Thomas unexpectedly arrives from a voyage bringing with him gifts for all plus a Terrible Turk and a Smiling Sultan. As a bonus, out of the cocoon hatches a zebra butterfly for Cousin Clement.

Newbery Winner 1952

Estes, Eleanor. *Ginger Pye*. Illustrated by the author. Harcourt, 1951, $17.00: 0-15-230930-6; pap., $5.95: 0-15-634750-4. (Grades 3–6)

Eleanor Estes (1906–1988) grew up in West Haven, Connecticut, a small town, which under the name Canbury became the setting for many of her novels including *Ginger Pye*. Her first book, *The Moffats* (Harcourt, 1941, $14.95; pap., Dell, $3.25), was the first of a trilogy of well-loved books about the closely knit family of four children and their seamstress mother who share a series of everyday experiences that would be common to any family even today. The other two titles were both Newbery Honor Books. They are *The Middle Moffat* (see "Honor Books," 1943, p. 122) and *Rufus M.* (see "Honor Books," 1944, p. 127). Much later a fourth volume, *The Moffat Museum* (Harcourt, 1983, $10.95; pap., Dell, $3.25), was also published. In all four, the innocent and naive eventually triumph over the pompous and powerful. Another of her books, *The Hundred Dresses* (see "Honor Books," 1945, p. 135), was also named a Newbery Honor Book. In an interview she was quoted as saying that, in her books, she is "holding up a mirror and I hope that what is reflected in it is a true image of childhood." Her many fans would agree that she has succeeded admirably. In all of her books, the only character that actually existed in real life was her dog, Ginger, who in her story becomes the pet of the Pye family. Mrs. Estes said that, one day, she saw in one of the windows of her ivy-covered school the dog Ginger, who, because he had a pencil in his mouth, was given the nickname, "the intellectual dog."

Plot Summary

The Pyes are a happy, loving, somewhat unusual family living in the town of Cranbury, somewhere between Boston and New York City. There is Mr. Pye, a birdman, such an expert that he is often called to Washington, D.C., for consultation (generally without pay). There is Mrs. Pye, who married at age 17 after she met Mr. Pye on an escalator in New York City. There is Jared, known as Jerry, age 10, and his sister Rachel, age 9, who, even though they are related, are very close companions. Because Mrs. Pye is such a young mother, Jerry and Rachel have the youngest grandmother in Cranbury and the youngest uncle, three-year-old Bennie, who is Mrs. Pye's baby brother. And there is Gracie-the-Cat, who has been in the household longer than either Jerry or Rachel and is considered a full-fledged member of the family.

Two problems are currently confronting the younger Pyes. Jerry has seen the new puppies over in Speedy's barn and has picked out the smartest and best of them all. More than anything in the world, Jerry wants that puppy. Mrs. Speedy says she will let Jerry have the puppy for one dollar, which must be paid by six o'clock on Saturday because someone else is also anxious to have that particular dog. However, Jerry doesn't have a dollar, and neither does Rachel. That is one problem; the other is Gracie-the-Cat. Will she be upset with a dog as a new member of the family?

Jerry and Rachel rack their brains for a solution to the first problem, even playing their favorite nighttime game of "Boombernickles," but no solution comes to them. However, the very next day the problem is solved. With three-year-old Uncle Bennie in tow, Rachel and Jerry go to town, still trying to come up with ways to earn a dollar. Jerry's offers to wash windows or do odd jobs have been turned down. Then comes the miracle in the form of 15-year-old Sam Doody. He lives just down the block and is good-natured and very tall. He is captain of the high school basketball team. Sam tells Jerry he must go to buy a new suit that very day, which means he has not time for his usual job of dusting the church pews, for which he earns one dollar! Does Jerry want the job?

Jerry cannot believe it! With Rachel and Uncle Bennie's help, the church pews get dusted, even though it takes a very long time. They do finish before the deadline for picking up the puppy, however. Off they rush to Mrs. Speedy, where they claim the most adorable and smartest brown-and-white puppy in all the world.

As they leave Speedy's barn, Jerry thinks he sees someone in the shadows wearing a sort of yellow-mustard-colored hat. On the way home in the growing darkness, the children think they are being followed. Could it be the person who wanted this same puppy? When they reach home and tell their mother, the story doesn't sound so scary anymore, and they soon forget all about the man in the hat and delight instead in the new puppy, whom they name Ginger.

The second problem is solved when Gracie-the-Cat takes an instant liking to Ginger and tries to wash him.

Ginger Pye is a welcome addition to the Pye household and proves, indeed, to be the smartest puppy around. The only cloud on the happiness of the Pye children is the occasional sightings of the man in the hat, whom they begin to call the "unsavory character." Once when Jerry, Rachel, and friends are at the reservoir, they find a discarded hat that looks very much like the one worn by the stranger. They mark it but leave it where it is so that if they see anyone wearing it again, they will know who has been following them.

Who is this stranger and why is he so interested in Ginger Pye?

As time goes on, Ginger proves what a smart dog he is. He even tracks Jerry's scent to school one day and enchants the whole class, all except Wally Bullwinkle, the big boy in Jerry's class. Wally is strangely unfriendly, which puzzles Jerry.

Total sadness hits the Pye household on Thanksgiving day, when Ginger disappears. No amount of searching and calling and asking everyone in town—including Wally Bullwinkle—turns up Ginger Pye. In fact, when they go to Wally's house, he is almost hostile. Opening the door just a crack, he tells them he hasn't seen Ginger and that they had better get away because he has a ferocious dog in the house, so they better not come knocking anymore.

Jerry and Rachel are inconsolable over the loss of Ginger. Weeks turn into months with still no sign of their beloved puppy. Although life goes on, it is never quite the same without their clever, loving little Ginger. The two children continue to be on the lookout for the man in the yellow hat, certain that if they find him, they will find Ginger. Now, it is May and nothing has happened. On Jerry's birthday, he and Rachel are picking wild strawberries near the railroad station. They are surprised when, instead of roaring through town, the Banker's Express train stops in Cranbury. This is quite exciting as it never stops there. To their surprise, they see Wally Bullwinkle standing on the rear platform. When they ask him if he is going to New York, Wally only gives a surly grimace in return. As the train pulls away, Wally puts on an old yellow hat, but the wind blows it off his head to the ground. Jerry and Rachel pick it up and discover the mark they had made many months ago. Then, Jerry remembers Wally boasting in school the other day that he and his father were going to join a vaudeville show. Perhaps they are planning an act with that fierce dog Wally had warned them about.

The thought occurs to both children at the same time. Perhaps the fierce dog is actually their own Ginger. With the help of the Cranbury police, a search of the Bullwinkle's vacated premises turns up circus posters featuring a dog doing tricks. The Pyes are now convinced that Wally has stolen Ginger and taken him to New York. Although the police are sympathetic, there is not much chance of recovering Ginger.

Imagine how surprised Jerry and Rachel are to return home to discover a strange, brown-and-white, full-grown dog at their house. They never figured on Ginger growing up. But it *is* Ginger, and little Uncle Bennie found him. Uncle Bennie is a hero. It seems that he and his mother were walking past the Bullwinkle's place on their way to the Pyes, with Uncle Bennie being pulled along in his squeaky cart. Ginger, tied up behind a fence, heard the familiar squeak, recognized it for Uncle Bennie's, and broke loose. What a smart dog! After Bennie convinced his mother that this grown-up dog really was Ginger, she decided to take him to the Pye's house to see if it was true. On the way they passed a trolley car. A man and a boy yelled out that she was taking their dog.

That was Wally and his father on the way to the train, Jerry thought. So, it *was* Wally who had taken Ginger. He knew what a smart dog Ginger was and figured that he and his ne'er-do-well father could make an act with him. All these months, Ginger had been tied up and no one had heard him bark or plead to be released. Ginger shows signs of being mistreated, and the Pye children cannot help but cry when they think of what the little dog has had to endure over the past months.

They will never forget what happened to their beloved Ginger, but they will try to make up for the bad times with all the love a family can possibly give the world's smartest dog.

Themes and Subjects

In this humorous but touching family story, the emotions of childhood are seen through the eyes and minds of children. The author presents real children having the kind of real childlike adventures that young readers understand and enjoy. Although the characters emphasize the importance of love and closeness in a family, and perhaps idealize the relationships between family members, there is bittersweet realism in the return of Ginger Pye. The realization by the children that their dog has been mistreated and that in a sense they can never take away the misery that the animal had to endure is convincingly shown. There is also much humor in the episodes written from Ginger Pye's point of view as he sets out to track his beloved Jerry at school or when he discovers that the household has another dog—who lives behind the mirror. The author has created a warm, sensitive, funny story of family, small-town life, and the gift of how childhood should be.

Incidents for Booktalking

The characters, human and animal, are the heart of this story and provide an appealing introduction to the Pye family. See: Jerry and Rachel discuss the possibility of a dog as well as Gracie's reaction, and end the evening playing Boombernickles (pp. 14–23); they use Uncle Bennie as a duster to help clean the church pews (pp. 36–39); Ginger Pye is accepted by Gracie and gets a name (pp. 62–76); they discover the hat at the reservoir (pp. 89–95); Ginger finds another dog in the house and goes to school (pp. 97–118); Ginger disappears (pp. 119–35); Ginger is found (pp. 234–38).

Related Titles

When a man announces that their house must be torn down, Poppa Whopper and his daughter Frannie take off in a camper in Marianne Busser and Ron Schroder's *On the Road with Poppa Whopper* (North-South, 1995, $13.95: 1-55858-373-4).

Dick King-Smith has written many books about plump, mischievous Sophie. In *Sophie Is Seven* (Candlewick, 1995, $14.95: 1-56402-542-X), she is intrigued with farm animals and is about to start riding lessons.

Being thrown out of the school chorus for burping and singing off-key are only two of Libby's problems in *Libby Bloom* (Holt, 1995, $14.95: 0-8050-3374-2) by Susan Rowan Masters.

In Richard Boughton's *Rent-a-Puppy, Inc.* (Atheneum, 1992, $13.95: 0-689-31730-1; pap., $3.95: 0-689-71836-5), Nikki hopes to keep all six of her beagle puppies by renting them out for an hour a day.

Mishmash, a dog that takes over a household, is featured in a series of dog stories by Molly Cone beginning with *Mishmash* (Houghton, 1962, $16.00: 0-395-06711-1).

About the Book and Author

Berger, Laura Standley, ed. *Twentieth-Century Children's Writers.* 4th ed. St. James, 1995, pp. 324–25.

Brown, Muriel W., and Rita Schoch Foudray. *Newbery and Caldecott Medalists and Honor Book Winners: Bibliographic & Resource Material Through 1990.* 2d ed. Neal-Schuman, 1992, pp. 127–28.

Cech, John, ed. "American Writers for Children, 1900–1960." In *Dictionary of Literary Biography.* Vol. 22. Gale, 1983, pp. 146–56.

Chevalier, Tracy, ed. *Twentieth-Century Children's Writers.* 3d ed. St. James, 1989, pp. 318–19.

Commire, Anne, ed. *Something About the Author.* Vol. 7. Gale, 1975, pp. 79–80.

Eleanor Estes. Profiles in Literature, 1971. Videocassette.

Evory, Ann, ed. *Contemporary Authors (First Revision Series).* Vol. 5. Gale, 1982, p. 181.

Estes, Eleanor. *Ginger Pye.* SRA McGraw-Hill, 1979. Audiocassettes. ($21.33)

Helbig, Alethea K., and Agnes R. Perkins, eds. *Dictionary of American Children's Fiction, 1859–1959.* Greenwood, 1986, pp. 150–51 (bio.), pp. 181–82 (book).

Hopkins, Lee Bennett, ed. *More Books by More People.* Citation Press, 1974, pp. 147–52.

Kunitz, Stanley J., and Howard Haycraft, eds. *The Junior Book of Authors.* Wilson, 1951, pp. 114–15.

Metzger, Linda, and Deborah A. Straub, eds. *Contemporary Authors (New Revision Series).* Vol. 20. Gale, 1987, pp. 150–51.

Miller, Bertha M., and Elinor Field, eds. *Newbery Medal Books: 1922–1955 with the Author's Acceptance Papers and Related Material.* Horn Book, 1955, pp. 372–87.

"Newbery Medal Acceptance Material, 1952." *Horn Book* 25, no. 4 (July/August 1952): 257–70.

Peterson, Linda K., and Marilyn L. Solt, eds. *Newbery and Caldecott Medal and Honor Books: 1922–1981.* Hall, 1982, pp. 117–18.

Riley, Carolyn, ed. *Children's Literature Review.* Vol. 2. Gale, 1972, pp. 72–77.

Silvey, Anita, ed. *Children's Books and Their Creators.* Houghton, 1995, pp. 226–27.

Ward, Martha, ed. *Authors of Books for Young People.* 3d ed. Scarecrow, 1990, p. 214.

Honor Books 1952

Baity, Elizabeth Chesney. *Americans Before Columbus*. Illustrated with photographs by C. B. Falls. Viking, 1951, o.p. (Grades 6–10)

This account traces the history of human life in North and South America before the Spanish invasion. Preceding the text are maps and charts showing where each Indian culture was located and a summary of the characteristics of each. There is also an attractive 30-page portfolio of photographs and text that illustrates and explains the art and architecture of each of these civilizations. The body of the work begins with the lives of the earliest Americans, those that crossed into North America during the Ice Ages some 10,000 years ago by way of the Bering Strait. It continues by chronicling the rise of what the archaeologists call Sandia Man and Folsom Man and their extinction with many of the great mammals of that time. There is a section that traces the history and culture of the Pueblos and Basketmakers, the cliff dwellers of the Southwest. That narrative is interrupted by a description of the Viking discovery of America, and the subsequent loss of Viking land claims. The life of the Mound Builders of the Mississippi and Ohio river systems is covered, followed by a description of "The Warrior Democracies of the Eastern Forests," the Iroquois and their League of Six Nations, and the Indians and Eskimos of the northern regions and West Coast. Included in the section on the Mayan civilization is a report on a day in Chichen Itza, which includes the story of a human sacrifice, the daughter of a priest, who is thrown down the Sacred Well to propitiate the Rain God. In the section on the Aztecs, we visit the city of Tenochtitlan, where Mexico City now stands, during the times of Montezuma, and see the thousands of human skulls neatly stacked in the streets. Lastly, there is a description of the Inca State of the Children of the Sun and an explanation of why these impressive civilizations fell under the domination of the invading Spaniards.

Buff, Mary, and Conrad Buff. *The Apple and the Arrow*. Illustrated by the authors. Houghton, 1951, o.p. (Grades 3–5)

This is a simple retelling of the legendary incidence that supposedly occurred more than 800 years ago when the Swiss gained their freedom from the oppressive Austrians who had occupied their country. This version of the story is told from the viewpoint of William Tell's older son, 11-year-old Walter, from whose head the apple was shot. The Tell family consists of father William, an impulsive, courageous fighter for freedom who is also a fine marksman with his crossbow; wife Hedwig, his loyal defender; and two sons, Walter and young Rudi. Rudi enjoys caring for the family's goats with Walter and their dog Prinz. The men of Uri, the canton in which the Tells live, have organized against the cruelties of the Austrian king Albrecht, and the governor, Gessler, their vicious overlord. In the company of his father, Walter visits a local fair and enjoys the sights and sounds, but when William refuses to bow to the king's hat that is displayed on a pole, the evil Gessler seizes him, promising him freedom if he can shoot an apple off his son's head. William succeeds in spite of his doubts and anxiety but Gessler sees that William has a second arrow. When questioned about its purpose, William says, "Had I killed my son, Governor, this arrow would have found your heart." He is immediately arrested, but later escapes in a boat, ambushes Gessler, and kills him. On New Year's Eve, Walter and Rudi see from a mountaintop the triumphant bonfires of the patriots. The next day, January 1, 1291, news reaches them that the Austrians have left and Switzerland has been born.

Holling, Holling C. *MINN of the Mississippi*. Illustrated by the author. Houghton, 1951, $20.00: 0-395-17578-X; pap. $9.00: 0-395-27399-4. (Grades 3–8)

In text and pictures, this folio-sized volume traces 25 years in the life of a huge snapping turtle. The first chapter describes the ancient waters of the north where a mud turtle and a crow are busy building their respective nests and laying eggs. The stages in the development of the fertilized turtle egg are also described. In the second, one of the newly hatched turtles accidentally loses her left rear leg to a hunter's bullet and manages to escape a roving pickerel. When a young Indian boy finds the three-legged turtle, he paints MINN on her back, which stands for Minnesota and is also the Indian word for water. In the third chapter, the turtle begins her amazing 2,552-mile journey down the Mississippi. During this odyssey, she has many adventures and the reader learns a great deal about the history of the river, its flora and fauna, the legends associated with it, the prehistoric animals like the mastodon and sabre-tooth tiger that once roamed its banks, and the lives of the Indians who relied on its waters for livelihood and transportation. Principal cities are mentioned and the workings of a dam explained. In the middle Mississippi, MINN lays her own eggs and soon they hatch to be her family. MINN, who has grown to weigh 48 pounds, ends her journey at the Gulf of Mexico, where she is caught by two Cajun fisherman. A woman pays the fishermen $20 to set the turtle free, and once again MINN joins the Mississippi and finds freedom. The 20 full-page color illustrations are complemented by hundreds of smaller, black-and-white marginal drawings with accompanying explanations. These supply great amounts of background technical information without interrupting the narrative flow.

Kalashnikoff, Nicholas. *The Defender*. Illustrated by Claire Louden and George Louden. Scribner, 1951, o.p. (Grades 4–7)

Before coming to the United States in 1924, the author spent four years as a political exile in northern Siberia, where this story is situated. Since the death of his wife and son, Turgen (who is a member of the Lamuts, a dying race), has lived a hermit's life in the mountains where he farms and cares for a herd of wild mountain goats. Because of his skill in medicine he has been called a sorcerer by the high priest of the Yakuts, the Shamanist. He is shunned by his superstitious neighbors who think his concern for the goats indicates that he has a pact with the devil. One day, he happens on the hut of a widow Marfa and her son and daughter, Tim and Aksa. They become friends and Turgen helps the destitute Marfa care for her family. One day, Turgen rescues an injured ram that calls him Tad. When it is domesticated, the neighbors say, "A wild ram has become tame . . . this really smells of the devil's work." Over a four-year period Marfa and Turgen grow closer, and one night he has a dream in which the Great Spirit visits him. When Turgen asks who will take care of his lambs when he is gone, the reply is that he should invite Marfa and his family to live with him. Although Marfa accepts his proposal of marriage, Turgen is fearful that she will also be shunned by the villagers. An esteemed merchant named Kamov suggests a solution. A Christian priest who lives

60 miles away is asked to come and perform the ceremony. This proves to the villagers that Turgen is not in league with the devil nor is he a sorcerer as the Shamanist had alleged. In keeping with Turgen's dream, young Tim, now Turgen's stepson, promises to be the defender of the sheep after Turgen is gone.

Sauer, Julia L. *The Light at Tern Rock*. Illustrated by George Schreiber. Viking, 1951, o.p. (Grades 3–5)

This story about discovering the true meaning of Christmas takes place in a lighthouse on the Atlantic coast, in the area of St. John's, New Brunswick. When the keeper of the lighthouse at Tern Rock, Bryan Flagg, says, "Why, Mrs. Morse, what boy wouldn't relish a holiday in a lighthouse?" Martha Morse must agree. For 14 years she and her husband had tended the light, and now living on land with her 11-year-old nephew, Ronnie, she thinks that substituting for Byron for the first two weeks in December while he visits his niece and her family will be a good idea. Ronnie agrees provided that the keeper returns by the 15th as promised so that the boy can take part in his school's Christmas activities. When Mr. Flagg does not appear, Ronnie is furious. On December 23, they find a sea chest full of gifts for them that proves Mr. Flagg had no intention of returning on time. Aunt Martha tries to make the best of things, but Ronnie broods and becomes disagreeable. On Christmas Eve, after Martha has arranged a festive table, she reads a letter of apology that Mr. Flagg left for them stating that he tricked them so he could fulfill a dream and spend one Christmas on shore with his niece's children while they were still young. Ronnie relents and realizes that helping others is the true spirit of Christmas. He says to his aunt,

All over the world, on Christmas Eve, people are putting little candles in their windows, to light the Christ child on His way. . . . We've lighted a candle tonight too—a big one. We've lighted the biggest candle we'll ever have a chance to light for Him—to help Him on His way.

He added, "Aunt Marty, Tern Rock's Light's the loveliest place in all the world to spend His birthday."

Newbery Winner 1953

Clark, Ann Nolan. *Secret of the Andes*. Illustrated by Jean Charlot. Viking, 1952, $14.99: 0-670-62975-8; pap., Puffin, $4.99: 0-145-030926-8. (Grades 5–7)

Ann Nolan Clark (1898–1995) is considered to be one of the great interpreters, through her writing, of the Native American experience. Her books also show a great respect for Native American traditions and beliefs, along with an appreciation of nature. At one time, she was a teacher for the United States Bureau of Indian Affairs, and worked for 10 years with Native American children. From these experiences came several books, including *In My Mother's House* (Viking, 1991, $15.95; pap., Puffin, $4.99). For this work, its illustrator, Velino Herrara, received the Caldecott Medal in 1941. Ann Nolan Clark also worked for the Institute of Inter-American Affairs in Central and South America, an experience that gave her insight into other native cultures. In her Newbery Award acceptance speech, she claims that growing up in a small town in New Mexico provided her with the raw material and stilmulus to write about Cusi, the Peruvian Indian boy who is the central character of *Secret of the Andes*. Cusi is an amalgam of many different boys that she had observed in many different settings. The book effectively contrasts the ancient Inca civilization with the newness of modern civilization. Its central subject is the way in which Cusi makes a choice whether to stay in his valley and foster his native traditions or venture into the outside world. As the author says, it is how Cusi comes into manhood and learns "to read his own mind." *Secret of the Andes* is a somewhat difficult book to read that requires some background knowledge of the Incas to appreciate it fully.

Plot Summary

High in the Andes Mountains of Peru in South America, in a valley hidden from the rest of the world, lives a young Indian boy called Cusi. His only companion is old Chuto, the Inca llama herder, who teaches Cusi how to care for the precious flock of llamas that they tend. Cusi has seen no other people in their remote valley for the eight years that he can remember living there. Before that, he has no knowledge of his life and Chuto does not speak of it.

Isolated though they are, Cusi is happy in his mountain home and with their wonderful llamas. His favorite is his special black pet llama called Misti. The walls of the llamas' corral are part of a temple left from the olden days when the great Inca Empire ruled Peru. Although the majesty of the Inca Empire is no more, Cusi knows how important the llama was to the Incas and how important these gentle animals still are, providing food, clothing, and warmth. Cusi regards his work of grazing, shearing, and training them as very important. Sometimes, however, when he looks down from his lofty mountain, he can see a family of Indians far below in a clearing as they work their land or cook their food. He wishes for an instant that he might meet them, that he might have another boy his own age with whom he could play. At those times, a strange look comes into old Chuto's eyes, though he says not a word.

One day, to Cusi's amazement, a stranger arrives. He is a wandering minstrel who has stumbled upon their mountain world. In exchange for their hospitality, the minstrel agrees to watch the flock for a short time while Chuto takes Cusi for his first trip down the mountain. They will make the journey to the Salt Pits. Cusi trembles with excitement for Chuto has never taken him before.

After preparations for their journey, Cusi and Chuto begin their descent down the mountain. The trail is steep and treacherous, but to Cusi everything is strange and fascinating. In time they come to Condor Kuncca, where a family that knows Chuto lives. They spend the night there and the next morning travel on to the Valley of the Salt, an open flat valley where men work in the hot sun of the afternoon. Chuto bargains for food and supplies, making a good trade in return for the llama yarn they have brought down from the mountain.

The man and boy return from their trip and before long Cusi has difficulty remembering that he even made the journey out of their valley. But their remote home seems a little lonely now with the minstrel gone and with the memories of other places filling his mind at unexpected times. Cusi is glad when shearing time comes and he is busy all day.

Then one day comes another surprise, for a tall Indian enters their remote valley. Cusi senses that he is of royal blood. The stranger calls himself Amauta, the teacher. Although Chuto objects, saying the boy is too young, the stranger says, "It is ordered." So Chuto tells the bewildered boy that Amauta has come to train him in the things that he should know.

Cusi does not understand this strange happening, but he accepts it and is lonelier than before after the training time is over and the teacher has gone. He wants answers to his many unspoken questions. Where did he—Cusi—come from? Who were his parents? How did he get to this remote Andes valley?

Before Cusi can find the courage to ask for explanations, he is led by his pet llama, Misti, to a ruined temple that Cusi did not know existed in their mountain retreat. There in this long-ago place of the Incas, the boy finds a pair of golden sandals. When he returns with them and shows them to Chuto, the old man tells him that it is a sign. Cusi must go alone to the Holy City of Cuzco, and it is there that he will find the answers to his unspoken questions. It is there he will learn what his heart truly desires. Mystified but anxious to go, Cusi takes Misti and descends the mountain again. He thinks that what his heart desires is a family, his own family. He will become part of this wonderful family he finds. He carries the golden sandals with him.

Cusi and Misti reach the sacred city of Cuzco, Holy Place of the Ancients. "Find a family. Find a family," it seems to say to him. And Cusi does indeed find a family, a mother and father with many children who welcome him with kindness and warmth. Surely now Cusi has found his heart's desire. Yet, before the night ends, although these people are kind and loving, Cusi knows he does not belong to them. As surely as though he has been told, he belongs to the Inca and his heart is in the hidden valley of the Andes.

Cusi and Misti return to their remote mountaintop. There he tells Chuto that he could not stay with the family below because of the sandals. Cusi knew he could not share the sandals with the family in Cuzco, just as he knows that he can share them with Chuto or with Misti. They truly are his family. He is certain.

Chuto asks the boy if he is sure that he wishes to stay in their hidden valley. Cusi replies that he does. Having said that, Cusi takes the vow of the Incas from Chuto, his promise to serve, guide, and train the llama flock that will keep alive the destiny of the Incas. In this way Cusi will spend his life, and in time, he will guide and train and preserve the novice who will be sent to him to carry on this vow, just as Chuto has done. Then Cusi will be taken to rest in the place of his Ancients.

Now Chuto tells the boy of his past, how Cusi's father, Titu, had been sent to the old man to train. But Chuto had been too strict and Titu had run away, never to return. Instead, in time he sent his son Cusi to Chuto, and later Amauta, the teacher.

Chuto tells the boy that he is free to roam over the trails for the old man knows he will return. Cusi says that perhaps some day he will go, but not tomorrow or tomorrow or tomorrow.

Themes and Subjects

The *Secret of the Andes* is part history, part legend, and part imagination. It portrays a sense of the majesty of the Andes, the steep canyons, lovely pastures, and wildflowers, as well as the quiet dignity of the descendants of the great Inca people of long ago. It is especially effective in its depiction of how certain values and ways of living are passed with pride from generation to generation, and how even though the grandeur that was the Inca Empire is no more, the traditions live on in the hearts of the Inca descendants. Cusi is portrayed as a thoughtful, intelligent boy who is quite naturally tempted by the desire to be a normal child in a normal family. The steps by which he comes to terms with his true heart's desire, to take his place in the long line of those who carry on the teaching of his ancestors are effectively depicted. The author shows the Incas' love for the llama and for other creatures of the wild that are so important to their well being. This is a sensitive, quiet story of a people far removed from the modern world who keep about them a sense of purpose and dignity throughout their lives. And it is the story of one young boy as he expands his awareness of the world's beauty and his knowledge and understanding of a great heritage.

Incidents for Booktalking

Almost every page gives a vivid picture of this strange (to modern eyes) life in a hidden, remote valley of the Andes. Use any of the following to contrast the life of Cusi with the more familiar trappings of the twentieth century: Cusi wakes to the beautiful sound of llama humming and follows Chuto to greet the sun (pp. 18–21); the minstrel sings of Inca Kings of long ago (pp. 24–26); Cusi and Chuto prepare for their journey down the mountain (pp. 31–34); they cross the swinging bridge (pp. 40–43); the first night with a family (pp. 47–49); the llama shearing time and the arrival of the teacher (pp. 63–69); Cusi finds the golden sandals (pp. 77–82); Cusi finds a family but returns to his mountain (pp. 111–15).

Related Titles

David N. Blair's *Fear the Condor* (Dutton, 1992, $15.00: 0-525-67381-4) explores the lives of poor farmers and their families in 1932 Bolivia.

Told in both English and Spanish, Lois Ehlert's *Moon Rope* (Harcourt, 1992, $17.99: 0-15-255343-6) is a Peruvian folktale about Fox who persuades his friend Mole to go with him to the moon.

In Kevin McColley's *The Walls of Pedro Garcia* (Delacorte, 1993, $15.00: 0-385-30806-X), a poor Mexican boy named Pedro must work in the fields of a large estate.

A young Indian boy is angry when his father invites some white men to the harvest feast in *Guests* (Hyperion, 1945, $13.95: 0-7868-0047-X; pap., $5.95: 0-7868-1108-0) by Michael Dorris.

In the nonfiction *Indians of the Andes* (Rourke, 1987, $16.67: 0-86625-260-6) by Marion Morrison, the Andean Indians and their way of life are introduced in text and numerous color photos.

About the Book and Author

Berger, Laura Standley, ed. *Twentieth-Century Children's Writers*. 4th ed. St. James, 1995, pp. 208–10.

Brown, Muriel W., and Rita Schoch Foudray. *Newbery and Caldecott Medalists and Honor Book Winners: Bibliographic & Resource Material Through 1990*. 2d ed. Neal-Schuman, 1992, pp. 64–66.

Chevalier, Tracy, ed. *Twentieth-Century Children's Writers*. 3d ed. St. James, 1989, pp. 202–03.

Commire, Anne, ed. *Something About the Author*. Vol. 14. Gale, 1970, pp. 51–52.

Estes, Glenn E., ed. "American Writers for Children Since 1960: Fiction." In *Dictionary of Literary Biography*. Vol. 52. Gale, 1986, pp. 75–83.

Evory, Ann, ed. *Contemporary Authors (First Revision Series)*. Vol. 2. Gale, 1981, pp. 117–18.

Harte, Barbara, and Carolyn Riley, eds. *Contemporary Authors (First Revision Series)*. Vols. 5–8. Gale, 1969, p. 220.

Helbig, Alethea K., and Agnes R. Perkins, eds. *Dictionary of American Children's Fiction, 1859–1959*. Greenwood, 1986, p. 104 (bio.), pp. 459–60 (book).

Hile, Kevin S. ed. *Something About the Author*. Vol. 82. Gale, 1996, pp. 31–37.

Hopkins, Lee Bennett, ed. *More Books by More People*. Citation Press, 1974, pp. 83–87.

Kunitz, Stanley J., and Howard Haycraft, eds. *The Junior Book of Authors*. Wilson, 1951, p. 71.

Nakamura, Joyce, ed. *Something About the Author: Autobiographical Series*. Vol. 16. Gale, 1993, pp. 33–109.

"Newbery Medal Acceptance Material, 1953." *Horn Book* 29, no. 4 (July/August 1953): 248–62.

Peterson, Linda K., and Marilyn L. Solt, eds. *Newbery and Caldecott Medal and Honor Books: 1922–1981*. Hall, 1982, pp. 121–22.

Senick, Gerard J., ed. *Children's Literature Review*. Vol. 16. Gale, 1989, pp. 67–85.

Silvey, Anita, ed. *Children's Books and Their Creators*. Houghton, 1995, pp. 139–40.

Ward, Martha, ed. *Authors of Books for Young People*. 3d ed. Scarecrow, 1990, pp. 129–30.

Honor Books 1953

Dalgliesh, Alice. *The Bears on Hemlock Mountain*. Illustrated by Helen Sewell. Scribner, 1952, $13.95: 0-684-19169-5; pap., Aladdin, $4.95: 0-689-70497-6. (Grades 1–4)

This very simple chapter book is based on a tall tale "told by the people" that was given to the author by the State Archivist of Pennsylvania. Eight-year-old Jonathan lives with his mother and father on a farm at the base of a large hill known as Hemlock Mountain. Through the help of older Uncle James, Jonathan has grown to love nature and the wildlife around him, but to be afraid of bears even though he has never seen one. To prepare ample food for a family christening, Jonathan's mother needs a large iron pot. She sends the young boy over the mountain to Aunt Emma's house to borrow one. Assured by all including his mother that there are no bears on Hemlock Mountain, Jonathan is nevertheless apprehensive and maintains his courage during the walk by repeating to himself, "There are no bears on Hemlock Mountain." At his Aunt Emma's, the boy eats some of her crispy, crunchy cookies and has a long nap. Having stayed longer than expected, it is already getting dark when he sets out with the huge pot on his shoulders. Suddenly, he hears strange rustling sounds in the distance and sees two large figures approaching him. They are bears. Quickly Jonathan hides under the kettle. From inside his hiding place, he hears them sniffing around the pot. Soon he hears a new sound, voices shouting "Hello, Jonathan." When he is sure that the bears have left, he crawls out from under the pot, and is greeted by his father and some of his uncles who were worried when he had not arrived home on time. When he greets his mother back home Jonathan is able to say with certainty, "There *are* bears on Hemlock Mountain."

Foster, Genevieve. *Birthdays of Freedom: America's Heritage for the Ancient World*. Illustrated by the author. Scribner, 1952, o.p. (Grades 5–7)

This book chronicles the major milestones in ancient history that were important in mankind's struggle for freedom. A second volume (also out of print) continues the story through the Middle Ages and Renaissance. Each page is handsomely illustrated with colorful pictures representing scenes from the period plus decorative maps and a time line. Beginning with America's birthday of freedom, July 4, the author tells about the writing of the Declaration of Independence and its adoption in Philadelphia. Moving backwards into prehistory, she then traces some birthdays of freedom common to all humans. The first is when *Homo sapiens* learned to make and use fire, followed by the development of a spoken language. The growth of cities in Egypt and Sumer showed that humans could live together in cooperative societies. Learning to write freed man's mind to widen his knowledge and the development of the calendar gave a sense of time and order in the universe. Other landmarks are the use of metals for tools and the codification of ideas concerning justice represented by Hammurabi's Code of Laws.

Other important events include Moses and the festival of Passover, as well as the work of great prophets like Confusius and Zoroaster and the great philosophers of Greece. The beginnings of democracy in Athens are traced, along with Rome's great contributions to the world such as the 12 Tables of the Law, the Pax Romanum, and the work of the philosopher-king Marcus Aurelius. The teachings of Jesus who was to reveal "the way to Freedom as the way of Life" are also out-lined. The book ends with the barbarians overrunning the Roman Empire in the fifth century, which paved the way for a new order.

McGraw, Eloise. *Moccasin Trail*. Coward-McCann, 1952, o.p.; pap., Puffin, $4.99: 0-14-032170-5. (Grades 6–9)

　　This action-filled novel set in the pioneer West of the 1840s tells of a teen-ager's struggle for identity when torn between his own white culture and that of the Indians who raised him. At age 11, Jim Keath runs away from his family's Missouri farm to follow his uncle, Adam Russell, a trapper. After a near-fatal en-counter with a grizzly, he is nursed back to health by a group of Crow Indians with whom he lives for six years. Though he left the tribe two years ago to join trapper Tom Rivers, 19-year-old Jim looks more Indian than white with his long braids, scalp feather, his wolf-like dog Moki and stolen mare, Buckskin. After a year of lost contact, Jim receives a letter from his younger brother Jonnie asking for help. Both their parents are dead, and Jonnie along with sister Sally, 15, and younger brother Dan'l, 11, are heading for Willamette Valley in Oregon. Because none of them is old enough to claim homestead land, Jonnie asks Jim to accompany them. Jim agrees and heads west with this family he does not know.

　　Though Sally and many of the settlers resent this foreigner, young Dan'l grows to worship his newfound brother as a hero. Adventures during the west-ward trek include driving stock through the mountains, shooting rapids on the Co-lumbia, and in Oregon, the process of clearing land and cabin building, along with encounters with unfriendly Indians. Believing that he is unwanted in the pioneer settlement, Jim leaves. When a distraught Dan'l tries to follow him, he is captured by Indians. In a rescue attempt, Jim is wounded but eventually both are saved by the settlers. Realizing that he is really wanted and loved by both his family and the settlers, Jim symbolically takes out his knife and slashes off both his braids. Jim Keath is home again at last.

Weil, Ann. *Red Sails to Capri*. Viking, 1952, o.p.; pap. Puffin, $3.95: 0-14-032858-0. (Grades 5–7)

　　Told largely in dialogue, this novel fictionalizes the story of the rediscovery of the famous Blue Grotto on the Isle of Capri in the Bay of Naples in November 1826. While Angelo, nicknamed "the laziest fisherman in Capri" mends his nets, his young friend, 14-year-old Michele Pagano spies a beautiful boat with flaming red sails entering the main harbor. Three obviously rich young men alight and the garrulous Angelo persuades them to stay at the inn owned by Michele's parents. There, the elegantly dressed owner of the boat makes introductions. He is Mon-sieur Jacques Tiersonnier, a writer in search of adventure, and his companions are Lord Derby, an English painter, and Herr Erik Nordstrom, a philosophy student. Michele becomes so fascinated with these strangers that he cancels a long-awaited trip to Naples with his friend Pietro. While guiding Monsieur Jacques around the island in his boat, Pietro avoids entering a beautiful cove, claiming that the cove and the underwater cave in its center are, by superstition, considered evil and dangerous and are always avoided by the natives. Intrigued by these stories, the three strangers insist on exploring the cove. At their bidding, Angelo secretly plans an expedition, which eventually carries himself, Michele, Signor Pagano, Pietro, and the three tourists into the cove and through a narrow passageway to a magical cave aglow with blue reflections. Not only have Michele and Pietro had a wondrous experience, but the three foreigners have fulfilled their quests: Monsieur Jacques for adventure, Lord Derby for beauty, and Herr Nordstrom for truth.

White, E. B. *Charlotte's Web*. Illustrated by Garth Williams. Harper, 1952, $14.95: 0-06-026385-7; pap., Trophy, $3.95: 0-06-44055-7. (Grades 3–6)

> The cycle of life, friendship, loyalty, and acceptance of death are only four of the many themes successfully explored in this modern children's classic. Fern Arable reluctantly agrees to sell Wilbur, the runt pig that she has cared for since his birth, to her uncle, Homer Zuckerman, who lives on a neighboring farm. Because school takes up much of Fern's free time, she is unable to visit Wilbur often. Wilbur becomes lonely and despairing until he is befriended by a large gray spider, Charlotte A. Cavatica, who becomes his wise and trusty friend. Wilbur panics when he learns from the gossipy sheep that he is slated to become somebody's Christmas dinner. Fortunately, the resourceful Charlotte comes to his rescue by spinning messages above his pen to convince the world that Wilbur is special and must be saved. Using a malodorous and malevolent rat named Templeton to find suitable words from discarded magazines, she diligently spins such words as Some Pig, Radiant, and Terrific. People come from miles around to see Wilbur and Mr. Zuckerman decides to enter him in the fall county fair. Charlotte, now weary and nearing death, reluctantly accompanies Wilbur in his crate along with Templeton. There, Wilbur wins a special prize for attracting crowds because Charlotte, in one last gargantuan effort, has spun above his head the word Humble. Too weak to return to the farm, Charlotte dies after entrusting Wilbur with the sac of her newly laid eggs. With Templeton's help the peach-colored sac is placed in the barn cellar, where, in the spring, Wilbur becomes a good friend to Charlotte's children.

Newbery Winner 1954

Krumgold, Joseph. . . . *And Now Miguel*. Illustrated by Jean Charlot. Crowell, 1953, $16.00 (0-690-09118-4). (Grades 5–8)

> Joseph Krumgold (1908–1980) was the first person to win the Newbery Award two times: the first for . . . *And Now Miguel* in 1954 and the second in 1960 for *Onion John* (see "Newbery Winner," 1960, p. 225). These two novels and *Henry 3* (Atheneum, 1967, o.p.) form a trilogy about three boys reaching maturity in three vastly different settings found in contemporary America. The first is set in New Mexico and describes a tradition-bound society of sheep ranchers still attached to their Spanish roots. The author grew up in New Jersey, the son of a father who was involved in the early motion picture industry as a distributor and theater owner. Joseph Krumgold, who enjoyed writing, also was interested in films and in 1929 moved to Hollywood as a script writer. In 1953, he made a documentary film for the U.S. Department of State, *Miguel Chavez*, about the life of southwestern sheep ranchers. To record the life of one particular family, Mr. Krumgold and his wife lived with the Chavez family in Taos. The film was so impressive that he was commissioned by T. Y. Crowell Publishers to write a novelization. In 1966, the film was remade by Universal Pictures for commercial

release. Of the book, the author states in his acceptance speech, "If only one person . . . joins the adventure that my hero has with his ego, from the thundering affirmation, 'I am Miguel,' to the only conclusion that permits one to grow, that 'Thy wish not mine be done,' then I shall have been beyond all measure rewarded."

Plot Summary

Twelve-year-old Miguel, who lives with his sheep-raising family near Taos, New Mexico, has an identification problem. He is not the oldest in the Chavez family—his brothers Young Blas and 19-year-old Gabriel, and his sisters as well, are older—nor is he the youngest—there is 7-year-old Pedro and Faustina, the littlest sister, for instance. In the middle, he has problems just getting noticed as Miguel.

In addition, Miguel has a secret wish. With all his heart, he yearns to accompany the men of his family when they go each summer to graze the sheep on the Sangre de Cristo Mountains. Grazing the sheep and caring for them are serious business for the Chavez family. They have guarded and protected the sheep for generations on their farm. It is the trusted job of the Chavez men to protect the flock.

When will Miguel be old enough to go to the mountains? He cannot say for sure, although he knows there will come a time when his father and the other men will know that he is ready. When that time comes, he will go along. But if they do not think he is ready, he must wait for another year and perhaps more.

But Miguel is determined that this year, at 12, he will accompany the men to the mountains to graze the flock. In the meantime, he goes to school and helps with the never-ending chores on the farm. As he does, he constantly tries to make his father and the other men notice him, not just as another farmhand who does his chores well, but as Miguel who is ready for the summer on the mountains. Usually, he succeeds only in annoying his father or perplexing him with endless questions.

In desperation, Miguel confides in Pedro and Faustina that he has a big plan that will ensure his trip to the mountains this summer. He is a little ashamed at their excitement because in truth he has no plan at all. But he feels better just having told someone of his secret desire.

Feeling guilty because he has lied to his brother and sister, Miguel finally does come up with an idea at least. He plans to get himself appointed to a particular chore on the farm instead of just helping wherever extra hands are needed. Miguel gets his Grandfather to teach him the job of branding the sheep and their newborns with numbers so that they do not get separated from one another. This is a very important job because if newborn and mother are separated, the newborn may die. Losing newborn sheep is a very serious business on the Chavez farm. Even so, there are always a few orphan sheep during the year, cared for by Miguel's sisters. Miguel performs his branding, which is done not with irons but with a special kind of paint, very well, and he soon becomes known as the bookkeeper.

When the branding is over, no one takes much notice of Miguel once more. Then his brother Blas announces one morning that many sheep have been lost. Miguel's father and the other men organize a search party. Miguel wants to help, but he is told to go to school as usual. Outside the schoolhouse, Miguel's best friend, Juby, tells him that wandering sheep have been spotted heading toward Arroyo Hondo, in the opposite direction from where Miguel's father and the other men are heading. Miguel decides to skip school and find the sheep. He locates them and herds them back to the farm.

Miguel is a hero—to everyone but his father, who is glad for the return of the sheep but unhappy because Miguel disobeyed and skipped school. Miguel promises never to do so again. Because he knows his father is secretly pleased that he was able to find the sheep, Miguel finds the courage to ask him if he can go to the mountains. His father says he cannot go because the arrangements have already been made and cannot be changed. Brother Gabriel is going. For Miguel it is not yet time, although his father does give him the special job for the summer of taking care of the little orphan sheep called Jimmy.

Miguel's dream seems lost. There is no one to appeal the decision of his father—except perhaps San Ysidro, the patron saint of Miguel's village of Los Cordovas. Miguel appeals to San Ysidro to arrange it in any way that he can so that Miguel will be able to go up on the mountain.

Nothing happens with his request except that Miguel becomes aware that his father has begun to notice him—as Miguel. He often asks the boy how he would solve such and such a problem on the farm. Miguel is surprised, then happy, and determined to show how grown he is.

Near the end of shearing time, a good thing happens to Miguel. All the men eat together at day's end around the big kitchen table. All the women and children eat together. On this evening, a stool is drawn up for Miguel next to his father. It is a proud moment. Then a bad thing happens. During the shearing, it is Miguel's job to hang up the huge sack for gathering the wool. It is an important job and he takes it seriously; however, he makes a mistake and falls into the sack itself. He is rescued quickly, but his father is angry at what he calls "playing games" when there is work to be done.

Then, about a week later, the miracle happens. Miguel learns that he is to go to the mountains with the men after all! Why? Because Gabriel cannot go; he has received a letter from the government to go into the military. He did not expect to go until the fall. Miguel is sorry his brother must go but happy for himself. Yet, Miguel feels it is his fault that Gabriel must go away because of what he asked San Ysidro.

Miguel appeals to San Ysidro once again, asking him to take back the letter that Gabriel received. When it does not happen, he tells Gabriel what he has done and how it is all his fault that his brother must go away. But he learns that Gabriel is not at all unhappy about the chance to see the world. Gabriel also tells Miguel that if he is to do a man's job this summer, he must stop acting as a child. Making wishes and expecting a fairy godmother to grant them are child's play. To get something you want, you must give something in return. You must earn it. Miguel has earned his chance at the mountains by his hard work.

Gabriel leaves for the service and gives Miguel his own jackknife. And then it is Miguel's turn to leave with the men for a summer on the mountain. He takes Jimmy along with him.

Themes and Subjects

With humor and simplicity, this is a poetic telling of a boy's yearning to grow up and to be taken seriously. As he shares his innermost desires and feelings, Miguel's world comes alive to the reader, who shares the closeness and simplicity of the boy's life in a sheep-raising southwestern family. The searching spirit of a child growing into adulthood and the realization that he has earned his reward are skillfully and touchingly handled. The growing bond between father and son as the older man slowly becomes aware of the boy's struggle for maturity is well portrayed. The concept of all working together for a common goal is explored in this intimate depiction of sheep farming and the hard work and responsibilities it entails for all members of a family, young and old.

Incidents for Booktalking

The yearnings and feelings of young Miguel will serve as an excellent introduction both to the growth of a boy and to the inner workings of a sheep-raising farm and family. See: Miguel talks to his brother about "being Gabriel" (pp. 6–9); Miguel tells his secret plan (pp. 35–37); Miguel describes the birth of a lamb (pp. 38–42); Miguel takes on the branding job (pp. 45–50); Miguel finds the lost sheep (pp. 79–89); he appeals to San Ysidro for help to get to the mountains (p. 116); Miguel gets to eat with the men (pp. 153–58).

Related Titles

In *A Sunburned Prayer* (Simon, 1991, $14.95: 0-689-80125-4) by Marc Talbert, A Mexican American boy living in New Mexico walks to a shrine 17 miles away in an effort to save his grandmother from cancer.

In Nicholasa Mohr's *Felita* (pap. Dell, $4.50: 0-440-41295-1), a Puerto Rican family moves to an area where Spanish is not spoken.

Thirteen-year-old Lupita and her older brother illegally cross the border at Tijuana to seek work in the United States in Patricia Beatty's *Lupita Manana* (Morrow, 1981, $12.88: 0-688-00359-1).

A young Mexican boy, illegally smuggled into the United States, discovers the cruelty and hardships of migrant worker labor camps in Theodore Taylor's *The Maldonado Miracle* (pap., Avon, $4.50: 0-380-70023-9).

The plight of illegal aliens in the United States is the subject of *Journey of the Sparrows* by Frank L. Buss (pap., Dell, $4.50: 0-440-40785-0).

About the Book and Author

Berger, Laura Standley, ed. *Twentieth-Century Young Adult Writers*. St. James, 1994, pp. 366–67.

Brown, Muriel W., and Rita Schoch Foudray. *Newbery and Caldecott Medalists and Honor Book Winners: Biographic & Resource Material Through 1990*. 2d ed. Neal-Schuman, 1992, pp. 225–26.

Chevalier, Tracy, ed. *Twentieth-Century Children's Writers*. 3d ed. St. James, 1989, pp. 547–48.

Commire, Anne, ed. *Something About the Author*. Gale, 1971, Vol. 1, pp. 136–38; 1987, Vol. 48, pp. 149–55.

Evory, Ann, ed. *Contemporary Authors (First Revision Series)*. Vol. 7. Gale, 1982, pp. 293–95.

Fuller, Muriel, ed. *More Junior Authors*. Wilson, 1963, p. 128.

Helbig, Alethea K., and Agnes R. Perkins, eds. *Dictionary of American Children's Fiction, 1859–1959*. Greenwood, 1986, pp. 278–79 (bio.), pp. 20–21 (book).

————. *Dictionary of American Children's Fiction, 1960–1985*. Greenwood, 1986, pp. 365–66.

Joseph Krumgold. Profiles in Literature, 1971. Videocassette.

Krumgold, Joseph. . . . *And Now Miguel*. SRA McGraw-Hill, 1985. Audiocassettes. ($21.33)

Miller, Bertha M., and Elinor Field, eds. *Newbery Medal Books: 1922–1955 with the Author's Acceptance Papers and Related Material*. Horn Book, 1955, pp. 405–23.

"Newbery Medal Acceptance Material, 1954." *Horn Book* 30, no. 4 (July/August 1954): 221–37.

Peterson, Linda K., and Marilyn L. Solt, eds. *Newbery and Caldecott Medal and Honor Books: 1922–1981*. Hall, 1982, pp. 125–26.

Silvey, Anita. ed. *Children's Books and Their Creators*. Houghton, 1995, p. 382.

Ward, Martha, ed. *Authors of Books for Young People*. 3d ed. Scarecrow, 1990, p. 407.

Honor Books 1954

Bishop, Claire Huchet. *All Alone*. Illustrated by Feodor Rojankovsky. Viking, 1953, $15.00: 0-670-11336-0. (Grades 2–5)

Both picture and text combine in this simple story to produce a realistic Alpine atmosphere. The motto of the fiercely independent and competitive farmers in the town of Monestier in the French Alps of Savoie is "Every man for himself." Thus Pere Mabout's last words to his 10-year-old son Marcel, as he sends the boy up Little Giant Mountain to graze the family cattle for the summer, is to mind his own business and speak to no one. At first, therefore, Marcel ignores the friendly yodeling that comes from Pierre Pascal, who tends his cows across the ravine on Big Giant Mountain. When Pierre's cows wander into his territory, Marcel reluctantly returns them and the two boys, defying convention, become friendly. A sudden blinding rainstorm causes a giant landslide that leaves the two boys and all the cows marooned on a high, steep cliff with the path below blocked by rocks. For seven days, the two boys live by using cow dung for fire fuel and rationing their meager provisions for food. During this time, they learn the meaning of cooperation and sharing. Finally, the villagers rescue them by breaking through the rock barrier with their picks and shovels. The boys are greeted joyously by their two fathers. When Pere tells Marcel that the Little Giant grazing ground has been destroyed in the landslide, M. Pascal insists that the two families share his meadow. This ushers in a new era of cooperation in the village. Old suspicions are forgotten as the villagers decide to tear down their fences and work the whole valley together. At the town meeting announcing this new policy, friends Marcel and Pierre graciously take a bow.

Buff, Mary, and Conrad Buff. *Magic Maize*. Illustrated by Conrad Buff. Houghton, 1953, o.p. (Grades 3–5)

The traditions and folklore of the ancient Maya are recaptured in this short, well-illustrated tale of a poor family of farmers living in modern rural Guatemala. Fabian is growing up on a small farm with his parents, two younger sisters (10-year-old Tsnuk and 5-year-old Caterina), and a mischievous parrot named Chichi. His older brother, 16-year-old Quin, has become disenchanted with his father's rigid, archaic ways and left home to become an itinerant peddler. One day, while Fabian's parents are away praying for a good crop, Quin visits briefly and gives his brother 20 kernels of maize he has received from two gringo archaeologists. He claims they are of a new strain that produce more and better corn like magic. Late one night, Fabian steals away with his friend, Augustin, and secretly plants the kernels in a clearing close to the City Up Yonder, the abandoned ruins of a Mayan temple. While digging he unearths a beautifully carved ancient ear plug, which he hides. When the two archaeologists who had helped his brother arrive, Fabian works for them at their excavations in spite of his father's suspicions about foreigners. The archaeologists uncover the mate of the valuable ear plug Fabian had unearthed, and he proudly shows them its companion piece. Happy at finding such a treasure, they buy it for several pieces of silver, enough to cover the loss Fabian's family suffers after a sudden rainstorm destroys their new crop. When Fabian shows his father the rich, new strain of corn, he not only befriends the strangers but also agrees with them that such a fine boy as Fabian should be given the chance to attend school like his friend Augustin.

DeJong, Meindert. *Hurry Home, Candy*. Illustrated by Maurice Sendak. Harper, 1953, $14.89: 0-06-021486-1. (Grades 4–7)

This touching story of a fearful puppy's search for a home and security is told from many viewpoints, including that of the dog. When only two months old and hardly weaned, the little dog is purchased by a family with two children, 10-year-old Catherine and 9-year-old George. The youngsters love the little pup they name Candy, but both parents are overly severe, particularly the mother who terrifies the pup and punishes him with a broom. One day on an outing to visit the children's grandparents, the family is delayed on the way home by a flat tire followed by a severe rainstorm. Candy hides under a bridge and the family, afraid that the road will be washed out, leaves him behind. The next day, the children unsuccessfully search for him, and Candy, alone and afraid, begins several months of wandering and scavenging to survive. After being chased by a pack of savage dogs, he takes refuge under a wagon driven by an eccentric old lady who is returning home after selling a litter of pigs. When the wagon accidentally overturns, Candy stays with the old lady until help arrives but at the hospital he is frightened by a broom-wielding nurse and flees into the street. Here he is found by a kindly retired seaman, Captain Carlson, who adopts him and cares for him tenderly. One evening, when in the woods, the two are accosted by bank robbers trying to escape the police. In the ensuing shoot-out, Candy is wounded and once again becomes lost. Captain Carlson offers a reward, and Catherine and George, recognizing the portrait of the dog in the local papers, join the search hoping to use the reward money for new bicycles. The dog is spotted in the neighborhood of the children's grandparents, and soon the dog and the Captain are reunited. Candy has found a real home at last.

DeJong, Meindert. *Shadrach*. Illustrated by Maurice Sendak. Harper, 1953, $14.89: 0-06-021546-1. (Grades 3–5)

This gentle story takes place in the countryside of Holland early in the twentieth century. Because Davie is recovering from a serious illness, the six-year-old boy spends each afternoon with his grandparents instead of going to school each day. When Grandfather promises to get him a pet rabbit in a week's time from the traveling peddler, Maartins, Davie becomes impatient with anticipation. He continually visits the little hutch his grandfather has made, and even though Shadrach (he has already given his pet a name!) is not due for several days, Davie risks his life to gather three bags of clover from the steep banks of a canal. His older brother, Rem, who is ordinarily a tease and nuisance, helps Davie hide the details of this adventure from his parents. Unfortunately, the clover rots and the boy is forced to bury it in his grandfather's compost heap. As a diversion, Grandfather, a retired schoolteacher, shows Davie a "secret" one-room school attached to the barn. Finally the long week is over and the Maartins deliver a beautiful black rabbit to Davie. The boy dotes on his pet, continually feeding and showering love on little Shadrach, yet the pet continues to lose weight. Davie becomes increasingly alarmed because Shadrach is now so thin that he is able to squeeze through the slats of his hutch. One day, Davie discovers that Shadrach is missing. He searches the barn, and in a dark corner grabs a small animal that is actually a rat. Davie proudly displays his catch and is praised for his bravery but is still disconsolate at the loss of Shadrach. One night, he creeps into the barn for another search and finds Shadrach in the schoolroom eating oats. Grandfather now explains to Davie that rabbits need a variety of foods for a good diet. Now reunited with his pet, Davie is sure that both he and Shadrach will thrive.

Judson, Clara Ingram. *Theodore Roosevelt*. Follett, 1953, o.p. (Grades 4–7)

The adventurous life of this famous American politician, statesman, naturalist, writer, humanitarian, and family man are vividly re-created in this biography, which adroitly combines details of both his public and private life. It begins in 1866 in New York City when Theodore, called Teddy, is a sickly boy of eight fighting respiratory problems. In spite of these physical problems, he exercised strenuously and in time was able to conquer them. As a youth he also showed great interest in the natural sciences, and using an empty hall bookcase, displayed his many collected specimens under the sign "Roosevelt Museum of Natural History." Born into wealth, he and his family made several excursions to Europe and the Near East when he was still a youngster, which kindled his love of nature and history. During his college years at Harvard, he extended his interests to boxing and hunting. On his 22nd birthday, he married Alice Lee, and later entered Republican politics by becoming the state assemblyman for New York City's 21st

District. The sudden deaths of both his mother and wife devastated him and he retreated to his large Elkhorn Ranch in the Dakota Territory where, among other adventures, he participated in bringing to justice some horse thieves. Later, he returned to the East, reentered politics, and remarried. As a volunteer during the Spanish American War, he helped organize the famous Rough Riders and led the victorious charge on San Juan Hill. His political activity increased, culminating in his two-term presidency, his retirement, and a later unsuccessful attempt to reenter politics as a candidate of the New Progressive party. This American original died at his home in Oyster Bay, Long Island, on January 6, 1919.

Newbery Winner 1955

DeJong, Meindert. *The Wheel on the School*. Illustrated by Maurice Sendak. Harper, 1954, $15.00: 0-06-021585-2. (Grades 4–7)

Meindert DeJong (1906–1991) was born in the Netherlands but came to the United States with his family when he was eight. He began writing children's books for a very practical reason.

> I started writing children's books because during the depression the little magazines to which I was contributing my adult short stories died off like flies . . . and since at that time I kept a pet goose on my poultry farm . . . I was persuaded by local librarians to write a child's book about him.

This became *The Big Goose and the Little White Duck* (1938, o.p.). In addition to a Newbery Medal, four of DeJong's other books have been Honor Books: *Hurry Home, Candy* (see "Honor Books," 1954, p. 193); *Shadrach* (see "Honor Books," 1954, p. 194); *The House of Sixty Fathers* (see "Honor Books," 1957, p. 210); and *Along Came a Dog* (see "Honor Books," 1959, p. 223). *The Wheel on the School* tells how six children set out to bring back the nesting storks to their Dutch village, Shora. In his Newbery acceptance speech, DeJong addressed the young reader when he said, "You are important, and all that matters is that in these six children of Shora are you and all the children of the world. I know, for I have been back, and I have been a child again."

Plot Summary

In the town of Shora, a little fishing village in Holland, there are six school-age children and no storks. Storks never come to Shora to build their nests as they do in other villages all over the country. This sets Lina, the only girl in school, to thinking. Why do the storks not come to Shora to build their nests? Why do they go instead to other Dutch towns?

Lina thinks about the storks and absence from Shora so much that she writes a composition about them. The teacher is so pleased that Lina has written a composition without any prompting from him that he allows her to read it to the entire class of five boys. After Lina has read her composition, which is rather short and not filled with many facts about storks (because Lina does not know much about storks seeing as they never come to Shora), the teacher asks each of the other students what *they* know about storks. Nobody—not Jella, the biggest; or Eekla, the most clumsy but with swift mind; or Auka, a nice, everyday sort of lad; or the brothers, Pier and Dirk—knows much about storks either.

The teacher sends all the children home an hour early that day asking them to wonder about storks and why they never come to Shora. For as the teacher says, if you wonder, sometimes things begin to happen.

Lina's wonderings get her into a conversation with Grandmother Sibble III, an old lady in town to whom she has never talked much. To Lina's great surprise, a conversation with Grandmother Sibble III is much like having a conversation with a girlfriend her own age, if she had such a girlfriend. Lina learns that storks never came to nest in Shora because the roofs of the houses are too pointed. However, that can be remedied as other villages do, by putting a wagon wheel on top of the roofs in which the storks can nest.

Lina can hardly wait for school the next day to tell what she had learned. She is very surprised, however, to find that quiet Eelka has found another answer. He says storks never come because Shora has no trees. The storks used to come because there used to be trees in the little village. Storks like trees and shade and that is why they do not come anymore.

No, no, Lina cries. It just has to be the pointed roofs because no one can do anything about no trees in the village—not for ages and ages anyway. But they *can* do something: find a wheel for the roof of the school. If they can do that, they will surely find out if the lack of a wheel is causing the storks to fly past their village.

And so the schoolchildren of Shora begin the hunt for a wheel for the school. This is far easier said than done, for nowhere in the small village is there a wheel that is not in use. But the search has been set in motion, and nothing can stop it now.

Like ripples that spread across a calm lake from a pebble thrown into the water, the search for a way to bring the storks to Shora begins to involve everyone in town. The six children explore all the surrounding countryside looking for a wheel of any kind. Sometimes the search gets them into trouble, as when Jella makes off with a wheel from the farmer's shed. Jella leaves a note saying he will return it as soon as the storks are through nesting. However, the farmer needs the wheel for his wagon now. He can let Jella have it in about a week, but by then it will be too late—nesting time will be over.

Pier and Dirk's search for a wheel leads them to legless Janus, who is confined to a wheelchair and known as the meanest man in Shora. Although Janus has no wheel, to the boys' great surprise, he is not the meanest man in town at all and becomes their friend.

In Eelka's search, he comes upon a farmer who tells him of an ancient wheel in the hayloft of his barn. The problem is getting it down from the hayloft. In so doing, Eelka manages to smash the wheel in pieces. However, the rim is still intact, so he gathers up the pieces and rolls the rim back to town.

Lina has luck too, for she finds an old wheel under a forgotten overturned boat. It seems as though everyone in town, including mean old Janus, gets involved in the wheel projects. Janus also helps to restore the broken wheel that Eelka found.

It is almost time for the storks to come, but instead the little fishing village is hit by a tremendous storm that lasts for days. Lina is worried that the terrible storm will scatter the storks from their usual flight path and they will miss flying over Shora altogether. And how will they ever get a wheel up on the schoolhouse in this howling storm?

But the teacher promises a day free from school if that will help in getting the wheel on top of the schoolhouse. The fathers come to the rescue even in the storm. With Janus instructing them from below, the wheel is put in place. Soon after, the ancient, broken wheel is fixed and set up on Janus's roof. They await the storks.

But the storm has caused terrible damage. The newspapers say no storks will come to the fishing villages of Holland at all. The whole town waits. There are no storks in sight.

As luck would have it, it is Lina's little sister, Linda, and Auka's little brother, Jan, who first see two white storks. However, they seem to still be standing in the sea. With the help of Janus, Lina, and the others they manage to rescue the two storks who have become mired in a sand bar as a result of the terrible storm. When the small rescue party returns with two very tired storks in tow, the whole town is lined up waiting on the dike.

The next problem is how to get the two half-dead storks up on the wheel of the schoolhouse. The quicker they get up there, the more likely they will remain when their strength comes back.

It is a difficult and perilous journey up the ladder with storks under one's arm. Finally, Jella is able to stretch high enough to place the female stork on the wheel on top of the schoolhouse. But the male looks angry. What will he do?

Everyone watches as the male stork circles the wheel as though inspecting it. Suddenly, he spreads his wings and flies down to the schoolyard. All the townspeople hush. Then, he picks up a twig in his long bill, flies to the roof, and drops it on the wheel in front of his mate.

Janus whispers to everyone, "They've shown that they will stay and build their nest. Now, let's get away from here and leave them alone."

And that is the story of the impossible dream, of how the storks returned to the little Dutch fishing village of Shora.

Themes and Subjects

In this telling of an adventure filled with excitement and vivid characterizations of children, the author is particularly successful in showing how one small idea can, with encouragement and the willingness to pursue a dream, spread from one person to many until, as in this case, it involves all the people of one village. They come together in pursuit of the same goal—to bring the storks back to their small fishing village. As the village people band together, they begin to look at each other as they have not before. They begin to see the true worth of their neighbors instead of only what they thought was true about them. The reader knows at the end that not only have the storks returned to Shora, and presumably will again, but the people of this small Dutch village are forever changed as well. The interactions of the children, by an author who spent his childhood in Holland, are portrayed with both warmth and humor, rendering them especially vivid, real, and touching.

Incidents for Booktalking

Any of the following incidents will serve as fine introductions to the eventual dream-come-true when the storks return to Shora. See: Lina's composition (pp. 206); Lina talks with Grandmother Sibble III (pp. 15–25); Jella takes a wheel from the farmer (pp. 50–57); Pier and Dirk meet up with Janus (pp. 59–77); Eelka finds an ancient wheel (pp. 80–101); Lina finds another wheel (pp. 128–43); getting the wheel on the schoolhouse (pp. 215–32).

Related Titles

Hans and his sister Gretel receive a single pair of skates and Hans insists that Gretel enter the silver skates competition in *Hans Brinker; or The Silver Skates* (pap., Apple, $3.99: 0-590-4129-7) by Mary Mapes Dodge.

An introduction of the history, geography, and the people of the Netherlands is given in Dennis B. Fradin's *The Netherlands* (Children's, 1982, $32.00: 0-516-02779-4).

A young boy and his little brother spend a summer with relatives on a farm in Sweden while their parents build a home in town in Ulf Nilsson's *If You Didn't Have Me* (McElderry, 1987, $15.00: 0-689-50406-3).

In Rjarne Renter's *Buster's World* (Dutton, 1989, $12.95: 0-525-44475-0), Buster, who comes from a poor family, gets in and out of trouble in a series of humorous escapades growing up in Copenhagen.

Twenty orphan girls in France are afraid that they will be separated by adoption in Natalie Savage Carlson's *The Happy Orpheline* (pap., Dell, $2.75: 0-440-43455-6).

About the Book and Author

Berger, Laura Standley, ed. *Twentieth-Century Children's Writers*. 4th ed. St. James, 1995, pp. 285–87.

Block, Ann, and Carolyn Riley, eds. *Children's Literary Review*. Vol. 1. Gale, 1976, pp. 54–62.

Brown, Muriel W., and Rita Schoch Foudray. *Newbery and Caldecott Medalists and Honor Book Winners: Bibliographic & Resource Material Through 1990*. 2d ed. Neal-Schuman, 1992, pp. 98–100.

Chevalier, Tracy, ed. *Twentieth-Century Children's Writers*. 3d ed. St. James, 1989, pp. 275–76.

Collier, Laurie, and Joyce Nakamura. *Major Authors and Illustrtors for Children and Young Adults*. Gale, 1993, 6 vols., pp. 654–57.

Commire, Anne, ed. *Something About the Author*. Vol. 2. Gale, 1971, pp. 89–90.

DeJong, Meindert. *The Wheel on the School*. Read by Anne T. Flosnik. Listening Library. Audiocassettes. ($29.98)

Estes, Glenn E., ed. "American Writers for Children Since 1960: Fiction." In *Dictionary of Literary Biography*. Vol. 52. Gale, 1986, pp. 115–32.

Fuller, Muriel, ed. *More Junior Authors*. Wilson, 1963, pp. 62–63.

Helbig, Alethea K., and Agnes R. Perkins, eds. *Dictionary of American Children's Fiction, 1859–1959*. Greenwood, 1986, p. 125 (bio.), pp. 258–59 (book).

———. *Dictionary of American Children's Fiction, 1960–1985*. Greenwood, 1986, p. 153.

Kinsman, Clare D., ed. *Contemporary Authors*. Vols. 12–16. Gale, 1976, pp. 210–11.

Miller, Bertha M., and Elinor Field, eds. *Newbery Medal Books: 1922–1955 with the Author's Acceptance Papers and Related Material*. Horn Book, 1955, pp. 424–38.

"Newbery Medal Acceptance Material, 1953." *Horn Book* 31, no. 4 (July/August 1953): 244–53.

Peterson, Linda K., and Marilyn L. Solt, eds. *Newbery and Caldecott Medal and Honor Books: 1922–1981*. Hall, 1982, pp. 129–30.

Silvey, Anita. ed. *Children's Books and Their Creators*. Houghton, 1995, pp. 192–93.

Ward, Martha, ed. *Authors of Books for Young People*. 3d ed. Scarecrow, 1990, pp. 177–78.

Honor Books 1955

Dalgliesh, Alice. *The Courage of Sarah Noble*. Illustrated by Leonard Weisgard. Scribner, 1954, $15.00: 0-684-18830-9; pap., Aladdin, $4.95: 0-689-71057-7. (Grades 2–4)

This brief, easily read pioneer story is based on an actual incident in the summer of 1707 when John Noble took his eight-year-old daughter, Sarah, with him from the Massachusetts Colony to New Milford, Connecticut to cook for him and keep him company while he constructed a house on his newly purchased property. For various reasons none of Sarah's brothers or sisters, nor their mother, are able to leave the Noble household, and so Sarah gallantly volunteers to accompany her father into the wilderness. Many times during the trip, she remembers her mother's parting words as she fastened her warm red cloak around her, "Keep up your courage, Sarah Noble." At the settlement, John finds a cave in which they can live temporarily. He enlarges it, builds a storage shed, and surrounds both with a fence. When some Indian children visit one day, Sarah is at first frightened, but later makes friends with them and reads them from the only book she owns, the Bible. John hires the strongest and most friendly of the Indians, Tall John, to help him construct his cabin and by the end of the summer, the house is completed. Sarah's courage is once more tested when her father asks her to stay with Tall John and his family while he returns to Massachusetts to bring back Sarah's mother and the rest of the family. Again Sarah's spirit and determination triumph and soon she becomes part of her adopted family. When her father returns there is a joyous family reunion. Atop Tall John's broad shoulders the courageous Sarah Noble enters the house that she already feels is her home.

Ullman, James Ramsey. *Banner in the Sky*. Lippincott, 1955, $14.95: 0-397-32141-4.; pap., Pocket, $2.95: 0-685-00477-5. (Grades 7–9)

This is a fictionalized account of the 1865 scaling of the last unconquered peak in the Alps, in reality, the Matterhorn but renamed the Citadel in this adventure novel. Secretly and against his mother's wishes, 16-year-old Rudi Matt has been practicing mountaineering on the approaches to the mountain. Fifteen years ago, Rudi's father, who was a renowned alpine guide, froze to death trying to conquer the Citadel, a giant peak that hovers majestically over the village of Kurtal. Rudi's mother fears that her son one day might suffer a similar fate. The only encouragement Rudi gets is from Teo Zurbriggen, himself crippled by the Citadel and now the chef in the hotel where Rudi works. After Rudi saves the life of the famous English mountaineer, Captain John Winter, after he had fallen into a frozen crevice, Rudi becomes involved in Winter's plan to climb the Citadel. Because of local opposition, Winter hires a guide, Emil Saxo, from the neighboring town of Broli, but Kurtal's local pride is so injured that Franz Lerner, Rudi's uncle and the best guide in town joins the party. Near the top, Emil leaves the group to continue the climb alone. Fearful that Emil will reach the peak first, Matt sets out to find him. During their violent encounter, Emil falls and is injured and Matt must choose between reaching the summit or saving Emil's life. Choosing the latter, he completely exhausts himself taking Emil back to the camp. Winter and Franz continue the climb, and at the summit, plant Rudi's staff with his father's red shirt on it, flying like a victory banner in the sky. Afterward the Citadel becomes known as Rudisberg, Rudi's Mountain, in honor of the boy who became a man trying to conquer it.

Newbery Winner 1956

Latham, Jean Lee. *Carry On, Mr. Bowditch*. Illustrated by John O'Hara Cosgrave, II. Houghton, 1955, $15.95: 0-395-06881-9; pap., Sandpiper, $6.95: 0-395-13713-6. (Grades 5–8)

Jean Lee Latham (1902–1995) is one of the most prolific writers of biography for children and young adults. Her first was *The Story of Eli Whitney* (o.p.), published in 1953. Among her subsequent subjects have been Samuel Morse, Sir Francis Drake, Sam Huston, David Farragut, Elizabeth Blackwell, and Rachel Carson. In each, she has been able to distill difficult technical and historical information into interesting, simple prose. Latham became interested in the career of Nathaniel Bowditch when she read an introduction he wrote when he was not yet 30 years old to a book published by the U.S. Navy Department. In this re-creation of his life, she has been faithful to the known facts, but has invented some characters, conversations, and incidents to flesh out the story. For example, characters such as Captain Prince and Nathaniel's sister Lizza, who died when she was 17, actually lived, but few details are known about them. These and other gaps have been filled in this "fictionalized" biography. This is a moving story of a man who, despite many disadvantages, achieved a place of eminence in the world of navigation. In speaking of Bowditch, an unnamed eulogist said, "His name will be revered as one who helped his fellow men in time of need, a man who was a guide to them over the pathless ocean."

Plot Summary

It is 1779 in the port of Salem, Massachusetts, well into the Revolutionary War. Nathaniel Bowditch has been born into a sailing family, although his frail frame does not make him rugged enough for the sea. The Bowditch family has fallen on hard times. Father has lost his ship, and he and the others, including Nat, Mary, Hab, Lizza, William, Mother, and Granny, have recently returned to their Salem home where Father will go back to his former trade as a cooper (a maker of barrels).

Young Nat learns that money can be made by buying expectations from a sailor, which means investing in the money a sailor expects to make on the voyage of a privateer. If the privateer captures a British ship, the cargo and vessel are sold and the money divided among the ship's owner, captain, and crew. If you buy an expectation, you will get some of that reward when the sailor returns—if he is lucky. Nat uses all the money he has saved to buy an expectation from a sailor named Tom Perry.

Time passes and the family fortunes grow no better, nor does Tom Perry return. Nat goes to school and impresses his teachers with his brilliance in mathematics. He begins to dream that his expectation will come one day and he will be able to go to Harvard to study. Instead, more misfortune hits as Mother dies and brother Hab goes off to sea. Then, Nat learns that Tom Perry has been killed at sea with no bounty recovered. There goes the expectation.

Another terrible blow comes to Nat when he is 12 years old and his father indentures him to a ship chandler. That means that until he is 21, he must work at keeping the books of the chandler and learning the business. It seems much like slavery except that someday he can think of obtaining his freedom, and perhaps there will still be time for an education at Harvard, if he works hard enough.

Despite the years of servitude, those to whom Nat is indentured are kind enough and the young man proves adept at his work, especially at figures. Night after night in his attic room, Nat learns everything he can about mathematics and astronomy, about ships and the sea. When he is given Issac Newton's book *Principia* so that he can study astronomy, he is dismayed to see that it is written in Latin. And so he learns Latin in order to understand the book. Nat also keeps a notebook that he entitles *Navigation*.

Slowly the years pass, and the boy begins to dream of his freedom, still hoping that he can further his education. But when he is 21 and his indentured days are over, he has little choice but to go to sea. The war is over and the United States is a free nation, but times are hard. Nat knows that many a ship's captain will pay for his ability to figure the buying and selling of cargo.

Nat Bowditch ships out on the *Henry* as ship's clerk under Captain Prince. By the time the first voyage ends, he has astounded the captain with his grasp of navigation. Also on this voyage, Nat begins to try to explain the rudiments of navigation to crew members, who know little or anything of it. He is frustrated at first by his inability to make things clear to those who have such need of this information. As he adds to the notebook begun so many years before, Nat realizes that he is beginning to find a way to explain facts of navigation to uneducated seaman. When the captain asks why he is spending his free time in such a pursuit, Nat replies that he is repaying a debt to all those who helped him when he needed to learn. He tells the captain that all of his crew could be first-rate seamen if they understood navigation.

By the time he is 30 years old, Bowditch's collection of notebooks has become *The American Practical Navigator*. This amazing book, which instructs the uneducated in how to navigate on the sea, is today still the "sailor's bible" and is a standard text at the U.S. Naval Academy at Annapolis.

Nat Bowditch was not only a teacher but a doer as well. On his third voyage, Captain Prince prepares to enter Manila Harbor in the Philippines, one of the biggest land-locked harbors in the world. Nat astounds everyone by navigating the ship safely into harbor in the midst of a monsoon. But it is the last voyage of Nathaniel Bowditch that sailors still talk about.

In 1802, Bowditch receives a letter from Harvard University granting him a degree of Master of Arts. He jokingly tells his wife, Polly, that he is the only Harvard man who has never set foot in its halls, but he is very proud all the same. He also learns that his book on navigation has become a best-seller in England, where his work has pointed out the numerous errors found in the navigational book called the *Practical Navigator* that had been in general use. And now he will set out on a ship called the *Putnam*, sailing on this voyage as captain and part owner.

On.the voyage to Sumatra, the awful responsibility of being the captain of ship and crew really hits him. The voyage is filled with difficulties and bad weather and takes many months. Although he had expected to return in late October, it is early December before the ship reaches the North Atlantic. They have been sailing for days through rugged storms. By mid-December they are off the island of Nantucket where at last the skies clear. But storms quickly strike again and for three days the rain pours down. When they let up, the fog rolls in—a sailor's dread.

As the crew waits to crash into anything in the ship's path, Captain Bowditch takes over, and to the amazement of the men he guides the ship by what he calls "simply a matter of mathematics." Without being able to check the ship's position for the past three days, Bowditch brings his ship into Salem harbor on Christmas night in a pea-soup fog.

How could he have possibly done this? "It's simple mathematics," he says again. "At such a speed, in so many hours, you log so many miles in a given direction."

Carry on, indeed, Mr. Bowditch!

Themes and Subjects

Although this is a fictionalized account, Nathaniel Bowditch, 1773–1838, was a real-life American mathematician and astronomer and a self-educated math prodigy. The author makes vivid the often dreary details of his sad personal youth and proves that the subject of mathematics can be exciting and human as well. The book also chronicles the exciting, although dangerous history of life at sea in the days of a young America. Bowditch is portrayed as a young man with extraordinary gifts and his quiet determination to succeed, even when faced time and again with adversity, is well depicted. An inspiring story of courage, bravery, and genius.

Incidents for Booktalking

A number of incidents can serve as an interesting introduction to both the character of Nathaniel Bowditch and the life of a seaman in the early days of the nation. See: Nat buys an expectation (pp. 10–14); Hab goes to sea and warns Nat not to blubber (pp. 26–28); Nat is indentured (pp. 40–42); Nat starts his navigation notebook (pp. 55–56); he begins the study of the *Principia* and Latin (pp. 64–66); he ships out on the *Henry* (pp. 100–14).

Related Titles

In the nonfiction *Clippers and Whaling Ships* (Crestwood, 1993, $11.95: 0-89686-735-8) by Tim McNeese, early American shipping and commerce are discussed, along with the ships that made them possible.

The story of the inventor and navigator whose steamboat, *Clermont,* made history is told in Elaine Landau's *Robert Fulton* (Watts, 1991, $21.00: 0-531-20016-7).

In John Lawson's humorous *If Pigs Could Fly* (Houghton, 1989, $13.95: 0-395-50928-9), Morgan James must deliver documents to Andrew Jackson during the War of 1812.

Dr. Peale and his apprentices help fight a yellow fever epidemic in 1793 Philadelphia in Paul Fleischman's *Path of the Pale Horse* (Harper, 1983, $13.89: 0-06-021905-X).

West follows his mother's dying words and heads seaward to his father in Susan Cooper's *Seaward* (Macmillan, 1983, $14.95: 0-689-50275-3).

About the Book and Author

Berger, Laura Standley, ed. *Twentieth-Century Children's Writers*. 4th ed. St. James, 1994, pp. 373–76.

Brown, Muriel W., and Rita Schoch Foudray. *Newbery and Caldecott Medalists and Honor Book Winners: Bibliographic & Resources Material Through 1990*. 2d ed. Neal-Schuman, 1992, pp. 229–31.

Chevalier, Tracy, ed. *Twentieth-Century Children's Writers*. 3d ed. St. James, 1989, pp. 554–56.

Collier, Laurie and Johce Nakamura. *Major Authors and Illustrators for Children and Young Adults*. Gale, 1993, 6 vols., pp. 1404-47.

Commire, Anne, ed. *Something About the Author*. Vol. 21. Gale, 1971, pp. 171–72.

Evory, Ann, and Linda Metzger, eds. *Contemporary Authors (First Revision Series)*. Vol. 7. Gale, 1982, pp. 303–5.

Fuller, Muriel, ed. *More Junior Authors*. Wilson, 1963, pp. 131–32.

Harte, Barbara, and Carolyn Riley, eds. *Contemporary Authors (First Revision Series)*. Vols. 5–8. Gale, 1969, pp. 675–76.

Hopkins, Lee Bennett, ed. *More Books by More People*. Citation Press, 1974, pp. 250–56.

Kingman, Lee, ed. *Newbery and Caldecott Medal Books: 1956–1965 with Author's Acceptance Papers, Biographies and Related Material*. Horn Book, 1965, pp. 13–30.

"Newbery Award Acceptance Material, 1956." *Horn Book* 32, no. 4 (July/August 1956): 283–99.

Olendorf, Donna, ed. *Something About the Author.* Vol. 68. Gale, 1992, pp. 123–26.

Peterson, Linda K., and Marilyn L. Solt, eds. *Newbery and Caldecott Medal and Honor Books: 1922–1981.* Hall, 1982, pp. 132–33.

Silvey, Anita. ed. *Children's Books and Their Creators.* Houghton, 1995, p. 392.

Ward, Martha, ed. *Authors of Books for Young People.* 3d ed. Scarecrow, 1990, p. 418.

Honor Books 1956

Lindquist, Jennie. *The Golden Name Day.* Illustrated by Garth Williams. Harper, 1955, o.p. (Grades 4–6)

    The author has used her childhood experiences and the remembrances of her Swedish heritage and its traditions as the basis for this affectionate, sentimental portrait of family life in rural America during the presidency of Theodore Roosevelt. Because of her mother's serious illness, nine-year-old Nancy Bruce has been sent to live with her grandparents, Albertina and Eric Benson, for a year in a small New England town. She is welcomed not only by her loving grandparents, but also by her three delightful cousins, Elsa, Sigrid, and Helga, daughters of Aunt Anna and Uncle John, and the Benson's menagerie, a coffee-drinking cat named Teddy, Oscar, the dog, and the family horse, Karl the Twelfth. Nancy's arrival coincides with the happy celebration of Grandmother Albertina's name day, a traditional Swedish custom. Although Swedish almanacs and the town wise man, Mr. Sanborn, are consulted, no one can discover a name day for Nancy. Although she hopes to have her own name day, Nancy is soon preoccupied by the happy everyday life in this Swedish community. She enjoys visiting Uncle Swen's nearby farm where kindly Aunt Martha, Swen's unmarried sister, also lives. Nancy picks new wallpaper and helps repaper her room at the Bensons, and finds a tiny kitten the family names Cuckoo Clock, after the beloved children's book by Mrs. Molesworth. She also loses her feelings of self-pity when she befriends a crippled boy, Alex Brown, and finds a new companion in a young Polish girl, Wanda, whose family has recently moved to the area. In spite of these diverting and often joyous experiences, Nancy still longs for her own name day. At last Grandpa finds a solution. In the Swedish almanacs, there is no name day on January 1, so in the future this will be Nancy's special day.

Rawlings, Marjorie Kinnan. *The Secret River.* Illustrated by Leonard Weisgard. Scribner, 1955, o.p. (Grades 2–4)

    When Marjorie Rawlings died in 1953, she left among her papers the manuscript of the only book she wrote specifically for children: this charming fantasy set in the author's home territory, rural Florida. The simple text contains a number of delightful poems made up by its heroine. Within a deep forest where redbirds sing and squirrels scamper among the trees, a little girl, Calpurnia, and her dog, Buggy-horse, live with Calpurnia's mother and her father, the local fish seller.

Unfortunately, hard times have come and nobody is catching fish. To help her father, Calpurnia decides to catch her own fish. She consults the local wise woman, Mother Albirtha, to find a suitable stream. She heeds Mother Albirtha's advice to follow her nose, and soon finds herself by a magical river where she catches many large catfish. On the way home, she is confronted in turn by a hoot owl, a bear, and a panther, each of whom she pacifies with a gift of fish. Although night is falling, she also pauses long enough at Mother Albirtha's to share some of the catch with her. Both her mother and father are astonished at Calpurnia's gift of fish and soon her father has money once again. However, when Calpurnia and Buggy-horse start out to revisit the secret river, they are unsuccessful. Again Calpurnia goes to Mother Albirtha for advice. The old woman explains that, "You caught catfish when catfish were needed. So you will not find that river again." But, as consolation, Calpurnia realizes that the secret river is in her mind and that she can close her eyes anytime and see the river again.

Shippen, Katherine B. *Men, Microbes, and Living Things*. Illustrated by Anthony Ravielli. Viking, 1955, o.p. (Grades 6–9)

This overview of the discoveries of the world's great biologists attempts to trace mankind's attempts to find the links that bind all living things. Beginning with prehistory, humans sought answers to the great questions of life and death, but it was the ancient Greeks who were first scientifically interested in living things. Aristotle studied catfish in the waters off the coast of Lesbos in the Aegean Sea. He hoped to come to an understanding of the meaning of life. Later through his study of mammals he devised the theory of the essence that distinguishes all living things. He called this principle of life the psyche or soul. Later, Pliny the Elder created *Natural History*, an encyclopedia of then-known scientific knowledge. After the Middle Ages, there was a reawakening of interest in science. Vesalius explored human anatomy, and Harvey pioneered the study of the heart and blood circulation. The hidden world of microbes was uncovered by pioneers of the microscope: Malpighi, Swammerdam, and most important, Anton van Leeuwenhoek. The classification and cataloging of living things was begun by Linnaeus and continued with the work of Baron Cuvier and Lamarck, the scientist who invented the term *biology*. Darwin made a landmark contribution with his theory of evolution, and Von Baer, through his study of embryos and his discovery of the mammalian ova, founded the study of embryology. Also highlighted are the work of Schwann and Schleiden who studied cells, and Gregor Mendel, the Augustine monk whose botanical research led to the theory of dominance in genetics. The final chapter, "We Are Still at the Beginning," outlines many of the challenges still faced by the world's biologists.

Newbery Winner 1957

Sorensen, Virginia. *Miracles on Maple Hill*. Illustrated by Beth Krush and Joe Krush. Harcourt, 1956 o.p.; pap., Odyssey, $6.95: 0-15-254561-1. (Grades 4–6)

Virginia Sorensen (1912–1991) divided her writing talents almost equally between fiction for adults and children with more than half a dozen novels completed for each audience. Her juvenile works are characterized by wholesome family relationships filled with kindness, understanding, mutual love, and respect. Her first book for children was *Curious Missie* (Harcourt, 1953, o.p.) about a young girl who cannot stop asking questions. In *Lottie's Locket* (Harcourt, 1964, o.p.), a young Danish girl faces conflicts when she is taken from the land she loves to live in the United States, and in *Plain Girl* (pap., Harcourt, $3.95), a young Amish girl, who is different in dress and behavior from her schoolmates, must resolve the conflict between her cultural background and the world around her. *Miracles on Maple Hill*, told from the viewpoint of 10-year-old Marly, exhibits Miss Sorensen's major strengths: believable characters, warm human relationships, positive attitudes, poetic writing, and a wonder at the marvels of nature. At the time of her death, Sorensen was planning a sequel.

Plot Summary

Ten-year-old Marly and her 12-year-old brother Joe are on their way with their mother and father to Maple Hill in rural Pennsylvania. They are planning to reopen the small farmhouse, which has been deserted for many years, where Marly's mother grew up with her brother and Grandma. But as the whole family knows, the real reason that they are going to Maple Hill is to help Marly's father. A soldier and then a prisoner of war, whom many thought would never return, he has been a changed man since his homecoming. Gone is the loving father that Marly remembers; in his place is a tired, discouraged, and often angry man who, this past Christmas, for instance, did not even come downstairs to see the presents.

In Maple Hill, a place of miracles that begin when the sap starts to rise in the maple trees and it is time to make syrup, Marly hopes that the miracle of her father's recovery will take place, too. Almost at once, he does seem to relax somewhat in the easygoing, friendly atmosphere of the pastoral community. Their neighbor, Mr. Chris, has a lot to do with that, and Marly is instantly drawn to the kindly old man who promises her that the countryside has many miracles to show her as winter changes into spring and then to summer.

Until summer comes and school is out, Marly, Joe, and her mother can visit Maple Hill only on weekends or school holidays, but their father stays in the farmhouse, renovating it and continuing to appear more relaxed than in the city. Marly finds almost complete joy in this place, although she is upset by the attitude of many of the rural people toward nature. For instance, after she talks about a nest of baby foxes she and Joe discover, she is horrified when the men of the community make plans to kill them the following morning because foxes kill their chickens. Although her mother and brother try to tell her that she must accept such things, she is inconsolable. Finally, Joe gives in to her grief and together they sneak out and frighten the baby foxes away so that they will not be killed.

However, Marly also learns of the great beauty of nature when Mr. Chris shows her the lush fields of wildflowers heralding the coming of spring and summer. That, too, is a miracle of Maple Hill.

When school is out, the family moves into the farmhouse for the summer. One day when they are discussing how people used to live off the land, Mr. Chris tells them about the man called Harry the Hermit who lives at the end of the mountain. Joe is determined to meet him. When he takes off the next morning, Marly is sure he is going to try to find the hermit and so she follows him. Joe finds a small barn, obviously the hermit's home, although he is not there. When Marly shows herself, the two cautiously look into the hermit's home and are nearly scared out of their wits when the man returns. He shouts after them, but the children run away.

That night there is a knock on the farmhouse door, and Joe and Marly are amazed to find the hermit standing there. Instead of being angry, he offers them some of his homemade cheese and honey and asks them to visit him again. Joe is in awe of Harry the Hermit and declares that he will get a house just like Harry's and live just like him when he grows up.

Thoughts of the hermit fly out of the window, however, when Marly overhears her parents discussing the possibility of not returning to the city in the fall, but moving permanently to this rural spot. Marly is charmed, but Joe is furious. He does not want to go to a dinky little school, especially when he has plans for being in the big school band back in the city this fall. The family talks over the pros and cons, and in the end it is decided that they are going to live in Maple Hill.

Although Joe is unhappy with the decision, his growing friendship with Harry the Hermit makes up somewhat for his new life in Maple Hill. Harry shows Joe how to make butter and cheese, how to milk cows, and a million other fascinating ways of getting along in the country.

When fall comes and Marly and Joe go to the little red schoolhouse in the country, Marly makes a new best friend and Joe gets to be in the school band after all. What with father improving and becoming his own self more and more, it does look as though Maple Hill has indeed worked its miracles, just as Mr. Chris promised.

One night near Christmas, Joe disappears. Mr. Chris and Father look for him, but he cannot be found. Then, Marly remembers that Joe told her he was going to visit Harry because one of his teachers had said that Christmas is a time to think about people who are lonely. Mr. Chris says he never thought about going to Harry's because he figured that Joe knew the hermit never spent the winter in Maple Hill but went to the Old Folks Home in Erie through the cold months. When Mr. Chris and father go to the hermit's home, they not only find Joe but also Harry, who has fallen and hurt his leg. Without Joe, Harry would have frozen to death. Joe is a hero!

As Marly says, "What a Christmas-thing to do!"

However, a problem develops the next morning when Joe wants Harry to recuperate in the farmhouse and his mother protests because he is a dirty old man and smells. Joe says Harry can have his room. Mother gives in when father for the first time tells them about the dirty conditions in which he was forced to live when in prison camp.

Harry recuperates, goes back to his home, and a new year begins. Now it is sap time again, and Marly is excited at the prospect until her beloved Mr. Chris has a heart attack, his second.

With Mr. Chris in the hospital, how can he finish the syrup run? He needs the money that this year's sap will bring in. Father, Mother, Joe, Marly, and others will do the job, but that means the children cannot go to school until it is done. The work is hard, long, and tiring, but very satisfying, except to the county truant officer, Annie-Get-Your-Gun, who arrives the next morning to find out where the children are. Not only is she sympathetic to what they are trying to do, but she convinces the school authorities that it would be a good idea for the boys and girls from Joe's class to come out and help with the sap run. And so they do . . . another miracle on Maple Hill.

When Mr. Chris is well enough to come home in the spring, he gets to taste the first of their syrup crop. He pronounces it as good as he ever could have made himself!

Themes and Subjects

This story of family and country life extols the virtues of love, friendship, kindness, and the beauty of nature. Strangely enough, although written in 1956, the book seems far more modern because of the father who is a former prisoner of war. Although this father would presumably have been in the military during the Korean War, his change of personality upon his return home will evoke closer memories of returning veterans from Vietnam. Marly's struggle to understand the transformation of her father and her subtle fear that the man she knows will never return are well presented. The other main theme is relevant to modern times. The character of Harry the Hermit points out the difficulties of being different in a world of conformity. This is a theme to which children of our times can easily relate.

Incidents for Booktalking

Surrounding the story of a family struggling to regain its closeness are the beauty and therapeutic properties of the changing rural countryside. See the following: Marly sees Maple Hill and meets Mr. Chris (pp. 12–13); bringing in the sap (pp. 35–45); Mr. Chris shows Marly the miracle of flowers (pp. 56–62); Marly meets the cows (pp. 63–69). For a discussion of nature in the country, see: Marly finds the baby mice (pp. 29–32); the baby foxes (pp. 70–86).

Related Titles

Lisa is overprotective of her younger brother, who has special needs, in a tender novel about growing up, *Commander Coatrack Returns* (Houghton, 1989, $13.95: 0-395-48295-X; pap., Dell, $4.95: 0-440-40479-7) by Joseph McNair.

In England during the Great Depression, a lonely boy named Lennie finds a friend in a deserted house in Ann Turnbull's *No Friend of Mine* (Candlewick, 1995, $15.95: 1-56402-565-9).

In Betty Ren Wright's *Nothing But Trouble* (Holiday, 1995, $15.95: 0-8234-1175-3), Vannie is forced to stay on a farm with her aged aunt who objects to her dog.

Susan Patron's *Maybe Yes, Maybe No, Maybe Maybe* (Orchard, 1993, $14.95: 0-531-05482-9) is a warm family story about three girls and their mother told by the middle child, PK.

In Robin Klein's *All in the Blue Unclouded Weather* (Viking, 1992, $11.95: 0-670-83909-4), four girls learn about themselves as they grow up in Australia during the late 1940s.

About the Book and Author

Berger, Laura Standley, ed. *Twentieth-Century Children's Writers*. 4th ed. St. James, 1995, pp. 896–97.

Brown, Muriel W., and Rita Schoch Foudray. *Newbery and Caldecott Medalists and Honor Book Winners: Bibliographic & Resource Material Through 1990.* 2d ed. Neal-Schuman, 1992, pp. 394–95.

Chevalier, Tracy, ed. *Twentieth-Century Children's Writers.* 3d. ed. St. James, 1989, pp. 907–08.

Commire, Anne, ed. *Something About the Author.* Vol. 2. Gale, 1971, pp. 233–34.

Fuller, Muriel, ed. *More Junior Authors.* Wilson, 1963, pp. 188–89.

Helbig, Alethea K., and Agnes R. Perkins, eds. *Dictionary of American Children's Fiction, 1859–1959.* Greenwood, 1986, pp. 480–81 (bio.), pp. 346–47 (book).

———. *Dictionary of American Children's Fiction, 1960–1985.* Greenwood, 1986, p. 616.

Kingman, Lee, ed. *Newbery and Caldecott Medal Books: 1956–1965 with Acceptance Papers, Biographies and Related Material.* Horn Book, 1965, pp. 31–49.

Nakamura, Joyce, ed. *Something About the Author: Autobiographical Series.* Vol. 15. Gale, 1993, pp. 267–76.

"Newbery Award Acceptance Material, 1957." *Horn Book* 33, no. 4 (July/August 1957): 273–81.

Peterson, Linda K., and Marilyn L. Solt, eds. *Newbery and Caldecott Medal and Honor Books: 1922–1981.* Hall, 1982, pp. 134–35.

Straub, Deborah A., ed. *Contemporary Authors (New Revision Series).* Vol. 22. Gale, 1988, pp. 434–35.

Ward, Martha, ed. *Authors of Books for Young People.* 3d ed. Scarecrow, 1990, pp. 662–63.

Honor Books 1957

de Angeli, Marguerite. *The Black Fox of Lorne.* Illustrated by the author. Doubleday, 1956, o.p. (Grades 5–7)

This historical adventure set in tenth-century Europe authentically re-creates the seafaring ways of the Vikings and the clan life in Scotland. Jan and Brus are 13-year-old identical twins whose father, the Viking Harald Redbeard, decides to move his family and followers from Norway to Britain where their Danish relatives have already settled. One ship, *Raven of the Wind,* carries the boys, their father, and their mother, along with their household belongings. The ships become separated in a violent storm and the *Raven of the Wind* is wrecked on the northern coast of Scotland in the land controlled by Began Mor, a savage clansman. He invites the survivors to a dinner where his followers slaughter all the men. Jan is spared and his brother Brus escapes by hiding. Later Brus finds his wounded father and drags him to a cave. While Brus is seeking water, someone enters the cave, kills his father, and steals his talisman, a jeweled brooch. Jan becomes a servant to the greedy, cruel Gavin Dhu, the Black Fox of Lorne, who begins wearing the breastpin to indicate that he is the murderer. Brus is able to contact his brother and soon they are secretly changing identities. Among Gavin Dhu's retinue are a nephew, Alan MacDugal, who hides the hatred he feels toward his uncle for killing his father. The party moves south supposedly to join King Malcolm in an attack against the British. Actually the Black Fox has plotted with the British to betray his king. Both Brus and Jan help in foiling these plans and reveal that they are twins. As a reward they receive from King Malcolm the land's of Began and Alan becomes the new lord of Lorne. To add to their happiness, the boys are reunited with their mother.

DeJong, Meindert. *The House of Sixty Fathers*. Illustrated by Maurice Sendak. Harper, 1956, $15.89: 0-06-021481-3; pap., Trophy, $4.95: 0-06-440200-2. (Grades 5–8)

This action-filled story is based on the author's experiences in China during World War II. Young Tien Pao is living on a sampan with his parents who have fled the advancing Japanese troops. One day, the boy ferries a young Air Force officer from a nearby base across the river. The impressionable boy considers this golden-haired, blue-eyed man to be a river god. The next day, a water buffalo accidentally loosens the rope that moors the sampan to the shore, and Tien Pao and his pet pig, Glory of the Republic, are carried downstream into Japanese-occupied territory. When the tiny boat comes to rest, the boy takes refuge in the surrounding hills. He endangers his own life to warn an American airman, whose plane has been shot down, that there are Japanese nearby. It is Tein Pao's river god, and together they begin their journey home. They are found by Chinese guerrillas who smuggle the boy into the city of Hengyang. When the Japanese attack, there is a mass flight from the city. Tien Pao and his little pig accidentally fall from the refugee train but are found by two Air Force men who take the boy to their base. There he is nursed back to health and adopted by the men. Soon the barracks become his home complete with 60 fathers. Lieutenant Hamsun, the real name of Tien Pao's river god, arrives at the base and through an interpreter the boy convinces the lieutenant to fly his plane low over the refugee encampment in an effort to find his family. Miraculously the plan works: the boy sees his mother working on the construction site of a neighboring airfield. Soon Tien Pao is joyfully reunited with his real family.

Gipson, Fred. *Old Yeller*. Harper, 1956, $23.00: 0-06-011545-9. (Grades 5–10)

This touching, often humorous story of a boy and his dog re-creates pioneer life in the Texas hill country after the Civil War with authentic details. Fourteen-year-old Travis Coates becomes the man of the house when his father joins a massive cattle drive to Abilene, Kansas, 600 miles away. One day, a mangy yellow dog with independent, thieving ways moves in on the family. Only the pleas of Travis's pesky young brother, Arliss, saves the dog from being sent away. He is named Old Yeller partly because of his color but principally because of his strange voice. Gradually the dog earns his rightful place in the family. He saves Arliss's life during a bear attack. In time, Old Yeller becomes Travis's dog; they hunt together and are soon inseparable. When Travis is engaged in lassoing the young in a herd of savage wild pigs that Old Yeller has driven in a ravine, the bank on which Travis is perched gives way and he falls into the midst of the herd.

Though wounded himself, Old Yeller routs the pigs, allowing Travis to reach safety. A plague of hydrophobia breaks out and the dog is bitten while driving off a rabid wolf who has attacked Travis's mother and a neighbor girl. It means eventual death to the dog and perhaps danger to the family when his brain becomes infected, so Travis must shoot him. He is inconsolable at Old Yeller's death, even when his father returns with a present of a horse. One day, Travis sees a puppy sired by Old Yeller steal cornbread just like his father did and realizes he has a new pet. He takes him out on his first squirrel hunt because, as Travis says, "If he was big enough to act like Old Yeller, he was big enough to earn his own keep." The story of the new dog is told in the sequel *Savage Sam* (pap. Harper, $5.50).

Judson, Clara Ingram. *Mr. Justice Holmes*. Illustrated by Robert Todd. Follett, 1956, o.p. (Grades 5–8)

This biography of the famous Supreme Court Justice and humanitarian concentrates on his boyhood and youth. It is filled with fascinating details of life in nineteenth and early twentieth-century America. Oliver Wendell Holmes, Jr. was born in 1841 to a distinguished Beacon Hill family in Boston. His father was a renowned doctor, teacher, and author. As a youngster, Wendell became interested in legal concepts, when, in spite of popular protests, the escaped slave Anthony Burns is returned to his master because of legal technicalities. He received a general education at several prestigious schools including Boston's Latin School and later at Harvard. Although he was not a brilliant student, he completed his undergraduate studies in the top quarter of his class. His hatred of slavery led him to volunteer for the Union forces at the outbreak of the Civil War. He was wounded in three different battles and each time returned to active service after recuperating at home until he had completed three years of service. After the war he studied law at Harvard despite his father's less than enthusiastic endorsement of his profession of choice. There he followed a distinguished career, first as a counselor of law, then as a law professor at Harvard and a member of the Massachusetts supreme judicial court. President Theodore Roosevelt appointed him to the U.S. Supreme Court in 1902 where he served courageously and unselfishly. He resigned in 1932, three years before his death. As the author states, Holmes's "outstanding contribution was in showing that law is not a dull, static thing, but experimental, fluid and realistic. He was honored as a wise philosopher, an honest judge, and a great man."

Rhoads, Dorothy. *The Corn Grows Ripe*. Viking, 1956, o.p.; pap., Puffin, $4.99: 0-14-036313-0. (Grades 3-5)

This is a brief, simple story of one year in the life of a peasant family whose home is in a primitive Maya settlement in the Yucatan where life revolves around ancient religious ceremonies and cultivating corn. It is also the story of how a young boy achieves maturity and manhood through work and adversity. Twelve-year-old Dionisio, nicknamed Tigre, is a lazy, mischievous child who is inclined to shirk his responsibilities until his father is seriously injured one day when a tree falls and breaks his leg as he is working on the family's milpa (cornfield). Because of this accident, the boy must suddenly assume responsibility for his family's welfare. Without hesitation, he walks the 17 kilometers to the nearest village to bring the medicine man back to set his father's broken bone. Single-handedly, Tigre clears the remaining trees and vegetation from the plot, and when the brush has been dried by the sun, he burns it in March. Later he plants the precious corn kernels in the newly prepared ground. Though so tired he can scarcely move, he visits the schoolteacher, Don Alfonso, nightly to keep up with his studies. In May, the tiny community comes alive with the annual Fiesta, three days of merrymaking that climax with the youths and men facing the charge of raging bulls in the hastily constructed bull ring. Tigre is skillfully able to jump out of danger onto one of the ring's tree posts just in time.

Unfortunately the rains do not come, and everyone is fearful that there will be no harvest. A "Chac Chac ceremony" is held to bring rain and Tigre participates. Three days later everyone is convinced that the rain god, Chac, has heard their prayers when the rains begin. Late in September, Tigre and his recently recovered father work together to harvest the ears of fat, yellow corn.

Newbery Winner 1958

Keith, Harold. *Rifles for Watie*. Crowell, 1957, $14.95: 0-06-9070181-0; pap., Harper, $4.95: 0-06-447030-X. (Grades 7–10)

Though not a prolific writer, Harold Keith (1903–1990) was famous for a series of historical novels noted for their exciting stories and accurate details. After winning the Newbery Award in 1958, he wrote two other fine novels. The first, *Komantica* (Cowell, 1965, o.p.) is based on the true story of a young Spaniard, Pedro, who is captured by the Comanches in 1865. He adjusts so completely to this Native American culture that he becomes part of the tribe. The second, *The Obstinate Land* (Crowell, 1977, o.p.), is set in northern Oklahoma in 1893 during the days of the Oklahoma land run into the Cherokee Strip. It centers on one pioneer family, the Rombergs, and their 14-year-old son, Fritz, who is forced to assume responsibility for the family's welfare after his father's death. Both these novels are currently available in reprint editions from Levite Apache Press in Norman, Oklahoma.

The research and writing on *Rifles for Watie* (pronounced way-tee) took many years. While working on his Master's degree in History at the University of Oklahoma, Keith became fascinated with the Civil War, particularly with the history of the western campaign in the Indian territory. He spent two summers (1940–1941) traveling around Oklahoma collecting data. During this time, he interviewed 22 Civil War veterans. The time and effort that the author spent resulted in this rich historical panorama created with intricate attention to the smallest detail.

Plot Summary

With its scorching drought, the year 1860 was a terrible year for the Bussey family and the other pioneer farmers trying to eke out a living from the soil of Linn County in Kansas. At last, in the spring of 1861, there is rain. However, another equally destructive force has emerged in the form of frequent raids from the abolitionist Kansas side of the territory by parties of proslavery Missouri bushwhackers. In one such raid, the Busseys lose their two horses, leaving only their mules to help farm the land.

One day, their 16-year-old son Jeff is working in the fields when he hears the warning sounds of his father's large sea horn. Rushing home, he finds that his parents and two sisters are being held at gunpoint by two marauding bushwhackers. Only when their guard is momentarily down are they routed by the combined attack of several family members including Jeff with a pitchfork and a sister with a pot of boiling water.

For Jeff this is the last straw. With his family's blessing he leaves the following morning to join the Union forces to fight in the impending Civil War that he hopes will rid the West of both these outlaws and the oppressive human slavery for which they stand. While walking to Fort Leavenworth to enlist, Jeff is joined by two of his friends, John Chadwick and Dave Garner, who also decide to join the Kansas Volunteers.

Though war has been declared, the first months in the army are something of an anticlimax. They consist of army drills, tiring marches, and a few foraging operations. Jeff is well-liked and makes many friends, including Noah Babbitt, a tramp printer from Illinois, and Jimmy Lear, a 14-year-old drummer boy. He also makes an enemy—Captain Asa Clardy, a sadistic army officer who delights in persecuting the boy. Jeff discovers that Captain Clardy's villainy extends beyond making his life miserable. He is convinced that Clardy robs innocent civilians and that the discovery of these crimes was the reason that their drunken cook, Sparrow, was killed.

Dave Gardner becomes so homesick that he deserts, but luckily Jeff is given a furlough home where he talks Dave into returning to his unit.

After marching to Springfield, Missouri, the Union forces are engaged in a battle at Wilson's Creek. Jeff, who is anxious to be tested in combat, instead is commanded by an officer to go to the rear of the action to fetch the quartermaster. By the time he returns, the battle has been fought and lost. Jeff discovers that some of his dearest comrades have either been killed or seriously maimed. Suddenly the thrill and glamour he felt about warfare disappears.

While occupying the rebel town of Tahlequah, the capital of the Cherokee Indian nation, Jeff meets the Washbourne family and is impressed with their kindness and quiet dignity even though they are supposedly the enemy. He is particularly attracted to Lucy, the youngest daughter. Lucy's father and her brother, Lee, are both serving in General Stand Watie's Confederate Cherokee Cavalry unit. In conversation with the Washbournes and other Southerners, Jeff realizes that the issues involved in the war are not as well defined as he once thought—there are good and bad on both sides.

At last, Jeff sees combat action. He and Noah distinguish themselves at the Battle of Prairie Grove by manning a deserted cannon and helping to repel the enemy charge. Much to Jeff's amazement, each is awarded the Congressional Medal of Honor.

The inhumanity and savagery of war become apparent to Jeff when he witnesses the execution of a Confederate spy caught behind Northern lines. When the soldier's personal belongings are collected, Jeff discovers that the boy was Lee Washbourne, Lucy's brother.

Because of his fine combat record, Jeff is chosen to act as a spy behind enemy lines. While in Confederate territory, he is captured by a group of Watie's men. To hide his real identity, he volunteers to serve in the Southern army. Just when Jeff has collected important information about Southern troop movements, he is stricken with an attack of malaria and is unable to return to his unit at Fort Gibson. Instead, he gives the information to a runaway slave, Leemon Jones, who manages to cross the battle lines and complete Jeff's mission.

During his illness, Jeff stays with the Jackmans, a kindly Southern family who nurse him back to health. While at the Jackmans, Jeff learns that Watie's men are receiving smuggled rifles for Fort Gibson. The identity of the Union officer who is selling them to the South is unknown. Jeff is determined to remain until he finds out the name of the traitor.

After his recovery, the boy rejoins Watie's unit and is welcomed back by the men. When he thinks of the warmth and kindness shown him by his supposed enemies, Jeff feels shame and guilt about the nature of his mission. At one point, he contemplates remaining with his friends in the South. However, an incident occurs that takes the decision out of Jeff's hands.

While engaging in a scouting expedition, the boy witnesses the delivery of a shipment of smuggled rifles. The Northern traitor is his hated enemy, Captain Clardy. Clardy recognizes the boy. To escape a Southern firing squad, Jeff is forced to flee to the North. For days, he endures incredible hardships and many narrow escapes. Finally, he stumbles into a Union encampment and is greeted by his friend Noah. As a result of his mission the arms shipments end. Mysteriously, Clardy disappears never to be heard of again.

When the war ends, Jeff and his two friends, John Chadwick and Dave Gardner, march back to their homes together. The three men are very different from the young boys who had left four years earlier.

Jeff has many thoughts about the future. He plans one day to return to the South and find Lucy Washbourne. Together, he hopes, they will find happiness and a chance to help reunite their divided country.

Themes and Subjects

Like *The Red Badge of Courage*, this is a coming-of-age story in which boys become men through the ordeal of war. It offers a realistic indictment of war with its filth, deprivation, horror, but at times, heroism. An equally important theme is well stated by the author when he said that a person sometimes finds that "one's enemies are often the same as one's friends." The discovery by Jeff that people and causes are often a mixture of both good and evil is the central conflict in the novel. Other themes involve an exploration of the meaning of courage, and the price of loyalty to a cause. The author makes history come alive with the accuracy and attention to detail he uses in describing this period of life on the western frontier.

Incidents for Booktalking

Some of the incidents that can be used to arouse interest are: the bushwhacker's raid on the Bussey farm (pp. 9–13); Jeff and his friends leave their homes to enlist (pp. 15–19); Jeff meets Captain Asa Clardy (pp. 23–26); the furlough and bringing Dave back to camp (pp. 32–38); the Battle of Wilson's Creek (pp. 61–67); Jeff works in a field hospital (pp. 69–72); the battle of Prairie Grove (pp. 127–34); the death of Jimmy Lear (pp. 143–46).

Related Titles

When Pa joins the Union army as a soldier, 11-year-old Willie goes along as a drummer boy in G. Clifton Wisler's *Mr. Lincoln's Drummer* (Dutton, 1994, $15.99: 0-525-67463-2), for young readers.

A teenage boy is involved in the building of a ship for the Confederate Navy in Scott O'Dell's *The Two Hundred-Ninety* (Houghton, 1976, $15.95: 0-395-24737-3).

The Slopes of War (pap., Houghton, 1984, $5.95: 0-395-54979-5) by N. A. Perez tells how young Buck Summerhill, a private during the Civil War, and his sister experience the horror of this war.

A young Southern girl during the Civil War learns about the evils of slavery in Ann Rinaldi's *The Last Silk Dress* (Holiday, 1988, $15.95: 0-8234-0690-3; pap., Bantam, $4.99: 0-553-28315-4).

For younger audiences, John Donahue's *An Island Far from Home* (Carolrhoda, 1994, $21.27: 0-87614-859-3) tells how 12-year-old Joshua wants to avenge the death of his father in the Civil War and finds instead a friendship with a young Confederate prisoner.

About the Book and Author

Berger, Laura Standley, ed. *Twentieth-Century Young Adult Writers*. St. James, 1954, pp. 341–43.

Brown, Muriel W., and Rita Schoch Foudray. *Newbery and Caldecott Medalists and Honor Books Winners: Bibliographic & Resource Material Through 1990*. 2d ed. Neal-Schuman, 1992, pp. 219–20.

Chevalier, Tracy, ed. *Twentieth-Century Children's Writers*. 3d ed. St. James, 1989, pp. 513–14.

Collier, Laurie, and Joyce Nakamura. eds. *Major Authors and Illustrators for Children and Young Adults*. Gale, 1993, 6 vols., pp. 1302-04.

Commire, Anne, ed. *Something About the Author*. Vol. 2. Gale, 1971, pp. 159–60.

Evory, Ann, ed. *Contemporary Authors (New Revision Series)*. Vols. 2. Gale, 1981, p. 373.

Fuller, Muriel, ed. *More Junior Authors*. Wilson, 1963, pp. 120–21.

Harte, Barbara, and Carolyn Riley, eds. *Contemporary Authors (First Revision Series)*. Vols. 5–8. Gale, 1969, p. 627.

Helbig, Alethea K., and Agnes R. Perkins, eds. *Dictionary of American Children's Fiction: 1859–1959*. Greenwood, 1986, p. 270 (bio.), pp. 431–32 (book).

———. *Dictionary of American Children's Fiction: 1960–1985*. Greenwood, 1986, p. 3652.

Hopkins, Lee Bennett, ed. *More Books by More People*. Citation Press, 1974, pp. 224–33.

Kingman, Lee, ed. *Newbery and Caldecott Medal Books: 1956–1965 with Acceptance Papers, Biographies and Related Material*. Horn Book, 1955, pp. 50–69.

"Newbery Medal Acceptance Material, 1958." *Horn Book* 34, no. 4 (July/August 1958): 285–301.

Peterson, Linda K., and Marilyn L. Solt, eds. *Newbery and Caldecott Medal and Honor Books: 1922–1981*. Hall, 1982, pp. 138–39.

Telgen, Diane, ed. *Something About the Author*. Vol. 74. Gale, 1993, pp. 140–42.

Ward, Martha, ed. *Authors of Books for Young People*. 3d ed. Scarecrow, 1990, p. 387.

Honor Books 1958

Enright, Elizabeth. *Gone-Away Lake*. Illustrated by Beth Krush and Joe Krush. Harcourt, 1957, o.p.; pap., Harcourt, $6.00: 0-15-231649-3. (Grades 3–6)

This appealing story of families and intergenerational friendship is set in a rural part of the northwestern United States during the 1950s. While their parents are in Europe, 11-year-old Portia Blake and her brother, Foster, age 6, are sent to the country to spend the summer with their aunt and uncle, Hilda and Jake Jarman and their 12-year-old son Julian, Portia's cousin. One day, equipped with nature guides, a collecting jar, a net, and other paraphernalia Julian and Portia go butterfly hunting and find, instead, a large, reed-covered swamp where there are a number of large, shabby, turn-of-the-century houses that are seemingly abandoned. In one, they find two occupants, Minnehaha Cheever, formerly Mrs. Lionel Cheever, and her brother Pindar Payton. The elderly people are friendly and begin telling the two youngsters of the golden days in the area when there was a thriving wealthy community and the swamp was Lake Tarrigo, before it was drained after a dam was built in 1903. In remembrance of what was, they now call the place Gone-Away Lake. Portia and Julian decide to keep their new friends a secret. The youngsters visit the old people regularly, hear more stories of the good old days, and make a clubhouse in one of the homes. One day, Foster follows them and is rescued by Pindar after being caught in quicksand. Pindar returns Foster in his old car and the Jarmans learn about this congenial pair that live in the swamp. Soon other youngsters join Portia and Julian's Gone-Away Lake group. When the Blakes return from their trip, they decide to refurbish one of the houses and keep it as a summer home. A sequel is *Return to Gone-Away* (Peter Smith, 1988, $17.25; pap., Harcourt, $4.95)

Gurgo, Leo. *Tom Paine: Freedom's Apostle*. Illustrated by Fritz Kredel. Crowell, 1957, o.p. (Grades 7–10)

Through the use of flashbacks and generous excerpts from Thomas Paine's writings, the entire life of this influential political writer and fighter for liberty is depicted. Born in 1737 in Norfolk, England, to a poor family that could not afford to give him an extensive education, Paine lived his first 37 years there. As an adult, he had only lowly, poor-paying jobs. After meeting Benjamin Franklin, he decided to emigrate to America, and armed with letters of introduction from his mentor, he arrived in 1774. His pamphlet "Common Sense," in which he argued that the colonies no longer needed English domination, caused a sensation. Other pamphlets followed, each increasing his fame. After the Revolutionary War, he returned to England in 1787, and wrote *The Rights of Man*. Although English politicians had hoped to use Paine to help reestablish relations with America, this work dashed these hopes because of its open support of the French Revolution. It stated that all people had natural rights, and only a democracy could ensure them. Before being arrested for treasonous activities, he fled to France, where he was greeted as a hero and took an active part in French politics. When the radical Jacobin took control, he was imprisoned during the Reign of Terror. During his 10-month stay in prison, he wrote the last part of the *Age of Reason*, a work that attacked religion and alienated many people. Because of his reputation in America and because he was known as a friend of the common man, he was freed. He returned to the United States in 1802, where his unorthodox opinions made him increasingly unpopular. He died in poverty in 1809.

Lawson, Robert. *The Great Wheel*. Illustrated by the author. Viking, 1957, o.p.; pap., Walker, $7.95: 0-8027-7392-3. (Grades 4–7)

This lighthearted, lively historical novel tells of the construction of the first Ferris Wheel for the Chicago World's Columbian Exposition of 1893, and recreates a period of unlimited hope and ambition in American history. At the bidding of his uncle Michael Gilbin, a prosperous builder of curbs and sewers in New York City, 18-year-old Cornelius (shortened to Conn) Kilroy leaves his County Mayo home in Ireland to seek his fortune in America. Before he leaves, his Aunt Honors predicts that one day he will ride the biggest wheel in the world. On the steamship, he meets Trudy, an attractive German girl who is going to Wisconsin to be with her Uncle Otto. Unfortunately, Conn fails to learn her last name.

In New York, Conn first works for Michael Gibin and there meets Uncle Patrick, the construction supervisor for the bright, imaginative engineer, George Washington Gale Ferris, who has been commissioned to create a huge wheel for the exposition in Chicago. Conn is hired by this company and moves west where he witnesses every aspect of the construction from digging the foundations to putting each car in place. The first ferris wheel became the world's largest ever. It was higher than a 20-story building and had 36 luxurious cars that held as many as 2,160 people. Not only does Conn fulfill his aunt's prophecy, but after the great wheel's fabulous inauguration, he remains on as a guard, hoping one day that Trudy will visit the fair. That day comes, and Conn discovers that she is a member of an extremely wealthy family of pork magnates. The two marry happily and begin farming in Wisconsin.

Sandoz, Mari. *The Horsecatcher*. Westminster, 1957, o.p.; pap., University of Nebraska, $7.95: 0-8032-9160-4. (Grades 6–12)

This historical novel deals with the lives, struggles, and culture of the American Indians living in the great western plains in the middle of the nineteenth century when herds of buffalo still roamed these vast grassy expanses. In spite of his father's wish that he become a warrior, Young Elk, the son of a Cheyenne chief, loves the wild horses that are now found on the plains and dreams of becoming a horsecatcher and tamer. Young Elk hates killing, and when his brother is killed by the Comanches, he refuses to join the war party that will avenge the death. After traveling alone into enemy territory, Young Elk returns with 15 horses including several highly prized ones. Realizing that he cannot change his son, his father allows him to join Old Horsecatcher who adopts him and offers to teach the boy his skills. Young Elk is anxious to learn. He gains experience with the northern Cheyenne who live along the Yellowstone and with a tribe of friendly Sioux. He infiltrates Comanche territory to watch two fabled sisters use their skills in taming wild mustangs. During his many solitary hunts, he endures great hardships and captures a variety of horses. He is intrigued by talk of a beautiful stallion, the White One, which he is later able to capture. While traveling home with his herd of 20 horses, he sees a Comanche war party moving toward his village. He must warn his clan quickly and is forced to release the horses to gain speed. In gratitude for saving them, his people honor him, and his father and the Old Horsecatcher rename him Elk River, the Horsecatcher.

Newbery Winner 1959

Speare, Elizabeth George. *The Witch of Blackbird Pond.* Houghton, 1958, $16.00: 0-395-07114-3; pap., Dell, $5.50: 0-440-99577-9. (Grades 6–9)

Elizabeth Speare (1908–1994) has an unusual record of success in the field of children's literature. Of her four historical novels written for young people, two of them, *The Witch of Blackbird Pond* and *The Bronze Bow* (see "Newbery Winner," 1962, p. 236), have won Newbery Awards and a third, *The Sign of the Beaver* was chosen as an Honor Book (see "Honor Books," 1984, p. 358). Her first book was *Calico Captive* (Houghton, 1957, $13.95; pap., Dell, $3.25). It is based on the diary of Susanna Johnson, published in 1807, which tells of a family of New England settlers who are captured by Indians in 1754 and later bartered to French captors. The novel's narrative concentrates on Susanna's high-spirited younger sister, Miriam, who was also one of the prisoners. In time, Susanna persuades the Chief to sell her husband, children, and Miriam to the French in Quebec while she remains behind with her son as prisoners. Eventually the family is reunited. The story gets its title from a beloved blue dress worn by Miriam during her captivity.

Speare was born in Massachusetts but moved to Connecticut where she lived for many years. She choose Wethersfield, a town on the Connecticut River about 10 miles south of Hartford, as the setting of *Witch of Blackbird Pond* for two main reasons: she had lived there and was therefore familiar with its geography and history, and because it once was a bustling river port in Colonial Connecticut similar to the one she wished to depict in the novel.

Plot Summary

In mid-April 1687, 16-year-old Kit (short for Katherine) Tyler stares disconsolately from the deck of the brigantine *Dolphin* at the gray hostile coast of Connecticut. She mentally compares this forbidding, inhospitable place with the sunny beaches of Barbados, her former home that she left five weeks ago. Kit's mother Margaret, an Englishwoman, had met her future husband after he arrived in England from Barbados to continue his education. They married and returned to the family's prosperous plantation on Barbados. Unfortunately, when Kit was only two, both her parents drowned in a boating accident. She was raised by her devoted grandfather, Sir Francis Tyler, the once-wealthy owner of one of the island's largest plantations. Upon his death Kit was forced to sell the plantation and its slaves to pay off the family's debts. She was able to save enough money to buy a passage to Wethersfield, Connecticut, where her only living relatives reside. Rachel, the sister of Kit's mother, had married a Puritan named Matthew Wood while she was still living in England and had run away with him to America. It is to her Aunt Rachel's home that Kit is now headed, hoping to begin a new life.

At the coastal town of Saybrook, many of the passengers leave the *Dolphin,* but a few new ones come on board to make the last lap of the journey to Wethersfield, 42 miles upstream. Kit meets a quiet but pleasant divinity student named John Holbrook, who, unable to afford tuition at Harvard, is going to study at Wethersfield with the Reverend Bulkeley. Other passengers include the Cluff family—Goodwife Cluff, a dour unfriendly woman, her husband Goodman Cluff, and their peaked, completely dominated young daughter, Prudence. When Kit jumps overboard to save a doll Prudence has accidentally dropped in the water, some of the passengers show amazement. Others, like the Cluffs, are hostile and suspicious because the captain's son, Nat Eaton, has said that only witches are supposed to have the ability to swim. Thus, the origin of the infamous trial by water.

Because of a number of setbacks, principally a lack of wind, it takes nine days to make this relatively short river journey. During this time Kit gets to know both John and Nat better. She is particularly attracted to Nat, who tries to be friendly but has difficulty adjusting to Kit's liberated, high-spirited ways that seem so different from the submissive, restrained behavior of the native Puritan girls. The Cluffs maintain their hostile, disapproving attitude during the entire trip.

No one is at the dock to meet her, and Kit is forced to confess to Captain Eaton that her uncle and aunt are unaware that she has left Barbados to live with them. However, when she arrives, her aunt welcomes her warmly while also expressing amazement at the amount of luggage and number of luxurious dresses that Kit has bought with her. They present a glaring contrast to the spartan drab clothing that the residents of Wethersfield wear.

Although she tries her best, independent and animated Kit finds it difficult to fit into the joyless, puritanical Wood household. Her aunt tries to be friendly, as do her two daughters—Judith, a rather selfish girl of Kit's age, and the older Mercy, who is a gentle, withdrawn cripple. All in the family are dominated by Matthew Wood, who regards Kit's elegant wardrobe as a sign of sloth and paganism. Kit lacks both the skill and patience to do her share of such household chores as carding wool, cooking, and soap making. Soon she feels both awkward and unwanted.

At Sabbath Meeting, Kit meets Mistress Ashly and her 19-year-old son William, the most eligible bachelor in Wethersfield. He begins to visit Kit, who is not really attracted to the reserved, too-proper young man. Nevertheless, she does nothing to discourage his attentions. Another frequent visitor to the Wood household is John Holbrook. Judith and the entire family mistakenly interpret this as paying court to Judith, but it is actually Mercy with whom John is secretly in love.

Kit enjoys helping Mercy at the dame school for young children that Mercy conducts in the Wood home. However, Kit's advanced teaching methods, such as role-playing, run afoul of the priggish supervising school master, Eleazer Kimberley, and Kit is severely reprimanded.

Her only real joy is to wander alone in the beautiful Great Meadow outside of town. Here she meets Hannah Tupper, an aged Quaker woman who lives in an isolated shack in the meadow. Because of her religion, Hannah was branded and driven out of Massachusetts. She sought refuge on the outskirts of Wethersfield, but here too she is regarded as a witch by the townspeople. Kit grows to love this gentle kindly woman, and she secretly visits her whenever possible. In addition to Kit, Hannah has two other visitors. The first is Nat Eaton who spends time with her whenever his ship, *Dolphin,* is docked in town. Kit becomes increasingly fond of this charming, good-natured young man. Prudence Cluff also begins to visit Hannah, and soon Kit is able to teach this hapless waif how to read and write.

A mysterious disease strikes Wethersfield, causing the death of several children and young people. Mercy is stricken, and only by the application of some poultices prescribed by Reverend Bulkeley is she able to recover. At the height of the epidemic, the superstitious townspeople decide that Hannah's witchcraft is the cause of their misery. Kit overhears a plan to burn Hannah's house and take her prisoner. Miraculously, Kit is able to reach her friend in time and with Nat's help, smuggle her safely on board the *Dolphin*.

The wrath of the townspeople now turns against Kit. Because of her association with Hannah, she is dragged to a filthy prison, and the next day, tried as a witch. Goodwife Cluff is the principal witness against her. A notebook containing Prudence's name has been found at Hannah's house, and the Cluffs maintain that Kit has bewitched their daughter. Nat appears, carrying Prudence. Before the assembled court, the little girl reads a passage from the Bible and writes her own name, thus showing to all that Kit's only crime was to educate her. Kit is freed.

Back home, Kit decides that she cannot, in honesty, marry William. She tells him so, and William turns his attention to Judith. Within the next few months there are two important weddings in town—Judith and William's and John and Mercy's.

During the summer, the *Dolphin* once more docks at Wethersfield. Nat Eaton, learning that Kit is now free of her attachment to William, joyously claims her as his bride.

Themes and Subjects

The term "witch-hunt," although associated with the cruel persecution of innocent women in the past, has taken on a broader meaning and is still present in different guises today. This novel illustrates how innocence and goodness can be interpreted as evil by the ignorance and intolerance of others. It also shows how religious beliefs can be perverted into attitudes that breed bigotry and persecution. The contrast between the life of a liberated, free spirit anxious to find truth, represented by Kit, and that of minds closed to reason and knowledge is well portrayed. The story shows how the powers of enlightenment and mercy can triumph over those of repression and ignorance. Kit emerges as a thoroughly convincing character: her charm, honesty, and vivacity intensify the interest in her struggle to help her friends and combat the fanaticism around her. Also touched on are such themes as self-reliance, perseverance, and the importance of acceptance and understanding in human relations. The story is filled with many fascinating details of everyday life and the political unrest found in Colonial New England.

Incidents for Booktalking

A brief description of Kit's lifestyle in Barbados as contrasted with the barren, sterile Puritan atmosphere of New England will serve to introduce the basic conflict found in the book. Some specific passages are: Kit saves Prudence's doll (pp. 7–10); she learns from Nat about witches and the trial by water (pp. 13–14); Kit meets John Holbrook (pp. 10–12); the trip from Saybrook to Wethersfield and getting to know the Cruffs (pp. 14–17); Kit tells John about her past (pp. 19–20); her reception at the Wood's home (pp. 30–35); Kit's dresses (pp. 39–44) and her teaching methods (pp. 86–90); Nat tells Kit about Hannah's past (pp. 130–31).

Related Titles

In *Priscilla Foster: The Story of a Salem Girl* (Silver Burdett, 1997, $14.95: 0-382-29640-5) by Dorothy and Thomas Hoobler, a grandmother takes her granddaughter to Salem and tells her about the witch trials of 1692.

Patricia Clapp's *Witch's Children* (pap., Puffin, $3.95) tells about the Salem witch trials from the standpoint of one of the afflicted girls.

Ann Petry's *Tituba of Salem Village* (Harper, 1988, $14.89) traces the life of Tituba from being sold as a slave in the Barbados to the Salem witch trials.

In John Bellairs's *The Ghost in the Mirror* (pap., Puffin, $4.50: 0-14-034934-0) 14-year-old Rose and white witch Mrs. Zimmerman are transported back in time to 1828 on a secret mission.

For a younger audience. Monster hunters Darcy and her friends travel back in time to the Salem witch trials to solve a modern-day problem in Nancy Garden's *The Monster Hunters: Mystery of the Watchful Witches* (Random, 1998, $11.99: 0-679-98575-1; pap. $3.99: 0-679-88575-7).

About the Book and Author

Apseloff, Marilyn. *Elizabeth George Speare*. Twayne, 1992.

Berger, Laura Standley, ed. *Twentieth-Century Young Adult Writers*. St. James, 1994, pp. 606–8.

Brown, Muriel W., and Rita Schoch Foudray. *Newbery and Caldecott Medalists and Honor Book Winners: Bibliographic & Resource Material Through 1990*. 2d ed. Neal-Schuman, 1992, pp. 395–96.

Chevalier, Tracy, ed. *Twentieth-Century Children's Writers*. 3d ed. St. James, 1989, pp. 910–11.

Collier, Laurie, and Joyce Nakamura. eds. *Major Authors and Illustrators for Children and Young Adults*. Gale, 1993, 6 vols., pp. 2182-84.

Commire, Anne, ed. *Something About the Author*. Gale, 1973, vol. 2, pp. 176–79; 1991, vol. 62, pp. 163–68.

Cosgrave, Mary Silva. "Elizabeth George Speare." *Horn Book* (July/August 1989): 465–68.

Gallo, Donald R. *Speaking for Ourselves, Too*. National Council of Teachers of English, 1993, pp. 201–2.

Helbig, Alethea K., and Agnes R. Perkins, eds. *Dictionary of American Children's Fiction, 1859–1959*. Greenwood, 1986, pp. 483–84 (bio.), p. 573 (book).

————. *Dictionary of American Children's Fiction, 1960–1985*. Greenwood, 1986, pp. 618–19.

Kingman, Lee, ed. *Newbery and Caldecott Medal Books: 1956–1965 with Acceptance Papers, Biographies and Related Material*. Horn Book, 1965, pp. 68–81.

"Newbery Award Acceptance Material, 1959." *Horn Book* 35, no. 4 (July/August 1959): 265–74.

Peterson, Linda K., and Marilyn L. Solt, eds. *Newbery and Caldecott Medal and Honor Books: 1922–1981*. Hall, 1982, pp. 143–44.

Senick, Gerard J., ed. *Children's Literature Review*. Vol. 8. Gale, 1985, pp. 204–11.

Silvey, Anita, ed. *Children's Books and Their Creators*. Houghton, 1995, pp. 615–17.

Speare, Elizabeth George. "Laura Ingalls Wilder Award Acceptance." *Horn Book* (July/August 1989): 460–64.

Ward, Martha, ed. *Authors of Books for Young People*. 3d ed. Scarecrow, 1990, p. 664.

Honor Books 1959

Carlson, Natalie. *The Family Under the Bridge*. Harper, 1958, $14.89: 0-06-020991-7; pap., $4.95, Trophy: 0-06-440250-9. (Grades 3–6)

This simple, brief story of a homeless family in modern Paris has been a favorite of youngsters for almost 40 years. High rents in post-World War II Paris force poor Madame Calcet to relocate her family to a cozy nook under a bridge. Unfortunately this also happens to be the home of a happy hobo, Armand, who uses a baby carriage as a trunk. He resents these interlopers, particularly the three red-headed children—Suzy, Paul, and tiny Evelyne, as well as their dog Jojo. Gradually his hostility abates and he grows to love his little "starlings." While Madame Calcet works he takes care of his young charges and shares some innocent adventures with them.. They visit a department store where Armand's friend is playing Father Christmas and attend a unique Christmas Eve party given by the Ladies of Notre Dame for the hobos of Paris. When it appears that the children will be separated from their mother by well-meaning people who want them placed in a conventional home, he hides them with gypsies who, unlike their forefathers, travel in cars and trucks. Unfortunately when the police arrive, the gypsies flee, and the children return to the bridge. Armand is so ashamed when he learns that young Paul has been looking for a job that he decides to make the supreme sacrifice and go job hunting. He believes that his application is for a night watchman's position but it is as a caretaker for several apartments. When he learns that in addition to wages the job provides living quarters, he accepts. Posing as "grandpa" Armand, he moves his surrogate family into a real home.

DeJong, Meindert. *Along Came a Dog*. Illustrated by Maurice Sendak. Harper, 1958, o.p.; pap., Trophy, $4.95: 0-06-440114-6. (Grades 4–7)

Joe, who works on a farm, raises a few chickens on his own small piece of land. In the all-white flock, there is a single red hen that has been crippled by losing toes that froze during the severe winter. One day a large black dog comes along, but Joe, fearful that the dog will cause trouble with the chickens, decides to drive him into the country and dump him. The crippled hen who is vulnerable to attacks by other chickens also comes in the car, and during the drive, the two animals form an unusual attachment. Back at the farm, the dog reappears and seems anxious to guard the little hen. Once again, Joe disposes of him in the country and once again the dog returns. This time he hides from Joe, but when the man is away working, the dog acts as the hen's protector. When the hen disappears, Joe thinks she has been killed, but actually she has created a nest far from the coop near a swamp and laid her eggs. Though half starved, the dog remains by the hen's side as her guardian. Unfortunately, Joe sees him once again, and this time, he drops the dog in the middle of a busy town where he becomes confused and directionless. Two weeks elapse. During that time the lingering scent of the dog at the nest helps protect the hen, but she is fearful of leaving the nest to find food because the hawks that are circling above will swoop down and destroy her eggs. She is near starvation on the day that the eggs hatch and the dog returns. Proudly, she hobbles back to Joe's place with five chicks and the dog. Joe relents and decides to provide a home for all of them.

Kalnay, Francis. *Chucaro: Wild Pony of the Pampa*. Illustrated by Juian de Miskey. Harcourt, 1958, o.p. (Grades 4–7)

This simple story gives an interesting picture of life on a mid-twentieth century estancia, or large cattle and horse ranch, in Argentina, where the owner and his family live in grandeur and luxury while the gauchos, or the simple cowboys, are housed in windowless adobe huts. One day 12-year-old Pedrito, who lives with his drunken father, an old vaquero, finds a beautiful pink- colored pony in an open field. Juan, a gaucho who has become Pedrito's guardian, lassos the pony whom he names Chucaro after a similar horse he had as a child. With Juan's help Pedrito breaks in the high-spirited animal and learns to ride him. When the owner of the ranch wants a horse for his spoiled, undisciplined son, Armondo, the mayordomo, or manager, orders Pedrito to give up Chucaro. At first the boy refuses, but Pedrito's father suggests that the pony be allowed to chose who should be his master. Chucaro resists all approaches from Armondo and kicks him. Angrily, the boy uses his bolas (heavy cowhide balls) on the frightened horse. Juan intervenes and scolds the boy for such cruel behavior. Outraged, the patron fires Juan and orders him and Chucaro off the property. The next day Juan on his horse, Gitana, and Pedrito on Chucaro leave the estancia. Far from being disheartened or despondent, Juan sees this as an opportunity for new adventures. They head in the direction of the massive waterfalls of Iguaza, a sight Juan has always wanted to see.

Steele, William O. *The Perilous Road*. Illustrated by Paul Caldone. Harcourt, 1958, o.p.; pap., Odyssey, $3.95: 0-15-260647-5. (Grades 4–7)

This is a simple historical novel about the Civil War and its effects on ordinary Tennessee mountain people. Although the issues of divided loyalties and family discord that the book deals with are complex, they are neither trivialized nor oversimplified. In 1863, on Signal Mountain in Tennessee, 11-year-old Chris Brabson is dismayed when Union soldiers confiscate his family's supplies and their horse. Before he and his friend Silas Agee, an older squirrel-hunting companion, can effect an ambush they are frightened off by the Yankees. Alone, Chris almost falls off a cliff but is rescued by his older brother Jethro. Chris is dismayed to learn that Jethro plans to join the Union forces. To prove his allegiance to the Confederacy, Jethro releases the Union mules from their corral one night. When he sees Silas loitering nearby, he thinks he might be a Confederate spy. Later, Chris tells Silas about a Yankee supply train he has seen in the area. Later, afraid that his brother might be assigned to the wagon train as a driver, he goes to the camp to warn him. He does not find him but he is welcomed by the soldiers who treat him with kindness. Tired, he falls asleep and is placed in one of the wagons when the Confederate Cavalry attacks. Chris is sickened by the carnage he witnesses. At the end of the terrible battle, he escapes back home and guiltily confesses all to his father. Mr. Brabson reassures his son on two accounts—first, Jethro was not part of the wagon train, and second, Silas is not a spy and could not have passed on Chris's information. Chris agrees with his father when he says, "War is the worst thing that can happen to folks."

1960s

Newbery Winner 1960

Krumgold, Joseph. *Onion John*. Illustrated by Symeon Shimin. Crowell, 1959, $15.89: 0-690-04698-7. (Grades 5–8)

Joseph Krumgold (1908–1980) is the first author to be awarded the Newbery Medal twice for the first two novels in a trilogy that explores three boys reaching maturation in three different contemporary American settings. The first is ... *And Now Miguel* (see "Newbery Winner," 1954, p. 188), which takes place in New Mexico and involves a family close to its Spanish heritage. The second is *Onion John*, which is set in a town in New Jersey similar to Hope, the one where the author lived for many years. The third, *Henry 3* (Antheneum, 1967, o.p.), is set in the suburbs of a modern big city, New York, and tells of the problems of super-bright Henry Lovering III adjusting to his new environment, making friends, and coping with modern social problems like advanced technology and the threat of war. In writing about receiving his first medal, which coincided with the writing of *Onion John*, the author said, "Curiously, I was writing about two characters who found themselves overwhelmed, as I was, by a substantial gift. Andy was being given an abstract future he didn't know anything about. Onion John was being dragged out of a meaningful past into a mechanical present he also didn't know anything about." How each of the two characters reacts to his gift forms the substance of this intriguing novel.

Plot Summary

Twelve-year-old Andrew J. Rusch, Jr., lives in the town of Serenity, where his father runs the local hardware store. Andy plays center field on the local Little League team and is the first to admit that he is not the best player, except for that one day when Serenity played Rockton Township for the pennant. It was also the beginning of his special friendship with Onion John.

Onion John could be called the local character. He lives up on Hession Hill in a broken-down shack that has four bathtubs lined up side by side and no running water. He got his name because he eats a lot of raw onions. John, at six feet three inches tall with a mustache, walks around town collecting things. No one pays much attention to him, partly because no one can understand a word he says.

On the day of the big game, Onion John is at his usual place out in the dump in the back of center field. Andy yells hello to him and Onion John yells back, but of course Andy does not understand him. Although Andy drops a ball and puts his team behind, he later wins the game on a home run and becomes the hero.

After all the hoopla dies down, Andy meets Onion John and understands him to say "cows in the sky." Then John says "mayglubpany," which means friends. Amazingly, Andy understands Onion John's conversation!

The two become fast friends and Andy finds himself somewhat in demand. If ever anyone wants to learn anything from or about Onion John, Andy becomes the interpreter. In this manner, Andy learns Onion John's remedy for the terrible drought affecting the area. Andy and his friend Eech agree to try Onion John's proposal of a procession through town carrying smoking torches. Andy's father tries to explain to his son that the idea is crazy, but the boys go ahead with it anyway. It does not rain then, but it does about three days later.

Andy runs into trouble with his father over Onion John. He and his friends invite John to their Halloween party and get so involved with his plan for making gold that Andy forgets to meet his father as planned at the Rotary Club. Soon after, Onion John arrives at the hardware store to pick up some hinges for the door on his broken-down home. Despite himself, Andy's father gets involved. Andy and his father accompany Onion John to his house and are astounded to see the four bathtubs lined up in the building's only room. The bathtubs are filled with newspapers, dust that John saves for his vegetable garden, beets and cabbages, and onions and potatoes. For bathing, he uses a bucket. He also has a wide hole in the floor at one corner of the room so that he can toss cans and other things right down into the cellar in case he wants them for future use.

From this visit comes the idea of building Onion John a new home. Andy's father reasons that this will be a great project for the Rotary Club. Onion John has been around for years and is a character that everyone likes. It is time, says Mr. Rusch, that Onion John had a decent home in which to live, with running water and electricity. What a marvelous idea! Onion John seems a little dubious at first, but when Andy explains it to him, he goes along.

The idea takes fire. Everyone in town is eager to contribute to the building of a fine new home for Onion John. And out of this enthusiasm grows the idea for Onion John Day, with a parade and all. The celebration will be as big as anything in Serenity since the Seventh National Guard returned from Korea.

Andy becomes more important and busy than ever. Because he is the only one who can understand Onion John, he is in great demand every time the electrician or another worker wants to converse with Onion John about his new home. There is some trouble, of course, as when Onion John refuses to give up Frolka, which is what John calls his wood stove. He insists on keeping it even though an electric stove will be installed. And he wants the new bathtub to be placed next to the four bathtubs in the living room. Mr. Rusch patiently explains that the four bathtubs have to go; there will be only one bathtub in the new house. Andy explains to his father that Onion John is not going to like this.

It is a grand day, indeed, when the new house is ready. By this time a reporter has discovered that Onion John's real name is Claiblin. He found that out at the immigration office.

While Mr. Rusch and Onion John are becoming the best of friends with this new project, Andy and his father are having a problem. Andy has always been interested in science and his father, who had dreams of becoming an engineer himself, envisions college for his son at the Massachusetts Institute of Technology (MIT) and perhaps later a scientific career that will even put Andy on the moon. He suggests to Andy that perhaps this summer, instead of working at the hardware store as usual, he should take a summer job at General Magneto, to get ready for his future career. Andy, who had been looking forward to the time with his father and is not at all positive about his future, is not happy with the suggestion.

However, there is another problem to worry about now. Onion John's beautiful new home burns down and John barely escapes. He feels especially bad because he started the fire by trying to treat his new electric stove as though it were a wood burner.

At first it seems as though Onion John is badly injured, but it turns out that he will recover. But what about his home? Mr. Rusch and the townspeople want to rebuild it. Andy objects, telling his father that Onion John just cannot live the way everyone else expects him to live. Mr. Rusch thinks that is nonsense, but in the end is dissuaded from rebuilding the house.

Instead of being delighted, Onion John is not happy with the news for he fears that people can change their minds and will soon want to "help him" again. Andy says that perhaps the only out for Onion John is just to run away from the town. Andy decides to go with him. He thinks the whole mess is his fault anyway and he is upset about the prospect of spending the summer with General Magneto.

Onion John has a new idea. Perhaps he can stay in town if he can make sure that the townspeople will not rebuild his house and will let him live as he wants to. His idea is to smoke the evil spirits right out of Serenity. It is evil spirits that prompted the people to build his new home, and if he can smoke out the spirits, all will be well.

Andy makes him see the folly of that idea, and the two make plans to run away. But Andy's mother and father interrupt his plans and Andy and his father have a heart-to-heart talk about General Magneto and his future. In the end, his father says that Andy's career should be up to Andy, no matter what he decides. Andy thinks that perhaps, for now, he will stick around the hardware store.

Yet, there is sadness in Andy's heart for Onion John has gone. When he does not show up for Fish Drive Day, Andy knows for sure that he has left. However, when Andy and his father are heading home, they round a corner and see a thin column of smoke rising above the hill west of Serenity. Looks like Onion John is smoking out the evil spirits after all.

Themes and Subjects

The key theme of *Onion John* is relationships—the affection between Andy and his father, and the growing friendship and trust between a young boy and an eccentric man. It is Andy's genuine feeling for Onion John and their mutual respect that allows the boy to understand the strange talk of the older man. Onion John is presented as an oddball but not a figure of ridicule. He is not to be feared or pitied. Onion John is a character, but a character who knows his own mind and desires and is a loyal friend. An underlying theme is the desire of Andy's father to achieve his own dreams of becoming an engineer through his son, something he realizes is both unfair and impossible.

Incidents for Booktalking

Young readers will enjoy Andy's conversations with Onion John; see: Andy first understands him (pp. 19–20); Onion John comes up with the plan for rain (pp. 28–33);

the rain procession (pp. 44–53); the Halloween party (pp. 62–79). Also of interest are the scenes describing Andy's relationship with his father; see: talk of MIT and the moon (pp. 34–37); Mr. Rusch and Andy visit Onion John's home (pp. 85–93); Andy and his father talk about his future (pp. 236–43).

Related Titles

Tino becomes so friendly with elderly Mrs. Sunday that he gives her the family's television in Leo Buscaglia's *A Memory for Tino* (Stack, 1988, $12.95: 1-55642-020-X).

In James Duffy's *Uncle Shamus* (Scribner's, 1992, $13.95: 0-684-19434-1), two children form an unusual friendship with a black man who has just been released from 30 years in prison.

A lonely, old neighbor teaches two boys that their own mother really cares for them in *Mrs. Abercorn and the Bunce Boys* (Macmillan, 1986, $13.95: 0-02-735460-1) by Liza Fosburgh.

Wilma must take care of a grandmother whom she really dislikes in Vera and Bill Cleaver's *Dust of the Earth* (Harper, 1975, $13.95: 0-397-31650-X).

Abby's attitudes toward her her stepfather gradually change from resentment to love in Evan Hunter's *Me and Mr. Stenner* (Harper, 1976, 0-397-31689-5).

About the Book and Author

(See also "About the Book and Author," 1954, p. 191.)

Kingman, Lee, ed. *Newbery and Caldecott Medal Books: 1956–1965 with Acceptance Papers, Biographies and Related Material.* Horn Book, 1965, pp. 82–96.

"Newbery Medal Acceptance Material, 1960." *Horn Book* 36, no. 4 (August 1960): 310–14.

Peterson, Linda K., and Marilyn L. Solt, eds. *Newbery and Caldecott Medal and Honor Books: 1922–1981.* Hall, 1982, p. 147.

Honor Books 1960

George, Jean. *My Side of the Mountain.* Dutton, 1959, $15.99: 0-525-44392-4. (Grades 5–8)

This first-person narrative is the story of Sam Gribley, a modern adolescent Thoreau, and his year alone in the Catskill Mountains. In addition to fascinating details about wildlife and survival skills, the story depicts a boy's courage, perseverance, and growing maturity. Equipped only with some simple tools, $40, and a vast knowledge of outdoor lore garnered from books, Sam sets out from New York City to rough it on the family's uncleared upstate track of land. He fashions a home in a decaying tree trunk, and learns to fish and set traps. With the help of books supplied by the local library, he is able to train a nestling hawk, whom he names Frightful, to hunt for him. He also befriends many woodland creatures including Baron Weasel and Jessie Coon James, a raccoon, and has a visit from an unusual traveler, Bando, a college professor, who teaches Sam pottery making. In the autumn, Sam prepares for the cold winter months by laying away a supply of smoked venison, fashioning warm clothes from hides, building an earthenware fireplace, and laying aside a cache of firewood. The loneliness of the winter months is broken by visits from Bando and from Sam's father, who is suitably impressed with his son's accomplishments. When spring comes, he realizes that his days on the land are numbered because news of his feat is spreading. Soon reporters, anxious for a story, begin arriving. He is also joined by his parents, brothers, and sisters who bring the news that the family plans on building a home on the property. Sam's saga of courage and survival is over. A sequel is *On the Far Side of the Mountain*.

Johnson, Gerald W. *America Is Born*. Illustrated by Leonard Everett Fisher. Morrow, 1959, o.p. (Grades 4–8)

This is the first volume of the author's acclaimed trilogy on American history. It is followed by *America Grows Up* (Dutton, 1960, $14.95; pap. Puffin, $14.95) and *America Moves Forward* (see "Honor Books," 1961, p. 235). Volume One traces American history from Columbus to 1787, when Congress approved a report recommending action to improve the Articles of Confederation. After the king of Portugal refused to support Columbus and his plan to sail westward to the Orient, the Italian navigator went to Spain, and received aid from Ferdinand and Isabella, King and Queen of Spain. Columbus's discoveries lead to national rivalries in exploiting the newfound land, named America after Amerigo Vespucci. The English concentrated on the middle geographical areas and founded the first permanent English settlement at Jamestown, Virginia, in 1607. Under the leadership of John Smith and through the work of such entrepreneurs as John Rolfe, the colony prospered and tobacco became an important crop. Originally headed for Virginia, the Pilgrims landed farther north on the shores of a bay that they called Massachusetts, after an Indian name. Under the leadership of such men as William Penn, Roger Williams, and James Oglethorpe, other colonies were founded. As they grew and prospered, conflicts arose between England, these colonies, and other European countries for control of what is now America. With the end of the French and Indian Wars (or Seven Years' War) in 1763, both the Indians and the French ceased to be serious threats and English became the language that helped unite the colonies. Unjust taxation, mismanagement, and a fundamental misunderstanding of the nature of the colonists led to protests, and later revolution against the British. When the revolution was successful, America was born.

Kendall, Carol. *The Gammage Cup*. Harcourt, 1959., o.p.; pap., Odyssey, $3.95: 0-15-230575-0. (Grades 4–7)

This intricately detailed fantasy takes place on the banks of the Watercress River in the Land Between the Mountains where a race of little people known as the Minnipins live in 12 almost-identical villages. These quiet, conservative people have lived in peace for more than 800 years since their leader, Gammage, brought them into the valley far from their traditional enemies the evil Mushrooms, also known as the Hairless Ones. The village of Slipper-on-the-Water, ruled by the Period family of whom Limited is their mayor, is buzzing with the news that the villages will have a contest, the winner of which will gain control of the prized relic from their founder, the Gammage Cup. The three nonconformists in the village—Walter the Earl, the town's archaeologist, who has secretly uncovered a cache of ancient buried weapons; Curly Green, the female artist; and Gummy, a writer of nonsense verses—object to the intimidating methods the Periods use to win the contest and are banished from the village. They are joined by the timid Muggles, the lady museum curator, and the town treasurer, Mingy, who fears that the cost of the contest will bankrupt the town. The five leave town with Walter the Earl's treasure of swords and armor and move to a new mountain home. There, they find that the swords begin to glow, a sign that danger is near. Investigations show that the hated Mushrooms have tunneled through the mountain and are about to attack. While Walter the Earl rouses the village and brings back a band of villagers, the remaining outcasts hold off the invaders. In a final battle, the Minnipins are successful, and the outsiders return to their village in triumph. As a final honor, Slipper-on-the-Water receives custody of the Gammage Cup. A sequel is *The Whisper of Glocken* (pap. Harcourt, $4.95).

Newbery Winner 1961

O'Dell, Scott. *Island of the Blue Dolphins*. Houghton, 1960, $13.45: 0-395-06962-9; pap., Dell, $5.50: 0-440-94000-1. (Grades 5–8)

Scott O'Dell (1898–1989) was a prolific author of historical novels for young adults, many of which took place around his native California and explored various aspects of the Spanish and Native American cultures. As well as the Newbery Medal, three of his novels were Honor Books: *The King's Fifth* (see "Honor Books," 1967, p. 265), *The Black Pearl* (see "Honor Books," 1968, p. 271) and *Sing Down the Moon* (see "Honor Books," 1971, 289). As a child growing up in San Pedro, he could almost see San Nicolas island, where a historical figure known as "The Lost Woman of San Nicolas" was left behind by her tribe. She lived there alone, like Robinson Crusoe, from 1835 to 1853. Fascinated by this story and inspired by the memory of a young Tarascan girl of 16, one of nine children of Pedro Flores who cared for the small home that the O'Dells once rented, the author created Karana, the valiant, resourceful young woman who conquered loneliness and privation to emerge triumphantly from her ordeal. Of this character, O'Dell wrote, "In her brief lifetime, Karana made the change from a world where everything lived only to be exploited, to a new and more meaningful world. She learned first that we each must be an island secure unto ourselves. Then, that we must 'transgress our limits,' in reverence for all life."

Plot Summary

In this story woven around the few facts known about Karana, San Nicolas is called the Island of the Blue Dolphins. It is shaped like a big fish sunning itself in the sea. Like a dolphin lying on its side, its tail points toward the sunrise, its nose toward the sunset, and its fins make reefs and ledges along the shore.

As the story opens, 12-year-old Karana lives on the Island of the Blue Dolphins with her father Chowig, chief of Ghalas-at, their village; an older sister, 14-year-old

Ulape; a 6-year-old brother, Ramo; and other members of her Indian tribe. Karana's mother died some time before the story opens.

One day an Aleut ship comes to the island to hunt the sea otter. Chief Chowig gives reluctant permission for the Russian hunters to stay on the island while they hunt in return for goods that are worth half of their catch. However, he is wary of these men because another Aleut hunting party had caused trouble in the past by trying to cheat the natives. But this Russian leader, Captain Orlov, assures Chief Chowig that he and his men will keep their part of the bargain.

The Aleuts kill many sea otters. When they prepare to leave the Island of the Blue Dolphins, the Aleut captain drops one chest on the shore in payment for the otter skins. Karana's father demands three more chests as proper payment to complete their bargain. As Karana and her sister watch in horror from a hidden ledge, a fight breaks out between the Aleuts and the Islanders. Although the Indians fight bravely, they are no match for the greater number of Aleuts and for the firepower from their ship. Many die, including Karana's father.

The villagers, especially Karana and her brother and sister, are in great sorrow for each has lost a member of the family. A new chief is chosen to replace Chowig. He is Kimki, a good man in his youth and a good hunter, but now he is old. Kimki realizes that with so many young hunters now gone from the tribe, the survivors will have great trouble finding enough food. Eventually, the old man decides to sail alone to locate another island that will be a better home for the tribe, where there will be more food and where the survivors will not be constantly reminded of their great loss. Kimki is gone for many moons. When a ship does finally appear, the Islanders are at first fearful that the Aleuts have returned. Matasaip, who is acting as chief in Kimki's absence, sends a messenger out to the ship to investigate. The runner returns with the news that the ship carries white men who have been instructed by Kimki to take them all to the new home he has found for them.

When the villagers board the ship and it begins to sail, Karana discovers that Ramo is missing. She sees him running along the beach, but Matasaip will not allow the ship to return to shore for the boy for fear of slamming against the rocks in the rough sea. He tells Karana that they will return to pick him up on another day, and until then the boy will be safe. But Karana will not leave him. Instead, she leaps overboard and swims back to the Island of the Blue Dolphins.

The two children wait for the ship to return for them. Although Karana knows that it may be some time before that happens, she is content with Ramo for company and with plenty of food and drink for just the two of them on the island. However, her life changes drastically when Ramo is killed by the wild dogs that also inhabit their island home. Karana is left completely alone.

Time passes slowly for the young girl on the deserted island. She must use all her courage and resourcefulness to feed herself and fend off the wild dog predators. With great difficulty she fashions a bow and arrows to protect herself if she must and a spear with which to catch fish.

Once the first storm of winter comes, Karana knows that she cannot expect a rescue ship until at least the next spring. So she decides to leave the island in a canoe and head east, in the direction Kimki had gone. It is a monumental task for the young girl to get a canoe that carries six people into the water. When she does, she watches the Island of the Blue Dolphins disappear from her view with fear in her heart for the first time. Karana soon knows more fear when she discovers that the canoe is leaking. When she makes a decision to return to the island, a swarm of blue dolphins appear.

She is heartened by their company and credits them with giving her the strength to paddle hard enough to return to her island home.

Realizing that she must remain on the island for possibly a long time until help comes, Karana builds a home for her protection and a place to store food. Winter is half over before she finishes the task. Then she determines that she must somehow manage to kill one of the sea elephants around the island. She will need the tusklike teeth of the bull sea elephant for spear points to defend and feed herself. In this, however, Karana is not successful and she returns to her cave without the desired tusks.

Karana does not realize how truly lonely she is until she rescues a dog wounded from one of her arrows. He had been the leader of the wild dog pack, but because Karana had never seen him before, she thinks that this animal with the yellow eyes and thick fur must have been left on the island by the Aleuts who had hunted the sea otters. She nurses him back to health and names him Rontu, which in her language means Fox Eyes. He becomes her constant and cherished companion. Now she has someone to talk to. Together they hunt and fish and battle a dangerous giant devilfish.

Winter turns to spring and the seasons pass. Always, Karana keeps an eye out for the arrival of more Aleuts, or perhaps members of her own tribe who will surely come for her. If Aleuts arrive, she and Rontu will hide from them in wait for her own people. Then, one day the Aleuts do arrive. Karana and Rontu hide away in their cave home, fearful of being found. They are not discovered by the Aleut men, but are found instead by a young Aleut girl about Karana's age who is with them. She stumbles upon their home and tries to make friends. When the girl leaves after the hunting trip is over, the island seems more lonely than before.

The years pass in endless isolation. Finally, old Rontu dies and Karana buries him with great sorrow that is not lifted until she is able to capture a young dog she had seen sometime earlier. He has the same yellow eyes and heavy fur of Rontu and she is sure that he is Rontu's son. With a mixture of ground-up seashells and wild tobacco, Karana entices the young dog to eat. When he falls asleep from the potion, she is able to capture him and take him to her home. Like Rontu, he becomes her cherished companion. She names him Rontu-Aru, Son of Rontu.

Karana and Rontu-Aru experience a terrifying earthquake, but when she is assessing the damage the next day, Karana sees a more startling sight. A ship is coming! A quick glance tells her that these are not Aleuts. The ship anchors and a man without a beard jumps into the water and walks along the beach. Karana hides, although she is certain that she hears her name being called. Yet, she is afraid and remains silent. The ship sails away.

Another two years pass until one morning the ship returns. This time, Karana knows it is time to leave. "We are going away," she tells Rontu-Aru, "away from our island."

When the men come ashore, Karana steps out to greet them. Although she cannot speak their language, she tries to ask them what happened to the ship that took her people away. In time, when Karana is taken to Mission Santa Barbara under the care of Father Gonzales, she will learn that the ship sank in a great storm, which was the reason no one ever returned for her. But for now, with Rontu-Aru beside her, she prepares at last to leave her lonely, beautiful home on the Island of the Blue Dolphins.

Father Gonzales of Mission Santa Barbara learned relatively little of Karana's 18 years spent on the island. She spoke to him only in sign language for the Indians of her village had long disappeared and no one, even among the many Indians at the mission, could understand her strange speech.

Themes and Subjects

Based on historical fact, this is a thoughtful story of courage, resourcefulness, perseverance, and a reverence for life. Not for all young readers perhaps, but its hint of melancholy will capture the heart of many. Karana is a stoic young girl who wastes little time in despair. She makes the best of her desperate situation, calling upon all she has learned from her elders during her young years to ensure her safety and protect her dog companions. This is a basic story of survival, both physical and psychological.

Throughout the book is the recognition of how humans are dependent upon animal and plant life and how all life must be nurtured. Although most of her young years have been lonely, there is a hint of sadness as Karana prepares to leave her island home and a recognition that even in isolation, her life had been happy.

Incidents for Booktalking

For a good introduction to life on the Island of the Blue Dolphins, see: the Aleut ship arrives (pp. 4–8); the fight between Aleuts and the islanders (pp. 20–24). For the flavor of life alone on a deserted island, see: Karana finds her dead brother (pp. 46–48); she sets out in the canoe (pp. 61–68); the sea elephant fight (pp. 81–85); Karana finds Rontu (pp. 94–98); Karana captures Rontu's son (pp. 161–64).

Related Titles

Walt Morey's *Kavik the Wolf Dog* (Dutton, 1977, $15.99: 0-525-33093-3) is a story of courage and survival in the Far North.

Teenage Brian survives a plane crash in the Canadian wilderness in Gary Paulsen's *Hatchet* (Macmillan, 1987, $12.95: 0-02-527403-1; pap., Simon, $4.50: 0-689-80882-8).

In a contemporary setting, crippled 12-year-old Koby begins a new life when she saves two injured whales near her home in Florida in Ben Mikaelsen's *Stranded* (Hyperion, 1995, $15.95: 0-7868-0072-0).

Tonight, by Sea (Orchard, 1995, $15.95: 0-531-06899-4) by Frances Temple tells about some Haitian boat people and their harrowing voyage to Florida.

In *The Iceberg Hermit* (pap., Scholastic, $4.50: 0-590-44112-4) by Arthur Roth, Allan Gordon survives a sinking ship that leaves him alone in the Arctic wilds.

About the Book and Author

Berger, Laura Standley, ed. *Twentieth-Century Children's Writer*. 4th ed. St. James, 1994, pp. 500–01.

Bock, Ann, and Carolyn Riley, eds. *Children's Literary Review*. Vol. 1. Gale, 1976, pp. 145–49.

Brown, Muriel W., and Rita Schoch Foudray. *Newbery and Caldecott Medalists and Honor Book Winners: Bibliographic & Resource Material Through 1990*. 2d ed. Neal-Schuman, 1992, pp. 313–15.

Chevalier, Tracy, ed. *Twentieth-Century Children's Writers*. 3d ed. St. James, 1989, pp. 735–36.

Collier, Laurie, and Joyce Nakamura, eds. *Major Authors and Illustrators for Children and Young Adults*. Gale, 1993, 6 vols., pp. 1790–94.

Commire, Anne, ed. *Something About the Author*. Vol. 12. Gale, 1977, pp. 161–64.

Estes, Glenn E., ed. "American Writers for Children Since 1960: Fiction." In *Dictionary of Literary Biography*. Vol. 52. Gale, 1986, pp. 278–95.

Fadool, Cynthia, ed. *Contemporary Authors*. Vols. 61–64. Gale, 1976, p. 402.

Fuller, Muriel, ed. *More Junior Authors*. Wilson, 1963, pp. 161–62.

Gallo, Donald R. *Speaking for Ourselves*. National Council of Teachers of English, 1990, pp. 154–56.

Garrett, Agnes, and Helga P. McCue, eds. *Authors and Artists for Young Adults*. Vol. 3. Gale, 1990, pp. 185–96.

Hipple, Ted. ed. *Writers for Young Adults*. Vol. 2. Scribner's, 1997, pp. 431–54.

Metzger, Linda, ed. *Contemporary Authors (New Revision Series)*. Vol. 12. Gale, 1984, pp. 346–47.

Petersen, Linda K., and Marilyn L. Solt, eds. *Newbery and Caldecott Medal and Honor Books: 1922–1981*. Hall, 1982, pp. 150–51.

O'Dell, Scott. *Island of the Blue Dolphins*. VHS Library Video, 1964. Videocassette, 99 min. ($59.95)

———. *Island of the Blue Dolphins*. Read by Tantoo Cardinal. BDD Audio Publishing, 1995. Audiocassettes, 240 min. ($19.99)

———. *Island of the Blue Dolphins*. Read by Christina Moore. Recorded Books, 1994. Audiocassettes. 270 min. ($26.00)

Scott O'Dell. Profiles in Literature, 1976. Videocassette.

Senick, Gerard J., ed. *Children's Literature Review*. Vol. 16. Gale, 1989, pp. 159–80.

Silvey, Anita, ed. *Children's Books and Their Creators*. Houghton, 1995, pp. 496–97.

Ward, Martha, ed. *Authors of Books for Young People*. 3d ed. Scarecrow, 1990, p. 534.

Honor Books 1961

Johnson, Gerald. *America Moves Forward: A History for Peter.* Illustrated by Leonard Everett Fisher. Morrow, 1960, o.p. (Grades 4–8)

In this third volume of the author's history of the United States (see *America Is Born*, under "Honor Books," 1960, p. 229), Johnson traces movements and events from the end of World War I to the mid-1950s. President Wilson suffered both defeat and heartbreak when the American people turned down the Covenant of the League of Nations that he fought for as part of the peace treaty after World War I. The 1920s brought a series of troubles both outside and inside America. International strife was caused by the Russian Revolution, inflation, poverty, and social unrest. At home we fought Prohibition, racketeers, the Ku Klux Klan, and unsafe business practices that led to the stock market crash. Franklin Roosevelt attempted to combat the hardships of the Great Depression through a series of reforms known as the New Deal. Abroad, insidious forces—Mussolini's Black Shirts and Hitler's Brown Shirts—were setting up repressive regimes in Italy and Germany while Japan was increasing its aggression in the Pacific. A chapter, "The Agony of War," describes America's role in World War II and another, "The Mushroom Cloud," tells of the consequences of Truman's decision to drop the atomic bomb. Other important decisions of the Truman administration are described in a chapter that deals with the Truman Doctrine, the Marshall Plan, Point Four, the North Atlantic Treaty Organization, and the Korean War. The book ends with the hope that America's future will be secure. The author states, "There is little reason to doubt that it will remain great and grow greater as long as the strong, the brave and the wise keep trying."

Schaefer, Jack. *Old Ramon.* Illustrated by Harold West. Houghton, 1960, o.p.; pap., Walker, $6.95: 0-9027-7403-2. (Grades 5–9)

Told in deceptively simple, spare prose, this is a powerful story of a few days in a boy's life that taught him the meaning of wisdom and manhood. The boy's father has entrusted him to the care of an old shepherd, Ramon, while the two drive the family's herd of sheep to summer pasture in the Southwest accompanied by a burro and two sheepdogs, the veteran Pedro and young Sancho, who like the boy is untrained and inexperienced but eager to please. As the boy says to Ramon, "You are to be my book about sheep," and during the few days of the sheep run he learns a great deal about sheep handling such as how to get them to ford rivers, protect them during a charro or sandstorm, kill a threatening rattlesnake, and get rid of deadly sheep ticks by blowing tobacco smoke into the infected areas. He also learns about Ramon's past. For example, as a young man, Ramon had carried the boy's grandfather on his back to safety while crossing the Mojave desert, and how he had foolishly succumbed to liquor, women, and gambling. Once while drinking, Ramon neglected his duties and caused the accidental death of some lambs. Filled with shame and humiliation, he left the ranch, returning only when he felt proper penance had been paid. At the summer pasture, a wolf attacks the flock and Pedro wakens Ramon and the boy. When they investigate, they discover the body of Sancho who died attacking the wolf. The boy grieves at his dog's death and blames Pedro for not staying to fight. Ramon explains that the dog was wise in rousing them first and that, years ago, Pedro had saved his life by confronting an attacking grizzly. To console the boy, Roman promises the young boy a dog from the litter fathered by Pedro. As a remembrance of his recent experiences with his wise and unforgettable teacher, he decides to name him Sancho.

Selden, George. *The Cricket in Times Square*. Illustrated by Garth Williams. Farrar, 1960, $15.00: 0-374-31650-3; pap., Dell, $4.99: 0-440-41563-2. (Grades 3–6)

On a Saturday night in June in the Times Square subway station, Tucker Mouse is watching poor Mario Bellini tend his family's business, the station's unprofitable newsstand. Through the din of trains and people, both Tucker and Mario hear an unusual sound. Mario investigates and finds, in a pile of wastepaper, a little cricket. In spite of his parents' objections, Mario puts the cricket in a tiny match box to keep as a good luck pet. After the stand is closed, Tucker investigates and learns from the cricket, Chester, that in his home in Connecticut, he had jumped into a picnic basket in search of food, and by the time he escaped, he had been transported to New York City. Along with Harry Cat, Tucker's friend and fellow tenant in an unused drainpipe, the mouse and Chester explore Times Square. To make his pet comfortable, Mario takes Chester to Chinatown where he purchases an elegant, pagoda-shaped cricket cage from the friendly merchant, Sai Fong. Chester accidentally eats a two dollar bill, but unselfish Tucker gallantly sacrifices his accumulated savings of loose change to reimburse the Bellinis. The family is mystified but delighted to find this gift that has appeared seemingly from nowhere. During a party thrown by Tucker and Harry Cat, his friends discover that Chester can play any tune he hears. In their excitement, they accidentally set the newsstand on fire. The Bellinis are heartbroken at the damage until they discover Chester's amazing talent. Soon the repaired newsstand becomes the most popular spot in town with Chester giving regular concerts. The cricket, however, longs for the quiet of the countryside and so, sadly, Tucker and Harry take him to Grand Central Station put him on a train bound for Connecticut. Before he leaves, Tucker and Harry promise to visit him, as they do in several sequels to this delightful fantasy including *Tucker's Countryside*.

Newbery Winner 1962

Speare, Elizabeth George. *The Bronze Bow*. Houghton, 1961, $16.00: 0-395-87769-5; pap., Sandpiper, $6.95: 0-395-13719-5. (Grades 8–10)

In 1962, Elizabeth George Speare (1908–1994) was awarded her second Newbery Medal for *The Bronze Bow*. Her first was for *The Witch of Blackbird Pond* (see "Newbery Winner," 1959, p. 218) just three years before. In her acceptance speech, Speare gives some interesting sidelights on how *The Bronze Bow* came to be. As a Sunday School teacher, she had always had the desire to write a book about the land of the New Testament, one in which Jesus would be portrayed as a dynamic leader that youngsters could admire, not just as the Messiah, but as a believable person who inspired both love and loyalty. At first both the characters and the plot were shadowy, but during a service at the Riverside Church in New York City immediately after being presented with her first medal, she suddenly realized how the book should end. With this in mind she began writing. Initially the main character was the girl Malthace, but as the story progressed, she found that Daniel, the renegade outlaw who was consumed with hatred for the

Romans and driven obsessively to avenge the death of his parents, began to dominate her thoughts. It was his story that eventually became the focus of this novel that depicts the internal struggle of a young man choosing between a life motivated by the negative emotions of destructive hatred and the peace that can result from faith and the power of love.

Plot Summary

Daniel bar Jamin is an 18-year-old Galilean who, for the past five years, has lived in hiding in the mountain stronghold of a gang of outlaws led by Rosh. He spent the first years of his life in the village of Ketzeh, a few miles from the city of Capernaum. When Daniel was only eight, his father was crucified by the Romans and his mother, unable to cope with this great loss, died of grief. The boy was later sold into slavery as an apprentice to the cruel blacksmith Amalek. Unable to stand the harsh treatment from this sadistic master, he escaped, leaving behind his grandmother and his pathetically withdrawn sister, Leah. Since then he has lived in hiding with Rosh and his gang, who are dedicated to harassing and destroying the Romans and their friends. They plan for the day when all of Israel will rise and rid itself of its hated conquerors.

One day while on a scouting expedition, Daniel sees two young acquaintances from his village hiking up the mountain. They are Joel bar Hezron, the studious son of the town scribe, and his twin sister, Malthrace, nicknamed Thracia. Daniel is overcome with curiosity for news from Ketzeh, so he questions the pair about his family and the fate of his friend Simon, called Simon the Zealot, who although six years older than Daniel, was apprenticed to Amalek at the same time as Daniel. Joel and Thracia know little about Daniel's grandmother and sister, but they tell him that Simon now has his own shop and is prospering.

A caravan from Damascus is passing through the valley and while the two intruders hide in the rocks, Rosh, Daniel, and the others raid the caravan and free a slave to join them. He is a black colossus of a man, who seems unable to speak or hear. The gang nicknames him Samson. Joel meets Rosh and immediately wants to join the cause, but Rosh dissuades him, particularly when he learns that Joel and his family are soon moving to Capernaum. A contact there might be very useful.

In time Samson becomes attached to Daniel, and with his mighty strength operates the bellows at the forge. Having heard through Joel about Daniel, Simon visits the camp and tells Daniel that because Amalek has just died, the boy is now free to visit his family in the village. He does so and is shocked at their poverty and Leah's complete seclusion. With Simon, he visits the synagogue and hears a sermon from a gentle, kindly preacher named Jesus.

Rosh orders Daniel to Capernaum to make contact with Joel, but Joel's father fears that he will lose his son to a gang of reckless extremists, and he orders Daniel out of the house. Leaving town, Daniel, becoming forgetful of his own safety, allows his temper and fierce hatred of the Romans to overcome natural caution and common sense, and insults a Roman soldier. Daniel manages to escape, but with a gaping spear wound in his side. He crawls back to Joel's house and Thracia hides him in a basement storage room. Brother and sister secretly minister to Daniel and heal his wound. They read scriptures together and are particularly impressed by the Song of David which reads:

> God is my strong refuge
> He trains my hands for war
> So that my arms can bend a bow of bronze.

By the sign of the bronze bow, the three swear dedication to freeing Israel from its oppressors.

Daniel is scarcely back in the mountain retreat when he is once more sent on a mission to Capernaum, this time to secure a rivet to repair Rosh's favorite talisman, a dagger. In a small town near Capernaum, Daniel and Joel see Simon, who has closed his blacksmith shop to become a disciple of Jesus. The boys listen in wonder to Jesus's teachings and watch him perform healing acts that some call miracles.

Daniel's grandmother dies. To take care of Leah, he regretfully leaves Rosh and his friends and accepts Simon's offer to take over his shop at home and become the town blacksmith. But he has lost none of his hatred for the Romans. When a young Roman soldier begins bringing work to his shop and one day happens to gaze fondly at Leah, Daniel, ignoring possible consequences, orders him off his property.

Daniel begins to organize some of the young boys in town as a force to work against the Romans. They meet frequently, and whenever possible Joel travels from Capernaum to join them. They use as their password the Bronze Bow. However, Daniel begins to wonder if violence is the only solution. He begins making more and more journeys to Bathsaida to hear Jesus speak.

Soon Joel is given his own assignment from Rosh. He is to find out the names of the wealthy men of Capernaum who will be attending a large banquet for the Romans so that Rosh and his men can rob their houses while they are away. Joel does so by disguising himself as a fish peddler and picking up information as he travels from kitchen to kitchen. The robbery is a success, but in the following investigation, Joel is arrested and sentenced to deportation.

Rosh reveals his true harshness and severity when he ignores Daniel's pleading to help rescue Joel. The young boys under Daniel, therefore, decide that they must be Joel's rescuers.

Knowing that Joel and the other prisoners will be led by their captors through a mountain gorge, the boys plan to hide in the hills and divert the soldiers by throwing stones while Daniel frees Joel. At the site, the boys find they are hopelessly outnumbered, but the unexpected appearance of Samson with his mammoth rock-throwing ability carries the plan to success. Joel is saved but not without casualties: one of the boys is killed, Samson is mortally wounded, and Daniel is severely injured.

Leah accidentally reveals that during Daniel's frequent absences, she has been having secret conversations with Marcus, the soldier whom Daniel ordered from his property. Daniel flies into a rage and so upbraids his sister that once again she becomes withdrawn. Soon she becomes ill with a fever, and Daniel is afraid she will die. Marcus comes to see Daniel. He says he is not a Roman but a native of Gallia who has been pressed into service. He is soon to be transferred to Corinth and he begs to see Leah one last time. Daniel threatens to kill him if he sets foot in the house.

When Leah's death seems certain, Daniel thinks of Jesus. The young man sends a message to Simon telling him of Leah's condition. After three days of waiting, Jesus appears at Daniel's house. He enters and gazes at Leah. She opens her eyes and appears well once more. After Jesus leaves, Daniel again sees Marcus waiting. This time he invites him into his home to say farewell to Leah. Perhaps it is only love that has the strength to bend the bow of bronze.

Themes and Subjects

In her Newbery Award acceptance speech, the author said that in this book she hoped "to show the change wrought in just one boy who came to know the teacher in Galilee. This is the story of *The Bronze Bow*." Two divergent methods of achieving goals are presented and contrasted in this book—the way of Rosh, by force and violence, and the way of Jesus, by acceptance and love. In many of today's causes, these same opposing methods are advocated. Daniel's conversion from one to the other is convincingly handled. The concept that courage and faith are powerful weapons in the fight against injustice is explored. The bonds of friendship, family responsibility, and loyalty to a cause are well depicted. Speare re-creates the Holy Land of biblical times with authenticity and color.

Incidents for Booktalking

Some interesting excerpts are: Daniel meets Joel and Thracia on the mountain (pp. 1–5); they share lunch and talk about politics and the coming of the Messiah (pp. 6–12); the capture of Samson (pp. 17–20); Daniel's first encounter with Jesus (pp. 45–49); Daniel's temper gets him into trouble (pp. 69–72); he tells his family's tragic story (pp. 80–83); he waylays a wealthy merchant (pp. 106–10).

Related Titles

The life of Jesus Christ is told through text from the King James Bible and illustrations from Washington's National Gallery in *Jesus of Nazareth: A Life of Christ Through Pictures* (Simon, 1994, $16.00: 0-671-88651-7).

In Uri Orlev's *Lydia, Queen of Palestine* (Houghton, 1993, $13.95: 0-395-65660-5), a young girl leaves her Romanian home during World War II to stay at a kibbutz in Palestine.

Barbara Dana brilliantly re-creates the daily life of Joan of Arc before she leads the French army in *Young Joan* (Harper, 1992, $17.95: 0-06-0211422-8).

A novel set in thirteenth-century Italy involving St. Francis of Assisi is Scott O'Dell's *The Road to Damietta* (pap., Fawcett, $4.50: 0-449-70233-2).

Mollie Hunter tells the story of Mary, Queen of Scots, in her historical novel *You Never Knew Her As I Did!* (Harper, 1981, $13.95: 0-06-022678-1).

About the Book and Author

(See also "About the Book and Author," 1959, p. 221.)

Helbig, Alethea K., and Agnes R. Perkins, eds. *Dictionary of American Children's Fiction, 1960–1985*. Greenwood, 1986, pp. 616–19 (bio.), pp. 757–56 (book).

Kingman, Lee, ed. *Newbery and Caldecott Medal Books: 1956–1965 with Acceptance Papers, Biographies and Related Material*. Horn Book, 1965, pp. 109–15.

"Newbery Acceptance Material, 1962." *Horn Book* 38, no. 4 (July/August 1963): 336–41.

Peterson, Linda K., and Marilyn L. Solt, eds. *Newbery and Caldecott Medal and Honor Books: 1922–1981*. Gale, 1982, pp. 156–57.

Honor Books 1962

McGraw, Eloise Jarvis. *The Golden Goblet.* Coward-McCann, 1961, o.p.; pap., Puffin, $4.99: 0-14-030335-9. (Grades 5–8)

In this exciting adventure novel set in ancient Egypt, a youngster named Ranofer eventually achieves his goal of becoming an apprentice to Zau, the famous goldsmith of Thebes. At his father's death, Ranofer is claimed as the property of his elder half-brother, the wicked, scheming Gebu who forces the boy to work as a humble porter for the goldsmith, Rekh. Here he becomes friendly with the apprentice Heqet. This job ends abruptly and Ranofer begins working in Gebu's stone-cutting business. When Ranofer discovers a valuable golden goblet concealed in Gebu's clothes, he begins to suspect his half-brother and his henchman, the mason Wenamon, of robbing tombs. He elicits the help of his friends, Heqet, and an old reedcutter named the Ancient, to spy on the two villains. During the High Nile Festival, Ranofer follows Gebu and Wenamon from the city to the Valley of the Tombs of the Kings across the river. Here, he sees them entering the tomb of the queen's parents by a secret passage. Although discovered, he manages to escape and trap the robbers in the tomb by rolling a stone across the entrance. While Heqet and the Ancient guard the blocked entrance to the shaft, Ranofer rushes to the palace, where with the help of the queen's dwarf, he tells the queen about the robbery. At first no one believes him, but his accurate description of the golden goblet in Gebu's possession convinces them that robberies have occurred. After the thieves are captured, the queen grants Ranover's wish for a donkey. With this donkey, he can make a living cutting and transporting papyrus and in time realize his lifelong ambition of becoming a pupil of the great Zau.

Stolz, Mary. *Belling the Tiger.* Illustrated by Beni Montresor. Harper, 1961, $12.89: 0-06-025863-2. (Grades 2–4)

In this charming variation of the ancient Aesop fable, two timid cellar mice, Asa and brother Rambo, are appointed by the Steering Committee of the mouse community, led by tyrannical Portman, to become heroes and bell the dreaded cat, Siri. They manage to steal a blue collar with a bell attached from a hardware store but are chased by another cat. Seeking safety, they scurry up a rope onto a ship and within minutes find themselves at sea.

When the ship lands on a tropical island, Asa and Rambo go exploring and come across a huge cat many times the size of Siri. Undaunted, they bell this huge cat's tail because its neck is much too large. The tinkling of the bell awakens this giant, friendly creature, who explains he is a tiger. Although the tiger has never seen mice before, he has heard that elephants are afraid of them. With Asa and Rambo on his back, he confronts an elephant who immediately runs away waving his trunk wildly. Asa and Rambo are impressed with their newfound power but the wise tiger tells them that everybody is afraid of something and that they should never become braggards. He then takes them back to their ship and returns to the jungle proudly swishing his bell-attired tail to and fro. Ada and Rambo decide to heed the tiger's advice and remain silent about their adventures lest they be considered blowhards. However, they have learned the meaning of bravery, and at a general meeting of the mice, they gallantly face Portman and instead of apologizing for their absence, request to be promoted to pantry mice. The rest of the mice are delighted that their dictator has been challenged and unanimously vote for the promotion.

Tunis, Edwin. *Frontier Living*. Illustrated by the author. World, 1961, o.p.; Crowell, $26.00: 0-690-0106408. (Grades 7–12)

With lucid prose and more than 200 detailed black-and-white drawings, the author re-creates significant aspects of life on the American frontier in this oversized book. He chronicles early American life as it changed from the Colonial and Revolutionary days in the East, through the eighteenth and early nineteenth century in the Midwest, ending with the post-Civil War period of the western cowboys and farmers. The first chapters tell of life in the eighteenth-century Piedmont regions. Clothing, food, pastimes, and common household utensils are described. Details are given on the construction of log cabins. Early modes of transportation west are described including keelboats, freight wagons, coach lines, and frontier inns. In later chapters there are sections on the Pony Express, famous trails like the Santa Fe and Oregon, and the early days of railroads. In a chapter titled *The Old Northwest*, farm life is described, including methods of farming, crops, and implements. Various types of settlers and their characteristics are detailed such as missionaries, religious groups like the Mormons, Mexican caballeros, gold seekers, and ordinary people intent on finding a new life. Throughout the book, information about important historical events like the Black Hawk War and the Louisiana Purchase are integrated into the text with emphasis on their effects on the westward movement. The book closes with chapters on the life and work of cowhands and sodbusters, and of the phenomenon known as the cattle drive, but in a postscript the author states that frontier life has not ended because even today, "men and women still build log cabins on homesteads in Alaska and live rugged lives in them."

Newbery Winner 1963

L'Engle, Madeleine. *A Wrinkle in Time*. Farrar, 1962, $17.00: 0-374-38613-7; pap., Dell, $3.50: 0-440-80054-4. (Grades 5–8)

The novels of Madeleine L'Engle (1918–) fall roughly into three series whose characters and settings often intersect and overlap. The first consists of several adventure stories such as *The Arm of the Starfish* (Farrar, 1965, $13.95; pap., Dell, $3.25), known collectively as the Cannon Tallis mysteries. A second group, beginning with the 1959 title *Meet the Austins* (pap., Dell, 1981, $3.25), features the Austin family. *A Ring of Endless Light*, one title in this series, was an Honor Book for 1981 (p. 342). The Time Fantasy series now contains five titles, each dealing with members of the Murry-O'Keefe family. The first is *A Wrinkle in Time*. It is followed by *A Wind in the Door* (Farrar, 1973, $13.95; pap., Dell, $3.25), in which Meg becomes concerned about the health and school problems of her precocious younger brother Charles Wallace. In the company of friend Calvin O'Keefe and their school principal Mr. Jenkins, Meg embarks on a galactic voyage and a trip into an unimaginably small world in order to save her brother's life. In *A Swiftly Tilting Planet* (Farrar, 1978, $13.95; pap., Dell, $3.25), Meg is now married to Calvin and Charles Wallace is 15 years old. In this story, a great white unicorn named Gaudior transports Charles Wallace through time and space and together with Meg he solves an age-old mystery and restores peace to the endangered Earth. These three novels, known collectively as the Time Trilogy, are complemented by *Many Waters* (Farrar, 1986, $13.95; pap., Dell, $3.25), in which Meg's teenage brothers, the twins Sandy and Denns, are transported in time to the days of Noah and the ark, and *An Acceptable Time* (Farrar, 1989, $16.00; pap., Dell, $3.50), which is the story of Polly O'Keefe, daughter of Meg and Calvin, and her adventures with a Celtic tribe that lived 3,000 years ago. Since its publication in 1962, *A Wrinkle in Time* has continued to attract an enthusiastic audience. It is amazing that it was turned down by 26 publishers before John Farrar of Farrar Strauss had enough faith in the manuscript to publish it.

Plot Summary

Twelve-year-old Meg Murry is not a happy person. She is approaching adolescence convinced that she is a completely plain girl with the additional physical liabilities of thick eyeglasses and heavy metal braces on her teeth. To add to her dwindling self-esteem, she has been told by one of her teachers that she may have to repeat a grade if her academic record does not improve. In addition, on the way home from school, she has been bruised (but not beaten) in a fight with a boy who called Charles Wallace her "dumb baby brother." All this and a prediction of hurricane-type weather in the offing have contributed to Meg's generally unsettled frame of mind.

The major worry and source of stress in Meg's life, however, is not her own personal problems, but the lack of information about her beloved father, a world-renowned physicist who disappeared without a trace about a year earlier while working on a top-secret government space project.

Through all these months of waiting and hoping, Meg's mother, also a famous research scientist, has been incredibly brave in keeping her family strong and calm during this crisis. There are four Murry children. The oldest is Meg, who in spite of poor school performance is actually extremely bright, particularly in math and science; followed by her 10-year-old twin brothers, Sandy and Denns, who are average in interests and appearance; and lastly, Meg's favorite, five-year-old Charles Wallace. He is a most unusual child—precocious, highly intelligent, clairvoyant, and so otherworldly that some find him strange.

Late that night, while the storm rages outside, Meg is so beset with her worries that she is unable to sleep. She leaves her warm bed to think her problems through over a cup of hot chocolate in the kitchen. She finds that her brother Charles has preceded her, and soon they are joined by Mrs. Murry. Charles Wallace begins telling them about an unusual woman named Mrs. Whatsit, and her two friends who have mysteriously appeared in the neighborhood and are now living in a nearby deserted "haunted" house. Their conversation is interrupted by the growling of their dog, Fortinbras. Mrs. Murry goes to investigate and returns with a strange-looking old lady completely bundled in several layers of clothing and wearing large rubber boots. It is Charles Wallace's new friend, Mrs. Whatsit. After resting a few moments and eating a sandwich,

Mrs. Whatsit leaves as mysteriously as she arrived while murmuring to herself something about a tesseract.

At school the next day, tired and somewhat irritable from lack of sleep, Meg is sent to the principal's office for being rude to her teacher. After school, she is happy to accompany Charles Wallace to visit Mrs. Whatsit. On the way they meet and talk to Calvin O'Keefe, a freckle-faced 14-year-old boy who is two grades ahead of Meg at her school. In spite of being extremely popular and a basketball star, Calvin is very self-effacing and not at all snobbish as Meg thought he might be. At the house, the three youngsters talk to Mrs. Whatsit's friend, Mrs. Who, whose speech is peppered with famous quotations from several languages. She tells them that an important event involving all three of them will soon occur. Meg instinctively feels that this event is related to her missing father.

Meg invites Calvin home for dinner and afterwards the two, who are drawn to each other by their similar sensitive dispositions, walk in the woods and talk about their lives and interests. Meg tells Calvin about Mr. Murry and of her growing fears concerning his safety. They are joined by Charles Wallace and, an instant or two later, by Mrs. Whatsit, Mrs. Who, and a third shimmering apparition named Mrs. Which, whose voice seems to emanate from an echo chamber.

Without warning the group suddenly travels though space and within seconds the youngsters find themselves on another planet. Mrs. Whatsit explains that they have traveled using a fifth dimension, a tesseract, which reduces the distance between two points by creating a tuck or wrinkle in time. They are also told that Mr. Murry is being held prisoner on a more distant planet named Camazotz where he had also traveled by means of a tesseract. In the distance, they spy their adversary, the Power of Darkness, a giant black cloud that represents all the evil and dehumanizing aspects in life. Camazotz has already surrendered to it, and the youngsters see, by looking into the crystal ball of the Happy Medium, that the people on Earth are also threatened by its power.

Before leaving the children to accomplish the rest of their mission, the ladies issue warnings of the dangers that lie ahead. Mrs. Who gives Meg her magic eyeglasses, to be used, she says, only in an extreme emergency.

Another tesser and the children, now alone, reach Camazotz. They find that here the people have given up their identities to live in mechanical, robot-like conformity where the slightest spark of individuality is repressed by harsh punishments. In the huge CENTRAL Central Intelligence Building, the three are confronted by the Prime Coordinator. In a duel of wits, he seduces the brain of the most vulnerable of them, Charles Wallace, and turns him into another dehumanized citizen of Camazotz.

Meg finds her father entrapped behind a transparent wall. Using Mrs. Who's spectacles, she is able to pass through the wall and free him. However, when they encounter the chief power on the planet, a large pulsating brain named IT, Meg is so close to submitting that Mr. Murry tessers Meg, Calvin, and himself to a nearby friendly planet. Charles Wallace, now a slave of IT's power, remains behind.

Meg slowly recovers from her ordeal. She is nursed by one of the planet's huge faceless inhabitants, whom she calls Aunt Beast. The three ladies return and tell Meg that she alone controls enough of the necessary power to save her brother. Meg does not understand what this power can be, but she consents to return to Camazotz.

When she confronts Charles Wallace once more, she suddenly knows that power that can save him is the power of love. In a climactic scene she repeats "I love you" to her brother over and over again until she frees him from the Power of Darkness. Together, they rejoin Mr. Murry and Calvin, and, with one more tesser, all return to Earth.

Themes and Subjects

This is a complex novel that combines elements of the quest fantasy, science fiction, philosophy, and religion. It explores such moral and ethical considerations as the nature of good and evil, the power and demands of loving, the possibility that evil can exist absolutely, and the place of the individual in society. This novel suggests that the most insidious form of evil is one where individuality is suppressed through thought control and coercion, chillingly portraying a society where this has taken place. The Murrys are a closely knit, intelligent, and supportive family and through the character of Meg there is an exploration of various aspects of courage, the importance of moral values, adolescent concerns, a search for identity, family allegiances, and friendship.

Incidents for Booktalking

This novel contains many fine incidents that can be read or retold: the first appearance of Mrs. Whatsit (pp. 16–17); Meg has a hard day at school (pp. 24–27); Charles Wallace and Meg meet Calvin and Mrs. Who (pp. 30–37); Meg tells Calvin about her father (pp. 48–52); the first tesser (pp. 56–62); a glimpse of the Power of Darkness (pp. 71–73); the Happy Medium's crystal ball (pp. 86–89); Camazotz (pp. 103–6); the CENTRAL Central Intelligence Building (pp. 115–20). An explanation of a tesseract is given on pages 75–78.

Related Titles

In Sid Hite's *Answer My Prayer* (Holt, 1995, $15.95: 0-8050-3406-4), ordinary Lydia Swain sets out with an angel named Ebol to save the jeefwood forests from an evil plot.

Playing Beatie Bow (pap., Puffin, $3.99: 0-14-031460-1) by Ruth Park uses an Australian setting and tells how 14-year-old Abbie travels back in time to Victorian Sydney.

Zoe moves to her grandmother's house and finds a playmate already there who lived in a previous century in Pam Conrad's *Stonewords: A Ghost Story* (Harper, 1990, $14.89: 0-06-021316-7).

In *Collidescope* (Bradbury, 1990, $14.95: 0-02-718316-5) by Grace Chetwin, three young people from different times and places team up in this time-travel novel.

In Anne Lindbergh's *The Shadow on the Dial* (pap., Avon, $2.75: 0-380-70545-1) Dawn and Marcus have many adventures as they travel back and forth in time.

About the Book and Author

Berger, Laura Standley, ed. *Twentieth-Century Children's Writers*. 4th ed. St. James, 1995, pp. 562–64.

———. *Twentieth-Century Young Adult Writers*. St. James, 1994, pp. 386–88.

Block, Ann, and Carolyn Riley, eds. *Children's Literary Review*. Vol. 1. Gale, 1976, pp. 129–34.

Brown, Muriel W., and Rita Schoch Foudray. *Newbery and Caldecott Medalists and Honor Book Winners: Bibliographic & Resource Material Through 1990.* 2d ed. Neal-Schuman, 1992, pp. 245–48.

Estes, Glenn E., ed. "American Writers for Children Since 1960: Fiction." In *Dictionary of Literary Biography.* Vol. 54. Gale, 1986, pp. 241–49.

Ethridge, James M., ed. *Contemporary Authors (First Revision).* Vols. 1–4. Gale, 1967, pp. 582–83.

Evory, Ann, and Linda Metzger, eds. *Contemporary Authors (New Revision Series).* Vol. 3. Gale, 1981, pp. 331–32.

Fuller, Muriel, ed. *More Junior Authors.* Wilson, 1963, pp. 137–38.

Gallo, Donald R. *Speaking for Ourselves.* National Council of Teachers of English, 1990, 116–19.

Garrett, Agnes, and Helga P. McCue, eds. *Authors and Artists for Young Adults.* Vol. 1. Gale, 1989, pp. 115–28.

Gonzales, Dolreen. *Madeleine L'Engle: Author of "A Winkle in Time."* Dillon, 1991.

Herne, Betsy. "A Mind in Motion: A Few Moments with Madeleine L'Engle." *School Library Journal* (June 1998): 28–33.

Hettinger, Donald R. *Presenting Madeleine L'Engle.* Twayne, 1993.

Hipple, Theodore W. ed. *Writers for Young Adults.* Scribners, 1997, 3 vols. Vol. 2, pp. 237–46.

Hopkins, Lee Bennett, ed. *More Books for More People.* Citation Press, 1974, pp. 257–66.

Kingman, Lee, ed. *Newbery and Caldecott Medal Books: 1956–1965 with Acceptance Papers, Biographies and Related Material.* Horn Book, 1965, pp. 116–28.

L'Engle, Madeleine. "1998 Margaret Edwards Award Acceptance Speech." *Journal of Youth Services in Libraries* (Fall 1998): 11–13.

———. *Trailing Clouds of Glory: Spiritual Values in Children's Books.* Westminster, 1985.

———. *Two Part Invention: The Story of a Marriage.* Farrar, 1988.

———. *A Wrinkle in Time.* Read by the author. Chivers Children's Audio Books, 1997. Audiocassettes. ($29.98)

———. *A Wrinkle in Time.* Listening Library, 1993. Audiocassettes, 345 min. ($22.95)

———. *A Wrinkle in Time.* Read by Barbara Caruso. Recorded Books, 1994. Audiocassettes, 390 min. ($42.00)

Madeleine L'Engle. Profiles in Literature, 1970. Videocassette.

McMahon, Thomas, ed. *Authors and Artists for Young Adults.* Vol. 28. Gale, 1999, pp. 137–44.

Nakamura, Joyce, ed. *Something About the Author: Autobiographical Series.* Vol. 15. Gale, 1993, pp. 187–99.

"Newbery Medal Acceptance Material, 1963." *Horn Book* 39, no. 4 (July/August 1963): 351–60.

Peterson, Linda K., and Marilyn L. Solt, eds. *Newbery and Caldecott Medal and Honor Books: 1922–1981.* Hall, 1982, p. 156.

Senick, Gerard J., ed. *Children's Literature Review.* Vol. 14. Gale, 1988, pp. 132–57.

Silvey, Anita, ed. *Children's Books and Their Creators.* Houghton, 1995, pp. 401–02.

Straub, Deborah A., ed. *Contemporary Authors (New Revision Series).* Vol. 21. Gale, 1987, pp. 240–43.

Ward, Martha, ed. *Authors of Books for Young People.* 3d ed. Scarecrow, 1990, p. 427.

Honor Books 1963

Nic Leodhas, Sorche. *Thistle and Thyme: Tales and Legends from Scotland.* Illustrated by Eveline Ness. Holt, 1962, o.p. (Grades 4–10)

In this companion volume to Nic Leodhas's *Heather and Broom,* the author has produced another excellent collection of Scottish folktales. This volume contains 10 stories that she remembers hearing from her childhood. They are of several types: two are legends, one is a "true" folktale (i.e., one made up by a common person and told around fires in the evening), five are sgeulachdans (i.e., stories made up by professional storytellers for special occasions), and two are seanachie stories or tales told by wandering storytellers that contain elements of all of the above types. The first and longest in this collection is a sgeulachdan from the Highlands called "The Laird's Lass and the Gobha's Son." In it, the beautiful, self-willed daughter of the village laird sees one day, from her bedroom window in the castle, the handsome son of the local blacksmith (gobha) when he comes to fetch her father's new mare for shoeing. She is so attracted to him that, disguised as a dairy maid, she visits the smithy's shop to get a better look. She is now convinced that this comely lad must be her future husband. However, her father refuses to have his well-bred daughter marry a lowly tradesman and instead arranges a marriage to a nobleman. In a desperate search for a solution to her troubles, the lass follows directions given to her by a kindly dwarf-like wizard she meets in the woods, and swallows two berries that he gives her. These magic berries turn her into a little dog. Her father tries every way possible to break this spell but to no avail. In the meantime, the wizard gives the gobha's son two more berries and tells him he must feed them to the little dog after receiving assurances from the laird that, if he breaks the spell, he may marry his daughter. The laird agrees. Eating the berries returns the girl to her original state and the two marry, presumably to live happily ever after. Other stories also deal with transformations and magic spells, some dating back to medieval times.

Coolidge, Olivia. *Men of Athens*. Houghton, 1962, o.p. (Grades 6–12)

After a brief introduction on the Golden Age of Athens, Coolidge, an Oxford-educated classical scholar, presents 13 biographical anecdotes that portray incidents in the lives of many famous and a few fictitious persons who lived in the Ancient World roughly between 500 and 400 B.C. Told in a series of stories, these sketches provide intimate glimpses into the history of the period, everyday life, and an introduction to such people as Pericles, Euripides, Darius, Xerxes, and Socrates. Although the title mentions only "men," women, such as Aspasia, Pericles' mistress, and Socrates's wife Xanthippe, also play prominent roles in these stories. The book is divided into three parts. The first contains five stories on Greek history before the Golden Age. They chronicle incidents in the history of the Greek conflict with Persia. One of these stories, *The Birth of a Lion*, tells about the joyful day when a son is born to Xanthippos and his decision to name him Pericles, meaning "Exceeding Glory."

The five stories in the second part feature Athenians of the Golden Age. One of these, *The Athenian*, features the great Athenian athlete, Criton, and tells of his training, hardships, and disappointments; his eventual triumphs in the Olympiad; and his untimely death in a battle defending Athens against the Corinthians. The three stories in the last part feature characters and incidents in the post-Golden Age when the 30-year Peloponnesian War was fought. The most moving of these tells of the trial and death of Socrates as seen through the eyes of one of the jurors. This book, which requires significant background knowledge to appreciate it fully, provides a panorama of this period and supplies flesh and blood to round out historical fact.

Newbery Winner 1964

Neville, Emily. *It's Like This, Cat*. Harper, 1963, $15.89: 0-06-024391-0. (Grades 6–8)

Emily Neville (1919–) was born in Manchester, Connecticut, to a family that was extremely interested in the arts, particularly writing and reading. The families of both her parents moved in a social circle that included Mark Twain. After graduating from Bryn Mawr, she became a journalist in New York and later turned to writing for children. In the 1970s she began a new career as a practicing lawyer after studying for her law degree and being admitted to the New York Bar in 1977. Her first novel was *It's Like This, Cat*, the story of a young teenager, Dave Mitchell, his adventures in New York City, his friends, and his often stormy relationship with his father. *Berries Goodman* (pap., Harper, $3.95), a later novel, takes the form of a reminiscence by a teenage boy as he recalls the two years when he and his family lived in the suburban town of Olcott Corners, In this town, through his friendship with a Jewish boy, he encounters the ugliness of anti-Semitism for the first time. Commenting on her writing, Neville said,

This, then, is what seems to me to be the job for a writer of junior novels: to shine the flashlight on good things, and on bad things. It is not our job to preach that this is right and that is wrong. It is ours to show how and when and why Wrong can be so overwhelmingly attractive at a given moment—and how Right can be found in some very unlikely corners.

Plot Summary

An only child, Dave Mitchell is having trouble getting along with his argumentative father. Although that is not too surprising in the life of a teenager, Dave has an added burden in that he feels that their frustrating relationship might be the cause of his mother's repeated asthma attacks. The Mitchells live in a New York City apartment, which has been home to Dave all of his 14 years. Dave and his father can argue about almost anything, but one constant source of irritation is the subject of a pet. His father thinks he should have one, not just any pet but a dog. His father had a rabbit-chasing dog when he was a youngster, which is probably why Dave rebels against the idea. It does not help their relationship any when Dave points out that you cannot chase rabbits on Third Avenue.

Dave gets some consolation about his rocky home life when he discusses his problems with Crazy Kate, a neighbor. She has that nickname because of all the cats she lives with. Kate is sympathetic—to a point—with Dave's problems. However, she occasionally lets him know that, in fact, he acts a good deal like the father he constantly harps on.

In time—and after another fight—Dave unexpectedly takes his father's advice and gets a pet. It is a cat, so that is what Dave names the animal. He is one of Crazy Kate's tomcats and is given to wandering about the apartment building and neighborhood, especially at night.

While searching for Cat in the basement of an adjacent building one day, Dave sees a young man he believes to be a burglar. Dave reports him to the superintendent and later discovers that the supposed burglar has been arrested. He is 19-year-old Tom Ransom. Dave immediately feels guilty about the young man's arrest because Tom helped him to locate Cat. As though to atone for what he has done, Dave writes Tom a letter and encloses his address.

Sometime later Tom appears at the Mitchells' apartment. He is on parole from the Youth Board. In a conversation with Dave, Tom points out that some of his own troubles may stem from the fact that his own father has rejected him. Tom says that Dave should be grateful that his father takes an interest in his comings and goings. Dave is not so sure, but he is surprised when his father offers to help Tom.

When he is not chasing after Cat or arguing with his father, Dave and his pal Nick bike around the city during vacation time. On one trip to Central Park, Cat unwillingly comes along in the bike basket. When they plan a trip to Coney Island, Nick is annoyed because Dave insists on taking Cat there too. Nick thinks this spoils their fun because Dave obviously cannot leave the animal unattended. But Dave insists and they bike to Coney Island, where they meet three girls at the beach. Even with Cat along, Dave enjoys the afternoon because he meets Mary, who pets Cat and seems to like him.

Cat's repeated fights and wanderings prompt Crazy Kate to suggest that it is time to have him neutered. Dave is very worried about the operation, but Cat survives and acts as though nothing very important has happened.

When school begins again, Dave enters senior high. With a new friend, Ben, he explores the city. When the Columbus Day holiday rolls around, he spends an enjoyable day with Mary. They promise to meet at Coney Island at the next holiday from school. But when the next holiday arrives, Dave has the flu and is not able to keep his date. Too embarrassed to call her when he recovers, Dave almost forgets their pleasant relationship as the Christmas holiday approaches.

In the meantime, Crazy Kate has some crazy news. Her rich brother has left her a good deal of money. The whole Mitchell family gets involved in helping Kate to deal with financial matters.

Surprisingly, Mary calls Dave. She needs his help because she is in a department store and has no money. Dave goes to the store and rescues her and at his father's suggestion, brings her home to dinner.

Once again, Tom visits the Mitchells. He tells Dave of his plans to join the army and he thanks Dave's father for taking an interest in him. All three give a toast to Cat, who brought them together. Before he leaves, Tom tells Dave that the reason he and his father quarrel so much is that they are so alike. This was a sentiment Crazy Kate had often expressed. Slowly, it begins to dawn on Dave that perhaps what he feels is overprotection is really a sign of his father's deep feelings for him. He thinks of Tom's rejection by his father and the deep pain it has caused him. He remembers a conversation with Mary in which she talks about the fact that her parents seem concerned only with how well she does in school, for instance, but never about how happy or well adjusted she might be. With these contrasts to his own family life, an appreciation of what he has begins to seep into Dave's view of his world and his relationship with his father.

Themes and Subjects

It's Like This, Cat is a story of growing up. Although it is very much a book of the sixties in its tone and teenage attitudes, it points out both the negative and positive aspects of the often-troubled teenage years. Contrasted with the anger Dave often feels toward his father or the unhappy experiences of Tom and Mary with their families is the happy enthusiasm of young adulthood. This is underscored by the delightful adventures that Dave and his friends have as they explore the sights and sounds of bustling New York City. Even in the changing world of the century's last decade, teenagers can relate to the typical teenager struggling toward adulthood in a typical American middle-class home. At the story's end is the sense that although Dave and his father will continue to have their problems, Dave has started on the road toward more understanding about his father's concern and love for him.

Incidents for Booktalking

Beside Dave, the main characters in this young adult novel are Dave's father, Crazy Kate, and, of course, Cat. Introductions to these characters can serve as a springboard for discussing Dave's rocky relationship with his father. See: Mr. Mitchell (pp. 2–4), meeting Crazy Kate and her cats (pp. 3–9); marvelous, independent Cat (pp. 10–12). Two other important characters are Tom and Mary. See: Dave mistakes Tom for a burglar when he searches for Cat (pp. 14–22); Dave enjoys his date (pp. 34–42). Readers might also enjoy sharing in Crazy Kate's inheritance (see pp. 151–60).

Related Titles

Jesse and his old and forgetful grandfather have a special relationship in Ron Koertge's *Tiger, Tiger Burning Bright* (Orchard, 1994, $17.95: 0-531-06840-4).

Thirteen-year-old Chrissa and her mother do not communicate, particularly about Chrissa's father, whom the girl has not seen in three years in Phyllis Reynolds Naylor's *Ice* (Atheneum, 1995, $16.00: 0-689-80005-3).

Harry is losing contact with his parents until he meets 70-year-old Amelia in John Donovan's *Remove Protective Coating a Little at a Time* (Harper, 1973, $12.89: 0-06-021720).

In Theresa Nelson's *Earthshine* (Orchard, 1994, $16.95: 0-531-06867-6), Slim lives with her charming actor-father—who is dying of AIDS—and his devoted partner, Larry.

For a younger audience, Dean Hughes's *The Trophy* (Knopf, 1994, $13.00: 0-679-84368-X) is about 10-year-old Danny, who is enjoying his first season of basketball and has trouble with his alcoholic father.

About the Book and Author

Berger, Laura Standley, ed. *Twentieth-Century Young Adult Writers*. St. James, 1994, p. 487.

Brown, Muriel W., and Rita Schoch Foudray. *Newbery and Caldecott Medalists and Honor Book Winners: Bibliographic & Resource Material Through 1990*. 2d ed. Neal-Schuman, 1992, pp. 309–10.

Chevalier, Tracy, ed. *Twentieth-Century Children's Writers*. 3d ed. St. James, 1989, p. 718.

Collier, Laurie, and Joyce Nakamura. *Major Authors and Illustrators for Children and Young Adults*. Gale, 1993, 6 vols., pp. 1761–63.

Commire, Anne, ed. *Something About the Author*. Vol. 1. Gale, 1971, p. 169.

de Montreville, Doris, and Don Hill, eds. *Third Book of Junior Authors*. Wilson, 1972, pp. 207–08.

Emily Cheney Neville's "It's Like This, Cat." Profiles in Literature, 1975. Videocassette.

Helbig, Alethea K., and Agnes R. Perkins, eds. *Dictionary of American Children's Fiction, 1960–1985*. Greenwood, 1986, pp. 470–71 (bio.), pp. 316–17 (book).

Hopkins, Lee Bennett, ed. *More Books by More People*. Citation Press, 1974, pp. 283–87.

It's Like This, Cat. SRA, n.d. Videocassette.

Kingman, Lee, ed. *Newbery and Caldecott Medal Books: 1956–1965 with Acceptance Papers, Biographies and Related Material.* Horn Book, 1965, pp. 129–39.

"Newbery Medal Acceptance Material, 1964." *Horn Book* 40, no. 4 (August 1964): 400–07.

Peterson, Linda K., and Marilyn L. Solt, eds. *Newbery and Caldecott Medal and Honor Books: 1922–1981.* Hall, 1982, pp. 158–59.

Sarkissian, Adele, ed. *Something About the Author: Autobiographical Series.* Vol. 2. Gale, 1986, pp. 157–74.

Silvey, Anita, ed. *Children's Books and Their Creators.* Houghton, 1995, p. 485.

Ward, Martha, ed. *Authors of Books for Young People.* 3d ed. Scarecrow, 1990, p. 523.

Honor Books 1964

North, Sterling. *Rascal: A Memoir of a Better Era.* Illustrated by John Schoenerr. Dutton, 1963 o.p.; pap., Avon, $2.75: 0-380-01518-8. (Grades 5–8)

> Arranged by months, this nostalgic picture of a gentle period in our history chronicles the year (May 1918 to April 1919) during which 11-year-old Sterling North's life was graced by the presence of his pet raccoon, Rascal. Sterling is growing up in Brailsford Junction, Wisconsin, almost completely without adult control; his mother is dead, his father often absent, and his two sisters, Theo and Jessica, live away from home and visit only occasionally. Meanwhile Sterling does the shopping, cooking, and household chores, builds a canoe in the living room, and keeps a menagerie of pets. After finding a baby raccoon, he brings him home and soon the two are inseparable and share many adventures. With Rascal's help, Sterling defeats his rival Sammy Stillman at the local fair's pie-eating contest and they witness a race in which a horse defeats a Model T. During a Spanish influenza epidemic, Rascal accompanies Sterling in a prolonged visit to out-of-town relatives. As Rascal grows, so do the problems of raising him. Attracted to bright objects, the animal steals Theo's engagement ring. Fortunately, Sterling is able to retrieve it. In a nature study class, Rascal bites his tormentor, Sammy Stillman, and a rabies scare hits town. Rascal begins raiding farmer's sweet corn patches and Sterling is forced to build a cage and keep Rascal locked up. When his father hires a housekeeper who is unsympathetic to Rascal, Sterling makes a heartbreaking decision to let Rascal return to the wild. One night he takes Rascal by canoe to the far bank of a creek. Soon, the crooning of a female raccoon is heard. At first Rascal hesitates, and then runs into the woods.

Wier, Ester. *The Loner.* Illustrated by Christine Price. McKay, 1963, o.p. (Grades 5–8)

> Boy—he has no real name—scarcely remembers his mother or father, although he thinks he is now about 14 years old. He is a migrant worker, scrounging a living moving from camp to camp. He becomes fond of a young girl, Raidy, and her family, but when Raidy is killed in a harvesting accident in Idaho, Boy wanders off. In the Montana hill country, he is found near death from exhaustion and starvation by Boss, a gargantuan woman who has lived alone in a trailer tending

her flock of sheep with her collies Jup and Juno. She, too, is a loner, still bitter about the death of her son Ben two years ago. Boss nurses Boy back to health and names him David from the Bible. At first, David is far from being the fine shepherd his namesake was. On one occasion he gives the wrong command to Jup, and almost drives the flock over a precipice. At another time, while trying to rescue a lost sheep, he falls down a mine shaft. David also interprets Boss's gruffness as resentment. However, when David runs away and Boss leaves her flock to bring him back, he realizes that she really cares for him. Gradually David begins to learn the skills of shepherding. He helps rescue some of the sheep when they are trapped in a snowstorm, saves Boss's friend Tex when he is caught in a bear trap, and kills a grizzly bear that is threatening the flock. In the spring, Boss moves the flock back to her ranch and decides to stay there so that David can go to school. The two have found a home, and as David says, "Home is a special word to a loner."

Newbery Winner 1965

Wojciechowska, Maia. *Shadow of a Bull*. Atheneum, 1964, $16.00: 0-689-30042-5. (Grades 5–8)

Maia Wojciechowska (1927–) was born in Warsaw, Poland, and emigrated to the United States in 1942. *Shadow of a Bull*, her second novel for young people, began as a short story aimed at an adult audience. When it was rejected for publication by a prominent magazine, the author rewrote and expanded the original manuscript, converting it into a novel for young readers. It explores one of the author's favorite themes—courage—in one of her favorite locales, southern Spain. Another of her novels that uses as a setting an Andalusian village and explores the similar theme is *A Single Light* (Atheneum, 1968, o.p.), in which a lonely, motherless girl, who is a deaf-mute outcast being raised by a priest, centers her love on a statue of the young Jesus. When an American visits her village looking for art treasures, she runs away with her statue to protect it, causing an eruption of violence in the village. *Shadow of a Bull* is an equally somber tale, one in which the author captures the rhythm of Spanish life, the importance of bullfighting in this culture, and the personal conflict of a young boy. A glossary of bullfighting terms is included on pages 157–65.

Plot Summary

Manolo Olivar, the son of the revered dead matador, Juan Olivar, dreads his 12th birthday. On that day everyone in the town of Arcangel expects him to fight his first bull and follow in his father's footsteps. Nine-year-old Manolo considers himself a coward. He cannot even bring himself to jump off a hay wagon with the other boys or ride a bicycle.

One day, after jumping back in fright from an approaching automobile, Manolo cowers while six village men chide him. They remind him that his long nose—a sign of bravery—is just like his father's. They also remind him that he better not jump away from the bull. These six aficionados (devotees of the bullfighting art) begin to instruct him. They take him to Cordova and Seville for the Sunday bullfights and on Thursdays they go to the local arena. When Manolo sees his first bullfight, he wants to leap out and rescue the bull, not kill him. Manolo is momentarily swept up in the hysteria of the crowd when the matador dedicates the bull to him, but at the "moment of truth" (the kill), the old terror returns.

Manolo knows that a gypsy fortune-teller said that his father would be a great *torero*. He also knows that no fortune-teller came to celebrate his birth. He permits himself to hope that his mother will not let him fight, but overhears her tell a neighbor, "It is his fate." He goes to the local museum to see his father's *traje de luces* (the "suit of lights" or ceremonial costume) and the mounted head of Patatero (his father's killer): he goes to look at his father's statue in the park, but nowhere is there an answer to his overwhelming fear. Knowing that his poor Andalusian people suffer all the plagues of mankind, Manolo realizes that for a few moments in the bull arena they watch Death being cheated and find comfort for their dreary lives. However, this knowledge does not allay his own fear.

Manolo is certain that the elderly Count de la Casa will have a bull ready for him to fight on his 12th birthday, just as he did for his father. So Manolo starts practicing with his grandfather's cape and muleta. He becomes very proficient at the veronicas, medias, and other bullfighting passes. He begins to gain confidence until the men remind him the kill is all-important. Discouraged, Manolo finds out from his classmate, Jaime Garcia, that he should practice running backwards to strengthen his leg muscles and should squeeze a ball to develop his sword hand in the same way Jaime's brother Juan does. Although he practices faithfully, his feeling of success is short-lived. When Count de la Casa visits Arcangel on Manolo's 10th birthday, he decides that the boy will fight a three-year-old bull at the annual spring *tienta* (bullfight). Manolo is desperate: now even the extra year has been taken away from him.

Manolo learns that Jaime's brother has been caping bulls in the pastures at night for practice and decides to visit him. During the visit, Juan's crippled father tells him that he watched Manolo's father fight his first bull at the *tienta*. Manolo feels very sorry for both Mr. Garcia, who wanted only to be a bullfighter, and his son, Juan, who has the same "*afición*." He promises to ask the Count to let Juan come to the *tienta*.

He and Juan go to the local arena one night to practice with the bull that the 18-year-old El Magnifico will fight the following day. Manolo is humble before Juan's confidence and dexterity in the moonlit ring. Suddenly, the bull topples Juan. Without hesitating, Manolo rushes in and successfully distracts the bull. While Juan leads the bull back to its stall, Manolo's fear returns. He cannot understand Juan's aplomb, although Juan explains that it does not take much to be brave if you have *afición*. He offers Juan his honored place at the coming *tienta*. Though tempted, Juan refuses because he does not want to deprive Manolo of this glorious privilege.

Stricken with fear and guilt, Manolo goes with his tutors to visit El Magnifico who has been seriously gored by the enraged bull. When the local doctor arrives, he commands Manolo to help him treat the wound. He listens attentively as the doctor laments that the "tragedy is that boys like him (El Magnifico) know of nothing else they want to do."

Manolo finds that he wants to help the doctor and learn to be like him. Before Manolo only knew he was afraid to fight the bull, but now he knows that here is some other work he really wants to do. Still, he has to face the ordeal of the *tienta*. He wonders if his father had been afraid, too. When Manolo asks his mother about his father, she tells him that his father was a man of honor and principle who "would never do anything he really did not want to." With this knowledge, Manolo comes to a decision.

After a prayer to the patron saint of bullfighting, Manolo leaves for his "moment of truth."

Manolo generally makes a good showing in the bull ring but realizes that he cannot finish. He tells the Count he can do no better and the Juan Garcia should take over to carry on the tradition of Arcangel. As Juan takes his place in the ring, Manolo goes to the stands and sits with his new friend, the doctor. He no longer lives under the shadow of the bull.

Themes and Subjects

This is the story of how a boy faces a conflict between his fear of bullfighting and the need to live up to the expectations bequeathed him through his father's reputation. It explores the nature of fear and of various kinds of courage ranging from physical courage, represented by bullfighting, to the more subtle types such as being true to oneself. Many youngsters live in the shadow of real or imaginary fears and resolving them is often a huge task. Realizing that one cannot run away from crises is a difficult reality to face. These situations involving fear and its resolution are depicted effectively in this novel. The author's spare writing style is reminiscent of Hemingway, who also wrote effectively on Spain and bullfighting. This novel also gives the reader an introduction to the atmosphere of the Andalusian countryside and to the ritual known as bullfighting.

Incidents for Booktalking

Some interesting passages are: the townspeople speak of their expectations involving Manolo and of his father's reputation (pp. 3–8); Manolo sees attributes his father that he does not remember (pp. 9–12); Manolo decides he is a coward (pp. 17–19); the six aficionados tell Manolo about bullfighting (pp. 23–28); Manolo's first introduction to a bullfight in the local arena (pp. 29–42); Juan and Manolo cape El Magnifico's bull (pp. 83–95).

Related Titles

In Aileen Friedman's *A Cloak for the Dreamer* (Scholastic, 1995, $14.95: 0-590-48987-9) Misha sets out to find his fortune in an amazing cloak designed by his father and brothers.

World War I Pittsburgh is the setting of Gloria Skurzynski's *Good-bye, Billy Radish* (pap., Macmillan, 1992, $2.99: 0-689-80443-1), the story of a friendship between a young American boy and the son of Ukrainian immigrants.

A young boy with spina bifida is transformed when he takes up horseback riding in *Colt* (pap., Puffin, $3.99: 0-14-036480-3) by Nancy Springer.

In Gary Soto's *The Pool Party* (Delacorte, 1992, $13.95: 0-385-308906; pap., Dell, $3.50: 0-440-41010-X), Rudy, part of a Mexican American family, has problems growing up.

Robby ends up running away when he cannot communicate with his father in *A Friend Like That* (Lippincott, 1988, $11.95: 0-397-32310-7) by Alfred Slote.

About the Book and Author

Berger, Laura Standley, ed. *Twentieth-Century Young Adult Writers*. St. James, 1994, pp. 711–13.

Block, Ann, and Carolyn Riley, eds. *Children's Literary Review*. Vol. 1. Gale, 1976, pp. 196–201.

Brown, Muriel W., and Rita Schoch Foudray. *Newbery and Caldecott Medalists and Honor Book Winners: Bibliographic & Resource Material Through 1990*. 2d ed. Neal-Schuman, 1992, pp. 458–59.

Chevalier, Tracy, ed. *Twentieth-Century Children's Writers*. 3d ed. St. James, 1989, pp. 1058–59.

Collier, Laurie, ed. *Authors and Artists for Young Adults*. Vol. 8. Gale, 1999, pp. 197–204.

Collier, Laurie, and Joyce Nakamura. *Major Authors and Illustrators for Children and Young Adults*. Gale, 1993, 6 vols. pp. 2489–91.

Commire, Anne, ed. *Something About the Author*. Gale, 1971, Vol. 1, pp. 228–29; 1982, Vol. 28, pp. 222–28.

de Montreville, Doris, and Don Hill, eds. *Third Book of Junior Authors*. Wilson, 1972, pp. 303–5.

Evory, Ann, ed. *Contemporary Authors (First Revision Series)*. Vol. 4. Gale, 1981, pp. 602–3.

Hedblad, Alan, ed. *Something About the Author*. Vol. 104. Gale, 1999, pp. 208–25.

Helbig, Alethea K., and Agnes R. Perkins, eds. *Dictionary of American Children's Fiction, 1960–1985*. Greenwood, 1986, p. 737 (bio.), pp. 589–90 (book).

Hile, Kevin S. ed. *Something About the Author*. Vol. 83. Gale, 1996, pp. 229–33.

Hopkins, Lee Bennett, ed. *More Books by More People*. Citation Press, 1974, pp. 381–86.

Kingman, Lee, ed. *Newbery and Caldecott Medal Books: 1956–1965 with Acceptance Papers, Biographies and Related Material*. Horn Book, 1965, pp. 140–52.

Kinsman, Clare D., and Mary Ann Tennenhouse, eds. *Contemporary Authors*. Vols. 9–12. Gale, 1974, pp. 974–75.

"Newbery Medal Acceptance Material, 1965." *Horn Book* 41, no. 4 (July/August 1965): 349–57.

Peterson, Linda K., and Marilyn L. Solt, eds. *Newbery & Caldecott Medal and Honor Books: 1922–1981*. Hall, 1982, pp. 160–61.

Sarkissian, Adele, ed. *Something About the Author: Autobiographical Series*. Vol. 1. Gale, 1986, pp. 307–25.

Silvey, Anita, ed. *Children's Books and Their Creators*. Houghton, 1995, p. 688.

Ward, Martha, ed. *Authors of Books for Young People*. 3d ed. Scarecrow, 1990, p. 762.

Wojciechowska, Maia. *Shadow of a Bull*. Read by Francisco Rivela. Listening Library. Audiocassettes, 210 min. ($16.98)

Honor Books 1965

Hunt, Irene. *Across Five Aprils*. Folett, 1964, o.p.; pap. Berkley, $4.99: 0-425-0241-6.

> Based on the memoirs of the author's grandfather, this is the story of the Creighton family of southern Illinois and their life during the five years of the Civil War from April 1861 to April 1865. Jethro Creighton is only nine when talk of a civil war ignites the feelings of everyone around him. Two of his older brothers, John and Tom, along with their cousin, Eb Carron, and the local schoolteacher, Shadrack Yale, join the Union forces, but middle brother, Bill, travels to Kentucky and joins the Confederate Army. As a result, the family is labeled Copperhead and suffers scorn and antagonism from many locals, leading to their well being poisoned and their barn burned. When his father suffers a crippling heart attack, Jethro assumes many adult chores. In 1863, some army deserters pass through the area. Among them is Eb. Realizing that Eb faces a firing squad when he returns to his unit, Jethro writes a letter to President Lincoln and in return receives a reply giving deserters amnesty. The family learns that Tom Creighton has been killed in battle and Bill is being held in a Yankee prison camp. Jethro's sister Jenny, who has fallen in love with Shadrack, goes east to nurse him when he is wounded in battle. When the war ends, Shad and Jenny, now married, come back to the homestead for a visit and take Jethro east to school. Time and the war have inflicted great changes on the Creighton family. During the five years of Jethro's adolescence, he has done a man's work and learned some painful lessons. Now there must come a time for healing.

Newbery Winner 1966

de Trevino, Elizabeth Borton. *I, Juan de Pareja*. Farrar, 1965, $16.00: 0-374-33531-1. (Grades 5–8)

> Elizabeth Borton de Trevino (1904–) was born and grew up in California and attended Stanford University. Her career as a journalist took her to Mexico, where she married and established a new home. This part of her life is covered in the charming autobiography *My Heart Lies South: The Story of My Mexican Marriage* (Farrar, 1953, o.p.). She became fascinated with both Spanish and Mexican cultures and from this interest came a number of books, including *The Greek of Toledo* (Farrar, 1959, o.p.), a novel about the artist El Greco, and *El Guero* (Farrar, 1989, $14.00; pap., $3.95), a tribute to her husband's grandfather, Judge Cayetano Trevino. Set in seventeenth-century Spain, *I, Juan de Pareja* tells of the

touching friendship between the court painter Velazquez and his slave, the talented Juan de Pareja, who is later granted his freedom. In writing about this book, the author says:

> Everything I have written deals with some form of love. The difficulties of loves across racial barriers can give rise to strong and loyal devotion. This was the theme of my story. [It] foreshadows, in the lifetime of the two men, what we hope to achieve a millionfold today. Those two, who began in youth as master and slave, continued as companions in their maturity and ended as equals and friends.

Plot Summary

This biographical novel concerns the great Spanish painter, Velazquez, and a young black boy who became his assistant. Diego Rodriguez de Silva y Velazquez (1599–1660) was born in Seville, Spain, and is considered a leading painter of the Spanish school. Among his most famous works are: *Adoration of the Magi, Christ and the Pilgrims of Emmaus*, and *Venus with a Mirror*.

Juan de Pareja, who would become the great painter's assistant, was born into slavery in the seventeenth century. By the age of five, Juan is an orphan and the personal slave of Dona Rodriquez, who is the wife of a wealthy merchant in Seville. The boy is taught how to read and write and because he is eager to learn and has a bright mind, he soon begins to answer all of the personal correspondence for his mistress. Juan is well cared for in the household, but his quiet, sheltered existence comes to an abrupt end when the dreaded plague strikes the city of Seville. The city is shattered by the number of deaths, including those of Juan's master and mistress.

For a time Juan is placed in the care of a Franciscan friar, kindly Brother Isidro. The friar explains to the boy that he is to go to Madrid. All of the Rodriguez's property, including Juan, has been inherited by their nephew, Don Diego Velazquez.

Juan is taken to Madrid by a cruel gypsy named Carmelo. He is beaten savagely by Carmelo and forced to beg for his food. By the time he arrives in Madrid and the home of Velazquez, he is more dead than alive.

Juan recovers and fits well into the new household. Both the mistress of the house, Dona Juana, and her daughter, Paquita, are fond of the young boy. He becomes the personal servant of Velazquez, who is a painter, and Juan helps him mix his colors, arrange his palette, and frame the canvases. Velazquez is a taciturn but gentle man, and a strong attachment develops between him and his eager, devoted young slave. As time passes, Juan longs more and more to learn how to paint. Spanish law, however, forbids slaves to engage in the arts.

The fame of Velazquez grows. He becomes the official court painter of the Spanish king, Philip IV. As court painter, Velazquez completes many portraits of the king, his family, and his advisors. He also helps to welcome the famed Flemish painter, Rubens, to the Spanish court. Along with Rubens as part of his entourage is a pretty slave girl named Miri. Juan falls in love with her and is heartbroken when they must part.

Sometime later, Juan accompanies Velazquez when he is sent to Italy by Philip IV to buy and copy artworks for the court gallery. While on the trip, Juan secretly tries his hand at painting. After their return, Juan helps to promote a romance between Paquita and one of Velazquez's apprentices. The two are eventually united in a happy marriage.

Juan continues to paint in secret but feels increasingly guilty. Finally, he confesses his guilt to his master's new apprentice, Bartolome Murillo. The apprentice assures Juan that he has talent and should not stifle it.

On a second visit to Italy, Velazquez's right hand becomes seriously infected. Juan is able to nurse the painter back to health and restore his confidence. Velazquez resumes painting by creating a magnificent portrait of Juan. When the art patrons of Rome see this masterpiece, commissions pour in. Before he leaves Rome, Velazquez completes several portraits, including one of Pope Innocent X.

Back in Madrid, Juan can no longer keep his secret from his master. When he confesses, Velazquez reacts by declaring Juan a free man and offering him a post as his assistant. He also gives freedom to a maidservant, Lolis, so that she and Juan may marry and have a family free of slavery.

Juan continues to work at the studio until Velazquez's death. Posthumously, King Philip confers knighthood on the painter. Juan de Pareja guides the king's hand as he paints the red cross of Santiago on Velazquez's only self-portrait.

Themes and Subjects

The author describes the principal theme in an afterword: "The story of Juan de Pareja and Velazquez foreshadows, in the lifetime of the two men, what we hope to achieve a millionfold today. Those two, who began in youth as master and slave, continued as companions in their maturity and ended as equals and as friends."

Incidents for Booktalking

If possible, display some of the paintings of Velazquez; well-known *Las Meninas* includes the famous self-portrait with the Cross of Santiago as well as a study, in the distance, of the painter's royal patron. Incidents for reading aloud include: Juan learns of his change of ownership (pp. 13–16); his journey with Carmelo (pp. 29–32); he leaves Carmelo and works in a bakery (pp. 33–36); Juan learns his duties (pp. 40–45); the apprentices (pp. 47–51); Rubens visits the Madrid Woodcutters (pp. 62–66); the first trip to Italy (pp. 84–90); Juan paints a Virgin and confesses to Murillo (pp. 122–27).

Related Titles

A brief biography and 15 color reproductions are found in Ernest Raboff's *Diego Rodriguez de Silva y Velasquez* (Lippicott, 1988, $11.95: 0-397-32219-4).

Following a discussion of the language of art are many projects in Moy Keightley's *Investigating Art: A Practical Guide for Young People* (Facts on File, 1984, $17.95: 0-87196-973-4).

Two excellent books on the history of art are Piero Ventura's *Great Painters* (Putnam, 1984, $24.95: 0-399-21115-2) and H. W. Janson's *History of Art for Young People* (Abrams, 1987, $29.95: 0-8109-1098-5).

Justin Denzel's *Boy of the Painted Cave* (Putnam, 1988, $14.95: 0-399-21559-X) is the story of a boy who longs to become a cave artist.

On the remote Scottish island of Sula, young Magnus's artistic talents are recognized by a schoolmaster in Lavinia Derwent's *Sula* (pap., Trafalgar Square, $6.95: 0-86241-068-1).

Left alone for a time by her artist father, Lily tries her hand at painting in *Catch the Sea* (Bradbury, 1989, $13.95: 0-02-743451-6) by Mary Haynes.

About the Book and Author

Berger, Laura Standley, ed. *Twentieth-Century Children's Writers*. 4th ed. St. James, 1995, pp. 297–99.

Brown, Muriel W., and Rita Schoch Foudray. *Newbery and Caldecott Medalists and Honor Book Winners: Bibliographic & Resource Material Through 1990*. 2d ed. Neal-Schuman, 1992, pp. 104–5.

Chevalier, Tracy, ed. *Twentieth-Century Children's Writers*. 3d ed. St. James, 1989, pp. 285–87.

Collier, Laurie, and Joyce Nakamura. *Major Authors and Illustrators for Children and Young Adults*. Gale, 1993, 6 vols, pp. 2335–37.

Commire, Anne, ed. *Something About the Author*. Gale, 1971, Vol. 1, pp. 216–17; 1982, Vol. 29, pp. 216–21.

de Montreville, Doris, and Elizabeth D. Crawford, eds. *Fourth Book of Junior Authors and Illustrators*. Wilson, 1978.

Evory, Ann, and Linda Metzger, eds. *Contemporary Authors (New Revision Series)*. Vol. 9. Gale, 1983, p. 499.

Helbig, Alethea K., and Agnes R. Perkins, eds. *Dictionary of American Children's Fiction, 1960–1985*. Greenwood, 1986, p. 67 (bio.), pp. 307–8 (book).

Hopkins, Lee Bennett, ed. *More Books by More People*. Citation Press, 1874, pp. 126–32.

I, Juan de Pareja. Profiles in Literature, 1977. Videocassette.

Kingman, Lee, ed. *Newbery and Caldecott Medal Books: 1966–1975 with Acceptance Papers, Biographies and Related Material*. Horn Book, 1975, pp. 3–19.

Kinsman, Clare D., ed. *Contemporary Authors*. Vols. 17–20. Gale, 1976, pp. 736–37.

"Newbery Medal Acceptance Materials, 1966." *Horn Book* 42, no. 4 (July/August 1966): 333–42.

Peterson, Linda K., and Marilyn L. Solt, eds. *Newbery and Caldecott Medal and Honor Books: 1922–1981*. Hall, 1982, pp. 162–63.

Sarkissian, Adele, ed. *Something About the Author: Autobiographical Series*. Vol. 5. Gale, 1989, pp. 287–302.

Silvey, Anita, ed. *Children's Books and Their Creators*. Houghton, 1995, p. 201.

Trevino, Elizabeth Borton de. *My Heart Lies South*. Crowell, 1953.

———. *Where the Heart Is*. Doubleday, 1963.

———. *The Hearthstone of My Heart*. Doubleday, 1977.

Ward, Martha, ed. *Authors of Books for Young People*. 3d ed. Scarecrow, 1990, p. 708.

Honor Books 1966

Alexander, Lloyd. *The Black Cauldron*. Holt, 1965, $16.95: 0-8050-0992-2; pap., Dell, $5.50: 0-440-40649-8. (Grades 5–8)

Readers first meet Taran, the assistant pig-keeper to Dallben, the great wizard of Prydain, in *The Book of Three* (Holt, $16.95, 1964) when Taran searches for Hen-Wen, the oracular pig. In this second adventure, he is appointed guardian of the pack animals in Prince Gwydion's quest for the magical black cauldron, used by the wicked Arawn, Lord of Annuvin, to bring slain warriors back to life for use in his army. With Taran's rear guard group are the proud, ambitious Prince Ellidyr and the brave Adaon. From Doli, a dwarf with the power to become invisible, the group learns that the cauldron is being guarded in a remote marsh by three enchantresses, Orddu, Orwen, and Orgoch. During an attack by Arawn's Huntsmen, Adaon is mortally wounded. Before his death, he gives Taran a magic brooch that bestows gifts of wisdom and insight on the wearer. In the land of the enchantresses, the brooch is the price paid to Orddu to release the cauldron. She informs them that the cauldron and its powers will be destroyed only when someone willingly sacrifices his life by jumping into it. The band is captured by a former ally, King Morgant, who has turned traitor. He seizes the cauldron and plans to use its powers to become Overlord of Prydain. Using his invisibility, Doli frees the group, and a mortally wounded Ellidyr sacrifices himself by throwing himself into the cauldron and destroying its powers. At that moment, Gwydion's army arrives and defeats Morgant, who is killed in the ensuing battle. Taran's adventures are continued in the three other Chronicles of Prydain, culminating in the last volume *The High King*, the Newbery Award winner for 1969 (p. 273).

Jarrell, Randall. *The Animal Family*. Illustrated by Maurice Sendak. Harper, 1985, $16.95: 0-06-205088-5. (Grades 4–8)

This poetic fantasy about a strong, handsome hunter who lives alone on an island and longs for a family with whom he can share the beauty of life is told in a series of deceptively simple vignettes. Each is prefaced with a drawing of a pastoral scene by Maurice Sendak. The hunter is continually disturbed by dreams of his dead parents and yearns for companionship. He first hears the voice of a shy mermaid who, at his bidding, joins him in his cottage. She gradually adjusts to life on land and delights in simple things like language, fire, and new foods. One day the hunter is forced to kill a mother bear. He brings the bear's cub home and he and the mermaid raise it as their child. In time, however, they are saddened by the absences caused by hibernation. Later the hunter brings home a baby lynx and again, the couple watch the cycle of growth and development in amazement. The hunter teaches the little animal to play ball and to box. One day, after a violent storm, the lynx finds a lifeboat containing a dead woman and her young son, miraculously alive after his ordeal. With the help of the bear, the lynx brings the boy to the hunter's house. The hunter now feels happy and complete with his family. He and the mermaid teach the boy about their worlds and he becomes the offspring of both the sea and the earth. As the mermaid and the hunter sit in the meadow one day, she is so overcome with the joy that the hunter has brought her that she sings a song of praise of her adopted home, the land. At that moment the hunter discovers for the first time that mermaids can cry. This gentle fable teaches the lesson that even disparate beings can live together peacefully as a family.

Stolz, Mary. *The Noonday Friends*. Illustrated by Louis S. Glansman. Harper, 1965, $14.89: 0-06-025946-9. (Grades 3–6)

This warm, sentimental story about a wholesome, if somewhat unconventional, family takes place in Greenwich Village in New York City during the early 1960s. The noontime friends are Franny Davis, an 11-year-old girl, and her classmate, Simone Orgella, whose large family came originally from Puerto Rico. Because Franny must rush home after school to fetch four-year-old brother, Marshall, from their baby-sitter, Mrs. Mundy, and care for him until Mrs. Davis gets home from her job in the laundry, Franny has only lunchtimes plus occasional weekend visits to spend with her dear friend. The two girls share many interests including working on their scrapbooks and envying Lila Wimbleton, a school acquaintance whose family is financially well-off. Not so Franny's family. Her father is a caring but basically irresponsible struggling artist who has recently and reluctantly taken a job as a salesman in Mr. Harney's shoe store hoping that, as a fringe benefit, he can buy much-needed shoes for his family at a discount. Completing the Davis family are Franny's mother, who emigrated from Ireland 15 years before, and Franny's twin brother, Jim, who unlike Franny seems to accept the family's precarious existence without strain or stress. Franny's world suddenly comes crashing around her when she and Simone quarrel and Mr. Davis loses his job for insulting a customer. There is, however, a happy ending. Mr. Davis's portrait of Mr. Harney arouses the interest of Mr. Wheeler, a gallery owner who agrees to display other paintings. Later, he gets Mr. Davis a job in an advertising agency. Through Mr. Davis's efforts, Francisco, Simone's job-hunting cousin, fills the vacancy at Mr. Harney's shoe store, leading to a reconciliation between the two friends. Even Marshall prospers. At his fifth birthday party, he receives presents from every member of his loving family.

❀ Newbery Winner 1967

Hunt, Irene. *Up a Road Slowly*. Follett, 1966, o.p.; Silver Burdett, 1990, $10.95: 0-382-24366-8; pap., Scholastic, $1.95: 0-590-03171-6. (Grades 6–9)

Born in Newton, Illinois, and educated at the universities of Illinois and Minnesota, Irene Hunt (1907–) was a public school teacher and a lecturer in psychology before she turned to writing books for young readers. Her first, *Across Five Aprils*, tells the story of the Creighton family split in allegiances during the war, but reunited afterward and hoping to rebuild their lives. It was a Newbery

Honor book (see "Honor Books," 1965, p. 256) and winner of the Charles W. Follett Award. Her second novel, the Newbery Award winner *Up a Road Slowly*, covers 10 years in the life of Julie Trelling, from age seven when she is sent to live with her strict but loving Aunt Cordelia to her graduation from high school. Two other important novels by Miss Hunt are *No Promises in the Wind* (pap., Berkley, $3.50), in which two young brothers run away from home during the Great Depression, and *The Lottery Rose* (1976, Scribners, o.p.), the story of family abuse and cruelty as seen through the experiences of a sensitive youngster, Georgie Burgess. Concerning the function of children's books, Miss Hunt has written, "Great books do not have to preach. But they do speak to the conscience, the imagination, and the heart of many a child. And they speak with very clear and forceful voices."

Plot Summary

Julie Trelling is just seven years old when her mother dies. *Up a Road Slowly* is the story of her next 10 years, which she spends in the home of her strict but kind Aunt Cordelia, a proper spinster lady and a schoolteacher. Set in the early decades of the twentieth century, automobiles are in use but roads are poorly maintained in the rural area where Aunt Cordelia teaches through the eighth grade. There is no bus transportation to the high school in town, and the one-room school that Julie and her brother Christopher attend and where her aunt teaches will soon be on the way out.

Told by Julie as her life's story, this is a tale of maturing and understanding as Julie recovers from the tragedy of her mother's death and begins life in a new setting. Through the small, day-to-day happenings of her home life, she gains a new understanding and appreciation of her aunt and comes to a sense of independence and maturity on her own.

Julie learns that Aunt Cordelia does not really have to teach to earn a living, for her income from the farm is sufficient. But Aunt Cordelia truly feels that *her* teaching is the best to be had anywhere. And so she goes back year after year to the one-room schoolhouse.

Julie must also get used to Uncle Haskell, Aunt Cordelia's brother, who has a drinking problem. He lives in a renovated carriage house out in back of the farmhouse. He prefers the privacy of his own establishment and in this manner does not have to share responsibility for the farm and for Julie with his sister. Besides getting used to a new life, Julie misses her older sister Laura, who has remained in the home with their father.

The years pass and soon Julie is ready for high school. The summer before, her father remarried. Her new stepmother is Alicia, an attractive woman who teaches English at the high school. Alicia and her father ask her to stay in town with them so that she can attend school. Instead, Julie decides to remain with Aunt Cordelia, who will quit teaching after all for the one-room school is no longer fashionable. As Julie tells her aunt:

> You wouldn't mind if I stayed here then—if I lived with you while I'm in high school. I'll try to be mature, Aunt Cordelia, honestly I'll try. I don't want to be a burden, but when you get down to brass tacks, this is *home* as far as I'm concerned.

Aunt Cordelia closes her eyes and shakes her head ever so slightly. but she smiles.

And so the high school years begin for Julie. Instead of living in town, she commutes to school with a neighbor boy named Dan Trevort. As she matures, Julie thinks more and more that she would like to become a writer when she is grown. She becomes very conscious of the beauty of words, especially the poems of Edna St. Vincent Millay and Sara Teasdale. Their views of the world and their feelings often reflect her own outlook on life and those about her. Were it not for the realism of Aunt Cordelia and her home life, Julie would probably be lost in the romance of words.

But there *is* much realism about Julie's life, as in the character of a mentally retarded child, Aggie Kilpin, who attends the one-room school with Julie. Repulsive in her hygiene, Aggie is often ignored by the other children, including Julie. After Aggie's death, Julie feels heavy remorse for the way she treated the young girl.

When Julie is a junior in high school, she falls in love. He is a handsome transfer student named Brett Kingsman. Wonder of wonders, Brett seems to return her feelings. He tells Julie, however, that Alicia, Julie's stepmother, is surely going to flunk him in English. Julie promises that that will not happen, for she will help the young man to pass. Indeed, she does, only to learn a harsh lesson—handsome Brett is interested in passing English and getting Julie to write his compositions, not in her.

As the high school years come to a close, Julie is well on the way to growing up. She and Dan make a tremendous discovery, too. They find their love for one another and vow that they will marry. First, however, Aunt Cordelia wants Julie to attend the State University, but Julie wishes to remain home for the next four years. However, Aunt Cordelia persuades Julie of the rightness of her decision. Dan and Julie part, vowing to keep their love alive and return in four years.

At Julie's high school graduation, she gives a speech. After it is over, Aunt Cordelia, always proper, says of her niece, "Within certain limits, I am quite proud of her." It is fine praise, indeed!

Themes and Subjects

This episodic quiet story of growing up gives an authentic flavor of rural life in the early decades of the twentieth century. It also incorporates some taboos generally avoided in children's books, especially of that time. Uncle Haskell, for instance, is obviously an alcoholic. Aggie Kilpin is mentally retarded and an overall repulsive figure because of her lack of personal cleanliness. Another character, Katy Eltwin, is insane. The characters, through the observations of Julie, are presented in a sympathetic but realistic manner. The growing relationship between Julie and her proper aunt is nicely and lovingly presented as well.

Incidents for Booktalking

Many scenes give both a flavor of the times and an indication of a young girl's slow progress through the tragedy of her mother's death to maturity and a new life of independence and responsibility. See, for example: the first time Julie sees Aunt Cordelia cry (p. 18); enter Aggie (pp. 23–26); Julie's 12th birthday (pp. 50–68); Julie makes the decision to stay with Aunt Cordelia (pp. 106–7); Julie and Brett (pp. 123–44); the graduation speech (pp. 190–92).

Related Titles

Sara finds a caring family after a series of unhappy foster homes in Julie Johnson's *Adam and Eve and Pinch-Me* (Little, Brown, 1994, $15.95: 0-316-46990-4; pap., Puffin, $4.99: 0-14-037588-0).

In Sarah Ellis's *Out of the Blue* (Simon, 1995, $15.00: 0-689-80025-8), Meegan suddenly discovers she has a 24-year-old sister who was given up for adoption many years before.

Jane would like to meet the family that her absent father had when he married years ago in Nina Bawden's *The Outside Child* (pap., Puffin, $3.99: 0-14-036858-2).

Sixteen-year-old Leenie is visited by a mother she does not know in Patricia Calvert's *Yesterday's Daughter* (pap., Avon, $2.75: 0-380-70470-6).

After a terrible radiation leak, 13-year-old Nyle and her grandmother try to continue a normal life on a Vermont farm in *Phoenix Rising* (Holt, 1994, $15.95: 0-8050-3108-1; pap., Puffin, $4.99: 0-14-037638-3) by Karen Hesse.

About the Book and Author

Berger, Laura Standley, ed. *Twentieth-Century Children's Writers*. 4th ed. St. James, 1944, pp. 312–14.

Block, Ann, and Carolyn Riley, eds. *Children's Literary Review*. Vol. 1. Gale, 1976, pp. 109–11.

Brown, Muriel W., and Rita Schoch Foudray. *Newbery and Caldecott Medalists and Honor Book Winners: Bibliography & Resource Material Through 1990*. 2d ed. Neal-Schuman, 1992, pp. 195–96.

Chevalier, Tracy, ed. *Twentieth-Century Children's Writers*. 3d ed. St. James, 1989, pp. 481–82.

Collier, Laurie, and Joyce Nakamura. *Major Authors and Illustrators for Children and Young Adults*. Gale, 1993, 6 vols, pp. 1191–93.

Commire, Anne, ed. *Something About the Author*. Vol. 2. Gale, 1971, pp. 146–47.

de Montreville, Doris, and Don Hill, eds. *Third Book of Junior Authors*. Wilson, 1972, pp. 139–40.

Estes, Glenn E., ed. "American Writers for Children Since 1960: Fiction." In *Dictionary of Literary Biography*. Vol. 52. Gale, 1986, pp. 207–8.

Evory, Ann, and Linda Metzger, eds. *Contemporary Authors (New Revision Series)*. Vol. 8. Gale, 1983, p. 259.

Helbig, Alethea K., and Agnes R. Perkins, eds. *Dictionary of American Children's Fiction, 1859–1985*. Greenwood, 1986, p. 303 (bio.), pp. 691–92 (book).

Hopkins, Lee Bennett, ed. *More Books by More People*. Citation Press, 1974, pp. 221–23.

Hunt, Irene. *Up A Road Slowly*. SRA McGraw Hill, 1979. Audiocassettes. ($21.33)

Kingsman, Lee, ed. *Newbery and Caldecott Medal Books: 1966–1975 with Acceptance Papers, Biographies and Related Material*. Horn Book, 1975, pp. 20–33.

Kinsman, Clare D., ed. *Contemporary Authors*. Vols. 17–20. Gale, 1976, p. 363.

"Newbery Medal Acceptance Material, 1967." *Horn Book*. 43, no. 4 (July/August 1967): 340–48.

McMahon, Thomas, ed. *Authors and Artists for Young Adults*. Vol. 18. Gale, 1999, pp. 161–68.

Peterson, Linda K., and Marilyn L. Solt, eds. *Newbery and Caldecott Medal and Honor Books: 1922–1981*. Hall, 1982, pp. 166–67.

Silvey, Anita, ed. *Children's Books and Their Creators*. Houghton, 1995, p. 331.

Ward, Martha, ed. *Authors of Books for Young People*. 3d ed. Scarecrow, 1990, p. 355.

Honor Books 1967

O'Dell, Scott. *The King's Fifth*. Harcourt, 1966, $17.00: 0-395-06963-7. (Grades 7–10)

This novel deals with the corrosive changes that greed and avarice can cause when humans sacrifice honor and their morals in the quest for gold. It is told in flashbacks by Estaban de Sandoval, a 17-year-old mapmaker who, in 1541, is awaiting trial in the prison at Vera Cruz for withholding the Spanish king's share of one-fifth of the gold seized in the ill-fated expedition to Cibola. Upon arrival in the New World, Estaban had joined Captain Mendoza and several others, including a 13-year-old Indian girl, Zia, and the devout priest, Father Fransisco, to find the army of Coronado. This accomplished, the group is given permission to leave the main force and head north to seek gold. They find it in the waters of a chasm of the Grand Canyon, but one of their companions, the treacherous Torres, steals their accumulated treasure and escapes. Later, the expedition, now crazed with gold fever, finds a lake whose bottom is covered with the gold dust accumulated from the bodies of the Indian's chieftains who entered the lake covered with gold dust during religious ceremonies. (Unknown to Zia and Father Fransisco, the only two not possessed by the lust for gold, a dike on the banks of the lake is weakening, which causes a disastrous flood.) After loading the mules with sacks of gold, the group hastily departs. One by one, all but three members of the original expedition—Zia, Father Fransisco, and Estaban—leave or are killed. Sickened by changes the gold fever has made in her beloved Estaban, Zia departs. Father Fransisco dies while crossing the desert known as the "Inferno." Now alone, Estaban comes to his senses and throws the sacks of gold into a bubbling hot spring, from which they can never be recovered. Later arrested and sent to jail, Estaban is comforted by the reappearance of Zia, who testifies for him at his trial. His sentence is either to spend three years in jail or to lead another expedition north. Sickened with the quest for gold, he chooses jail. He still has many maps to draw, and Zia has promised to wait for him.

Singer, Isaac Bashevis. *Zlateh the Goat and Other Stories*. Illustrated by Maurice Sendak. Harper, 1966, $15.99: 0-06-025699-0. (Grades 4–7)

Most of the seven short stories in this volume had their origins in middle-European Jewish folktales that the author heard while growing up in Poland early in the twentieth century. Many are centered on the festival of Hanukkah, some tell of the amiable fools of Chelm and others deal with angels and demons. In the title story, Reuven the furrier finds that the weather is still summery at Hanukkah and his business is suffering terribly. He decides to sell the family's ancient goat, Zlateh. His son, 12-year-old Aaron, reluctantly sets off for town with the goat. When they encounter a fierce blizzard, Aaron takes refuge in a haystack where he and the goat stay for three days until the storm subsides. During this time, Aaron is kept alive by Zlateh's warmth and her milk. In gratitude after the rescue, nobody ever again mentions selling Zlateh, who has now taken an honored place in the family circle. In another story, *Fool's Paradise*, young Atzel believes that he is dead and despite the pleadings of his father, Kadish, and girlfriend, Aksah, refuses to leave his bed. A great doctor is called in for consultation and under his guidance an elaborate scheme is hatched in which "dead" Atzel is blindfolded and taken to a room designed to look like Paradise. Here he is waited on by servants with wings and wearing long robes. However, Atzel discovers that in Paradise there is nothing to do and no change in the daily menu. On the eighth day, a servant announces that a mistake has been made and that Atzel is not really dead. A relieved Atzel rejoins Aksah and his family. The atmosphere of each of the stories is brilliantly complemented by Maurice Sendak's full-page, black-and-white illustrations.

Weik, Mary Hays. *The Jazz Man*. Illustrated by Ann Grifalconi. Atheneum, 1966, o.p.; pap., Aladdin, $3.95: 0-689-71767-9. (Grades 3–6)

This is a bleak, somber story about a young helpless boy who is trapped in a cycle of poverty. Though the ending is a happy one on the surface, there is no assurance that the reunion of the boy's family is anything more than a temporary one. On a positive note, the story also shows how the human spirit can rise above despair and be exalted and enriched by outside forces like music. Zeke, a nine-year-old crippled black boy, lives with his parents on the top floor of an old brownstone in Harlem. His favorite pastime is looking out of his bedroom windows into the apartments of his neighbors. He is particularly intrigued by the closed window of a vacant apartment and wonders if it will ever be rented. One day, he sees a piano being moved into the room and soon his courtyard is filled both night and day with wonderful music produced by the new tenant whom they call the Jazz Man. Some nights, Zeke, along with his mother and father, sits for hours as the Jazz Man's music encloses them in a circle of happiness.

Unfortunately, this joy does not last. Zeke's parents are poor and his father's drinking and inability to keep a steady job cause tensions and quarrels in the family. One day his mother leaves. His father becomes despondent, begins drinking more heavily, and stays out nights. Even the Jazz Man is silent and the blinds on his apartment are pulled. One night, weak from lack of food, Zeke becomes delirious and dreams of visiting a nightclub with his parents where the Jazz Man is playing. He is reliving the joyous music of the past when he is awakened by his father, who has a present for him. His mother has returned, and to make the evening perfect, across the courtyard can be heard the music of the Jazz Man.

Newbery Winner 1968

Konigsburg, Elaine L. *From the Mixed-up Files of Mrs. Basil E. Frankweiler*. Illustrated by the author. Atheneum, 1967, $16.00: 0-689-20586-4; pap., Dell, $3.99: 0-440-22802-6. (Grades 3–6)

The year 1968 was a banner year for Elaine Konigsburg (1930–). Not only was her first novel for youngsters, *Jennifer, Hecate, Macbeth, William McKinley and Me, Elizabeth*, designated as a Newbery Honor Book (see p. 271), but her second, *From the Mixed-Up Files . . .* was chosen as the year's Medal Winner. These were great surprises for a budding writer who had originally planned on pursuing a career in chemistry. A graduate of the Carnegie Institute of Science in Pittsburgh, she changed her occupational goals after "a few minor explosions, burned hair, and stained and torn clothes." She taught high school science for some years, married, and began raising a family of three (her children later served as models for her illustrations).

When her son Paul began to play baseball, she became fascinated with the sport and the result was *About the B'nai Bagels* (Atheneum, 1971, $14.95; pap., Dell, $3.50), the story of 12-year-old Mark and his consternation when his mother becomes the coach of his Little League baseball team. Two other excellent novels by Konigsburg are: *Journey to an 800 Number* (Atheneum, 1982, $13.95; pap., Dell, $3.50), in which a snobbish boy learns about life when he is forced to spend time with his estranged father, an itinerant camel keeper, and *Father's Arcane Daughter* (Atheneum, 1976, $13.95; pap., Dell, $3.50), the story of the Carmichael household and the sudden appearance of Caroline, who claims to be the daughter who was kidnapped 17 years before.

Plot Summary

If you are bored at school and nobody appreciates you at home anyway, what do you do if you are 11 years old? Well, naturally you run away. That is, if you are Claudia Kincaid of Greenwich, Connecticut. Still, the knapsack-on-your-back routine is not for Claudia. She is not striking out on the open road. She wants a place to go to and a comfort level she can tolerate. Therefore, her runaway destination is the Metropolitan Museum of Art in New York City. Claudia also does not like the idea of running away alone, so which of her three younger brothers should she choose as companion? Actually, the decision is based on practicality. Nine-year-old Jamie has saved money from his allowance. So begins Claudia's week in New York City.

After much planning and some reluctance on Jamie's part, Claudia reaches her destination. They arrive at the museum on Wednesday afternoon and it is very busy. Although Claudia's plans are not fully formed as yet, the two children do manage to spend the night in the Hall of English Renaissance. On the second day, however, they are better organized and map out a plan of cover and study. Yet, even with all this planning—at which Claudia excels—there is a problem. Claudia had wanted to run away because she needed to feel *different* somehow, important maybe. But even here at the museum, she feels much the same as always.

Yet it is not long before even the adventure of running away and the feeling of being the same are forgotten because of the museum's newest acquisition, a small and beautiful statue called Angel. Is it by Michelangelo? No one seems to know. To Claudia, it is so beautiful that she must learn more about it.

By reading someone else's *New York Times*, the children discover that the previous owner of the statue is 82-year-old Mrs. Frankweiler, who lives on an estate in Farmington, Connecticut, and is immensely rich. She bought the statue in Bologna, Italy, before World War II.

Claudia decides she must find out for certain who created Angel. First, she concentrates on finding out all she can about Michelangelo. Convinced that they have found a clue, Claudia and Jamie send a helpful letter to the museum and are quite disappointed when told that the museum has its own experts who are arriving from Italy to inspect the statue and identify its maker.

There is nothing to do but to spend their last money on train tickets back to Connecticut—but this time to Farmington! They are going to see Mrs. Frankweiler,who makes a deal with them because she admires their spirit of adventure. She will allow them to search her mixed-up files, whose order is known only to her, if they do not change the mysterious order and if they complete the search in one hour. In return, the children will tape their entire adventure in detail for the elderly lady. Claudia agrees and Mrs. Frankweiler, who narrates the children's adventure, is glad to see that she is not dealing with a beetleheaded child.

In their allotted time, Claudia first decides to spend a few minutes in planning. She chooses the file marked Bologna, Italy, as a logical starting place. Inside she finds a very old piece of paper with a sonnet written in Italian. The other side of the paper shows a sketch of the statue of Angel. The signature says Michelangelo. Mrs. Frankweiler admits that she knew the statue was done by the master. She explains that a rich Italian nobleman needed money for an operation for his daughter. In return, Mrs. Frankweiler got the statue and kept the secret. Now, she tells the children that in return for their keeping her secret of the statue's identity, she will leave the sketch to them in her will. She knows the children will keep the secret—Jamie because not to do so will mean that he will lose a lot of money later on, and Claudia for the same reasons as Mrs. Frankweiler herself. Claudia needs to have a secret. It will make her return to Greenwich *different*. As for Mrs. Frankweiler, even if there is the slightest doubt that the statue is not Michelangelo's, she just does not want to know at this stage in her life.

The children return home. Jamie is thrilled to tears because he gets a ride in Mrs. Frankweiler's chauffeured limousine.

But Mrs. Frankweiler has the last secret. She sends the narrative of the children's adventure to her long-time lawyer. He just happens to be the children's grandfather, something she knew all along.

Sometime later, according to newspaper reports, the museum will beef up their security guards. It seems that some mysterious items were left throughout the museum and no one can figure out how they got there. Something about gray-washed underwear and a cheap transistor radio.

Themes and Subjects

This funny story of two children leaving home for an adventure in the Metropolitan Museum presents well-rounded characters who are realistic, with faults and virtues. Claudia is intelligent, cautious, and a careful planner except where money is concerned. She is also somewhat bossy and a fusspot. Young Jamie is the financial expert, a willing participant in adventure but somewhat of a skinflint. Together, their lavish adventure in the museum brings them closer together and gives them experiences in the city that further their maturity. Their relationship with Mrs. Frankweiler is humorous and unusual, and their days in the museum provide a delightful romp and some funny events for the reader.

Incidents for Booktalking

The relationship between Claudia and Jamie is a pivotal focus of the book and offers some delightful moments. See, for example: planning to run away (pp. 14–18); Claudia announces their destination (pp. 24–27); the first night in the Hall of English Renaissance (pp. 36–42); the statue (pp. 56–64); learning about Michelangelo (pp. 57–75); the bath in the fountain (pp. 80–87); meeting Mrs. Frankweiler (pp. 125–49).

Related Titles

In Althena Lord's *Z.A.P., Zoe and the Musketeers* (Macmillan, 1992, $13.95: 0-02-759561-7), the four friends nicknamed Z.A.P., who are led by 12-year-old Zach, share experiences in Albany, New York.

Hillary McKay has written a clever combination time-travel and ghost story in her *The Amber Cat* (McElderry, 1997, $15.00: 0-689-81360-0).

A loving family including sixth-grader Koya Delaney, who loves to make people laugh, are portrayed in Eloise Greenfield's *Koya Delaney and the Good Girl Blues* (pap., Scholastic, $13.95: 0-590-43299-0).

Marie and her unexpected friend Lena cope with discrimination and abuse in *I Hadn't Meant to Tell You This* (Delacorte, 1994, $14.95: 0-385-32031-0; pap., Dell. $4.99: 0-440-91087-0) by Jacqueline Woodson.

Unlike his namesake, this present-day Hercules messes up the most ordinary jobs in John Bendall-Brunello's *The Seven-and-One-Half Labors of Hercules* (Dutton, 1992, $10.95: 0-525-44780-6).

About the Book and Author

Berger, Laura Standley, ed. *Twentieth-Century Children's Writers*. 4th ed. St. James, 1995, pp. 533–34.

Block, Ann, and Carolyn Riley, eds. *Children's Literary Review*. Vol. 1. Gale, 1976, pp. 118–23.

Brown, Muriel W., and Rita Schoch Foudray. *Newbery and Caldecott Medalists and Honor Book Winners: Bibliography & Resource Material Through 1990.* 2d ed. Neal-Schuman, 1992, pp. 224–25.

Chevalier, Tracy, ed. *Twentieth-Century Children's Writers.* 3d ed. St. James, 1989, pp. 541–42.

Collier, Laurie, and Joyce Nakamura. *Major Authors and Illustrators for Children and Young Adults.* Gale, 1993, 6 vols., pp. 1347–51.

Commire, Anne, ed. *Something About the Author.* Gale, 1973, Vol. 4, pp. 137–39; 1987, Vol. 48, pp. 140–47.

de Montreville, Doris, and Don Hill, eds. *Third Book of Junior Authors.* Wilson, 1972, pp. 164–65.

E. L. Koningsburg. Profiles in Literature, 1983. Videocassette.

Estes, Glenn E., ed. "American Writers for Children Before 1900." In *Dictionary of Literary Biography.* Vol. 42. Gale, 1985, pp. 214–29.

Gallo, Donald R., ed. *Speaking for Ourselves, Too.* National Council of Teachers of English, 1993, pp. 113–14.

Garrett, Agnes and Helga P. McCue, eds. *Authors and Artists for Young Adults.* Vol. 3. Gale, 1990, pp. 123–34.

Hanks, Dorrel Thomas. *E. L. Konigsburg.* Twayne, 1993.

Hedblad, Ian, ed. *Something About the Author.*Vol. 94. Gale, 1998, pp. 126–32.

Helbig, Alethea K., and Agnes R. Perkins, eds. *Dictionary of American Children's Fiction, 1960–1985.* Greenwood, 1986, pp. 364–65 (bio.), pp. 227–28 (book).

Hopkins, Lee Bennett, ed. *More Books by More People.* Citation Press, 1974, pp. 234–38.

Jones, Daniel, ed. *Contemporary Authors (New Revision Series).* Vol. 59. Gale, 1998, pp. 220–24.

Kingman, Lee, ed. *Newbery and Caldecott Medal Books: 1966–1975 with Acceptance Papers, Biographies and Related Material.* Horn Book, 1975, pp. 34–44.

Konigsburg, E. L. *From the Mixed-up Files of Mrs. Basil E. Frankweiler.* Read by Jan Miner. Listening Library, 1990. Audiocassettes, 219 min. ($16.98)

———. *From the Mixed-up Files of Mrs. Basil E. Frankweiler.* Starring Lauren Bacall. Library Video, 1995. VHS videocassette, 92 min. ($9.95)

Metzger, Linda, and Deborah A. Straub, eds. *Contemporary Authors (New Revision Series).* Vol. 17. Gale, 1968, pp. 249–54.

"Newbery Medal Acceptance Material, 1968." *Horn Book* 44, no. 4 (August 1968): 391–98.

Peterson, Linda, K., and Marilyn L. Solt, eds. *Newbery and Caldecott Medal and Honor Books: 1922–1981.* Hall, 1982, pp. 169–70.

Silvey, Anita, ed. *Children's Books and Their Creators.* Houghton, 1995, pp. 377–78.

Trosky, Susan M., ed. *Contemporary Authors (New Revision Series).* Vol. 39. Gale, 1982, pp. 207–11.

Ward, Martha, ed. *Authors of Books for Young People.* 3d ed. Scarecrow, 1990, p. 403.

Honor Books 1968

Konigsberg, Elaine L. *Jennifer, Hecate, Macbeth, William McKinley and Me, Elizabeth.* Illustrated by the author. Atheneum, 1967, $15.00: 0-689-30007-7. (Grades 3–6)

This humorous novel about the meaning of friendship takes place in a contemporary New York City suburb over a period of six months. Ten-year-old Elizabeth and her family are recent arrivals in a newly constructed apartment complex. At the William McKinley Elementary School, where she is in the fifth grade, Elizabeth has yet to make any friends, but one day while returning to school from lunch, she meets Jennifer, a most unusual black girl who claims to be a witch. Also a fifth grader but in a different class, Jennifer impresses Elizabeth with her unconventional habits and dress. Elizabeth accepts an offer from Jennifer to become an apprentice witch, an honor that involves their studying books on witchcraft every Saturday at the library. For Elizabeth, it also means undergoing a series of rites and rituals that usually involve food, such as eating one raw egg per day for a week. When Elizabeth progresses from apprentice to journeyman witch, the requirements proscribed by the domineering Jennifer become tougher. For example, at the birthday party of snobby Cynthia, a pretty but obnoxious fellow student, Elizabeth is forbidden to eat cake or play musical chairs. Again the persevering Elizabeth passes each trial successfully. However, when Jennifer is about to throw their pet toad, Hilary Ezra, onto a cauldron of "hot fat a la witches" in *Macbeth* to create a magic brew, Elizabeth rebels at the thought of this cruelty and breaks off their friendship. After the passage of several days, a humbled Jennifer visits Elizabeth. There will be no more witchcraft, no more spells, just a real friendship based on mutual love and trust.

O'Dell, Scott. *The Black Pearl.* Illustrated by Milton Johnson. Houghton, 1967, $16.00: 0395-06961-0; pap., Dell, $4.50: 0-440-90803-5. (Grades 6–9)

This allegorical novel is set in the town of LaPaz in the Baja California section of Mexico and is narrated by 16-year-old Ramon Salazar. Ramon, the son of a successful pearl dealer, disobeys his father, and with an old Indian, Soto Luzon, dives for the legendary black pearl. Legends say that the pearl is guarded jealously by a giant sea ray, Manta Diablo. Much to the distress of the renowned pearl diver and town braggart, Gaspar Ruiz, a.k.a. The Sevillano, Ramon is successful and the huge pearl is placed as a sacrifice in the hand of the town's statue of the Madonna-of-the-Sea. Later, when the local fishing fleet is destroyed at sea, Ramon believes that his theft of the pearl caused the tragedy and decides to return the pearl to the sea ray's cave. He is followed by the treacherous Ruiz, who wants the wealth that the pearl will bring when sold. Ruiz forces Ramon at knifepoint to row away from the cave. However, the aroused Manta Diablo follows them, and after Ruiz wounds it with a harpoon, he jumps on the giant manta's back to administer the coup de grace with his knife. However, Ruiz becomes entangled in the rope and is pulled underwater to his death by the mortally wounded sea monster. When Ramon enters LaPaz alone early the next morning, he returns the pearl to the hand of the Madonna. It is now given not as a sacrifice but as a gift of love. Reminiscent of both *Moby Dick* and John Steinbeck's *The Pearl*, this simply written novel uses the giant fish and the pearl as symbols for abstract ideas while supplying the reader with fascinating details about pearl diving and life in this part of Mexico.

Singer, Isaac Bashevis. *The Fearsome Inn*. Illustrated by Nonny Hogrogian. Scribners, 1967, o.p.; pap., Aladdin, $4.95: 0-689-70768-X. (Grades 5–7)

In this engrossing story, Singer has used his extensive knowledge of folklore to create an eerie tale of adventure and the supernatural. In a remote, barren area in rural Poland, there was an inn run by the witch Doboshova and her husband, a half-man, half-devil named Lapitut. These two evil beings plied their witchcraft on hapless innocent travelers who happened by. Under the thrall of these evil creatures were three captive girls named Reitze, Leitze, and Neitze. Under threat of severe punishments, the three girls were forced to act as servants. One night during a severe blizzard, three young men seek shelter at the inn. They are Hershel, a traveler who has lost his way; Velvel, a merchant who has slipped off his sleigh; and Leibel, a student of the cabala. After completing his studies, Leibel's teacher gives him a magic piece of chalk. If used to draw a line around people, the chalk will imprison them within the circle. The witch bakes a loaf of poisoned bread that deprives those who eat them of their willpower. Fortunately, Leibel senses the danger in time, and draws a circle with the magic chalk around Doboshova and Lapitut. He also draws circles around the inn's doors, windows, and chimneys, so that other evil spirits will be unable to enter. Throughout the night, the inn is besieged by devils and witches in various shapes and forms. Meanwhile, inside the inn, the two captives use threats and blandishments in vain to try to break Leibel's spell. In the morning, exhausted and defeated, the two sign an agreement in blood promising to return to the netherworld forever. The three travelers marry the three servant girls, and in time the once-fearsome inn becomes a great academy of the cabala as well as a welcome haven for all travelers who lose their way.

Snyder, Zilpha K. *The Egypt Game*. Illustrated by Alton Raible. Atheneum, 1967, $17.00: 0-689-30006-9; pap., Dell, $3.50: 0-440-80245-0. (Grades 6–8)

This realistic novel on the maturation of a misfit combines a suspenseful, unusual plot with a multiracial story about friendship. Eleven-year-old April is a reluctant transplant sent to a California city to live with her grandmother. She shows her contempt for her surroundings by dressing in outlandish clothes, wearing her hair in an untidy upsweep, and donning false eyelashes. Luckily she is befriended by a sixth-grade classmate, a black girl named Melanie Ross, and Melanie's four-year-old brother Marshall, who distracts April from her personal problems. Both girls are imaginative and interested in ancient Egypt. They stumble into the fenced-in backyard of an antique store run by a crotchety old man known as the Professor. It is filled with fascinating junk like crumbling columns and a bust of Nefertiti—perfect for make-believe activities and rituals involved in their developing "Egypt game." Later they are joined by two other sixth-graders, Tom and Toby, and nine-year-old Elizabeth Chung, who has recently lost her father. When a neighborhood youngster is murdered, people begin to suspect the Professor and the youngsters are forced to halt their ceremonies temporarily. One evening when April and Marshall are searching for April's lost math text in the backyard, she is nearly strangled by a stranger. The cries of the Professor frighten off the assailant who is later identified by Marshall as a local shopkeeper's assistant. Now exonerated, the Professor, with a renewed interest in life, repairs the backyard fence and gives each youngster a key. April, too, has changed and found maturity and contentment in her new life. Together with Melanie, she plans newer and more elaborate games.

Newbery Winner 1969

Alexander, Lloyd. *The High King*. Holt, 1968, $16.95: 0-03-089504-9; pap., Dell, $3.99: 0-440-93574-1. (Grades 6–9)

This is the fifth and last volume in the Chronicles of Prydain by the much-honored writer Lloyd Alexander (1924–). The second volume, *The Black Cauldron*, was an Honor Book in 1966 (see p. 260). Work begun on the series after the research for his book *Time Cat* (Peter Smith, 1992, $16.25) led the author to re-read Welsh legends, including the *Mabinogion*. This "awakened a long-sleeping love of heroic tales and legends [and] the original goal of merely retelling these ancient legends grew into something much more ambitious." The Prydain books trace the career of youthful Taran from his job as assistant pig-keeper to assuming the leadership of a newly formed kingdom. During his quest, Taran learns about the meaning of courage and love. He realizes that "every man is a hero if he strives more for others than for himself alone." In the end, Taran hopes for universal peace and a kingdom where the rights of all, whether rich or poor, will be honored. About his writing, Alexander has said,

> Even though I can't analyze what led me to children's literature, I do know what I found there. For me, a true form of art that not only helped me understand something of what I wanted to say but also let me discover ideas, attitudes, and feelings I never suspected were there in the first place.

Plot Summary

This is the last of five books of the Chronicles of Prydain. In 1966, the second volume, *The Black Cauldron*, was a Newbery Honor Book. (See "Honor Books," 1966, p. 260.)

The magical black sword, Drynwyn, which is the greatest weapon in Prydain, has been stolen from Prince Gwydion of the House of Don. The thief is Arawn, Lord of Annuvin, the land of death. The prince, along with the now-grown Taran, the assistant pig-keeper who wanted to be a hero, and the beautiful Eilonwy, and others set out to effect its return. They are stopped in this pursuit, however, when they learn that Arawn has amassed a superior force of Huntsmen and the Cauldron-Born battalions.

The prince and his companions go to the home of the High King, Math, at the golden castle of Caeth Dathyl. They are dismayed when King Pryderi and his army arrives. Although the king has superior forces, he has sided with Arawn and now demands Prince Gwydion's surrender! In the following dreadful battle, Gwydion's side loses. However, King Math is killed when Caeth Dathyl is attacked, and Gwydion becomes the High King.

The new High King plans an attack of revenge. He gathers his warlords together to explain his scheme. Arawn is now unprotected because the legions of the Cauldron-Born are away. However, the western shore of Prydain is quite near to Annuvin, so Gwydion decides to march his troops to the sea and then sail to the western shore. To make sure that the Cauldron-Born do not return before Gwydion and his men arrive, Taran will go after them with a small force.

Taran and his small band meet much misfortune in their pursuit of the Cauldron-Born. It is rough tracking through the winter snow in the mountains. When they try a shortcut through a mine that the dwarves, led by Doli, had abandoned, there is a cave-in and they must go back. But finally, Taran and his men are able to destroy many Huntsmen using a great pile of brush that the dwarves light on a frozen waterfall. When the water melts, it drowns the Huntsmen in their camp below.

Meanwhile, Gwydion and his men have arrived at Annuvin. Unfortunately, so have the Cauldron-Born. At this time, Taran and his weary warriors have reached Mountain Dragon, near Annuvin. They are spotted by the Cauldron-Born who start up the mountain to pursue them. Their assent is stopped by Taran, who snatches a stone loose from the mountain and sends it crashing down on the enemy. As he does, he sees the sword Drynwyn where the rock had been.

Taran quickly grabs the now-flaming sword and immediately kills a Cauldron-Born warrior. Other Cauldron-Born men fall as well. Arawn is killed and Annuvin is captured.

The terrible Lord of Annuvin has been destroyed. Gwydion declares that the Sons of Don and all their kinsmen and kinswomen must sail on the Golden Ship for the Summer Country, the land from which they came.

They will rejoin the never-ending life. This means that all magic will leave Prydain and all men will be in charge of their own destiny.

Taran is dismayed when he hears this news. "How soon shall you return?" he asks. "Shall you not first rejoice in your victory?"

But Gwydion replies that their victory is itself the reason for their voyage. It is a destiny long laid upon them. He speaks of the Summer Country, a land without suffering, where even death itself is unknown.

As Taran's reward for his bravery in battle, he is to go to the Summer Country with Gwydion. Even the Princess Eilonwy, daughter of Angharad, will go.

When Taran hears this news, he asks Eilonwy to marry him, if she would have an assistant pig-keeper. "I wondered if you'd ever get round to asking," Eilonwy replies.

But that night, Taran does not sleep well. In the morning, he has made a decision. Although he dearly loves Eilonwy, he cannot accompany her to the Summer Country. He must remain in Prydain. Although he once wanted to become a hero, he is now well content to be a pig-keeper.

But he is a pig-keeper no more, for now he is to be the High King of Prydain. His parentage has been kept a secret. His queen will be Eilonwy, who renounces her enchantment powers to remain with him. As King Taran and Queen Eilonwy, they live many happy years in the their land and accomplish much that is good.

Themes and Subjects

This is a fantasy inspired by ancient heroic legends and the folklore of Wales. It speaks of a great conflict between the forces of good and of evil. Young Taran is a believable character whose growth to manhood is an important thread of the story. Eilonwy, however, is not the classical traditional heroine. Although she is beautiful with traditional queenly qualities, she is also an energetic lass, which seems more in keeping with modern-day heroines. In general, *The High King* is heroic fantasy on an epic scale.

Incidents for Booktalking

There are many epic adventure scenes in this fantasy. See: the prophecy (pp. 42–55); they reach Caer Cadarn (pp. 59–67); the coming of Pryderi (pp. 127–40); Eilonwy taken prisoner (pp. 189–96); the snowstorm (pp. 222–33); Taran uses the magic sword (pp. 249–50); Taran makes his decision and earns his heritage (pp. 273–85).

Related Titles

In Norman Juster's *The Phantom Tollbooth* (Knopf, 1961, $15.95: 0-394-81500-9; pap., $3.95: 0-394-82199-8), Milo goes off in his toy car through the magic tollbooth on a quest to an imaginary country.

In an exciting story of Arthurian romance, Margaret Hodge's *Dealing with Dragons* (Harcourt, 1990, $17.00: 0-15-222900-0; pap., Point, $3.95: 0-590-45722-5), a poor lad woos his lady love.

A wizard agrees to raise the heir of a country at war in Patricia McKillip's *The Forgotten Beasts of Eld* (Atheneum, 1974, $14.95: 0-689-30434-X).

Jean Ure's *The Children Next Door* (Scholastic, 1996, $14.95: 0-590-22293-7) is a time-travel fantasy in which Laura discovers the truth about two mysterious children who play in the garden next door.

When an ancient stone monster threatens the home of his cousins, Simon seeks help from other supernatural beings in Patricia Wrightson's *The Nargun and the Stars* (McElderry, 1986, $13.95: 0-689-50403-9).

About the Book and Author

Alexander, Lloyd. "Fools, Heroes and Jackasses: The 1995 Anne Carroll Moore Lecture." *School Library Journal* (March 1996): 114–16.

Berger, Laura Standley, ed. *Twentieth-Century Children's Writers*. 4th ed. St. James, 1994, pp. 14–15.

Block, Ann, and Carolyn Riley, eds. *Children's Literary Review*. Vol. 1. Gale, 1976, pp. 11–18.

Brown, Muriel W., and Rita Schoch Foudray. *Newbery and Caldecott Medalists and Honor Book Winners: Bibliographic & Resource Learning Material Through 1990.* 2d ed. Neal-Schuman, 1992, pp. 5–9.

Collier, Laurie, and Joyce Nakamura. *Major Authors and Illustrators for Children and Young Adults.* Gale, 1993, 6 vols. pp. 60–64.

de Montreville, Drois, and Don Hill, eds. *Third Book of Junior Authors.* Wilson, 1972, pp. 6–7.

Estes, Glenn E., ed. "American Writers for Children Since 1960: Fiction." In *Dictionary of Literary Biography.* Vol. 52. Gale, 1986, pp. 3–61.

Ethridge, James M., ed. *Contemporary Authors.* First rev. Vols. 1–4. Gale, 1967, p. 17.

Gallo, Donald R. *Speaking for Ourselves.* National Council of Teachers of English, 1990, pp. 5–7.

Helbig, Alethea K., and Agnes R. Perkins, eds. *Dictionary of American Children's Fiction, 1960–1985.* Greenwood, 1986, p. 8 (bio.), pp. 286–87 (book).

Hile, Kevin S. *Something About the Author.* Vol. 81, 1995, pp. 1–8.

Hipple, Theodore W. ed. *Writers for Young Adults.* Scribners, 1997, 3 vols. Vol. 1, pp. 21–33.

Hopkins, Lee Bennett, ed. *More Books by More People.* Citation Press, 1974, pp. 10–17.

Jacobs, James S., and Michael O. Tunnell. *Lloyd Alexander: A Bio-Bibliography.* Greenwood, 1991.

Kingman, Lee, ed. *Newbery and Caldecott Medal Books: 1966–1975 with Acceptance Papers, Biographies and Related Material.* Horn Book, 1975, pp. 45–55.

Lesniak, James G., ed. *Contemporary Authors (New Revision Series).* Gale, 1988, Vol. 24, pp. 7–10; 1993, Vol. 38, pp. 10–14.

Lloyd Alexander. Profiles in Literature, 1972. Videocassette.

May, Jill. *Lloyd Alexander.* Twayne, 1991.

McMahon, Thomas, ed. *Authors and Artists for Young Adults.* Vol. 27. Gale, 1999, pp. 17–26.

Nakamura, Joyce, ed. *Something About the Author: Autobiographical Series.* Vol. 19. Gale, 1995, pp. 35–52.

"Newbery Medal Acceptance Material, 1969." *Horn Book* 45, no. 4 (August 1969): 378–84.

Peterson, Linda K., and Marilyn L. Solt, eds. *Newbery and Caldecott Medal and Honor Books: 1922–1981.* Hall, 1982, pp. 164–66.

Senick, Gerard J., ed. *Children's Literature Review*. Vol. 5. Gale, 1983, pp. 13–26.

Straub, Deborah A., ed. *Contemporary Authors (New Revision Series)*. Vol. 24. Gale, 1988, pp. 7–10.

Tunnell, Michael O. *The Prydian Companion*. Greenwood, 1989.

Ward, Martha, ed. *Authors of Books for Young People*. 3d ed. Scarecrow, 1990, p. 9.

Honor Books 1969

Lester, Julius. *To Be a Slave*. Illustrated by Tom Feelings. Dial, 1968, $16.99: 0-8037-8955-6. (Grades 5–10)

Using his own connecting narrative, the author quotes principally from two original sources to explore various aspects of slavery in America. First, he uses the stories of slaves that escaped from the South in the first half of the nineteenth century. These accounts were collected and transcribed by various northern antislavery groups. Secondly, he cites narratives of ex-slaves collected through a Federal Writers' project during the 1930s. Beginning with a chapter that chronicles the inhuman methods used by slave traders and tribal chieftains to collect and ship their human cargo to the New World, the author then explores the life that awaited the slaves upon arrival. The business of slave trading is described, including the practice of slave auctions where families were torn apart to the highest bidder and the forced marches or "coffles" where thousands died before being parceled out to their new owners. The barbarous living conditions on the plantations, the dawn-to-dusk work regime, and the ever-present use of force are explored. As the author states, "To the sound of the whip and the shrieks of black men and women, the slave owner and America grew wealthy." As well as force, brainwashing, in which blacks were taught to believe in their genetic inferiority, was used to keep slaves in their place. In two chapters titled "Resistance to Slavery," the author explores ways in which slaves defied their masters from sly forms of sabotage to overt rebellion. The final chapters tell of emancipation, post-Civil War segregation, and the rise of the Ku Klux Klan. The use of first-person accounts and effective charcoal drawings add immediacy and power to this tragic, often heartbreaking account.

Singer, Isaac Bashevis. *When Shlemiel Went to Warsaw*. Illustrated by Margot Zemach. Farrar, 1968, $16.00: 0-374-38316-2. (Grades 4–7)

Of the eight delightful stories in this collection, three are original and the rest are genuine folktales about eastern Jewish life and traditions. Two of the folktales involve Shlemiel, one of the fools of Chelm. In the title story, Shlemiel decides to leave his wife and children and venture out of Chelm to explore the world. Before long he gets turned around and returns to Chelm, thinking that it is a twin city to the one he left. He finds in this town a house with a family in it that are exact duplicates of the ones he left behind. When he insists that they belong to another Shlemiel, the elders of Chelm, all numskulls like himself, are called in to decide the fate of Shlemiel. They decide to award Schlemiel four groschen a day to care for the supposedly abandoned family until the real Shlemiel returns. Amazingly enough, he never does.

In another folktale, "Shrewd Todie and Lyzer the Miser," a crafty pauper outwits the town skinflint. He borrows one silver spoon from the miser and returns two, claiming that the original had a baby. When this is repeated two more times, Lyser lends Todie eight silver candlesticks hoping to get more in return. However, Todie sells them, and tells the miser that they have died. When the town's wise rabbi is called in to adjudicate, he states that anyone who would believe that spoons could have children, should also believe that candlesticks could die.

One of the original tales, "Rabbi Leib and the Witch Cunegunde" tells how a gentle rabbi uses the divine forces to outwit and banish forever the wicked Cunegunde, who has feigned a desire to marry the rabbi in order to usurp his power.

1970s

Newbery Winner 1970

Armstrong, William. *Sounder*. Harper, 1969, $14.00: 0-06-020243-6; pap., $3.95: 0-06-440020-4. (Grades 6–10)

William Armstrong (1914–1999) was born in Virginia, graduated from Hampton-Sydney College, and later did graduate work at the University of Virginia in Charlottesville. For most of his adult life, he was a history teacher, first in the South, and from 1945 on, at the Kent School in Connecticut. His interests in the past, the course of social changes, and the role that individuals play in history have influenced his writing of both fiction and biographies. In his preface to *Sounder*, he states that he originally heard the story of the coon dog, Sounder, and his master from a gray-haired black schoolteacher who worked for Armstrong's father after school and during the summers. Although the novel is set in the South in the late years of the nineteenth century and deals with a poor black sharecropper and his family, its theme, the endurance and invincibility of people, is ancient. Some critics have accused the author of racial stereotyping, principally because none of the characters are identified by name. For most readers, the anonymity of the protagonists and the deliberate vagueness of the setting tends to heighten the universality of the theme. The author's sparse, simple style adds to the effectiveness of the work. A sequel, *Sour Land* (Harper, 1971, $13.89; pap., $3.50), was published in 1971.

Plot Summary

The main characters in this novel set in the American South in the nineteenth century are a black sharecropper, his wife, and their four young children, none of whom can read or write. The oldest child, a boy, has tried for two years to walk the eight miles to school, but each year he has been forced to give up when the severe cold of winter has set in. The boy is deeply attached to Sounder, a stray hunting dog who followed the boy's father home one day from the fields. Sounder is a mixture of Georgia redbone hound and bulldog and is well named because of his loud and clear bark.

During the winter months when the crops have been picked, it is only the sale of the pelts of possum and raccoon, plus the few pennies received for walnut kernels painstakingly picked by the mother from obstinate shells, that keep the family from starvation. But one cold November day, despite a disastrous hunting season, the boy sees pork sausages frying in the skillet and smells a ham boiling in the possum pot. He also notices that his mother is humming, a sure sign that she is worried and agitated. That day the family has good meals, but two days later, a white sheriff and his two deputies arrive and accuse the father of being a "thievin' nigger" who has stolen food from the local smokehouse. The father is handcuffed and thrown into the back of a horse-drawn wagon. Sounder tries to protect his master and has to be restrained by the boy, but as the wagon leaves he pulls himself free and is shot by one of the deputies. The dog drags himself under the house, presumably to die. The boy finds Sounder's ear in the road and that night puts it under his pillow, making a wish that the dog will not die.

The next morning the mother walks into town to return the remnants of the ham and sausages. The boy tries to find Sounder under the house and discovers that he is gone. When the mother returns that evening, she speculates that the dog has gone into the woods seeking oak leaves to draw out the pus and heal his wound.

By Christmas there is still no sign of Sounder. The mother bakes a cake and sends the boy into town to deliver it to his jailed father. It is a fearsome trip for the boy, who passes homes festooned with Christmas ornaments. When he arrives at the jail, he is cruelly rebuffed by the keeper, who destroys the cake while looking for a saw or file. Finally the youngster is allowed to visit with his father, who tells him not to grieve and assures him that he will try to get word to the family through the visiting preacher after the court hearing.

The following day Sounder returns with a shattered shoulder, the use of only three legs, and only one eye and one ear. He no longer barks, but instead emits a dull whine. Despite the dog's state, the boy is overjoyed to welcome him home. Weeks later, the mother learns from townspeople that her husband has been sentenced to a labor gang that works in road camps and quarries.

When summer comes the boy takes his father's place in the fields, but when the harvest is over he sets out wandering from town to town and visiting work camps in the hope of catching a glimpse of his father. When word reaches the family that there has been a terrible explosion in one of the quarries and that 12 men have been killed and many others injured, they are relieved to learn that the father is not one of the dead.

Years pass. The boy continues working during the summer and when possible, searching for his father. One day, after having been driven away from a work camp by the guard who throws a piece of iron at him and badly injures his hand, the boy finds a book in a trash barrel, and although not able to read it, clings to it as though it were a treasured possession. When he stops at the pump in a schoolyard to wash the blood from his hand, he meets a kindly schoolmaster who tells him that the author of the book is Montaigne. Hearing the boy's story and realizing how desperately he wants to learn, the schoolmaster offers to house and feed him and allow him to attend school during the winter months in exchange for his help with the chores. The mother agrees.

More years pass, and soon the boy is able to share his new knowledge with his younger brother and sisters. One August afternoon when Sounder becomes unusually nervous, the family sees a man in the distance slowly hobbling toward their cabin. For the first time since his return, Sounder barks. His master has come home.

The return is tinged with tragedy, however, because the husband is now a completely broken man. One half of his body is paralyzed from the mine explosion that killed so many. Within weeks the man dies and shortly afterward so does Sounder. Although deeply saddened, the boy remembers what Montaigne wrote in one of his essays, "Only the unwise think that what has changed is dead," and he remembers his father walking upright and strong with Sounder barking at his side.

Themes and Subjects

This is an agonizing story of tragedy and pain, but is also one of great dignity and inspiration. The family, although shackled by poverty and ignorance, now has some glimmer of hope because of the boy's new knowledge. The cruelty, loneliness, and injustice suffered by the family are not underplayed, but in their acceptance of tragedy, there is an aura of strength and endurance and a reassurance of survival.

Incidents for Booktalking

With small groups, James Barkley's illustrations, such as his portrait of Sounder (p. 72) and the cabin (facing p. 1), could be used in a booktalk. Specific passages are: a description of Sounder (pp. 4–5); the father being taken to jail (pp. 21–26); the boy's trip to the jail (pp. 55–58); his visit with his father (pp. 62–64).

Related Titles

Virginia Hamilton's *Many Thousand Gone: African Americans from Slavery to Freedom* (Knopf, 1992, $18.00: 0-394-82873-9) combines general history with personal slave narratives to describe the story of slavery in America. By the same author, use *Drylongso* (Harcourt, 1992, $18.95: 0-15-224241-4), the story of how a young boy ended a terrible drought on a farm in 1975.

In Ouida Sebestyen's *Words by Heart* (Little, Brown, 1979, $14.95: 0-316-77931-8; pap., Dell, $3.95: 0-440-41346-X), race relations are explored when a black family moves into an all-white community during the Reconstruction era.

Tom Bee gets into trouble when he refuses to call a white man "mister" in Mildred D. Taylor's *The Friendship* (Dial, 1987, $14.89: 0-8037-0418-6; pap., Puffin, $3.99: 0-14-038964-4).

In Karen English's *Francie* (Farrar, 1999, $16.00: 00-374-32456-5), a young black girl bides her time in a small-minded Alabama town while waiting for her Pullman porter father to send for his family.

Leon's Story (Farrar, 1997, $14.00: 0-374-34379-9) by Leon Walter Tillage is an autobiographical account of growing up in the Jim Crow South as the son of North Carolina sharecroppers.

About the Book and Author

Armstrong, William. *Sounder*. Read by Avery Brooks. Recorded Books, 1997. Audiocassettes, 180 min. ($17.50)

————. *Sounder*. SRA/McGraw Hill, 1970. Audiocassettes. ($20.00)

————. *Sounder*. Starring Cicely Tyson. Library Video, 1974. VHS videocassette, color, 105 min. ($14.95)

Berger, Laura Standley, ed. *Twentieth-Century Young Adult Writers*. St. James, 1994, pp. 22–23.

Block, Ann, and Carolyn Riley, eds. *Children's Literary Review*. Vol. 1. Gale, 1976, pp. 22–25.

Brown, Muriel W., and Rita Schoch Foudray. *Newbery and Caldecott Medalists and Honor Book Winners: Bibliography & Resource Material Through 1990*. 2d ed. Neal-Schuman, 1992, pp. 15–16.

Chevalier, Tracy, ed. *Twentieth-Century Children's Writers*. 3d ed. St. James, 1989, pp. 33–34.

Commire, Anne, ed. *Something About the Author*. Vol. 4. Gale, 1973, pp. 11–13.

de Montreville, Doris, and Donna Hill, eds. *Third Book of Junior Authors*. Wilson, 1972, pp. 20–21.

Ethridge, James M., and Barbara Kopa, eds. *Contemporary Authors*. Vols. 19–20. Gale, 1968, p. 22.

Evory, Ann, and Linda Metzger, eds. *Contemporary Authors (New Revision Series)*. Vol. 9. Gale, 1983, pp. 21–22.

Hopkins, Lee Bennett, ed. *More Books by More People*. Citation Press, 1974, pp. 18–23.

Kingman, Lee, ed. *Newbery and Caldecott Medal Books: 1966–1975 with Acceptance Papers, Biographies and Related Material*. Horn Book, 1975, pp. 56–65.

Kinsman, Clare D., ed. *Contemporary Authors (First Revision Series)*. Vols. 17–20. Gale, 1976, p. 35.

McMahon, Thomas, ed. *Authors and Artists for Young Adults*. Vol. 18. Gale, 1996, pp. 9–16.

Nakamura, Joyce, ed. *Something About the Author: Autobiographical Series*. Vol. 7. Gale, 1989, pp. 1–16.

Peterson, Linda K., and Marilyn L. Solt, eds. *Newbery and Caldecott Medal and Honor Books: 1922–1981*. Hall, 1931, pp. 178–79.

Silvey, Anita, ed. *Children's Books and Their Creators*. Houghton, 1995, pp.30–31.

Ward, Martha, ed. *Authors of Books for Young People*. 3d ed. Scarecrow, 1990, p. 22.

Honor Books 1970

Ish-Kishor, Sulamith. *Our Eddie*. Knopf, 1969, $15.00: 0-394-81455-X. (Grades 7–10)

 In the dedication to this moving tragedy, the author has written a poem that begins, "The children of the poor and troubled/rarely do come to full growth; like/forced fruit, they blossom too early and/wither before they ripen." This describes the short, unhappy life of Eddie Raphel. At age 14, when the novel begins, he is growing up with his family in a modest house in London in the early part of the twentieth century. His father, a devout Zionist and scholar is a dedicated teacher in a Hebrew school. At home, he is a martinet who rules his family, including a loving wife, with an iron hand. Although Eddie tries, he is unable to please or even communicate with his stern father. When Mr. Raphel leaves to seek a better position in New York, Eddie leaves school to help the family finances. He takes a job in a department store but loses it when he is caught stealing presents to give to his sisters and mother at Hanukkah. When the family moves to New York, Eddie continues to be a loser. Unable to persuade his father to let him return to school, he again looks for work but a strange crippling disease (perhaps multiple sclerosis) begins attacking his body and he loses one position after another. The estrangement from his father, who denies the seriousness of his physical problems, increases and the two rarely speak. Through the intervention of his sisters and an uncle, Eddie, now barely 17 and still unreconciled with his father, is seen by a doctor, who performs a critical operation that Eddie does not survive. His family and his guilt-ridden father grieve at his passing. This novel is particularly notable for its sensitive portrayal of Jewish life and effects of a fatal disease on a family, as well as its exploration of a corrosive father-son relationship.

Moore, Janet Gaylord. *The Many Ways of Seeing: An Introduction to the Pleasures of Art*. Illustrated. World, 1969, o.p. (Grades 5–10)

 The author, a painter, museum curator, and teacher states as her purpose in writing this book, "to suggest ways of sharpening visual awareness and of cultivating perception in the visual arts." She begins by exploring various points of view possible in observing objects and recording them on a canvas and then moves on to an exploration of such basics as line, color, and form. Explanations are given for such concepts as line contours, hot and cold colors, and the effects of tone placement. Many examples are used to show how artists give expression and reflect the time and place in which they live, and thus, why artistic styles change sometimes causing problems with the understanding of "modern" art. A center section, "A Collage of Pictures and Quotations," consists of several large color reproductions of paintings from different historical periods with quotations from literature to amplify the artist's message. To encourage the amateur to try new ways of expression through art, there are chapters on the various materials and techniques used by the artist. Included are sections on drawing and painting in such media as watercolors, fresco, tempera, and oil. Explanations and examples are given for various printmaking techniques including etching, lithograph, woodcut, and engraving. In the area of sculpture, text and illustrations are used to introduce types of carving and modeling and the material used. The book ends with further hints on how to increase our ways of seeing and explore the art around us. This is both a beautiful book and a fascinating introduction to art appreciation.

Steele, Mary Q. *Journey Outside*. Illustrated by Rocco Negri. Viking, 1969, o.p; pap., Puffin, $4.99: 0-14-030588-2. (Grades 4–7)

Dilar is a young member of the Raft People. The group consists of several families who, for generations, have lived on an interconnected network of rafts navigating subterranean rivers and living entirely on the fish that they catch. Although Dilar's grandfather assures him that they are on a voyage to "a better place," Dilar is convinced that they are actually traveling in circles. To prove his point he leaves his raft one night determined to live on a rocky ledge until the rafts reappear. However, when he is attacked by thousands of ravenous rats, Dilar escapes through a cracked rock into the green world above. He sets out to seek information about his people. During his quest Dilar encounters a number of unusual humans like Dorna and her doctor mother, Norna, who nurse him through a painful sunburn. He learns nothing from them because they live only in the present without thoughts of the future or the past. He also learns nothing from the giant Wingo, a hermit with whom he stays for one winter, nor from the Desert People, a race that experiences neither pain nor pleasure but instead live like sleepwalkers and seek nothing from life. Finally, Dilar meets an old goatherd named Vigan who, on the promise of telling Dilar about the origins of his people, sends him on a perilous climb to steal an eagle's egg. Finally Vigan reveals that the Raft People had once lived along the seacoast but after an unusually severe winter had retreated underground, planning to return later. Dilar now leaves with a map that Vigan gives him. The boy is determined to return to his people and bring them to "a Better Place." This unusual fantasy, like *Gulliver's Travels,* can also be interpreted as an allegory on human life and values.

✿ Newbery Winner 1971

Byars, Betsy. *Summer of the Swans*. Viking, 1970, $15.99: 0-670-68190-3; pap., Puffin, $4.50: 0-14-031420-2. (Grades 4–7)

Betsy Byars (1928–) is one of the most honored and enjoyed writers for young people. Her books now number about 50 and include two delightful series, one about the flaky Blossom family and the other about the fortunes and misfortunes of young Bingo Brown. In her refreshingly candid and unassuming Newbery Award acceptance speech in 1972, she amusingly outlines the four stages in the creation of a book. They are: sitting around for days thinking about ideas and characters; a stage of wild enthusiasm when the words pour out; a period when they dry up and personal discipline is needed to complete a rough draft; and finally, the part that is "the longest and the most trying. It involves reading what I have written and trying to make something of it." During this stage she asks her children to read the manuscript because she finds they are the most critical and most truthful of all her critics. Obviously this process works amazingly well because Betsy Byars is one of today's most proficient and popular writers of juvenile fiction. Her childhood is delightfully recalled in her autobiography for young readers, *The Moon and Me* (Simon, 1992, $14.95). *Summer of the Swans* is more serious than most of her works. It tells of a fateful day in the lives of 14-year-old Sara and her mentally retarded younger brother Charlie.

Plot Summary

For 14-year-old Sara Godfrey, this is truly the summer of her discontent. Although she tells her sister, Wanda, that she is neither popular nor pretty—"I'm not anything," (p. 49)—her unhappiness stems from more than growing pains. Sara's life is marred by tragedy. Her 10-year-old brother, Charlie, suffered a severe illness that left him mentally retarded and speechless. Sara's mother died, and her father, once a smiling, attractive person, has retreated into a shell of remoteness and indifference. He now lives several hours away from the small West Virginia town where the children are being raised by Aunt Willie (short for Wilhelmina).

Sara's "nothing" summer consists mainly of visiting her friend, Mary Weicek, watching television, and taking care of Charlie. She has developed a lovely relationship with her brother. Mindful of his needs and protective of him with outsiders, she neither pampers him nor is condescending. However, she is so incensed that her schoolmate Joe Melby has taken Charlie's prized possession, a loud-ticking wristwatch, that even though he returns it, Sara not only refuses to speak to Joe but also tries to turn others against him.

A minor diversion breaks the monotony of the summer—six swans are sighted on a wooded lake within easy walking distance of Sara's home, and she decides to take Charlie to see them. They feed the swans, and Charlie becomes so enchanted by the birds that Sara actually has to drag him away when it is time to go home.

Charlie is unable to sleep that night because he remembers the swans and wants to see them again. Dressed in pajamas and slippers, he leaves the house and wanders into the woods looking for the lake. He is chased by dogs and becomes hopelessly lost.

In the morning, the family discovers that Charlie is missing. Sara runs to the lake, but Charlie is not there. A distraught Aunt Willie calls the police, who organize a search party. She also calls Sara's father, who promises to drive down that night if Charlie is not found. Sara thinks he should come immediately, but Willie defends his actions.

Sara decides to search for Charlie in the woods. On the way to pick up Mary, she meets Joe Melby, who volunteers to help. But Sara cannot hide her continued anger and once again accuses him of stealing Charlie's wristwatch.

When Sara tells Mary about the meeting, she learns that Joe did not steal the watch. Some boys thought it would be amusing to tease Charlie by hiding his watch. Then they were too embarrassed to return it. Joe learned about the trick, found the watch, and returned it himself. Sara is ashamed of the way she has treated him.

Searching in the woods, Sara and Mary meet Joe. In spite of Sara's anger, he has joined the search team. He has just found a slipper, which Sara recognizes as Charlie's. While they search on, Sara apologizes to Joe.

As they scour the woods, they shout Charlie's name. This awakens Charlie, who has fallen asleep in the woods. There is a joyful reunion, and as the search party returns to town, the swans are seen in the sky. They are leaving the lake and going home.

Joe invites Sara to a party that night. After this dreadful ordeal, could things be getting better?

Themes and Subjects

One of the most interesting themes developed in the novel is the family's wonderful attitude toward Charlie, an open and complete acceptance based on love, not pity.

Other important themes are Sara coping with adolescence; her adjustment to what is really a foster home; the acceptance of personal tragedy and loneliness; and her developing sense of responsibility toward Charlie.

Incidents for Booktalking

Some incidents that could be used to introduce the book are: Charlie's first appearance in the novel and the moment when the reader begins to realize his problem (pp. 13–19); getting Charlie to visit the swans (p. 30); the visit (pp. 40–45); Charlie wanders away (pp. 58–60). Some indications of Sara's problems are given in a monologue with her brother (pp. 31–32); a talk with her sister (pp. 47–50). Ted McConis' excellent illustrations also could be used, such as the drawing of Charlie on page 36.

Related Titles

In *Ellen Grae* (Lippincott, 1967, $12.89: 0-397-30938-4) by Vera Cleaver and Bill Cleaver, an engaging young heroine and persistent liar is friends with a mentally handicapped young man.

Twelve-year-old Solly develops a friendship with a mentally ill boy in Karen Acherman's *The Broken Boy* (Putnam, 1991, $14.95: 0-399-22254-5).

When his mother dies suddenly and his father disappears, privileged David finds himself in a foster home in Susan M. Brown's *You're Dead, David Borelli* (Atheneum, 1995, $15.00: 0-689-31959-2).

Yolanda is convinced that her younger brother, who still cannot read, is a musical genius in Carol Fenner's *Yolanda's Genius* (Simon, 1995, $17.00: 0-689-80001-0; pap., Aladdin, $4.50: 0-614-29086-4).

In Marlene Fanta Shyer's *Welcome Home, Jellybean* (pap., Aladdin, $3.95: 0-689-71213-8), 12-year-old Neil encounters a near tragedy when his older retarded sister comes home to stay.

About the Book and Author

Berger, Laura Standley, ed. *Twentieth-Century Young Adult Writers*. St. James, 1994, pp. 96–97.

Block, Ann, and Carolyn Riley, eds. *Children's Literary Review*. Vol. 1. Gale, 1976, pp. 35–36.

Brown, Muriel W., and Rita S. Foudray. *Newbery and Caldecott Medalists and Honor Book Winners: Bibliographic & Resource Material Through 1971*. 2d ed. Neal-Schuman, 1992, pp. 56–58.

Byars, Betsy. *The Moon and I*. Messner, 1992.

———. *Summer of the Swans*. Read by Christina Moore. Recorded Books, 1995. Adiocassettes, 165 min. ($18.00)

———. *Summer of the Swans*. New Kids Home Video (After School Special Series), 1974. VCR Videocassette, color, 45 min. ($38.95)

Callaway-Schaefer, Judith. "Betsy Byars: Techniques and Themes." *The Alan Review* (Fall 1997): 20–22.

Chevalier, Tracy, ed. *Twentieth-Century Children's Writers*. 3d ed. St. James, 1989, pp. 166–68.

Collier, Laurie, and Joyce Nakamura. eds. *Major Authors and Illustrators for Children and Young Adults*. Gale, 1993, 6 vols., pp. 405–08.

Commire, Anne, ed. *Something About the Author*. Vol. 46. Gale, pp. 36–47.

de Montreville, Doris, and Donna Hill, eds. *Third Book of Junior Authors*. Wilson, 1972, p. 52.

Estes, Glenn E., ed. "American Writers for Children Since 1960: Fiction." In *Dictionary of Literary Biography*. Vol. 52. Gale, 1986, pp. 52–66.

Evory, Ann, ed. *Contemporary Authors (First Revision Series)*. Vols. 33–36. Gale, 1978, pp. 164–65.

Hedblad, Alan, ed. *Something About the Author*. Vol. 108. Gale, 2000, pp. 23–39.

Helbig, Alethea K., and Agnes R. Perkins, eds. *Dictionary of American Children's Fiction, 1960–1984*. Greenwood, 1986, pp. 83–84 (bio.), pp. 634–35 (book).

Hile, Kevin S., ed. *Something About the Author*. Vol. 80. Gale, 1995, pp. 29–35.

Hipple, Theodore W., ed. *Writers for Young Adults*. Vol. 1. Scribners, 1997, pp. 199–208.

Hopkins, Lee Bennett, ed. *More Books by More People*. Citation Press, 1974, pp. 68–73.

Kingman, Lee, ed. *Newbery and Caldecott Medal Books: 1966–1975 with Acceptance Papers, Biographies and Related Material*. Horn Book, 1975, pp. 66–78.

Lesniak, James G., ed. *Contemporary Authors (New Revision Series)*. Vol. 36. Gale, 1992, pp. 68–70.

McMahon, Thomas, ed. *Authors and Artists for Young Adults*. Vol. 19. Gale, 1996, pp. 63–74.

Meet the Newbery Author: Betsy Byars. SRA/McGraw-Hill, 1990. Videocassette.

Metzger, Linda, and Deborah A. Straub, eds. *Contemporary Authors (New Revision Series)*. Vol. 18. Gale, 1986, pp. 72–75.

"Newbery Award Acceptance Material, 1971." *Horn Book* 47, no. 4 (August 1971): 354–62.

Peterson, Linda K., and Marilyn L. Solt, eds. *Newbery and Caldecott Medal and Honor Books: 1922–1981*. Hall, 1982, pp. 181–82.

Sarkissian, Adele, ed. *Something About the Author: Autobiographical Series*. Vol. 1. Gale, pp. 63–68.

Scales, Pat. "Betsy Byars' *The Summer of the Swans*." *Book Links* (November 1996): 16–22.

Silvey, Anita, ed. *Children's Books and Their Creators*. Houghton, 1995, pp. 111–12.

Senick, Gerard J., ed. *Children's Literature Review*. Vol. 16. Gale, 1986, pp. 41–66.

Ward, Martha ed. *Authors of Books for Young People*. 3d ed. Scarecrow, 1990, pp. 104–5.

Honor Books 1971

Babbitt, Natalie. *Kneeknock Rise*. Illustrated by the author. Farrar, 1970, $15.00: 0-374-34257-1; pap., $3.95: 0-374-44260-6. (Grades 3–6)

> Egan is on his way to the village of Instep to visit his Aunt Gertrude, his Uncle Anson, their lively, somewhat bratty daughter, Cousin Ida, and Gertrude's brother, the eccentric Uncle Ott. Instep lies in the shadow of a large, craggy hill, Kneeknock Rise. According to legend, a giant savage monster, the Megrimum, lives on the hill. On stormy nights his moaning voice "like a lonely demon, like a mad despairing animal" strikes terror into the hearts of the townspeople, none of whom have ever seen this fabled beast. It is fair time, and tourists are coming from miles around hoping to hear the Megrimum or perhaps, best of all, catch a glimpse of him. On Egan's arrival in Instep, he is greeted by the family, including Ida's unfriendly cat, ironically named Sweetheart, and Uncle Ott's dog, Anabelle. Uncle Ott has once again pulled one of his frequent, unexplained disappearances. One rainy night, when the terrifying voice of the Megrimum can be heard through the valley, Ada goads Egan into climbing Kneeknock Rise with only Anabelle as a companion. There he is surprised and relieved to find Uncle Ott, who has come to this humid place seeking relief from his asthma. Ott also explains that there is no Megrimum, but only an eerie sound produced by the steam from a hot spring when rain hits it. When Egan returns alone to Instep leaving Anabelle with her master, he tries to reveal the truth about the Megrimum but no one will believe him. The next day, he departs for home, leaving the townspeople still gossiping about the young boy who single-handedly confronted the monster and lived to tell about it. It has been rumored, however, that his dog did not survive. This delightful fantasy proves once again that humans prefer fantasy to fact.

Engdahl, Sylvia Louise. *Enchantress from the Stars*. Atheneum, 1970, o.p. (Grades 7–10)

> This novel depicts the clash on the planet Andrecia of three different cultures representing three different stages in human social development. The most primitive, represented by Georyn, a woodcutter's son, is that of the native inhabitants, the Younglings, who still live in a feudal society. They are being conquered by

the technologically oriented Imperialists, whose giant earth-moving machine so impresses the Younglings that they refer to it as the Dragon. To help save the Younglings, a third highly advanced civilization, the Federation, sends a rescue mission to teach the hapless Younglings sufficient psychic powers to frighten away the Imperialists. On the mission are Elana, an intelligent, courageous young woman, and her father, the Starwatcher, who leads the expedition. Elana pretends to be an enchantress and begins teaching Georyn how to use some of the commonplace resources that her people possess, such as a use of psychokinesis, by pretending that they are magical powers that can be evoked by using a "magic" stone that she gives him. Georyn and Elana are captured by the Imperialists and scheduled to be sent to their Research Center, when Elana secures Georyn's release by appealing to the better nature of Jarel, a doctor with the Imperialists. Rather than face life as a prisoner, Elana rushes to the Dragon as it is about to drop a huge load of rocks. Georyn suddenly appears, and using his magical power of psychokinesis, he stops the avalanche of stone in midair. The Imperials are so awestruck and frightened that they leave the planet. Because their mission has been accomplished, Elana and her father also board their spaceship for departure. Before they leave Georyn returns the stone to Elana—his new world will not need magic to produce progress. A sequel to this novel is *The Far Side of Evil* (pap., Macmillan, $3.95).

O'Dell, Scott. *Sing Down the Moon*. Houghton, 1970, $16.00: 0-395-10919-1; pap., Dell, $4.99: 0-440-97975-7. (Grades 6–9)

   Based partly on fact, this is the story of the Navajos and their inhuman treatment by white men during the 1860s. Narrated by a 15-year-old Navajo girl, Bright Morning, the story is divided into two parts. In the first, Bright Morning and her friend Running Bird are caring for their sheep in what is now northeastern Arizona when they are kidnapped and taken south by Spanish soldiers who sell them into slavery. They become household servants and meet Nehana, a Nez Percé girl who is also a slave eager to escape. Nehana is able to steal three horses and the girls make a break for freedom. While trying to elude their Spanish pursuers, they are helped by two other Navajos, Tall Boy, Bright Mornings's betrothed, and his friend, Mando. All successfully escape but Tall Boy is shot in the shoulder, which leaves him with a permanently crippled arm. Their lives are once more disrupted when news arrives that the American soldiers, nicknamed the Long Knives, plan to relocate the Navajo people. Before their capture, their villages, orchards, and gardens are destroyed. Then begins the 300-mile death march to Fort Sumner. Now married and pregnant, Bright Morning does not want to have a child in captivity. At first, Tall Boy is fearful of trying to leave the fort, but after being unjustly sentenced to a term in the white man's jail, he realizes that he and Bright Morning must escape. With amazing luck they are eventually able to make their way back to the canyon that was their home. They find some of Bright Morning's sheep and with aching hearts, try again to repair their broken lives. This novel not only re-creates a shameful period in our history but also is a moving tribute to the human spirit.

❀ Newbery Winner 1972

O'Brien, Robert C. *Mrs. Frisby and the Rats of NIMH*. Illustrated by Zena Bernstein. Atheneum, 1971, $14.95: 0-689-20651-8; pap., Aladdin, $3.95: 0-689-82966-3. (Grades 4–8)

In order to prevent conflicts with his full-time position as a senior editor at *National Geographic* magazine, Robert Leslie Conley (1918–1973) decided to use the pseudonym Robert C. O'Brien when he began writing books for young people. He came to this field rather late—he was about 50 when he began work on his first novel *The Silver Crown* (pap., Collier, 1988, $3.95). At the time of his death only five years later, he had almost completed his third, *Z for Zachariah* (Atheneum, 1975, $14.95; pap., Collier, $3.95). This novel, which deals with the aftermath of a nuclear holocaust, was completed by his wife and daughter from his notes. Between these two books came *Mrs. Frisby and the Rats of NIMH*, winner of the Newbery Award as well as the 1972 Lewis Carroll Shelf Award.

All three explore the conflict that exists between modern technology when it exploits and threatens the environment, and the forces that wish to preserve both the earth's natural resources and the dignity of the individual. In his Newbery Medal acceptance speech, O'Brien states that he is unable to pinpoint exactly when the idea for this book came to him although he had speculated many times on what would happen to civilization if humans were exterminated and only intelligent rats survived. From this germ of an idea, the novel slowly emerged. O'Brien's daughter, Jane Leslie Conley, has continued the saga of this rat colony in two successful sequels. In the first, *Racso and the Rats of NIMH* (Harper, 1986, $13.00; pap., $3.95), Mrs. Frisby's son and his friend, the young rat Racso (Oscar spelled backwards) try to thwart the plans of human developers to build a dam that will flood Thorn Valley, the home of the rats. The second, *R-T, Margaret, and the Rats of NIMH* (Harper, 1990, $12.95; pap., $3.50) tells how Racso and his friends, Christopher and Isabella, struggle to save the rat colony from possible destruction after it has been discovered by two human children. All three of these novels combine fantasy, a touch of science fiction, and love of nature.

Plot Summary

Since her husband's death, Mrs. Frisby, a field mouse, is responsible for the care of her four children—Teresa, the oldest; Martin, the biggest; pretty Cynthia, a bit light-headed and overfond of dancing; and Timothy, the youngest, smartest, and most frail. The family lives in a slightly damaged but cozy cinder block house in Mr. Fitzgibbon's vegetable garden. With hard work and luck, Mrs. Frisby manages to keep her family happy and well fed.

But one morning as she calls the children to breakfast, she learns that Timothy is ill. He has a high fever and a rapid heartbeat. Mrs. Frisby is worried, because of all her children, he is the one most likely to come down with colds or flu. When Timothy grows worse, Mrs. Frisby seeks Mr. Ages, a white mouse who lives across the farm in a brick wall. Some time ago, Timothy had been bitten by a poisonous insect and Mr. and Mrs. Frisby had taken him to Mr. Ages, who administered a medicinal powder that cured him.

After Mrs. Frisby describes her son's symptoms, Mr. Ages diagnoses pneumonia and gives her medicine to cure Timothy. However, he warns that the youngest Frisby will have a long recuperation and must be kept warm and quiet for some time. On the trip home, clutching the medicine, Mrs. Frisby comes upon a crow that has gotten itself tangled on a fence. The Fitzgibbon's huge orange cat, named Dragon, has spotted the crow. Mrs. Frisby quickly untangles the bird, whose name is Jeremy. In turn, he invites her to hop on his back, out of the advancing Dragon's way, and he flies her safely home. Jeremy also tells her that if ever she needs help to call on him.

With the aid of Mr. Ages's medicine, Timothy does begin to recover slowly, so slowly that Mrs. Frisby has a new worry. Although it is still early in the year, the weather shows some signs of approaching spring. That means that Mr. Fitzgibbon will soon begin to plant his garden, which means a tractor, which means that the Frisby field mice must move to their summer home. They move each year because the Fitzgibbon's plow wrecks their winter place, which they rebuild when they return. But the summer home is far away at the brook's edge, and Timothy is not strong enough to travel. And even if he were, the summer home will not be warm enough for him to recuperate for quite some time.

What should she do? Mrs. Frisby remembers Jeremy's offer of assistance. When she explains her problem to the young crow, he offers to fly her to the home of the wise owl. It is a very frightening trip for Mrs. Frisby, who has certainly never been so high before. Besides, mice do not usually like to be in the company of owls. To her relief, the owl listens patiently, but he cannot come up with a workable solution to her predicament. However, when he learns Mrs. Frisby's name, he asks if she is related to Jonathan Frisby. She explains that Jonathan was her late husband. The owl immediately tells her that she must go to the rats.

"To the rats?" Mrs. Frisby asks in bewilderment. "I don't know any rats."

Nonetheless, the owl insists that she go see the rats, who live in the rosebush. She must ask for Nicodemus or Justin.

Mrs. Frisby does find the home of the rats and when she gives her name and explains her problem, Nicodemus promises that the rats will move her cinder-block home that very night to a spot in the garden where it will be so cleverly disguised that the farmer will never find it and the plow will never hurt it. Then the family can stay there until Timothy is well enough to travel to their summer home. The only problem is that Dragon the cat prowls around at night, so the rats will be in danger. If only someone were small enough to sneak into the Fitzgibbon kitchen and put a small powder in Dragon's food, that would make him drowsy so that he would not prowl the garden. Although she is very frightened, Mrs. Frisby bravely volunteers.

Why are these extraordinary rats willing to help her? Mrs. Frisby, whose husband could read and who taught her to read just a little, recognizes that these are no ordinary creatures. Besides their reading ability, they have electric lights and running water in their underground home, and books in the library. While they wait for nightfall, Nicodemus tells their story.

Years before, Nicodemus, Justin, and other rats who lived in a marketplace at the edge of a big city were captured and taken to a huge lab complex called NIMH. There, over a long period of time, they were the subjects of an extraordinary experiment headed by a Dr. Schultz. The rats were injected daily with DNA material to see if their intelligence could be enchanced. The experiment worked far better than the doctor realized. The rats of NIMH not only grew as intelligent as humans, if not more so, but their life spans were so lengthened that today Nicodemus and the others seem as young as when the experiment started. No one knows how long they will live or even if their children will be as intelligent as they.

The rats of NIMH grew so smart that they figured out a way to escape from the lab. Escaping with them were some of the mice who had also been captured and had become part of the experiment. One of them was Mrs. Frisby's husband, Jonathan. He had not yet told his wife of what had happened in the lab because he knew that while Mrs. Frisby grew old, he would stay young, and he did not want to frighten her. Nicodemus also tells Mrs. Frisby that the rats are planning to move from their rosebush home out to Thorn Valley in the wilderness. They have been planning the move for some time. They want to live a new life—no longer stealing for their food, as rats normally do, but growing their own food and living without taking something from someone else. They have been reading books on farming and watching Mr. Fitzgibbons each spring. That is what they call The Plan—to live without stealing.

That evening Mrs. Frisby sneaks into the farmhouse and puts the sleep medicine in Dragon's dish. She is captured for a time by one of the farmer's sons, and during that period she overhears some frightening news. Humans have found some rats that have been electrocuted. It looks as though they were trying to move an electric motor. Mrs. Frisby remembers that Nicodemus told her of one of the rats, Jenner, and his followers who refused to join them in the move to Thorn Valley. Could the dead rats have been Jenner and his group?

The news of the rats' deaths has apparently reached the doctor and staff at NIMH. They have, of course, long been searching for the intelligent rats, in the hope of either recapturing them or destroying them before the secret experiments are uncovered. The rats from NIMH live in fear of this. Mrs. Frisby learns that the following morning a crew is coming out to the farm to exterminate any rats they can find.

With the help of Justin, Mrs. Frisby is freed and warns Nicodemus and the others of the impending danger. The rats move the Frisby home to safety that evening, and they establish a complicated ploy to convince the exterminators that they are just "normal" rats whose home they have destroyed. Two rats are killed during the escape, but the others are free to make their journey to their new home in Thorn Valley.

Mrs. Frisby wishes that she could see her new friends once again, but she realizes that is probably not possible. She is grateful to the rats of NIMH for making their home safe. Timothy recovers fully, although he will always be a little on the frail side. When the warm days of May arrive, the Frisby mice move to their summer home at the brook's edge. And it is there that Mrs. Frisby tells her children about their amazing father and the intelligent rats of NIMH.

Themes and Subjects

In his Newbery acceptance speech, author Robert O'Brien wrote—he was unable to attend the award ceremony because of poor health—that the rats in his highly original novel where "saner and more pleasant" than humans. Amidst growth and change, the rats do, indeed, establish a society in which family values are respected and where justice triumphs. One of the main and most compelling aspects of this suspenseful and often humorous social allegory is that despite and beyond the fact that the rats of NIMH can talk and read and reason, they remain, otherwise, rats. They live as rats live and react as rats react. Although they understand nature and the seasons as experienced by humans, they do so from a rat's viewpoint. They do not like living in a human home, for instance, although they must for a period of time, because rats naturally like to live underground. Their environment, despite their unusual capabilities, remains natural to what is natural for any rat. The environment portrayed in this novel, then, remains realistic and believable at all times. The rats may exhibit human thought, but they do so without challenging human existence—they are still rats. It is this constant thread that makes the story so believable. Also part of the basic thread of the novel is the rats' decision to move to Thorn Valley, the desire for a "back-to-basics" life instead of one filled with gadgets and "easy living," which has destroyed a sense of worth and fulfillment for these intelligent animals. The author shows a sensitive observance of the natural world. Interwoven with the story of the rats of NIMH is the tender tale of Mrs. Frisby, a frightened but determined and very brave mouse who risks all to protect her family.

Incidents for Booktalking

Any of a number of realistic though imaginative passages will delight the reader as an introduction to the wonderful rats of NIMH. See: Mrs. Frisby is taken into the rats' underground home and gets her first ride in an elevator (pp. 77–79); Nicodemus takes Mrs. Frisby into his elegantly furnished library and tells her the story of how the rats became prisoners in NIMH (pp. 98–111); Nicodemus explains their escape and how he meets Jonathan Frisby (pp. 129–41); Justin and Nicodemus explain The Plan (pp. 157–70); Nicodemus and Jenner disagree over The Plan (pp. 174–75); the rats escape (pp. 221–26).

Related Titles

Water Rat, affectionately known as Ratty, is a forceful character who worries (with cause) about his friend, the foolish Toad, and experiences a series of adventures along with Mole and Badger in Kenneth Grahame's classic *The Wind in the Willows*. E. H. Shepard, Arthur Rackham, and more recently Michael Hague and John Burningham have illustrated recommended editions of this book. The Shepard illustrations appear in the 75th edition (Scribner, 1983, $18.95: 0-684-19345-0).

In *Stuart Little* (Harper, 1945, $14.95: 00-06-026395-4; pap., Trophy, $3.95: 0-06-022378-2) by E. B. White, a mouse child is born to a human New York family. After a series of humorous adventures at home, Stuart sets out to find Margola, a bird to which he is attracted.

Russell Hoban's *The Mouse and His Child* (Harper, 1967, $14.95: 0-06-022378-2) tells how a broken windup mouse child and his father, also a tin toy, are captured by an enormous rat, Manny.

Amos, a poor church mouse, makes himself invaluable to Benjamin Franklin in the humorous novel that combined fiction and history, *Ben and Me* (Little, Brown, 1939, $16.95: 0-316-51732-1; pap., Little, Brown, $5.95: 0-316-51730-5) by Robert Lawson.

The Mouse and the Motorcycle (Morrow, 1965, $16.00: 0-688-21698-6; pap., Avon, $4.50: 0-380-72799-4) by Beverly Cleary is the story of an unusual mouse named Ralph who is given a toy motorcycle by a visitor to his home, the somewhat shabby Mountain View Inn.

About the Book and Author

Berger, Laura Standley, ed. *Twentieth-Century Young Adult Writers*. St. James, 1994, pp. 499–550.

Brown, Muriel W., and Rita S. Foudray. *Newbery and Caldecott Medalists and Honor Book Winners: Bibliographic & Resource Material Through 1991*. 2d ed. Neal-Schuman, 1992, pp. 312–13.

Chevalier, Tracy, ed. *Twentieth-Century Children's Writers*. 3d ed. St. James, 1989, pp. 733–34.

Collier, Laurie, and Joyce Nakamura, eds. *Major Authors and Illustrators for Children and Young Adults*. Gale, 1993, 6 vols. pp. 552–54.

Commire, Anne, ed. *Something About the Author*. Vol. 23. Gale, 1981, pp. 45–47.

de Montreville, Doris, and Elizabeth D. Crawford, eds. *Fourth Book of Junior Authors and Illustrators*. Wilson, 1978, pp. 275–78.

Evory, Ann, ed. *Contemporary Authors (First Revision Series)*. Vols. 41–44. Gale, 1979, p. 148.

Garrett, Agnes, and Helga P. McCue, eds. *Authors and Artists for Young Adults*. Vol. 6. Gale, 1991, pp. 173–80.

Helbig, Alethea K., and Agnes R. Perkins, eds. *Dictionary of American Children's Fiction, 1960–1985*. Greenwood, 1986, p. 481 (bio.), pp. 441–42 (book).

Kingman, Lee, ed. *Newbery and Caldecott Medal Books: 1966–1975 with Acceptance Papers, Biographies and Related Material*. Horn Book, 1975, pp. 79–92.

Locher, Frances C., ed. *Contemporary Authors*. Vols. 73–76. Gale, 1978, p. 130.

"Newbery Award Acceptance Material, 1972." *Horn Book* 48, no. 4 (August 1972): 343–51.

O'Brian, Robert C. *Mrs. Frisby and the Rats of NIMH*. Chivers Children's Audio Books. Audiocassettes, 240 min. ($32.95)

———. *Mrs. Frisby and the Rats of NIMH*. Read by Barbara Caruso. Recorded Books, 1993. Audiocassettes, 435 min. ($42.00)

———. *Mrs. Frisby and the Rats of NIMH*. SRA/McGraw-Hill, 1990. Videocassette.

Peterson, Linda K., and Marilyn L. Solt, eds. *Newbery and Caldecott Medal and Honor Books: 1922–1981*. Hall, 1982, pp. 185–86.

Riley, Carolyn, ed. *Children's Literature Review*. Vol. 2. Gale, 1976, pp. 127–30.

Silvey, Anita, ed. *Children's Books and Their Creators*. Houghton, 1995, pp. 495–96.

Ward, Martha, ed. *Authors of Books for Young People*. 3d ed. Scarecrow, 1990, p. 533.

Honor Books 1972

Eckert, Allan W. *Incident at Hawk's Hill*. Peter Smith, 1971, $19.50: 0-8446-6848-6; pap. Little Brown, $5.95: 0-319-20948-1. (Grades 5–9)

Based on an actual incident, this novel takes places in 1850 and is set in the sprawling prairie land of what is now Manitoba, Canada. Six-year-old Ben, the shy, undersized youngest of the MacDonald clan has an unusual talent of mimicking the actions and sounds of the animals around his family's farm. This gift comes in handy when one night alone on the prairie during a wild electric storm, the boy takes shelter in a badger's burrow. When the badger returns she adopts this strange creature who is able to convince her that he is really one of her kind. The novel tells the amazing story of the two months that Ben lived with the badger while successfully eluding the settlers who were looking for him. Finally the boy is found by his brother and returned home and the badger, in a tragic ending, is fatally shot by a dishonest trapper.

Hamilton, Virginia. *The Planet of Junior Brown*. Macmillan, 1971, $17.00: 0-02-742510-X. (Grades 6–9)

This unusual and compelling story takes place during one week in the lives of two black eighth-grade friends, Junior Brown and Buddy Clark. Junior is a disturbed youngster who weighs almost 300 pounds, is a talented musician, and finds it increasingly impossible to cope with his neurotic mother. Buddy, who enjoys science and math, is a homeless waif who lives by his wits and is the leader of a group of boys who live in the basement of an abandoned building that they call their planet. For the past two and a half months, the two boys have been skipping classes and instead spending their days in the school in a room hidden behind the broom closet with Mr. Pool, the school janitor. There, Buddy tries to help Junior retain his fragile grip on reality particularly after the boys are caught by the assistant principal. This story of compassion, interdependence, and friendship is a challenging book for better readers.

LeGuin, Ursula. *The Tombs of Atuan*. Atheneum, 1971, $18.00: 0-689-31684-4. (Grades 6–9)

In the first of the Earthsea fantasies, *The Wizard of Earthsea* (pap., Bantam, $3.95), readers were introduced to an imaginary magical archipelago traveled by a novice wizard, Ged, in his quest to find and destroy an evil beast. In *Tombs*, Tenar, a child, is taken from her family to become Arha, a priestess to the Nameless Ones, ancient priests who are buried under the Tombs of Atuan. Her training proceeds through her adolescence during which she becomes familiar with the Labyrinth beneath the Tombs. One day in this maze, Arha encounters the wizard Ged, who has come to steal the treasure of the Tombs. The treasure is half of a magic ring, which with the half that he already owns, will bring peace to the land and allow kings to rule justly. Urha, whom Ged calls by her real name, Tenar, must decide whether to face possible death by helping this young man or let him die of thirst and starvation in the Labyrinth.

Miles, Miska. *Annie and the Old One*. Little, Brown, 1971, $16.45: 0-316-57117-2. (Grades 1–4)

This brief (44 pages) story introduces the concept of death through a simply told story of a Navajo girl and her grandmother, called the Old One. The many full-page drawings by Peter Parnall add to the poignancy of the story. Annie, a contemporary Navajo girl, lives with her parents and the Old One in a happy and secure life encompassed by love and the traditions of the past. This calm is shattered when one evening the Old One tells the family that when the rug that she is weaving is complete, she will die and go to Mother Earth. Annie is unable to face the inevitability of death and tries various schemes to prevent the rug's completion, including secretly unraveling the day's work at night. Only when the Old One takes her away and explains that it is impossible to hold back time does Annie understand.

Snyder, Zilpha K. *The Headless Cupid*. Atheneum, 1971, $17.00: 0-689-20687-9. (Grades 5–7)

Although 11-year-old David and the three other younger Stanley children are eagerly awaiting the arrival of their stepsister, 12-year-old Amanda, they are not prepared for her unusual appearance and the consequences of her strange behavior. Amanda, claiming to be a psychic, dresses outlandishly, has a triangle on her forehead, and carries a cage in which her crow, Rolor, resides. The children, fascinated by Amanda and her way-out behavior, obey her wishes and submit to a series of rituals and trials to become part of the occult world. It is only when a truly terrifying incident occurs at the Stanley home that Amanda admits that her behavior has been a cleverly devised hoax to gain attention. Several other entertaining stories about the Stanley family are in print including *The Famous Stanley Kidnapping Case* (Atheneum, 1979, $14.95).

Newbery Winner 1973

George, Jean Craighead. *Julie of the Wolves*. Illustrated by John Schoenherr. Harper, 1972, $15.95: 0-06-021943-2; pap., $3.95: 0-06-440573-7. (Grades 4–8)

It seemed natural for Jean George (1921–) to turn to nature writing. Her father was an entomologist and her twin brothers became wildlife ecologists. As a child her home was filled with pets—from such commonplace animals as dogs to the more exotic such as owls, raccoons, and falcons. After a career as a reporter and magazine author-illustrator, she wrote a series of nature stories with her ex-husband John George. This novel grew out of the author's experiences in Alaska doing research on wolves for an article that later appeared in the *Reader's Digest*. She was impressed with the amazing similarities between human behavior and that of the wolves. As she said in her acceptance speech, both "have leaders, population problems, and live together all year round. Both have language." She also found that wolves care for each other in times of trouble. All the facts about the wolves in this novel have been authenticated by the author. This book, however, is more than just a nature story. It tells of the conflict of cultures as experienced by a young girl torn between the two. It is also a novel of human survival and courage. The story of Julie, or in her native language, Miyax, is continued in *Julie* (Harper, 1994, $14.95). Another of Ms. George's novels, *My Side of the Mountain,* was a Newbery Honor Book in 1960 (p. 228).

Plot Summary

Julie's amazing story recounts the journey of a courageous young Eskimo girl as she crosses miles of Arctic tundra alone. Part of the story describes her life up to her decision to leave the town of Barrow, Alaska, on this trek that she hopes will lead to a new life in San Francisco.

Julie, also called by her Eskimo name of Miyax, lives her first four years in the settlement of Mekoryak on Nunivak Island in Alaska. When her mother dies, her father, Kapugen, gives up the ways of the white settlers and leaves his home and possessions to live with his daughter in the true Eskimo way in a remote seal camp. There Miyax absorbs the language and culture of her people. She develops an affinity and respect for nature. Kapugen helps her to understand and love all wildlife, including the wolves whom he says love each other and "if you learn to speak to them, will love you too."

Shortly after her ninth birthday, Miyax is forced by Aunt Martha to return to Kekoryak to attend school. Before Miyax leaves, Kapugen arranges that she will be married at age 13 to David, son of Kapugen's hunting partner, Naka. After her departure, Kapugen grows more despondent. Within a month, Miyax receives news that her beloved father has not returned from a seal hunt and is presumed dead.

In her non-Eskimo environment, Miyax gradually becomes Julie. She makes friends with her schoolmates and becomes pen pals with Amy Pollack, a San Francisco girl of Julie's age. Julie becomes envious of Amy's life of prosperity and ease, and she hopes one day to accept her friend's invitation to visit San Francisco.

Life with her stern, unfeeling Aunt Martha becomes increasingly difficult. But when she reaches 13, Miyax is summoned by Naka to Barrow to marry David. Her life in Barrow is even more intolerable. Naka is frequently drunk and quarrelsome, to the point of physically abusing his wife, Nuson. David proves to be retarded, and their marriage remains one in name only. Julie becomes a household drudge, forced to spend hours each day sewing boots and parkas for the tourists.

One day David tries to attack her sexually. She escapes and with the help of her friend Pearl gathers together a few essentials in her backpack. She leaves Barrow to trek the 300 miles to Point Hope, where she thinks she can get work on a ship heading for San Francisco.

Julie is traveling during the arctic summer, the time of the midnight sun. After five days, or "sleeps," away from Barrow, when she is completely lost and almost without food, she happens upon a small pack of wolves. Remembering her father's words, she tries to communicate with them and tell them of her plight. She builds a sod house at the bottom of the frost heave that separates her from the wolves' den and begins to observe them closely. At first she is unsuccessful in her attempts to imitate the sounds and body language of the wolves, but within a few days she learns the basic vocabulary and to her surprise, becomes an adopted member of the pack. Miyax grows to love and respect her new family, and she even gives them names. The leader, who becomes her wolf-father, is Amaroq (Eskimo for "wolf"). The other adult members are Silver, the mother of the pups, a second male, Nail, and Jello, the last adult, who for some reason is treated like an outcast. He lives physically and socially outside the pack's close family circle. There are five pups. Miyax names the liveliest and most friendly of the pups after her father, Kapu. The others are Sister, Zing, Zat, and Zit.

With her full acceptance by the wolves, Miyax no longer has to worry about her food supply. The wolves take care of her through their frequent caribou kills. Miyax begins to cure and store a supply of meat because she realizes that when summer ends the wolves will move on and she will be alone once more. She and the wolves share their lives and livelihood for several weeks, but when summer ends, the wolves leave.

When Miyax returns to her sod house, she discovers that Jello, now a complete outcast, has attacked her camp, destroyed her sleeping gear, and eaten most of her food supply. That evening she hears the howling of her wolves and knows that they cannot be far ahead, but by morning Jello has attacked again, this time stealing her pack filled with equipment and the remaining food. In the morning, close to her camp, Miyax finds the torn body of Jello. Amaroq has turned on him and killed him.

Miyax rejoins the wolves and constructs a makeshift sled with which she is able to travel fast enough to keep up with them. She also finds a sick golden plover whom she adopts and names Tornait, the bird spirit. At the first sign of civilization—some empty oil cans—Miyax becomes fearful for the wolves in an area where the white hunters have placed a bounty on their skins.

One day a small plane carrying hunters spots the wolves in a clearing. From the air, they shoot and kill Amaroq and seriously wound Kapu. To Miyax the plane suddenly represents the white civilization—no longer something to be sought after but a hateful monster that has killed her beloved protectors. Miyax slowly nurses Kapu back to health. He becomes the leader of the pack and at Miyax's insistence, leaves her while he leads the pack back to the wilderness and safety.

Instead of traveling to San Francisco, Miyax decides to live truly like an Eskimo. She builds a snow house and begins to live off the land. One day an Eskimo family on their way to hunt caribou visits Miyax and tells her of a village, Kangik, they have left and of the mighty hunter who lives there, Kapugen. She sets out for the village with dreams of a reunion with her father untainted by the white civilization. Her father, as kindly and loving as before, is overjoyed to see his daughter. But Miyax soon realizes that Kapugen has adopted many of the gussack ways; he has even married a white woman.

Crushed, Miyax returns to her ice house. Her pet, Tornait, dies and she is once more alone. In her complete solitude, she wonders if it is still possible to live as in the olden days, or if one must make compromises with the changes that time brings. Slowly she realizes that "the hour of the wolf and the Eskimo is over," and with resignation, leaves her ice house to join her father in Kangik.

Themes and Subjects

The facts about wolves in this novel have been authenticated by the author, who had spent time in Alaska doing research for an article on the habits of Arctic wolves. From the vast amount of data she collected came the inspiration for this novel. But *Julie* is more than a nature story rich with fascinating details of animal life in the Arctic. It contains a wealth of other themes, the most important being the conflict within a young girl between modern culture and the primitive life of the Eskimo. Julie's resolution of this conflict reflects her growing maturity. The novel also explores relationships and responsibilities within an animal family and suggests parallels and applications in our own lives. Perhaps most of all, this is a novel of human survival in spite of extreme adversity, and of the courage and self-will that make this victory possible.

Incidents for Booktalking

Young people can be introduced to the "first" Julie (pp. 342–43) or to the typical home life of the wolf as seen by the author (p. 344). Some interesting passages are: Miyax's first successful attempt at talking to the wolves (pp. 21–22); she becomes one of the pack (pp. 24–26); the wolves save her from a grizzly attack (pp. 131–33).

Related Titles

Recommended sequels to *Julie of the Wolves* include *Julie* (Harper, 1994, $14.89: 0-06-023529-2) and *Julie's Wolf Pack* (Harper, 1997, $15.89: 0-06-027407-7).

The relationship between man and nature, and the fear of wolves are interwoven in the modern fairy tale by Bebe F. Rice, *The Year the Wolves Came* (Dutton, 1995, $14.99: 0-525-45209-5).

Peter Grayson spends a winter in a remote mountain valley in Walt Morey's *Canyon Winter* (pap., Puffin, $3.99: 0-14-036856-6).

The Inuit culture and their practice of making homes out of snow are described in Ulli Steltzer's *Building an Igloo* (Holt, 1995, $14.95: 0-8050-3753-5).

Phillip and an old black West Indian man survive on a coral island after their boat is torpedoed in Theodore Taylor's *The Cay* (Doubleday, 1969, $15.95: 0-385-07906-0; pap., Avon, $4.99: 0-380-01003-8).

Mary and other foster children spend a summer in a remote cabin with a sick adult in Jean Thesman's *When the Road Ends* (Houghton, 1992, $14.95: 0-395-59507-X; pap., Avon, $3.99: 0-380-72011-6).

About the Book and Author

Berger, Laura Standley, ed. *Twentieth-Century Young Adult Writers*. St. James, 1994, pp. 239–42.

Brown, Muriel W., and Rita S. Foudray. *Newbery and Caldecott Medalists and Honor Book Winners: Bibliographic & Resource Material Through 1991*. 2d ed. Neal-Schuman, 1992, pp. 164–66.

Chevalier, Tracy, ed. *Twentieth-Century Children's Writers*. 3d ed. St. James, 1989, pp. 381–83.

Collier, Laurie. *Authors and Artists for Young Adults*. Vol. 8. Gale, 1992, pp. 61–72.

Collier, Laurie, and Joyce Nakamura, eds. *Major Authors and Illustrators for Children and Young Adults*. Gale, 1993, 6 vols. pp. 935–41.

Commire, Anne, ed. *Something About the Author*. Vol. 2. Gale, 1971, pp. 112–14.

Estes, Glenn E., ed. "American Writers for Children Since 1960: Fiction." In *Dictionary of Literary Biography*. Vol. 52. Gale, 1986, pp. 168–74.

Gallo, Donald R. *Speaking for Ourselves*. National Council of Teachers of English, 1990, pp. 74–76.

George, Jean Craighead. *Journey Inward: An Autobiography*. 1982, o.p.

———. *Julie of the Wolves*. Read by Christina Moore. Recorded Books. Audiocassettes, 270 min. ($27.00)

———. "Taking Care of Our Planet Through Books." *Horn Book* (March/April 1994): 170–77.

Helbig, Alethea K., and Agnes R. Perkins, eds. *Dictionary of American Children's Fiction, 1960–1984*. Greenwood, 1986, p. 236 (bio.), pp. 344–45 (book).

Hipple, Theodore W., ed. *Writers for Young Adults*. Vol. 2. Scribners, 1997, pp. 47–57.

Hopkins, Lee Bennett, ed. *More Books by More People*. Citation Press, 1974, pp. 178–86.

Kingman, Lee, ed. *Newbery and Caldecott Medal Books: 1966–1975 with Acceptance Papers, Biographies and Related Material*. Horn Book, 1975, pp. 93–112.

May, Hal, and Deborah A. Straub, eds. *Contemporary Authors (New Revision Series)*. Vol. 25. Gale, 1989, pp. 156–58.

"Newbery Acceptance Material, 1973." *Horn Book* 49, no. 4 (August 1973): 337–50.

Olendorf, Donna, and Diane Telgen, eds. *Something About the Author*. Vol. 68. Gale, 1992, pp. 78–85.

Peterson, Linda K., and Marilyn L. Solt, eds. *Newbery and Caldecott Medal and Honor Books: 1922–1981*. Hall, 1982, p. 192.

Silvey, Anita, ed. *Children's Books and Their Creators*. Houghton, 1995, pp. 268–70.

Ward, Martha, ed. *Authors of Books for Young People*. 3d ed. Scarecrow, 1990, p. 264.

Honor Books 1973

Lobel, Arnold. *Frog and Toad Together*. Illustrated by the author. Harper, 1972, $14.00: 0-06-023960-3; pap., Trophy, $3.00: 0-06-444021-4. (Grades Preschool–3)

This sequel to *Frog and Toad Are Friends*, (Harper, 1970, $13.00. pap. $3.50) another "I Can Read" book, contains five short, simple-to-read stories about the daily activities of these two humanized friends. Each story is enriched with several illustrations that nicely complement the stories and their genial often comic mood. In the first, "The List," Toad writes a list of all the activities he plans for the day beginning with "Wake Up." Unfortunately after "Take Walk with

Frog," he loses the list and must sit doing nothing until it's time to do the only other thing on the list he remembers, "Go to Sleep."

"The Garden" tells how Toad, under Frog's guidance, plants a garden. He becomes impatient when nothing seems to be happening so he tries various tactics like talking to the seeds, shouting at them, telling them stories, and keeping them company at night. When the seeds sprout, he believes it was his hard work rather than just sunshine and rain.

In "Cookies," the two friends are unable to exercise the necessary willpower to stop eating Toad's delicious cookies. Finally, in desperation, they feed them to some hungry birds who are grateful for the treats. Frog and Toad learn about courage when they confront a big snake, a hungry hawk, and a deadly avalanche in "Dragons and Giants."

Lastly, "The Dream" tells of Toad's dream of excelling as a performer, first as a pianist, then as a high-wire aerialist, and lastly as a dancer. With each accomplishment, he brags to Frog in the audience who, with each boast, becomes smaller and more distant. At the point where Toad is fearful that Frog has disappeared forever, his faithful friend wakes him up in time for them to spend another happy day together.

Reiss, Johanna. *The Upstairs Room.* Crowell, 1972, $15.00: 0-690-85127-8; pap., Trophy, $3.95: 0-06-440374-X. (Grades 5–9)

In a slightly fictionalized form and using different names for the characters, this is the true story of Ms. Reiss's family and their experiences in hiding during World War II as seen through the eyes of young Annie de Leeuw. When the story opens in 1938, Annie is only six but becoming aware from her home in Holland of the increasing menace from Nazi Germany. After the invasion and occupation, her family—father, sickly mother, and two older sisters, Rachel and 16-year-old Sini—manage to exist somehow. But in October 1942, they receive a letter ordering them to work camps. The family separates and goes into hiding. Annie and Sini are first taken in by the Hannink family, but when this becomes too dangerous, they are moved to the home of a poor farmer, Johan Oosterveld, who lives with his wife Dientje and his mother. The girls spend their days in the couple's upstairs bedroom and later, when searches are anticipated, in a tiny adjoining closet specially constructed by Johan. These become their quarters for almost two and a half years. During this time tempers sometimes flare and the monotony often becomes unbearable despite infrequent diversions like visits from friends and listening to foreign radio broadcasts. News arrives that an informer is active in town and Johan is given the assignment of killing him. He is successful but the Germans take reprisal by shooting some townspeople. For a time, German soldiers use the farmhouse as an office, creating many suspenseful moments of near-discovery. Finally, in April 1945 after the Allied invasion, the Germans evacuate and the town is freed. When the townspeople assemble to greet their liberators, many wonder who are the two girls with Johan and his family. This story of courage and endurance is continued in *The Journey Back* (1976, Crowell, $12.95; pap., Harper, $3.95).

Snyder, Zilpha K. *The Witches of Worm.* Illustrated by Alton Raible. Atheneum, 1972, $16.00: 0-689-30066-2. (Grades 4–8)

This story of an imaginative and neglected 12 year old and her retreat into a world of witchcraft and demonology is effectively illustrated with eerie full-page black-and-white drawings. Jessica Ann Porter is a lonely, plain girl who is grow-ing up with her frequently absent attractive mother in an apartment building in a California city. Her best friends Diane and a co-resident, the trumpet-playing Brandon Doyle, seem to have deserted her and she has increasingly immersed herself in books about the occult. In a secret cave behind the apartment house that Brandon and she used to explore, Jessica finds a newborn, still-sightless kitten whom she names Worm and nurses to health with the help of Mrs. Fortune, the building's owner. As Jessica's actions become more spiteful and destructive, she claims she is being possessed by the "witchcat," Worm, who secretly talks to her and directs her to commit such malicious acts as getting Diane into trouble, ruin-ing her mother's expensive new dress to keep her from visiting her fiancée, and pushing Brandon's trumpet from a third-story window. Mrs. Fortune realizes that these events are really symptoms of Jessica's inner unhappiness but suggests that an exorcism should be performed on Worm to end Jessica's troubles. After the rit-ual, Worm runs away but Jessica, with Brandon's help, finds him stunned after a fall from scaffolding. Later she confides to Brandon that it was she who was re-sponsible for damaging his trumpet and promises to pay for repairs. Jessica, now more in touch with reality, welcomes back both Brandon and Worm as friends.

Newbery Winner 1974

Fox, Paula. *The Slave Dancer*. Bradbury, 1973, $16.00: 0-02-735560-8; pap., Dell, $3.99: 0-440-80203-2. (Grades 6–9)

In her Newbery Medal acceptance speech, Paula Fox (1923–) traces the genesis of this novel to a footnote in a forgotten history book, which stated that of-ten, to preserve the physical health of their wretched cargo, the crews of slave ships kidnapped young street musicians to serve as slave dancers. About slavery, the author states,

> When I read the records of the past, I sometimes wanted to turn away from what I was learning—to sleep. But as I read on and heard the words of the captive people themselves, as I began to feel the power of their endurance, I perceived that the people who had spoken so long ago of every conceivable human loss were not only survivors, but pioneers of the human condition in inhuman circumstances.

She also said that "it is not the victim who is shamed. It is the persecutor, who has refused the shame of what he has done." When reading this novel one re-alizes that slavery diminishes the oppressors as well as the oppressed. Though graphic in its scenes of horror and inhumanity, the author neither sensationalizes nor exploits the material. Paula Fox writes fiction for both adults and young read-ers. In the latter area, she has been a frequent recipient of major literary prizes. Her novel *One-Eyed Cat* was named a Newbery Honor Book in 1985 (see p. 363).

Plot Summary

Jessie Bollier is a 13-year-old boy who earns a few pennies each day playing his fife on the docks of New Orleans for the amusement of sailors and passersby. He lives with his widowed mother, a seamstress, and a nine-year-old sister, Betty, in poverty in the Vieux Carre, now called the French Quarter. It is 1840 and although slavery is still legal, by law no American ship may engage in this odious practice.

One evening Jessie is sent to his Aunt Agatha's to borrow some candles so that his mother and Betty can work into the night on a special sewing assignment. On his way home he is grabbed from behind by two men who throw a canvas bag over him. He is first transported by wooden raft to a marshy area and then the three walk to a small sailboat. When the canvas is removed, he recognizes his captors, Claudius and Purvis, as part of the group he had entertained that afternoon. They soon arrive at a sailing ship with many masts, *The Moonlight*, where the boy is brought before Captain Cawthorne, a cruel, corrupt man who, in his characteristic sarcastic way, nicknames the boy Bollweevil. With satanic coldness, he explains that the ship is bound on a four-month voyage to a Spanish contact in Cuba. There they will purchase molasses and then return to Charleston. Jessie realizes with horror that he has been press-ganged onto a slaver.

He finds life on the ship filled with misery and hardship and is amazed at the indifference and cruelty of the crew, even toward each other. Thirteen crew members—an unfortunate number—are aboard, including the brutal Captain and his equally hated and feared mate, Nicholas Spark. Jessie soon gets to know them all. At first he is mistakenly deluded by the friendliness of one seaman, Ben Stout, but soon finds that Stout is even more calculating and cunning than the rest. Clay Purvis is the most enigmatic—moody, unpredictable, taciturn—but in time Jessie realizes that he is the only one to be trusted. Because of the menial jobs he is given, Jessie often also works with the cynical ship's carpenter, Ned Grime, and the cook, Adolph Curry.

One night Stout steals an egg from the Captain's stores. Purvis is falsely accused and without protesting his innocence, he is publicly flogged before being hung on the shrouds for the night. Jessie finds this lassitude and stoicism incomprehensible, but he is filled with loathing and disgust for Stout.

At the Bight of Benin, the ship is harassed by a British naval vessel whose crew destroys the barracoon, or compound where the slaves were imprisoned while awaiting the arrival of *The Moonlight*. Captain Cawthorne makes new deals with the local slave brokers, and in the dead of night the human cargo, shackled and terrified, is brought to the ship and herded in the hold. Cawthrone, who is known as a "tight packer," squeezes almost 100 slaves in the ship before it leaves Africa.

Jessie now learns his real function on the journey. Each day the slaves are exercised and fed on deck. He must play the flute while the seamen prod the hapless prisoners into a macabre dance to keep their muscles strong. Jessie watches the slaves carefully and is particularly intrigued by a quiet wide-eyed boy of his own age.

The homeward journey is a nightmare of degradation, hardship, and death. Several of the slaves develop a fever and are pitched overboard while still alive. Stout is the only one who seems to thrive on these conditions. Fed up with the bestiality and horror of the situation, Jessie rebels and refuses to play his pipe. Under Captain's orders, he is flogged into submission.

The mate, Nicholas Spark, takes pleasure in tormenting and abusing the slaves. After one strikes out against him, the mate has the black man flogged unmercifully and then shoots him in the back. The Captain has Spark thrown overboard, not to serve justice but because the mate destroyed a valuable piece of cargo.

Stout, who takes Spark's place, turns his sadistic nature against Jessie, the one crew member who has openly shown his scorn and loathing. He steals Jessie's flute, drops it into the hold, and forces the boy to clamber among the half-dead slaves to retrieve it. The wide-eyed boy finds it for him, but in spite of this kindness, Jessie begins to hate even the slaves because it is they and their plight that are slowly eroding his sense of conscience.

They reach Cuba and the night before the slaves are to be taken ashore, the Captain holds his customary "farewell party." He brings the slaves on deck, feeds them rum, and dresses them in strange costumes and bits of finery for a final dance. Both slaves and sailors become drunk, but panic breaks out when an American naval ship is spotted on the horizon lowering landing boats. Fearful of being caught with evidence aboard, the seamen begin flinging the slaves into the ocean. Jessie and the wide-eyed boy hide in the hold. Before a landing can be made, a tropical squall develops and for hours, perhaps days, the terrible storm batters the ship. When it begins to list badly, the boys emerge and find the entire crew dead or missing. They grab a piece of boom and attempt to swim to safety.

They are successful and come ashore on the coast of Mississippi, close to the cabin of an escaped slave, Daniel, who befriends and nurses them. Daniel makes arrangements to have Ras, the black boy, sent north by way of the Underground Railroad, and gives Jessie food and directions for his journey home to New Orleans.

In a postscript, Jessie tells how, after spending some time at home, he travels north and becomes an apothecary in Rhode Island. He survives service in the Civil War and three months in the Andersonville prison. Throughout his later life, he tries to erase the memory of the events of 1840 but is only partially successful. When he hears music, he often thinks of the slaves, their joyless dances, and the clanking of their chains.

Themes and Subjects

This is a graphic, realistic picture of one of the most shameful aspects of our history. Although the story is grim and often horrifying, it is never sensationalized to exploit the material. In the self-hatred and abhorrence that the crew feels for each other, one realizes that slavery diminishes the oppressors as well as the oppressed. Jessie's character is well developed, and one feels both the physical and mental agonies he suffers, particularly in his outburst against the slaves (p. 91) when his conscience can no longer bear the burden of his guilt and shame.

Incidents for Booktalking

An explanation of the title plus the "history" page (p. 1) could be used to introduce the book. Also use Eros Keith's dark and forbidding illustrations in the hardcover edition. Specific passages are: Jessie is kidnapped (pp. 11–14); he meets Captain Cawthorne (pp. 24–26); Purvis is flogged (pp. 52–56); the first slaves arrive (pp. 72–75).

Related Titles

Eleven-year-old Genevieve, forced to care for her penniless family, is tempted to turn in an escaped slave to collect the bounty in *On Winter's Wind* (Little, Brown, 1995, $15.95: 0-316-35978-5) by Patricia Hermes.

Two young girls run away from slavery in 1855 and learn the true meaning of being free in Jennifer Armstrong's *Steal Away* (pap., Apple, $3.99: 0-590-46921-5).

In Joyce Hansen's novel *Which Way Freedom* (Walker, 1986, $13.95: 0-8027-6636-6; pap., Avon, $4.99: 0-380-71408-6), former slaves help Union soldiers during the Civil War.

Raisha, renamed Angelica, is a slave on a plantation on St. John, then part of the Danish West Indies in Scott O'Dell's *My Name Is Not Angelica* (Houghton, 1989, $18.00: 0-385-51061-9).

Escape from Slavery: The Boyhood of Frederick Douglass in His Own Words (Knopf, 1995, $15.00: 0-679-84652-2; pap., $4.99: 0-679-84651-4), edited and illustrated by Michael McCurdy, is a shortened version of Douglass's autobiography.

About the Book and Author

Berger, Laura Standley, ed. *Twentieth-Century Young Adult Writers*. St. James, 1994, pp. 214–21.

Block, Ann, and Carolyn Riley, eds. *Children's Literary Review*. Vol. 1. Gale, 1976, pp. 59–65.

Brown, Muriel W., and Rita S. Foudray. *Newbery and Caldecott Medalists and Honor Book Winners; Bibliographic & Resource Material Through 1991*. 2d ed. Neal-Schuman, 1992, pp. 142–45.

Chevalier, Tracy, ed. *Twentieth-Century Children's Writers*. 3d ed. St. James, 1989, pp. 357–58.

Commire, Anne, ed. *Something About the Author*. Vol. 17. Gale, 1979, pp. 59–60; 1990, Vol. 60, pp. 29–38.

de Montreville, Doris, and Elizabeth D. Crawford, eds. *Fourth Book of Junior Authors and Illustrators*. Wilson, 1978, pp. 135–36.

Estes, Glenn E., ed. "American Writers for Children Since 1960: Fiction." In *Dictionary of Literary Biography*. Vol. 52. Gale, 1986, pp. 143–56.

Fox, Paula. "On Language." *School Library Journal*. March, 1995, pp. 122–26.

———. *The Slave Dancer*. Read by Peter MacNicol. BDD Audio Publishing, 1996. Audiocassettes, 240 min. ($18.99)

————. *The Slave Dancer*. Read by George Guidall. Recorded Books, 1993. Audio-cassettes, 255 min. ($26.00)

Gallo, Donald R. *Speaking for Ourselves*. National Council of Teachers of English, 1990, pp. 69–70.

Garrett, Agnes, and Helga P. McCue, eds. *Authors and Artists for Young Adults*. Vol. 3. Gale, 1990, pp. 95–106.

Helbig, Alethea K.,and Agnes R. Perkins, eds. *Dictionary of American Children's Fiction, 1960–1983*. Greenwood, 1986, p. 222–23 (bio.), pp. 604–05 (book).

Hipple, Theodore W., ed. *Writers for Young Adults*. Vol. 1. Scribners, 1997, pp. 397–420.

Kingman, Lee, ed. *Newbery and Caldecott Medal Books: 1966–1975 with Acceptance Papers, Biographies and Related Material*. Horn Book, 1975, pp. 113–25.

Lesniak, James G., ed. *Contemporary Authors (New Revision Series)*. Vol. 36. Gale, 1992, pp. 140–44.

Locher, Frances C., ed. *Contemporary Authors*. Vols. 73–76. Gale, 1978, pp. 214–15.

Metzger, Linda, ed. *Contemporary Authors (New Revision Series)*. Vol. 20. Gale, 1987, pp. 116–68.

"Newbery Acceptance Material, 1974." *Horn Book* 50, no. 4 (August 1974): 345–53.

Paula Fox. Profiles in Literature, 1987. Videocassette.

Peterson, Linda K., and Marilyn L. Solt, eds. *Newbery and Caldecott Medal and Honor Books: 1922–1981*. Hall, 1982, pp. 196–97.

Silvey, Anita, ed. *Children's Books and Their Creators*. Houghton, 1995, pp. 249–52.

Ward, Martha, ed. *Authors of Books for Young People*. 3d ed. Scarecrow, 1990, p. 242.

Honor Books 1974

Cooper, Susan. *The Dark Is Rising*. Illustrated by Alan Cober. Atheneum, 1973, $17.00: 0-689-30317-3; pap., Aladdin, $3.95: 0-689-70420-8. (Grades 5–8)

    This is the second of a five-part series with the overall title of The Dark Is Rising. The author relies on a mingling of Celtic folklore and contemporary settings to create an epic struggle between good, the Light, and the forces of evil, the Dark. The first volume *Over Sea, Under Stone* (Harcourt, 1966, $14.95; pap., Collier, $3.50) featured Merriman Lyon as the central character and the fourth, *The Grey King* was awarded the 1976 Newbery Medal (p. 314).

    Will Stanton, who is the seventh son in a large prosperous English family living in rural Buchinghamshire, receives an unusual gift from neighbor Farmer Dawson three days before Christmas, on Will's eleventh birthday. It is an iron circle with a cross inside. The next day, Will is mysteriously transported through time and meets one of the Old Ones, Merriman Lyon, a fighter for the Light, who tells him that the forces of Dark are rising. Lyon also says that Will, the appointed Sign-Seeker, must find the six great Signs of the Light, which when forged together can conquer the Dark. He already has the first, the iron ornament. Now he must acquire the signs of bronze, wood, stone, water, and fire. After getting the Sign of Bronze from a former servant of Merriman's, he collects the Sign of Learning (Wood) from another Old One, Miss Greythorne, a neighbor, and the Sign of Stone from a niche in the local church. The Dark begins its attack with penetrating cold and violent snowstorms and Will still has not found the two remaining Signs. In Miss Greythorne's manor, Will places an icicle into a magical candlestick and the combination produces a gold object, the Sign of Fire. Immediately the cold stops and a thaw begins that produces terrible flooding. Will finds the last sign, Water, on the body of an ancient king whose burial ship is unearthed during the floods. The forces of the Light have been strengthened by Will's successful quest, and under Merriman's guidance, the boy returns home to his family who is unaware of his exploits.

Newbery Winner 1975

Hamilton, Virginia. *M. C. Higgins, the Great*. Macmillan, 1974, $17.00: 0-02-742480-4; pap., $3.95: 0-689-82168-9. (Grades 6–9)

Since her first children's book appeared in 1967, Virginia Hamilton (1936–) has produced an astonishing total of more than 30 titles and has won many of the major awards in children's literature. For example, *M. C. Higgins, the Great* was awarded not only the Newbery Medal but also the Boston Globe-Horn Book and the National Book awards. In her Newbery Award acceptance speech, she comments on the great difficulties this book caused. "No book of mine was ever in more danger of being a failed labor of love. . . . None was to give me more pleasure and pain in the writing." After writing several chapters, nothing more came and she put the book aside for many years, before returning with renewed inspiration to complete it. Through the central character, M. C., the author explores the themes of survival and the affirmation of life. As she says:

> . . . young people reading *M. C.*, particularly the poor and the blacks, have got to realize that his effort with his bare hands to stay alive and save his way of life must be their effort as well. For too long, too many have suffered and died without cause. I prefer to write about those who survived.

The novel is not a conventional one of plot, but instead deals with feelings and emotions that transcend time and place. Like the Ohio land it describes, it gives up its wealth slowly and sometimes grudgingly. Hamilton is the author of three Newbery Honors also described in this text. They are *In the Beginning* (see "Honor Books," 1989, p. 381), *The Planet of Junior Brown* (see "Honor Books," 1972, p. 295) and *Sweet Whispers, Brother Rush* (see "Honor Books," 1983, p. 351).

Plot Summary

Mayo Cornelius Higgins is the 13-year-old great-grandson of an escaped slave named Sarah, who fled from the South with her baby and settled on the slope of what later became known as Sarah's Mountain, in a mining area close to the Ohio River. There are many reasons why M. C. could be called "the Great": he is considered one of the best swimmers in the area; he comes from a wonderful family; he has a mother, Banina, whose voice matches the sweetness of her temperament; and when he sits atop the 40-foot pole his father gave him, he feels like an emperor surveying his dominions. Inwardly, he also feels great because to him his thoughts are more great and daring than those of others, and he is willing to take risks that would confound anyone else.

By economic standards, the Higgins family would be considered poor. Jones, M. C.'s father, works in the mine only when a regular hand is absent, and Banina does cleaning jobs in town. There are three other children, all younger than M. C.: two boys, Lennie Pool and Harper, and a girl, Macie Pearl. Their modest cottage is built on an overlap on the mountainside, but thanks to Jones' ingenuity, they at least have hot and cold running water. What is most troubling to M. C. is that a huge spoil heap left by the mining company above them on the mountains seems to be moving glacier-like down the mountain and will soon engulf their house and property. Despite M. C.'s warnings, Jones refuses to admit to the danger because he knows it means eventual loss of his family's property.

Apart from his family, M. C. has only one friend, Ben Killburn, who belongs to a large clan of social outcasts who live together in an enclave on Kill's Mound. They are known as the "witchy" people. Not only are the Killburns supposed to have supernatural powers to heal wounds and drive out devils, but their physical appearance is startling. Each has six fingers and toes, pale yellowish skin, and red hair. In spite of his parents' warnings, M. C. meets Ben away from home, but he has never had the courage to cross the swinging rope bridge that leads to Kill's Mound.

At one of their meetings, Ben tells M. C. that there is a man in town who is recording folk songs and because he has been told of Banina's lovely voice, he will soon be calling on the Higgins family. M. C. begins dreaming that his mother will become a big recording star and take them away from the danger of the mountain. He rushes up the trail to await the coming of the "dude" and sees a stranger on the path, a young girl who runs away when she sees him.

At home, he climbs his 40-foot pole and engages in his pastime of viewing the countryside. The pole was part of an array of junk that his father has dragged up the mountain to their yard. Jones gave it to M. C. as a prize for swimming, and the boy attached a bicycle seat and two tricycle wheels and pedals before erecting it in the front yard. Here, past and present meld, and he often imagines that Sarah is down below working her silent way through the underbrush to freedom.

M. C. sees the man with the tape recorder in the distance and runs to meet him. His name is James K. Lewis. On their way to the Higgins home, they pass the spoil heap. Lewis reaffirms M. C.'s deepest fears about the impending landslide. Because Banina is not yet home from work, Lewis leaves, promising to come back that evening.

At dinner that evening, through speech and action, M. C. reveals how much he loves each of his parents but how differently he feels toward them. With his father he has a surface, physical relationship that is competitive at times, but with his mother, there is a deeper emotional bond of felt—but often unspoken—understanding love.

After dinner, M. C. tries to explain to his mother the importance of her getting a record contract and of their leaving the mountain. She gently explains that Jones's roots are here and that, at her insistence, years ago he had removed the external signs of the family graveyard in front of their house. However, it had been his intention to use the 40-foot pole as a suitable monument for all his ancestors.

Ben reports that the girl M. C. saw on the trail is camping in the valley. M. C. investigates and although he finds her attractive, she is so defiant and unfriendly that he returns home.

Lewis comes back and tape records Banina, but there is no mention of a contract. Early the next morning before Banina must go to work, M. C. goes swimming with her in the cirque, a small lake in a deep hollow. They notice that the unfriendly girl is camped on the bank. After Banina leaves, M. C. displays his swimming prowess by negotiating a dangerous underwater tunnel. The girl, who is older than M. C., is wordless and totally enthralling to him. She insists that he take her through the tunnel. After she almost drowns, she confesses that she cannot swim!

M. C. takes the girl, whose name is Lurhetta Outlaw, home for lunch. There, she tells Jones something about herself. With her mother's permission, during her summer vacation, she leaves home to explore the countryside.

After lunch M. C. takes her to see his rabbit traps, and on the trail they meet Ben. Lurhetta is fascinated by him and consents to go to Kill's Mound. M. C., not wishing to be branded a coward, tags along. The commune is far from the witchy place that M. C. expected. The Killburns are a closely knit, industrious group who are friendly to their guests even though they have been ostracized from the community by suspicion and prejudice.

M. C. invites Lurhetta to dinner, but she does not appear. Lewis does drop by, however, to give the Higginses a cassette of Banina's voice. Before leaving, he tells M. C. that his mother is too pure, too natural ever to withstand the rigors of the commercial music field. The next morning, M. C. finds Lurhetta's camp deserted, but she has left him her knife. Dejectedly, M. C. returns home. Suddenly, he has one of his great notions—he will not sit passively by and see his family's home destroyed. He starts to dig up the earth and uses all the junk in their yard to create a wall to shield them against the oncoming spoil pile. Some family members help. At M. C.'s insistence, Ben is allowed for the first time on the Higgins property to help, too. Quite unexpectedly, Jones crawls under the house and drags out Sarah's gravestone. That will surely make M. C.'s wall strong.

Themes and Subjects

M. C. Higgins is not a conventional novel of plot, but instead is one of feelings, sensations, and emotions that transcend time and space. The novel is a reaffirmation of life, a hymn to those who help us survive, a tribute to the human spirit that never passively accepts fate. There are many other themes in the complex novel, such as conflicts between the past and the present and between illusion and reality. The novel also portrays many family relations and tells how physical differences in people can make them objects of fear and suspicion. Finally, it is also the story of a boy's maturation.

Incidents for Booktalking

A description of the central character, his family, and his amazing 40-foot pole might be used to interest readers. Individual passages are rather difficult to isolate; however, one could use: M.C. finds Lurhetta on the trail (pp. 18–20); atop the 40-foot pole (pp. 25–28); meeting with the dude (pp. 38–40); M. C. remembers a past birthday (pp. 84–87).

Related Titles

In Judy Blume's *Iggie's House* (Macmillan, 1970, $14.00: 0-02-711040-0; pap., Dell, $3.99: 0-440-44062-9), a black family moves into Iggie's old house.

A black boy, eight-year-old Thomas, spends a day fishing with his grandfather on the Gulf of Mexico in *Go Fish* (Harper, 1991, $14.89: 0-06-025822-5) by Mary Stolz.

William H. Hooks's *Circle of Fire* (Macmillan, 1982, $15.00: 0-689-50241-9) tells how three friends—a white and two black boys—try to thwart an attack on some Irish gypsies by Klan members.

Farm life in Ohio in 1946 is one of the subjects in Patricia Willis's *Out of the Storm* (Clarion, 1995, $15.00: 0-395-68708-X) in which a 12-year-old girl adjusts to the death of her father during World War II.

Louis Fitzhugh's *Nobody's Family Is Going to Change* (pap., Farrar, $4.95: 0-374-45523-6) focuses on a middle-class black family in which young Willie wants to become a tap dancer.

About the Book and Author

Berger, Laura Standley, ed. *Twentieth-Century Young Adult Writers*. St. James, 1994, pp. 267–69.

Block, Ann, and Carolyn Riley, eds. *Children's Literary Review*. Vol. 1. Gale, 1976, pp. 103–7.

Brown, Muriel W., and Rita S. Foudray. *Newbery and Caldecott Medalists and Honor Book Winners: Bibliographic & Resource Material Through 1991*. 2d ed. Neal-Schuman, 1992, pp. 182–84.

Chevalier, Tracy, ed. *Twentieth-Century Children's Writers*. 3d ed. St. James, 1989, pp. 442–44.

Collier, Laurie, and Joyce Nakamura, eds. *Major Authors and Illustrators for Children and Young Adults*. Gale, 1993, 6 vols., pp. 1047–52.

Commire, Tracy, ed. *Something About the Author*. Vol. 4. Gale, 1973, pp. 97–99.

de Montreville, Doris, and Elizabeth D. Crawford, eds. *Third Book of Junior Authors*. Wilson, 1978, pp. 162–64.

Estes, Glenn E., ed. "American Writers for Children Since 1960: Fiction." In *Dictionary of Literary Biography*. Vol. 52. Gale, 1986, pp. 174–84.

Gallo, Donald R. *Speaking for Ourselves*. National Council of Teachers of English, 1990, pp. 90–92.

Garrett, Agnes, and Helga P. McCue, eds. *Authors and Artists for Young Adults*. Vol. 2. Gale, 1989, pp. 53–64.

Hamilton, Virginia. "Laura Ingalls Wilder Medal Acceptance." *Horn Book* (July/August 1995): 436–41.

———. "Looking for America." *School Library Journal* (May 1999): 28–31.

———. *M. C. Higgins, the Great*. Read by Roscoe Browne. Recorded Books, 1993. Audiocassettes, 510 min.

———. "1995 Laura Ingalls Wilder Award Acceptance Speech." *Journal of Youth Services in Libraries* (Summer 1995): 355–60.

Helbig, Alethea K., and Agnes R. Perkins, eds. *Dictionary of American Children's Fiction, 1960–1984*. Greenwood, 1986, p. 269 (bio.), pp. 411–12 (book).

Hipple, Theodore W., ed. *Writers for Young Adults*. Vol. 2. Scribners, 1997, pp. 79–92.

Hopkins, Lee Bennett, ed. *More Books by More People*. Citation Press, 1974, pp. 199–207.

Kingman, Lee, ed. *Newbery and Caldecott Medal Books: 1966–1975 with Acceptance Papers, Biographies and Related Material*. Horn Book, 1975, pp. 126–40.

Lesniak, James G., ed. *Contemporary Authors (New Revision Series)*. Vol. 37. Gale, 1992, pp. 231–35.

McMahon, Thomas, ed. *Authors and Artists for Young Adults*. Vol. 21. Gale, 1997, pp. 81–92.

Meet the Newbery Author: Virginia Hamilton. SRA/McGraw-Hill, 1990. Videocassette.

Metzger, Linda, and Deborah A. Straub, eds. *Contemporary Authors (New Revision Series)*. Vol. 20. Gale, 1987, pp. 207–12.

Mikkesen, Nina. *Virginia Hamilton*. Twayne, 1992.

Nasso, Christine, ed. *Contemporary Authors (New Revision Series)*. Vol. 25. Gale, 1977, pp. 25–28, 299.

"Newbery Award Acceptance Material, 1975." *Horn Book* 51, no. 4 (August 1975): 337–48.

Peterson, Linda K., and Marilyn L. Solt, eds. *Newbery and Caldecott Medal and Honor Books: 1922–1981.* Hall, 1982, pp. 198–99.

Senick, Geerard J., ed. *Children's Literature Review.* Vol. 11. Gale, 1986, pp. 94–95.

Silvey, Anita, ed. *Children's Books and Their Creators.* Houghton, 1995, pp. 293–95.

Sweet Whispers, Brother Rush. SRA/McGraw-Hill, 1990. Videocassette.

Virginia Hamilton. Profiles in Literature, 1978. Videocassette.

Ward, Martha, ed. *Authors of Books for Young People.* 3d ed. Scarecrow, 1990, p. 527.

Honor Books 1975

Collier, James Lincoln, and Christopher Collier. *My Brother Sam Is Dead.* Four Winds, 1974, $17.00: 0-02772980-7; pap., Scholastic, $3.50: 0-590-37362-5. (Grades 5–9)

This powerful novel recounts the tragic effects of the American Revolutionary War on the Meeker family of Redding, Connecticut. It spans a four-year period from 1775 to 1779. Eleven-year-old Tim Meeker is confused about his loyalties in the gathering crisis in the Colonies. His parents, tavern owner Eliphalet (also known as Life) Meeker and wife Susannah are Tory sympathizers but Tim's older brother, 16-year-old Sam has already joined the rebel army. When Sam visits his home in April 1775, he and his father clash violently and Sam leaves after secreting stealing his father's blunderbuss, Brown Bess. The uncertainty of the future coupled with hard times and the occupation of their town by one side and then the other makes life difficult for the Meekers. In the fall of 1776, when Life and Tim go to Verplanks Point on the Hudson River for provisions, the two become separated and Life is kidnapped by rebel thieves. In the spring, after British troops have raided their town killing rebel sympathizers, Tim learns that his father has died aboard a prison ship. At the end of 1778, Sam's regiment is sent to Redding. When he intercepts two soldiers stealing the family's cattle, Tim is accused of being the cattle thief, court-martialed, and sentenced to die. In spite of personal pleas by Susannah and Tim, no reprieve is granted and Tim sees his innocent brother executed by a firing squad of his fellow soldiers. Years later Tom, now a prosperous merchant, thinks about the tragic events that destroyed his family and wonders if the same objectives could not have been achieved by more peaceful means. But now it is too late; those troubled times have become history.

Greene, Bette. *Philip Hall Likes Me, I Reckon, Maybe.* Illustrated by Charles Lilly. Dial, 1974, o.p.; pap., Dell, $4.99: 0-440-45755-6). (Grades 4–6)

This humorous saga of an 11-year-old black girl's declaration of sexual independence is set near the town of Pocahantas in rural Arkansas and takes place over a period of one year. Beth Lambert is bright and talented but is so infatuated with Philip Hall, who is "number-one best" in everything including all the subjects at school, that she allows herself to be number two for fear of losing him if she were best. Although this situation troubles her, her life is otherwise a happy one with a loving family and four girlfriends who jointly call themselves the Pretty Pennies. With some help from a fearful Philip, Beth courageously helps capture thieves who have been stealing her father's turkeys. Through painful experiences, Beth discovers that she is allergic to dogs, but this does not deter her in her plans to become a veterinarian. She is named number one scholar in her class, and when the Pretty Pennies buy T-shirts that shrink after washing, she and her friends successfully picket the local Busy Bee Bargain Store with some help from Philip and his gang, the Tiger Hunters. At the fall church picnic, Beth rescues Philip when he becomes lost on a nearby mountain, and in September at the 4-H fair, her calf, Madeline, wins first prize while Philip's Leonard is second. Although she is proud of and happy about being the best, Beth is still fearful that this will alienate Philip and end their friendship. However, in the past year Philip has also changed and realizes that only the person who has rightfully gained the honor should be considered number one. As they enter a square dance contest together as partners not rivals, Philip says, "Sometimes I reckon I likes you, Beth Lambert."

Pope, Elizabeth Marie. *The Perilous Gard*. Illustrated by Richard Cuffari. Houghton, 1974, o.p.; pap., Puffin, $5.99: 0-14-034912-X. (Grades 7–10)

This novel combines an accurate picture of life in Tudor England with details of an ancient Celtic religion. It tells of the fortunes of courageous Kate Sutton and her growing love for Christopher Heron. In July 1558, Kate, a lady-in-waiting to Princess Elizabeth, is falsely accused of causing trouble and is banished to Elvenwood Hall. Once known as the Perilous Gard, the Hall is a castle in Derbyshire owned by Sir Geoffrey Heron, the recently widowed lord of the manor. There she meets Sir Geoffrey's younger brother, Christopher, a young man slightly older than herself. Because of his negligence, his charge Cecily, Sir Geoffrey's four-year-old daughter, has disappeared and is feared dead. Guilt-ridden and miserable, he has become a recluse on the estate. After Sir Geoffrey is called away to his property in the south, Kate learns about the strange People of the Hill or Fairy Folk that live phantom lives in connecting caves on the property. They take a mind-numbing drug and practice a strange primitive religion in which they make a human sacrifice every seven years to appease the gods. The manor's simple-minded minstrel Randal shows Kate and Christopher, who have become friendly, a child's slipper given to him by a young girl dancing with the Fairy Folk. They recognize it as belonging to Cecily and realize that Cecily has been kidnapped to be the next sacrifice. Christopher frees Cecily by substituting himself, but Kate is found spying and is taken prisoner by the Fairy Folk. Two months later, on All-Hallows Eve, the night of the sacrifice, she escapes and rescues Christopher. Believing that they have lost their power, the Fairy Folk flood the caves and disappear. When news arrives that Elizabeth has been made queen, Kate and Christopher make plans to marry.

Raskin, Ellen. *Figgs and Phantoms*. Illustrated by the author. Dutton, 1974, o.p.; pap., Puffin, $5.99: 0-14-032944-7. (Grades 5–8)

This inventive romp, part mystery story and part slapstick comedy, stretches both the reader's imagination and sense of humor. The residents of the town of Pineapple are fed up with the antics of the Figg family particularly when young Mona Lisa Newton, daughter of Sister Figg Newton, wanders around town dressed in billowed oversized clothes balanced on her Uncle Florence's shoulders pretending to be a fearsome giant. Mona's family, the Fabulous Figgs, settled in Pineapple after a less-than-illustrious career in show business and the town has never recovered. Along with Mona's tap-dancing, baton-twirling mother, her relatives include Uncle Truman, "the Human Pretzel" who is able to bite his own toenails but now makes a living painting signs with misspelled words; Uncles Romulus, "the Walking Book of Knowledge" and Remus, the "Talking Adding Machine," who bills himself as "the world's greatest C.P.A."; and Uncle Kadota Figg, formerly part of an act with his Nine Performing Kanines, but now a practicing veterinarian with a mail order degree; and a son named Fido, who is Mona's age. Mona, a sullen, moody girl, loves only her midget Uncle Florence Italy Newton, a tenderhearted, loving bookseller, and an aspiring pianist. When the old man dies, and supposedly goes to Capri, the Figgs' idea of heaven, Mona is inconsolable. Isolated in her room, she develops a psychosomatic illness. In one of her feverish nightmares, she searches for Flo in Capri and after exploring many fears and wishes from her subconscious, finally finds him well and happy. When she is awakened from her dream by the sound of her mother's tap-dancing, she is surrounded by loving relatives. Cleansed by the experience, she is now able to face reality.

Newbery Winner 1976

Cooper, Susan. *The Grey King*. McElderry, 1975, $17.00: 0-689-50029-7; pap., Aladdin, $3.95: 0-689-50029-7. (Grades 4–8)

> Susan Cooper (1935–) spent the first 18 years of her life about 20 miles from London in Buckinghamshire. Her other home was Aberdovey in North Wales, where her grandmother was born. During the blitz of World War II, she found that she enjoyed writing and turned to the old tales of England and Wales for inspiration. About her books she says, "They simply appear and grow, out of the great jumble of English and Celtic myth and legend that my subconscious has acquired over the years." Her major contribution has been a five-volume series, The Dark Is Rising, which is also the title of the second book and a Newbery Honor Book (see "Honor Books," 1974, p. 306). About the series, the author said in her Newbery Award acceptance speech:

>> The underlying theme of my Dark Is Rising sequence, and particularly of its fourth volume *The Grey King*, is, I suppose, the ancient problem of the duality of human nature. The endless coexistence of kindness and cruelty, love and hate, forgiveness and revenge—as inescapable as the cycle of life and death, day and night, the Light and the Dark.

In the fifth and final volume, *Silver on the Tree* (McElderry, 1980, $14.95), the Dark rises for the last time and produces a final confrontation with the forces of the Light. All of the Drew children are involved in the complex plot during which Bran bids farewell to Arthur when he chooses mortal life and humanity instead of myth and legend.

Plot Summary

Will Stanton, an 11-year-old English boy, is the last born of the Old Ones, servants of the Light, who are immortals dedicated to saving the world from domination by the evil force known as the Dark. In this fourth of The Dark Is Rising series, Will goes to Wales to recover from a severe case of hepatitis. According to an old North Wales tradition, a boy followed by a white dog with silver eyes will find a harp of gold within a certain hill. The dog can see the wind. Will seeks to recover the harp of gold, whose song will rouse the Sleepers by the Pleasant Lake. The Sleepers will ride forth as part of the host of the Light and engage in the last great battle between the Light and the Dark.

Will is aided in his quest by Bran Davies, a boy his own age whose father herds sheep on the farm of Will's uncle David Evans. Bran has golden eyes and his eyebrows and hair are white. Will soon learns that Bran has been told by the first of the Old Ones, Merriman, that he must help Will in his quest. First, they must battle the Grey King who lives in the peaks of Cader Idris, one of the highest mountains in Wales. The Grey King is one of the Great Lords of the Dark, the Brenin Llwyd.

The boys are guided in their search by verses that have been put into Will's head. They travel to the Grey King along an old pilgrim trail, Cadfan's Way, accompanied by Bran's dog Cafall. When they enter the oldest of the hills through Bird Rock, they are confronted by three figures, one of whom is Merriman, robed in different shades of blue. They are the Lords of the High Magic. After answering three riddles put to them by the robed figures, the boys open a carved chest to discover the golden harp, which means that the first part of the quest has been completed.

But the Grey King is another matter entirely. He puts many obstacles in their way such as the North Wind in all its fury, but it is stopped by the song of the harp. Next, the foxes—seen only by Will and Bran—attack them and the sheep. They take over the body of a mean neighboring farmer, Caradog Prichard, who is induced to kill Bran's beloved dog with the silver eyes.

With the help of a kind shepherd, John Rowlands, Will is able to rouse the Sleepers. The boys learn Bran's true identity. He is Pendragon, the true son of King Arthur and Queen Guinevere. He has been brought forward in time as a baby to grow up in the twentieth century. Will understands that it is his destiny to support and aid Bran.

In a last battle, Will meets the Grey King at Llyn Mwyngil, or Pleasant Lake, below his stronghold. The Grey King tries to win by channeling his immense power through Caradog Prichard, but Will is able to play the harp and awaken the Sleepers. Six horsemen clad in silver-grey speed from the slopes of Cader Idris. They ride over the lake without touching the water. After saluting Bran, they ride into the sky and away from the valley. Prichard, however, is able to grab the harp and fling it into the lake. As he does, his mind snaps and the Dark's powers are gone forever. The quest is completed.

Themes and Subjects

Celtic folklore strengthens the plot, and fantasy and realism are blended into a compelling drama that relies more on setting and atmosphere than on action for its appeal. The characters are well drawn and the incidents are plausible, with the excitement of the drama building at the end. Although Will is the protagonist, Bran is by far the more interesting character. The powerful theme of the struggle between good and evil is woven throughout the book. Folklore, setting, and mythic atmosphere blend to permeate the story with a sense of timelessness.

Incidents for Booktalking

Many scenes will give the folklore flavor of the story. See: Will meets Bran and his dog (pp. 31–33); they meet Prichard (pp. 43–46); fire on the mountain (pp. 65–79); they meet the hooded figures (pp. 89–98); Will and the Grey King (pp. 134–38).

Related Titles

Doug and his younger sister discover a hidden tunnel where a race of weird underground people live in William Sleator's *The Beasties* (Dutton, 1997, $15.99: 0-525-45598-1).

When Laurel Wang moves to a new house, she wants the guardian spirit of the great grandfather to accompany her in *The Golem and the Dragon Girl* (Dial, 1993, $14.89: 0-8037-1281-2) by Sonia Levitin.

In the charming fantasy *The Warm Place* (Orchard, 1995, $15.95: 0-531-06888-9) by Nancy Farmer, a young giraffe named Rura finds her way back to Africa from a zoo near San Francisco.

In John Bellairs's *The Doom of the Haunted Opera* (pap., Viking, $4.99: 0-14-037657-7), Lewis and his buddy Roe Rita Pottinger let loose an evil spirit in an abandoned theater.

Nine familiar stories about King Arthur and the Knights of the Round Table are retold in Michael Morpurgo's *Arthur: High King of Britain* (Harcourt, 1995, $22.00: 0-15-200080-1).

About the Book and Author

Berger, Laura Standley, ed. *Twentieth-Century Young Adult Writers*. St. James, 1994, pp. 150–52.

Brown, Muriel W., and Rita S. Foudray. *Newbery and Caldecott Medalists and Honor Book Winners: Bibliographic & Resource Material Through 1991*. 2d ed. Neal-Schuman, 1992, 182–84.

Chevalier, Tracy, ed. *Twentieth-Century Children's Writers*. 3d ed. St. James, 1989, pp. 231–32.

Commire, Anne, ed. *Something About the Author*. Vol. 4. Gale, 1973, pp. 56–57.

de Montreville, Doris, and Elizabeth D. Crawford, eds. *Fourth Book of Junior Authors and Illustrators*. Wilson, 1978, pp. 98–99.

Evory, Ann, ed. *Contemporary Authors (First Revision Series)*. Vols. 29–32. Gale, 1978, p. 138.

Gallo, Donald R. *Speaking for Ourselves*. National Council of Teachers of English, 1990, pp. 54–56.

Hile, Kevin S., and E. A. DesChenes, eds. *Authors and Artists for Young Adults*. Vol. 13. Gale, 1994, pp. 47–56.

Helbig, Alethea K., and Agnes R. Perkins, eds. *Dictionary of American Children's Fiction, 1960–1984*. Greenwood, 1986, p. 130 (bio.).

Kingman, Lee, ed. *Newbery and Caldecott Medal Books: 1976–1985 with Acceptance Papers, Biographies and Related Material*. Horn Book, 1985, pp. 3–17.

Lesniak, James G., ed. *Contemporary Authors (New Revision Series)*. Vol. 37. Gale, 1992, pp. 99–102.

Metzger, Linda, ed. *Contemporary Authors (New Revision Series)*. Vol. 15. Gale, 1985, pp. 88–89.

Nakamura, Joyce, ed. *Something About the Author: Autobiographical Series*. Vol. 6. Gale, 1988, pp. 67–86.

"Newbery Award Acceptance Material, 1976." *Horn Book* 52, no. 4 (August 1976): 361–72.

Peterson, Linda K., and Marilyn L. Solt, eds. *Newbery and Caldecott Medal and Honor Books: 1922–1981*. Hall, 1982, pp. 205–6.

Senick, Gerard J., ed. *Children's Literature Review*. Vol. 4. Gale, 1982, pp. 41–49.

Silvey, Anita, ed. *Children's Books and Their Creators*. Houghton, 1995, pp. 168–69.

Ward, Martha ed. *Authors of Books for Young People*. 3d ed. Scarecrow, 1990, p. 149.

Honor Books 1976

Mathis, Sharon Bell. *The Hundred Penny Box*. Illustrated by Leo Dillon and Diane Dillon. Viking, 1975, $15.00: 0-870-3878-8; pap., Puffin, $4.99: 0-14-032169-1. (Grades 3–6)

This short story, beautifully illustrated with full-page drawings in sepia tones, tells of the loving relationship between a young black boy, Michael John Jefferson, and his great-great-aunt Dewbet Thomas. Aunt Dew, who raised Michael's father John as a child, is now frail at 100 years of age and has been brought from Atlanta to live with the Jeffersons. Among her possessions is a scratched wooden box with a broken top that contains a penny for each year of her life. Although she is growing senile and sometimes confuses Mike with John as a child, Mike adores the old lady and is fascinated with the stories she tells associated with each penny beginning with 1875. As Aunt Dew says, "Year I was born. Slavery over. Black men in Congress running things. It was Reconstruction." She tells Mike of her deceased husband Henry Thomas, and how he put the first 56 pennies in the box before his death. Other stories involve her own five sons and John as a young boy. Mike's mother, Ruth, who is totally ignored by Aunt Dew, wants to burn the ugly box, but as Dew tells Mike, "When I lose my hundred penny box, I lose me." In an angry confrontation with his mother, Mike saves the box and later curls up in bed with his aunt. The old lady is so fragile and weak that Mike is fearfull he will not have the privilege of placing the one-hundred and first penny in the box. He gently asks Aunt Dew, "How do you get to be a hundred years old?" and her answer is "First you have to have a hundred penny box."

Yep, Laurence. *Dragonwings*. Harper, 1975, $14.89: 0-06-026738-0. (Grades 6–9)

Based on a actual incident in which a Chinese immigrant made a flying machine and flew it on September 22, 1909, this novel re-creates a fascinating period in San Francisco history and describes the customs and culture of Chinese Americans. The narrator, Moon Shadow Lee, is only eight when he leaves China to join his father, Windrider, whom he has never known. His escort is Hand Clap, part-owner of the laundry in San Francisco where his father works. In America, Moon Shadow meets the other owners, White Deer, a cook, and Uncle Bright Star, whose son Black Dog is a vicious opium addict. After Black Dog robs and beats Moon Shadow, Windrider seeks revenge. In the ensuing melee he kills a man, which results in father and son being banished from the Tang community, Chinatown, to find lodgings with the white people, known as "demons." They take up residence in a stable behind Miss Whitlaw's boarding house on Polk Street, where Windrider becomes a general repair man and janitor and spends his spare time building and flying gliders. Miss Whitlaw's niece, Robin, teaches Moon Shadow to read and write and helps him construct a letter to the Wright brothers that results in their sending plans to help his father build his own flying machine. During the earthquake of 1906, both the boarding house and the laundry are destroyed and father and son help dig out survivors from the wreckage. Windrider decides to build an airplane, *Dragonwings,* to fulfill a vision he once had in which the Dragon King granted him wings. After three years of obsessive work, he is successful, and now feels free to devote time to his real love, the family. He accepts a partnership in the laundry and the next summer goes to China to bring back Moon Shadow's mother.

Newbery Winner 1977

Taylor, Mildred D. *Roll of Thunder, Hear My Cry*. Dial, 1976, $15.00: 0-8037-7473-7; pap., Puffin, $4.99: 0-14-034893-X. (Grades 6–10)

Mildred Taylor (1943–) was born in Jackson, Mississippi, but has lived most of her life in the North. While doing graduate work in journalism at the University of Colorado, she organized their first Black Studies program and later served as a teacher of English and history in the Peace Corps in Ethiopia. Her major contribution to children's literature is the creation of a series of novels about the Logan family. The series reflects the southern black experience from the economic depression of the 1930s into the 1950s. *Roll of Thunder* is the second installment. It was preceded by a book for a younger audience, *Song of the Trees* (Dial, 1975, $13.95) and followed by *Let the Circle Be Unbroken* (Dial, 1981, $15.95). In the latter, several plot threads of *Thunder* are resolved and new ones introduced. Some highlights are: T. J. is tried and sentenced to death, another victim of Southern white justice; Stacey has a harrowing experience on a sugar-cane plantation and comes back more dead than alive; and old Miss Lee Annie tries unsuccessfully to register to vote. In her Newbery Award acceptance speech, Taylor comments on the similarity between the Logans and her own family.

> Through David Logan have come the words of my father, and through the Logan family the love of my own family. If People are touched by the warmth of the Logans, it is because I had the warmth of my own youthful years from which to draw. . . . I have tried to make the Logans an embodiment of the spiritual heritage; for contrary to what the media relate to us, all Black families are not father-less or disintegrating. Certainly my family was not.

Plot Summary

The Logan family consists of mother and father; grandmother, who is called Big Ma; and Cassie and her three brothers, Stacey, Christopher-John, and Clayton, the baby who is nicknamed Little Man. It is the height of the Depression. High taxes and the mortgage on their house and land have forced the father to take a job away from home on the railroad. The family makes ends meet with his salary, plus what Mrs. Logan earns as schoolteacher, and the small amount they get from their cotton crop.

In many ways, however, the Logans are more fortunate than their sharecropper neighbors, who work on the plantation owned by Harlan Granger and who are en-slaved by debt to the local store, operated by the three redneck Wallace brothers and controlled by Granger. The black adults live in economic and social slavery, and in constant fear of night riders, usually led by the Wallaces. The most recent raid on the Berry property left one dead and two others badly burned.

The children also suffer discrimination and prejudice—they must walk to their rundown, segregated school while white children ride on a bus to the attractive, well-equipped Jefferson Davis school. The black children receive only outdated textbooks and their school year is shortened so they can be sent to work in the cotton fields.

During one of his stays at home, Mr. Logan brings with him a giant of a man, Mr. Morrison, to work for them and help protect the family. He is quickly welcomed into the warm family circle.

Although they know that Granger is anxious to own their property, the Logans courageously decide to help the sharecroppers by putting up their land as collateral for establishing credit so their neighbors can buy supplies at lower interest in the city of Vicksburg. A liberal white lawyer and friend, Mr. Jamison, knows that this will make them vulnerable to a takeover by Granger. Instead, he volunteers to underwrite the credit note. Soon the Logans have organized 30 families in the cooperative venture, and each week they take orders and travel to Vicksburg to do their buying. When the white establishment hears of this, the harassment begins.

T. J. Avery, one of the sharecropper's sons, is a pupil in Mrs. Logan's seventh-grade class. His cheating and bad behavior constantly get him into trouble. When he fails his first-term examination, he tells everyone at Wallace's store that the cause is Mrs. Logan's poor teaching. Granger uses this as an excuse to have her fired.

Through eviction and foreclosure threats, families are forced to drop out of the cooperative. Finally, only seven families remain. Mr. Logan, along with Morrison and Stacey, decide to make the trip by horse and wagon to Vicksburg. One of their enemies has tampered with the wagon and as a result, Mr. Logan's leg is broken. They are attacked and shot by night riders, but Morrison drives them off. In a final effort to get the Logans, Granger arranges to foreclose on their mortgage, but an appeal to Mr. Logan's brother in Chicago brings a visit from Uncle Hammer who brings the necessary cash.

In the meantime, Cassie is fighting her own battles. She is publicly humiliated by being forced unjustly to apologize to a spiteful white girl, Lillian Jean, for an imagined slight. Cassie then gains the confidence of Lillian Jean, who tells her about her boyfriends and all the local gossip. One day Cassie forces an apology from Lillian Jean by threatening to tell all the girl's secrets. Revenge is sweet for Cassie.

Ignored by the black children because of his role in Mrs. Logan's dismissal, T. J. begins to associate with two cynical white boys, Lillian Jean's brothers R. W. and Melvin. The three make a robbery attempt on a local store. When it fails and the owner and his wife are beaten, the boys blame T. J. A lynch mob visits the Averys. To save T. J. and divert the crowd, Mr. Logan sets fire to his own cotton fields. Fearing that the fire will spread, the men rush off to fight it, and T. J. is whisked off to jail. When the fire is put out, Mr. Logan has lost one-quarter of his crop, but their homestead has been saved and another crisis has passed.

Themes and Subjects

The qualities of indomitability and dignity pervade this novel. In the preface, the author explains how she learned from her own family to respect her own heritage and her people, who, although not free, would not allow their spirits to be enslaved. The reader will also enjoy getting to know the wonderful Logan family, especially the courageous Cassie.

Incidents for Booktalking

A description of the period, setting, and the Logans themselves will introduce the novel. Some representative passages are: Little Man receives his first textbook (pp. 22–25); the school bus incident (pp. 50–55); Cassie is humiliated (pp. 114–16); Mr. Jamison backs the credit note (pp. 160–65); Stacey tells of the attack on the wagon (pp. 214–17).

Related Titles

Junebug lives in the projects and takes care of his little sister, Tasha, while his mother works in Alice Mead's *Junebug* (Farrar, 1995, $14.00: 0-374-33964-3; pap., Dell, $4.99: 0-440-91275-X).

With the help of her family and housekeeper, 10-year-old Rachel copes with problems of friendship and racism in *Learning by Heart* (Houghton, 1993, $14.95: 0-395-65369-X) by Ronder Thomas Young.

Ludell (Harper, 1975, $14.89: 0-06-026492-6) by Brenda Wilkinson is the tender story of a girl's year in the fifth grade in a southern segregated school during in the mid-1950s.

In the Civil War novel *Pink and Say* (Philomel, 1994, $15.95: 0-399-22671-0) by Patricia Polacco, a former slave is killed after saving the life of a young white soldier.

A young Vietnamese woman is forced to leave her homeland in this novel that spans 50 years, *Lotus Seed* (Harcourt, 1993, $15.00: 0-15-249465-0; pap., $6.00: 0-15-201483-7) by Sherry Garland.

About the Book and Author

Berger, Laura Standley, ed. *Twentieth-Century Young Adult Writers*. St. James, 1994, pp. 635–36.

Brown, Muriel W., and Rita S. Foudray. *Newbery and Caldecott Medalists and Honor Book Winners: Bibliographic & Resource Material Through 1991*. 2d ed. Neal-Schuman, 1992, pp. 413–14.

Chevalier, Tracy, ed. *Twentieth-Century Children's Writers*. 3d ed. St. James, 1989, pp. 951–52.

Collier, Laurie, and Joyce Nakamura, eds. *Major Authors and Illustrators for Children and Young Adults*. Gale, 1993, 6 vols., pp. 2275–77.

Commire, Anne, ed. *Something About the Author*. Vol. 15. Gale, 1979, pp. 275–77.

Estes, Glenn E., ed. "American Writers for Children Since 1960: Fiction." In *Dictionary of Literary Biography*. Vol. 52. Gale, 1986, pp. 364–68.

Helbig, Alethea K., and Agnes R. Perkins, eds. *Dictionary of American Children's Fiction, 1960–1984*. Greenwood, 1986, pp. 648–49 (bio.).

Hile, Kevin S. *Authors and Artists for Young Adults*. Vol. 10. Gale, 1993, pp. 201–08.

Holtze, Sally Holmes, ed. *Fifth Book of Junior Authors and Illustrators*. Wilson, 1983, pp. 307–9.

Kingman, Lee, ed. *Newbery and Caldecott Medal Books: 1976–1985 with Acceptance Papers, Biographies and Related Material*. Horn Book, 1985, pp. 18–34.

Locher, Frances C., ed. *Contemporary Authors*. Vols. 85–88. Gale, 1980, p. 579.

Meet the Newbery Author: Mildred Taylor. SRA/McGraw-Hill, 1990. Videocassette.

"Newbery Acceptance Material, 1977." *Horn Book* 53, no. 4 (August 1977): 401–14.

Olendorf, Donna, and Diane Telgen, eds. *Something About the Author*. Vol. 70. Gale, 1993, pp. 222–26.

Sarkissian, Adele, ed. *Something About the Author: Autobiographical Series*. Vol. 5. Gale, 1988, pp. 267–86.

Senick, Gerard J., ed. *Children's Literature Review*. Vol. 9. Gale, 1985, pp. 223–29.

Silvey, Anita, ed. *Children's Books and Their Creators*. Houghton, 1995, pp. 638–39.

Taylor, Mildred. "Acceptance Speech for the 1997 ALAN Award." *The Alan Review* (Spring 1998): 2–3.

Taylor, Mildred D. *Roll of Thunder, Hear My Cry*. Read by Lynne Thigpen. Penguin Audiobooks, 1996. Audiocassettes, 480 min. ($21.33)

———. *Roll of Thunder, Hear My Cry*. Starring Claudia McNeil and Morgan Freeman. Library Video Co. 1976. VHS videocassette, 115 min. ($14.95)

———. *Roll of Thunder, Hear My Cry*. SRA/McGraw-Hill, 1978. Audiocassette. ($21.33)

Ward, Martha, ed. *Authors of Books for Young People*. 3d ed. Scarecrow, 1990, pp. 1091–92.

Honor Books 1977

Bond, Nancy. *The String in the Harp*. Atheneum, 1976, $19.00: 0-689-500360-X; pap., Aladdin, $4.95: 0-689-80445-8. (Grades 6–9)

This fantasy combines a story of friendship and family problems with interesting elements of Welsh folklore. Fifteen-year-old Jen Morgan is excited at the prospect of spending Christmas in Wales with her widowed father, David, an American university professor who is there on a one-year visiting professorship at the coastal university in Aberystwyth. She will also be reunited, if only for three weeks, with her two younger siblings, 12-year-old Peter and 10-year-old Becky who have accompanied their father. After Jen arrives in the small village of Borth, where her family is living, she discovers tensions in the family. Becky has adjusted to the new environment and made some friends including the loner Gwilym Davies, a boy fascinated with local birds, and Rhian Evans, a schoolmate who lives on a nearby sheep farm. Peter, however, feels lonely and wants to go home. He constantly quarrels with his father who is distant and wrapped up in his work.

Peter finds a magic key on the seashore that hums on contact and produces visions of a Wales of long ago. In consecutive episodes, he witnesses important episodes in the life of an ancient bard, Taliesin. Without revealing his secret, Peter learns from Dr. Rhys, a folklorist, that Taliesin was a famous sixth-century bard and that the Key is actually a tuning instrument for an ancient harp. When Taliesin's story is told, the Key loses its magical powers and Peter places it in the bard's sacred burial cairn. These experiences plus Jen's guiding hand help Peter adjust to Wales. When Mr. Morgan is offered a contract for the following year, the entire family, including Jen and even Peter, enthusiastically decides to stay on.

Steig, William. *Abel's Island*. Illustrated by the author. Farrar, 1976, $15.00: 0-374-30010-0; pap., $4.95: 0-374-40016-4. (Grades 3–7)

Written in formal, Victorian style with witty, cartoon-like drawings, this is a charming takeoff on the survival story popular with children since *Robinson Crusoe*. Abelard Hassam di Chiroco Flint of the Mossville Flints is a gentlemanly mouse used to the idle life including croquette playing with his beloved wife, Amanda. One day, during a violent rainstorm he gallantly tries to retrieve Amanda's scarf, and, instead is swept away by a surging river. He finds himself alone on an island. Being a resourceful mouse, Abel tries various ways to escape, such as constructing two types of boats, building a rope bridge, and fashioning a rock causeway. All fail and Abel must adjust to a solitary life on the island. He collects and stores a variety of foods, learns to make a fire, weaves clothes of grass, and builds himself a comfortable home in a hollow log. His artistic instincts lead to sculpting a series of clay statues of loved ones including Amanda. A narrow brush with a ravenous owl makes him careful of predators. In the spring, he has a visitor, Gower Glackens, an old frog with a faulty memory. Gower leaves in June but forgets to send Abel the help he promised. During the driest part of late summer, Abel swims to the mainland. During his year on the island, he has indeed proven himself able. When freedom seems assured, he is caught by a marauding cat, but again he uses his ingenuity to escape. Amanda is out when he arrives home. When she returns, she finds a freshly bathed, elegantly dressed husband awaiting her. Before they embrace, Abel, in a classic understatement says, "I've brought you back your scarf."

⟨⟩ Newbery Winner 1978

Paterson, Katherine. *Bridge to Terabithia*. 1977, Crowell, $15.95: 0-690-01359-0; pap., Trophy, $3.95: 0-06-44184-7. (Grades 5–8)

Katherine Paterson (1932–) was born and spent her childhood in the Orient, the locale of her first three novels for young people. Her fourth, *Bridge to Terabithia*, has a contemporary setting and tells about the special friendship between Leslie and Jess, two fifth-graders, and how after Leslie's tragic and unexpected death, Jess passes painfully through the various phases of grieving until acceptance comes. The story is based on fact. Ms. Paterson's young son David had a close friendship with a young girl, Lisa Hill, who was struck and killed by lightning. As the author states in her Newbery Award acceptance speech, "David went through all the classical stages of grief, inventing a few the experts have yet to catalog. In one of these he decided that because Lisa had been good, God had not killed her for her sins but as a punishment for him." Distressed and at times overwhelmed by this situation, Ms. Paterson decided to write out the problem in novel form. This process was also painful and upsetting, particularly when she reached the point of Leslie's death. The final result was catharsis for the author and a moving reading experience that, over the years, continues to touch the hearts of youngsters. The author's *The Great Gilly Hopkins* was a Newbery Honor Book (see "Honor Books," 1979, p. 332) and she received a second Newbery Medal in 1981 for *Jacob Have I Loved* (p. 338).

Plot Summary

Terabithia is a secret place, a magic world inhabited only by best friends Jess and Leslie. For Jess, it opens up a world far more glorious than his own or even Terabithia itself. It comes about in this way:

Ten-year-old Jesse Aarons is a loner who likes to draw and would like to become an artist. Neither parent approves of that ambition, and Jess knows that his father regards him as somewhat of a sissy. They live in rural Virginia. His father is a construction worker and his mother has her hands full with Jess and his four sisters. The two older sisters are bossy and the youngest is only an infant. Six-year-old May Belle adores Jess and he tolerates her. Jess's only other interest is in running, which he practices daily in the cow pasture. He is going to be the best runner in the fifth grade. Jess knows his father will be proud of that.

It does not work out that way. Just before school begins, a new family moves into the old Perkins place on the adjoining farm. When Jess first sees his new neighbor, he does not know whether she is a boy or girl. Leslie Burke has short hair and wears jeans and sneakers and does not seem to care what she looks like. She is also a runner—the only girl runner in the whole class—and she beats everybody.

After Jess defends Leslie from a seventh-grade bully, they become fast friends. He learns that her life is very different from his own. Her parents are writers who have moved to the country to "reassess their values." They have no money worries and no television, and scuba diving is Leslie's favorite pastime. Leslie's vivid imagination opens up an entirely new world to Jess, who is astounded and delighted by the scope of her reading and knowledge. He is introduced to her world of books and the people who live in them. She, in turn, admires his ability to draw and encourages it.

Leslie decides that what they need is a special place of their own. They find Terabithia, their hut in the woods, which is reached by swinging on a rope tied to a tree across a ditch. Leslie develops a special language for Terabithia. As she says, "Even the rulers of Terabithia come into it only at times of greatest sorrow or of greatest joy. We must strive to keep it sacred. It would not do to disturb the Spirits."

Jess's world expands to become more exciting and fun-filled than it has ever been. Leslie benefits from his friendship, which makes school bearable for her. They manage to get even with fat Janice Avery, a seventh-grader who picks on little May Belle. They write a love note to her, supposedly from a boy she really likes, but later Leslie discovers Janice crying in the girls' room and learns that her father beats her. Influenced by Jess's kindness toward people, Leslie now befriends the girl.

Adding to his happiness comes a perfect day for Jess. His music teacher takes him to Washington, D.C., where he visits the Smithsonian and the National Gallery. It is a day he will never forget, partly because of the tragedy that confronts him when he returns home. His beloved Leslie is dead. She was crossing over to Terabithia on the rope, it broke, and she was killed by the fall.

Jess goes through various stages of reaction to her death. He is shocked and does not believe it. He realizes that now he will be the best runner in the fifth grade and then is filled with guilt for the thought. He is stricken with sobbing, stormy grief, but realizes how proud he is to have been singled out as her friend. She has shaped his life forever and he will never forget her. When her parents move away, they give him Leslie's books.

At Terabithia, Jess builds a pine memorial to his friend. When he hears May Belle's voice, he realizes that she has followed him, but she is stuck crossing the ditch to Terabithia and nearly falls in. Jess rescues her and takes her home.

Days later, Jess returns to Terabithia and builds a plank across the ditch. He will share this most secret place with his little sister. He puts flowers in her hair and takes her across the plank. "Look," he says. "Where?" she answers. "Can't you see 'um? All the Terabithians standing on tiptoe to see you." "Me?" "Shhh, yes," he replies. "There's a rumor going around that the beautiful girl arriving today might be the queen they've been waiting for."

Themes and Subjects

Love, friendship, death, sorrow, and growing up are all part of this tender story. Most moving are Jess's many reactions to Leslie's death as he tries to come to grips with his horrifying loss. His maturing and healing begin as he leads his little sister to their secret place to share that world with her. Jess will always be a better person for having known Leslie, and the world she has opened up to him will never be closed again. The reactions of two totally different families are well portrayed as the Burkes try to deal with their loss partly by giving Leslie's beloved books to her friend, and the awkward but sincere attempts by Jess's parents to console him for his loss.

Incidents for Booktalking

The strong theme of this book is the friendship between Jess and Leslie in its different, maturing forms. See: Jess does not know whether the newcomer is a boy or girl (pp. 16–18); Leslie wins the race (pp. 26–28); Terabithia (pp. 38–43); Jess visits the Burke home (p. 45); getting even with Janice (pp. 50–56); Jess gives Leslie a present (pp. 60–64); Jess deals with Leslie's death (pp. 103–10).

Related Titles

Thirteen-year-old Phoebe Harte describes the effects of her brother Mick's death on her family in *Mick Harte Was Here* (Knopf, 1995, $15.00: 0-679-87088-1) by Barbara Park.

In Barbara Garland Polikoff's *Life's A Funny Proposition, Horatio* (Holt, 1994, $14.95: 0-8050-1972-3), a boy grieves his father's death and finds renewal in a small Wisconsin town.

Carol L. Williams's *Adeline Street* (Delacorte, 1995, $18.95: 0-385-30998-8), a sequel to *Kelly and Me* (pap., Dell, $3.50: 0-440-41069-X), chronicles the life of the Orton family for one year after the death of the youngest daughter, Kelly.

Jenny Rutherford confronts the meaning of her mother's death in Patricia Reilly Giff's *Gift of the Pirate Queen* (pap., Dell, $3.99: 0-440-43046-1).

In a story of dreams and imagination, Jamie believes that shadows have helped him save the life of his grandfather in Dennis Haseley's *Shadows* (Farrar, 1991, $12.95: 0-374-36761-2).

About the Book and Author

Berger, Laura Standley, ed. *Twentieth-Century Young Adult Writers*. St. James, 1994, pp. 515–17.

————. *Twentieth-Century Children's Writers*. 4th ed. St. James, 1995, pp. 740–42.

Brown, Muriel W., and Rita S. Foudray. *Newbery and Caldecott Medalists and Honor Book Winners: Bibliographic & Resource Material Through 1991*. 2d ed. Neal-Schuman, 1992, pp. 321–24.

Chevalier, Tracy, ed. *Twentieth-Century Children's Writers*. 3d ed. St. James, 1989, pp. 758–60.

Collier, Laurie, and Joyce Nakamura, eds. *Major Authors and Illustrators for Children and Young Adults*. Gale, 1993, 6 vols., pp. 1828–32.

Commire, Anne, ed. *Something About the Author*. Vol. 13. Gale, 1978, pp. 176–77; Vol. 53, pp. 118–29.

Estes, Glenn E., ed. "American Writers for Children Since 1960: Fiction." In *Dictionary of Literary Biography*. Vol. 521. Gale, 1986, pp. 296–314.

Garrett, Agnes, and Helga P. McCue, eds. *Authors and Artists for Young Adults*. Vol. 1. Gale, 1989, pp. 203–14.

Harte, Barbara, and Carolyn Riley, eds. *Contemporary Authors (First Revision Series)*. Vols. 23–24. Gale, 1970, p. 322.

Helbig, Alethea K., and Agnes R. Perkins, eds. *Dictionary of American Children's Fiction, 1960–1984*. Greenwood, 1986, pp. 501–02 (bio.).

Hipple, Theodore W., ed. *Writers for Young Adults*. Vol. 2. Scribners, 1997, pp. 443–54.

Holtze, Sally Holmes, ed. *Fifth Book of Junior Authors and Illustrators*. Wilson, 1983, pp. 236–38.

Katherine Paterson. Profiles in Literature, 1979. Videocassette.

Kingman, Lee, ed. *Newbery and Caldecott Medal Books: 1976–1985 with Acceptance Papers, Biographies and Related Material*. Horn Book, 1985, pp. 35–49.

McMahon, Thomas, ed. *Authors and Artists for Young Adults*. Vol. 31. Gale, 2000, pp. 85–94.

Meet the Newbery Author: Katherine Paterson. SRA/McGraw-Hill, 1990. Videocassette.

Nasso, Christine, ed. *Contemporary Authors (New Revision Series)*. Vols. 21–24. Gale, 1977, p. 662.

"Newbery Award Acceptance Material, 1978." *Horn Book* 54, no. 4 (August 1978): 361–71.

"Newbery Award Acceptance Material, 1978." *Top of the News* 34, no. 4 (summer 1978): 353–58.

Paterson, Katherine. *Bridge to Terabithia*. Children's Television International. 1989. VHS Videocassette, 15 min. ($24.95)

———. *Bridge to Terabithia*. Starring Annette O'Toole. Public Media, 1990. VHS Videocassette, 55 min. ($29.95)

———. *Bridge to Terabithia.* Read by Tom Stechschulte. Recorded Books, 1997. Audiocassettes, 240 min. ($26.00)

———. *Bridge to Terabithia.* SRA/McGraw-Hill, 1986. Audiocassette. ($21.33)

———. "Confusion at the Crossroads: The Forces that Pull Children and Reality Apart (1997 Anne Carroll Moore lecture)." *School Library Journal* (May 1998): 34–37.

———. "In Search of Wonder (May Hill Arbuthnot Honor Lecture)." *Journal of Youth Services in Libraries.* (Summer 1997): 378–91.

Peterson, Linda K., and Marilyn L. Solt, eds. *Newbery and Caldecott Medal and Honor Books: 1922–1981.* Hall, 1982, pp. 212–13.

Schmidt, Gary D. *Katherine Paterson.* Twayne, 1990.

Senick, Gerard J., ed. *Children's Literature Review.* Vol. 7. Gale, 1984, pp. 224–43.

Silvey, Alita, ed. *Children's Books and Their Creators.* Houghton, 1995, pp. 507–09.

Ward, Martha, ed. *Authors of Books for Young People.* 3d ed. Scarecrow, 1990, p. 551.

Honor Books 1978

Cleary, Beverly. *Ramona and Her Father.* Illustrated by Alan Tiegreen. Morrow, 1977, $16.00: 0-688-22114-9; pap., Dell, $3.25: 0-440-47241-5. (Grades 2–5)

    Set in a small Oregon town in the early 1970s, this is part of the continuing saga of the loving Quimby family. Seven-year-old Ramona Quimby is now in the second grade and her sister, Beezus (short for Beatrice) is in the seventh, and feeling the first pangs of grouchy adolescence. Family relations become somewhat strained when Father loses his job, and Mrs. Quimby must switch from a part- to a full-time job at the doctor's office. Ramona notices that her usually affable father is becoming irritable, smokes nervously, and anxiously awaits phone calls. Hoping to earn a million dollars through television commercials, Ramona begins practicing for a career in show biz, but that ends disastrously when her father cuts the burrs out of her hair that she has used to fashion a crown. When Picky-Picky, Ramona's cat, refuses to eat cheap cat food, Beezus angrily questions the expense. She also comments on the health problems involved in her father's smoking. To help their father quit, Ramona and Beezus begin a campaign by placing "No Smoking" signs around the house and holding their noses when Father lights up. Father gives up the habit only after the campaign is abandoned. Ramona has other diversions in her life: she and her friend Howie Kemp make tin can stilts and parade around town singing "99 Bottles of Beer." After volunteering to be a sheep in the Sunday School Christmas pageant in which Beezus is Mary, Ramona has costume problems. Conditions at home improve when, a few days before Christmas, Father gets a job as a supermarket checker. Ramona is particularly happy during the pageant, when Father gives her a reassuring wink from the audience. In response, she "baas" joyfully and wiggles her seat to make her tail wag. A continuation, *Ramona Quimby, Age 8,* is a 1982 Honor Book (p. 345).

Highwater, Jamake, *Anpao: An American Indian Odyssey*. Illustrated by Fritz Scholder. Lippincott, 1977, $14.00: 0-397-31750-6; pap., Trophy, $6.95: 0-06-440437-4. (Grades 6–10)

This epic narrative chronicles the adventures of Anpao as he pursues his quest to find his love, the beautiful Ko-ko-mik-e-is. In an afterword, "The Storyteller's Farewell," the author supplies valuable background information. Anpao is a fabrication, a hero that has been created to make a connecting thread that links the retellings of a number of North American Indian myths and legends. The author says that he "created Anpao out of the many stories of the boyhood of early Indians . . . in order to make an Indian 'Ulysses' who could become the central dramatic character in the saga of Indian life in North America." No single tribe is represented nor any particular time period. The stories come from many sources; many are ancient but some date to the period after the white man's appearance. Collectively they tell of a journey to manhood and at another level supply an account of the American Indian through history. Ko-ko-mik-e-is, the proud and stunningly beautiful maiden, refuses to marry because the Sun has told her that she belongs to him. When the poor, scarred Anpao boldly requests her hand in marriage she replies that if the Sun grants permission, she will comply. Thus begins Anpoa's long, arduous journey. From an old woman he learns about his origins, that he actually came into being after the union involving the Sun and an Earth mother. As he travels through mountains, prairies, and deserts, he learns from others about himself and his people. In the country of the Sun, he makes friends with Morning Star, the handsome, favored son of the Sun and the Moon. When Anpao saves his half-bother from monstrous birds, the Sun recognizes Anpao as his son and, in gratitude, removes his scar and gives him the permission he requires. After their marriage, Anpao and Ko-ko-mik-e-is live happily ever after in a village below the great water.

Newbery Winner 1979

Raskin, Ellen. *The Westing Game*. Dutton. 1978, $15.95: 0-525-42320-6; pap., Puffin, $4.99: 0-14-038664-5. (Grades 5–8)

Ellen Raskin (1928–1984) began her professional life as an artist and illustrator. The first book she wrote and illustrated was the delightful 1966 picture book, *Nothing Ever Happens on My Block* (pap., Macmillan, $3.95). Its success encouraged her to expand her writing talent into full-length novels for older children. Among these is the amusing *Figs and Phantoms* (see "Newbery Honor Books," 1975, p. 313). Her writing is unique and unconventional in many ways. For example, her style incorporates wonderful plays on words, puns, puzzles, and allusions, and her plots are usually intricate and filled with eccentric characters. This is certainly true of *The Westing Game,* a sophisticated, densely plotted, zany mystery about a strange assortment of heirs trying to uncover the secret of their relative's disappearance and solve the puzzle of his will. Along with an ingenious, intricate plot, it is filled with shifting identities, riddles, complex word plays, literary allusions, and bizarre oddballs. The complexity of the story even confounded the author, who confessed during her Newbery Award acceptance speech, "The plot thickens and thickens but refuses to jell, and I refuse to give up. . . . Knitting and unraveling, knotting and unknotting, I rewrite the manuscript again. And again. At last I find the answer." For readers, the answer is a challenging, entertaining roller-coaster ride of a story that forces one to hang on for dear life.

Plot Summary

Certain specially selected people rent apartments in a glittery, glassy, luxury apartment house in Milwaukee, Wisconsin. Sunset Towers on Lake Michigan is strangely named, for the sun sets in the west and towerless Sunset Towers faces east. A 61-year-old delivery man named Otis Amber hand-delivered invitations to rent to Jake and Grace Wexler, who have two daughters: lovely, dutiful Angela and skinny, pig-tailed, undutiful and teenaged Turtle; to Sydelle Pulaski; to the Theodorakis family and to the Hoos; to Flora Baumbach, a dressmaker; and to J. J. Ford.

From their windows, the tenants can see a mansion on the north cliff. Their apartment is built on land adjoining the old Westing house, which supposedly has not been occupied for 15 years. But Turtle sees smoke coming from it, and soon others see it too. On Halloween night, Turtle enters the old house and finds a dead man tucked in a four-poster bed. The dead man turns out to be millionaire Samuel W. Westing, who disappeared 13 years ago and left an estate of more than $200 billion! Apparently, he has no heirs.

Soon after, the tenants of Sunset Towers are summoned to the south library of the Westing mansion for the reading of the will. They are somewhat surprised to see Westing's corpse in an open coffin dressed as Uncle Sam, even wearing the tall hat. They are even more stunned to hear that Westing calls them his "nearest and dearest, my sixteen nieces and nephews." They are shocked to hear that Westing claims to have been murdered—by one of them! " My life was taken from me," says the will, "by one of you." Whoever finds the murderer will become the heir of his great fortune. "My soul shall roam restlessly until that one is found."

So begins the Westing game. The 16 players are divided into eight pairs. Each pair is given $10,000 and a set of clues. The pairs are Madame Sun Lin Hoo, who does not speak English, and Jake Wexler; Turtle Wexler and dressmaker Flora Baumbach; Christos Theodorakis, who is in a wheelchair, and D. Denton Deere, an intern; doorman Alexander McSouthers, and Judge J. J. Ford, the first black and first woman elected to the state supreme court; Grace Wexler and James Shin Hoo, who owns the restaurant in Sunset Towers; Berthe Erica Crow of the Good Salvation Soup Kitchen, and deliveryman Otis Amber; Theo Theodorakis, brother of Chris, and high-school athlete Doug Hoo; secretary Sydelle Pulaski and Angela Wexler, who is not employed but is engaged to be married.

The players have no idea what to do and no idea what the clues mean. But as the Westing game continues, the players learn that each of them in some way is connected with the deceased Westing, who disappeared after surgery for damage to his face suffered in an automobile accident 13 years earlier. Grace Windsor Wexler, for instance, is Westing's niece. Judge Ford owes her education to the millionaire.

When a severe winter snowstorm makes the 16 tenants housebound, they devote themselves entirely to solving this strange puzzle. Despite all their efforts, plus some thefts and bombings in the apartment, they cannot unravel the mysterious and maddening clues. As they work at this mystery, the tenants discover something vital about themselves, and their lives are changed. Judge Ford, for instance, discovers a way to repay Westing for her education, and dutiful Angela discovers that she is not quite so dutiful after all.

It is up to young Turtle, who suffers from the fact that her mother ignores her, who likes to play the stock market, and who has a nasty habit of kicking in the shins anyone whom she dislikes, to solve the mystery in the end. She learns that Samuel Westing was actually alive when the will was read and was, in fact, their doorman at the apartment house! She also learns that Samuel Westing was a man suffering from a fatal disease, who disguised himself as different personalities and played a game of mystery with these 16 people who all were connected to him in some way before he died.

Themes and Subjects

The theme of *The Westing Game* is a puzzling mystery. The plot and clues are clever but complicated. The tone is witty and fast-paced. Even though the author leaves many clues throughout the book, few readers will unravel the complications of the plot until they are uncovered at the end. However, it is a merry romp with strange, funny, and clever characters. One is unlikely to meet them in real life, but they are fun to read about.

Incidents for Booktalking

Almost any scene sets the tone for this lively, improbable mystery romp. Any of the scenes can set free one's wild imagination. See, for example, the reading of the will (pp. 28–31); the tenants are paired (pp. 32–35).

Related Titles

In P. J. Peterson's *Liars* (Simon, 1992, $15.00: 0-671-75035-6; pap., Aladdin, $3.95: 0-689-800130-0), Sam learns that he has the unusual gift of detecting when people are not telling the truth.

Jane and Dinah have a rocky relationship until they become involved in a mystery about robberies in *Don't Call Me Toad!* (Putnam, 1987, $14.95: 0-399-21706-1; pap., Avon, $2.95: 0-380-70496-X) by Mary Francis Shura.

The amateur sleuth Heruleah Jones and Meat, his sidekick, solve a mystery in the suspenseful *Tarot Says Beware* (Viking, 1995, $13.95: 0-670-85575-8), a sequel to *The Dark Stairs* (Viking, 1994, $13.95: 0-670-85487-5), both by Betsy Byars.

A seven-year-old boy befriends a young ghost after he and his older sister explore Halcyon House, a deserted mansion, in Zilpha Keatley Snyder's *The Trespassers* (pap., Dell, $4.50: 0-440-41277-3).

Zoe Brook is convinced that the new girl in the eighth grade is really an alien in Catherine Dexter's *Alien Game* (Morrow, 1995, $15.00: 0688-11332-X).

About the Book and Author

Berger, Laura Standley, ed. *Twentieth-Century Young Adult Writers*. St. James, 1994, pp. 548–50.

Block, Ann, and Carolyn Riley, eds. *Children's Literary Review*. Vol. 1. Gale, 1976, pp. 155–57.

Brown, Muriel W., and Rita S. Foudray. *Newbery and Caldecott Medalists and Honor Book Winners: Bibliographic & Resource Material Through 1991*. 2d ed. Neal-Schuman, 1992, pp. 337–39.

Chevalier, Tracy, ed. *Twentieth-Century Children's Writers*. 3d ed. St. James, 1989, pp. 808–9.

Collier, Laurie, and Joyce Nakamura, eds. *Major Authors and Illustrators for Children and Young Adults*. Gale, 1993, 6 vols., pp. 1936–39.

Commire, Anne, ed. *Something About the Author*. Gale, 1971, Vol. 2, pp. 209–10; 1985, Vol. 38, pp. 172–80.

Estes, Glenn E., ed. "American Writers for Children Since 1960: Fiction." In *Dictionary of Literary Biography*. Vol. 52. Gale, 1986, pp. 314–24.

Helbig, Alethea K., and Agnes R. Perkins, eds. *Dictionary of American Children's Fiction, 1960–1984*. Greenwood, 1986, p. 542 (bio.), pp. 708–9 (book).

Kingman, Lee, ed. *Newbery and Caldecott Medal Books: 1966–1975 with Acceptance Papers, Biographies and Related Material*. Horn Book, 1975, pp. 50–61.

Lesniak, James G., ed. *Contemporary Authors (New Revision Series)*. Vol. 37. Gale, 1992, pp. 370–73.

May, Hal, ed. *Contemporary Authors*. Vol. 113. Gale, 1985, p. 388.

Nasso, Christine, ed. *Contemporary Authors (New Revision Series)*. Vols. 21–24. Gale, 1972, p. 708.

"Newbery Award Acceptance Material, 1979." *Horn Book* 55, no. 4 (August 1979): 385–89.

"Newbery Award Acceptance Material, 1979." *Top of the News* 35, no. 4 (summer 1979): 401–15.

Olson, Marilyn Strasser. *Ellen Raskin*. Twayne, 1989.

Peterson, Linda K., and Marilyn L. Solt, eds. *Newbery and Caldecott Medal and Honor Books: 1922–1981*. Hall, 1982, pp. 215–16.

Raskin, Ellen. *The Westing Game*. Read by Jeff Woodman. Recorded Books, 1998. Audiocassettes. ($47.00)

Senick, Gerard J., ed. *Children's Literature Review*. Vol. 12. Gale, 1987, pp. 213–29.

Silvey, Anita, ed. *Children's Books and Their Creators*. Houghton, 1995, pp. 549–50.

Honor Books 1979

Paterson, Katherine. *The Great Gilly Hopkins.* Crowell, 1978, $14.95: 0-690-03837-2; pap., Trophyr, $3.95: 0-06-440201-0. (Grades 6–8)

The power of love and the need to face reality are two important themes in this moving often humorous novel about a defiant, imaginative 11-year-old girl who has built emotional defenses around her as impregnable as Gibraltar. Her name is Gilly (Galadriel) Hopkins, and she is being escorted to her umpteenth foster home by Miss Ellis. This home is different from the others. Her foster mother is a large, almost illiterate woman named Maime Trotter who also cares for a timid, sensitive seven-year-old black boy, William Earnest (W. E.) Teague, and feeds blind black neighbor, Mr. Randolph. At first Gilly showers contempt on both her foster home and her new school, where Miss Harris, her teacher, is able to call her bluff. Gilly writes to her absent, ex-flower-child mother, Courtney, in San Francisco begging her to come and rescue her. She receives no answer. In time, Gilly grudgingly responds positively to the love and understanding that Trotter and friends show her, but in one final act of defiance she steals money from Mr. Randolph and Trotter to buy a bus ticket to California. Apprehended at the bus station, she is sent back, and to her astonishment is welcomed lovingly by Trotter. On Thanksgiving day after Gilly has been complimented on the dinner she cooked, Mrs. Rutherford Hopkins arrives. She is Gilly's grandmother and has come at Courtney's request to take Gilly to her home in Virginia. Gilly resists but eventually leaves with the grandmother she's never known. Further disillusionment comes when Courtney visits Gilly at Christmas and proves to be an over-the-hill hippie, who is really not interested in her daughter. Gilly phones Trotter who tells her that though they love one another deeply, Gilly must stay with her lonely grandmother who needs her. Gilly accepts the situation hoping Trotter will be proud of her.

1980s

☙ Newbery Winner 1980

Blos, Joan W. *A Gathering of Days: A New England Girl's Journal, 1830–32*. Scribner, 1979, $15.00: 0-684-16340-3; pap., Aladdin $3.95: 0-689-71419-X. (Grades 4–7)

This novel had its beginnings in a simple event that occurred to Joan Blos (1928–) in 1941. In that year, the parents of her husband bought an old farmhouse in Holderness, New Hampshire. She became interested in tracing the history of the house, and began haunting libraries. In addition to finding that it was built in 1827, she collected a mass of information about the period and became particularly interested in how children lived during those times. She began a fictional journal of Catherine Hall, a girl growing up on a New England farm in the early 1830s. Work progressed slowly and she continued her research and writing even when she moved west to Ann Arbor, Michigan in 1970, where she taught children's literature at the University of Michigan. The book, finally published in 1979, shows the painstaking research and attention to detail that the author lavished on it. Even the writing style is in accurate post-Colonial English, an element that might cause difficulties for some readers. Though rooted in the past, it deals with such universal problems as understanding race relations, adjusting to a stepparent, and coping with the death of a friend. Its central theme, religion versus humanism, as represented by Catherine's authoritarian father and her more sophisticated stepmother, is a struggle that is widespread in contemporary society.

Plot Summary

This is the journal of Catherine Hall, who is 13 years old in October 1830 when she begins to record her life on a small New Hampshire farm. Many years later, when she is nearly 86 years old, she experiences the joy of sharing her journal with her great-granddaughter, also named Catherine. The book title comes from Catherine's last journal entry, made on New Year's Day 1832. It says, "This year, more than others, has been a lengthy gathering of days wherein we lived, we loved, were moved, learned how to accept."

Although Catherine Hall records such small things as recipes and meals, things she learns at school, games she plays outdoors on summer evenings, and stories her elders tell, most of all she writes about her family. Her father, Charles, is a farmer. Her mother, Hannah, died of a fever four years earlier. Catherine has a younger sister, Mary Martha (Matty) and an unmarried Uncle Jack.

333

Catherine's best friend is Cassie Shipman who lives on a neighboring farm with her parents and brothers, David, Asa, and Willie, the baby. Catherine and Cassie tell each other everything.

In November, Cassie's aunt arrives on a visit from Salem. Everyone, including Catherine, calls her Aunt Lucy. Cassie's mother keeps reminding Catherine's father that Lucy is unmarried, but he seems not to respond. By the end of November, even young Matty is speculating on whether their father will marry the woman, but Catherine is more preoccupied with the fact that her lesson book has turned up missing. By early December the lesson book turns up mysteriously with a stranger's words on the cover: "Pleez miss take pitty I am cold."

In this manner, young Catherine first becomes aware of the plight of slaves and the evils of slavery. She and Cassie's brother, Asa, learn that a black man, perhaps a slave, is hiding in the woods. With the help of Cassie, they leave food and an old quilt of Catherine's mother for the stranger. Slowly, Catherine becomes more aware of the plight of slaves and the prejudice of the people around her.

The following spring, Catherine's father and Mr. Shipman make a trip to Boston to trade goods. Principal among their goods is the work of many hours on the farm—maple sugar cut and packed in blocks. Father returns in a week and Catherine and Matty are overjoyed to see him, except for one thing. He brings a letter from Mistress Ann Higham. The note says that Mistress Higham is to marry their father. It also says she has a son Daniel who is Catherine's age!

Although their father is eager for Mistress Higham's arrival, Catherine is not. The two are married in Boston in May, and when they return to the farm, Catherine notes that her stepmother is smaller than expected and plainer. Matty's comment is that young Daniel has freckles inside his ears. Catherine knows that she will not call this woman mother.

Time passes, and the family unit slowly knits. Even as they grow closer, Catherine refuses to call her father's new wife by name. Finally, Daniel comes up with the perfect name by which Matty and Catherine may address his mother. It is "Mammann." That night, Catherine uses it for the first time.

That August, Catherine's dear friend Cassie becomes ill. Catherine thinks that perhaps she got a chill when they were out picking berries the day before. Cassie gets worse, and the doctor must be called. He applies the recommended remedy of leeches, but Cassie grows even more weak and pale. Mammann becomes distressed because another doctor is not called. When she mentions this to Catherine's father, he merely tells her "this is not Boston." Mammann, although upset by this attitude, retains her composure and writes a letter to Boston. She says that she is in need of more knowledge of remedies. "If somewhere in a book, there is knowledge to combat such an illness," should they, she asks, "not inform ourselves against another occasion?"

Cassie improves and everyone is relieved. Then, quite unexpectedly, on the night of August 20, 1831, she dies. Catherine learns the pain of grief.

That September, the issue of slavery comes back into Catherine's life as news reaches New Hampshire of a slave revolt led by Nat Turner. Increasingly there is talk of slavery unrest. Soon, Catherine receives a package in the post. In it are two pieces of crocheted lace, with this message: "Sisters bless you. Free now. Curtis." In this way Catherine knows that the man she, Cassie, and Asa helped was indeed a slave and is now free in Canada. For a time she is puzzled by the two pieces of lace, and then she realizes that he meant one of them for dear, dead Cassie.

Later that year when there is trouble involving physical punishment by the schoolteacher, Mammann decides to resume her own teaching duties. She sends to

Boston for books. Although Daniel and the Shipman boys will continue at the school-house, Catherine and Matty will be taught at home.

Late in December 1831, Aunt Lucy, now married and with a baby due, writes to ask if Catherine would be allowed to come and stay with them for a time in Exeter where her husband teaches at an academy. Although girls cannot attend the school, Catherine will be taught at home, so in March 1832, Catherine leaves the New Hampshire farm for the first time.

Years later she writes a letter to her great-granddaughter after sending the journal to her. She tells young Catherine that often through the years she had hoped to hear from the runaway slave, Curtis, again but never did. Catherine is 86 now and most of the people she wrote about in her journal are dead, except for Cassie's brother, Willie, who just celebrated his 75th birthday! She tells young Catherine that the house and barn where the story takes place have been restored because she wanted to "reconstruct life as it was when the house was new."

Themes and Subjects

This is a quiet, loving, and satisfying story of old-fashioned ways and old-fashioned values. It reads much like a nonfiction journal because in a way it is. The author wove people around a handful of real-life facts plus interest in and knowledge of the region. As a result, the journal entries read true, telling of the simple joys of picking wildflowers or making maple sugar. Interspersed in the everyday happenings is a record of news events of the day—the slave revolt, the growing unrest, and talk about the morals of slavery. There is much hardship reflected in this life of early Americans, especially concerning the limited knowledge of human physical ailments. But there is joy and tranquility too, which is well-captured in this simple picture of people who rely on the love and caring of family and friends for happiness.

Incidents for Booktalking

Many of Catherine's journal entries can spark a discussion of life in early nineteenth-century America. See, particularly: Catherine's lesson book disappears (pp. 17–21); Catherine and Asa are aware of the stranger and decide to do something (pp. 23–30); slavery intrudes into Catherine's life (pp. 45–47); the maple sap is running (pp. 51–55); father goes to Boston and brings back news of a marriage (pp. 67–70); the new mother arrives (pp. 75–77); Catherine calls her stepmother by name for the first time (p. 96); Cassie's illness and death (pp. 106–14); Catherine hears from the runaway slave (pp. 125).

Related Titles

Joan Lowry Nixon has written a fine series about the Orphan Train in pioneer America. *Keeping Secrets* (Delacorte, 1995, $15.95: 0-385-32139-2) tells how 11-year-old Peg Kelly gets herself involved with a Union spy during the Civil War.

In 1888 rural Alabama, a young African American girl helps shelter a fugitive Apache boy in Patricia McKissack's *Run Away Home* (Scholastic, 1997, $14.95: 0-590-46751-4).

In *Stay Away from Simon* (Houghton, 1985, $13.95: 0-89919-343-9; pap., $5.95: 0-89919-849-X), a story set in Martha's Vineyard in the 1830s, Carol Carrick's Lucy finds that mentally retarded Simon is not as dangerous as people believe.

A New England white boy helps a black family escape on the Underground Railroad in F. N. Monjo's *The Drinking Gourd* (pap., Trophy, $3.95: 0-06-44042-7).

Based on fact, Dave Jackson's and Neta Jackson's *Abandoned on the Wild Frontier* (pap., Bethany, $5.99: 1-55661-468-3) tells the story of a young boy's search for his mother, who had been kidnapped by Indians after the War of 1812.

About the Book and Author

Berger, Laura Standley, ed. *Twentieth-Century Children's Writers*. 4th ed. St. James, 1994, pp. 107–8.

————. *Twentieth-Century Young Adult Writers*. St. James, 1994, pp. 58–60.

Blos, Joan W. *A Gathering of Days*. Read by Madeline Potter. Recorded Books, 1992. Audiocassettes, 225 min. ($29.00)

Brown, Muriel W., and Rita S. Foudray. *Newbery and Caldecott Medalists and Honor Book Winners: Bibliographic & Resource Material Through 1991*. 2d ed. Neal-Schuman, 1992, pp. 41–42.

Chevalier, Tracy, ed. *Twentieth-Century Children's Writers*. 3d ed. St. James, 1989, pp. 98–99.

Collier, Laurie, and Joyce Nakamura. *Major Authors and Illustrators for Children and Young Adults*. Gale, 1993, 6 vols. pp. 245–47.

Commire, Anne, ed. *Something About the Author*. Gale, 1982, Vol. 27, p. 35; 1983, Vol. 33, pp. 40–42.

A Gathering of Days. SRA/McGraw-Hill, 1990. Videocassette.

Hedblad, Alan, ed. *Something About the Author*. Vol. 109, Gale, 2000, pp. 29–32.

Helbig, Alethea K., and Agnes R. Perkins, eds. *Dictionary of American Children's Fiction, 1960–1984*. Greenwood, 1986, pp. 54–60 (bio.), pp. 231–32 (book).

Holtze, Sally Holmes, ed. *Fifth Book of Junior Authors and Illustrators*. Wilson, 1983, pp. 35–37.

Kingman, Lee, ed. *Newbery and Caldecott Medal Books: 1976–1985 with Acceptance Papers, Biographies and Related Material*. Horn Book, 1985, pp. 62–73.

Locher, Frances C., ed. *Contemporary Authors*. Vol. 101. Gale, 1981, p. 6.

Nakamura, Joyce, ed. *Something About the Author: Autobiographical Series*. Vol. 11. Gale, 1991, pp. 51–68.

"Newbery Award Acceptance Material." *Top of the News* 36, no. 4 (summer 1980): 393–96.

"Newbery Award Acceptance Material, 1980." *Horn Book* 56, no. 4 (August 1980): 369–77.

Olendorf, Donna, and Diane Telgen, eds. *Something About the Author.* Vol. 69. Gale, 1992, pp. 21–25.

Peterson, Linda K., and Marilyn L. Solt, eds. *Newbery and Caldecott Medal and Honor Books: 1922–1981.* Hall, 1982, pp. 218–19.

Senick, Gerals, ed., *Children's Literature Review.* Vol. 18. Gale, 1989, pp. 14–19.

Silvey, Anita, ed. *Children's Books and Their Creators.* Houghton, 1995, p. 65.

Straub, Deborah A., ed. *Contemporary Authors (New Revision Series).* Vol. 21. Gale, 1987, pp. 52–53.

Ward, Martha, ed. *Authors of Books for Young People.* 3d ed. Scarecrow, 1990, p. 68.

Honor Books 1980

Kherdian, David. *The Road from Home: The Story of an Armenian Girl.* Greenwillow, 1979, $15.95: 0-688-84205-4; pap., $4.95: 0-688-14425-4. (Grades 7–10)

This is a touching first-person narrative biography of the first 17 years of the life of the author's mother (1907–1924) during the barbaric persecution and attempted genocide inflicted on the Armenians by the Turks.

Veron Dumehjian's first seven years were happy ones. She was born into a caring extended family in Azizya, Turkey, where her father was a prosperous Armenian businessman. As a child she enjoys a comfortable life including such luxuries as weekly visits to the Turkish baths. In 1915, the Turks issue an order of deportation for all Armenians using as an excuse their questionable loyalty during World War I. A few fortunate family members are allowed to remain but most are herded together on a forced march to Syria. The inhumane conditions and lack of food take their toll. In the town of Adana, Veron's father, disguised as a Turk in order to purchase food, learns that more than 1 million Armenians have died through massacres and other atrocities. Cholera strikes and many members of Veron's family die. Shortly after the death of her brothers and sister, both her mother and father die of exhaustion and heartbreak. In Aleppo, Veron is cared for by distant relatives and eventually returned to Azizya and her surviving grandmother. During the post-war Greek invasion, Veron is seriously wounded and sent to Smyrna where she lives with her loving Aunt Lousapere. The Greeks are forced to evacuate Smyrna amid incredible scenes of carnage and looting. Miraculously, Aunt Lousapere and Veron are saved and sent to Athens. In time, Veron is contacted by an Armenian couple who are seeking a bride for their American son, Melkon Kherdian. After some hesitation and much negotiation, Veron accepts, looking forward to a new life in the United States. This amazing story of courage and survival is continued in *Finding Home* (Greenwillow, 1981, o.p.).

⚜ Newbery Winner 1981

Paterson, Katherine. *Jacob Have I Loved*. Crowell, 1980, $14.95: 0-690-04078-4; pap., Harper, $4.95: 0-06-447059-8. (Grades 6–10)

Katherine Paterson (1932–) is one of the few authors awarded the Newbery Medal twice. She received it first in 1978 for *Bridge to Terabithia* (p. 323), a tender story of a friendship interrupted by death. She also received Honor Book status for *The Great Gilly Hopkins* in 1979 (p. 332).

The title of *Jacob Have I Loved* is from Romans 9:13 in which the Lord says, "Jacob have I loved, but Esau have I hated," a reference to the bitter rivalry between the twin brothers Jacob and Esau. In the novel this verse is whispered to Louise by her spiteful grandmother and refers to the family situation where, like Esau and his brother Jacob, the narrator appears to have lost her birthright to her beautiful sister Caroline. Except for a brief opening prologue and a few closing pages, the story takes place on small, imaginary, windswept Rass Island in Chesapeake Bay and covers the teenage years of twin sisters during World War II and immediately after. About the emotional truth and appeal of this novel, Ms. Paterson said in her Newbery Award acceptance speech, "I have learned . . . that when I am willing to give myself away in a book, readers will respond by giving themselves away as well, and the book that I labored over so long becomes in our mutual giving something far richer and more powerful than I could have ever imagined."

Plot Summary

Growing up in the 1940s, Louise Bradshaw is a study in contrasts to Caroline, her younger, by a few minutes, twin sister. Caroline, who has given Louise the nickname of Wheeze, is blond, poised, pretty, and vivacious. She is always the center of attention and very aware of that role. Furthermore, she has so much musical talent that her parents have sacrificed financially, first for her piano lessons and later to send her across Chesapeake Bay each week from their home on Rass Island to Salisbury for voice.

Louise is the opposite. She is more thoughtful, withdrawn, and in appearance quite plain and ordinary compared to her twin. She tends to think of others before herself and as a result is often shunted into the background and ignored in spite of the efforts of her loving mother and father. She is an ugly duckling who is becoming increasingly aware of this status and miserable about it.

The girls' father, Truitt, is a sturdy, hardworking waterman, who, in his boat, the *Portia Sue*, combs the bay for crabs and oysters. Their mother, Susan first came to Rass as a young, idealistic schoolteacher and after marriage, remained to raise a family. The other member of the family is their cantankerous, Bible-thumping Methodist grandmother, who, although only in her sixties, is becoming more mean-mouthed and difficult. She openly favors Caroline.

Louise helps supplement the family income by crabbing in her skiff with her friend McCall Purnell, better known as Call. He is one year older than she, and although somewhat unimaginative and plodding, he is her best friend.

When the attack on Pearl Harbor occurs and the country enters World War II, Louise suggests to her teacher Mr. Rice that the school forgo its annual concert for the war effort. She is overruled and made to feel foolish. At the concert, Caroline is, of course, once again the star.

There is great excitement in the island community when one day a distinguished-looking man of about 70 arrives and moves into the deserted Wallace place close to the shore. He is Hiram Wallace, who more than forty years before left his island home after suffering endless humiliation and contempt from the residents because of an act of cowardice during a violent summer storm. At first, Louise imagines that he might be a spy, but when, out of curiosity, she and Call visit him one day, she realizes he is a wise and friendly man who, without family, has come back to Rass to live. She calls him Captain Wallace and all three become close friends and helpmates. Later, much to Louise's dismay, Caroline joins the circle.

In her search for individuality, Louise answers an advertisement and submits a poem to Lyrics Unlimited in the hope of untold riches. The ad proves to be a scam and she is once more frustrated and belittled.

A neighbor and former acquaintance of the Captain, Auntie Trudy Braxton, suffers a stroke and is taken off the island, leaving 16 wild cats to be cared for. Caroline has the brilliant idea of giving them a pacifier and peddling them door to door. The plan works through a combination of her charm, sweet talk, and some beautiful cats.

A hurricane hits the island in 1942, doing great damage and destroying the Captain's house. When he gets the news, in a comforting gesture, Louise puts her arms around the Captain and is alarmed at the feelings of love she experiences. Grandmother notices how Louise feels about the man and in her half-senile way, openly accuses the girl of an improper attachment.

After a short stay with the Bradshaws, the Captain moves into Auntie Braxton's vacant home on a temporary basis. When the old lady is well enough to return from the hospital, helpful Caroline alarms Louise by suggesting a marriage of convenience between the Captain and Auntie Trudy. Both parties agree and once more Louise loses.

As the war progresses, Call turns from a pudgy adolescent into an attractive young man, a phenomenon not unnoticed by Caroline. He quits school to help Mr. Bradshaw on his boat and later leaves to join the navy.

When Trudy Braxton dies, the Captain gives part of her bequest to the Bradshaws to enable Caroline to continue voice lessons up north. Louise suffers pangs of resentment she cannot hide.

While still only in her mid-teens and with the war half over, Louise drops out of school to help her father full-time on his boat while studying at home under her mother's tutelage. The work is sometimes unbearably harsh but is partly compensated for by the opportunity to work closely with her adored father and share his empathy with the sea, a quality that is revealed by his singing to the oysters. At the war's end, Call is demobilized and returns home to New York, where he spends some time with Caroline, now studying at the famed music institute Juilliard. He tells Louise and her family that he and Caroline are engaged and plan to marry soon. Louise valiantly stifles the renewed animosity she feels toward her sister.

Mr. and Mrs. Bradshaw attend the wedding at Christmas 1946, while Louise stays home and prepares a holiday dinner for her crotchety grandmother and the Captain.

As she sinks deeper into a life of bitterness and acrimony, Louise finally realizes she must help herself. With her parents' encouragement, she decides to enter college on the mainland. A climax in her life occurs when, after asking her mother if she will miss her as much as she does Caroline, the reply is "more."

In a brief epilogue, Louise describes her days of self-fulfillment and independence. She becomes a nurse-midwife in a small Appalachian community and meets Joseph, a widower with three small children and the almost unpronounceable last name of Wojtkiewicz. She marries him partly because he seems like the kind of man who would also sing to oysters.

She names her first child Truitt, and after the death of her grandmother and father, she returns to Rass Island to bring her mother back to live with her. Another cycle in life has been completed.

Themes and Subjects

This story tells of the crushing effects of growing up in the shadow of a beautiful, talented sibling, and how a person's fine qualities, if they are neither showy nor superficial, can remain unknown and unappreciated in the process. It also tells of a girl's struggle to conquer feelings of inferiority, resentment, and guilt in order to find a life of fulfillment, confidence, and self-reliance. The strength of family ties is well portrayed, as is the author's brilliant depiction of the hardships and joys of life in a tiny fishing village and of the perennial struggle of humanity against the sea. A youngster's first awakening to love is an interesting subtheme. The use of a World War II setting effectively coincides with Louise's internal war.

Incidents for Booktalking

The concept of the effects of sibling rivalry could lead into an introduction to Louise and Caroline. Some passages of note are: background information about the twins (pp. 14–21; pp. 20–25 pap.); Mr. Rice and the Christmas pageant (pp. 25–30; pp. 28–32 pap.); Call and Louise visit the Captain for the first time (pp. 54–62; pp. 51–57 pap.); a reply from Lyrics Unlimited (pp. 81–82; pp. 72–73 pap.); finding homes for the cats (pp. 92–99; pp. 81–86 pap.); the storm hits (pp. 103–9; pp. 89–94 pap.).

Related Titles

Through the terminal illness of her beloved grandmother, 14-year-old Emmie learns of a past family tragedy in *Toning the Sweep* (Orchard, 1993, $15.95: 0-531-0547604) by Angela Johnson.

When Keely's brother gets polio, she faces a terrible challenge in Julie Johnston's *Hero of Lesser Causes* (Little, Brown, 1993, $15.95: 0-316-46988-2).

La Vaughn takes a job as a baby-sitter and encounters a 17-year-old unwed mother who has two children in *Make Lemonade* (Holt, 1993, $15.95: 0-8050-2228-7) by Virginia Euwer Wolff.

A girl faces the challenge of losing both her mother and her childhood in Carolyn Coman's *Tell Me Everthing* (Farrar, 1993, $15.00: 0-374-37390-6).

Twelve-year-old Buhlaire Sims discovers that her father is not dead but is actually living in her home town in Virginia Hamilton's *Plain City* (Scholastic, 1993, $13.95: 0-590-47364-6).

About the Book and Author

(See also "About the Book and Author," 1978, p. 325)

Kingman, Lee, ed. *Newbery and Caldecott Medal Books: 1976–1985 with Acceptance Papers, Biographies and Related Material.* Horn Book, 1985, pp. 74–92.

"Newbery Award Acceptance Material, 1981." *Horn Book* 57, no. 4 (August 1981): 385–99.

"Newbery Award Acceptance Material, 1981." *Top of the News* 37, no. 4 (summer 1981): 367–73.

Paterson, Katherine. *Jacob Have I Loved.* Starring Bridget Fonda. Library Video Co., 1980. VHS videocassette, 55 min. ($14.95)

————. *Jacob Have I Loved.* Read by Moira Kelly. Harper Audio. Audiocassettes, 175 min. ($16.00)

Peterson, Linda K., and Marilyn L. Solt, eds. *Newbery and Caldecott Medal and Honor Books: 1922–1981.* Hall, 1982, pp. 220–22.

Honor Books 1981

Langton, Jane. *The Fledgling.* Harper, 1980, $15.89: 0-06-023679-5; pap., Trophy, $4.95: 0-06-440121-9. (Grades 4–7)

This satisfying fantasy, set in Concord, Massachusetts combines satisfying family relationships with the teachings of Thoreau and the adventures of a girl who longs to fly. Eleanor and Edward Hall, ages 14 and 12 (central characters in the author's three earlier fantasies), live with their Uncle Freddy Hall, master of the Concord College of Transcendental Knowledge, his wife Aunt Alex, and her eight-year-old daughter, tiny Georgie Dorian. Georgie is convinced she can fly, and after several unsuccessful attempts, she accepts an invitation from a talking Canadian goose to fly around Walden Pond on his back. Nightly the two repeat the same magical ritual with Georgie now able to leave the Goose Prince's back temporarily and glide in solo flight. Convinced that a dangerous goose is in the area, a meddling near-sighted neighbor, Ralph Preek, buys a gun. On the first day of the hunting season, in the predawn hours, he shoots Georgie in the arm and the Goose Prince in the leg while they are in flight. Georgie gradually mends, and believing the hunting season is over, she signals the Goose Prince to return. He does and gives her a present, a small rubber ball he has found at Walden Pond. Unfortunately, because of daylight savings time, Mr. Preek has an extra hour of hunting. After visiting with Georgie, the Goose Prince takes to the air. Believing the goose intends to harm the child, Mr. Preek shoots him. The Goose Prince falls dead at Georgie's feet. Uncle Fred buries the Goose Prince at Walden Pond. When Georgie cannot find the goose's present, she stays in bed for a week grieving both her losses. Later, the ball is located, and she discovers that in the dark it glows and expands into an image of the earth. The Goose Prince has bequeathed the whole world to Georgie.

L'Engle, Madeleine. *A Ring of Endless Light*. Farrar, 1980, o.p.; pap., Dell, $5.50: 0-440-97232-9. (Grades 7–10)

In this, the third of the Austin family series, Vicky Austin, now almost 16, and her mother, father, older brother John and younger sister and brother, are spending the summer at the New England island home of her Grandfather Eaton, a gentle retired man suffering from terminal leukemia. Soon, Vicky becomes involved with three men: the ne'er-do-well, rich playboy, Zachary Gray; Leo Rodney, the son of a recently deceased family friend; and Adam Eddington, an attractive 18-year-old college student who has a summer job studying dolphins under the supervision of Jed Nutteley at the local marine biology station. While juggling dates with her three friends, Vicky also spends precious moments talking and reading to her beloved grandfather. One poem that both love is by Henry Vaughan and contains the lines: "I saw Eternity the other night/Like a great ring of pure and endless light." With Adam, she discovers that because of her naive purity, she can communicate with the dolphins where others are unable to. Through these animals she receives amazing thought sensations and dream pictures that convey different concepts of life and time. Suddenly, her life turns bleak and miserable. Jed is struck by a motorcycle and lies in a coma, her Grandfather is sent to a mainland hospital after suffering several seizures, and the sick child that Vicky is caring for dies in her arms. Though Jed and Grandfather improve, Vicky is unable to shake the terrible melancholy she feels. Through her love for both Adam and her Grandfather as well as the life-giving gentleness of the dolphins, she improves and is once again able to face the future confidently.

Newbery Winner 1982

Willard, Nancy. *A Visit to William Blake's Inn: Poems for Innocent and Experienced Travelers*. Illustrated by Nancy Provensen and Martin Provensen. Harcourt, 1981, $16.00: 0-15-293822-2; pap., $5.95: 0-15-293823-0. (Grades Preschool–4)

Nancy Willard (1936–) began writing poetry at a very early age. Her first published poem appeared when she was seven, and while a high school senior, *Horn Book* published a children's book titled *A Child's Star*, that she both wrote and illustrated. *William Blake's Inn* was the first book of poetry to win the Newbery Award. The wonderful illustrations by the Provensens gained a Caldecott Award Honor Book citation the same year. The work first took shape over several years as a large model of the inn made out of cardboard that later was rebuilt using wood. This model still exists. As Ms. Willard says:

> I constructed most of William Blake's inn and the writing came out of that. . . . You learn about characters as you work on things that belong to them. That certainly happened with *William Blake's Inn*. I made all his companions before I ever found William Blake. But Blake was on my mind. Things came together: listening to Blake's poetry on a record and making a lot of characters for the inn.

The poetry is original, magical, and elegant, and the characters—tigers, lambs, and sunflowers—come directly from Blake. The great beauty of the poems is particularly evident when they are read aloud. In her Newbery acceptance speech, the author said, "The poet writes poems for people to listen to, poems to be heard as well as read. . . . children know the importance of hearing and saying poetry. . . . Do we ever really outgrow that wish to hear a story, to say a poem?"

Plot Summary

To date this is one of only two poetry winners of the Newbery Award. The other is the 1989 winner, *A Joyful Noise*. This book springs from the admiration the author felt for William Blake, who centuries before wrote these wonderful lines: "Tyger, Tyger, burning bright, in the forests of the night, / What immortal hand or eye, / Could frame thy fearful symmetry?" This book of poems centers on an imaginary inn that is run by the great Blake himself.

Marvelous creatures inhabit the inn, including dragons who spend the day brewing and baking so that guests may enjoy their bread with Mr. Blake himself. A wonder of a car brings passengers to the inn. The driver wears a dappled green hat and wings because the car flies. Once at the inn itself, a rabbit shows travelers to their rooms. Instead of a bed, one might find a shaggy old bear to rest upon. Of course there is a marvelous cat who has a prodigious appetite. Once, in the middle of the night, he ate a dozen lobster claws.

There is no end to the wonders of those, including two sunflowers who want a room with a view, that inhabit the marvelous inn of William Blake. As the author says in parting: "You whose journeys now begin, / if you reach a lovely inn, / if a rabbit makes your bed, / if two dragons bake your bread, / rest a little for my sake, / and give my love to William Blake."

Themes and Subjects

Whimsy, laughter, marvelous creatures, and clever verse light up this book of magical poems that create a fantasy world elevated by the enchanted illustrations. Readers of any age cannot help but wish to tarry a while at this inn.

Incidents for Booktalking

Turn to any page to start a discussion of the fantasy created by the William Blake Inn. Who could resist a bear instead of a bed or two dragons instead of bakers to make your morning bread?

Related Titles

New ways of looking at ourselves and our world are explored in the poems by Barbara Esbensen in *Who Shrank My Grandfather's House? Poems of Discovery* (Harper, 1992, $15.00: 0-06-021827-4).

Poems by 129 contemporary poets from 68 countries are arranged by themes such as "Families" and "Losses" in Naomi Shihab Nye's *This Same Sky: A Collection of Poems from Around the World* (Four Winds, 1992, $17.00: 0-02-768440-7).

A boyhood in a small town is celebrated in Paul B. Jancezko's book of poems *Brick-yard Summer* (Orchard, 1989, $14.95: 0-531-05846-8).

Runaway Opposites (Harcourt, 1995, $15.00: 0-15-258722-5) by Richard Wilbur is a fascinating compilation of challenging poems illustrated with collages by Henrik Drescher.

Thoughts and memories involving a variety of childhood activities are in *Remember-ing and Other Poems* (Macmillan, 1987, $13.95: 0-689-50489-6) by Myra Cohn Livingston.

About the Book and Author

Berger, Laura Standley, ed. *Twentieth-Century Young Adult Writers*. St. James, 1995, pp. 1026–28.

Brown, Muriel W., and Rita S. Foudray. *Newbery and Caldecott Medalists and Honor Book Winners: Bibliographic & Resource Material Through 1991*. 2d ed. Neal-Schuman, 1992, pp. 445–57.

Collier, Laurie, and Joyce Nakamura. *Major Authors and Illustrators for Children and Young Adults*. Gale, 1993, 6 vols., pp. 2476–78.

Commire, Anne, ed. *Something About the Author*. Vol. 37. Gale, 1985, pp. 214–23.

Estes, Glenn E., ed. "American Writers for Children Since 1960: Fiction." In *Diction-ary of Literary Biography*. Vol. 52. Gale, 1986, pp. 386–91.

Evory, Ann, and Linda Metzger, eds. *Contemporary Authors (New Revision Series)*. Vol. 10. Gale, 1983, pp. 522–23.

Greiner, Donald J. "American Poets Since World War II." In *Dictionary of Literary Biography*. Vol. 5. Gale, 1980, pp. 396–401.

Helbig, Alethea K., and Agnes R. Perkins, eds. *Dictionary of American Children's Fiction, 1960–1984*. Greenwood, 1986, p. 725 (bio.).

Holtze, Sally Holmes, ed. *Fifth Book of Junior Authors and Illustrators*. Wilson, 1983, pp. 326–27.

Kingman, Lee, ed. *Newbery and Caldecott Medal Books: 1976–1985 with Acceptance Papers, Biographies and Related Material*. Horn Book, 1985, pp. 93–104.

Locher, Frances C., ed. *Contemporary Authors*. Vols. 89–92. Gale, 1980, pp. 574–75.

"Newbery Award Acceptance Material, 1982." *Horn Book* 58, no. 4 (August 1982): 369–79.

"Newbery Award Acceptance Material, 1982." *Top of the News* 38, no. 4 (summer 1982): 351–55.

Senick, Gerard J., ed. *Children's Literature Review*. Vol. 5. Gale, 1983, pp. 243–50.

Telgen, Diane, ed. *Something About the Author*. Vol. 71. Gale, 1993, pp. 209–13.

Trosky, Susan M., ed. *Contemporary Authors*. Vol. 39. Gale, 1992, pp. 462–65.

Ward, Martha, ed. *Authors of Books for Young People*. 3d ed. Scarecrow, 1990, p. 753.

Willard, Nancy. *A Visit to William Blake's Inn*. SRA/McGraw Hill, 1985. Audiocassette. ($18.66)

Honor Books 1982

Cleary, Beverly. *Ramona Quimby, Age 8*. Illustrated by Alan Tiegreen. Morrow, 1981, $16.00: 0-688-00477-6; pap., Avon, $4.50: 0-380-70956-2. (Grades 3–5)

> The irrepressible, appealing Ramona Quimby, returns in this sequel to *Ramona and Her Father* (see "Honor Books," 1978, p. 327). Set again in a small Oregon city in the shadow of Mount Hood, this humorous novel features the Quimby family: Ramona; her older sister, adolescent Beezus; Mother, a full-time doctor's receptionist; and Father, now a student in a teacher training program with a part-time job in a food warehouse. Ramona is excited because it's her first day in the third grade in a new school with a new teacher. It is not as pleasant as expected because Danny, a boy on the school bus, teases her and steals her eraser, and her new teacher, Miss Whaley, makes a humorous comment about her squeaky sandals. After school, Ramona is cared for by Howie Kemp's grandmother. These sessions are difficult because of pesky Willa Jean, Howie's little sister who demands Ramona's complete attention. Through all these problems, Ramona is determined to be cheerful and not to complain, particularly when the family suffers financial problems. However, her sensitive feelings are hurt when, after accidentally breaking a raw egg over her head and being sent to the school office for a hair wash, she overhears Miss Whaley refer to her as a nuisance. When Beezus and Ramona rebel against eating inexpensive tongue, their punishment is to prepare the next dinner. Although it is not quite the disaster expected, it is a humbling experience. Ramona finds that Miss Whaley really loves her after the attention Ramona receives when she throws up in class and is sent home with stomach flu. One evening when the family's spirits are low, Father decides to splurge and take them to Whopperburger. An old man, sitting nearby, is so impressed with the Quimbys that he pays for their dinner, and afterward the four agree that they really are quite a family.

Siegal, Aranka. *Upon the Head of the Goat: A Childhood in Hungary, 1939–1944*. Farrar, 1981, $16.00: 0-374-38059-7; pap., Signet, $3.95: 0-451-12084-1. (Grades 7–12)

> The title of this moving autobiography about a Jewish family's life during the Holocaust refers to the passage in Leviticus in which Aaron is commanded by the Lord to place all of the iniquities of the children of Israel upon the head of the goat and send it into the wilderness. Told through the eyes of Peri Davidowiz, the book begins when, at age nine in 1939, she is sent by her parents, with an older sister, Rozsi, from their home in Beregszasy, Hungary to visit with Grandmother Rosner, their Babi, in Komjaty, Ukraine. This strong, religious woman, provides

a simple but stable home for her two grandchildren. While there, they first become aware of the war when Hungarian soldiers occupy the territory. News comes that Peri's father and Lajos, the husband of her eldest sister, Lilli, are in the army. After Peri returns to Hungary, there are growing signs of increased pressures to inflict German policies on the Jewish population. Curfews are imposed, and Jewish children are forbidden to attend regular schools. Alone and without substantial assets, Mrs. Davidowitz somehow is able to provide both physical and spiritual comfort for Peri, her older sister, Iboya, the youngster, Sandor, and baby Joli. When the Germans arrive, persecutions increase and all Jews are forced to wear the Star of David. Their dear friend Lujza, a member of a Zionist group, commits suicide, fearing that her activities will jeopardize her family's welfare. Soon the Jews are herded into a makeshift ghetto where, in spite of squalid, inhuman conditions, the determination and resilience of Peri's mother help make life bearable. Here, Peri experiences first love with a boy named Henri. In the middle of 1944, trains arrive and the inmates are shipped to Auschwitz where they believe they will do war work. In an afterword, the author states that of all the members of her family only she and her sister Iboya survived.

Newbery Winner 1983

Voigt, Cynthia. *Dicey's Song*. Atheneum, 1982, $17.00: 0-689-30944-9; pap., Fawcett, $4.50: 0-449-70276-6. (Grades 6–10)

Cynthia Voigt (1942–) has written seven novels about the Tillerman family and their friends, beginning with *Homecoming* (Atheneum, 1981, $15.95). In *Homecoming*, we meet the four Tillerman children, Dicey, the courageous, resourceful 13-year-old heroine who assumes family leadership when their mother abandons them; precocious, 10-year-old James; quiet, silent, Maybeth, age nine; and Sammy, a boisterous, somewhat stubborn boy of six. *Homecoming* recounts their adventures as they travel alone and virtually penniless from Provincetown, Massachusetts to Crisfield, a town on the tip of Maryland's eastern shore, where they hope to be given a home by their maternal grandmother, Mrs. Abigail Tillerman. When they arrive tired and destitute, they find Abigail to be an ornery, bad-tempered recluse who is inhospitable and unwelcoming. Gradually she comes around and allows her grandchildren to stay. The first sequel, *Dicey's Song*, begins "And they lived happily ever more. Not the Tillermans." and chronicles the adjustments the kids make to living with Gran, how difficult it is for Dicey to relinquish the maternal responsibilities she assumed, and also how Dicey learns to get along and make new friends at school. The story of one of these friends, Jeff Greene, is told in *A Solitary Blue*, a Newbery Honor book for 1984 (see p. 358). In the last of the series, *Seventeen Against the Dealer* (Antheneum, 1989, $14.95), Dicey, now 21, decides to become independent, and she begins a career as a boat builder. It ends with her making plans to marry Jeff after his college graduation.

Plot Summary

In the first book about the Tillerman children, *The Homecoming*, their mentally ill mother abandons them and is finally traced to an asylum. The children spend the summer searching for the grandmother they have never met. In this sequel, they have moved in with Gran in her rambling, old farmhouse on Chesapeake Bay in southern Maryland. The book tells of their first four months of adjustment. The family includes Dicey, the oldest at 13 and very independent; intelligent James, who is 10; musically gifted Maybeth, 8; and the youngest, 7-year-old Sammy. Dicey hopes their troubles are finally over and that they have found a home with feisty Gran, their maternal grandmother.

Adjustment to this new life is not easy, in spite of how much Dicey wants it. She has been watching over her younger siblings since their mother's crisis, and now she feels that she should have a little time to herself. She wants to earn some spending money and refinish the old sailboat she finds in Gran's barn. Quite frankly, Dicey feels that she has earned the right to be a little selfish and do what she wants to do. So what if she spends each day in the barn, sanding away at the old boat? She just wants to be left alone to be her own person. She wants to leave all the decisions of the younger children to Gran.

Gran, very different in personality from Dicey, has problems of her own. One of them is money. It is difficult for her to make ends meet and doubly so when four children enter her life and care. She very much wants to adopt them legally, but in the meantime she must swallow her considerable pride and apply for welfare. It is a difficult decision, but Gran knows she cannot possibly provide adequately for the children's needs without this help.

Through all the problems there is the thought of and the worry about Momma. None of the children, especially Dicey, can forget about what has happened to her. Even with a new life and new ties, the old worries and the old ties do not go away. When Dicey yearns to be free of her worries about her mother and about her siblings, Gran tells her that the attachment she feels is "for as long as you live. That's something I learned, even though I didn't want to. For as long as you live, the attachments hold."

As she strives to pull away, to have time only to herself, Dicey is held by family ties and by Gran's encouragement to reach out, to keep involving herself in the lives of her brothers and sisters. As she does, she begins to understand the needs and problems of the younger Tillermans. Intellectually gifted James, for instance, has always wanted to make friends but never really had the chance before because of his mother's condition. As strong as his need for acceptance is his worry that his intelligence will make people his own age back away from him. He is afraid to succeed in school for fear he will be rejected.

Both Gran and Dicey are aware of Maybeth's problems, too. Although she is highly gifted in music, she does not do well in her studies. The problem is aided, if in a somewhat contrived manner, by James beginning to tutor Maybeth in reading, urged on by Gran and Dicey. They also deal with the personality of the youngest Tillerman, Sammy, as he reacts to his mother's illness and his change in living by becoming docile and then returning to belligerence.

It is a slow and painful process of readjustment for all of the Tillermans, including Gran, who wants to do well by her grandchildren but is aware of the many problems that face them all. At Gran's urging, Dicey does try to reach out beyond herself by making a few friends in school and trying to get along with teachers that she finds difficult.

Slowly but surely, the two different personalities of Dicey and Gran come together and Dicey begins to gain respect for this older woman. They continue to clash, however. One day Dicey announces that in four and a half years she can get a full-time job, and then the welfare checks can stop. This infuriates Gran, who tells her that she's going to college, not to work after high school. No one in the family has done this, and Dicey, and the others are going to.

In the climax of the book, Gran and Dicey fly to Boston to see Momma. While they are there, Momma dies. They decide that they will take her body back to Maryland with them. The problem is that transporting Momma's body will cost many hundreds of dollars, which they don't have. The decision is made to have Momma's body cremated.

Dicey and Gran return home with Momma's ashes, which they bury in an intimate family ceremony beneath the old paper mulberry tree at the front of Gran's house, Momma's childhood home. The Tillerman family is together. In one way, they will always be together.

Themes and Subjects

This is a warm and moving family story with strong themes of love and hope, courage and perseverance, maturing, compassion, and understanding. Perhaps the most endearing character is doughty Gran. She is reluctant at first to take in the children because she knows the hardships that lie ahead, including the loss of her own independence. Yet she opens her heart to them and in so doing opens her own life toward the people in her community. In short, like Dicey, Gran grows. Dicey learns to reach out beyond herself in spite of her inclination to pull away from the responsibilities that have been forced upon her. In the end, Dicey learns that what Gran said is true: life brings problems, but they can be worked out as one goes along. The attachment to the ones you love is always there, and always will be.

Incidents for Booktalking

Interfamily relationships are the key to development of all the characters in this novel. See: Dicey and Maybell talk about fractions (pp. 13–14); James is worried about fitting in (pp. 18–19); Sammy and Dicey have a chat in the barn (pp. 28–31); James completes a report on the pilgrims (pp. 44–46); the Tillermans try to solve the problem of Maybeth and her studies (pp. 77–80).

Related Titles

Seventh-grader June and her mother move in with Franklin, an old man who needs their help, in Kristi Holl's *No Strings Attached* (Atheneum, 1988, $13.95: 0-689-431398-3; pap., Royal Fireworks, $6.99: 0-88092-434-9).

In Sheri Cooper Sinykin's *Next Thing to Strangers* (Lothrop, 1991, $12.95: 0-688-10694-3), two misfits, each visiting grandparents in a retirement trailer park, form an unusual friendship.

In Amy Hest's *The Private Notebook of Katie Roberts* (Candlewick, 1995, $14.95: 1-56402-474-1; pap., $4.99: 0-56402-859-3), Katie, age 11, hates the ranch in Texas where she and her mother have moved to from New York City.

Orphaned 12-year-old Nettie and younger brother, John Peters, are shunted from one relative to another until they land in Boston with an elderly grandfather, in Jan Marino's *The Mona Lisa of Salem Street* (Little, Brown, 1995, $15.95: 0-316-54614-3).

Patty, an eighth-grader, matures while working in a shelter for the homeless in Susan Wojciechowski's *Paty Dillman of Hot Dog Fame* (Orchard, 1987, $13.95: 0-531-05810-7).

About the Book and Author

Berger, Laura Standley, ed. *Twentieth-Century Young Adult Writers*. St. James, 1994, pp. 669–71.

Brown, Muriel W., and Rita S. Foudray. *Newbery and Caldecott Medalists and Honor Book Winners: Bibliographic & Resource Material Through 1991*. 2d ed. Neal-Schuman, 1992, pp. 427–28.

Collier, Laurie, and Joyce Nakamura. *Major Authors and Illustrators for Children and Young Adults*. Gale, 1993, 6 vols., pp. 2382–86.

Commire, Anne, ed. *Something About the Author*. Vol. 33. Gale, 1983, p. 226.

Cynthia Voight. Profiles in Literature, 1988. Videocassette.

Gallo, Donald R. *Speaking for Ourselves*. National Council of Teachers of English, 1990, pp. 217–18.

Garrett, Agnes, and Helga P. McCue, eds. *Authors and Artists for Young Adults*. Vol. 3. Gale, 1990, pp. 207–16.

Helbig, Alethea K., and Agnes R. Perkins, eds. *Dictionary of American Children's Fiction, 1960–1985*. Greenwood, 1986, p. 700 (bio.), pp. 156–57 (book).

Hile, Kevin S., ed. *Something About the Author*. Vol. 79. Gale, 1995, pp. 209–14.

Hipple, Theodore W., ed. *Writers for Young Adults*. Vol. 3. Scribners, 1997, pp. 329–38.

Holtze, Sally Holmes, ed. *Fifth Book of Junior Authors and Illustrators*. Wilson, 1983, pp. 320–21.

Kingman, Lee, ed. *Newbery and Caldecott Medal Books: 1966–1985 with Acceptance Papers, Biographies and Related Material*. Horn Book, 1985, pp. 105–19.

Lesniak, James G., and Howard Haycraft, eds. *Twentieth-Century Authors*. Vol. 37. Gale, 1992, pp. 439–42.

Locher, Frances C., ed. *Contemporary Authors*. Vol. 106. Gale, 1982, p. 508.

McMahon, Thomas, ed. *Authors and Artists for Young Adults*. Vol. 30. Gale, 1999, pp. 143-50.

Metzger, Linda, ed. *Contemporary Authors (New Revision Series)*. Vol. 18. Gale, 1986, p. 468.

"Newbery Award Acceptance Material, 1983." *Horn Book* 59, no. 4 (August 1983): 401–13.

"Newbery Award Acceptance Material, 1983." *Top of the News* 39, no. 4 (summer 1983): 360–65.

Reid, Suzanne. *Presenting Cynthia Voight*. Twayne, 1995.

Senick, Gerard J., ed. *Children's Literature Review*. Vol. 13. Gale, 1987, pp. 223–41.

Silvey, Anita, ed. *Children's Books and Their Creators*. Houghton, 1995, pp. 664–65.

Sutton, Roger. "A Solitary View—Talking with Cynthia Voight." *School Library Journal*. June, 1995, pp. 28-32.

Trosky, Susan M., ed. *Contemporary Authors*. Vol. 40. Gale, 1993, pp. 456–57.

Voigt, Cynthia. *Dicey's Song*. Read by Jodi Benson. BDD Audio Publishing, 1996. Audiocassettes, 360 min. ($19.99)

———. *Dicey's Song*. Read by Barbara Caruso. Recorded Books, 1992. Audiocassettes. ($49.00)

———. "1995 Margaret A. Edwards Acceptance Speech: Thirteen Stray Thoughts about Failure." *Journal of Youth Services in Libraries* (fall 1995): 23–32.

Ward, Martha, ed. *Authors of Books for Young People*. 3d ed. Scarecrow, 1990, p. 725.

Honor Books 1983

Fleischman, Paul. *Graven Images*. Illustrated by Andrew Glass. Harper, 1982, $14.89: 0-06-021907-6. (Grades 6–9)

This slim volume contains three stories, each involving a carved figure or graven image. In the first story, "The Binnacle Boy," the brig *Orion* arrives at its home port, New Bethany, Maine, with the entire crew mysteriously dead and no evidence of a struggle. As a monument, a life-sized carving of a sailor boy holding the iron binnacle, or compass housing, is taken from the ship and placed before the town hall. In time, this lifelike statue becomes a father confessor for the townspeople who come and whisper their innermost secrets into its ear. A deaf girl, adept at reading lips, watches the people as they confess their sins before the binnacle boy and is gradually able to unravel the mystery of the *Orion*. The ship's supply of tea had been poisoned by the respectable Miss Frye who was distraught when the orphan boy she had raised decided to leave her and become part of its crew. "St. Crispin's Follower," the second story, is set in colonial Charleston and involves a shoemaker's apprentice, Nicholas, and his faith in his master's copper weather vane of St. Crispin, the patron saint of cobblers. Nicholas is smitten with Juliana, the young helper in the grocery store. His many attempts to make contact are misunderstood or thwarted until one day he follows the direction the weather vane indicts, meets Juliana, and gets a partner for the public ball that evening. Zorelli, the master sculptor in medieval Genoa, is the central character in the final story, "The Man of Influence." Without commissions and facing poverty, he accepts an offer from a ghost to create a statue of a disreputable man feeding a baby. After he finishes, he learns that the man was a hired assassin who had been shot to cover up the crime of poisoning the child. The baby was murdered to ensure the future inheritance of the assassin's employer, one of the city's most prominent citizens and a man whom Zorelli has admired. The sculptor takes the tainted money he receives for his work and throws it into the sea.

Fritz, Jean. *Homesick: My Own Story*. Putnam, 1982, $15.95: 0-399-20933-6. (Grades 4–7)

This book covers two years—from October 1925 to September 1927—in the life of the prominent children's writer Jean Fritz when she was a young girl in China with her missionary parents. This is a period of turmoil in China, as Communists fight to gain control of the country from the Nationalists. Although Jean knows she is an American, there are many wonderful things to do in China, and she loves her amah, the Chinese woman who takes care of and teaches her. She is a curious, fun-loving girl who has a secret desire to become a writer. She realizes how serious the situation is becoming when she and her friend Andrea are called "foreign devils" and stoned by young boys. The family has an idyllic holiday in the mountains and Jean spends two unforgettable days traveling on the Yangtze. On their return, they are nearly killed by a mob of revolutionaries but are luckily saved by ricksha coolies. Tension mounts and the anger against foreigners increases. Word comes that Mr. Fritz will be replaced, but before their scheduled departure date, they are forced to flee with only three hours to pack. The journey is arduous and frightening, but at long last Jean and her family board the *President Taft* for the voyage home. When they pull into San Francisco harbor, Jean thinks, "This is my own, my native Land!" They drive across the United States and finally arrive at her grandmother's home in Pennsylvania where she is happy to hear the words, "Welcome home."

Hamilton, Virginia. *Sweet Whispers, Brother Rush*. Philomel, 1982, $17.95: 0-399-208894-1. (Grades 7–10)

Fourteen-year-old Teresa Pratt, nicknamed Tree, has many responsibilities for her age. Often left alone for days by her mother Vi, Tree has the burden of caring for her handsome, retarded, 18-year-old brother Dab, to whom Tree is devoted. Though outwardly independent and self-reliant, Tree is actually a fearful child who longs for love and security from the seemingly indifferent mother she adores. Several times on her way home from school, Tree sees an attractive, impeccably dressed stranger gazing at her and later, when Tree gazes into the surface of a table in her private walk-in closet, this man appears. In time, she realizes that he is Brother Rush, the ghost of Vi's deceased brother. He begins taking Tree back to witness scenes of her childhood that reveal Vi's cruelty towards Dab, and a father, Ken, who is a wanton spendthrift. In later visions she witnesses Brother Rush caring for her and Dab and his death in an automobile accident. After a lengthy absence, Vi returns home with plans to start a catering business with her current boyfriend, Silversmith. Dab become violently ill and Tree learns that he suffers from a hereditary disease, porphyry. Dab dies, and Tree, in a violent confrontational scene blames Vi and her neglect for Dab's death. Tree secretly decides to leave home after the funeral when, in one last encounter with Brother

Rush, she sees him and Dab laughing and enjoying themselves together. By funeral time, Tree has become more reconciled to her brother's death. Vi announces that when their business is established, she and Silversmith will marry and create a proper home for Tree. The young girl is torn about her future but finally decides to stay. Working things out will be difficult, but Tree is used to challenges.

McKinley, Robin. *The Blue Sword*. Greenwillow, 1982, $16.00: 0-688-00938-7; pap., Ace, $5.99: 0-441-06880-4. (Grades 7–10)

The setting for this adventure fantasy is the land of Daria, a country similar to India during the British occupation. The story involves three different peoples: the Homelanders or Outlanders, the conquerors; the Hillpeople who are natives of the northern province of Damar; and the half-human Northerners who live in the country beyond the mountains. Angharad Crewe, nicknamed Harry, an attractive young girl, leaves the Homeland after the death of her father and visits Istan, a northern military outpost in Daria where her brother Richard is stationed. Harry becomes impatient with the very proper life she is forced to live, and welcomes the diversion of a visit from the dynamic king of the province of Damar, Corlath, who has come to the fort in a futile effort to get help with repulsing an impending invasion of the Northerners. Guided by his kelar, an extrasensory gift of foretelling the future, Corlath secretly takes Harry to his kingdom because he believes she will help his cause. Harry enjoys the spirited, exciting life with the Hillpeople and finds she too has the power of kelar and can speak the Old Tongue of Damar. Corlath sets off to the eastern mountains where he believes the Northerners will strike, but Harry, using her power of kelar, sees the hordes coming through another access point, Ritgar's Gap. She is able to raise a small force of volunteers including her brother and some of the Homelanders. Invoking the spirit of a dead female warrior, Aerin, who centuries before had also saved Damar, and brandishing Aerin's magical blue sword, Gonturan, Harry unleashes powers that cause the mountains to collapse and destroy the enemy. Harry and Corlath are reunited and marry hoping their union will bring together the Homelanders and the Hillpeople. The story of Aerin is told in the author's *The Hero and the Crown* (see "Newbery Winner," 1985, p. 359).

Steig, William. *Doctor De Soto*. Farrar, 1982, $16.00: 0-374-31804-4; pap., $4.95: 0-374-41810-1. (Grades 1–3)

This story, told in simple, straightforward prose and illustrated with imaginative, witty drawings by the author, is a parable that tells how goodness, courage and quick thinking can outwit brute strength and evil. Doctor De Soto is a mouse dentist noted far and wide for his gentleness and professionalism. Though small animals like chipmunks use the regular dentist chair, the good doctor, with his equally proficient wife who acts as his nurse, has devised special tools and apparatuses, including ladders, to accommodate larger animals. His shingle states specifically that he will not treat cats and other animals dangerous to mice, but one day he takes pity on an ailing fox and pulls his rotten tooth. While under the anesthetic, the fox is heard murmuring that he loves to eat raw mice with just a pinch of salt, but the little doctor, a true professional, nevertheless promises to complete the procedure by inserting a new tooth of pure gold in the fox's mouth the next day. Aware that he might be the first course in the fox's luncheon plans, the good doctor devises a bold scheme. After the insertion, he paints each tooth with a special formula that supposedly will prevent tooth decay. It is actually glue, and when the fox tries to open his mouth, his jaws are locked solid. Doctor De Soto claims that this is all part of the treatment, and as he says goodbye to the fox, assures him that he will be able to open his mouth again in a day or two. As he says, "The secret formula must first permeate the dentine. But don't worry. No pain ever again."

Newbery Winner 1984

Cleary, Beverly. *Dear Mr. Henshaw*. Morrow, 1983, $17.00: 0-688-02405-x; pap., Dell, $3.99: 0-440-800008-0. (Grades 4–6)

Beverly Cleary (1916–) is perhaps best known for creating such memorable characters as Henry Huggins and Ramona Quimby. Two books about Ramona were Newbery Award Honor Books: *Ramona and Her Father* (see "Honor Books," 1978, p. 327) and *Ramona Quimby, Age 8* (see "Honor Books 1982," p. 345). In her Newbery Award acceptance speech she said that the stimulus for writing *Henshaw* came from two influences. The first was the recurring request from her readers to write a book about a boy's adjustment to his parent's divorce and the second was a desire to write something new and different. Through journal entries and a series of letters to the author Boyd Henshaw, Ms. Cleary takes her young protagonist, Leigh Botts, from the second to the sixth grade, during which time he accepts his parents' separation and the fact that his father really loves him. In its sequel, *Strider* (Morrow, 1991, $13.95), Leigh is 14 and continues to keep his journal entries. Although still troubled by the divorce, his spare time is taken up caring for an abandoned dog. Assuming this responsibility and achieving a fine track-team record help Leigh gain personal satisfaction and confidence. Many people have asked the author if there really is a Leigh Botts. To this she replies, "There is not one Leigh Botts; there are many. Leigh Botts is all the brave and lonely children I have ever known who have found books and libraries to be their best friends."

Plot Summary

Dear Mr. Henshaw is a series of letters written by Leigh Botts from his home in California to his favorite author, Boyd Henshaw. When the letters begin, Leigh is in the second grade and is apt to make spelling mistakes, such as "freind" for "friend." By the end of the book, he is a sixth-grader who writes rather well-composed letters and might also become a writer when he grows up.

Leigh occasionally gets replies from Mr. Henshaw, who encourages him to write (hence the diary). The letters reveal the often lonely life of a sensitive boy who misses his father and has trouble making friends.

Leigh's father is a long-distance trucker, away for long stretches of time on the highway. Leigh's mother says that was part of the reason why she and his father divorced; her husband, she tells Leigh, is in love with his truck, not his family. Leigh doesn't want to believe that, of course, and lives for the times when his father calls or sends postcards. They are few and far between.

Since the divorce, Leigh and his mother have lived in a small ramshackle house and his mother often works at night to support them, especially when his father is late sending checks. On those evenings Leigh amuses himself by putting down his feelings in his diary, still in the form of letters to Mr. Henshaw.

Leigh also misses his dog, Bandit, who went with his father. The boy understands that his father must get lonely too out on the road by himself, but he wishes Bandit were at home with him.

Besides loneliness, Leigh's other big problem is that someone keeps stealing things out of his lunch bag. His mother works for a catering business, so his lunches often contain very tasty and unusual items. But more often than not, they are missing by lunchtime. When Leigh complains about this to his one friend at school, Mr. Fridley the school custodian, Mr. Fridley suggests a burglar alarm. It sounds like a good idea, but how do you put an alarm in a lunchbag?

Now in the sixth grade, Leigh is sure his father will show up at Christmas. Instead, on Christmas Eve a stranger arrives at their door. He is another trucker who is passing through, and Leigh's father asked him to drop off a present. It is a jacket for Leigh.

In January, his father phones from Oregon, where he is waiting for a load of potatoes. He promises to call Leigh in about a week, but the call never comes. Finally, out of loneliness, Leigh calls his father at his trailer over in Bakersfield. To his surprise, his father answers. He isn't off on the highway somewhere, and he didn't even call! His father says he was just about to call him. Then he tells Leigh the bad news that Bandit ran off when his father left the cab door of the truck open.

For a while after that, lonely and bitter, Leigh hates his father. He talks to his mother about him. His mother says his father is not a bad man; he will just never grow up.

In February, an envelope arrives from Albuquerque, New Mexico. His father writes on a paper napkin that he is sorry about Bandit and encloses $20. Leigh spends some of the money for a lunch box of the type truckers carry and equipment to rig a burglar alarm. The alarm actually goes off, and although he never does catch the lunch burglar, the thefts stop and Leigh is much admired in his class for his cleverness. In fact, classmate Barry asks Leigh over to his house to help rig up an alarm for his bedroom to keep his pesky sisters out. At last, he has a friend.

One day in March, as Leigh is returning from mailing a letter to Mr. Henshaw, he sees a big rig in front of the house. There stands his father—and Bandit! His father heard on his CB that another trucker had picked up Bandit, so now he is returning him to Leigh. His mother comes home from work while they are talking and asks his father inside for a cup of coffee.

Much to Leigh's embarrassment, his father asks his mother if there is any chance they can get back together. "No," his mother replies, "there isn't a chance."

When his father leaves, he promises to write more often. "Sure, Dad," Leigh says, but he knows now that it isn't always possible to count on his father. However, before he leaves, Leigh tells him to take Bandit with him. His father needs Bandit a whole lot more than Leigh does.

Themes and Subjects

This is a sensitive, insightful story of a young boy growing up, often lonely without his father and with few friends, finding refuge and solace in words and expressing himself. Funny and wise in its observations, it shows the gradual changes that bring a young boy to his own niche in the world. Such changes help him to look at his parents with love, and a growing understanding of their achievements as well as their shortcomings. It is a compassionate, warm story.

Incidents for Booktalking

Some of the letters to Mr. Henshaw point at how Leigh matures and can serve as a good introduction to this sensitive story. See: third-grader Leigh writes to Mr. Henshaw and talks about Bandit (p. 2); as a sixth-grader, Leigh sends Mr. Henshaw a list of questions to answer (pp. 7–8); Leigh begins to reply to some of Mr. Henshaw's questions (pp. 14–17); the diary entries begin (pp. 39–53); Leigh builds the lunchbox alarm (pp. 93–98).

Related Titles

Ken Derby, age 12, learns about life when his teacher assigns him a week of charitable work during spring break in John Neufeld's *Almost a Hero* (Atheneum, 1995, $15.00: 0-689-31971-1).

Starting with a school assignment, Matt's contacts with reclusive Auntie Florrie develop into a friendship in Theresa Tomlinson's *Riding the Waves* (Macmillan, 1993, $13.95: 0-02-789207-7).

Martin, the underachiever, fantasizes about heroic adventures and finally proves his worth as a baby-sitter in Mary Stolz's *The Explorer of Barkam Street* (pap., Trophy, $3.95: 0-06-440207-7).

Three people adjust to loss and loneliness—Mr. Torkleson, a widower; Catherine, recently divorced; and Catherine's son Rodney—in Diane J. Hamm's *Second Family* (Macmillan, 1992, $13.95: 0-684-19436-8).

Rudy, part of a Mexican American family, has problems growing up in Gary Soto's *The Pool Party* (Delacorte, 1992, $13.95: 0-385-30890-6; pap., Dell, $3.50: 0-440-41001-X).

About the Book and Author

Ammon, Bette D., and Gale W. Sherman, eds. *Handbook for the Newbery Medal and Honor Books, 1980–1989*. Alleyside, 1991, pp. 97–102.

Berger, Laura Standley, ed. *Twentieth-Century Children's Writers*. 4th ed. St. James, 1995, pp. 215–18.

Beverly Cleary. Profiles in Literature, 1979. Videocassette.

Brown, Muriel W., and Rita S. Foudray, eds. *Newbery and Caldecott Medalists and Honor Book Winners: Bibliographic & Resource Material Through 1991*. 2d ed. Neal-Schuman, 1992, pp. 66–69.

Chevalier, Tracy, ed. *Twentieth-Century Children's Writers*. 3d ed. St. James, 1989, pp. 209–10.

Cleary, Beverly. *Dear Mr. Henshaw*. Read by George Guidall. Recorded Books, 1992. Audiocassettes, 120 min. ($18.00)

————. *A Girl from Yamhill: A Memoir*. Morrow, 1988.

Collier, Anita, and Joyce Nakamura. *Major Authors and Illustrators for Children and Young Adults*. Gale, 1993, 6 vols., pp. 492–97.

Commire, Anne, ed. *Something About the Author*. Vol. 43. Gale, 1986, pp. 53–61.

Dear Mr. Henshaw. SRA/McGraw-Hill. n.d. Videocassette.

Estes, Glenn E., ed. "American Writers for Children Before 1900." In *Dictionary of Literary Biography*. Vol. 52. Gale, 1987, pp. 85–91.

Ethridge, James M., and Barbara Kipala, eds. *Contemporary Authors*. Vols. 1–4. Gale, 1967, p. 181.

Evory, Ann. *Contemporary Authors (New Revision Series)*. Vol. 2. Gale, 1981, pp. 121–23.

Fuller, Muriel, ed. *More Junior Authors*. Wilson, 1963, pp. 49–50.

Garrett, Agnes, and Helga P. McCue, eds. *Authors and Artists for Young Adults*. Vol. 6. Gale, 1991, pp. 11–24.

Helbig, Alethea K., and Agnes R. Perkins, eds. *Dictionary of American Children's Fiction, 1960–1984*. Greenwood, 1986, p. 117 (bio.), pp. 150–51 (book).

Hile, Kevin S. *Something About the Author*. Vol. 78. Gale, 1995, pp. 43–49.

Kingman, Lee, ed. *Newbery and Caldecott Medal Books: 1966–1975 with Acceptance Papers, Biographies and Related Material*. Horn Book, 1985, pp. 120–35.

Metzger, Linda, and Deborah A. Straub, eds. *Newbery Medal Books (New Revision Series)*. Vol. 19. Gale, 1987, pp. 120–26.

Nakamura, Joyce, and Gerard J. Senick, eds. *Something About the Author: Autobiographical Series*. Vol. 20. Gale, 1995, pp. 65–82.

"Newbery Award Acceptance Material, 1984." *Horn Book* 60, no. 4 (July/August 1994): 429–43.

Riley, Carolyn, ed. *Children's Literature Review*. Vol. 2. Gale, 1976, pp. 44–51.

Senick, Gerard J., ed. *Children's Literature Review*. Vol. 8. Gale, 1985, pp. 34–62.

Silvey, Anita, ed. *Children's Books and Their Creators*. Houghton, 1995, pp. 145–47.

Ward, Martha, ed. *Authors of Books for Young People*. 3d ed. Scarecrow, 1990, p. 132.

Honor Books 1984

Brittain, Bill. *The Wish Giver: Three Tales of Cloven Tree*. Illustrated by Andrew Glass. Harper, 1983, o.p.; pap., $3.95: 0-06-107012-2. (Grades 4–6)

This is part of the author's Cloven Tree books which are set in a small New England town early in the twentieth century. Others include *Devil's Donkey* (Harper, 1981, $13.89) and *Dr. Dredd's Wagon of Wonders* (Harper, 1987, $13.89). Each combines folk story elements, fantasy and humor. This installment begins when Stew Meat (Stewart Meade), the narrator and owner of the local grocery store, attends the Coven Tree Church social and fair and sees a sign outside one of the booths: "Thaddeus Blinn, I can give you whatever you ask for only 50 cents." Only Stew Meat and three young inhabitants accept this offer. For 50¢, each receives a white card with a red spot on it and the assurance that when the spot is pressed the first wish uttered will be granted. Eleven-year-old Polly Kemp wishes for popularity and to become the center of attention within her limited social circle. Her wish comes true when her vocal sounds change to uncontrollable frog croaks. When the second purchaser, Rowena Jervis, wishes that the young traveling salesman she admires would take root and not leave town, this happens literally, and to her dismay the young man begins turning into a tree. The third, Adam Fiske, wishes for water for his parents' drought-stricken farm, and soon they are surrounded by a lake and have to take their furniture to higher ground by raft. Inevitably the three come to Stew Meat with their problems and ask for his help. He saves the day by using his wish to undo theirs, thus returning the status quo.

Lasky, Kathryn. *Sugaring Time*. Photographs by Christopher Knight. Macmillan, 1983, $15.00: 0-02-751680-6. (Grades 3–6)

The author uses a spare, informative text and the brilliant black-and-white photographs of her husband, Christopher Knight, to re-create an annual American tradition, the production of maple syrup. This account focuses on the Lacey family of rural Vermont and how the entire family, except their youngest child, becomes involved in this spring ritual. Even the children's grandmother makes her annual visit when the sap is running so that she can help. The process begins when Mr. Lacey, the town doctor, hitches up the family's two horses and breaks through the snow to reach the grove of maple trees located on the Lacey's many acres of farmland. When the sap begins to run, small holes are drilled in the tree trunks and spigots inserted. Each has a pail and a tiny protective hat attached. There are usually two spigots driven into each tree or, for the Laceys, about 200 of these tiny faucets. The pails of sap are then poured into large collection vats and transported to the boiling trays where the closely watched, around-the-clock process of reducing the sap to the consistency of syrup takes places. It requires 40 gallons of sap to produce 1 gallon of syrup. This is a delicate process that requires constant supervision because too much heat can turn the sap to sugar. When the operation is complete, the syrup is graded according to its color and the amount of maple flavor it contains. Though the entire process takes only a week or two, the results are savored long afterwards. Just ask the Lacey children!

Speare, Elizabeth George. *The Sign of the Beaver.* Houghton, 1983, $16.00: 0-395-33890-5; pap., Dell, $3.50: 0-440-80038-2. (Grades 5–8)

This novel takes place in 1768 over a six-month time period—June through December—in the Maine wilderness. Thirteen-year-old Matthew Hollowell is a little apprehensive when his father leaves him to guard their newly constructed log cabin while Mr. Hollowell returns to Quincy, Massachusets to bring back Matt's mother and family. Things go poorly for the boy. An unscrupulous man steals Matt's rifle, and a marauding bear ransacks the cabin and destroys his food supply. When Matt is severely stung by bees while trying to gather honey, he is found and nursed back to health by two Native American members of the Beaver tribe, the ancient Saknis and his grandson Attean who is about Matt's age. Through their help, Matt learns new ways to survive in the forest such as how to snare animals and spear fish. In exchange, he teaches Attean how to read and write using *Robinson Crusoe* as a text. Although Matt learns to respect and participate in the daily life of the Beaver people, there remains a cultural gap between him and Attean. These feelings gradually disappear, particularly after they share such adventures as being attacked by a bear which Attean is forced to kill, and Matt rescuing Attean's dog from a hunter's trap. Though invited to go with the tribe when they break camp to head north, Matt decides to stay and wait for his long overdue parents. The boys exchange their most prized possessions as gestures of their friendship and love. Matt receives Attean's dog and Matt gives Attean his father's watch. Just before Christmas, Matt's family arrives. They were delayed by an outbreak of typhus. As the family settles in, Matt looks forward to telling them about his beloved friend Attean and of the adventures they shared.

Voigt, Cynthia. *A Solitary Blue.* Atheneum, 1983, $17.00: 0-689-31008-0; pap., Fawcett, $3.95: 0-449-70268-5. (Grades 7–10)

This story about the maturation and family problems of a boy named Jeff Greene covers approximately 10 years and is linked with the Tillerman family saga (see *Dicey's Song*, "Newbery Winner," 1983, p. 346) by Jeff's friendship with Dicey after he and his father move to the Chesapeake Bay area. When he is seven years old, Jeff returns home from a day in the second grade in Baltimore to find his mother Melody gone and a note from her stating she has left to help others, like the starving children of the world, who need her more than he does. Feelings of guilt, abandonment, and insecurity persist during Jeff's later childhood as he continues to live with his father, a distant, preoccupied college teacher he calls the Professor. When Jeff is 12, he is summoned to visit his mother in Charleston and is enchanted by her charm and beauty and enthralled by his grandmother, a southern matriarch named Gambo. He is, however, totally disillusioned when he returns the next year and finds his mother again absorbed in her projects and occupied by a new boyfriend. Feeling deceived and rejected, he withdraws into a private world, until his father realizes the boy needs help. He buys a cabin on a marshy seashore at Chesapeake Bay, and he and Jeff begin renovating it. Slowly Jeff and the Professor start a new trusting life together. They make friends and begin to give and receive confidences and affection. Melody sues for divorce and wants custody of Jeff, but in a confrontational scene, Jeff firmly but compassionately tells his mother that he wants to stay with the Professor. One day, Jeff's new friend, Dicey, says that he reminds her of the solitary blue heron they see in a tidal marsh because he, too, is a self-sufficient loner. Though he will always feel the emotional damage caused by his mother, Jeff now has his interests in music, new friends, a caring father, and hope for the future.

Newbery Winner 1985

McKinley, Robin. *The Hero and the Crown*. Greenwillow, 1984, $16.00: 0-688-02593-5; pap., Ace, 5.99: 0-441-32809-1. (Grades 8-12)

Robin McKinley (1952–) first introduced readers to the fantastic land of Damar in *The Blue Sword*, a Newbery Honor Book in 1983 (p. 352). It tells how Harry (short for "Anghared") Crewe leads a battle against invading Northerners and is encouraged and guided by the spirit of a dead female warrior, Aerin. In *The Hero and the Crown*, Aerin's full story is told. This novel is divided into two parts. In the first, the reader is introduced to the court of King Arlbeth and his daughter Aerin in the mythical kingdom of Damar. In the second part, Aerin sets out on a mission to save her beloved kingdom. In her Newbery Award acceptance speech, the author wrote that *Sword* had its roots

> in Kipling and Haggard and P. C. Wren. . . . Perhaps the first real flicker of the tale that would become Damar—and even more particularly the kernel of what would become the story of Aerin—is from my passionate rereadings of *The Lord of the Rings*. . . . I wished for books like *Hero* when I was young: books that didn't require me to be untrue to my gender if I wished to fantasize about having my sort of adventures. . . . [It is hoped] that young readers who identify with Harry and Aerin and the others and wish to be like them will also realize that they are. And that this should be true of boy readers as well as the girls: both sides of our gender-specific event horizon need to be expanded.

Plot Summary

Aerin is the only child of widowed King Arlbeth whose wife, an enchanting witch woman from the North country, died shortly after Aerin's birth. Because of the mystery involved in her ancestry, Aerin is not fully accepted at the court, although her father and her older cousin, Tor, who has assumed the role of the king's successor, love her dearly. Her chief enemies, however, are two other cousins, Galanna and her husband, Perlith.

A high-spirited and brave young girl, Aerin tries to emulate the ways of the warrior knights around her, in spite of admonitions from her loyal and caring maidservant, Teka. When Aerin is 15, she succumbs to the goading of the jealous Galanna and eats some of the hallucinogenic surka plant, which is supposed to give superhuman strength and visions of royalty. To Aerin, it brings only convulsions and nightmares. During her long period of convalescence and while Teka ministers to her needs, Aerin begins creeping out of the castle to the pasture where the king's gallant but now very lame white stallion, Talat, is kept. The horse suffered a crippling wound while saving his master in battle. Aerin begins secretly riding this magnificent beast and bringing him back into shape. She also learns the rudiments of swordplay from Tor, who is beginning to view his redheaded, attractive cousin with more than a platonic interest.

In an old book on the history of Damar, Aerin discovers a recipe for kenet, an ointment that protects one from dragon fire. She begins collecting the herbs that are its ingredients and experimenting for long painstaking months to discover their correct proportions. When she thinks she is successful, she smears her body and clothes with the salve. Then, she bravely enters a bonfire and emerges unharmed.

About the time of her eighteenth birthday, Aerin learns that a nearby village is being troubled by a small dragon that has been killing chickens and frightening farmers. Without telling anyone, she gathers a supply of kenet and on her trusty steed, Talat, successfully vanquishes her first dragon. Soon she has gained a reputation within the kingdom as a dragon slayer, and now Aerin feels that her days of squiring are over and she is ready to fulfill her destiny.

She hasn't long to wait. Trouble begins to break out within the kingdom, and King Arlbeth blames it on the disappearance many years ago of the Hero's Crown, a magical talisman that brings power to its owner. As the king, Tor, and the army prepare to leave to quell an uprising in the North, there is news that in another part of the kingdom the fearful giant Black Dragon, Maur, has reappeared and is on a rampage destroying villages.

After the army leaves, Aerin decides to do battle with this savage monster, and she leaves with Talat and armed only with a supply of kenet and a sword her father has given her. But Maur is unlike the small dragons Aerin has encountered in the past; it is as big as a mountain and its teeth alone are as long as Talat's legs. In the ensuing battle, Aerins' face and body are severely burned when part of her clothing and her helmut fall off. Her mouth and lungs are scorched raw from breathing in dragon fire, and after Talat accidentally falls, her ankle is crushed. However, as the dragon leans toward her for the kill, she frees a dagger from her boot and before she faints, she stabs it through the right eye of the dragon into its brain. When she awakes, she finds Maur dead and on the ground a glowing red stone—the solidified last drop of its blood.

Aerin spends days at the site gaining strength for the journey home. In her feverish dreams, a tall, blond man appears and promises her aid. Still suffering great pain, she begins her journey back to the castle, but even there, under the tender care of Teka, Aerin fails to respond. As a trophy, Maur's head has been mounted in the great hall, and the girl senses that the evil power it represents is slowly destroying her.

Once again, the man in her dreams appears, promising help. In desperation, she once more mounts Talat and leaves the castle. After many days she arrives at a stone building where the tall, blond man greets her. He is Luthe, a soothsayer equipped with superhuman power. Through the enchanted magical waters of the nearby Lake of Dreams, he cures Aerin, but when she is well, Luthe informs her that she has one more mission to fulfill. He tells her that the evil power that controls the Hero's Crown and that has unleashed forces like Maur on the world is actually Aerin's uncle, the wizard Agsded. According to the ancient prophecy, only one of his own blood can destroy him. Fearful of Aerin's mother, Agsded had destroyed her. It is only Aerin who can kill him. Before she leaves, Luthe gives Aerin a magical blue sword called Gonturan.

On her journey, she recruits a strange army of followers: a group of folstza, catlike creatures, and pack of wild dogs called yerig. Together with Talat they are able to clear a passageway into the tower where Agsded lives. There, equipped with only a wreath of surka gathered outside the castle, the dragon's stone, and Gonturan, she confronts her wicked uncle. In the ensuing battle, good triumphs over evil and Aerin emerges victorious and in possession of the Hero's Crown.

Luthe once more appears to her. Although she loves him dearly and would like to stay with him, she tearfully says goodbye and returns to Damar. At the death of her father, Aerin marries Tor and together they reign over a now peaceful and prosperous land.

Themes and Subjects

While being entranced by this enthralling story, readers learn much about the elements of fantasy, such as the quest, the struggle of good versus evil, unusual beasts, and the use of magical powers. This is a story of great heroism, and in spite of its exotic trappings, a moral tale in which justice triumphs. The use of sometimes complex symbolism enriches the story and will deepen the rewards for the better, more perceptive readers. The character of Aerin is interesting, particularly for girls, as she represents a model of both physical and moral courage.

Incidents for Booktalking

A brief introduction to the land of Damar, its troubles, and the king's daughter should intrigue young readers. Specific passages of interest are: Aerin eats the surka plant (pp. 23–25; pp. 22–24 pap.); she first visits Talat in his pasture (pp. 27–29; pp. 26–27 pap.); Aerin finds the right recipe for kenet (pp. 60–62; pp. 57–59 pap.); Aerin tries the kenet (pp. 80–82; pp. 75–77 pap.); Aerin's first encounter with dragons (pp. 86–91; pp. 80–85 pap.); the fight with Maur (pp. 112–18; pp. 104–10 pap.).

Related Titles

When 13-year-old Joey, her older brother, Peter, and younger sister Liana are kidnapped, they believe that they have been abducted by aliens in Gillian Rubinstein's *Galax-Arena* (Simon, 1995, $15.00: 0-689-80136-X; pap., Aladdin, $3.99: 0-614-29087-2).

Princess Tesessa must assume control of her kingdom, and with friends like Wren, fight the powers of evil in Sherwood Smith's *Wren's War* (Harcourt, 1985, $17.00: 0-15-200977-9), a sequel to *Wren to the Rescue* (Harcourt, 1990, $15.95: 0-15-200975-2) and *Wren's Quest* (Harcourt, 1993, $16.95: 0-15-200976-0).

A 14-year-old girl is pulled into another world on a magical horse in Marilyn Singer's *The Horsemaster* (Atheneum, 1985, $13.95: 0-689-31102-8).

Sophie Hatter seeks refuge in Wizard Howl's castle after she has been turned into an ugly crone by the wicked Witch of the West in Diana Wynne Jones's *Howl's Moving Castle* (Greenwillow, 1986, $16.00: 0-688-06233-4).

Nine tales of medieval enchantment are told as dreams by the Arthurian magician in Peter Dickinson's *Merlin Dreams* (Delacorte, 1998, $19.95: 0-440-50067-2).

About the Book and Author

Berger, Laura Standley, ed. *Twentieth-Century Young Adult Writers*. St. James, 1994, pp. 442–44.

Brown, Muriel W., and Rita S. Foudray. *Newbery and Caldecott Medalists and Honor Book Winners: Bibliographic & Resource Material Through 1991*. 2d ed. Neal-Schuman, 1992, pp. 278–79.

Chevalier, Tracy, ed. *Twentieth-Century Children's Writers*. 3d ed. St. James, 1989, pp. 667–68.

Commire, Anne, ed. *Something About the Author*. Vol. 32. Gale, 1983, p. 136.

Estes, Glenn E., ed. "American Writers for Children Since 1960: Fiction." In *Dictionary of Literary Biography*. Vol. 52. Gale, 1986, pp. 262–66.

Garrett, Agnes, and Helga P. McCue, eds. *Authors and Artists for Young Adults*. Vol. 4. Gale, 1990, pp. 193–202.

Helbig, Alethea K., and Agnes R. Perkins, eds. *Dictionary of American Children's Fiction, 1960–1984*. Greenwood, 1986, p. 412 (bio.).

Holtze, Sally Holmes, ed. *Fifth Book of Junior Authors and Illustrators*. Wilson, 1983, pp. 212–13.

Lesniak, James G., ed. *Contemporary Authors (New Revision Series)*. Vol. 31. Gale, 1990, pp. 280–81.

May, Hal, ed. *Contemporary Authors*. Vol. 107. Gale, 1983, pp. 328–29.

McKinley, Robin. *The Hero and the Crown*. Read by Rosalyn Alexander. Recorded Books, 1992. Audiocassettes, 1,050 min. ($67.00)

———. *The Hero and the Crown*. SRA/McGraw Hill, 1988. Audiocassettes. ($34.66)

"Newbery Award Acceptance Material, 1985." *Horn Book* 61, no. 4 (July/August 1985): 395–409.

"Newbery Award Acceptance Material, 1985." *Top of the News* 41, no. 4 (summer 1984): 386–96.

Sanders, Lynn Moss. "Girls Who Do Things: The Protagonists of Robin McKinley's Fantasy Fiction." *The ALAN Review*. Fall, 1996, pp. 38–42.

Senick, Gerard J., ed. *Children's Literature Review*. Vol. 10. Gale, 1986, pp. 121–26.

Honor Books 1985

Brooks, Bruce. *The Moves Make the Man*. Harper, 1984, $15.89: 0-06-020698-5; pap., Trophy, $4.50: 0-06-440564-8. (Grades 7–9)

This novel about an interracial friendship, basketball, and an obsession with truth was the first young adult novel by Bruce Brooks. The narrator is Jerome Foxworthy—Jayfox—a brash, very intelligent boy who is the first black to attend Chestnut Junior High in Wilmington, North Carolina. Besides knowing all the social moves, Jayfox knows all the basketball moves. There is nothing he can't do with a basketball. He grows to admire a fellow student and equally talented basketball player, Braxton Rivers III, also known as Bix. Gradually they strike up a friendship and begin practicing together. Bix is a complex young man who wants only truth in his life. He never lies or fakes and abhors this characteristic in others. For example, when his class makes a mock apple pie but pretends it is real, Bix becomes emotionally upset. This obsession leads to tragedy. When Bix's neurotic mother asks him one day if he loves her, he answers truthfully "no." Shortly after, she attempts suicide and is confined to a mental hospital. Blaming himself, he begs his father, another basketball enthusiast, to allow him to visit her. When he is refused, Bix goads his father into a one-on-one on the basketball court. The prize: a visit to his mother. He wins, but the scene at the hospital is a disaster with his mother refusing to recognize him. Bix runs away and Jerome never sees him again although one day he receives an unsigned postcard from Washington, D.C. After Bix leaves, Jerome decides to stop playing basketball, but who knows, one day maybe he'll change his mind.

Fox, Paula. *One-Eyed Cat*. Bradbury, 1984, $14.95: 0-02-735540-3. (Grades 5–8)

This novel, set in upstate New York during the depression year of 1935, tells of young, introspective Ned Wallis growing up in the shadow of his saint-like father, the town's Congregational minister. His loving and imaginative mother is often confined to a wheelchair with severe arthritis. On the eve of Ned's 11th birthday, Uncle Hilary arrives and gives him a Daisy air rifle as a present, but Ned's father, a non-violent person, puts the gun in the attic promising Ned that he may use it when he is older. That night, Ned secretly steals out with the gun and shoots at a gray shadow by the barn. He is certain, however, that someone is watching him from the house. On a visit to his 80-year-old friend, Mr. Scully, Ned sees a gray feral cat with one eye. They begin feeding him and Ned, convinced that the cat is the victim of his disobedience, suffers growing feelings of guilt. He becomes preoccupied with caring for the cat. When Mr. Scully suffers a stoke and is confined to a nursing home, Ned secretly buys scrap food with his savings and continues the feeding. However, after Mr. Scully's death and the sale of his house, Ned no longer has access to the cat's feeding place. One night, Ned takes a walk and is joined by his mother. In the distance they see the one-eyed cat, his mate and two children. He confesses to the rifle incident and in turn his mother tells him it was she who witnessed the scene but wisely remained silent. She also tells him that she realizes Ned's problem of feeling unable to live up to his father's goodness and perfection because she had similar feelings when they first married. At home, they are welcomed by Papa who says he is glad that the two are back safely.

Jukes, Mavis. *Like Jake and Me*. Illustrated by Lloyd Bloom. Knopf, 1984, o.p.; pap., $7.99: 0-394-89263-1. (Grades 1–5)

This gentle story of family relationships, acceptance, and love is brightened by misty, full-page pastel illustrations that catch and reflect the delicate, tender emotions the story evokes. Alex, about seven years old, idolizes his stepfather Jake, but still feels insecure with him and is in awe of this huge man, a former cowboy, and his brute physical strength. By comparison, Alex is a quiet, sensitive child who enjoys his ballet lessons and is very attached to his mother, Virginia, who is expecting twins with her new husband. When Alex asks his mother if the twins will be like Jake, he is satisfied with the reply that they may be a little like both Jake and her. One day, while Alex is playing with a loose tooth that he lacks the courage to pull out, he and Jake watch Virginia in the yard. At the same time, Alex sees a large pregnant wolf spider crawling on Jake's neck. In the ensuing conversation, Alex's talk of the spider is misinterpreted by Jake as references to Virginia, until he realizes with panic that he has a furry thing crawling on him. Jake reacts with such fear and confusion, that Alex realizes his stepfather also has anxieties and fears. With Alex's help, Jake takes off his clothes and the spider is located. In gratitude, Jake picks up Alex and they dance around the porch. Virginia rubs her belly and says she feels that the twins are also dancing inside her. "Like Jake and me," says Alex as Jake whirls around the porch with Alex in his arms.

Newbery Winner 1986

MacLachlan, Patricia. *Sarah, Plain and Tall*. Harper, 1986, $14.90: 0-06-024101-2; pap., Trophy, $3.95: 0-06-440205-3. (Grades 4–7)

Patricia MacLachlan (1938–) was born in Cheyenne, Wyoming and grew up an only child in a loving family. Her experiences as a teacher and working with a family service agency have helped her with ideas for her books, which usually deal with family situations and interpersonal relationships. *Sarah, Plain and Tall* grew out of recollections of simple stories that her mother referred to as "the heroics of common life." She says, "My mother told me early on about the real Sarah, who came from the coast of Maine to the prairie to become a wife and mother to a close family member." When the author went back west with two of her children to the place where her parents lived (her father was born in a sod house) and where she was born, the story of Sarah took shape. It was first conceived as a picture book and grew into a short, miniature novel of less than 60 pages that conveys a strong emotional appeal in simple, touching prose. In her Newbery Award acceptance speech, the author recalls that at the time she began this novel, her mother was beginning to show symptoms of Alzheimer's disease, and it became the author's intent in the book "to wrap the land and the people as tightly as I could and hand this small piece of my mother's past to her." About the function of literature in children's lives, Ms. MacLachlan also wrote that it is "the daily grace and dignity with which we survive that children most need and wish to know about in books." A sequel is *Skylark* (Harper, 1994, $12.00).

Plot Summary

Jacob Witting and his two children, Anna and Caleb, are a prairie farm family. Life is hard and often lonely on the prairie, but for the Wittings it is doubly so. A few years before, the day after Caleb's birth, their mother died. Anna, who has taken over the cooking chores for the family, still feels the hurt of knowing that her mother did not even say good night to her before she died. Caleb, with no recollection whatsoever of his mother, constantly asks Anna to talk about her. Anna doesn't really mind the request, although it brings back the loss and the loneliness they all still feel.

The Witting children know that their neighbor, Matthew, once wrote a letter to obtain a bride. His reply came in the form of Maggie from Tennessee, whom both

Anna and Caleb like very much. Today, their neighbors are a family with two small daughters, Rose and Violet. Anna and Caleb are surprised but rather pleased when their father tells them that he, too, has written a letter for a "mail order" bride and mother for the children. Their expectations mount when a reply comes from Sarah Elizabeth Wheaton, a woman from Maine. She will visit them for one month as a trial and will bring along her cat, Seal.

When Jacob replies to Sarah Wheaton, Anna asks him to make sure to inquire if Sarah sings. Anna remembers that her mother used to sing a lot while doing her chores on the farm. Sarah writes back and answers various questions for all of them. She says that she can make fires and braid hair. She tells them of her fisherman brother named William. She says she is not certain if she snores. Sarah writes to Jacob that she will arrive for the trial month in the spring and will be wearing a yellow bonnet so he can recognize her. She describes herself as "plain and tall." She adds a postscript for the children: "Tell them I sing."

It is an exciting day when Jacob hitches up Wild Jack and Old Bess and goes to town. He returns with Sarah in the yellow bonnet—plain and tall. The children love her on sight.

So begins the trial month on the prairie. It is far from the Maine seacoast, which the children soon realize Sarah deeply loves. Even though they know how different life here must be for her, they desperately hope she will stay and become a family with them. During the month's trial, Sarah does many things with Anna and Caleb. They pick wildflowers and she cuts their hair. She draws pictures of Maine and teaches them to sing songs. She recounts stories of her family and they all go swimming in the old watering hole.

Sarah is not silent about the fact that she is a sturdy and independent woman. She helps Jacob with the farm chores, including plowing the fields and fixing the roof. She helps Anna with the cooking. She learns to ride a horse and visits with Maggie, the neighbor "mail order" bride. Maggie suggests that Sarah start a garden. Jacob brings her June roses.

Then, quickly, the month is up. Nothing has been said. No decision has been made. One day Sarah announces she is going into town, and she is gone. The day is endlessly long and worrisome. Anna and Caleb are dreadfully afraid she is leaving them. Jacob is worried, too. Is Sarah really going back to Maine? The long day passes, and Sarah returns. She has only been to town to buy colored pencils. They will help to make her prairie drawings more vivid and true to life.

Sarah, plain and tall, is going to stay. They will be a family again. Jacob promises that instead of saying yes at the wedding ceremony, he will say "ayuh," just as they do in Maine. When the time comes, Anna and Caleb decide they will silently say "ayuh" right along with Jacob. It will be a silent but heartfelt "ayuh" in gratitude for Sarah, plain and tall.

Themes and Subjects

Much of the beauty of this book lies in its simplicity and gentleness. The emotions of the three family members—Anna, Caleb, and Jacob—are simply and quietly expressed. At its center is the family structure. With their loving father, Anna and Caleb are able to grow and survive without the presence of a mother, but the loss remains with them, as does the longing. The person of Sarah, plain and tall, adds a new dimension to their family group. She completes their happiness and their closeness. This simple story also shows how love and sharing among family members can ease the loneliness of personal loss, whether it be the death of a loved one or leaving the environment one knows for something strange and uncharted.

Incidents for Booktalking

The first pages of this short book (pp. 1–15) introduce the four main characters—Anna, Caleb, Jacob Whitting, and Sarah Elizabeth Wheaton. For an interesting insight into the character of this independent Maine woman, see the letters (pp. 9, 11–13, 15).

Related Titles

Fifteen-year-old Francis joins a wagon train headed for Oregon, gets caught up in a buffalo stampede, and finds herself hopelessly lost in Gary Paulsen's *Call Me Francis Tucket* (Delacorte, 1995, $14.00: 0-385-32116-3; pap., Dell, $3.99: 0-440-41270-6), a sequel to *Mr. Tucket* (Delacorte, 1994, $15.95: 0-385-31169-9).

Based on published accounts, Jean Van Leeuwen's *Bound for Oregon* (Dial, 1995, $14.99: 0-8037-1526-9), describes a pioneer family's tumultuous, deeply moving journey westward.

The frail young wife of a doctor is unable to adapt to the harshness of prairie life in Pam Conrad's *Prairie Songs* (Harper, 1985, $14.00: 0-06-021336-1).

In Ann Warren Turner's *Grasshopper Summer* (Macmillan, 1989, $14.95: 0-02-789511-4), 11-year-old Sam and his family move from Kentucky to the southern Dakota Territory in 1874.

Nathan, age 11, runs afoul of a renegade killer known as Weasel when he is alone on the Ohio frontier in 1839, in Cynthia DeFelice's *Weasel* (Macmillan, 1990, $15.00: 0-02-726457-2).

About the Book and Author

Berger, Laura Standley, ed. *Twentieth-Century Children's Writers*. 4th ed. St. James, 1995, pp. 617–18.

Brown, Muriel W., and Rita S. Foudray. *Newbery and Caldecott Medalists and Honor Book Winners: Bibliographic & Resource Material Through 1991*. 2d ed. Neal-Schuman, 1992, pp. 279–80.

Chevalier, Tracy, ed. *Twentieth-Century Children's Writers*. 3d ed. St. James, 1989, pp. 622–23.

Collier, Laurie, and Joyce Nakamura. *Major Authors and Illustrators for Children and Young Adults*. Gale, 1993, 3 vols. pp.1550–53.

Commire, Anne, ed. *Something About the Author*. Gale, 1986, Vol. 42, p. 146; 1990, Vol. 62, pp. 115–21.

Hedblad, Alan, ed. *Something About the Author*. Vol. 107. Gale, 1999, pp. 128–32.

Helbig, Alethea K., and Agnes R. Perkins, eds. *Dictionary of American Children's Fiction, 1960–1984*. Greenwood, 1986, p. 393 (bio.).

Holtze, Sally Holmes, ed. *Sixth Book of Junior Authors and Illustrators*. Wilson, 1989, pp. 183–84.

Locher, Frances C., ed. *Contemporary Authors*. Vol. 118. Gale, 1986, p. 301.

———. *Sarah, Plain and Tall*. SRA\McGraw-Hill, 1990. Videocassette.

———. *Sarah, Plain and Tall*. Starring Glenn Close. Republic, 1991. VHS videocassette, 98 min. ($14.98)

McMahon, Thomas, ed. *Authors and Illustrators for Young Adults*. Vol. 18. Gale, 1999, pp. 169–78.

Newbery Acceptance Speech: Patricia MacLachlan. ALSC, 1986. Audiocassette.

"Newbery Award Acceptance Materials, 1986." *Horn Book* 62, no. 4 (July/August 1986): 407–15.

"Newbery Award Acceptance Material, 1986." *Top of the News* 42, no. 4 (summer 1986): 391–95.

Patricia MacLachlan. Profiles in Literature, 1989. Videocassette.

Senick, Gerard J., ed. *Children's Literature Review*. Vol. 14. Gale, 1988, pp. 177–86.

Silvey, Anita, ed. *Children's Books and Their Creators*. Houghton, 1995, pp. 427–29.

Trosky, Susan M., ed. *Contemporary Authors*. Vol. 136. Gale, 1992, pp. 261–63.

Ward, Martha, ed. *Authors of Books for Young People*. 3d ed. Scarecrow, 1990, p. 459.

Honor Books 1986

Blumberg, Rhoda. *Commodore Perry in the Land of the Shogun*. Lothrop, 1985, $17.00: 0-688-03723-2. (Grades 4–8)

   Through a well-written and lively narrative and dozens of fascinating, black-and-white period prints, drawings, and portraits, the author describes Commodore Perry's two visits to Japan and also gives an intriguing introduction to the Japanese society and culture of the period. On Friday, July 8, 1853, "giant dragons puffing smoke," arrived at the port city of Shimoda, in the Land of the Rising Sun. It was Commodore Perry and four ships of the U.S. Navy intent on delivering a letter from President Millard Fillmore to the Emperor requesting protection for American shipwrecked seamen and the right to use Japanese ports for refueling and obtaining supplies. He was ordered by the Japanese to go to Nagasaki, the only port open to foreigners where the Dutch, under humiliating conditions, operated a trading concession. Perry refused and on July 14 he successfully presented his papers and the letter to the Emperor before leaving Japan and retiring to the Chinese coast. He returned in February of the next year with an increased fleet and 1,500 men. He presented his hosts with a fine assortment of gifts including farm tools, a hose and folding ladder that could be used for fire fighting and a small telegraph operation that could transport messages from the building where negotiations took place to a nearby building. In turn, the Japanese were lavish in their gifts. Perry's show of pomp and power, impressed the insecure shogunate, and on March 31, 1854 near Yokohama, the Treaty of Kanagawa was signed opening the ports of Shimoda and Hakodate to U.S. trade. Though emphasizing the human side of these historical events, the account is a well-researched chronicle that is complemented by such appended material as the texts of President Fillmore's letter, the Japanese reply, and the final treaty plus lists of the gifts exchanged.

Paulsen, Gary. *Dogsong*. Bradbury, 1985, $16.00: 0-02-770180-8; pap., Puffin, $4.99: 0-14-032235-3. (Grades 7–9)

In this novel set in the frigid northland, the author captures the immensity of this barren wilderness while telling the story of a young Inuit teenager's real and symbolic journey to find himself and his past and come one step closer to maturity. It is winter and 14-year-old Russel Susskit is living in an Alaskan village with his father. During the summer, he and the community move to the fishcamps. Fascinated with his people's culture and traditions and upset that they are losing touch with their past, Russel moves in with a town elder, Oogruk, and learns from him the true Inuit ways. In his old home, Oogruk's walls are decorated with harpoons and bows, and the floors are covered with furs. The old man is the only one in town with a sleigh and dogs. On a seal hunt, the ancient Oogruk senses that his own death is near, so he follows ancient custom and leaves to die alone on the ice. Before departing, he tells Russel that the boy must take the dogs and sleigh on a journey to find himself and his own song. Later, Russel finds Oogruk dead sitting with arms outstretched in the old Inuit way, smiling in death. The boy heads north across the ice. During his travels he has a series of dreams bordering on visions and hallucinations that re-create the lore of the Eskimo. Russel endures incredible hardships including riding out a two-day fierce storm in his tent. In the tundra, he finds a young pregnant girl, Nancy, near death. Russel nurses her back to consciousness, but her baby is still-born. He feeds her from a polar bear he is able to kill, and when her strength returns, they head for a coastal settlement to get her medical attention. Russel's journey has been successful. He has survived in the ancestral way using old-fashioned instruments and adhering to Inuit traditions and practices. Through his ingenuity and bravery, he has also discovered himself and his dogsong.

Newbery Winner 1987

Fleischman, Sid. *The Whipping Boy*. Greenwillow, 1986, $16.00: 0-688-06216-4. (Grades 3–6)

Sid Fleischman (1920–) began his career writing for young people with a series of humorous, historical adventures that began with *Mr. Mysterious and Co.* (Little, 1962, o.p.), the story of a traveling magician and his family touring the

West in 1884. He is also known for his riotous tall tales with larger-than-life characters like McBroom, the New England farmer who, in a typical adventure, *McBroom Tells the Truth* (Little, 1981, $12.45), acquires land so rich that it produces four crops per day. While doing historical research for another project, the author encountered the phrase, "the whipping boy," which refers to a boy educated with a prince and punished in his stead. Mr. Fleischman found the practice outrageous, but in his imagination he now had the two main characters for a new novel. He worked on it, on and off for several years, first as a picture book, then as a short novel. It tells of royal derring-do and the exploits of Prince Roland, also known as Prince Brat, and Jemmy, his whipping boy. In writing about the boys' situation, the author says that both were denied their rightful childhood, "the prince by a smothering excess of privilege; Jemmy by none at all." At the time of the Newbery Awards, Paul Fleischman, the author's talented son, wrote, "you won't find a single cliché in my father's work . . . but lots of rich, visual imagery."

Plot Summary

Prince Brat was just that. He is a dreadful child. Not even black cats will cross his path, but he never gets spanked for any bad thing he does. That is because the bratty prince has a whipping boy. He is Jemmy, an orphan boy and son of a rat catcher, who had been yanked from the streets to serve as the royal whipping boy. It is, of course, forbidden to spank or smack or whip a prince, no matter what he does, so Jemmy gets whipped at least twice a day for things the bratty prince has done. Even that makes the prince angry because Jemmy never cries out, no matter how much it hurts. When the prince tells Jemmy that if he does not cry out, he will see that he's sent back to the streets, Jemmy thinks he has a plan of escape.

For awhile, things continue as before. Jemmy, dressed as the prince in fine silks and velvets, takes his whippings, especially during school sessions. The prince simply will not learn to read and write and do sums. He feels he can always get someone to do those things for him. Jemmy, who must stand by at all the lessons, learns instead.

One day the prince tells Jemmy that he is running away because he is bored. He commands Jemmy to go with him. They leave on a royal horse and get lost in the forest. Before long they are discovered by two cutthroats, Billy and Cutwater. Naturally, these two ruffians do not believe that the bratty boy is Prince Roland, but when they see the king's own crest on the saddle, they decide to hold the prince for ransom. They tell the prince to write a ransom note, but of course he cannot write. Over the prince's protests, Jemmy says he is the prince and will write the ransom note. Then he tells the ruffians to send the note to the castle by way of his whipping boy, who of course is the real prince. Jemmy cannot believe it when the real prince refuses to go! Could it be that he wants to protect Jemmy?

That notion is soon dispelled when the prince points to Jemmy as the real prince. Jemmy runs away, with the prince close behind. They run right into a bear in the forest! They discover that the bear's name is Petunia and is owned by Betsy. She points the boys in the direction of the river and runs off after Petunia.

When Jemmy realizes that he cannot leave the prince to fend for himself, he decides to do some rat catching to earn some money for food. Unhappily, they soon run into the cutthroats again. When the cutthroats begin to beat the prince, Petunia and Betsy come to the rescue.

Back in the city, Jemmy runs into his old rat catching friends. Suddenly, the news seller appears with this horrifying message: "Prince sold to gypsies! The true and genuine facts! Ink still wet! Whipping boy charged with dastardly scheme! King offers reward for the unspeakable rascal! Dead or alive! Full description! Get your copy! Keep your eyes peeled and catch the reward!"

Jemmy runs off to the only safe place he knows, the dark sewers. The prince follows and Jemmy accuses him of getting a price on his head. The prince protests, saying Jemmy is his friend. When the cutthroats appear again, the two boys take off through the water so as not to leave footprints. Jemmy leads them through the sewer tunnel, with the ruffians in pursuit. The boys are saved when the sewer rats attack the bad guys.

Once out in the sunshine again, the prince declares they are going back to the castle. Jemmy refuses, saying he does not fancy doing a jig from the end of a rope. But the prince asks him if he wants to spend the rest of his life in the sewers.

"You said you trusted me," the prince says. "But I can see you didn't mean it." He commands Jemmy to follow him. He also tells Betsy that she must turn the whipping boy in to the king for the reward. She refuses, but the prince commands it! For the first time, Jemmy sees that the royal prince is up to a bit of mischief.

Back at the castle, Jemmy waits anxiously while Prince Brat is alone with the king. When they appear, the king rewards Betsy for returning the prince and the whipping boy. But what about Petunia, who was helpful after all? Petunia is given the title of Official Dancing Bear to Your Royal Majesty.

Alone with the king and Prince Brat, Jemmy is told that he ought to be whipped. However, he will be placed under the prince's protection on one condition. The prince has sworn to do his lessons, blow out his night candle, and otherwise behave himself. Jemmy figures Prince Brat must really want him for a friend. One last warning from the king—if the boys run away again, they must take him with them!

The last heard of Billy and Cutwater was that they stowed away on a ship heading for a long voyage. It was a convict ship bound for a speck of an island in distant waters.

Themes and Subjects

A rollicking blend of humor, friendship, and compassion fills the pages of this high-spirited adventure in a long-ago kingdom in a faraway time. Prince Brat is a most obnoxious young man, but once he runs away with Jemmy and gets a taste of the world outside the castle walls, a world where people do not cater to his every whim, he begins to change and value such things as friendship and honor and bravery. By the book's end, Prince Brat has turned into a young man with a sense of humor and decency, rewarding his friends for their help when he needed it, and especially rewarding the friendship and bravery shown by the one who was his whipping boy. Suspense and rich, colorful characters highlight this comic romp and the growing friendship between two young boys of very different backgrounds.

Incidents for Booktalking

The scenes that point out the differences in the life of Prince Brat and everyone else around him, especially the whipping boy, are especially colorful. See, for example, the prince warns Jemmy about crying out when he is spanked (p. 4); the prince is bored and runs away (pp. 7–8); the prince and Jemmy meet the cutthroats (pp. 11–15);

writing the ransom note (pp. 22–26); the boys meet Petunia and Betsy (pp. 41–49); Jemmy is wanted! (p. 73); the chase in the sewers (pp. 77–84).

Related Titles

In Victorian London, a street urchin is forced to work on a river barge until he escapes in Berlie Doherty's *Street Child* (Orchard, 1994, $16.99: 0-531-08714-X).

There are nine wonderfully wise and witty stories about boys and girls in unusual situations in Tim Wynne-Jones's *Some of the Kinder Planets* (Orchard, 1995, $15.95: 0-8050-1142-0).

In Ann Cheetham's *The Pit* (Holt, 1990, $14.95: 0-8050-1142-0), a young boy in present-day England is drawn back to London in the days of the Great Plague.

Buried treasure and Dickensian derring-do are featured in Bruce Clements's *The Treasure of Plunderell Manor* (pap., Farrar, 1987, $3.95: 0-374-47962-3), in which a young maid serves a girl who is kept hidden by her wicked aunt and uncle.

The Writing on the Hearth (Viking, 1984, $9.95: 0-670-79119-9) by Cynthia Harnett deals with intrigue and witchcraft in fifteenth-century England.

About the Book and Author

Berger, Laura Standley, ed. *Twentieth-Century Children's Writers*. 4th ed. St. James, 1995, pp. 357–58.

Block, Ann, and Carolyn Riley, eds. *Children's Literary Review*. Vol. 1. Gale, 1976, pp. 73–76.

Brown, Muriel W., and Rita S. Foudray. *Newbery and Caldecott Medalists and Honor Book Winners: Bibliographic & Resource Material Through 1991*. 2d ed. Neal-Schuman, 1992, pp. 137–39.

Chevalier, Tracy, ed. *Twentieth-Century Children's Writers*. 3d ed. St. James, 1989, pp. 350–51.

Collier, Laurie, and Joyce Nakamura. *Major Authors and Illustrators for Children and Young Adults*. Gale, 1993, 6 vols., pp. 845–49.

de Montreville, Doris, and Don Hill, eds. *Third Book of Junior Authors*. Wilson, 1972, pp. 86–87.

Ethridge, James M., and Barbara Kopala, eds. *Contemporary Authors*. Vols. 1–4. Gale, 1967, p. 320.

Evory, Ann, ed. *Contemporary Authors (First Revision Series)*. Vol. 5. Gale, 1992, pp. 191–92.

Fleischman, Sid. "Reality of Laughing Gas." *Horn Book* (March/April 1994): 162–65.

———. *The Whipping Boy*. Read by Spike McClure. Recorded Books, 1993. Audiocassettes, 120 min. ($18.00)

———. *The Whipping Boy*. Read by Kerry Shale. Chivers North America. Audiocassettes. ($18.95)

———. *The Whipping Boy*. PBS Video, 1987. VHS videocassette, 15 min. ($35.00)

Hedblad, Alan. *Something About the Author*. Vol. 96. Gale, 1998, pp. 94–100.

Lesniak, James G., ed. *Contemporary Authors (New Revision Series)*. Vol. 37. Gale, 1992, pp. 191–92.

Meet the Newbery Author: Sid Fleischman. Pied Piper, 1987. Videocassette.

"Newbery Award Acceptance Material, 1987." *Horn Book* 63, no. 4 (July/August 1987): 423–32.

"Newbery Award Acceptance Material, 1987." *Top of the News* 43, no. 4 (summer 1987): 385–90.

Newbery-Caldecott Acceptance Speech: Sid Fleischman. ALSC, 1987. Audiocassette.

Senick, Gerard J., ed. *Children's Literature Review*. Vol. 15. Gale, 1988, pp. 101–13.

Silvey, Anita, ed. *Children's Books and Their Creators*. Houghton, 1995, pp. 245–47.

Ward, Martha, ed. *Authors of Books for Young People*. 3d ed. Scarecrow, 1990, pp. 230–31.

Honor Books 1987

Bauer, Marion Dane. *On My Honor*. Clarion, 1986, $15.00: 0-89919-439-7; pap., Dell, $3.25: 0-440-80216-4. (Grades 4–7)

Preteen Joel Bates gets permission from his father to go bike riding with his best friend Tony Zabrinsky after he promises on his honor that they will ride only to a park some eight miles away and come back immediately. On the way, they cross a bridge over the Vermillion River, and Tony suggests they have a swim. Joel realizes he is disobeying his father but agrees and challenges Tony to race him to a sandbar in the middle of the river. Joel finishes first, turns around and realizes that Tony has disappeared in the treacherous current. He dives many times but sees nothing. Panicking, he hails a passing car. The driver, an older boy, also dives into the water again without seeing Tony. The boy drives off after Joel promises to go immediately to the police. Instead, he goes home. Confused and guilt-ridden he lies and tells his parents that he left Tony behind in the park. At first everyone believes him including Tony's parents who live across the street from the Bates's. That evening Joel is miserable, torn between telling the truth and facing the consequences or remaining silent. That night, the Zabrinskys, now desperate for news of their son, call the police who discover Tony's clothes by the river. Under questioning Joel tells the truth and wants to be punished for his disobedience. His father takes him up to bed and there Joel breaks down and sobs uncontrollably from grief at the loss of his friend and shame at his behavior. Gently his father comforts him and tells him that they both are guilty because of choices they made. He says, "It's going to be a hard thing to live with, for both of us, but there is nothing else to be done." Joel asks his father if he will stay with him until he falls asleep and his father replies, "Of course."

Lauber, Patricia. *Volcano: The Eruption and Healing of Mount St. Helens.* Bradbury, 1986, $16.95: 0-02-754500-8. (Grades 3–6)

This before, during, and after account of the eruption of Mount St. Helens is made memorable by high-quality color photographs depicting the catastrophe and showing the gradual ecological recovery of the area with the return of the plant and animal life that seemed totally destroyed. For more than 100 years there had been no signs of life from the volcano named Mount St. Helens. Then on March 27, 1980, there was a tremendous explosion within the mountain that produced streams of smoke and ash. Smaller explosions occurred during April and May, and a large, growing bulge appeared on the north face. At 8:32 A.M. on May 18, the giant eruption occurred covering 230 square miles and killing 57 people and countless plants and animals. The next day it was reported that the mountain was 1,200 feet shorter than it had been the day before. The north side now looked like the surface of the moon. Somehow nature began healing its wounds. Some small animals and amphibians survived under the snow pack and frozen lakes, and many underground insects such as ants reappeared. Seeds germinated and plants grew, attracting larger animals such as deer. Birds were able to find holes for nests in fallen trees. By the end of the summer, plant and animal colonizers were arriving steadily and wildlife was returning to the volcano as it had many times before. The book ends with an explanation of the formation of volcanoes and of the plate theory of geology. The author describes the circle of active volcanoes surrounding the Pacific Ocean (the Ring of Fire) and reports both the positive and negative effects of volcanic eruptions. The phenomenon is another example of how nature survives disaster and can, with time, undergo a rebirth.

Rylant, Cynthia. *A Fine White Dust.* Bradbury, 1986, o.p.; pap., Dell, $3.50: 0-440-42499-2. (Grades 6–8)

It has been a year since Pete Cassidy underwent the traumatic experience that left him with painful memories and a bag in his bureau drawer containing a broken ceramic cross and some fine white dust. He was 13, fresh out of the seventh grade, and prepared for an uneventful summer palling around with his best friend, Rufus, in their small North Carolina town. Then the Preacher Man came to town for a series of four revival meetings. Pete is captivated by his presence, his impressive height and piercing blue eyes. Though Pete's parents rarely go to church, they respect Pete's devotion to his beliefs and his need to attend church regularly. Pete longs for the religious experience of being saved. This happens at the first revival meeting when the Preacher Man places his hands on Pete's hands and tells him he has been reborn. Filled with religious ecstasy, Pete faints. In the next days, Pete falls further under the spell of this messianic evangelist, who confesses privately to Pete that he still feels an inner loneliness and asks Pete to fill this gap by leaving town with him after the last gathering. Pete consents. He packs a duffel bag of clothes and mementos including a ceramic cross he had made. Reluctantly, he tells Rufus of his plans, but that night the Preacher Man does not appear. Angry and disillusioned, Pete kicks the duffel bag breaking the cross. Rufus appears and takes Pete home. Later it is discovered that the preacher had actually run off with a local cafe waitress. Pete feels lost, deceived, and forsaken, but with time and the help of his family and Rufus, these wounds heal. He realizes that he has learned a great deal from this experience, including the fact that he lives in a world "where somebody like the Man can work so hard to save a million doomed sinners but come near to killing the soul of one mixed-up kid."

Newbery Winner 1988

Freedman, Russell. *Lincoln: A Photobiography.* Clarion, 1987, $17.00: 0-89919-380-3); pap., $7.70: 0-395-51848-2. (Grades 4–9)

Russell Freedman (1929–) has written more than 30 books for young people and has made a significant contribution to both scientific and historical nonfiction. As an example of the former, there are such titles as *Animal Superstars: Biggest, Strongest, Fastest, Smartest* (pap., Prentice, $4.95) and of the latter, there are several books on American history like *Children of the Wide West* (Clarion, 1983, $14.95). Recently he has been concentrating on richly illustrated biographies of famous Americans, including *The Wright Brothers*, which was a Newbery Honor Book in 1992 (p. 399), and a book each on Franklin Roosevelt and Eleanor Roosevelt. In commenting on the writing of *Lincoln*, the author has stated that he "grew up during the cherry-tree era of children's biography" and that the Lincoln he encountered as a child was "a first cousin to Goody Two-Shoes," a sanitized paragon. When asked by his publisher to write a biography of a president, "I picked Lincoln as a subject because I felt I could offer a fresh perspective for today's generation of young readers, but mostly I picked him because I wanted to satisfy my own itch to know." Lincoln was a difficult and challenging subject; there are more books written about Lincoln than any other American. Extensive research was done, including visits to the actual historical sites. Archives were combed for suitable quotes, pictures, and political cartoons (there are more than 90 black-and-white photographs included). The result is a vivid, realistic portrait that brilliantly re-creates both the man and his times.

Plot Summary

This is a warm, lively, and appealing biography of the Civil War president whom many historians regard as our greatest—Abraham Lincoln—and is illustrated with photographs and prints. There are seven entertaining chapters.

Chapter 1 covers the "mysterious" Mr. Lincoln and tries to separate fact from myth, what is actually known about him and what is only surmised. He is many things to his country—an American folk hero, an admired president, and the man called the Great Emancipator. His critics, of course, had other names, such as hick and tyrant.

Chapter 2 covers the early life of the boy who would grow up to become the 16th president. He was indeed born in a Kentucky log cabin to parents who could not read or write. The author describes how Lincoln grew into a gangly youth who was smart and regarded as something of a bookworm. When he was 17, he left home for the first time to work for a few months as a ferryman's helper on the Ohio River. It opened his eyes to the conditions of slaves. He got a steady job in New Salem, Illinois, and worked in a store for a time. After doing whatever odd jobs he could find, Lincoln taught himself law and passed the bar exam on March 1, 1837.

Chapter 3 describes Lincoln's life as a young lawyer in Springfield, Illinois and his love for Mary Ann Todd, the pampered, temperamental daughter of a Kentucky banker. Although they seemed mismatched and relatives did not approve, the two were married in 1842 after a stormy courtship and broken engagements. They would have four sons, Robert Todd, Eddie, Willie, and Tad. Lincoln was elected to the House of Representatives in 1847 and moved his young family to the nation's capital. The Lincoln marriage may have been stormy, but they adored their children and spoiled them unmercifully. Someone once remarked that it was a miracle the Lincoln boys ever learned to walk because their father was always carrying them around on his shoulders.

Chapter 4 discusses the rising slavery issue. Although Lincoln made few public statements about slavery, he did take a stand, recording his belief that it was founded on "injustice and bad policy." After the Dred Scott court decision, a setback for those who opposed slavery, Lincoln became a leading antislavery spokesman in Illinois. He made an unsuccessful bid for the senate in 1855 and tried again in 1858. He said in a rousing speech, "A house divided against itself cannot stand." What followed were the challenging debates between Lincoln and his democratic opponent, Senator Stephen A. Douglas of Illinois. Lincoln lost the election but was chosen as the presidential nominee of the Republican party in 1860. He won that election and became the nation's 16th president. Before he took office, South Carolina announced it had seceded from the Union.

Chapter 5 covers emancipation and the beginning of the Civil War. It details Lincoln as the commander in chief of the armed forces of the North and covers his signing of the Emancipation Proclamation. He signed it with his full signature, although he usually signed documents just as "A. Lincoln." This time he said, "If my name ever goes into history, it will be for this act."

In Chapter 6, the dreadful war continues. Lincoln was a decisive leader who was deeply horrified by the tremendous toll in human suffering brought on during the long war. In Chapter 7, the country loses perhaps its greatest president as he is assassinated. The nation mourns.

Additional material includes samplings of Lincoln's writings and speeches as well as historic sites around the country that honor him.

Themes and Subjects

This is a lively and entertaining as well as informative biography of one of the nation's great leaders. It is also a look at the terrible war that tore apart the country.

Incidents for Booktalking

Any of the chapters can initiate a discussion of the type of man Lincoln was, the forces that drove him, and his leadership in guiding the country through its darkest hours. See, for example, Lincoln's young years (pp. 7–17); Lincoln as a young lawyer (pp. 27–43); as president at the beginning of the war (pp. 67–80); the war's end (pp. 112–18).

Related Titles

Jim Haskins's *The Day Fort Sumter Was Fired On: A Photo History of the Civil War* (pap., Scholastic, $6.95: 0-590-46397-7) is a short readable history of the Civil War and Reconstruction that emphasizes the contributions of women and blacks.

Zachary Kent's *Ulysses S. Grant* (Children's Press, 1989, $24.00: 0-516-01364-5) is an account of the life and career of the Civil War hero who became president.

In Jean Fritz's *Stonewall* (Putnam, 1979, $15.95: 0-399-20698-1), she tells of the amazing Southern general who was nicknamed Stonewall after his stand at Bull Run during the Civil War.

The Battle of Gettysberg is told from two different viewpoints, that of a Confederate lieutenant and that of a Union corporal in Jim Murphy's *The Long Road to Gettysburg* (Houghton, 1992, $17.00: 0-395-55965-0).

In addition to explaining the causes of the war, James I. Robertson Jr.'s *Civil War! America Becomes One Nation* (Knopf, 1992, $16.99: 0-394-92996-9) gives a year-by-year account of events.

About the Book and Author

Berger, Laura Standley, ed. *Twentieth-Century Young Adult Writers*. St. James, 1994, pp. 222–24.

Brown, Muriel W., and Rita S. Foudray. *Newbery and Caldecott Medalists and Honor Book Winners: Bibliographic & Resource Material Through 1991*. 2d ed. Neal-Schuman, 1992, 146–48.

Collier, Laurie, and Joyce Nakamura. *Major Authors and Illustrators for Children and Young Adults*. Gale, 1993, 6 vols., pp. 877–80.

Commire, Anne, ed. *Something About the Author*. Vol. 16. Gale, 1979, pp. 115–16.

Contemporary Authors (New Revision Series).Vol. 81. Gale, 1999, pp. 170–74.

Dear, Pamela S. *Contemporary Authors (New Revision Series)*. Vol 46. Gale, 1995, pp. 127–29.

Dempsey, Frank J. "An Interview with Russell Freedman." *Horn Book* (July/August 1988): 452–56.

Evory, Ann, ed. *Contemporary Authors (New Revision Series)*. Vol. 7. Gale, 1982, pp. 174–75.

Garrett, Agnes, and Helga P. McCue, eds. *Authors and Artists for Young Adults*. Vol. 4. Gale, 1990, pp. 95–106.

Hipple, Ted. ed. *Writers for Young Adults*. Vol. 2. Scribner's, 1997, pp. 1–10.

Holtze, Sally Holmes, ed. *Sixth Book of Junior Authors and Illustrators*. Wilson, 1989, pp. 889–90.

Kinsman, Clare D., ed. *Contemporary Authors*. Vols. 17–20. Gale, 1976, p. 258.

Lincoln: A Photobiography. SRA/McGraw-Hill, 1990. Videocassette.

McMahon, Thomas, ed. *Authors and Artists for Young Adults*. Vol. 24. Gale, 1998, pp. 113–22.

Meet the Newbery Author: Russell Freedman. SRA/McGraw-Hill, 1990. Videocassette.

"Newbery Award Acceptance Material, 1988." *Journal of Youth Services in Libraries* 1, no. 4 (summer 1988): 421–27.

"Newbery Medal Acceptance." *Horn Book* (July/August 1988): 444–51.

Newbery-Caldecott Acceptance Speech: Russell Freedman. ALSC, 1988. Audiocassette.

"1998 Laura Ingalls Wilder Medal Acceptance Speech." *Journal of Youth Services in Libraries* (summer 1998): 353–56.

Senick, Gerard J., ed. *Children's Literature Review*. Vol. 20. Gale, 1990, pp. 71–89.

Silvey, Anita, ed. *Children's Books and Their Creators*. Houghton, 1995, pp. 253–55.

Straub, Deborah A., ed. *Contemporary Authors (New Revision Series)*. Vol. 23. Gale, 1988, pp. 151–52.

Telgen, Diane, ed. *Something About the Author*. Vol. 71. Gale, 1993, pp. 69–72.

A Video Visit with Russell Freedman. Houghton, 1990. Videocassette.

Ward, Martha, ed. *Authors of Books for Young People*. 3d ed. Scarecrow, 1990, p. 244.

Honor Books 1988

Mazer, Norma Fox. *After the Rain*. Morrow, 1987, $16.00: 0-688-06867-7. (Grades 7–10)

The central character in this touching novel of love and loss is 15-year-old Rachel Cooper, a sophomore and an aspiring writer who feels with some justification that she is both physically and socially unfulfilled. Her working parents, soft, fat Manny and Shirley, both adore and overly protect her, their last child. Rachel has two, much older, absent brothers: Phil, married with family and her adored Jeremy, a brilliant misfit who has suffered emotional problems since the Vietnam War. Through her friend Helena, Rachel meets and begins dating shy, sensitive Lewis Olswanger. At last she begins to feel socially alive and wanted. Although Shirley's father, tough, crusty 83-year-old Izzy Shapiro, a retired stone mason, lives only a mile and a half away, Rachel scarcely knows her gruff, ill-tempered grandfather. However, when his health declines and his doctor tells the Coopers, in confidence, that Izzy has lung cancer and only a few months to live, Rachel agrees to visit him daily after school and accompany him on his walks. At first these visits are painful. Izzy is either grouchy and impolite or taciturn and distant. Slowly, however, a bond grows between the two to the point where he allows Rachel to kiss him and once he even calls her "darling." When Izzy enters the hospital, Rachel takes days off from school to stay with him and she is in his room when he dies. During her period of grieving, her moods swing from denial and disbelief to anger and despair. Slowly through the help of all her family, particularly Jeremy, comes acceptance and peace. One day, she and Lewis visit some of the small bridges Izzy had helped build and find his handprint in the hardened cement, a monument that no one can erase.

Paulsen, Gary. *Hatchet*. Bradbury, 1987, $16.00: 0-02-770130-1; pap., Puffin, $4.99: 0-14-03437107. (Grades 5–9)

Thirteen-year-old Brian Robeson, hurt and confused by the divorce of his parents, is flying north into Canada to spend the summer with his father, a mechanical engineer employed in the oil fields. Brian wants to tell his father The Secret, which is that his mother wanted the divorce because she was in love with another man. Before reaching their destination, the pilot of the tiny airplane suffers a fatal heart attack and the plane crashes into a lake and sinks. Brian survives with only the clothes he is wearing and a hatchet, a last minute gift from his mother. Through trial and error, he slowly masters the skills of survival. He learns how to catch both fish and birds and soon builds a shelter for himself and fashions a campfire to cook his food and keep wild animals at bay, but a deadly tornado hits the area destroying both his shelter and his morale. The heavy winds, however, dislodge the plane's wreckage, and Brian is able to salvage the survival kit inside, while trying not to look at the decomposing body of the pilot. The kit contains a sleeping bag, utensils, food, and a transmitter. He fiddles with the transmitter but decides it is broken and instead prepares his first decent meal in 54 days. Suddenly a plane appears—the transmitter had actually been operating. Brian is rescued and for a few days is a celebrity. Although things soon return to normal, Brian has been changed by his near-death experiences. He has gained maturity, inner strength and self-knowledge. One indication is that although he thinks about The Secret often, Brian never tells his father.

Newbery Winner 1989

Fleischman, Paul. *A Joyful Noise: Poems for Two Voices*. Illustrated by Eric Beddows. Harper, 1988, $14.95: 0-06-021852-5. (Grades 3–7)

Paul Fleischman (1952–), the son of the distinguished writer, Sid Fleischman, is known for both the quality and the variety of his writings. Among his many historical novels and short collections are *Graven Images*, a Newbery Honor Book for 1983 (p. 350), and *The Borning Room* (Harper, 1991, $14.00), a story that centers on a simple room off the kitchen in the Lott's family home in Ohio, a place that could be used for dying, for caring for the sick, and for giving birth. In the field of poetry, he is best known for two collections of "poems for two voices." The first, *I Am Phoenix* (Harper, 1988, $14.00), is the result of many hours watching birds. It consists of 15 free-verse poems about birdsongs and flight designed to be read aloud. Later, he cast about for material for a companion volume and through reading such works as Edwin Way Teale's *The Strange World of Familiar Insects*, settled on insects as subject matter. The writing went slowly and was often abandoned, but he persevered. The result is a book of 14 poems about the lives and dreams of insects that contain clear, spirited images and use many poetic devices such as alliteration, repetition, and onomatopoeia to produce such insect sounds as buzzing and droning. In an interview quoted in *Something About the Author, Autobiographical Series*, Mr. Fleischman says, "If insects seemed a strange choice of subject, two voices must seem an even stranger method. This method itself attracted me as a metaphor as much as a form. We all have more than one voice within us. A writer lives off these multiple voices."

Plot Summary

This winner of the Newbery Medal is an oddity—a book of poetry. In 14 poems of varying lengths the author re-creates the soaring, spinning, creeping, booming "joyful noise" of insects. The author instructs readers that the poems should be read aloud by two readers at once, hence the subtitle. The idea is to read the poems from top to bottom with the two parts meshing as though to music. When the lines to be read are on an equal horizontal level, they are to be spoken simultaneously. For example, note the beginning of this poem titled "Mayflies":

> Your moment
> Mayfly month
> Your hour
> Mayfly year
> Your trifling day
> Our life
> We're mayflies We're mayflies
> just emerging just emerging

The last two lines—"We're mayflies, just emerging"—are to be read by both readers at the same time.

The effect of these poems extolling the insect world is to bring the drone of the honeybee or the pulse of the cicada to vibrant life, at the same time creating a marvelous nature picture of the mysterious world of the insect.

Other poems tell about "leapfrogging, longjumping grasshoppers" and water striders, who are often asked to walk on water. And they do. Fireflies discuss the fact that they use the light as ink to write upon the night. Even the mostly shunned book lice are extolled as they discuss their lives in a world of dusty bookshelves where they pass their youth with Agatha Cristie, Mickey Spillane, or even Shakespeare. The moth prepares a love song for his serenade, and cicadas hum and buzz into a mighty chorus in the sweltering night. Honeybees, alas, must work their way through life, while whiligig beetles swim in circles.

The world of nature is a busy place as the author captures the uniqueness of each noisy insect.

Themes and Subjects

A love of poetry and a love of nature merge magically in this tribute to small creatures. These simple, spare rhymes, when read together, produce an atmosphere that allows the buzz, chirp, drone, and whirr of the insects to come to life as they speed on their busy ways.

Incidents for Booktalking

Any of these short poems, especially if read as the author intends, can spark an interest both in poetry, and the reading of it, through the fascinating world of insects.

Related Titles

Indian philosophy and a people living in harmony with the land are revealed in the beautifully illustrated book of free verse, *Navajo: Visions and Voices Across the Mesa* (Scholastic, 1995, $15.95: 0-590-46153-2) by Shonto Begay.

In *Meet Danitra Brown* (Lothrop, 1994, $16.00: 0-688-12073-3) by Nikki Grimes, poetry and art introduce you to "the most splendiferous girl in town."

In 27 previously unpublished poems, an animal alphabet is presented by Lanston Hughes in *Sweet and Sour Animal Book* (Oxford, 1994, $17.95: 0-19-509185-X).

All sorts of small things are highlighted in the 60 poems included in *These Small Stones* (Harper, 1987, $12.95: 0-06-024013-X) edited by Norma Farber and Myra Cohn Livingston.

Richard Wilbur's *Runaway Opposites* (Harcourt, 1995, $15.00: 0-15-258722-5) is an intriguing, involved book of poems that deal with synonyms and antonyms.

About the Book and Author

Berger, Laura Standley, ed. *Twentieth-Century Young Adult Writers*. St. James, 1994, pp. 214–16.

Brown, Muriel W., and Rita S. Foudray. *Newbery and Caldecott Medalists and Honor Book Winners: Bibliographic & Resource Material Through 1991*. 2d ed. Neal-Schuman, 1992, pp. 136–37.

Chevalier, Tracy, ed. *Twentieth-Century Children's Writers*. 3d ed. St. James, 1989, pp. 349–50.

Collier, Laurie, and Joyce Nakamura. *Major Authors and Illustrators for Children and Young Adults*. Gale, 1993, 6 vols., pp. 842–45.

Commire, Anne, ed. *Something About the Author*. Vol. 39. Gale, 1985, pp. 72–73.

Contemporary Authors (New Revision Series).Vol. 84. Gale, 2000, pp. 92–96.

Fleischman, Paul. "The Accidental Artist (1998 Anne Carroll Moore lecture)." *School Library Journal* (March 1999): 104–7.

———. *Joyful Noise*. SRA/McGraw-Hill, 1990. Videocassette.

Fleischman, Sid. "Paul Fleischman." *Horn Book* (July/August 1989): 452–55.

Gallo, Donald R. *Speaking for Ourselves, Too*. National Council of Teachers of English, 1993, pp. 68–69.

Hedblad, Alan, ed. *Something About the Author*. Vol. 110. Gale, 2000, pp. 89–92.

Hile, Kevin S. *Authors and Artists for Young Adults*. Vol. 11. Gale, 1993, pp. 65–72.

Lesniak, James G., ed. *Contemporary Authors (New Revision Series)*. Vol. 37. Gale, 1992, pp. 185–87.

May, Hal, ed. *Contemporary Authors*. Vol. 113. Gale, 1985, p. 158.

Nakamura, Joyce, and Gerald J. Senick, eds. *Something About the Author: Autobiographical Series*. Vol. 20. Gale, 1995, pp. 219–30.

"Newbery Award Acceptance Material, 1989" *Journal of Youth Services to Libraries* (summer 1989): 299–306.

Newbery-Caldecott Acceptance Speech: Paul Fleischman. ALSC, 1989. Audiocassette.

"Newbery Medal Acceptance." *Horn Book* (July/August 1989): 451–52.

Senick, Gerard J., ed. *Children's Literature Review*. Vol. 20. Gale, 1990, pp. 63–70.

Silvey, Anita, ed. *Children's Books and Their Creators*. Houghton, 1995, p. 245.

Telgen, Diane, ed. *Something About the Author*. Vol. 72. Gale, 1993, pp. 68–71.

Ward, Martha, ed. *Authors of Books for Young People*. 3d ed. Scarecrow, 1990, p. 231.

Honor Books 1989

Hamilton, Virginia. *In the Beginning: Creation Stories from Around the World*. Harcourt, 1988, $23.95: 0-15-238740-4; pap., $18.95: 0-15-238742-0. (Grades 6–10)

This book contains 25 creation myths representing various cultures, times, and locations. Each of the tales is illustrated by at least one full-page dramatic illustration in full color by Barry Mosher. There are a total of 42 of these impressively striking paintings. Both the author and the illustrator have researched each myth thoroughly, and each retelling is followed by a brief commentary on its origin and the culture represented. In the Inuit myth "The Pea-Pod Man," the first man falls out of a pea pod and is found by the great god, the Raven, who begins to create plants and animals to please Man. Lastly he makes a figure out of clay with watercress for hair and gives it life. It is a lively woman, who has been fashioned to be Man's helper and mate. Soon they have a child, and the world begins to prosper. In a Huron myth, the creator is a divine woman who produces the earth and places it on the back of the turtle. She has two sons, one evil and one good. The evil one creates frightening animal life such as giant mosquitoes while the good one creates gentle beasts such as doves. The brothers quarrel, and the evil one is killed, though his spirit still roams the land. A story from ancient Babylonia, "Marduk, God of Gods" tells how the great and good Marduk confronts the evil Tiamat, queen of the salt-sea waters. When she is destroyed, Marduk raises one-half of her body on high to create heaven and creates earth out of the other half. After producing the days of the year and the order of the planets, he makes constellations representing the gods and creates man to be their servants. The book ends with the story of Elohim the Creator based on the Bible's Book of Genesis.

Myers, Walter Dean. *Scorpions*. Harper, 1988, $14.95: 0-06-024364-3; pap., $2.95: 0-06-447066-0. (Grades 6–9)

This novel of violence, gang life, and death on the streets of Harlem deals with 12-year-old Jamal Hicks and his problems involving family loyalties, poverty, friendship, and social pressures. Jamal's family consists of a loving Mama, who cleans for white folks; an eight-year-old sister, Sassy; and two absent members: his father, Jevon Hicks, a shiftless heavy drinker; and his older brother, Randy, who is in prison for armed robbery and lacks the $2,000 for an appeal. Jamal is devoted to his best friend, the gentle, dreamy Tito Cruz who lives with his grandmother. Mack, a member of Randy's former gang, the Scorpions, gives Jamal a gun along with an offer to become their new leader. Jamal knows that with the gun he can stop the taunts of the school bully, Dwayne Parsons, and also illegally get enough money for his brother's appeal. When he brandishes the gun at school and gets into trouble, Jamal gives the gun to Tito for safe keeping. Two members of the Scorpions who oppose Jamal's possible leadership, attack him one evening in a park, and to stop his friend's possible death, Tito shoots them. One dies and the other is seriously wounded. Although the gun is disposed of and a crackhead confesses to the crimes, Tito is so miserable and conscience-ridden that he finally tells his grandmother the truth. At the police hearing, Tito is cleared of the charges, but he is sent to Puerto Rico to live with his father. At their last meeting together, the two boys realize that both their lives and their friendship are in tatters. They embrace and part.

1990s

Newbery Winner 1990

Lowry, Lois. *Number the Stars*. Houghton, 1989, $16.00: 0-395-51060-0; pap., Dell, $3.99: 0-440-91002-1. (Grades 4–7)

Lois Lowry (1937–) is usually associated with contemporary family stories that chronicle, often humorously, the problems of growing up. *Number the Stars* represents a change in time, locale, and mood. In tracing the roots of the novel in her Newbery Award acceptance speech, the author stated that she had a dear friend, Annelise, who grew up in Denmark during World War II. Annelise told Lowry about life during this period, particularly when Denmark was occupied by the Germans. Later Lowry traveled in Denmark with Annelise, talked to resistance workers, and gathered detailed material on life at this time, even to the point of finding out the nature of the boots worn by Nazi soldiers. In an afterward to the novel, the author lists the historical sources used and which incidents and characters are based on fact. The title comes from Psalm 147, which is read by Peter Neilson during the supposed wake for Great-Aunt Birte. The significant lines are:

> O praise the Lord
> It is he who heals the broken in spirit
> and binds up their wounds
> he who numbers the stars one by one.

Although the story is written in the third person, the events are seen entirely through the eyes of the young heroine, Annemarie Johansen. Lois Lowry was awarded a second Newbery Medal in 1994 for *The Giver*. (See "Newbery Winner," 1994, p. 405)

Plot Summary

It is September 1943, and Copenhagen is enduring its third year of Nazi occupation during World War II. Ten-year-old Annemarie Johansen is racing home after school with her friend and neighbor, Ellen Rosen, and Annemarie's five-year-old sister, Kirsti. They are stopped by two German patrolmen who engage in some bullying tactics before allowing them to continue on their way. All three are shaken by the experience, and at home both Annemarie's mother and Mrs. Rosen warn them to avoid that street in the future.

Mr. and Mrs. Johansen and their two daughters live in the same apartment building as their friends and neighbors the Rosens, a Jewish couple and their only child, Ellen. Annemarie's beloved older sister, Lise, was killed less than three years ago, at age 18, on the eve of her wedding to Peter Neilsen. Her parents rarely mention her death except to say it was caused by an automobile accident. Her unworn wedding dress has been carefully stored in a never-opened trunk in the room Annemarie and Kirsti now share. Peter Neilsen is still part of their lives. He occasionally delivers a copy of the underground newspaper *De Frie Danske* (*The Free Danes*) to the Johansens. Annemarie is convinced he is a member of the gallant freedom fighters who make up the Danish Resistance movement.

Everyday life is difficult under the occupation. Food, clothing, and fuel are scarce; young Kirsti wears shoes made of fish skins. However, Annemarie feels fortunate to have loving, patient parents who do their best and hope for a better future. Occasional gifts of food are welcome from Mrs. Johansen's bachelor brother, Uncle Henrik, a fisherman who lives on the north coast.

The Johansens begin to notice increased persecution of Jews. All shops owned by Jews are closed, including the tiny button shop run by their friendly neighbor, Mrs. Hirsch. The day of the Jewish New Year, Rosh Hashanah, the Rosens's rabbi tells his congregation that Jews will soon be rounded up for deportation. That evening, Annemarie's mother announces that Mr. and Mrs. Rosen have been called away suddenly and that Ellen will be spending a few days with them.

In the middle of the night, the Johansens are awakened by German soldiers who want to search the apartment for Jews. As they enter the girls' bedroom, quick-thinking Annemarie snatches an incriminating Star of David from Ellen's neck. Ellen is presented as daughter Lise, and when the officer questions the fact that she has dark hair when the rest of the family is fair, Papa Johansen cleverly shows them a baby picture of Lise from the family album, who, luckily for them, had been born with a temporary head of rich dark-brown hair. Reluctantly, the soldiers leave.

The next day, Annemarie overhears a mysterious conversation between Papa and Uncle Henrik with references to good fishing weather and a carton of cigarettes. Soon, the three young girls and Mama Johansen are on a train headed north to visit Uncle Henrik in the tiny fishing village of Gillelege, only a few miles from the coast of Sweden. To avert suspicion, Papa stays behind in Copenhagen.

After a close brush on the train with more suspicious Nazis, they arrive safely and walk to the promontory on which Uncle Henrik's home and small farm are located. Kirsti, Ellen, and Annemarie are enchanted by the house, by a little kitten they find whom Kirsti names Thor, and by the luxury of real cream and butter courtesy of Henrik's cow, Blossom.

The next day, Mama announces that in the evening a casket containing the body of recently deceased Great-Aunt Birte will arrive and that a wake is to be held at Uncle Henrik's. Annemarie knows there is no Great-Aunt Birte but remains silent.

The casket is placed in the living room, and soon the "mourners" appear. First, there is a young couple with a tiny baby, followed by an elderly man. Soon they are joined by another couple, Mr. and Mrs. Rosen! When Peter Neilsen also appears, Annemarie realizes this is part of an elaborate and dangerous rescue plan. They will use her uncle's boat to transport the fugitive Jews to neutral Sweden and safety.

The mock wake is interrupted by loud banging on the door. German soldiers enter. They are suspicious and demand that the coffin be opened. Ingeniously, Mama tells them that Birte died of a very infectious form of typhus and that the attending doctor had insisted the coffin remain closed. After they leave, Peter opens the coffin, which is filled with warm clothing for the refugees. Peter also gives Mr. Rosen a small package that he says must be delivered to Henrik at his boat. Peter leaves for the boat with the first group, and 20 minutes later Mama leaves with the Rosens. The rocky, root-covered path is extremely treacherous in the dark.

When Mama's return is long overdue, Annemarie sees her in the distance, painfully crawling toward the house. She has fallen and broken her ankle. Annemarie also sees on the ground the package Mr. Rosen was to deliver. He obviously has accidentally dropped it. After making her mother comfortable, Annemarie sets out to deliver the package alone. After outwitting Nazi guards, she reaches the boat in which her friends are now safely hidden. The package contains a special formula that will deaden the sense of smell of the guard dogs that the Germans use to sniff out humans hidden on fishing boats. Because of Annemarie's bravery, the boat is able to leave safely for Sweden.

The war ends and Denmark is awash in celebrations, but for Annemarie, sorrow is mixed with joy. Some months before, Peter Neilsen was caught and executed. She has also learned that her sister Lise was in fact a martyr in the Resistance. She will never forget her sacrifice, but now she awaits the return of her friend Ellen and the opportunity to give back the tiny necklace she has kept for her.

Themes and Subjects

This is not only a stirring re-creation of a bleak period in Western history but also a moving tribute to those who sacrificed themselves to save their friends and restore their country's liberty. Its child's-eye view enables young readers to understand the war and identify with those innocents caught in it. It also explores the meaning of courage and how even the young can perform acts of heroism and selflessness. Another theme is the power of friendship between individuals and families and how this can influence important moral choices even to the point of jeopardizing one's personal safety. Good family relationships, the terrible consequences of prejudice, the Holocaust, and everyday life in occupied Denmark are all well portrayed in this suspense-filled, simply written novel.

Incidents for Booktalking

This novel contains a number of exciting passages to read or retell: Annemarie and Ellen are stopped by soldiers on their way home from school (pp. 1–4); Mrs. Hirsch's store is closed (pp. 19–22); Kirsti and her fish shoes (pp. 28–30); German soldiers raid the Johansen apartment (pp. 43–49); and the train ride to Uncle Henrik's home (pp. 54–56).

Related Titles

Lisa and other teenage Jews in Nazi-occupied Denmark get involved in the underground resistance movement in *Lisa's War* (Scribners, 1989, $15.00: 0-684-19010-2) by Carol Matas.

Individual acts of heroism performed by righteous gentiles are chronicled in *Rescue: The Story of How Gentiles Saved Jews in the Holocaust* (Harper, 1988, $16.00: 0-06-024209-4) by Milton Meltzer.

The day-to-day life of a French boy, Jean-Louis, during World War II, first in Brittany, then in Paris, is told in Jean-Louis Besson's *October, 45: Childhood Memories of the War* (Harcourt, 1995, $22.00: 0-15-200955-8).

America's involvement in World War II is told through many eye-witness accounts in Kathlyn and Martin Gay's *World War II* (Twenty-First Century, 1995, $18.90: 0-8050-2849-8).

Cassie's young friend, Miko Yashimoto and her family, leave for a Japanese American internment camp during World War II in Allan M. Winkler's *Cassie's War* (Royal Fireworks, 1995, $15.00: 0-88092-107-2).

About the Book and Author

Andres, Linda R. *Children's Literature Review*, Vol. 46. Gale, 1998, pp. 25–74.

Berger, Laura Standley, ed. *Twentieth-Century Young Adult Writers*. St. James, 1994, pp. 408–10.

Bowden, Jane A., ed. *Contemporary Authors*. Vols. 69–72. Gale, 1978, p. 386.

Brown, Muriel W., and Rita S. Foudray. *Newbery and Caldecott Medalists and Honor Book Winners: Bibliographic & Resource Material Through 1991*. 2d ed. Neal-Schuman, 1992, pp. 271–72.

Chevalier, Tracy, ed. *Twentieth-Century Children's Writers*. 3d ed. St. James, 1989, pp. 610–11.

Collier, Laurie, and Joyce Nakamura. *Major Authors and Illustrators for Children and Young Adults*. Gale, 1993, 6 vols., 1525–7

Commire, Anne, ed. *Something About the Author*. Vol. 23. Gale, 1981, pp. 120–22.

Estes, Glenn E., ed. "American Writers for Children Since 1960: Fiction." In *Dictionary of Literary Biography*. Vol. 52. Gale, 1986, pp. 249–61.

Gallo, Donald R., ed. *Speaking for Ourselves, Too*. National Council of Teachers of English, 1993, pp. 125–26

Garrett, Agnes, and Helga P. McCue, eds. *Authors and Artists for Young Adults*. Vol. 5. Gale, 1990, pp. 129–40.

Haley-James, Shirley. "Lois Lowry." *Horn Book* (July/Aug., 1990): 422–24.

Hedblad, Alan, ed. *Something About the Author*. Vol. 111. Gale, 2000, pp. 102–10

Hipple, Ted, ed. *Writers for Young Adults*. Vol. 2. Scribner's, 1997, pp. 279–87

Lois Lowry. Profiles in Literature, 1990. Videocassette.

Lowery, Lois. *Number the Stars.* PBS Video, 1994. Videocassette, 15 min. ($39.95)

————. *Number the Stars.* Read by Christina Moore. Recorded Books, 1992. Audio-cassettes, 270 min. ($26.00)

Metzger, Linda, ed. *Contemporary Authors (New Revision Series).* Vol. 13. Gale, 1984, pp. 333–36.

"Newbery Award Acceptance Material, 1990." *Journal of Youth Services in Libraries* 3, no. 4 (summer 1990): 281–88.

"Newbery Medal Acceptance." *Horn Book* (July/Aug. 1990): 412–21

Newbery-Caldecott Acceptance Speech: Lois Lowry. ALSC, 1990. Audiocassette.

Olendorf, Donn, and Diane Telgen, eds. *Something About the Author.* Vol. 70. Gale, 1993, pp. 134–37.

Peck, Jackie S., and Judy Hendershot. "An Interview with Lois Lowry, 1994 Newbery Medal Winner." *Reading Teacher* (Dec./Jan. 1994–95): 308–9.

Sarkissian, Adele, ed. *Something About the Author: Autobiographical Series.* Vol. 3. Gale, 1987, pp. 189–204.

Senick, Gerard J., ed. *Children's Literature Review.* Vol. 6. Gale, 1984, pp. 192–94.

Silvey, Anita, ed. *Children's Books and Their Creators.* Houghton, 1995, pp. 419–21.

Trosky, Susan M., ed. *Contemporary Authors (New Revision Series).* Vol. 43. Gale, 1994, pp. 280–84.

Ward, Martha, ed. *Authors of Books for Young People.* 3d ed. Scarecrow, 1990, p. 451.

Honor Books 1990

Lisle, Janet Taylor. *Afternoon of the Elves.* Orchard Books, 1989, $15.95: 0-531-05837-9. (Grades 4–6)

Nine-year-old Hillary Lenox and her snooty friends regard Sara-Kate Connolly as a pathetic loner. Though 11, Sara-Kate is only in the fifth grade because of failing a year. Plain and unattractive, she dresses in old wrinkly clothes and oversized boots. She lives in a dilapidated old house with a reclusive mother who is never seen. Her father lives in Florida. Sara-Kate has a secret that she shares with Hillary. In her backyard, among the weeds, old tires, and assorted junk she has a miniature community of nine tiny houses made out of sticks, string, and wire with leaves for roofs. Sara-Kate claims it is a village inhabited by elves. Gradually, Hillary loses her distaste for the defiant, independent Sara-Kate, and the two build a friendship and a fantasy world around these structures. Other structures appear including a ferris wheel made of popsicle sticks and two bicycle tires. Impressionable Hillary wants to believe that they are actual manifestations of a fairy world, although in time she wonders if the elf-like Sara-Kate is really the secret builder. Sara-Kate won't talk about her family or allow Hillary inside her house, but one day, after Sara-Kate has been absent from school for several days, Hillary ventures inside the house and finds total disarray and squalor. Sara-Kate confesses that she is responsible for running the household and caring for a completely helpless, deranged mother. When the small checks from her father do not arrive, she is forced to steal and cheat to get enough food to survive. Her major form of escape has been the elf village. Hillary's mother learns of Sara-Kate's situation, and with other do-gooders in the community gets Sara-Kate's mother to a rest home, and in spite of protests from Sara-Kate, arranges for the girl to go to live with relatives in Kansas. Hillary is crushed when Sara-Kate leaves without saying goodbye, but as a remembrance of their magical moments together decides to move the little village to her backyard.

Paulsen, Gary. *The Winter Room*. Orchard Books, 1989, $15.95: 0-531-05839-5. (Grades 5–8)

This novel set on a northern Minnesota farm, probably in the 1930s, is narrated by 11-year-old Eldon whose family consists of a mother and father, a 13-year-old brother, Wayne, and two elder farm helpers, Uncle David and Nels. The action involves a calendar year in the lives of this loving, closely knit hardworking family. In the spring the earth on the 87-acre farm is prepared for the seeding that takes place during the early summer when such crops as wheat, oats, barley, corn, and potatoes are planted. The fall is a time of terror and sadness for Eldon because this is when the steers, pigs, and chicken are slaughtered. These scenes of death and blood are described graphically by the boy who is horrified at what he sees. In the evenings during the winter, the family moves into a downstairs room where there is a wood stove and each member of the family has an allotted seat. While father works on his wood carving and mother knits, Uncle David tells stories of his native Norway. Stories of how his young, beautiful bride, Alida, died with her baby during childbirth and of David's grief that finally led him to the New World to forget. He also tells of an ancient Viking warrior, Orud the Terrible, and of a wily prankster, the logger nicknamed Crazy Alen. When he tells of the marvelous feats of a woodcutter, Father says that these are thinly disguised stories of David's own accomplishments. One day, Uncle David overhears Wayne tell his brother that he thinks his uncle has made up the stories of his exploits and that he is a liar. That night there are no more stories and everyone sees how hurt and withdrawn Uncle David has become. Several days later, the boys see their uncle secretly take out his giant axes and try one of the deeds he has bragged about in his stories. Summoning all his strength, the old man is successful. The boys remain silent about what they have seen but that night the storytelling resumes.

Staples, Suzanne Fisher. *Shabanu: Daughter of the Wind*. Knopf, 1989, $18.00: 00-394-84815-2; pap., $4.99: 0-6788-81030-7. (Grades 7–9).

Set in contemporary Pakistan, this novel deals with a family of nomadic camel raisers who live in the desolate Cholistan Desert about midway between Karachi and Lahore. It brilliantly recaptures the atmosphere, customs, and hardship of life in this remote Muslim area. The narrator is 11-year-old Shabanu who lives in the desert with her father Dadi, Mama, a grandfather, an aunt, and her sister Phulan, now 13. Shabanu and Phulan have been promised in marriage to two young brothers, Murad and Hamir, who, since their father's death, have cared for their mother and sisters on their small farm some miles away. Shabanu, a lively, daring girl, accompanies her father on an adventurous journey to the town of Sibi where they successfully sell part of their herd of camels to raise money for both living expenses and the two marriage dowries. After their return, the family is forced to leave their desert encampment temporarily after a violent sand storm engulfs their watering hole and causes mortal injuries to their grandfather. After obeying grandfather's deathbed request to be buried at a fort where he had served gallantly in the army, the family continues on to the farm of their future in-laws. There, they run afoul of Nazir Mohammed, Murad and Hamir's lecherous landlord, and are forced to flee after a skirmish in which Hamir is killed. In a settlement with Nazir's family, the farm is returned to Murad and his family, and it is decided that Phulan will marry Murad and Shabuna, instead, will become the fourth wife of Rahim, the wealthy 50-year-old brother of Nazir. Shabuna is dismayed at this, even though it means she will have a life of comfort and luxury. She decides to run away but is caught by her father who reluctantly beats her for her disobedience. Shabanu now realizes that she must accept her fate and make the best of it.

Newbery Winner 1991

Spinelli, Jerry. *Maniac Magee*. Little, 1990, $15.45: 0-316-80722-2; pap., Harper, $3.95: 0-06-447151-9. (Grades 5–8)

Jerry Spinelli's (1941–) first books for young readers appeared in the early 1980s with such titles as *Space Station Seventh Grade* (Little, 1982, $14.95), the story of an early adolescent struggling with pimples, girls, and puberty. Mr. Spinelli claims that many of the ideas and situations in his novels come from real-life experiences with his children. The author's knack for realistically re-creating the irreverent vocabulary and concerns of today's young people is again evidenced in *Maniac Magee*, but here the material is handled with greater depth and scope. The central character in this novel, a pint-size contemporary version of Pecos Bill or Paul Bunyan, is, in the words of the author, "the kid as legendary hero." Although the story is set within a tall-tale framework, at its center is the reality of today's social concerns. Spinelli uses exaggeration, humor, and melodrama to tell a parable about racism and the homeless. This novel won both the Boston Globe-Horn Book Award and the Newbery Medal. Most of the story takes place in a small town in southeastern Pennsylvania similar to Phoenixville where the author currently lives. The novel covers a period of about one year.

Plot Summary

At age three, Jeffrey Lionel Magee (later nicknamed Maniac by those who witnessed his amazing feats) was orphaned when the trolley on which his parents were passengers left the tracks of the Schuylkil River trestle and plunged into the water. For the next eight years he lived with an ever-quarreling Aunt Dot and Uncle Dan until one day, unable to take it any longer, he ran away.

Now, one year later, he suddenly appears on the streets of Two Mills, a small Pennsylvania town just across the river from where he was born. Two Mills is divided geographically and emotionally by rampant racism. The blacks live in the East End and the whites, or fishbellies, live in the West End. The dividing line is the uncrossable Hector Street.

Unaware of this division, Maniac wanders aimlessly from one area to another. In the black neighborhood, he meets a high-spirited girl named Amanda Veale, who grudgingly lends him one of her precious reading books. It is on the white side of town, however, that Maniac performs his most talked about feats and is given his nickname. First, he outshines even James "Hands" Down in a high school football practice; next, he shows fantastic courage by entering the dreaded Finsterwald property to rescue a youngster who was there as a result of a cruel practical joke. His most important accomplishment occurs during his appearance at a Little League game when he scores several home runs at the expense of the invulnerable pitcher, John McNab. However, Magee still does not have a home. Sometimes he eats meals with the Pickwells, a family so large they often don't realize they have a guest, and sometimes in the evenings he climbs the fence at the zoo and sleeps in the lean-to in the buffalo enclosure.

Seeking revenge for his humiliating baseball defeat, John McNab and his street gang, known as the Cobras, chase Maniac who innocently seeks refuge in the East End. Here he is confronted by a big black bully named Mars Bar Thompson, but fortunately Maniac is rescued by Amanda who is as anxious to save her precious book as she is to help McGee. Amanda invites him to her home, and he instantly becomes a part of the family. The Beale family so adores him—even the younger children, Hester and Lester—that they invite him to stay.

His reputation in town increases when he is able to untie the fabled Cobble's Knot, a mass of tangled rope the size of a volleyball that has defied hundreds who attempted to undo it. His reward is a year's supply of pizza, a food to which Maniac is unfortunately allergic.

His stay with the Beales is cut short when racist threats by black extremists in the neighborhood make him fearful for the safety of the Beales. Regretfully, he leaves and moves back to the zoo.

He is found by an old park hand named Grayson who moves Maniac into the equipment room at the back of the bandstand. Grayson tells an enthralled Maniac about his career as a pitcher in the minor leagues, of such glories as striking out a young Willie Mays, and of the tragedy of his eventual discharge. They become such close friends that Grayson gives up his room at the YMCA and moves in with Maniac. One day the old man asks Maniac if he will help him learn to read, so every day after the old man is finished working at the park, Maniac gives instruction from old books, such as *The Little Engine That Could*, purchased from the discard pile at the local library. Their little home is the scene of wonderful feasts at Thanksgiving and Christmas. At the latter, Grayson gives Maniac a box of his favorite sweets, Krumpets, and Maniac gives Grayson a hand-printed book he has written called *The Man Who Struck Out Willie Mays*.

Just before the New Year, Grayson dies suddenly and Maniac is again without a home. Once more he begins wandering and one night takes shelter from the bitter cold in one of the cabins at Valley Forge that are replicas of the army shelters used during the American Revolution. In a neighboring shelter, he encounters two scruffy young brothers, Russell and Piper, who are runaways. Maniac persuades them to go back to their home in Two Mills. He accompanies them and finds himself in one of the dirtiest, roach-ridden hovels imaginable. Maniac meets the boys' older brother, John McNab, the once-ace pitcher whom he had humiliated at Little League months before, and the father, George McNab, a filthy redneck so obsessed with racial hate that he is building a mortar bunker in his living room in case the blacks cross Hector Street. In spite of these obvious inconveniences, Maniac stays with the McNabs to make sure that Russell and Piper remain in school. He does this by bribing the boys by performing physical feats that again enhance his reputation. One such exploit involves entering the East End where once again he encounters Mars Bar. To settle their old dispute, they engage in a road race. When Maniac wins, Mars Bar not only declares a truce but even extends the hand of friendship. Maniac reciprocates by inviting the black boy to the McNabs' for Piper's birthday party. When father George and John's gang, the Cobras, arrive, Maniac realizes his mistake and manages to escape with Mars Bar before violence erupts.

Once again, Maniac is on his own living with the buffalo. One day he again encounters Mars Bar. Together they wander toward the trestle where Maniac's parents were killed. There they see a stranded Russell McNab, who has wandered halfway out on the trestle and is now motionless with fright. Maniac is so traumatized by his memories that he walks away, leaving Mars Bar to effect the rescue.

In spite of Mars Bar's entreaties to come home with him, Maniac continues to stay at the zoo until one day forceful Amanada Beale accompanies Mars Bar. She demands that Maniac give up this unhealthy life and come back to live with the Beales. Maniac capitulates, secretly overjoyed that somebody wants him enough to give him a permanent home.

Themes and Subjects

Although this story uses many features of the tall tale, these elements not only amuse but also soften the poignant story of a vulnerable young boy looking for a home, family, and security. This is also a good-natured spoof of some of our folktales and myths, e.g., the variation of the Gordian knot story. Maniac is, in some respects, a present-day Candide, unable and unwilling to believe the ugly aspects of reality. Three of the contemporary problems addressed in this story are racial prejudice, homelessness, and illiteracy. In spite of the seriousness of these themes, this is a hopeful book, one in which optimism, innocence, and positive values prevail. The importance of getting to know one another as individuals in order to combat bigotry and misunderstanding is stressed. Other subjects dealt with are baseball, friendship, survival, and various kinds of family life.

Incidents for Booktalking

How Jeffrey Lionel became known as Maniac can provide a fine introduction to the book. Important episodes include: Maniac leaves Aunt Dot and Uncle Dan (pp. 5–7); he meets Amanda Beale (pp. 10–13) and saves a child from the Finsterwald backyard (pp. 16–19); the Little League game with John McNab as pitcher (pp. 22–27); Maniac first encounters Mars Bar and is invited to Amanda's house (pp. 33–40); and untying Cobble's Knot (pp. 70–73).

Related Titles

Humor and science fiction mix successfully in Richard Peck's *Lost in Cyberspace* (Dial, 1995, $14.99: 0-8037-1931-0; pap., Viking, $3.95: 0-14-037856-1) when Josh and best friend Aaron turn two computers into a time machine.

Two misfits, a 20-year-old punk artist named Angie, and a bullied 11-year-old boy find temporary happiness in Robin Klein's *Came Back to Show You I Could Fly* (Viking, 1990, $11.95: 0-670-82901-3).

Jessie and her older brother pick up an unusual hitchhiker, an elderly man who loves gambling, in *The Hitchhiking Vampire* (pap., Dell, $3.25: 0-440-40477-0) by Stephen Mooser.

In San Francisco's Chinatown, Teddy gives his younger, almost-perfect brother an alligator as a birthday present in Laurence Yep's *Later, Gator* (Hyperion, 1995, $13.95: 07868-0059-3).

Avi's *Poppy* (Orchard, 1995, $15.95: 0-531-09483-9) tells an exciting story about the territory ruled by Mr. Ocax the owl where Poppy, a young deer mouse, lives with his large extended family.

About the Book and Author

Berger, Laura Standley, ed. *Twentieth-Century Young Adult Writers*. St. James, 1994, pp. 611–12.

Brown, Muriel W., and Rita S. Foudray. *Newbery and Caldecott Medalists and Honor Book Winners: Bibliographic & Resource Material Through 1991*. 2d ed. Neal-Schuman, 1992, p. 401.

Collier, Laurie, and Joyce Nakamura. *Major Authors and Illustrators for Children and Young Adults*. Gale, 1993, 6 vols., pp. 2192–94.

Commire, Anne, ed. *Something About the Author*. Vol. 39. Gale, 1985, p. 198.

Gallo, Donald R., ed. *Speaking for Ourselves*. National Council of Teachers of English, 1990, pp. 198–99.

Hile, Kevin S. *Authors and Artists for Young Adults*. Vol. 11. Gale, 1993, pp. 209–16.

Hedblad, Alan. *Something About the Author*. Vol. 110. Gale, 2000, pp. 210–214.

Hipple, Ted, ed. *Writers for Young Adults*. Scribner's, 1997, 3 vols., pp. 193–202.

Holtze, Sally Holmes, ed. *Sixth Book of Junior Authors and Illustrators*. Wilson, 1989, pp. 284–85.

Jerry and Eileen Spinelli. Profiles in Literature, 1992. Videocassette.

Keller, John. "Jerry Spinelli." *Horn Book* (July/Aug. 1991): 433–35.

Lesniak, James G., ed. *Contemporary Authors (New Revision Series).* Vol. 30. Gale, 1990, p. 424.

May, Hal, ed. *Contemporary Authors.* Vol. 111. Gale, 1984, p. 435.

"Newbery Award Acceptance Material, 1991." *Journal of Youth Services in Libraries* (summer 1991): 335–39.

"Newbery Medal Acceptance." *Horn Book* (July/Aug. 1991): 426–32.

Newbery-Caldecott Acceptance Speech: Jerry Spinelli. ALSC, 1991. Audiocassette.

Senick, Gerard J., ed. *Children's Literature Review.* Vol. 26. Gale, 1992, pp. 201–7.

Silvey, Anita, ed. *Children's Books and Their Creators.* Houghton, 1995, pp. 619–21

Spinelli, Jerry. *Maniac Magee.* Pharaoh Audiobooks, 1992. Audiocassettes, 160 min. ($15.95)

Telgen, Diane, ed. *Something About the Author.* Vol. 71. Gale, 1993, pp. 180–83.

Honor Books 1991

Avi. *The True Confessions of Charlotte Doyle.* Orchard, 1990, $16.95: 0-531-05893-X; pap., Avon, $4.50: 0-380-71475-2. (Grades 6–9)

In 1832, after almost eight years working in England, Mr. Doyle is recalled to the head office of his shipping firm in Providence, Rhode Island. It is decided that his daughter Charlotte should remain behind to complete her school year and return in the summer as the sole passenger on the brig *Seahawk*. At the dock in Plymouth, she encounters the first indications that the trip is ill-fated when, at the mention of the captain's name, Jaggery, the stevedores refuse to handle her luggage. On board, she is befriended by an old black seaman named Zachariah who gives a reluctant Charlotte a dagger for protection. Captain Jaggery at first appears to Charlotte to be a perfect gentleman. Under his influence, she consents to report any suspicious actions by the crew. Because of her tattling, Jaggery tries to prevent a mutiny by killing one of the ringleaders and flogging Zachariah publicly. Charlotte realizes that her first impressions of Jaggery were actually a calculated hoax to win her confidence and that he is really a sadistic, cruel man whose crew is rightfully planning a retaliation to avenge past injustices. Although Charlotte is lead to believe her friend Zachariah has died of his wounds, he has been hidden and is being nursed back to health by the crew. Filled with remorse and guilt at her actions, Charlotte switches allegiances and joins the crew. Fearfull of the tales Charlotte will tell when they land, Jaggery murders the first mate, Hollybrass, using Charlotte's dagger, and thus, is able to blame the murder on her. Zarchariah secretly frees Charlotte from the ship before she is scheduled to be hanged. On deck she is found by Jaggery and in the ensuing chase, the captain falls overboard and is drowned. In Providence, Charlotte is unable to adjust to the dull life of again being a prim young lady who accepts the harsh regulations that her father imposes. One evening, she dresses in her sailor's togs, and creeps out to join Zachariah on the next voyage of the *Seahawk*. This rousing sea adventure is a first-person narrative that contains many fascinating details of life aboard a nineteenth-century sailing ship.

❀ Newbery Winner 1992

Naylor, Phyllis Reynolds. *Shiloh*. Macmillan, 1991, $15.00: 0-689-31614-3; pap., Dell, $3.50: 0-440-21991-4. (Grades 3–6)

As Phyllis Reynolds Naylor (1933–) states in her autobiography, *How I Came to Be a Writer* (pap., Macmillan, $4.95), she began writing as a teenager. Since then she has written approximately 60 books for children, among them the popular Alice series for middle-grade students. In a comment reprinted in *Twentieth-Century Young Adult Writers*, Ms. Naylor said about her writing, "If I spent the rest of my life working at the ideas I have already accumulated. . . . I would still not be able to finish them all. I will do anything possible to save time in which to write. I shamelessly order meals to be delivered, pay for secretarial and cleaning help, and if I could allocate my three-mile walk every morning to some- one else, I would probably even pay for that." Concerning the genesis of *Shiloh*, a more serious novel than her average, the author said in her Newbery Award ac- ceptance speech that she and her husband were visiting friends in West Virginia, and while on a long walk in the country, "we found a hungry, trembling—and strangely silent—dog. It was so frightened and beaten down, it kept slinking away from us but . . . when I whistled, it inexplicably came bounding over, leaping up to lick my cheek." This dog, later adopted by their friends, was the inspiration for *Shiloh*. It is a first-person narrative told by young Marty Preston in a frequently ungrammatical but authentic West Virginia dialect.

Plot Summary

Eleven-year-old Marty is the oldest of the three Preston children, who live with their parents in a humble four-room house in rural West Virginia close to a small town called Friendly. Their home, situated on wooded property surrounded by three hills, is isolated but beautiful in its peacefulness. The other children are Dara Lynn, age seven, and the baby, Becky, age three. Ray Preston, their father, is a rural mail deliverer, and although he has a steady job, much of his salary is used to support his ailing aged mother, who lives with her daughter and requires constant home care. Lou Preston, their mother, is therefore often hard-pressed to run a household of five on the meager amount of money available. She must often rely on Roy's prowess as a hunter to put meat on the table. Nevertheless, it is a loving, caring household in which simple things like being polite and considerate are stressed as important guidelines by which to live.

One Sunday after a noontime rabbit dinner, Marty takes his .22 rifle out for target practice. He has a great respect for living things and would never shoot an animal or bird. In the Shiloh woods he realizes he is being followed by a young beagle with black and brown spots. From its cautious, frightened behavior, Marty surmises the dog has been severely maltreated. Gradually the dog realizes he won't be harmed and allows Marty to pet and play with him. He follows the boy home and in spite of pelting rain, remains hunched outside the house until Marty sneaks out and feeds him an egg from the hen house. Marty decides to call him Shiloh after the area where he was found.

Mr. Preston is certain the animal is Judd Traver's new hunting dog. After supper, he loads Shiloh and Marty into their Jeep to return the dog. Although Marty does not know Judd Travers well, he has ample reason to dislike him. He has seen Judd cheat the local general store owner out of $10 and he knows Judd hunts out of season and is cruel to his hunting dogs. He also has the disgusting habit of spitting tobacco out of the side of his mouth. As Marty fears, the dog belongs to Judd, who, as a welcome home present, gives the dog a nasty kick and promises to cut his rations until he learns not to run away. Marty is heartbroken but helpless. He plans to start earning money so that one day he will be able to buy Shiloh for his own. The next day he begins collecting bottles and cans from roadsides, hoping to make some money from deposits. The pickings are very lean, and he becomes discouraged.

The following morning, Marty hears a strange but familiar sound from the direction of the sycamore tree in the yard. It is Shiloh, who has escaped from Judd again. Marty carries him into the woods, where he puts up a 4-x-6-foot pen using some fencing wire he finds in the barn and builds a lean-to of old planks to protect the dog from the rain. He also feeds Shiloh table scraps he manages to take from the house. He feels increasingly guilty about deceiving his parents, particularly when, the next evening, Judd drives by in his pickup looking for the dog, and Marty lies openly, saying he hasn't seen him. However, he feels that saving Shiloh's life is now his most important mission.

In the next few days, Marty's life is an agony of trying to keep Shiloh's whereabouts a secret. Once Dara Lynn almost happens on his hiding place, and on another occasion his father is asked by Judd to hunt on Preston's land, but luckily the request is refused. When Marty's best friend, David Howard, asks to visit and explore in the woods, Marty decides to hitch a ride to David's home in Friendly rather than face the possibility of discovery. Ironically, the man who gives him a ride is Judd Travers, who again threatens a terrible punishment on his dog when it is found.

The visit with David is fun. With the sandwich Mrs. Howard packs for his walk home and some scraps he buys from the local store with his deposit money, Marty now has enough food to feed Shiloh for the next few days.

Discovery comes. Ma, who has become suspicious of Marty's eating habits, follows him into the woods and sees Shiloh. Giving in to Marty's tearful pleas, she agrees to remain silent for 24 hours to see if Marty can work out a solution. However, that evening the household is awakened by loud yelping and barking from the direction of the pen. A savage German shepherd has jumped the fence and is attacking Shiloh fiercely. Marty and his father drive the intruder off, but Shiloh is badly injured and bleeding profusely. In the middle of the night Mr. Preston takes him to Doc Murphy, who stitches him up and cleans out the wounds, but the dog is unable to walk. On the way home, Marty once again begs to keep the dog. Reluctantly, Mr. Preston agrees to keep Shiloh until he has recovered. Then he must be returned to Judd.

The next day Doc Murphy brings Shiloh back to the Prestons, where he quickly captures the hearts of the entire family. Just when he is able to hobble about, Judd Travers appears at their door. Through acquaintances who saw Shiloh at the doctor's office, he has tracked down the dog. Judd refuses to sell the dog and demands that he be returned on Sunday, only three days away. Marty frantically tries to think of a way to keep Shiloh, but in vain.

Early on Sunday morning, he decides to walk over to Judd's, hoping for a last-minute reprieve. On the way he sees a grazing doe and a moment later hears rifle shots. The deer falls dead and Judd strides into the clearing to claim his illegal prize. Marty confronts him and threatens to expose him to the game warden for hunting out of season. Judd strikes a bargain. If the boy will keep silent about the deer and do 20 hours of labor around Judd's house weeding, stacking wood, and doing odd jobs, the dog is his. Marty gets a written contract from Judd and gleefully returns home.

The family is overjoyed that Shiloh is going to become a permanent member of the household, but guilt again overwhelms Marty because he can't tell his family the real cause of Judd's change of heart.

Each day Marty walks to Judd's to do two of his 20 hours of service, and Judd does everything he can to make the boy give up. Once he tells him the contract is invalid because there were no witnesses; on other occasions he pretends to be asleep, thinking Marty will steal off before his two hours are up. He also assigns him the most backbreaking chores—splitting large chunks of locust wood using a heavy wedge and sledge hammer. But Marty's body and spirit will not be broken, and by the last day Judd grudgingly feels something close to admiration for this gutsy boy who will not take no for an answer. As a parting gift, he gives Marty an old dog collar. It's pretty large, but in time, Marty knows, it will fit Shiloh snugly.

Themes and Subjects

This is the story of the great bond that can exist between a boy and a dog. It is also a plea to end cruelty to helpless animals and to respect all living creatures. Marty's feelings of guilt when he has to compromise his honesty, steal, and deceive his parents to save Shiloh introduce the question "Does the end ever justify the means?" The author has captured the atmosphere of rural West Virginia and the speech patterns of the residents authentically. Solid family relationships, animal rights, the courage to fight for a just cause, and a boy's first steps to independence are other subjects dealt with in this novel.

Incidents for Booktalking

Some of the following are interesting passages that could be read or retold: Dinner at the Prestons (pp. 11–12); Shiloh is first introduced (pp. 13–18); the reasons given why Marty doesn't like Judd Travers, Shiloh is returned (pp. 22–27); Shiloh re-appears (pp. 40–44); Marty lies to Judd (pp. 51–54).

Related Titles

In *Where the Red Fern Grows* (pap., Dell, $2.99: 0-440-22814-X) by Wilson Rawls, a young boy saves money to buy two coon dogs and is heartbroken when they die.

Daniel finds a dog that is near death and tries to give this fearful pet a good home in Jane Resh Thomas's *The Comeback Dog* (Clarion, 1981, $16.00: 0-395-29432-0).

Rowena turns a foul-mouthed cockatoo into a model pet in Morris Gleitzman's humorous *Sticky Beak* (Harcourt, 1995, $11.00: 0-15-200366-5).

In the 12 stories (three per season) in Sheila Kelly Welch's collection *A Horse for All Seasons* (pap., Dell, $3.99: 0-044-41174-2), young people tell about their horses.

Two dogs and a Siamese cat set out on a perilous trek to return to their original home in Shiela Burnford's *The Incredible Journey* (Amereon, 1994, $18.95: 0-88411-099-0).

About the Book and Author

Berger, Laura Standley, ed. *Twentieth-Century Young Adult Writers*. St. James, 1994, pp. 481–84.

————. *Twentieth-Century Children's Writers*. 4th ed. St. James, 1995, pp. 692–94.

Brown, Muriel W., and Rita S. Foudray. *Newbery and Caldecott Medalists and Honor Book Winners: Bibliographic & Resource Material Through 1991*. 2d ed. Neal-Schuman, 1992, pp. 305–7.

Chevalier, Tracy, ed. *Twentieth-Century Children's Writers*. 3d ed. St. James, 1989, pp. 710–12.

Collier, Laurie, and Joyce Nakamura. *Major Authors and Illustrators for Children and Young Adults*. Gale, 1993, 6 vols., pp. 1747–51.

Commire, Anne, ed. *Something About the Author*. Vol. 12. Gale, 1977, pp. 156–57.

Evory, Ann, and Linda Metzger, eds. *Contemporary Authors (New Revision Series)*. Vol. 8. Gale, 1983, pp. 380–81.

Gallo, Donald R. *Speaking for Ourselves, Too*. National Council of Teachers of English, 1993, pp. 146–47.

Garrett, Agnes, and Helga P. McCue, eds. *Authors and Artists for Young Adults*. Vol. 4. Gale, 1990, pp. 215–28.

Graham, Joyce. "An Interview with Phyllis Reynolds Naylor." *Journal of Youth Services in Libraries* (summer 1993): 392–98.

Hedblad, Alan. *Something About the Author*. Vol. 102. Gale, 1999, pp. 149–56.

Helbig, Alethea K., and Agnes R. Perkins, eds. *Dictionary of American Children's Fiction, 1960–1984*. Greenwood, 1986, p. 469 (bio.).

Hipple, Ted, ed. *Writers for Young Adults*. Scribner's, 1997, 3 vols., pp. 397–46.

Holtz, Sally Holmes, ed. *Fifth Book of Junior Authors and Illustrators*. Wilson, 1983, pp. 227–28.

McMahon, Thomas, ed. *Authors and Artists for Young Adults*. Vol. 29. Gale, 1999, pp. 149–60.

Nasso, Christine, ed. *Contemporary Authors (First Revision Series)*. Vols. 21–24. Gale, 1977, p. 634.

Naylor, Phyllis Reynolds. *How I Came to Be a Writer*. Macmillan, 1989.

————. *Shiloh.* Read by Peter MacNicol. Recorded Books, 1997. Audiocassettes, 180 min.

Naylor, Rex. "Phyllis Reynolds Naylor." *Horn Book* (July/Aug. 1992): 412–15.

"Newbery Award Acceptance Material, 1992." *Journal of Youth Services in Libraries* 5, no. 4 (summer 1992): 351–56.

"Newbery Medal Acceptance." *Horn Book* (July/Aug. 1992): 404–11.

Olendorf, Donna, ed. *Something About the Author.* Vol. 66. Gale, 1991, pp. 170–76.

Senick, Gerard J., ed. *Children's Literature Review.* Vol. 17. Gale, 1989, pp. 48–62.

Silvey, Anita, ed. *Children's Books and Their Creators.* Houghton, 1995, pp. 482–83.

Straub, Deborah A., ed. *Contemporary Authors (New Revision Series).* Vol. 24. Gale, 1988, pp. 344–45.

Ward, Martha, ed. *Authors of Books for Young People.* 3d ed. Scarecrow, 1990, p. 520.

West, Mark I. "Speaking of Censorship: An Interview with Phyllis Reynolds Naylor." *Journal of Youth Services in Libraries* (winter 1997): 177–83.

Honor Books 1992

Avi. *Nothing But the Truth: A Documentary Novel.* Orchard, 1991, $16.95: 0-7862-0131-2. (Grades 6–9)

This novel, which takes place in a four-week time span, is told entirely through the use of documents—memos, transcripts of conversations, and letters. It deals with an escalating crisis in the relationship of a 14-year-old high school freshman, Philip Malloy, and his dedicated and somewhat old-fashioned English teacher, Miss Margaret Narwin. Philip is a lazy, smart-alecky boy who tries to get along by personality rather than work. When he rightfully gets a failing grade in English from Miss Narwin, who is also his homeroom teacher, thus disqualifying him from the track team, he vows somehow to get out of Miss Narwin's clutches. His tactic is to disrupt homeroom period by humming during the playing of the national anthem, though the school rules require a "respectful silence." In spite of repeated warnings, he continues this confrontational behavior and is suspended for two days by the vice principal. His parents, unaware of Philip's true motives, appeal for help to their neighbor Ted Griffen, who is looking for a cause on which to bolster his campaign in the upcoming school board election. He reports the story to the local newspaper which prints a biased, inaccurate account under the headline *Suspended for Patriotism.* Soon the story receives national coverage in the news media and radio phone-in shows all supporting the gallant lad who stood up for his rights and love of country. The Molloy family is flooded with telegrams and letters of support while Miss Narwin gets her share of communications—all critical, many demanding her resignation. Miss Narwin and Philip, both increasingly miserable with each new development, become helpless pawns in a larger power conflict much of which is motivated solely by self-interest. Sickened by the crisis he has caused and ashamed for his part in destroying a fine teacher's reputation, Philip transfers to another school while Miss Narwin, now contemplating resignation, is forced to take a leave of absence. Ted Griffen, however, wins the school election. This powerful novel shows how truth can be manipulated sometimes innocently but often for personal gain. It also explores the concept, well-stated by Samuel Johnson, that "patriotism is the last refuge of the scoundrel."

Freedman, Russell. *The Wright Brothers: How They Invented the Airplane*. Holiday, 1991, $19.95: 0-8234-0875-2. (Grades 6–9)

Although separated in age by four years, Wilbur and Orville Wright grew up like twins. As Wilbur once said, "we lived together, played together, worked together and, in fact, thought together." As children in Dayton, Ohio, both Wilbur (b. 1867) and Orville (b. 1871) were interested in tinkering, repairing broken objects, and creating models. As young men they became successful publishers and soon were printing their own daily newspaper. They became so involved with the care and use of bicycles that they opened the Wright Cycle Company where they built, sold, and repaired all kinds of bicycles. Their fascination with the emerging science of flight lead to a study of the works of pioneers Lilienthal and Chanute in hang gliding and Langley in model airplanes. Soon they also began experimenting with gliders at Kitty Hawk, on the Outer Banks of North Carolina chosen because the winds were favorable and there were great open spaces. After designing and building a number of innovative gliders, they decided to experiment with aircrafts propelled by a motor. Through a series of amazing trial and error efforts using various wing and tail rudder configurations, as well as different lightweight motors and propellers, success came on December 17, 1903, with a 59-second solo flight with Orville at the controls. The age of flight had begun. Gradually their aircraft became more substantial and sophisticated and their flights longer and more daring. As people realized the momentous importance of their work, the fame of the brothers grew. When they went to Europe for a series of demonstration flights, they were feted by crowned heads and other dignitaries. Back home, they soon became wealthy entrepreneurs in the fledgling airplane industry. In 1912, Wilbur died at age 45 of typhoid fever but Orville lived until 1948, the eve of space travel. The exciting text in this volume, is perfectly complemented by more than 90 wonderful, well-chosen photographs, many of them full-page.

Newbery Winner 1993

Rylant, Cynthia. *Missing May*. Orchard, 1992, $14.95: 0-531-05996-0. (Grades 5–8)

Cynthia Rylant (1954–) frequently uses scenes from her childhood in her work. She grew up as part of a large family in Appalachia where she lived with several other family members in a four-room house without running water. She was eventually able to attend college and for a time worked as a college English teacher and a librarian. In the few years that she has been writing books for young people, she has scored amazing successes at various reading levels. For the primary ages, she has written several prize-winning texts for picture books, including two Caldecott Honor Books and a charming series of Henry and Mudge books about a boy named Henry, his dog Mudge, and their many adventures in everyday situations. One of her many books of poetry, *Waiting to Waltz: A Childhood* (Macmillan, 1984, $12.95), is a collection of 30 poems about growing up in a small town in Appalachia. *A Fine White Dust* was named a Newbery Honor Book for 1987 (p. 373). It is the story of a deeply religious boy who faces a personal crisis when the traveling Preacher Man first promises him a future with him and later rejects him. *Missing May* contains many elements typical of this author's innovative and powerful novels. It has a strong, sensitive central character that is trying to cope with disillusionment and difficult situations. Although there is no happy ending, there is a hopeful one in this forceful novel that deals with death, grief, and caring.

Plot Summary

Summer's mother died when she was just a baby. Since that time, her life has been a succession of stays with different relatives around the state of Ohio. All that changes one day when she is six years old and she meets elderly Aunt May and Uncle Ob. They are visiting from West Virginia. They offer to adopt Summer and take her back with them to their home in Deep Water.

For the next six years, Summer's life is filled with a love and affection she never knew existed. She adores her aunt and uncle; in return they adore her and each other.

May and Ob are poor. They live in a rusty old trailer. The trailer is perched on a West Virginia mountainside and surrounded by a garden that May cultivates religiously. Uncle Ob is a tall scarecrow of a man. A disabled war veteran, he spends his time building whirligigs. The whiligigs are pieces of delicate sculpture with wonderful names like Fire and Love. Summer marvels at his patience and his skill. Ob stores the whirligigs on shelves inside the trailer. When the overhead fan is turned on, their home becomes magically alive with a maze of beautiful spinning objects.

May and Ob love one another so wholly and completely that Summer thinks it is a miracle that they still have enough left over for her. But they do. May, who is best at articulating their feelings, tells Summer over and over that they regard her as a gift from above to brighten their declining years and that, like all precious gifts, she must be cherished and cared for with both devotion and love. For Summer, May becomes the symbol of all that is good, unselfish, and kind in this world.

When Summer is 12 and in the seventh grade, the impossible, the tragic occurs. While working in her garden, May suddenly dies. Neither Summer nor Ob can accept the fact that their loving May is gone. After the funeral, when all the relatives have returned home, the girl and the old man are left alone in the quiet of their lonely trailer.

The days go on in a trance-like existence for Ob, who is too numb even to grieve. Summer, herself hurting from her loss, is alarmed at his decline but powerless to help.

The intrusion of Cletus Underwood in their lives some months after May's death provides an unusual diversion. Cletus is a classmate of Summer's. Everyone has considered him to be odd, bordering on eccentric. His passion for collecting objects started with potato chip bags. It passed through stages involving spoons and buttons and is now focused on pictures he retrieves chiefly from old magazines and newspapers and saves in a battered suitcase.

One day Ob sees Cletus in their old car searching for newspapers. Much to Summer's distress, Ob invites him into the trailer. Ob finds Cletus and his pictures fascinating. To Summer he is a "kook" to be tolerated only because he diverts Ob's mind from thoughts of May. Cletus begins visiting fairly regularly.

One day when Ob and Summer are in the garden, Ob straightens up suddenly, claiming he has felt May's presence. He is so puzzled and excited by this mystical experience that he talks of getting a spiritual adviser to help him communicate with his beloved departed wife. When Cletus relates how he once had an amazing out-of-body experience and saw dead relatives when he was on the verge of drowning, Ob elicits his help. The three stand out one cold February afternoon, and while Ob tells stories of May's many wonderful qualities, all pray for some sign of her presence. Time passes and nothing happens. Finally, Ob slouches back to the trailer.

Ob's depression and lethargy increase to the point where he oversleeps and roams about the trailer during the day in his pajamas. The amazing Cletus comes up with another idea. He produces a clipping from a six-month-old newspaper announcing the services of the Reverend Miriam B. Conklin, who calls herself a Small Medium at Large, at the Spiritualist Church in Glen Meadows, a town some three hours away by car. He suggests that they visit her for help. Ob becomes very excited at the prospect of reaching May with help from the Reverend Conklin and plans are made to drive to Glen Meadows. They will spend the night at a motel and return by way of the state capital, Charleston. There they will tour the public buildings that Cletus in particular is anxious to visit.

Ob and Summer visit Cletus's parents to ask permission to take the boy with them. Summer has become increasingly fond of the strange youngster and his unusual insights into human feelings. When she meets his loving parents and sees how proud they are of their son and his gifts, her affection for him grows.

When the trio reaches Glen Meadow, a further disappointment awaits them. They are told at the church that the Reverend died some months before and that there is no one who can help them. Crushed and dejected, Ob decides to return immediately to the solitary and far-reaching place in his mind where he was before. Minutes seem like hours as they drive in silence. After they pass the exit to Charleston, Ob suddenly turns the car around and happily announces they will tour the capital after all. In that miraculous moment, through his love for Summer, he has finally accepted May's death and the necessity of continuing his life.

When they return to the trailer after a wonderful visit in Charleston, Summer now feels free to grieve for May. She sobs uncontrollably while Ob holds her close to him. Finally the morning arrives, bringing with it consolation, release, and hope. Together, Ob and Summer take Ob's whirligigs out of the trailer and into May's garden, where they fill it with movement and the spirit of life.

Themes and Subjects

This is a novel not only about accepting death and about the process of grieving but also about the need to care for people because they are all that is important in this world. This sense of caring proves to be the salvation of both Ob and Summer. In its simple style, sly humor, and depth of perception, this multilayered novel speaks forcefully about values, the nature of love and friendship, families, and the power of love to overcome loss.

Incidents for Booktalking

The following important passages could be used in a booktalk: Summer's first night in the trailer (pp. 5–8); Ob feels May's presence (pp. 11–14); introducing Cletus (pp. 17–18); Cletus shows Summer one of his newest acquisitions (pp.25–27); Cletus tells of his near-death experience (pp. 28–32); Ob, Cletus, and Summer try to reach May's spirit (pp. 33–37); and Ob and Summer visit Cletus's parents (pp. 60–66).

Related Titles

Three misfit children and a childlike aunt find that they are on their own in Jean Thesman's *When the Road Ends* (Houghton, 1992, $14.95: 0-395-59507-X: pap., Avon, $3.99: 0-380-72011-6).

When Lark's family adopts an abandoned baby, they are freed to talk about the loss of their own baby in Patricia MacLachlan's *Baby* (Delacorte, 1993, $13.95: 0-385-44623-3).

Chris Lynch's *Iceman* (Harper, 1993, $15.00: 0-06-023340-0; pap., Trophy, $4.95: 0-06-447114-4) is the portrait of a disturbed teenager caught up in a dysfunctional family.

Liam's father is dying of AIDS and the family lives through the terrible months of the illness in Paula Fox's *The Eagle Kite* (Orchard, 1995, $16.99: 0-531-08742-5).

Budge Wilson's *The Leaving* (pap., Point, $3.50: 0-590-46933-9) contains nine stories about growing up and change.

About the Book and Author

Berger, Laura Standley, ed. *Twentieth-Century Young Adult Writers*. St. James, 1994, pp. 570–72.

———. *Twentieth-Century Children's Writers*. 4th ed. St. James, 1995, pp. 835–36.

Chevalier, Tracy, ed. *Twentieth-Century Children's Writers*. 3d ed. St. James, 1989, pp. 903–5.

Collier, Laurie, and Joyce Nakamura. *Major Authors and Illustrators for Children and Young Adults*. Gale, 1993, 6 vols, pp. 1995–2001.

Commire, Anne, ed. *Something About the Author*. Vol. 50. Gale, 1988, pp. 182–88.

Gallo, Donald R. *Speaking for Ourselves, Too*. National Council of Teachers of English, 1993, pp. 177–78.

Hile, Kevin S. *Authors and Artists for Young Adults*. Vol. 10. Gale, 1993, pp. 163–68.

Holtze, Sally Holmes, ed. *Sixth Book of Junior Authors and Illustrators*. Wilson, 1989, pp. 255–56.

Meet the Author: Cynthia Rylant. SRA/McGraw-Hill, 1990. Videocassette.

Nakamura, Joyce, ed. *Something About the Author: Autobiographical Series*. Vol. 13. Gale, 1992, pp. 155–63.

"Newbery Award Acceptance Material, 1992." *Journal of Youth Services in Libraries* (summer 1992): 353–56.

"Newbery Medal Acceptance." *Horn Book* (July/Aug. 1993): 416–19.

Newbery-Caldecott Acceptance Speech: Cynthia Rylant. NLSC, 1992. Audiocassette.

Rylant, Cynthia. *But I'll Be Back Again.* Orchard, 1989.

———. *Missing May.* Read by Angela Jayne Rogers. Recorded Books, 1995. Audiocassettes, 120 min. ($18.00)

———. *Missing May.* Read by Frances McDormand. BDD Audio Publishing, 1996. Audiocassettes, 120 min. ($16.99)

Senick, Gerard J., ed. *Children's Literature Review.* Vol. 15. Gale, 1988, pp. 167–74.

Silvey, Anita, ed. *Children's Books and Their Creators.* Houghton, 1995, pp. 566–68.

Telgen, Diane, ed. *Something About the Author.* Vol. 76. Gale, 1994, pp. 193–99.

Trosky, Susan M., ed. *Contemporary Authors.* Vol. 136. Gale, 1993, pp. 357–60.

Ward, Diane. "Cynthia Rylant." *Horn Book* (July/Aug. 1993): 420–23.

Ward, Martha, ed. *Authors of Books for Young People.* 3d ed. Scarecrow, 1990, p. 616.

Honor Books 1993

Brooks, Bruce. *What Hearts?* Harper, 1992, $14.00: 0-06-44727-6; pap., $3.95: 0-06-02-1131-8. (Grades 7–12)

In four interrelated stories, scenes are portrayed in the childhood of Asa, a precocious, overly articulate boy who is both intelligent and sensitive beyond his years. When Asa returns home triumphantly from the end of the first grade with a report card of straight As and an armful of hardy radishes he has grown, he finds that his mother, an emotionally fragile woman, is divorcing Asa's father and marrying Dave, a childhood sweetheart. This involves the first of several moves for Asa to various parts of North Carolina. In their first evening together, the bullying, unsympathetic Dave forces Asa to ride alone on a scary roller coaster. Shrieking in panic, the boy is taken off the ride but later that night he returns alone and, conquering his fear, rides the roller coaster again. In the fourth grade, he and a classmate, Joel, a somewhat dull boy who adores Asa, prepare to recite the poem "Little Boy Blue" at parent's night. Asa becomes bored with its soppy sentiment and substitutes the more challenging "The Highwayman" by Alfred Noyes in spite of Joel's inability to memorize such complex lines. On performance night, rather than reciting it alone and depriving Joel of a small moment of glory, he gallantly returns to the original program. Dave and Asa maintain an uneasy truce, their relationship held together by their love for Asa's mother and their mutual love of sports. But even this causes competition, and Asa's mother, buckling under the continued strain of a stressful marriage, attempts suicide. After recovering in a mental institution, she decides to divorce Dave and move away with Asa. Paradoxically, this coincides with Asa's first pangs of love in the seventh grade. After he confesses his love for Jean Williams, she responds by sending him two candy hearts with the words "I love you" on each. She is hurt and confused when she learns of Asa's leaving and when he phones to bid her good-bye and thank her for the hearts, she coolly replies "What hearts?" Asa, however, is confident that in spite of these adversities, he will eventually find love and fulfillment.

McKissack, Patricia C. *The Dark-Thirty: Southern Tales of the Supernatural*. Illustrated by Brian Pinkey. Knopf, 1992, $16.00: 0-679-81863-4. (Grades 4–7)

The author explains that the dark-thirty was the half hour before nightfall when, as a child, she had "exactly half an hour to get home before the monsters came out." At this time, she and her friends often listened to Grandmama's hair-raising tales, some based on fact but embellished through the years. This collection of 10 original stories were inspired by those of Grandmama. They range in time from slavery and the Civil War to the present. "The Legend of the Pin Oak," a story set on a Southern plantation during slavery, tells of two half brothers both fathered by Amos McAvoy but each with a different mother, one white, the other black. The white man is weak, crafty Harper McAvoy who is consumed with jealous over his mulatto brother Henri, a handsome, capable man who actually runs the plantation. When Amos dies, Harper decides to sell Henri to pay for gambling debts, but when Henri reveals that he was born a free man, Harper says he will sell Henri's wife, Charlemae instead. Unable to face separation, Henri, with his wife and child, commits suicide by jumping off a cliff into raging river below. Miraculously, three beautiful birds arise from the churning water. In "The Woman in the Snow," a bigoted southern bus driver, Grady Bishop, refuses to give a ride, during a blinding snowstorm, to a penniless young black woman who is frantically trying to get her sick baby to a hospital. The next day he reads that the woman and child froze to death. One year later, while trying to avoid the ghostly apparition of the same woman in another blinding storm, the bus goes out of control and Grady is killed. Twenty-five years pass and Ray Hammond, the first black man hired by the bus company, takes over the route. When he confronts the same ghost in a terrible storm, he lets her ride free to the hospital. The woman says "thank you" and is never seen again.

Myers, Walter Dean. *Somewhere in the Darkness*. Scholastic, 1992, $14.95: 0-590-42411-4. (Grades 7–10)

Jimmy Little, an intelligent, sensitive, black 15-year-old 10th-grader, lives in a New York ghetto in a fourth floor walkup apartment with his loving maternal grandmother, Mama Jean, a domestic. Jimmy's mother died many years ago and his father is in jail. Life has become increasingly directionless for the boy, and he frequently plays truant to hang out with friends. One day he enters his building and is told by his neighbor Cookie that a man is upstairs waiting for him. The man introduces himself as Crab, Jimmy's father who, after almost nine years in jail, claims he has been paroled on condition that he accepts a job offer in Chicago. He has decided to take Jimmy with him in spite of Mama Jean's doubts and anxiety. Jimmy is also uneasy about traveling with this stranger but reluctantly accepts the offer. On the way to Chicago, Jimmy realizes that Crab has not told him the truth and has escaped from a prison hospital where he was being treated for a critical kidney disease. Now Crab's only aim in life is to establish a bond with his son. As he says, "You're all I got in this world that means anything to me." Though guilty of some minor crimes, he was sent to jail after being framed on a murder rap by an ex-friend, Rydell. In Chicago, he looks up an old girlfriend, Mavis Stokes, and her belligerent punky son, Frank, and tries unsuccessfully to persuade them to accompany him and Jimmy to his hometown of Marion, Alabama, where Rydell lives. Here he hopes to clear his name and start a new life. As the relationship between father and son grows, so does the seriousness of Crab's illness. In his hometown, he is once again betrayed by Rydell and captured by the police. Chained to his hospital bed, Crab dies. Jimmy, grieving for the loving father he scarcely knew, returns to New York and the comforting arms of Mama Jean.

🏵 Newbery Winner 1994

Lowry, Lois. *The Giver*. Houghton, 1993, $14.95: 0-395-64566-2; pap., Dell, $5.99: 0-614-22196-X. (Grades 6–10)

Lois Lowry (1937–) was awarded her second Newbery Medal for *The Giver*. Her first was for *Number the Stars* in 1990, (see "Newbery Winner," 1990, p. 383). In her Newbery Award acceptance speech Ms. Lowry tells of the many strands of thought that went into creating this thought-provoking novel about a young boy, Jonas, living in a seemingly perfect society where there is no pain or serious problems, but in reality there is a denial of the essence of life, struggle, truth, and a sense of the past. One of the strands was the friendship of a painter, Carl Nelson, who in later life, through blindness, lost his access to color. This man's face is on the cover of the novel. Other strands involve episodes in the author's life when she was part of a protected, select group shielded from the real world such as when she was growing up in a special American compound in Tokyo and when she was part of an exclusive group in her college dormitory. From these experiences she realized the danger in communities controlled by uniformity and order. In closing she said, "The man that I named the Giver passed along to the boy knowledge, history, memories, color, pain, laughter, love and truth. Every time you place a book in the hands of a child, you do the same thing. It is very risky. But each time a child opens a book, he pushes open the gate that separates him from Elsewhere. It gives him choices. It gives him freedom. Those are magnificent, wonderfully unsafe things."

Plot Summary

Jonas, who is nearing 12, lives in a perfect world. There is no poverty or divorce, no inequality or injustice, no conflict, no bad manners, no teenage rebellion, and the utmost in family values. He lives with Mother, Father, and sister Lily. They are not his blood relatives, of course. In this ideal world, there are birth mothers who have the children. When young people in the community reach the age when they might otherwise begin to feel romantically inclined, they are given a pill to dispel such feelings. Adults who wish to form a family unit may, however, apply for a newborn. Each family consists of just two children, a male and a female. Therefore, Jonas's family unit is complete.

About the only thing that frightens Jonas, although perhaps that is too strong of a word, is the thought of release. If one does not conform to the community or breaks too many rules too often, one is released. No one has ever heard of what has happened to anyone who has been released, but Jonas supposes that the person goes off to another community to live.

As December nears, Jonas begins to feel what he describes as apprehension. This is a very important time for him. All twelves are given their life assignment. Father, for instance, is a Nurturer. He loves newborns and spends his life seeing them through their first year, when they are eligible to join a family unit. Father is having a problem right now with a newborn called Gabriel who is not measuring up to the standards set by the community. Father does not want Gabriel to be released and has applied for permission to bring the infant into their family unit at night for the next year to give him some extra time to measure up.

When the life assignment ceremony takes place, Jonas watches with happiness as his best friend, happy-go-lucky Asher, gets the life assignment of Assistant Director of Recreation. The Elders, who determine life assignments, very rarely make mistakes in their choices. He is also pleased when his friend Fiona becomes Caretaker of the Old. But Jonas is frightened when his number is passed over and he receives no life assignment! Then he discovers that he has been singled out for what the Elders call a great honor. He is to become the Receiver. There is only one in the community and the current Receiver is growing too old for the job.

Jonas apprehensively begins his training under the Receiver, whom he calls the Giver. It is the Giver's assignment to give all the memories of the past to Jonas. He is to receive all the memories of the whole world, and with them will come the joy and the pain, the happiness and the sorrow, which none of the rest of the community know or experience. It is a great burden to become the Receiver, and it is often very painful.

Little by little, memories are transmitted from the Giver, whose burden is lightened each time he lets go of a memory to Jonas. For the first time, he knows snow; here in the community, the climate is controlled. For the first time, he sees color; there are no color designations in the community. For the first time, Jonas is made aware of many things that he never saw or knew before and that no one else will ever see or know.

The Giver insists that Jonas witness a "releasing ceremony." In this case, Father is to release a newborn who did not measure up and has been judged unfit for the community. Jonas watches unobserved while Father "releases" the child by injecting him with a fatal needle. Now Jonas understands what releasing means and why no one has ever returned. He is horrified at Father, but the Giver explains that Father has no understanding or feeling for what he has done. Only Jonas has been given that.

The daring decision is made for Jonas to leave the community and take his memories to find a new life. People felt things once, says the Giver. Jonas must go to find them again.

Jonas escapes into the night, but he takes the newborn Gabriel with him. Together, they will take memories and find a new place. He can see windows and colors and places where families live and love. For the first time, he hears what he knows to be music.

Themes and Subjects

This haunting novel has an aura of Orwell's *1984* in a modern setting. Jonas's ideal world is too perfect, too ordered, too safe, too careful, too rigid. But it is the only world people know in the community, a fact that slowly becomes painfully obvious to Jonas as he struggles with the memories that slowly are transmitted to him from the Giver. The themes of love and compassion, friendship, and caring for one another are made all too evident by their absence in the lives of the people who live in the community. This is a deceptively simple tale of a boy who has discovered the terrible truth about the life he lives and who sets out to find a less perfect world where there is love, color, and music.

Incidents for Booktalking

So many of the scenes that point up the stark realities of the world known only as the community will serve to introduce life in this other time. See, for example, the "feelings" talk (pp. 4–8); Father discusses the Ceremony of Twelve (pp. 13–19); the House of Old (pp. 27–33); Jonas feels "stirrings" (pp. 36–39); the Ceremony of Twelve (pp. 59–64); Jonas meets the Giver (pp. 74–79); Jonas witnesses a release (pp. 148–51).

Related Titles

In the year 1999, when the weather is out of control and conditions are getting worse, 13-year-old Telly discovers that she can be of great help in Lesley Howarth's *Weather Eye* (Candlewick, 1995, $16.95: 1-564-02-616-7).

Machine-like Tripods control society in John Christopher's celebrated science fiction trilogy that begins with *The White Mountains* (Macmillan, 1967, $11.00: 0-02-718360-2).

James travels to a future world where a fossilized dump is patrolled by vicious rats and giant seagulls in Peter Dickinson's *A Box of Nothing* (Delacorte, 1988, $14.95: 0-385-29664-9).

When little Jon falls to Earth from another planet, he encounters suspicion and hostility as well as sympathy in Alexander Key's *The Forgotten Door* (pap., Scholastic, 1986, $3.99: 0-590-43130-7).

There are two stories in Jean Keal's *Strange Tomorrow* (Dutton, 1985, $13.95: 0-525-44162-X), one about survivors after a holocaust on Earth, and the other about building a new society.

About the Book and Author

(See also "About the Book and Author," 1990, p. 386.)

Lorraine, Walter. "Lois Lowry." *Horn Book* (July/Aug. 1994): 423–26.

Lowry, Lois. *The Giver.* Read by Ron Rifkin. BDD Audio Publications, 1995. Audiocassettes. 270 min. ($19.99)

"Newbery Award Acceptance Material, 1994." *Journal of Youth Services in Libraries* 7, no. 4 (summer 1994): 361–68.

Newbery-Caldecott Acceptance Speech: Lois Lowry. ALSC, 1994. Audiocassette.

"Newbery Medal Acceptance." *Horn Book* (July/Aug. 1994): 414–22.

Honor Books 1994

Conly, Jane Leslie. *Crazy Lady!* Harper, 1993, $32.99: 0-06-02135; pap., Trophy, $4.95: 0-06-440571-0. (Grades 5–7)

Vernon Dibbs, a failing seventh-grade student, is growing up in a city slum known as Tenley Heights characterized by low, narrow, dilapidated houses and omnipresent poverty. Vernon is a poor student who has been lonely and confused since his mother's death a year ago. He is the third of five children who are taken care of by a loving, hardworking dad. The neighborhood oddity is Maxine Flooter, also known as Crazy Lady. She dresses and behaves strangely and is the butt of pranks played by Vernon and his friends. Maxine has a pathetic, retarded son, Ronald, whom she drags around with her. She is also an incurable drunk and, when soused, wanders through town shouting insults and obscenities at everyone. Vernon seeks help to boost his pitiful grades from a kindly retired school teacher, Miss Annie, who often helps the eccentric Maxine and her son. Through his friendship with Miss Annie, Vernon becomes attached to these misfits particularly Ronald, on whom Vernon showers attention and love as he would a mistreated pet. After Maxine is temporarily sent to jail for drunkenness, Vernon becomes fearful that the social service authorities, represented by the compassionate Miss Marlow, will be forced to place Ronald in a foster home. He begins a crusade to help the unfortunate boy by organizing a street fair to raise money for clothes and provisions, spending free time caring for him, and even taking him to the local Special Olympics. However, Maxine's alcoholism is uncontrollable, and she agrees to send Ronald to live with his uncle and aunt on a small farm in North Carolina. Vernon is devastated. When the relatives arrive to take Ronald, he tries in vain to prevent them. Alone and broken-hearted, he is found by his father who comforts him and takes him home where Vernon can start a new project, teaching his father the skill he has learned from Miss Annie, reading.

Freedman, Russell. *Eleanor Roosevelt: A Life of Discovery.* Clarion, 1993, $17.95: 0-89919-862-7. (Grades 5–10)

Like its companion volume, *Franklin Delano Roosevelt* (Clarion, 1990, $16.45), this book combines a lively, penetrating text including many quotations with more than 100 well-chosen photographs. The result is a fascinating well-rounded portrait of one of the most courageous and innovative figures in American history. Born in 1884 to a wealthy, socially prominent New York City family, Eleanor was an unattractive, sensitive child of whom her aunt Edith said prophetically, "the ugly duckling may turn out to be a swan." Her alcoholic father died when she was 10 and her mother was often sick. Therefore, Eleanor grew up with various sets of relatives, principally her Grandmother Hall. She spent three happy, self-fulfilling years in England at a private school whose headmistress was the nurturing Mlle. Souvestre. Back home, she made her social debut in 1902 and later was courted and wed by Franklin Roosevelt. She had six children during a marriage that, though outwardly happy, was rocked by tensions with her domineering mother-in-law, Sara, and the discovery of her husband's infidelity. When Franklin entered politics, Eleanor slowly adjusted to her new prominence and, after his crippling polio attack, she assumed more responsibilities becoming her husband's "legs and eyes." Gradually, she emerged as an important force in American life and politics who, when she spoke on behalf of the underprivileged and various minority groups, was considered America's conscience. After Franklin's death, she became a distinguished member of the U.S. delegation to the United Nations, while continuing to write many books and a popular newspaper column "My Day." This defender of the oppressed, and tireless political activist, continued to channel her abundant energy into numerous pursuits and crusades until her death in 1962.

Yep, Laurence. *Dragon's Gate*. Harper, 1993, $14.95: 0-06-022971-3; pap., Trophy, $4.95: 0-06-440489-7. (Grades 7–10)

This novel, a prequel to the author's *Dragonwings*, a Newbery Award Honor Book for 1976 (p. 318), covers a two-year period, from July 1865 through June 1867, and is set principally in China and in the Sierras of California. Fourteen-year-old Otter is growing up in Manchu-dominated China, the foster son of upper-middle-class land owners. Both of Otter's biological parents are dead. His father was killed in the Land of the Golden Mountain (America) while working on a railroad construction crew. Otter's foster father Squeaky and Uncle Foxfire, both of whom the boy passionately admires, return home for a visit from America with stories of wealth and of their accomplishments. Otter wants to accompany them back, but his new mother will not give permission. However, a short time later he is involved in the accidental death of a Manchu and is forced to flee by ship to America, where he finds incredible hardship and disillusionment. He becomes part of the railroad construction crew with his foster father and uncle and soon finds the work backbreaking and the living conditions inhumane, totally unlike what the two elders had led him to believe. In the incredible winter cold of the Sierras, the crews are scraping out a tunnel in a huge mountain called the Tiger. Their boss is the inhumane Kilroy who is driven each day to meet a stated goal regardless of the cost in human life and misery. During the winter, Otter's foster father is blinded in a blast, and Uncle Foxfire is killed, but through Otter's efforts an avalanche is diverted from destroying the camp's living quarters, and a strike is successfully carried out to give the same pay and benefits to the Oriental workers as white men receive. In the closing pages, Otter and his white friend Sean witness from afar the ceremony of the driving of the golden spike that symbolizes the completion of the transcontinental railroad.

Newbery Winner 1995

Creech, Sharon. *Walk Two Moons*. Harper, 1994, $14.95: 0-06-023334-6. (Grades 6–9)

Sharon Creech (1945–) lives a double life. For nine months of each year, she teaches literature in the American school in Surrey, England where her husband is headmaster. During the summer, she returns to a cottage on Lake Chautauqua in upstate New York and visits with her family and grown children. Although she has had novels published in England, this is her first American publication. It tells about 13-year-old Salamanca Tree Hiddle—proud of the "Indian-ness in her blood"—and a car trip she takes with her grandparents, retracing the route that her missing mother took. In her Newbery Award acceptance speech, the author told a little about the origins of the novel. The title came from a message in a Chinese fortune cookie that said, " 'Don't judge a man until you've walked two moons in his moccasins'—American Indian proverb." Perhaps the central character is part Sharon Creech. She says, "My cousins maintain that one of our ancestors was an American Indian. As a child, I loved the notion, and often exaggerated it by telling people that I was a full-blooded Indian. I inhaled Indian myths . . . [and] crept through the woods near our house reenacting these myths. In *Walk Two Moons*, I saw an invitation, from character to writer, and from writer to reader: come along and walk with us awhile, slip into our moccasins so that you might see what we think and feel, and so that you might understand why we do what we do, and so that you might glimpse the larger world outside your own."

Plot Summary

Thirteen-year-old Salamanca Tree Hiddle is proud of her Indian roots; she doesn't like the term "Native American." Her great-great-grandmother belonged to the Seneca tribe, but Sal's parents mistakenly thought it was the "Salamanca" tribe. As the story opens, Sal is on a cross-country driving trip from Ohio to Idaho with her eccentric—to say the least—paternal grandparents.

This is a trip that Sal does and does not want to make. She does not want to make it because she is not sure that Gram and Gramps, with Gramps's erratic driving habits and their desires for side trips, will ever reach Idaho, but she wants to go because of her mother. One April morning, Sal's mother left for Idaho and promised to return before the tulips bloomed. She has not returned and Sal wants to find her. She thinks that if they reach Idaho by the day of her mother's birthday, she will be able to persuade her to return. Sal's father tries to talk her out of it, but to no avail. Besides, Sal is not so sure that he will notice her absence. Of late, he has been spending most of his time with their neighbor, Margaret Cadaver. About a year ago, her father announced they were leaving their home in Kentucky, which is how they came to be living in Euclid, Ohio, next to Mrs. Cadaver, who lives with her blind mother, Mrs. Partridge. Despite her father's attempts to change her mind, Sal wants nothing to do with Margaret.

On the long trip, Sal begins to tell her grandparents stories about her life in Euclid and about her new friends. One of them is Phoebe Winterbottom, a girl with a very vivid imagination. Phoebe is certain that death and destruction are just around the corner and that every stranger is a potential ax murderer. She is sure that no good will come of the fact that Margaret Cadaver's last name means "dead body." She is convinced that Mrs. Cadaver has killed her absent husband and chopped him up, burying his body in the backyard.

As Sal and her grandparents make various stops across the country in what seems to be a never-ending trip, she continues the stories of her life in Euclid. She tells of the mysterious messages that keep appearing on Phoebe's doorstep, such as "Don't judge a man until you've walked two moons in his moccasins." A strange young man appears in the neighborhood and Phoebe is sure he is a lunatic and up to no good. She tells them of her unusual English teacher, Mr. Birkway, who turns out to be Margaret Cadaver's brother. She also tells them about Ben, who draws cartoons all day long in class and remarks to Sal that she "flinches" whenever someone touches her.

On the cross-country trip, Sal also learns a good deal about her eccentric grandparents and their 51-year marriage. She knows the story of their meeting and courtship and wonders if someday she will have such a warm, enduring marriage. One day during the drive, they stop at the Missouri River, and her grandparents wade in. Gram is bitten by a poisonous snake and ends up spending the night in the hospital. Although she is released and they continue on, Gramps is obviously disturbed by her continued raspy breathing.

But Sal keeps on with her stories of Phoebe. Oddly enough, Phoebe's mother, like Sal's, disappeared for a time. Phoebe is suspicious that this is the work of Margaret Cadaver again! Her mother has either been kidnapped or murdered! It takes Mr. Birkway to convince her otherwise. He explains that his sister would not have kidnapped or murdered anyone. He also explains the disappearance of Mr. Cadaver. He died in a car accident that also blinded Mrs. Partridge.

Phoebe's mother finally returns, and a young man is with her. He is her son, whom no one knew she had. The son, to the astonishment of both girls, turns out to be the "lunatic" they had seen in the neighborhood! Mrs. Winterbottom had given him up for adoption when she met Phoebe's father because she was afraid that she would be considered not "respectable." This will all take some working out, but Phoebe's father seems willing to try to make this a family once more. Phoebe is not quite so forgiving, and with Sal in hand leaves the house.

When they leave, they discover who has been planting the messages on Phoebe's door. They bump right into Mrs. Partridge as she is placing a white envelope on Phoebe's steps. Mrs. Partridge has known about the existence of Phoebe's half-brother for a time, and this has been her way of helping Phoebe to take another look at the situation and, perhaps, "walk two moons in someone else's moccasins." Phoebe goes back into her home to look at the situation once again. Sal decides that perhaps it is time to talk to Mrs. Cadaver.

What with all the delays, Sal is afraid they will not make their Idaho destination by her mother's birthday. Gram insists that they will and also insists that they stop to see Old Faithful, which they do.

When they arrive in Coeur d'Alene, Idaho, their destination is the hospital. Gram has had a stroke. Gramps must stay at her side, but he knows how anxious his granddaughter is to find her mother, so he gives Sal the keys to the truck. She has long ago learned to drive on the farm, although she of course has no license.

Sal sets off for Lewiston and her mother and learns the truth, which her father and her grandparents have known. Her mother was killed in a bus accident on that trip to Idaho. That is why she did not return. Her father knew the truth but could not bring himself to tell Sal. The one survivor in the bus crash was Margaret Cadaver, who had been sitting next to her mother and had become friendly with her during the six-day bus trip. When her father had gone to Idaho to identify his wife's body, he met Margaret and they began a friendship because she was the last person to talk to his beloved wife. Sal visits her mother's grave. She also realizes that her grandparents meant this trip as a way of allowing their granddaughter to find the truth in her own way. Sal returns to the hospital to find that Gram has died.

Sal and her father return to the farm in Kentucky and Gramps comes to live with them. Soon Phoebe and Ben and Mrs. Cadaver and her mother, Mrs. Partridge, are all coming to the farm to visit.

Sal and Gramps often play the game of "If I were walking in so-and-so's moccasins." They learn a lot about other people's feelings in this way. Sal begins to understand that no one told her of her mother's death when it happened because, for a while, she needed to believe that her mother would return to her. In a way, though, Sal figures her mother is not gone. She's just singing in the trees.

Themes and Subjects

Funny, touching, and very real, this is a warm, sometimes mysterious, eccentric story of a young girl and her trip to maturity. Sal is proud of her country roots and the "Indian-ness" in her blood, but she is having difficulty trying to come to terms with the disappearance of her mother. In some ways still a child wanting the comfort and knowledge of her mother's love, she is independent and self-reliant, too. She will not listen to her father's protestations about her mother's return. This trip is something that Sal must do for herself. When she learns the truth, she is strong in her acceptance and although saddened by the loss, richer for the memory of the woman who loved her.

Incidents for Booktalking

There are many both amusing and touching incidents that will serve as a fine introduction to this heartwarming story. See: Sal and Phoebe meet Mrs. Cadaver and her mother (pp. 18–19); Sal tells her grandparents about the lunatic (pp. 42–45); Sal meets Ben (pp. 48–49); Sal flinches when Ben touches her (pp. 65–66); Gramp's story of the marriage bed (pp.75–79); Gram gets bitten by a snake (pp. 93–97); Phoebe and Sal go to the police station to report the disappearance of Phoebe's mother; Mr. Birkway talks about his sister and the accident (pp. 218–20); Mrs. Winterbottom comes home with the lunatic (pp. 246–50); Sal learns the truth about her mother (pp. 264–68).

Related Titles

Two sisters and their alcoholic father move to an area in Washington State where Indian spirits roam, in Helen K. Passey's *Speak to the Rain* (Macmillan, 1989, $13.95: 0-689-31489-2).

A young Native American girl whose soul can enter the spirit of others is sent out into the wilderness to seek her own vision in Phyllis Root's *The Listening Silence* (Harper, 1992, $13.89: 0-06-025093-3).

Three generations of a North Plains Indian family are chronicled in Jamake Highwater's Ghost Horse trilogy, beginning with *Legend Days* (Harper, 1984, $14.95: 0-06-022303-0).

A Taino brother and sister describe their lives before the arrival of Columbus in *Morning Girl* (Hyperion, 1992, $12.95: 1-56282-284-5) by Michael Dorris.

Mary Lou, an average 13-year-old, keeps a journal about a summer during adolescence in Sharon Creech's *Absolutely Normal Chaos* (Harper, 1995, $14.89: 0-06-026992-8).

About the Book and Author

Creech, Sharon. *Walk Two Moons.* Read by Kate Harper. Listening Library, 1997. Audiocassettes. ($29.98)

Hedblad, Alan, ed. *Something About the Author.* Vol. 94. Gale, 1998, pp. 46–51.

Holtze, Sally Holmes. *Seventh Book of Junior Authors and Illustrators.*Wilson, 1996, pp. 67–69

"An Interview with Sharon Creech, 1995 Newbery Medal Winner." *Reading Teacher* (Feb. 1996): 380–82.

McMahon, Thomas, ed. *Authors and Artists for Young Adults.* Vol. 21, Gale, 1997, pp. 29–44.

Newbery Acceptance Speech: Sharon Creech. ALSC, 1995. Audiocassette.

"Newbery Award Acceptance Material, 1995." *Journal of Youth Services in Libraries* 8, no. 4 (summer 1995): 347–53.

"Newbery Medal Acceptance." *Horn Book* (July/Aug. 1995): 418–25.

Peacock, Sco, ed. *Contemporary Authors.* Vol. 159. Gale, 1998, pp. 82–85.

Rigg, Lyle D. "Sharon Cheech." *Horn Book* (July/Aug. 1995): 426–29.

Telgen, Diane, ed. *Children's Literature Review.* Vol. 42. Gale, 1997, pp. 36–44.

Honor Books 1995

Cushman, Karen. *Catherine, Called Birdy.* Clarion, 1994, $13.95: 0-395-68186-3; pap., Trophy, $4.95: 0-06-440584-2. (Grades 6–9)

This fascinating, often uproarious, series of diary entries chronicles one year in the life of high-spirited, imaginative Catherine, nicknamed Birdy because of the number of birds she has as pets. Birdy lives with the Lady Aislinn, her patient, understanding mother, and Rollo her ill-tempered, miserly father, who is a country knight. They occupy a modest manor house (only 10 servants) in Stonebridge, Lincolnshire. Birdy's pious brother, Edward, a monk in a scriptorium, has suggested she keep a diary to gain self-knowledge and maturity. The first entry is for Sept. 19, 1290 and the last is for Sept. 23, 1291. Each entry is preceded by a daily comment about a saint such as, "3rd day of February—Feast of St. Ia, who sailed across the Irish Sea on a leaf." Birdy's days are usually taken up by avoiding boring household tasks dictated to her by her nurse, Morenna, or by spending time with her best friend, clever, wily, Perkin, a crippled goat boy. She also is involved in the lives and fortunes of the beautiful Aelis who lives nearby, Birdy's dashing Uncle George who is a returned crusader, and another brother, the "abominable" Robert, who later reforms and marries the fair Aelis. Birdy is 14, of marriageable age, and continually beset by suitors secured by her father, each more odious and unattractive than the last. Birdy's ingenuity is shown in the imaginative ways she disposes of them using such methods as feigning extreme ugliness or setting the privy (known today as a toilet) afire while an obnoxious candidate is relieving himself. However, she seems unable to escape the clutches of the latest wooer, Murgau Lord of Lithgow, whom she nicknames Shaggy Beard and describes as "a smelly, broken tooth old man." Fortunately, at the last moment, Shaggy Beard is killed in a tavern brawl, and Birdy becomes affiancéd to his handsome son, Stephen, the first suitor to gain her approval. Her last entry ends, "I leave in October. Only one month until Stephen!"

Farmer, Nancy. *The Ear, the Eye and the Arm*. Orchard Books, 1994, $18.95: 0-531-06829-3. (Grades 6–9)

This fast-paced adventure fantasy combines quick action, scary situations, and a measure of humor with undertones of the spirit world of primitive African religions. It is 2194 in Zimbabwe's capital city of Harare. For security reasons, General Amadeus Matsika, the Chief of Security, has deliberately isolated his three children—13-year-old Tendai, 11-year-old Rita, and 4-year-old Kuda—from the outside world. He is particularly afraid of his children being kidnapped by the fearsome underworld gang known as the Masks because of their frightening headgear. With the help of a family servant, the Mellower, a Praise Singer hired to build egos through his constant fawning and compliments, the three girls venture out into the city one day when their parents are away. They are promptly seized by Fist and Knife, two henchman of a gigantic woman named She Elephant whose domain is a former toxic garbage dump being mined for recyclable material. Before they can be sold to the Masks, the three led by Tendai who has found a magical amulet, a ndoro, in the waste heaps, escape with the help of Trashman, a childlike innocent who has befriended Kuda. By accident they enter a huge walled country called Resthaven where the inhabitants live in ancient tribal ways raising cattle and believing in a vast spirit world. The youngsters are accused of witchcraft by the tribe's religious leader, the Spirit Medium, and once more make a perilous escape. Meanwhile, General Matsika has hired three detectives known as Ear, Eye, and Arm, because of their special radiation-produced abilities. More dangers occur when the children are first taken in by Mrs. Horsepool-Worthingham who is intent on collecting a ransom from their father and later when they fall into the clutches of the Masks who are revealed to be agents of a neighboring country eager to infiltrate Zimbabwe. Through the work of the three detectives, the help of mystical powers, and the courage of Tendai, the children are eventually returned unharmed to their parents.

Newbery Winner 1996

Cushman, Karen. *The Midwife's Apprentice*. Clarion, 1995, $10.95: 0-395-69229-6; pap. Trophy, $4.95: 0-06-440630-X. (Grades 7–10)

Karen Cushman (1941–) was more than 50 years of age when she decided to become a writer. Her keen interest in history (she teaches graduate courses in Museum Studies at John F. Kennedy University in Orinda, California) and her memory of reading eagerly and voraciously as a child led her to an interest in juvenile historical fiction. She says, "I grew tired of hearing about kings, princes, generals, presidents. I wanted to know what life was like for ordinary young people in other times." She immersed herself in the works of such masters as Rosemary Sutcliffe and Patricia MacLachlan, sought advice from other practitioners, and began work. She used as a setting the Middle Ages on the brink of the Renaissance, a period that reminded her of a child growing into adolescence. The original sources she consulted included such fascinating tips on etiquette as "Don't blow your nose in the tablecloth." Her first book, *Catherine Called Birdy*, a story told in diary form about a rambunctious 14-year-old trying to achieve an identity while warding off the suitors her father has chosen for her, was a Newbery Honor Book in 1995 (p. 413). The second, *The Midwife's Apprentice*, also deals with a young girl, this time the homeless Brat/Alyce and her search for meaning in her life. About these two characters, the author said in an interview in *Children's Book Review*, "I wanted to write about issues a young person is interested in—issues of identity, responsibility, limitation and what it means to be human in this world. Who knows? Birdy and Brat might even live in the same village—one rich and the other poor. Each girl deals with issues facing all young people, but in the context of the century." About her remarkable success in her new writing career, Ms. Cushman said, "I'm a late bloomer. It takes some time, but I always bloom."

Plot Summary

In fourteenth-century England, a girl known only as Brat sleeps in a dung heap because she has no other place to go. She is probably about 12 or 14 years old, but she doesn't know for sure and neither does anyone else. One rainy cold morning, she is kicked awake by a woman who turns out to be the village midwife. The midwife christens the girl "Beetle" and has her come to the cottage to work in exchange for food and a place to sleep.

So begins Beetle's new life in the home of Jane the midwife. Her only friend is a cat who at first is not friendly at all, but when Beetle saves his life from the hands of the village roughneck boys, she and the cat become fast friends.

Jane the midwife is not a compassionate or even friendly woman, but at least Beetle has food and somewhere to stay out of the cold and rain. Little by little, almost without her knowing it, Beetle begins to pick up small bits of information in the art of midwifery. She even takes to watching through the cottage windows as Jane the midwife helps to deliver babies in the village.

Then one day the miller's wife is in trouble; her baby is coming and the midwife is off on another delivery. Beetle is too terrified to help the woman and is severely scolded when the midwife returns in time for the delivery.

When it is summer, the midwife prepares for a trip to the Saint Swithin's Day Fair, but she breaks a leg and must send Beetle instead who is thrilled by this chance. At the fair, Beetle is given a comb and a new name. A man mistakes her for a girl named Alyce, and Beetle adopts the name.

Alyce it is, and cat becomes Purr. Back in the village, life becomes a little more bearable when Alyce comes to the aid of one of the village roughneck boys named Will. From then on, Will offers to protect her from the others. Great pride comes to Alyce when she helps in the delivery of a baby to the bailiff's wife. The child is named Little Alyce.

After this, Alyce tries harder to study the ways of the midwife. She understands that it is easy to be a midwife when the birth is without complications, but much skill is needed when something goes wrong.

One day in November, Alyce comes upon a small homeless boy who says his name is Runt. She calls him Edward. She sends him up the road to the manor where they are hiring boys to help with the threshing.

One day Alyce is summoned by Emma Blunt to help with the delivery of her baby. The midwife is angry not to be called herself, but Emma had heard of Alyce's skill in delivering Little Alyce and will have no other. When Alyce arrives, she sees that the delivery is in trouble, and she cannot help. Instead, she becomes frightened and runs away, turning her back on the village and the midwife and the only home she remembers. Purr the cat accompanies her.

Alyce tells herself that she is too stupid even to be a midwife's apprentice and will never amount to anything. Finally, she comes to an inn where she is taken in by innkeeper John Dark and his wife, Jennet. Alyce must work hard, but at least she and Purr have found a new home.

As the days lengthen into months, Alyce notices a man hunched over a table at the inn. He spends long hours writing. He tells Alyce he is writing his master work, an encyclopedic compendium. Alyce enjoys listening to him and little by little begins to learn the letters that make up the words he is writing. Once she has mastered that, he begins to teach her many bits of wisdom from the encyclopedia about the Roman Empire and heavenly planets circling the earth and even how to plant corn by moonlight. When the man, whose name is Magister Reese, asks her what she wants out of life, she replies, "A full belly, a contented heart, and a place in this world." But she adds that she is too stupid even to be a midwife's apprentice.

One day in spring, Jane the midwife arrives at the inn asking for Alyce. The girl overhears Jane telling Magister Reese that perhaps it is best that she ran away because she is not what the midwife needed. "Because I failed," Alyce says to herself. "Because she gave up," says the midwife.

Alyce decides to go to the manor to see how young Edward is doing. She thinks that perhaps she will rescue Edward from his life and take care of him, but she finds that the boy is reasonably happy and has found a life of his own and a place for himself.

Alyce returns to the inn, and one warm evening a couple arrives. The man says his wife is being devoured by a stomach worm, but Alyce sees that the woman is about to deliver a child. The man says that is impossible because his wife has been barren since the day of their marriage. Using all her skills that she learned from the midwife, Alyce helps the astonished man and his wife deliver a baby boy.

Magister Reese offers Alyce a place in his home with his sister back in Oxford. Although Alyce knows she would enjoy such a home, she also knows that she has found her own place in the world. She and Purr leave the inn and head back to the village where she knocks on the door of Jane the midwife. She tells Jane that she has returned and she will be a fine midwife's apprentice now because she has learned so much. "Is that all?" Jane asks. "That is all," Alyce replies, "and I am here."

Jane the midwife sends her away. It never occurred to Alyce that she would not be wanted. Alyce tells Purr that she does not wish to leave, but there is no place for her here. Even as she speaks, a thought comes to her.

Alyce and Purr return to the cottage and once again she knocks on the door. This time Alyce says that she has returned, and if she is not allowed in, she will return time and again because she has learned how to try and risk failure, and she will not give up. She will not go away. The door opens, and Alyce and Purr enter.

Themes and Subjects

This is a story of compassion and love and of finding one's niche in the world. Alyce cannot believe in herself, and when she is confronted with a difficult task, such as assisting in a complicated birth, she loses confidence and runs away from the experience. It is only when she realizes that one must take a chance and risk failure if one is to learn and grow that she truly finds a place for herself. She has earned the title of midwife's apprentice.

Incidents for Booktalking

This story is sad, funny, moving, and compassionate, and many incidents demonstrate these qualities. See, for example, Jane the midwife finds Brat and names her Beetle (pp. 3–5); Beetle rescues the cat (pp. 7–10); Beetle runs from the miller's wife (pp. 21–24); Beetle goes to the fair and changes her name (pp. 29–32); Alyce helps with the delivery of Little Alyce (pp. 54–60); she meets Edward (pp. 63–66); Alyce runs away (pp. 70–71); Alyce meets Magister Reese and learns to read (pp. 78–81).

Related Titles

In Elizabeth Alder's *The King's Shadow* (Farrar, 1995, $17.00: 0-374-34182-6), a Welsh orphan is sold into slavery but eventually finds a place at the throne of the last Saxon king of England.

On a pilgrimage to Spain during the fourteenth century, 14-year-old Elenor and her betrothed hear many engrossing stories that are told by their fellow pilgrims in Frances Temple's *The Ramsay Scallop* (Orchard, 1994, $18.95: 0-531-06836-6).

In Rosemary Sutcliffe's historical tale set in coastal England, *Flame-Colored Taffeta* (Farrar, 1986, $11.95: 0-374-32344-5; pap., $4.95: 0-374-42341-5), 12-year-old Damaris rescues a wounded stranger and hides him in a deserted cottage in the forest.

In the Middle Ages, orphaned Ceridwen is accused of witchcraft because of her knowledge of herbal healing in Bertha Amoss's *Lost Magic* (Hyperion, 1993, $14.95: 1-56282-573-9).

Information on the social structure and everyday living conditions are highlighted in Sarah Howarth's *The Middle Ages* (Viking, 1993, $14.99: 670-85098-5), and the history and culture of medieval Europe are covered in Mike Corbishley's *The Middle Ages* (Facts on File, 1989, $17.95: 0-8160-1973-8).

About the Book and Author

Cushman, Karen. *The Midwife's Apprentice.* Read by Jenny Sterlin. Recorded Books, 1996. Audiocassettes, 165 min. ($18.00)

Cushman, Philip. "Karen Cushman." *Horn Book* (July/Aug. 1996): 420–23.

"Flying Starts." *Publishers Weekly* 24 (July 4, 1994): 36–40.

Hedblad, Alan, ed. *Something About the Author.* Vol. 89. Gale, 1997, pp. 43–47.

Hendershot, Judith, and Jackie Peck. "Interview with Newbery Medal Winner Karen Cushman." *Reading Teacher* (Nov. 1996): 198–201.

Holtze, Sally Holmes, ed. *Seventh Book of Junior Authors and Illustrators.* Wilson, 1996, pp. 72–73.

McMahon, Thomas. ed. *Authors and Artists for Young Adults.* Vol. 22. Gale, 1997, pp. 37–44.

Morad, Deborah J. *Children's Literature Review.* Vol. 55. Gale, 1999, pp. 55–75.

"Newbery Award Acceptance Material, 1996." *Journal of Youth Services in Libraries* (summer 1996): 351–57.

"Newbery Medal Acceptance." *Horn Book* (July/Aug. 1996): 413–19.

O'Neill, Alexis. "Birdy, Brat and Books: An Interview with Karen Cushman." *Children's Literature Review* 1 (winter 1995): 42–43.

Rooney, Terrie M., ed. *Contemporary Authors.* Vol. 155. Gale, 1997, pp. 143–47.

Honor Books 1996

Coman, Carolyn. *What Jamie Saw*. Front Street, 1995, $13.95: 1-886910-02-2; pap., Penguin, $3.99: 0-14-038335-2. (Grades 5–7)

One wintery night Jamie, a sensitive third-grader, witnesses an event that both scars his psyche and changes his life. Van, his mother's lover, becomes so enraged at the prolonged crying of his baby daughter, Nin, Jamie's half-sister, that he yanks her out of her crib and throws her across the room. Luckily she is caught by Jamie's mother, Patty, who within minutes bundles up her children, collects their belongings, including Jamie's prized book of magic tricks, and drives them to the home of her dear friend Earl to ask for his help. Although Earl wants them to use his comfortable home while he will move to his trailer on the outskirts of their town of Stark, New Hampshire, Patty insists that she will move into the tiny, isolated trailer. Still dazed and emotionally rung, Patty and Jamie retreat psychologically and physically and remain isolated in the trailer for a week until Mrs. Desrochners, Jamie's understanding and supportive teacher, finds out their whereabouts and visits them. She is able to convince Patty that they must resume their lives. Jamie goes back to school, and Patty returns to her job at a local supermarket. Though almost penniless, Patty takes her children to the Christmas Fair at the local high school where Jamie is delighted to eat a hot dog and win a small stuffed animal at the ring toss game. They leave hurriedly when Patty believes that she sees Van. On another occasion, Patty plans a small shopping trip for Christmas presents, but the car won't start and they return to the trailer defeated and instead decorate a tiny evergreen nearby. Just before Christmas, the trailer is sealed tight by an ice storm, but the family is once again rescued by Earl who delivers presents, including ice skates, for Jamie. The young boy secretly wishes Earl was his father. On Christmas Eve when Jamie is alone in the trailer with Nin, Van suddenly appears. Alarmed and fearful, Jamie hastily hides his sister under the bed. Van looks tired and contrite. Patty returns, and in a tense confrontational scene, she bravely tells him that they are through and a defeated Van leaves quietly. With his departure, the fearful tension is broken. Jamie sobs uncontrollably. Patty takes her son tenderly in her arms and holds him until his crying stops.

Curtis, Christopher Paul. *The Watsons Go to Birmingham: 1963*. Delacorte, 1995, $15.95: 0-385-32175-9; pap., Bantam, $2.99: 0-440-22836-0. (Grades 5–7)

During a cold, wintery Saturday in 1962, the African American Watson family of Flint, Michigan is trying to keep warm and defy an unresponsive landlord by bundling together under blankets on their living room sofa. This loving, tightly knit family consists of Dad, an auto worker; Mama, originally from Birmingham, Alabama; and their three children: older brother, mischievous Byron, age 13 who is still only in the sixth grade; young sister, Wilona now of school-age; and the narrator, 10-year-old Kenny, a bright, sensitive boy. Kenny's overly trusting nature makes him a vulnerable target for exploitation when, for example, his friend LJ Jones tricks him out of his plastic dinosaur collection, and the school bully, Larry Dunn, steals his new leather gloves. Luckily Kenny has Byron to act as his protector and sometime avenger. However, Byron's overly fertile imagination and his ability to get into trouble cause many household crises. At the beginning of summer, Mamma and Papa decide to visit Grandma Sands, in Birmingham where the family can enjoy a vacation and Byron can simmer down and find new interests. The family car, a 1948 Plymouth nicknamed the Brown Bomber, is spruced up and a special record player, the Ultraglide, is installed so the family can have music on the trip. The 1,000 miles pass quickly and the family is given a true southern welcome by Grandma Sands, her male companion, Mr. Robert and the dog, Toddy. At first Kenny has a little trouble adjusting to the heat, the southern accents, and rural ways. He narrowly escapes drowning when, uncharacteristically, he disobeys his parents and swims in a swampy lake. Their familiar peace is shattered one Sunday when racial bigots firebomb the local church. Kenny is so shocked and disturbed at witnessing the deaths and senseless violence that, back home he begins withdrawing from life and spending time in isolation hiding behind a couch. With Byron's help and understanding, Kenny gradually works through his trauma and is able to assimilate the horror he has seen. Slowly he emerges from his sanctuary and rejoins his family.

Fenner, Carol. *Yolanda's Genius*. McElderry, 1995, $17.00: 0-689-80010-0. (Grades 5–7)

When Yolanda'a mother, an African American businesswoman whose husband, a police officer, was killed while on duty, hears that there has been a shooting at the school where her daughter is a fifth-grader, and, later her other child, six-year-old Andrew, brings home a packet of cocaine, a gift from a drug pusher, Mrs. Blue decides its time to move her family from Chicago to the relative safety of Grand River, Michigan. Yolanda is a bright, precocious girl who is so big, heavy, and strong that she soon is nicknamed "Whale" by her new classmates. By comparison, Andrew is a silent, angel-faced youngster, who possesses an unusual talent for expressing himself and his feelings through creative music making on his wooden whistle and the harmonica that his father gave him years ago when he was teething. Not only is Yolanda able to ward off her own tormentors she is also usually able to protect her younger brother from harm and temptation. However, one day when she leaves Andrew unguarded, three youthful drug pushers cruelly ambush him and smash his harmonica. Yolanda is so full of guilt and remorse that she uses her own money and ingenuity to get him a new one. Because Yolanda is so brilliant and knowledgeable, her only friend, Shirley Piper, a white girl, calls her a genius, but when Yolanda explores the meaning of this word, she realizes that it is her quiet brother, Andrew, with his uncanny creative musical talent who is really a genius. Yolanda, however, finds it impossible to convince others that Andrew possesses a phenomenal talent. Even her supportive Aunt Tiny, who visits from Chicago, remains skeptical. When Tiny, so-named because she weighs 300 pounds, invites Yolanda and her family to attend the June Blues Festival in Chicago, Yolanda realizes that this is a golden opportunity to reveal Andrew's talent to the world. At one of the concerts Yolanda, with Andrew in tow, leaves her mother and Aunt Tiny and pretending that they are lost, persuades the MC to allow them on stage to help find their mother. As a dividend, the MC lets Andrew play his harmonica. His song is one about Yolanda, her daily activities and his love for her—"Yolanda, Big Sister! Big Queen in the World." He finishes to rapturous cheering and applause. When the MC calls him "a brand-new Chicago musician," Yolanda beams with pride.

Murphy, Jim. *The Great Fire*. Scholastic, 1995, $16.95: 0-590-47267-4. (Grades 5–9)

The great Chicago fire of 1871 was one of the great disasters of the nineteenth century. This awesome event is chronicled and re-created vividly and accurately through a narrative using exhaustive research involving original documents, eyewitness accounts, and selected secondary sources. In addition, there are many illustrations, maps, drawings, photographs, and reproductions of newspaper accounts. One particularly effective part of this book is the seven double-page city maps that allow the reader to follow the course of the fire almost on an hourly basis. Interspersed with the factual reports, are accounts of several survivors. Through them, the reader becomes involved in the lives of such people as Julia Lemos, a widow who saved her five children and elderly parents; James Hildreth, a politician who tried unsuccessfully to contain the fire by destroying buildings in its path; Joseph E. Chamberlin, a youthful reporter for the *Chicago Evening Post* and; Claire Innes, a 12-year-old who spent a nightmarish three days separated from her family while struggling to survive. There are stories of greed and incompetence mingled with those of heroism and sacrifice. The fire began in the barn of Catherine and Patrick O'Leary on Sunday night, October 8, 1871 (the myth of the cow kicking over a lantern was invented after the fact). Through a series of unfortunate circumstances, mistakes and well-intentioned miscalculations such as a prolonged hot, dry stretch of weather, faulty fire alarms, and misguided firefighters, the fire spread quickly and raged for 31 hours without any significant way of containing it. Finally it was doused by a miraculous rain storm that drenched the area. More than 100,000 people were left homeless and about 300 were killed, many of whom drowned in the city's river while trying to escape the fury of the fire. After the tragedy, most of the residents returned to rebuild their shattered city. Outside help poured in and within a few days reconstruction began that resulted in the rebirth of a new and different Chicago.

❀Newbery Winner 1997

Konigsburg, Elaine L. *The View from Saturday*. Atheneum, 1996, $16.00: 0-689-80993-X; pap., Aladdin, $4.50: 0-689-81721-5. (Grades 5-8)

When E. L. Konigsburg (1930–) was awarded the Newbery Medal in 1997 for *The View from Saturday*, she became the fifth author in the history of the award to receive it twice. The others are Joseph Krumgold (1954, 1960), Elizabeth Speare (1959, 1962), Katherine Paterson (1978, 1981), and Lois Lowry (1990, 1994). Konigsberg's previous award was in 1968 for *From the Mixed-up Files of Mrs. Basil E. Frankweiler* in 1968 (p. 267). Konigburg's *Jennifer, Hecate, Macbeth, William McKinley and Me, Elizabeth* was also an Honor Book in 1968 (p. 271). *The View from Saturday* tells of four sixth-grade friends, Noah, Nadia, Ethan, and Julian, who call themselves the Souls; their devoted teacher, Mrs. Eva Marie Olinski, who is a paraplegic; and their collective pursuit of winning New York State's scholastic contest, the Academic Bowl. The novel is complex in structure. While the central narrative traces the Soul's ultimate victory in the state championship contest in Albany, New York, there are many flashbacks that give important background information on each of the Souls and trace the growing friendship and devotion they feel toward one another and toward their teacher.

Plot Summary

To almost everyone's surprise, four sixth-graders from Epiphany Middle School are in the Academic Bowl finals in Albany, New York. They actually have a chance to beat an eighth-grade team! This has never been done before. How did it happen? Here is the tale of four individuals, each with his or her own story, and of their teacher and how she comes to choose each one for a member of the team.

Noah's story concerns his trip to Century Village in Florida, a place he looks upon with great disdain as being an "old people's home." He doesn't want to be there in the first place and wouldn't be if his mother hadn't won a cruise and decided to share it with her husband, Noah's father, instead of with Noah and his brother! Once at Century Village, Noah gets involved, against his will, in the wedding of Margaret Draper and Izzy Diamondstein. Nate's grandmother volunteered to do the wedding cake. Someone, of course, has to write the invitations. Tillie of Century Village volunteers to do that. Noah notices that she writes in calligraphy, and she offers to teach him. To his surprise, Noah likes it. But things really get involved when Allen Diamondstein hurts his ankle and can't be best man for his father. However, after Bella, a former artist, paints Noah's T-shirt to look like a tuxedo, he is ready and able to be best man at the wedding. All in all, it is a spectacular vacation.

Nadia goes on a trip to Florida, too, to spend some time with her father. Her parents are newly divorced. That's why she lives in upstate New York now, with her mother. Unhappy with the divorce, unhappy with her father whom Nadia feels hovers over her, she is not about to cooperate and have a good time. Worse still, her grandfather, Izzy, has just married a ditzy blond. Nadia can't believe it. Despite herself, Nadia has to admit that her grandfather's new wife, Margaret, is dedicated to the sea turtles she helps to rescue. Along with her father, Nadia is slowly drawn into the community of those who care about these helpless creatures. She learns about the kindness of others and what it means to give. Perhaps she'll come back and visit her father after all.

Ethan saw Nadia down in Florida on the turtle rescue missions, but he didn't say much. His story concerns his return when he gets on the school bus and runs into Julian, a boy from India. Always in the shadow of his perfect, older brother, Ethan stays silent. Julian is friendly, but Ethan thinks he's weird. Yet, when some of the school tough guys pick on Julian, Ethan comes out of his shell and learns something about friendship.

The fourth member of the team is Julian. New to the United States and often the victim of prejudice, which he endures in quiet fashion, he and his father have opened a bed and breakfast inn in town and soon the members of the team begin to find a new closeness and friendship there. Julian was confronted with malice when he started the sixth grade, but endured it to find acceptance and genuine warmth among his peers.

It is these four youngsters that Mrs. Olinski chooses to represent Epiphany at the finals in Albany. From disbelief that a sixth-grade team could make it, the school is turning into believers and excitement grows. But even before they reach that final contest, it all seems lost when, in one of the preliminary matches, the judges refuse Julian's explanation of an acronym. Epiphany loses points, despite Julian's protest, which in itself shocks the judge. However, at the finals, some better research turns up Julian's answer as correct, and the source is adjusted. When Julian answers the match point question correctly—What was the real name and occupation of Lewis Carrol?—Epiphany wins!

Themes and Subjects

This is a book about competition in its best sense as these young people compete for the big prize. The book makes heroes of "ordinary" kids who are intelligent, decent, and kind youngsters. Each of the four team members learns how good it feels to be part of family and friends. The themes of tolerance, prejudice, and dealing with a bully are well drawn. The social politics of sixth-graders come to life in the relationships between the students and with their teacher, Mrs. Olinski. Her struggle to overcome her disability and take charge of her classroom is sensitively depicted. Through humor, the book explores how the bonds of friendship are forged. At the back of the book are 15 questions (with 36 answers) presented to the Academic Bowl team. They may be used as an introduction to these types of contests and as a way to measure one's knowledge against Konigsburg's four.

Incidents for Booktalking

Any of the following scenes will provide insight into the growing-up process of four delightful characters. See: Noah wears his T-shirt tuxedo to the wedding (pp.12–20); Nadia and her father help to rescue sea turtles during a storm and discover a new kind of closeness (pp. 52–57); Ethan doesn't want to get involved but finds a way to even the score with those who torment his friend Julian (pp. 106–18); Julian challenges the committee on his answer (pp. 126–27, 132–33). For a discussion on bullies, see pp.72–73, 94–95. For how to deal with bullies, see pp. 128–31. For a discussion on why Mrs. Olinski chose the Souls, see pp. 155–159.

Related Titles

In *Arly* (Walker, 1989, $16.95: 0-8027-6856-3) by Robert Newton Peck, a young hero has little hope of learning to read until a teacher named Miss Binie appears in this story set in Florida during 1927.

Three new students become close friends when they join Mrs. Ten Broeck's sixth-grade class in a West Virginia town in Andrea Wyman's *Faith, Hope, and Chicken* (Holiday, 1994, $15.95: 0-8234-1117-6).

The Tulip Touch (Little, Brown, 1997, $15.95: 0-316-28325-8) by Anne Fine is set in a plush hotel and tells of the attraction a good girl feels toward a dangerous outsider.

In *Preacher's Boy* (Clarion, 1999, $15.95: 0-395-83897-5) by Katherine Paterson, the reader meets precocious Robbie growing up in turn-of-the-twentieth-century Vermont.

A bossy, insecure sixth-grader and a defender of weaker students are both sentenced to the school's Special Discussion Group in *The Twinkle Squad* (Scholastic, 1992, $13.95: 0-590-45249-5) by Gordon Korman.

About the Book and Author

(See also "About the Book and Author," 1968, p. 269)

Hendershot, Judy, and Jackie, Peck. "The View from Saturday—A Conversation with E. L. Konigsburg, Winner of the 1997 Newbery Medal." *Reading Teacher* (May 1998): 676–80.

Konigsburg, E. L. *The View from Saturday.* Read by various actors. Listening Library, 1997. Audiocassettes, 287 min. ($23.98)

"Newbery Medal Acceptance." *Horn Book* (July/Aug. 1997): 404–14

"1997 Newbery Acceptance Speech." *Journal of Youth Services in Libraries* 10, no. 4 (summer 1997): 365–72

Todd, Laurie Konigsburg. "E. L. Konigsburg." *Horn Book* (July/Aug. 1997): 415–17.

Honor Books 1997

Farmer, Nancy. *A Girl Named Disaster.* Orchard, 1996, $19.95: 0-531-08889-8. (Grades 6–8)

Nhamo, the girl named disaster, is not yet 12 years old and lives in a small village in Mozambique. Her father is long gone, and her mother was killed by a leopard when Nhamo was just an infant. Although it is the custom for girls to be raised by the father's family, in this case Nhamo is being cared for by her mother's relatives, especially her grandmother Ambuya who is the only one who shows Nhamo any tenderness. Nhamo's Aunt Chipo is jealous and gives her all the hardest household chores to do. When Nhamo's aunt and uncle decide that Nhamo should marry a cruel man who already has three wives, her grandmother sends her alone on a boat journey to Zimbabwe in search of her father. With great courage, Nhamo fights loneliness and terror and even joins a baboon troop on a island for a time. Throughout her journey, her conversations with her ancestors, including her dead mother, give her the will to endure. As she nears Zimbabwe, Nhamo faces a new kind of terror: border patrols. Starving and delirious, at last Nhamo stumbles into a strange village run by scientists in the middle of the wilderness. One of them is a woman, Dr. Everjoice Masuku, whom Nhamo at first calls Mother. After many months, Nhamo's relatives are located. Her grandfather recognizes her ability to communicate with the spirits and welcomes her into the family. She learns that her father is dead, and her grandfather believes it was his spirit that protected Nhamo on her long journey. Nhamo returns to the village in the wilderness. She learns that her grandmother Ambuya has died and left her gold nuggets, which will pay for an education. During the summers, she will work at the wilderness village with the woman she now calls Aunt Everjoice. The last evening of that summer vacation, with a new life ahead of her, Nhamo once more communicates with the spirits of her ancestors.

McGraw, Eloise. *The Moorchild.* McElderry, 1996, $16.00: 0-689-80654-X. (Grades 6-9)

The Folk are small people who live in a cavern beneath the moor. Saaski (Moql) lives with them. However, she is not one of them because her mother was Folk, but her father was human. Nonetheless, she is happy with her life until it is discovered that she cannot make herself invisible to humans, something all Folk must do to survive. She is neither one nor the other and is cast out into the human world. In exchange, the Folk snatch a human baby, who will be trained as a Folk servant. Saaski, now a changeling child, struggles to fit into her new life in the village as the daughter of Yanno and Anwara. Although protective and loving, even Anwara senses something different in this child. The villagers also regard her as not one of them. Not understanding why she is different, Saaski finds her only happiness on the moor with the boy Tam and the goat herd and while playing the bagpipes. She finds the bagpipes that belonged to Yanno's father hidden in the loft and immediately knows how to play them. Yanno is shocked and does not want this brought to the attention of the people in the village, who are already curious about this child, so Saaski is allowed to take the pipes up on the moor to play. As she grows older and is increasingly taunted by the children of the village, she slowly begins to realize, with the help of Old Bess her supposed grandmother, that she is not a human child but a changeling. More trouble comes when all the children of the village fall sick except for Saaski. When Midsummer's Eve comes, the villagers vow to rid themselves of the changeling. However, Saaski decides what she must do. With the help of Tam and one of the Folk, Saaski returns to the Folk cavern under the moor where she finds the real-life child of Yanno and Anwara and rescues her. Saaski and Tam leave the little girl at the door of her parents' home. Saaski knows that she does not belong in this village; nor does she belong with the Folk. Tam doesn't belong anywhere either; they belong together. As Saaski leaves Yanno and Anwara's house, she sees Old Bess holding her grandchild and waving back. The child, Leoran, grows up happy and healthy and loved. Once in a while, Anwara thinks she hears the distant sound of bagpipes, and sometimes the sound of two shepherd's pipes playing in unison, but she can't really be sure.

Turner, Megan Whalen. *The Thief.* Greenwillow, 1996, $15.00: 0-688-14627-9. (Grades 5-8)

Gen is sitting in the king's prison in Sounis when the king's scholar, the magus, arrives to release him. The magus has discovered what he believes to be the site of an ancient treasure, and he needs a skilled thief to get it for him. Gen is the best thief around, even he admits that, so, they begin a dangerous and difficult journey. The journey is brightened with the tales they tell of old gods and goddesses, and Gen and the magus learn much about the world and each other. They enter the mountain country of Eddis, and Gen learns that the treasure they seek is a stone called Hamiathes's Gift, supposedly hidden by the former king of Eddis—but no one knows for sure. However, the magus thinks he knows where to find it. The magus will take the stone to the king of Sounis and he, the magus, will be known as the king's thief. This annoys Gen. When they reach the site of the treasure, Gen discovers that it is in a temple that is now underwater because of a dam and reservoir upstream. The water flows out of the temple for four nights each year. The magus has calculated that this is the time. The clever Gen, after some hazardous and fruitless trips, is able to steal the stone. However, as they prepare to return home, they are attacked by horsemen, and the magus loses Hamiathes's Gift. Gen, the magus, and their party are put in prison. Gen is brought before his captor, the queen of Eddis, who addresses him as Eugenides. Gen pulls the stone from his braided hair, where he had hidden it after the magus lost it, and presents it to his queen. As it turns out, Gen's father is the queen's minister of war. In the end, the queen will climb the sacred mountain and throw the stone into Hephestia's fire. It doesn't belong to the world, she says, and Eugenides agrees. In the months that follow, he writes down all of his adventures in the quest for the stone. Soon he will show his writings to the queen. There is even some hint that they might marry, although Eugenides insists that a sovereign is not supposed to marry a thief.

White, Ruth. *Belle Praeter's Boy.* Farrar, Straus & Giroux, 1996, $16.00: 0-374-30668-0; pap., Dell $4.99: 0-374-30668-0. (Grades 6-9)

Just like everyone else in Coal Station, Virginia, 12-year-old Gypsy Praeter wonders what really happened to her Aunt Belle who disappeared, leaving her son, Woodrow, and her husband. Woodrow, who is Gypsy's age and has crossed eyes, comes to Coal Station to live with Granny and Grandpa. Gypsy discovers that Woodrow is a wonderful companion. He is witty and kind, but she is disappointed that he seems to have little information about his mother's disappearance and little curiosity. Their sixth-grade year passes during which Gypsy and Woodrow become best friends. This is a trying time for Gypsy who cannot come to terms with the death of her own father in a fire accident years ago and refuses to accept the presence of her stepfather, Porter. By the end of the year, both youngsters learn to face the truth, no matter how painful. Woodrow confesses that he has always known in his heart that his mother is not dead, that she has simply run away because she could not stand her confining life. He will never see her again. Gypsy faces the fact that her father committed suicide because the burn accident he suffered so disfigured his face that he could not accept the way he looked beside Gypsy's beautiful mother.

⚜ Newbery Winner 1998

Hesse, Karen. *Out of the Dust*. Scholastic, 1997, $15.95: 0-590-36080-9. (Grades 6-9)

In addition to several picture books and novels for older children that are set in the present, Karen Hesse (1952–) has written one book with a futuristic setting—*Phoenix Rising* (Holt, 1994, $14.95), which tells of a nuclear disaster and its aftermath—and three historical novels, including *Out of the Dust*. The first of these, *Letters from Rifka* (Holt, 1992, $14.95) is based on experiences of her great aunt and tells of the trials and hardships of a young Russian Jew who is separated from her family as they flee across Europe in 1919 to escape the persecutions that followed the Russian Revolution. The second, *A Time of Angels*, is set in Boston at the time of the influenza epidemic that followed World War II. It deals with Hannah, her sisters, and Hannah's recovery from the flu thanks to the kindness and help of an old German farmer who is considered an outcast because of his former nationality. The third, *Out of the Dust*, is told in the form of free verse diary entries that cover a two-year period (January 1934–December 1935) in the life of teenage Billie Jo who is growing up on a wretched farm in the Oklahoma Panhandle. There are two central conflicts. The first involves Billie Jo's growing pains and adjustment to her mother's death and its aftermath, and the other tells of the never-ending battle against the forces of nature that include drought and the relentless encroachment of a sea of dust that kills everything including the body and the spirit. In commenting on the grimness of her subject matter, Hesse said in her Newbery Award acceptance speech, "Young readers are asking for substance. They are asking for respect. They are asking for books that challenge, and confirm, and console. The are asking for us to listen to their questions and to help them find their own answers."

Plot Summary

Told in free verse by 14-year-old Billie Joe Kelby, this book covers the period of winter 1934 through December 1935 and tells the story of a family caught in the heartbreak of the Oklahoma dustbowl. Ma has just told Daddy and Billie Joe that she is expecting another baby. Daddy keeps saying that it's bound to rain soon, and Ma keeps reminding him that it hasn't rained enough to grow wheat in three years. They go back and forth like that all the time, but now that Ma is carrying another child, Daddy goes out to the barn so they won't fight about the weather.

Billie Joe is a pretty fair pianist, although not as good as Ma, who insists that her school work is more important than piano playing. Billie Joe thinks that maybe Ma thinks Billie Joe will follow the music one day and get away from there. Is that what Ma wants for herself?

Rain does not come. There are few crops and no work and everyone is poor. A young boy comes by the house one day and offers to work for food. They give him biscuits and milk and a pair of Daddy's mended overalls before he leaves. Ma says that somewhere a mother is wishing for that boy to come home.

One day Daddy leaves a pail of kerosene by the stove, which Ma thinks is filled with water. When she goes to make Daddy's coffee using the pail, she catches fire. Billie Joe catches her as she runs and tries to beat out the flames with her hands. After long grueling, pain-wracked days, Ma dies giving birth to a son. Soon after, the baby dies and is buried with her. Billie Joe's hands are badly burned and she doesn't play the piano quite as well anymore. She is horrified when she later overhears some ladies talking. They say that it was Billie Joe that threw the pail of kerosene.

Billie Joe and Daddy find it difficult to communicate now, not that they ever did very much. Often when they talk, Billie Joe finds that she is optimistic about the weather and Daddy talks much like Ma used to.

One Sunday night in the winter of 1935, Billie Joe is in bed when she hears the first drops. It is still raining on Monday morning when she walks to school soaked to the skin. Then one day the government sends in food—bread and canned meat, and lots of milk—and everyone eats well for one meal at least.

One day a couple comes by with their kids and everyone in town helps to feed and take care of them before they pull out for the next trek of their journey to somewhere. Billie Joe finds herself longing to go with them, anywhere, just to get away from here. She is tired of the dust, the hunger, the sadness, the loneliness. She is tired of her scarred and stiff hands that make her piano playing sound terrible. She is tired of seeing the red spots on her father's nose, knowing what they are and knowing he won't see a doctor. She is tired of seeing people die. Billie Joe knows she doesn't want to die. She just wants to get away, out of the dust.

And one day she does. In the summer of 1935 she hops a train west, out of the dust. When she gets off in Flagstaff, Arizona, a lady from a government agency is there. She gives Billie Joe water and food, and Billie Joe calls home. She's going back.

Billie Joe realizes that getting away wasn't any better, just different. Her father meets her at the station and promises to see the doctor about his face. Doc cuts out the skin cancer and hopes it was done in time. He gives Billie Joe ointment for her stiff hands and says they'll heal up fine. The government has promised money for planting. It rains again.

And now Louise has come into their lives, a fine lady who was Daddy's teacher at night school class. She leaves Billie Joe and Daddy alone when it comes to things about Ma, but otherwise she makes the farm a brighter place every time she visits. Billie Joe begins to hope she'll visit more often and maybe one day stay for good. In the meantime, Billie Joe is content as she sits down once more to play the piano.

Themes and Subjects

Here is a book of sadness and hope, of family loyalty and loss, of a longing for a better life and the realization that one makes one's own happiness. Set in the Depression era when times were hard anyway, the lives of these people are made more miserable by the lack of the rain and by the eternal dust that is everywhere. It chokes not only the lives and livelihood of the people, but their spirit as well. Billie Joe is portrayed as a 14-year-old made mature beyond her years by the reality of poverty and dashed hopes. Daddy, always suffering under the guilt of not being able to provide for his family, endures by optimism and hope that tomorrow will be better. Ma, her own dreams gone under the burden of this harsh life, refuses to sustain that optimism. Deep in personal feeling and underscored with hope, this is a triumphant look into the inner spirit.

Incidents for Booktalking

Any of the following scenes well illustrates the joys and despairs of life in the tortured dust bowls of the 1930s. See: killing rabbits (pp. 6–7); Billie Joe exalts in piano playing (pp. 13–14); playing (pp. 13–14); Daddy and Ma on the weather (pp. 26–27); the accident (pp. 60–61); the first rain (pp. 104–6); Billie Joe can't play (pp. 134–35); Daddy goes to night school (pp.138–39); the trip west (pp. 197–203).

Related Titles

Using a diary format, Barry Denenberg's *So Far from Home* (Scholastic, 1997, $9.95: 0-590-92667-5) tells the story of Mary Driscoll's Journey from Ireland to American and her ordeal as a mill worker in Massachusetts in the 1800s.

During the Depression, clubfooted Talmadge and his family lose their home and must become cotton pickers in Arkansas, in Emily Crofford's *A Place to Belong* (Carolrhoda, 1994, $19.95: 0-87614-808-9).

Abandoned by his mother, Harley connects with some fellow outcasts to build a new family in Ouida Sebestyen's *Out of Nowhere* (Orchard, 1994, $16.95: 0-531-06839-0).

In Jessie Haas's *Unbroken* (Greenwillow, 1999, $15.00: 0-688-16260), Harriet copes with her mother's death and her unyielding aunt while training an unruly colt.

Tracey Porter's *Treasures in the Dust* (Harper, 1997, $14.89: 0-06-027564-2) tells, in alternating points of view, the story of two girls from poor family's in Oklahoma's Dust Bowl.

About the Book and Author

Andres, Linda R. ed. *Something About the Author: Autobiographical Series.* Vol. 25. Gale, 1998, pp. 117–37.

Bowen, Brenda. "Karen Hesse." *Horn Book.* (July/Aug 1998): pp. 428–32.

Hedblad, Alan, ed. *Something About the Author.* Vol. 103. Gale, 1999, pp. 80–86.

Hendershot, Judy, and Jackie Peck. "Newbery Medal Winner Karen Hesse Brings Billie Jo's Voice *Out of the Dust.*" *Reading Teacher* (May 1999): 856–58.

Hesse, Karen. "Karen Hesse, Newbery Award Winner and Scott O'Dell Award Winner, on Receiving the 1998 Scott O'Dell Award." *Alan Review* (Fall 1998): 5.

———. *Out of the Dust.* Read by Marika Mashburn. Listening Library, 1998. Audiocassettes, 240 min. ($16.98)

McMahon, Thomas, ed. *Authors and Artists for Young Adults.* Vol. 27. Gale, 1999, pp. 120–27.

Morad, Deborah J. ed. *Children's Literature Review.* Vol. 54. Gale, 1999, pp. 26–42.

"Newbery Medal Acceptance." *Horn Book* (July/Aug. 1998): 422–27.

"1998 Newbery Medal Acceptance Speech." *Journal of Youth Services in Libraries* 11, no. 4. (summer 1998): 341–45.

Peacock, Scot, ed. *Contemporary Authors.* Vol. 168. Gale, 1999, pp. 133–38.

Telgen, Diane, ed. *Something About the Author.* Vol. 74, Gale, 1993, pp. 120–21.

Honor Books 1998

Levine, Gail Carson. *Ella Enchanted.* Harper, 1997, $15.95: 0-06-0127510-3. (Grades 5-8)

> In this amusing tale of enchantment Ella is but a few hours old when a fool of a fairy named Lucinda puts a curse on her. Lucinda doesn't mean it to be a curse when she declares, "Ella would always be obedient," but that's how it turns out. Every time anyone gives an order, such as "eat your dinner" or "sit up straight," Ella has to obey.
>
> After Mother dies, Father, who is a trade merchant and away all the time, decides to send Ella to finishing school along with Dame Olga's daughters, Hattie and Olive, dreadful girls whom Ella can't stand. These two quickly figure out the enchantment under which Ella must live. Things go from bad to worse when Father marries Dame Olga and is himself given an enchantment by Lucinda that he will have eternal love. Before she left for school, Ella formed a close attachment to Char, prince and eventual king of the realm. Now Char is away for a year learning matters of state in another kingdom. Although they are in love and wish to marry, Ella realizes that if she marries Char, she will just transfer the curse to him, so she tells him that she has run off to marry another. As a consequence, when the prince returns three balls are to be held at which he will pick a bride. Ella, who is being treated little better than a scullery maid in the home of her stepmother and stepsisters, decides to disguise herself and go to the ball so she can at least see her beloved. Once there, her secret is uncovered. Char recognizes her and knows her letter was false. He asks her to marry him. Although she loves him dearly, she knows she cannot cast him under the curse, so she refuses. In so doing, the curse is broken. Ella rescued herself from the curse when she rescued her beloved prince, and so they live happily ever after.

Giff, Patricia Reilly. *Lily's Crossing.* Delacorte, 1997, $15.95: 0-385-32142-2; pap., Dell, $4.95: 0-440-41453-9. (Grades 5-8)

> Lily can hardly wait to get out to Rockaway, her family's house on stilts over the Atlantic Ocean. They go there every year. But this is 1944. World War II is still raging in Europe, and Lily soon learns that nothing is the same, even in Rockaway. For one thing, Poppy, her father, insists on having her piano shipped out to the summer house so that she can practice. Lily hates to practice. Then her best friend at the shore, Margaret, with whom she planned to spend the entire summer, announces that her family is going to Detroit. Her father has gotten a job building airplanes for the war effort. Margaret gives Lily a key to her family's boarded-up home so she will have a place to go when she wants to get away from Gram. Lily's mother is dead and Gram cares for her and Poppy. Sometimes Lily thinks Gram is too strict. Then comes the biggest blow of all: Poppy, an engineer, must go overseas. Suddenly, there is no one left to talk to until she meets Albert, a

refugee boy from Hungary, whose sister Ruth is still in Europe. Lily and Albert become friends when they rescue a cat named Paprika which they care for in Margaret's house. When Albert talks about missing his sister, Lily, who is given to telling tall stories, assures him that not only can she teach him to swim, but that he will be able to row over to France and find his sister. Albert later admits that he did not tell the truth about Ruth. He is ashamed because he feels he abandoned her to save himself. Lily finally admits that she also lied, but Albert does not believe her and tries to row out to sea. Lily saves him when his boat capsizes. Both of them vow to tell the truth from then on. The next summer, with Poppy now home, the family returns to Rockaway. There, a delighted Lily once again meets not only Paprika but also her best friend Albert and his sister Ruth.

Spinelli, Jerry. *Wringer*. HarperCollins, 1997, $14.95: 0-06-024913-7. (Grades 4-7)

No nine-year-old in the entire town of Waymer, perhaps in the entire world, dreads another birthday more than Palmer LaRue. Just nine when the story opens, he is already counting the days until that dreadful birthday. Why? Because in Palmer's hometown, when a boy becomes 10 he gets the privilege and honor of becoming a wringer at the annual weeklong Family Fest, which is a very big deal in Waymer. At the end of the week of celebration, some 5,000 pigeons are released. Hundreds of sharpshooters get their chance to kill the birds. For those that are only wounded, young boys called wringers race to pick up the wounded birds and wring their necks—to put them out of their misery. The town makes a lot of money from this event, but Palmer doesn't care. He doesn't see why the birds are put into misery in the first place, but he can't tell anybody how he feels. He can't tell his father who was once a wringer himself. He can't tell his newly found friends—Beans, Mutto, and Henry. They've only just started to pay attention to him; they even gave him a nickname—Snots. He doesn't want them to call him sissy or throw him out of the group. Then the strangest thing happens: a pigeon appears on his bedroom sill. The dumb bird just won't go away. Eventually, even though he doesn't want to, Palmer takes him in—a pigeon of all things. He even names him Nipper. As his 10th birthday approaches, Palmer lives in growing fear that Beans and the others will discover Nipper. Finally he confides his fears to Dorothy who lives across the street. Even though she's a girl, she seems to understand. No matter how he tries, Palmer can't stop becoming 10 years old. As the day nears, he realizes he must release Nipper because Beans and the others are suspicious. Dorothy says she and her family will take him somewhere far enough so that he won't return. On the day of the pigeon release, Palmer learns that they have released Nipper near the railroad yards. That's where the pigeons are trapped for Family Fest! Palmer goes to find his beloved pigeon. Eventually he does because Nipper has a habit of landing right on Palmer's head! As soon as the bird lands, Palmer realizes he has doomed Nipper. Beans snatches the pigeon off Palmer's head and throws him to the ground for the hunters. Palmer makes his choice. He screams at the hunters and runs to Nipper, who is unharmed. Palmer cradles his bird in his hands and walks through the field of hunters and wringers and lookers-on. Palmer is not a wringer. Palmer will never be a wringer. Palmer and Nipper are going home.

❀ Newbery Winner 1999

Sachar, Louis. *Holes*. Farrar, 1998, $16.00: 0-374-33265-7. (Grades 6-8)

Louis Sachar (1954–) was born in East Meadow on Long Island but spent most of his youth in California. While attending undergraduate school and later law school at the University of California, he began writing fiction for children. By the time *Holes* was published, Sachar had more than a dozen books in print including the popular series about Wayside School and several books about young Marvin Redpost and his problems growing up. *Holes*, written for an older audience, tells the story of Stanley Yelnats (a palindrome), a young boy without direction or any feelings of self-esteem, who is wrongfully sent to a correctional institution in rural Texas where he and other inmates must dig holes in the desert to fulfill the sadistic warden's dream of uncovering a buried treasure. Through extreme adversity and hardship, Stanley gains confidence and a sense of identity. The story is told through such unusual plot twists, incredible coincidences, flights of fancy, and infectious humor that it becomes at times part tall tale and part magic realism. When asked by a newspaper reporter what young readers should learn from the book, Sachar replied, "The best morals kids get from any book is just the capacity to empathize with other people, to care about the characters and their feelings." In Stanley Yelnats, the author has indeed created a character about whom readers will care; they will cheer his triumphs over misfortune and his growing sense of self-worth.

Plot Summary

Stanley Yelnats—his name reads the same backward and forward—has the choice of going to jail or going to Camp Green Lake, a juvenile detention center. Even though he is innocent of the crime of stealing sneakers, he's not so sure that Camp Green Lake was the right choice. In the first place, there's nothing green in this part of Texas and there certainly isn't a lake. There is, however, a great big dry bed where the lake used to be, and that's where the boys at Camp Green Lake are told to dig a five by five hole every single day. They have no idea for what, if anything, they're digging. Stanley is also told to watch out for rattlesnakes, spiders, and above all, the lizards. If a lizard bites you, there is no cure. You die.

Stanley's family has a history of bad luck, so he isn't surprised that bad luck put him in the camp. His father is an inventor whose inventions just never pan out. Stanley had bad luck with the sneakers, too. They dropped on his head from an overpass one day. Stanley thought it was a sign of good fortune, and he was taking the sneakers home when a policeman stopped him. Seemed the sneakers belonged to Clyde "Sweet Feet" Livingston, famed basketball star, who was auctioning them off to build a homeless shelter. Nobody believed that they had just fallen on Stanley's head. But whenever misfortune befalls the family, they just blame it on Stanley's "no-good-dirty-rotten-pig-stealing-great-great-grandfather." It's a family joke.

All the boys have nicknames at Green Lake, which is run somewhat like a concentration camp. Stanley's nickname is Caveman. Overweight when he arrives, Stanley finds it difficult to keep up with the relentless digging in the hot Texas sun. One day he digs up a small gold tube with the initials "KB" on it. If the boys dig up anything interesting, they are promised the day off, but Stanley has promised to give one of the boys, X-ray, his first interesting find. X-ray drops the tube in his hole, some distance away from Stanley and announces it as his discovery. This brings the Warden, as well as Mr. Sir and Mr. Pendanski, who oversee the boys. Now the digging goes on in earnest. Stanley soon realizes that these people are in search of something, but of course he also knows they are digging in the wrong place.

As the digging goes on without reward, the treatment of the boys becomes more and more cruel. Finally the smallest of the boys, Zero, who has asked Stanley to teach him to read, runs away. Fearing that Zero cannot survive in this parched land, Stanley escapes to find him, which he does. The two boys face starvation out in the Texas wasteland until Stanley discovers wild onions. Stanley now recalls some of the stories his family has kept repeating through the years about his pig-stealing great-great-grandfather and how he lost his fortune when he was robbed by the outlaw Kissin' Kate Barlow. KB—the initials on the small tube he had dug out of his hole.

Stanley tells Zero they have to return and dig one more hole. The boys find their way back to the dry lake bed, where Stanley finds the original hole that unearthed the small tube, and the boys begin digging for what they realize must be a treasure. They dig up a battered suitcase just in time to be caught in the act by the Warden, Mr. Sir, and Mr. Pendanski. These three are serious about killing the boys for the suitcase, but they feel they don't have to, for also in the hole, and now sitting on the boys, are the deadly lizards. All they have to do is wait.

Strangely enough, the lizards don't bite. Eventually the boys are rescued by Ms. Morengo, a lawyer who has learned that Stanley is innocent. The evil plot of the three would-be killers is uncovered. It turns out that the suitcase has the name Stanley Yelnats on it. It belonged to the first Stanley Yelnats, and it contains jewels worth about $20,000 plus stock certificates and promissory notes. They turn out to be worth about $2 million, which the boys will share.

The three would-be killers are taken to jail. The correction center is destined to become a Girl Scout Camp, and Stanley's father has invented a cure for foot odor! The curse, if it ever existed, is over.

Why didn't the deadly lizards bite the boys? As it turns out, lizards hate onion blood. All the onions the boys ate when they were lost made them distasteful to the deadly creatures!

Themes and Subjects

This is a book about crime and punishment and redemption with an air of folklore and tall tales. Stanley is portrayed as an optimistic youngster who takes his family's travails in stride and tries to look at better things to come. Even the injustice of being sent to the correction center does not bury him in doom. In his quiet way, he endures the cruelty of the Warden and overseers, forming friendships with the other boys, especially Zero. When he senses that Zero will die if he does not get water or help, Stanley does not hesitate to go after him. The other boys are portrayed as normal youngsters who have gotten themselves into trouble and are trying to survive in a harsh environment. Those who run the correction center are larger-than-life characters in cruelty, obviously willing to kill if necessary for greed. The story is nicely embroidered with flashbacks to Stanley's and Zero's ancestors as they make their way to the New World and a fortune. The themes of friendship, loyalty, trust, and a fine sense of humor in adversity are well portrayed.

Incidents for Booktalking

The following incidents illustrate some of the major themes of the book. Stanley accepts his unjust encampment with stoic silence (pp. 11–15); a flashback to Stanley's great-great-grandfather and Zero's great-great-great grandmother, Madame Zeroni (pp. 28–31); Stanley becomes Caveman (pp. 46–47); Stanley finds the tube (pp. 59–63); Zero wants to learn to read (pp. 80–82); Zero runs away (pp. 132–40); Stanley goes after him (pp. 146–48); they find the treasure (pp. 200–30).

Related Titles

Through friendship with a Quaker boy and the adjustment to his grandfather's stroke, a smug jock learns lessons in maturation in Jerry Spinelli's *Crash* (Knopf, 1996, $16.00: 0-679-87957-9)

Orphan Harry Potter learns he is a wizard in *Harry Potter and the Sorcerer's Stone* (Scholastic, 1998, $16.95: 0-590-35340-3) the first of a brilliant fantasy series by J. K. Rowling.

In Lynne Rae Perkins's *All Alone in the Universe* (Greenwillow, 1999, $16.00: 0-688-16881-7), Debbie feels lonely and bewildered when her best friend suddenly dumps her.

A 12-year-old clairvoyant runs away from vaudeville and a drunken father to live with a cousin he has never met in *The Mind Reader* (Putnam, 1997, $15.95: 0-399-23150-1) by Jan Slepian.

A 10-year-old girl tries to fight the power of an evil usurper in *A City in Winter* (Viking, 1996, $22.50: 0-670-86843-4) by Mark Helprin.

About the Book and Author

Berger, Laura Standley, ed. *Twentieth-Century Children's Writers*, 4th ed. St. James, 1995, pp. 837–38.

Commire, Anne, ed. *Something About the Author.* Vol. 63. Gale, 1991, pp. 137–40.

Hedblad, Alan, ed. *Something about the Author.* Vol. 104. Gale, 1999, pp. 157–61.

Holtze, Sally Holmes. *Seventh Book of Junior Authors and Illustrators.* Wilson, 1996, pp. 274–76.

Lesniak, James G. *Contemporary Authors (New Revision Series).* Vol. 33. Gale, 1991, p. 386.

Locher, Frances Carol, ed. *Contemporary Authors.* Vols. 81–84. Gale, 1979, p. 491.

"Newbery Medal Acceptance." *Horn Book* (July/August 1999): 410–17.

"The 1999 Newbery Medal Acceptance Speech." *Journal of Youth Services in Libraries* 12, no. 4 (summer, 1999): 12–15.

Sachar, Louis. *Holes.* Read by Kerry Beyer. Listening Library, 1999. Audiocassettes. ($23.98)

Sachar, Shere, and Carla Sachar. "Louis Sachar." *Horn Book* (July/August 1999): pp. 418–22.

Senick, Gerard J. ed. *Children's Literature Review.* Vol. 28. Gale, 1992, pp. 200–205.

Honor Books 1999

Peck, Richard. *A Long Way From Chicago.* Dial, 1998, $19.99: 0-8037-2290-7. (Grades 6-9)

From 1929 to 1935, Joey and Mary Alice make seven summer trips from Chicago to visit Grandma Dowdel in her sleepy Illinois town. This warm, funny, nostalgic book recounts seven extraordinary experiences with eccentric Grandma. In 1929, Joey and Mary Alice, nine and seven years old, get their first look at a dead body when Grandma decides to impress an out-of-town reporter by staging a wake for Shotgun Cheatham. In 1930, Grandma gets back at the Cowgills for destroying her mailbox. In 1931, Grandma goes against the town policy of not feeding drifters by using the sheriff's boat to catch illegal fish and set up banquet tables for anyone drifting through. In 1932, Grandma is not above switching cards at the gooseberry pie judging contest if it gets Joey a ride in a barnstormer. In 1933, Grandma helps out with an elopement. In 1934, Grandma's best friend—whom she can't stand—loses her home and must leave town, but Grandma finds a devious solution! In 1935, Joey and Mary Alice find old clothes in the attic and bring a tear to Grandma's eye for the Centennial Celebration. That was the last year of their visits to Grandma. But in 1942, Joey—now Joe—is on a troop train leaving for army basic training. His train will go right through Grandma's sleepy town, although it will not stop. He telegrams Grandma—she never got a phone—just to tell her that the train will be going through. At an hour before dawn, the train passes Grandma's house, the last house in town. It is lit up like a jack-o'-lantern and there she is, waving from the door.

2000s

Curtis, Christopher Paul. *Bud, Not Buddy*. Delacorte, 1999, $15.95: 0-385-32306-9. (Grades 5-8)

As though foreshadowing future distinctions for African American writer Christopher Paul Curtis (1954–), *The Watsons Go to Birmingham—1963*, his first book for young readers, was designated as a honor book for both the Newbery and Coretta Scott King Awards (See "Honor Books," 1996 p. 419). *Bud, Not Buddy*, his second novel, won both of these awards and, as such, was the first book in the history of these awards to be thus honored. Set in 1936 at the height of the Great Depression in and around Flint, Michigan, *Bud, Not Buddy* tells of orphaned 10-year-old Bud Caldwell ("not Buddy" he insists) and his escape from a cruel foster home. His subsequent odyssey takes him to a hobo Hooverville and with the help of Lefty Lewis—a Pullman porter and labor organizer—to the beginning of a search for jazz musician Herman E. Calloway, leader of the Dusky Devastators of the Depression, whom Bud mistakenly thinks is his father. In an afterword, Curtis tells that the characters Lewis and Calloway are based loosely on the lives of his two grandfathers. Curtis's odyssey to becoming an award-winning author is as fascinating and inspiring as Bud's. Unable to complete his college degree at the University of Michigan because of financial reasons, Curtis spent 10 years working on the assembly line of Fisher Body Works. Later with his wife's help, he took a year off to write, using a table at the children's room of the local public library as his writing desk. Every night his young son typed the hand-written manuscript pages into the family computer. The result was *The Watsons* and the beginning of his amazing career.

Plot Summary

Bud Caldwell's Momma died when he was six. Since then he's been in the Home, with occasional short trips to a foster home, which never seem to work out. At age 10, Bud is wise in the ways of the world, especially wise in the ways of an orphaned black child in Flint, Michigan, during the Great Depression of the 1930s. One of the ways that Bud keeps on top of things is to follow his own rules, such as "Rules and Things Number 83: If an Adult Tells You Not to Worry, and You Weren't Worried Before, You Better Hurry Up and Start Cause You're already Running Late."

Besides his rules, Bud has two things he holds dear. The first is something his mother once told him: "Bud is your name and don't you ever let anyone call you anything outside of that either. Buddy is a dog's name or a name that someone's going to use on you if they're being false-friendly. Your name is Bud, period." Bud, not Buddy always remembers that. The second thing Bud holds dear is his suitcase, which he keeps stashed under his bed at the Home. The most important things in the suitcase are the rocks Momma gave him and the flyers—blue flyers worn out from use. They show a man standing next to a giant fiddle with two men on either side, one playing drums and the other blowing a horn. The flyers are advertising "Herman E. Calloway and the Dusky Devastators of the Depression!!!!!!" (including six exclamation points). Bud, not Buddy has a pretty good idea that Herman E. Calloway is his father even though he's never seen him and Momma never talked about him. Just when Bud was going to ask some questions, Momma died.

As the story opens, Bud is sent to a new foster home. This family has a 12-year-old son, and right away Bud knows there's going to be trouble. He is right. When the mother threatens to return him to the Home, Bud figures he's had enough. He slips away, and carrying his suitcase, he sets out to find Herman E. Calloway whom he thinks lives in Grand Rapids.

After some adventures at a hobo camp (known as a Hooverville), Bud gets a lift on the road from a character named Lefty Lewis. Bud tells Lefty that he has actually run away from his father in Grand Rapids, figuring that's the way to ensure Lefty will see that he gets there. It works, and it turns out that Lefty even knows Bud's father, although he remembers that Calloway's wife died many years ago, not just four years ago when Bud's mother died. They figure that Calloway was married more than once.

Bud begins to suspect that the strangely behaving Lefty is some kind of criminal on the lam, although it turns out that he is a union organizer, something that could get you in a lot of trouble in those days. Lefty deposits Bud at the place where Calloway and his band are currently playing. To say that his father is not pleased to see him is an understatement. Calloway is rude, surly, and standoffish. Bud is not at all pleased to think that this man is actually his father. However, he is taken in by the rest of the band members and allowed to stay at the Grand Calloway Station, the house where Calloway and the band members live. It is presided over by Miss Thomas, the band's singer.

Bud begins to settle in to life at Calloway Station, still unhappy with the reaction of the man he believes is his father. Things change when Calloway sees some of the rocks that Bud has carried in his suitcase. His Momma gave them to him. The writing on the rocks says "Flint, Michigan, August eighth 1911" and "Gary, Indiana, July thirteenth, 1912." When Calloway sees them, he looks like a man in shock.

Bud learns that Herman Calloway is not his father, but is his grandfather. The man is his mother's father, and he recognizes the rocks. Momma ran away years ago and Calloway never could find her and never knew what happened. Miss Thomas explains that Calloway loved his daughter very much. It will take him some time to get over this shock and to look at Bud as his grandson. In the meantime, Bud can wait, and when the boys in the band give him a saxophone, Bud, not Buddy knows he's come home.

Themes and Subjects

This is a story of different kinds of love and longing, Bud's love for his mother and his longing for a solid base in his life, and Calloway's love for his long-lost daughter. It also shows how circumstances, such as the death of Bud's mother and his years in a home, can make a child old beyond his years, yet still longing for a family to love. More than most children his age, Bud seems to understand that it will take his grandfather will some time to adjust to his daughter's death and accept the boy as his own grandchild.

Incidents for Booktalking

The story lends itself to two excellent subjects for booktalking. One is life in a foster home, where Bud encounters the animosity of the natural child and his unwillingness to accept a newcomer (pp. 9–20). The other is life in a Hooverville, one of the makeshift towns that sprouted up all over the United States during the Great Depression (pp. 63–87).

Related Titles

Francisco Jimenez's. *The Circuit: Stories from the Life of a Migrant Child* (University of New Mexico, 1997, pap., $10.95: 0-688-14321-0) consists of a series of short stories based on the author's experience as a child in a migrant farm worker family.

Trevor is sent to stay on an island off the coast of Maine with two eccentric great aunts in *The Original Freddie Ackerman* (Simon, 1992, $15.00: 0-689-50562-0) by Hadley Irwin.

Down in the Piney Woods (Knopf, 1992, $14.00: 0-679-80360-2) by Ethel Footman Smothers tells of the daily life of a black sharecropper family in Georgia during the 1950s.

In Jean Sparks Ducey's *The Bittersweet Time* (Eerdmans, 1995, $13.00: 0-8028-5096-0), a seventh-grade girl must get a job to help support her family during the Great Depression.

From a sheltered rich-kid life, David is suddenly thrown into a foster home in a rough neighborhood when his mother dies and his father disappears in Susan M. Brown's *You're Dead, David Borelli* (Simon, 1995, $15.00: 0-689-31959-2).

About the Book and Author

Contemporary Authors (New Revision Series). Vol. 80. Gale, 1999, pp. 60–62.

"From Assembly Line to Book Awards." *New York Times* Jan. 22, 2000, p. 17.

Hedblad, Alan. *Something About the Author.* Vol. 93. Gale, 1997, pp. 60–62.

Lamb, Wendy. "Christopher Paul Curtis." *Horn Book* (July/August 2000): 397–401.

"Newbery Medal Acceptance." *Horn Book* (July/August 2000): 386–96.

Peacock, Scott. *Contemporary Authors.* Vol. 159. Gale, 1998, pp. 87–89.

"2000 Newbery Medal Acceptance Speech." *Journal of Youth Services in Libraries* 13, no. 4 (summer 2000): 9–12.

Honor Books 2000

Couloumbis, Audry. *Getting Near to Baby*. Putnam's, 1999, $17.99: 0-233890-X. (Grades 6-8)

Willa Jo is up on the roof of Aunt Patty's house. She went up there to see the sunrise and she's still there. Little Sister has followed her up there, too, and Aunt Patty is frantic because neither of them will come down. So, begins a sensitive, tender tale of dealing with sorrow and loss. Willa Jo and Little Sister, who hasn't spoken a word for some time, have come to stay with Aunt Patty for a spell. Things have gotten bad at home. Dad lost his job and went away to find work, and now he doesn't even call anymore. Mom just can't seem to deal with the loss of Baby, their infant sister who died after they all went to a carnival and she apparently drank some tainted water. Mom blames herself and Little Sister won't talk. Staying with Aunt Patty hasn't been easy either. She's a woman who wants her own way. Frustrated and frantic when the girls won't come down and annoyed when her own husband follows them, Aunt Patty climbs out on the roof herself and demands an answer. To everyone's surprise, Little Sister says, "We were getting near to Baby." Each in their own way finally comes to grips with a terrible loss, and at story's end, Mom has come back, too, ready to put aside her grief to care for the two people who need her most.

dePaola, Tomie. *26 Fairmount Avenue*. Illustrated by the author. Putnam's, 1999, $13.99: 0-399-923246-X. (Grades 4-6)

Well-known author/artist Tomie dePaola will never forget the "Big Hurricane of 1938." He was four years old, and his mom and dad were starting to build the family's first—and only—house. This is the story of the year of the building. First there is the hurricane, a truly unforgettable event when Tomie sees a boy carrying an umbrella who floats down the stairs just like Mary Poppins. The year was also memorable for the long-awaited premier of *Snow White and the Seven Dwarfs*, although Tomie becomes quite upset at what he views as Mr. Walt Disney's inability to get the story right. There are all sorts of building problems with the new house, and sometimes it seems as though it will never come to pass. Other things happen, too: Tomie starts school, Christmas comes, and then a new year, but finally, finally it is moving day. Mom and Dad send the kids away for the day to be removed from the all the packing, unpacking, and bustle, but at the end of this long day, Tomie and his brother march right up the steps of 26 Fairmount Avenue, their new home.

Holm, Jennifer L. *Our Only May Amelia*. Harper, 1999, $15.95: 0-06-027822-6. (Grades 5-7)

In this historical fiction based on the diary of the author's Finnish American grandaunt, May Amelia is the only daughter in a family of seven brothers. Kaarlo, the second oldest, is actually a cousin, but he counts as a brother. May Amelia is said to be a miracle because she is the only girl to be born on the Nasel River in rural Washington State during the nineteenth century. Now her mother is expecting another child, and May Amelia desperately hopes she will have a sister. Being a miracle and the only girl has its drawbacks. Sometimes May Amelia even forgets that she is a girl, being around so many brothers. At other times, Pappa singles her out for running around the logging camp or causing more trouble than all the boys put together. Through the months while the family waits for the new arrival, Pappa's mother, Grandmother Patience, moves in with them. It is not a happy move because May Amelia's grandmother is anything but patient and anything but kind. The oldest son, Matti, disappears and there are rumors that he is long gone on a fishing boat. Finally the baby is born, and to May Amelia's delight, it is a girl, whom she is allowed to name—Amy. Tragedy strikes when, sometime later, the baby just stops breathing. Grandmother Patience heartlessly blames May Amelia who was caring for the child while Mamma recuperated. Horrified and angry, May Amelia vows that she will stay in her home no longer and goes to live with her aunt and uncle in the much bigger town of Astoria where, for the first time in her life, she has a girlfriend to talk to. May Amelia learns that her oldest brother is not on a ship but has eloped and is living in San Francisco. One day Pappa shows up with the news that Grandmother Patience has died and the family wants May Amelia to return. She does, to find that her brother Wilbert is ill with the fever. Everyone thinks he will die, but while May Amelia was in Astoria she learned something about Chinook medicine, and she saves him. Wilbert recovers and May Amelia is home to stay.

✿❀Newbery Winner 2001

Peck, Richard. *A Year Down Yonder.* Dial, 2000, $16.99: 0-8037-4618-3. (Grades 5–8)

On the morning of January 15, 2001, during the American Library Association conference in Washington, D.C., a large, crowded roomful of librarians and publishing personnel heard the announcement that Richard Peck (1934–) had won the Newbery Award for *A Year Down Yonder.* The audience immediately broke into enthusiastic cheering and applause to express their approval and admiration. When one reviews Richard Peck's distinguished career, it is amazing that in more than 30 years of full-time writing, during which he has produced approximately 25 highly praised novels for young people and has been the recipient of many prizes and honors including the Margaret Edwards Young Adult Author Achievement award in 1990, the Newbery Medal has always eluded him. He came closest in 1999 when this book's prequel, *A Long Way from Chicago*, was named an Honor Book (See "Honor Books," 1999, p.434). Mr. Peck's work falls roughly into two categories. The first includes his many novels for teenagers that explore such adolescent concerns as loneliness, family problems, and relationships with peers, as well as emotional situations such as rape or the death of a friend. The second group is for a slightly younger audience. These are lighter and filled with humorous situations and, often, eccentric characters. Some are adventure/fantasies; many are set in America in the first half of the twentieth century. The 2001 medal winner falls into the second group of novels.

It is not necessary to be familiar with its prequel to understand and appreciate *Down Yonder*, but *A Long Way from Chicago* does introduce the locale and the principle characters. The first novel covers one week in each of seven summers from 1929 to 1935 when Joey, the narrator, and his younger sister Mary Alice visit their amazing Grandma Dowdel in her sleepy rural Illinois town. The sequel opens in 1937 while the country is still wracked by the Great Depression. Mary Alice, now 15, is sent to spend one year with her Grandma while her father looks for work. Although Mary Alice relates the events of this year, the star of the novel remains the feisty, resourceful, indomitable and unscrupulous Grandma Dowdel who has a sharp tongue but an understanding heart. She will be remembered as one of Mr. Peck's greatest creations.

Plot Summary

Fifteen-year-old Mary Alice is not thrilled with the prospect of spending an entire year living with her eccentric Grandma in rural Illinois. She is used to spending summers there, but her brother Joey was always along to share Grandma's odd ways. Now it is the Depression, Joey is working with the Civilian Conservation Corps, and their mother and father can't afford to keep her at home. So, with her cat Bootsie and her radio, Mary Alice travels to Grandma's small town.

She is hardly off the train when Grandma trots her right to the schoolhouse, so she doesn't miss out on any lessons. The other students regard her as a city girl, although she dresses as poorly as the rest of them. For Mary Alice, it is going to be a long, long year.

Each day, however, becomes an adventure as Mary Alice is alternately appalled, terrified, and bemused by the unique character that is her grandmother. Right off, Grandma doesn't want Bootsie inside, so her cat must live in the cob house. Although this distresses Mary Alice, Bootsie seems to take to it quite nicely and is soon running the yard as though she'd been a country cat all her life. In time, Bootsie appears with a kitten that Mary Alice names April.

While Mary Alice struggles with math and a new school, Grandma goes about her business, which apparently is running the town. People are either terrified or in awe of her, and Grandma doesn't care which. At Halloween, for instance, when the local boys think they'll play some tricks around the old cob house, Grandma devises a plan that includes a lot of glue, and she sends the would-be pranksters running. It's a Halloween they won't soon forget! Then there is the time Grandma takes Mary Alice pecan picking in Old Man Nyquist's yard. Old Man Nyquist said she could have any pecans that fell on the ground, but they can find only a few. This highly annoys Grandma until she drives Old Man Nyquist's old tractor out of the barn and smack into a tree. The impact shakes down enough pecans for a wagonload of Grandma's special pies!

In spite of her grandmother's eccentric ways, Mary Alice begins to notice how much Grandma helps those less fortunate than she. Her manner may be gruff, but in her no-nonsense way she dispenses just the right amount of caring without embarrassing anyone.

Mary Alice's school days are brightened when a new boy comes to town. His name is Royce McNabb, and she thinks he's the best looking boy in the county. She even gets him to come over and help her with her math work. That turns out to be the day when the snake Grandma keeps in the attic to "keep down the birds" decides to make an appearance. Mary Alice figures she'll never see Royce again.

When the year is up and times are improving, Mary Alice doesn't want to go home. But Grandma knows better. As she tells her granddaughter, "I don't lock my doors." That is her way of saying Mary Alice is always welcome.

As the book ends, World War II is nearing an end. Brother Joey is flying B-17s, Mother and Father are doing war work in Seattle, and Mary Alice marries soldier Royce McNabb in Grandma's house. Grandma bakes the wedding cake.

Themes and Subjects

This "Valentine of a book" creates a realistic but sympathetic atmosphere of the Depression years in America. It speaks of family values and a quieter, gentler time in the "good ole days." In the character of Grandma, Peck captures the Yankee stereotype of decency and independence. Her granddaughter, Mary Alice, is a spunky version of the eccentric Grandma, and the relationship between them is portrayed with just the right amount of humor, respect, and love. This is a funny, warm book that captures another era.

Incidents for Booktalking

The heart of this story is found in the eccentricities of Grandma and her relationship with Mary Alice. See: Grandma teaches Mary Alice about fighting battles (pp. 15–18); the Halloween trick (pp. 25–28); Grandma and Mary Alice go pecan picking (pp. 29–32); Grandma teaches a lesson in making money (pp. 47–54); Royce meets the snake in the attic (pp. 104–9).

Related Titles

In *No Strings Attached* (Royal Fireworks, 1998, $6.99: 0-88092-434-9) by Kristi D. Holl, June has difficulty adjusting when she and her mother move in with crabby old Franklin Cooper.

Trish's political campaign for junior class president turns out to be a model of inefficiency in Lael Littke's *Trish for President* (Harcourt, 1984, o.p. 0-15- 290512-x).

In Nina Bowden's *Granny the Pag* (Clarion, 1996, $15.00: 0-395-77604-X), Catriona is left by her parents with her grandmother who embarrasses the young girl with her eccentric ways, such as riding a motorcycle and wearing a leather jacket.

The four Sutton kids find a new and most unusual housekeeper in Robert Burch's *Ida Early Comes over the Mountain* (Puffin, 1990, pap., $3.99: 0-14-034534-5).

In David Almond's Printz Award winning novel, *Kit's Wilderness* (Delacorte, 2000, $15.95: 0-385-32665-3), set in an English mining town, Kit Watson mixes such real-life problems as his grandfather's memory loss with visions of long-gone ancestors.

About the Book and Author

Berger, Laura Standley, ed. *Twentieth-Century Young Adult Writers*. St. James, 1994, pp. 523–26.

Chevalier, Tracy, ed. *Twentieth-Century Children's Writers*, 3d ed. St. James, 1989, pp.768–69

Commire, Anne, ed. *Something About the Author*. Vol. 18. Gale, 1980, pp. 242–44; updated, Vol. 55, 1989, pp. 126–38.

Gallo, Donald. *Presenting Richard Peck*. Twayne, 1989.

————. *Speaking for Ourselves*. National Council of Teachers of English, 1990, pp. 165–67.

Garrett, Agnes, and Helga P. McCue, eds. *Authors and Artists for Young Adults*. Vol. 1. Gale, 1989, pp. 215–30.

Hedblad, Alan, ed. *Something About the Author*. Vol. 97. Gale, 1998, pp. 181–87.

————. *Something About the Author*. Vol. 110. Gale, 2000, pp 159–70 (autobiographical).

Hotze, Sally Holmes, ed. *Fifth Book of Junior Authors and Illustrators*. Wilson, 1983, pp. 238–40.

Kirkpatrick, D. L., ed. *Twentieth-Century Children's Writers*, 2d ed. St. Martin's, 1983, pp. 610–11.

Metzger, Linda, ed. *Contemporary Authors* (New Revision Series). Vol. 19. Gale, 1987, pp. 366–70.

"Newbery Acceptance Speech." *Horn Book* (July/August 2001): not yet published.

Peck, Richard. "Interview." *School Library Journal*. (June 1990): pp. 40–42

————. *A Year Down Yonder*. Read by Lois Smith. Listening Library, 2000. Audiocassettes (3hrs. 25 min). ($23.00)

Sarkissian, Adele, ed. *Something About the Author: Autobiographical Series*. Vol. 2. Gale, 1986, pp. 175–86.

Senick, Gerard J., ed. *Children's Literature Review*. Vol. 15. Gale, 1988, pp. 146–65.

Silvey, Anita. *Children's Books and Their Creators*. Houghton, 1995, pp. 512–14.

"The 2001 Newbery Acceptance Speech." *Journal of Youth Services in Libraries*, 14, no. 4 (summer, 2001): not yet published.

Honor Books 2001

Bauer, Joan. *Hope Was Here*. Putnam's, 2000, $16.99: 0-399-23142-0. (Grades 8–10)

Sixteen-year-old Hope, who lives with her diner cook extraordinaire Aunt Addie, is used to moving around. Aunt Addie is always off to the next diner to make the eating better. Hope herself has learned to be a highly competent waitress, although always adjusting to a new town and new school sometimes can be difficult. Hope sees her mother once in a while but has never met her father and doesn't even know who he is. She dreams of the day when she will meet him. The most recent move is especially hard on Hope because she has grown fond of living in Brooklyn. Now she and Addie are off to rural Mulhoney, Wisconsin, to take over the cooking in G.T. Stoop's Welcome Stairways Diner. G.T. turns out to be a straight-talking bald guy who is suffering from leukemia. He and Addie immediately disagree on food, but in a good-natured way. As Hope and Addie settle in, much to everyone's surprise, G.T. decides to run for mayor against corrupt Eli Millstone. Who is going to vote for a man with a fatal illness or vote against the long-time mayor? It seems hopeless at first, but throughout the summer, Hope is drawn more and more into G.T.'s campaign, along with other workers at the diner including Braverman, whom Hope secretly likes. At every turn their efforts are hindered by obvious treachery from the mayor's side. Hope learns about the staging of a campaign and learns about honesty and strength from G.T. When the election results are in and G.T. loses by 114 votes, they are stunned. Not long after, however, Hope uncovers the fraud behind the tally. When the fraudulent votes are thrown out, G.T. is fairly installed as mayor. Even better, his leukemia is in remission, and he and Addie marry. Hope discovers for the first time what it really means to have a father. Two years later, G.T. dies and Hope leaves for college, but she knows now that she can return to a home. This is a funny, sad, and sensitive story about people at their very finest.

Creech, Sharon. *The Wanderer*. Harper-Collins, 2000, $15.95: 0-06-027730-0. (Grades 5–9)

Thirteen-year-old Sophie is thrilled beyond belief when her parents give permission for her to leave their Kentucky home and accompany her bachelor uncle Dock on his two-masted sailing ship, *The Wanderer*, for a transatlantic voyage to visit her ailing 72-year-old grandfather, Bompie (real name Ulysses). Sophie is a sensitive but tough youngster who has always had a powerful, sometimes frightening attraction to the sea. Accompanying her and Dock as crew and passengers are Dock's two brothers, Stu and Mo; Stu's son, Brian; and Mo's son, Cody. Both Brian and Cody are older than Sophie. Brian is like his father: priggish, controlling, overly organized, and difficult to like. Cody is the total opposite: charming and attractive but also flighty and irresponsible. The story is told through two journals. The first, kept by Sophie, is, like her, thoughtful, pensive, and observant; the other, written by Cody, is terse, matter-of-fact, and sometimes flip. On their three- to four-week voyage, they make stops at Block Island, Martha's Vineyard, and an island that is part of Nova Scotia. Later, Sophie learns that these are places that Dock associates with Rosalie, the girlfriend he loved and lost. On the open ocean, each performs regular chores and also shares his or her special knowledge. For example, Mo teaches radio code, Cody teaches juggling skills, and Sophie retells stories about the childhood of Grandpa Bompie. Everyone is convinced that Sophie is making up these stories because, as we learn from Cody's journal, Sophie was adopted only three years before. When Brian cruelly confronts Sophie with questions about her origins, she retreats into silence, unwilling or unable to confront her past. A wild storm that lasts for days hits *The Wanderer* with such severity that everyone thinks the ship will sink. A gigantic 50-foot wave almost capsizes their boat. This traumatic experience triggers Sophie's memory of another violent storm and a huge wave in which her parents drowned while saving her. After weeks at sea, the ship limps into an Irish port where, miraculously, Dock is reunited with Rosalie. The six adventurers travel to England where there is a joyful reunion with Bompie, and it is revealed that, through a three-year correspondence, Bompie told Sophie the stories she narrated on the ship. As their pilgrimage ends, the six travelers realize that each has profited from the experience. The three brothers know each other better, Dock has found Rosalie, Brian has learned some social skills, Cody has gained maturity and a sense of responsibility, Sophie has come to accept her past, and all have visited with the beloved Bompie.

DiCamillo, Kate. *Because of Winn-Dixie*. Candlewick, 2000, $15.99: 0-7636-0776-2. (Grades 4–6)

In this touching story of loneliness and friendship, 10-year-old India Opal Buloni moves to Naomi, Florida, with her preacher father. Neither of them are doing well at forgetting the wife and mother who left when Opal was three. But Opal's lonely life with her busy, reclusive father is suddenly brightened when she befriends a stray dog that she names for the grocery store where she found him: Winn-Dixie. Winn-Dixie, who can smile and listen better than anybody, becomes her constant companion, even going to the Baptist church where Opal's father preaches on Sundays. Winn-Dixie also wins over the preacher, who begins to talk to his daughter about her long-gone mother. The only problem is Winn-Dixie's terror of the thunderstorms that occur frequently in Florida. Opal's father warns her that she must watch over the dog carefully when a storm comes up. Little by little, Winn-Dixie helps to expand Opal's world. When she wants to buy him a red leash but doesn't have the money, she does chores for Otis at the pet store, and the two become friends. She makes another friend of Miss Franny Block at the Herman W. Block Memorial Library where Winn-Dixie is allowed inside, and she especially makes a friend of elderly Gloria Dump, who some say is a witch; Winn-Dixie doesn't think so, and neither does Opal. Opal even develops an understanding of pinch-faced Amanda Wilkinson and the bald-headed Dewberry boys. Finally, Opal gathers all her new friends together at a party, which goes well until an unexpected storm occurs. Winn-Dixie disappears, and Opal is frantic. After a long search with her father through town, they return to the party at the Dump house only to find that Winn-Dixie has been there under the bed all along. With her dog and her new friends, Opal decides she doesn't feel quite so lonely anymore.

Gantos, Jack. *Joey Pigza Loses Control*. Farrar, 2000, $16.00: 0-374-39989-1. (Grades 4–8)

For a grade-schooler, young Joey Pigza, the narrator of this novel, has more than his share of problems. Although he is basically a well-meaning, honest, and good-natured boy, his fits of erratic behavior have led to a diagnosis of attention deficit disorder, and he wears a medical patch to keep his hyperactivity in check (See *Joey Pigza Swallowed the Key*, Farrar, 1998, $16.00: 0-374-33664-4). Joey's loving, caring mother, who operates the Beauty and the Beast Hair Salon in Lancaster, Pennsylvania, has been raising him, but now she is driving him to Pittsburgh to spend six weeks with his absentee dad who he scarcely knows. Joey dreams that he will be loved by this stranger and perhaps succeed in getting his mother and father back together. His pet Chihuahua, Pablo, accompanies him. Joey's father, Carter, who is a janitor, lives alone with Joey's grandma, a self-willed, eccentric, often maddening chain smoker. In spite of her emphysema, Joey's grandmother grabs puffs from her cigarettes when she isn't attached to an oxygen machine. At first, Joey is attracted to his affable, charming father and refuses to face the mounting evidence that his father is a born loser suffering from the same moods swings as Joey once had. He is an alcoholic fast talker and bar brawler who has a record of failure. However, he has a lovely girlfriend, Leezy, whom Joey grows to like, and he coaches a junior league baseball game where he hopes Joey will become a star. Joey tries in every way to please his father and discovers that he has a natural talent for pitching. His competitive father soon makes him the official pitcher for the team. In one of his hyperactive moods, Carter claims every one should be self-sufficient and flushes his nicotine patches and Joey's medication down the toilet. Joey is at first frightened of the consequences. He pretends that all is well but gradually begins to unwind. An afternoon in a video game store and a bungee jumping excursion with his father further unsettle him, and soon he is running out of control. At the championship game, he becomes emotionally unstable and throws wild pitches at everyone. He escapes his angry father and takes refuge in a shopping mall where he phones his mother to take him home. As Joey and his mother leave Pittsburgh with Pablo, Joey tries to put his disappointment and disillusionment behind him and find comfort in the love they feel for each other.

# Bibliography

Ammon, Bette D., and Gale W. Sherman, eds. *Handbook for the Newbery Medal and Honor Books, 1980–1989*. Alleyside, 1991.

Association for Library Service to Children. *The Newbery and Caldecott Awards: A Guide to the Medal and Honor Books, 2000*. American Library Association, 2000.

Atkinson, Joan Lyon. "Oh, the Places You'll Go! (and Won't) with Newberys." *Journal of Youth Services in Libraries* (fall 1996): 46–57.

Authors and Artists for Young Adults. Gale, 1989– (continuing series).

Berger, Laura Standley, ed. *Twentieth-Century Children's Writers*. 4th ed. St. James, 1995.

—————. *Twentieth-Century Young Adult Writers*. St. James, 1994.

Brown, Muriel W., and Rita S. Foudray. *Newbery and Caldecott Medalists and Honor Book Winners: Bibliographies & Resource Material Through 1991*. 2d ed. Neal-Schuman, 1992.

Cech, John, ed. "American Writers for Children, 1900–1960." In *Dictionary of Literary Biography*. Vol. 22. Gale, 1983.

Children's Literary Review. Gale, 1976– (continuing series).

Collier, Laurie, and Joyce Nakamura. *Major Authors and Illustrators for Children and Young Adults: A Selection of Sketches from Something About the Author*. Gale, 1993, 6 vols.

Comfort, Claudette H. *Distinguished Children's Literature: The Newbery and Caldecott Winners: The Books and Their Creators*. Denison, 1990.

Contemporary Authors. Gale. 1962– (continuing series).

Darton, F. J. Harvey. *Children's Books in England: Five Centuries of Social Life*. 3d ed. Cambridge, 1982.

de Montreville, Doris, and Elizabeth D. Crawford, eds. *Fourth Book of Junior Authors and Illustrators*. Wilson, 1978.

de Montreville, Doris, Elizabeth D. Crawford, and Donna Hill, eds. *Third Book of Junior Authors*. Wilson, 1972.

Edwards, Ronald G. "John Newbery: Bookseller, Entrepreneur, and Advocate for Children's Literature."*Journal of Youth Services in Libraries* (fall 1996): 64.

Estes, Glenn E., ed. "American Writers for Children Before 1900." In *Dictionary of Literary Biography*. Vol. 42. Gale, 1985.

———. "American Writers for Children Since 1960: Fiction." *Dictionary of Literary Biography*. Vol. 52. Gale, 1986.

Fuller, Muriel, ed. *More Junior Authors*. Wilson, 1963.

Gallo, Donald R. ed. *Speaking for Ourselves*. National Council of Teachers of English, 1990.

———. *Speaking for Ourselves, Too*. National Council of Teachers of English, 1993.

Gillespie, Cindy S. et al. "A Look at the Newbery Medal from a Multicultural Perspective."*Reading Teacher* (Sept. 1994): 40–50.

Hadlow, Kathy, et al. "What the Newbery Has Meant to Me." *Journal of Youth Services in Libraries* (fall 1996): pp. 68–84.

Helbig, Alethea K., and Agnes R. Perkins, eds. *Dictionary of American Children's Fiction, 1859–1959*. Greenwood, 1986.

———. *Dictionary of American Children's Fiction*, 1960–1985. Greenwood, 1986.

Hipple, Theodore W., ed. *Writers for Young Adults*. Scribners, 1997, 3 vols.

Holtze, Sally Holmes, ed. *Fifth Book of Junior Authors and Illustrators*. Wilson, 1983.

———. *Sixth Book of Junior Authors and Illustrators*. Wilson, 1989.

Hopkins, Lee Bennett, ed. *More Books by More People*. Citation Press, 1974.

Horn Book (various annual issues of Newbery acceptance material).

Houdyshell, M. L., and J. J. Kirkland. "Heroines in Newbery Medal Award Winners: 75 Years of Change." *Journal of Youth Services in Libraries* (spring 1998): pp. 252–62.

Hunt, Peter, ed. *Children's Literature: An Illustrated History*. Oxford, 1995.

Journal of Youth Services in Libraries (various annual issues of Newbery acceptance material).

Kerby, Ramona Nolan. "Happy Seventy-Fifth Birthday, Newbery Award! Newbery Authors Share Their Thoughts." *Journal of Youth Services in* Libraries (fall 1996): pp. 25–34.

Kingman, Lee, ed. *Newbery and Caldecott Medal Books: 1956–1965 with Acceptance Papers, Biographies and Related Material*. Horn Book, 1965.

———. *Newbery and Caldecott Medal Books: 1966–1975 with Acceptance Papers, Biographies and Related Material*. Horn Book, 1975.

———. *Newbery and Caldecott Medal Books: 1976–1985 with Acceptance Papers, Biographies and Related Material*. Horn Book, 1985.

Kleuser, Susan R., et al. "A Comparison of the Level of Difficulty of Newbery Award Books for the Decades 1950–1959 and 1980–1989." *Current Studies in Librarianship* (spring/fall 1991): pp. 71–89.

Kunitz, Stanley J., and Vineta Cloby, eds. *European Authors 1000–1900*. Wilson, 1967.

Kunitz, Stanley J., Vineta Cloby, and Howard Haycraft, eds. *The Junior Book of Authors*. Wilson, 1951.

———. *Twentieth-Century Authors*. Wilson, 1942.

Littlejohn, Carol. "Number the Stars: Booktalking the Newbery Winners." *Journal of Youth Services in Libraries* (fall 1996): pp. 92–95.

McGowan, Sue. "Choosing the Newbery Winners." *Book Report* (March/April 1997): pp. 22–23.

Mealy, Virginia. *Newbery Books*. Book Lures, 1991.

Meigs, Cornelia, et al. *A Critical History of Children's Literature*. Macmillan, 1969.

Miller, Bertha M., and Elinor Field, eds. *Newbery Medal Books: 1922–1955 with the Author's Acceptance Papers and Related Material*. Horn Book, 1955.

Miller, Bonnie. "What Color Is Gold? Twenty-One Years of Same-Race Authors and Protagonists in the Newbery Medal." *Journal of Youth Services in Libraries* (fall 1998): pp. 34–39.

Muir, Percy H. *English Children's Books—1600–1900*. Batsford, 1954.

Noblett, William. "John Newbery: Publisher Extraordinary." *History Today* (April 1972): pp. 266–73.

Parravano, Martha V. "Alive and Vigorous—Questioning the Newbery." *Horn Book* (July/Aug. 1999): pp. 434–44.

Parravano, Martha V., and Lauren Adams. "A Wider Vision for the Newbery." *Horn Book* (March/April): 1996, pp. 4–5.

Peltola, Bette J. "Newbery and Caldecott Medals: Authorization and Terms." *Top of the News* (fall 1979): pp. 49–54.

Peterson, Linda K., and Marilyn L. Solt, eds. *Newbery and Caldecott Medal and Honor Books, 1922–1981*. Hall, 1982.

Pickard, Patricia W. "The Newbery Award and Tehnology." *Journal of Youth Services in Libraries* (fall 1996): pp. 85-91.

Quale, Eric. *Early Children's Books: A Collectors Guide*. Barnes and Noble, 1983.

Sharkey, Paulette B. *Newbery and Caldecott Medal and Honor Books in Other Media*. Neal-Schuman, 1992.

Silvey, Anita, ed. *Children's Books and Their Creators*. Houghton, 1995.

Smith, Irene. *A History of the Newbery and Caldecott Medals*. Viking, 1957.

Something About the Author. Gale, 1971– (continuing series).

Something About the Author: Autobiographical Series. Gale, 1986– (continuing series).

Staerkel, Kathleen. *The Newbery and Caldecott Mock Election Kit: Choosing Champions in Children's Books*. ALSC/ALA, 1994.

Sullivan, Peggy. "Victim of Success? A Closer Look at the Newbery Award." *School Library Journal* (May 1972) pp. 40–43.

Sutherland, Zena. "The Newbery at 75: Changing with the Times." *American Libraries* (March 1999): pp. 34–36.

Thwaite, M. F. *From Primer to Pleasure in Reading*. Library Association, 1972.

Top of the News (various issues).

Townsend, John Rowe, ed. *John Newbery and His Books: Trade and Plumb Cake Forever, Huzza!* Scarecrow, 1995.

———. *Written for Children: An Outline of English-Language Children's Literature*. 4th ed. Harper, 1990.

Wadham, Tim. "The Part you Carry with You: A Personal Journal through Seventy-Five Years of Newbery Books." *Journal of Youth Services in Libraries* (fall 1996): pp. 35–45.

Ward, Martha, ed. *Authors of Books for Young People*. 3d ed. Scarecrow, 1990.

Welsh, Charles. *A Bookseller of the Last Century, Being Some Account of the Life of John Newbery*. Griffith, 1885.

Woolman, Bertha, and Patricia Litsey. *The Newbery Award Winners: The Books and Their Authors*. Denison, 1992.

Index